Springer Texts in Business and Economics

For further volumes:
http://www.springer.com/series/10099

Guido Candela • Paolo Figini

The Economics of Tourism Destinations

Guido Candela
Paolo Figini
Department of Economics
University of Bologna
Bologna
Italy

Translated and revised from the book "Economia del Turismo e delle Destinazioni", published by McGraw-Hill Companies Inc. Publishing Italia, 2nd edition 2010.

Translation by Mirco Soffritti and Patric J. Walton (Chaps. 2–11) and Riccardo Leo (Chaps. 13–16).

ISSN 2192-4333 ISSN 2192-4341 (electronic)
ISBN 978-3-642-20873-7 ISBN 978-3-642-20874-4 (eBook)
DOI 10.1007/978-3-642-20874-4
Springer Heidelberg New York Dordrecht London

Library of Congress Control Number: 2012943717

Printed on acid-free paper

Springer is part of Springer Science+Business Media (www.springer.com)

To Benedetta, my true *Blessed Candle* (Guido)
From an Economist of Tourism to all Tourists of Economics (Paolo)

Preface to the English Edition

This book was originally thought of as the translation of "Economia del Turismo e delle Destinazioni" (Candela and Figini 2010a), a well-known Italian textbook of Tourism Economics, into English. The book originates from the long experience of the authors (given the age, particularly one of the two authors!) in teaching and investigating tourism-related issues at the Rimini Campus of the University of Bologna, one of the main centers in Italy for the study of Tourism Economics. Candela published his first textbook on Tourism Economics in 1996 (Candela 1996, but also see Candela 1988). Candela and Figini published their first book together in 2003 (Candela and Figini 2003).

However, the project was completely changed since its conception two years ago and, from what should have been a mere translation of the Italian version, the book was completely revisited and updated. Although its structure was not changed, the book needed to adapt to the different styles used in English, to adapt to the different and heterogeneous background of the international audience, and last but not least, to correct some mistakes that were found and some explanations that were not satisfying. To sum up, the book was basically rewritten. Although the exerted effort was considerable, errors and mistakes certainly remain, for which the authors are the sole responsible.

Bologna, Italy

Guido Candela
Paolo Figini

Acknowledgements

An academic text, whatever teaching or research oriented, is always the outcome of a collaborative effort of socialization of knowledge, whereby scholars, researchers, students, and professionals play a key, although often unaware, role. Apart from all the students and colleagues whom we have met in our professional life, we want to explicitly thank those who actively gave a contribution to the preparation of this textbook.

Mirco Soffritti and Patric J. Walton for translating Chaps. 2–11 and Riccardo Leo for translating Chaps. 13–16 of the Italian version of the textbook and that have been used as the base on which this textbook was written. The work of the translator is a tricky one, particularly when the academic style used in Italian and English textbooks are so different.

Isabel Cortès-Jiménez for carefully reading and working on the first three chapters of the book, for which she might almost be considered a co-author.

The editor of Springer, Barbara Fess, for the encouragement and for the patience while she was waiting for the final version of the book. Although we sign the book with the date of January 2012, the readers might want to know that originally the book was expected to be delivered by the end of 2010. A special thanks goes to Marion Kreisel, the editorial assistant, and Sylvia Schneider, the production editor, who took care of the book in the publishing process.

Some colleagues helped us in setting the Italian edition, in particular: Rainer Andergassen, Patrizia Battilani, Massimiliano Castellani, Roberto Cellini, Roberto Dieci, Simone Giannerini, Maurizio Mussoni, Marco Savioli, Antonello E. Scorcu, Matteo Troilo, and Laura Vici.

An infinite thanks to Barbara Ravagli who helped us in the equation editing and for a careful checking of mistakes, errors, or incongruities. We know that many typos and mistakes will be found in this book but much less of what would have been without her precious work. Moreover, she gave us the assurance that, by working with her, what you start, you will bring it to the end.

Finally, thanks to all who will read the book, particularly to those who will provide us with their feedback, comments, or suggestions. There are always possibilities to improve.

Bologna, Italy
January 2012

Guido Candela
Paolo Figini

Contents

Chapter 1
Introduction: Economics of Tourism, Economics of Destinations, Tourism Studies and Other Related Issues

1.1 Introduction

In the early days, research in tourism was mainly stimulated by investigations commissioned by business associations and policy makers rather than by scientific curiosity on open issues and by a clear research agenda (Ashworth 1989). At that time, the research was acritically descriptive and inadequate in the methodology, instruments, and approaches used.

The delay of tourism studies at the academic level, and of Tourism Economics in particular, is acknowledged by the literature when one of the most popular international textbooks (Cooper et al. 2008) affirms, at the beginning of the new millennium, that the development of tourism as a field of study is relatively new, a young discipline that only recently has been considered worthy of a serious research effort.

> Tourism does suffer from an image problem in academic circles. Indeed, many are attracted to it as an exciting vibrant subject and an applied area of economic activity—which we believe that it is. But to be successful, tourism demands very high standards of professionalism, knowledge and application from everyone involved. This is sometimes felt to be in contrast to the image of jet-setting, palm-fringed beaches and a leisure activity.
>
> (Cooper et al. 1998, p. 3)

According to Sinclair and Stabler (1997), research in tourism has developed only since the second half of the 1980s in terms of scientific methodology, with the birth of specialized scientific journals, University departments, research centers, and undergraduate and postgraduate degrees. In the last 25–30 years, tourism has greatly benefited from the strong development of both research and teaching in this subject and, in one of the most popular textbooks of Tourism Economics (Stabler et al. 2010), the authors conclude that the topics belonging to this field of study can be classified into three groups: established research, emerging themes, and themes under-researched.[1]

[1] An interesting analysis of current research themes can be found in Tribe and Xiao (2011).

G. Candela and P. Figini, *The Economics of Tourism Destinations*, Springer Texts in Business and Economics, DOI 10.1007/978-3-642-20874-4_1,

The established research interests and the emerging themes are mainly topics of applied research: the Tourism Satellite Account, the modeling of demand and forecasting, the Computable General Equilibrium, the Cost–Benefit Analysis, some microeconomics issues (such as the hedonic price approach and the discrete choice analysis applied to tourism), and some macroeconomic issues (such as the relationships between tourism, growth, development, globalization, and international trade), all issues that have been pushed by the recent increase in data availability.

The themes under-researched can further be classified into three categories (1) the relationship between tourism and the environment, with related consequences in terms of sustainability and intragenerational equity; (2) the crisis management, called upon many terrible terrorism acts and natural events; (3) the definition and conceptualization of tourism (on which we will return in Sect. 1.4).

> With all these elements of tourism, research into their effect is still in its infancy: a fundamental requirement is for more empirical research to be undertaken.
>
> (Stabler et al. 2010, p. 429)

At the beginning of 2012, this classification is the best proof that Tourism Economics has built its own history and, although one might disagree with Stabler et al. on the classification of research topics within one group or another, everyone should agree that Tourism Economics is now sufficiently grownup to allow for a systematic organization, which is one of the goals that a textbook has. In fact, in the international literature, there are many popular, well structured, and interesting textbooks of Tourism Economics. Together with the ones already quoted in this introduction (Cooper et al. 2008; Stabler et al. 2010), we also mention Tribe (2011), Lundberg et al. (1995), and Vanhove (2005).

Was there a need for another textbook?

1.2 Was There a Need for Another Textbook?

Being the authors, our answer is obviously "yes." Let us explain why. Some of the existing textbooks mainly focus on describing the economic activity of the different sectors composing tourism, and only a general sketch of the economic principles, problems, and open issues of tourism is provided. On the other hand, other textbooks are general introductions to economics and to economic theory, thereby focusing on perfect competition markets which, however, do not appropriately describe the way in which tourism works in the real world. Finally, some other textbooks are very business-oriented, well dealing with real-world practices, case studies, and marketing and management policies but with a blurring economic theory approach.

We believe our book is different.

First, it is mainly a book of Applied Economics specifically built on the characteristics of the tourism sector. In doing so, we follow the *fundamentum divisionis* between Pure Economics and Applied Economics proposed by Pareto.

Our approach is then to consider Tourism Economics as an applied field of study in which assumptions of bounded rationality are largely used and where models of perfect competition are only marginally employed, since they are not particularly relevant for this sector. Tourism markets are then treated as imperfect markets, with asymmetric and incomplete information among agents and with strong presence of externalities and public goods.

Second, although the economic issues discussed in the book are approached intuitively, by largely using examples and case studies, they are also formally treated, by using the proper economic toolbox and modeling to approach the problems (with mathematical formalizations often added in special boxes, for the most demanding readers). In this way, we treat tourism with the same methodology and care as used in other fields of applied economic research.

Third, the structure of the book is tailor made on the organization of the tourism markets, with discussion of both microeconomic and macroeconomic issues. On top of that, since one of the main and peculiar features of tourism is the role played by tourism destinations (see Sect. 1.4) so that one can affirm that competition in tourism is between destinations, not (only) between firms, our analysis of tourism destinations is very detailed. Although we specifically dedicated a whole chapter to the economic analysis of destinations (Chap. 4), destination-related issues are widespread throughout the book (particularly in Chaps. 5, 11, 13, 15, and 16) such that their role is emphasized in the book's title.

In this way, we aim at providing a whole and unifying framework in which Tourism Economics can be coherently analyzed. The book focuses on the economic problems faced by agents such as tourists, firms, destinations, the public sector, thus leaving marketing and management issues to textbooks of other disciplines. Among the many examples analyzed in the book, we recall here the tourist's choice on whether to buy a package holiday or self-organize it, the choice of the hotel's size when there is seasonality in demand, how the tour operator sets the price in an oligopoly market structure, the economic growth in an economy specialized in tourism, etc.

As a downturn of this approach, this book requires the knowledge of some basic economics. Although many elementary notions are explained throughout the text and, in some cases, described in special boxes, it is advisable that the reader has taken an introductory course in Economics (including both parts of Microeconomics and Macroeconomics). The student should know the concept of demand, supply, and price; how the market works; some basics of national accounting; and a few other topics. An introductory course in quantitative methods can also be of help (the student should know the meaning of function and of first-order condition, the concept of probability, the distribution function, the mean and the variance).

1.3 The Organization of the Textbook

The book is divided into three parts. The first part (including Chaps. 2–4) introduces to the main concepts, definitions, and measurement issues of tourism, of the tourism sector, and of its impact on the economy. A comprehensive economic analysis of the tourism destination is mainly carried out in Chap. 4, thus highlighting that the destination has a key role in the tourism markets and that, from an economics perspective, there are specific aspects of the destination that cannot be traced back neither to Microeconomics nor to Macroeconomics.

The second part (including Chaps. 5–12) is the microeconomic analysis of tourism, divided into the analysis of the tourism demand (Chaps. 5–6), the analysis of the tourism producers (Chaps. 7–9 and 12), and the analysis of tourism markets (Chaps. 10 and 11). Particular emphasis is given to the interaction between different types of tourism suppliers and to the contractual solutions provided for their problems (Chap. 11) and to the economic strategies undertaken by tourism firms to increase market power (Chap. 10).

The third part (including Chaps. 13–16) is the macroeconomic analysis of tourism, where the typical distinction between closed economy (Chap. 13, analysis of the impact of tourism on the economy in the short run and in the long run) and open economy (Chap. 14, analysis of the real and financial aspects related to tourism in an international context) is carried out. Moreover, the key role of the public sector in dealing with externality issues and with the provision of public goods in tourism is underlined in Chap. 15, while Chap. 16 concludes the book by investigating into the relationship between tourism and the environment, thus discussing the issue of sustainability.

Every chapter starts with an Introduction and ends with a Chapter Overview that, in our hope, help facilitate the comprehension and the study. The textbook includes tables, figures, and three types of boxes (1) Theory in Action, to formally treat some of the theoretical models recalled in the main text; (2) Notes, to deepen the knowledge of specific topics; (3) Case study, to back the theory with real-world examples. Finally, on the companion Web site, exercises, questions, and slides will be available for both students and teachers.

Our hope is that the organization of the book and the treatment of the issues under discussion will be useful to students, practitioners, and researchers. Although the book is mainly addressed to students enrolled in Schools of Business and Economics, with major in Tourism, Travel, or Hospitality Management, both at the undergraduate and postgraduate level and taking a course of "Tourism Economics", it can successfully be used in shorter courses or modules, particularly at the postgraduate level (M.A., Ph.D.), or by scholars and professional new to the study of Tourism Economics. For these "advanced students," the book offers, together with a systematic treatment of the whole field of study, an updated list of references of the specific literature on each topic, so that the book might also be the starting point for the necessary literature overview which constitutes the beginning of each research.

1.4 On the Research and Teaching of Tourism Economics

We start by recalling one of the under-investigated themes cited by Stabler et al. (2010) and listed in Sect. 1.1: the conceptualization of tourism and tourism studies. As Wanhill (2007) reminds us, very few articles on the definition and conceptualization of tourism have been submitted to the tourism journals. We find it necessary, therefore, to unfold our position on the issue, which is key to understand the rationale and the vision behind the book.[2]

1.4.1 Genus and Species Disciplines

In identifying the content of a discipline we find, in the literature, both de facto definitions and definitions which meet epistemological criteria:

> Three main paths are available for delineating the subject matter [of a discipline]. (1) The *historical*, whereby we seek through study of the classic writing to find the central traditional concerns and interests [of a discipline] as an intellectual discipline. In brief, we ask: "What did the founding fathers say?" (2) The *empirical*, whereby we study current work [of a discipline] to discover those subjects to which the discipline gives most attention. In other words, we ask: "What are contemporary scholars [of a discipline] doing?" (3) The *analytical*, whereby we arbitrarily divide and delimit some larger subject matter and allocate it among different disciplines. We ask, in effect: "What does reason suggest?".
>
> (Inkeles 1964, p. 2)

Accordingly, when answering the question as to whether a complex of studies is a discipline (that is to say, an autonomous form of knowledge) or a field of study (where knowledge from different disciplines meets), both empirical and analytical answers can be found. A de facto discipline could be considered to exist if it is recognized by a community which guarantees its communication and habits and which develops its values and research criteria (King and Brownell 1966). A scientific discipline, on the other hand, might be considered to exist if it satisfies the conditions under which the philosophy of science recognizes a discipline of scientific knowledge. If the conditions are satisfied, one can conclude that we are not facing a field of study but dealing with:

> A distinct way in which our experience becomes structured around the use of accepted public symbols.
>
> (Hirst 1974, p. 44)

1.4.2 What Is Tourism?

What happens if the object of study is tourism? At the threshold of the twenty-first century, we feel confident in affirming that tourism is a de facto discipline, since there exists a community which is specialized in studying it:

---

[2] The remaining of Sect. 1.4 is mainly borrowed by Candela and Figini (2009) and (2010b).

> Tourism as a subject is showing signs of maturity with a growing academic community, increasing numbers of both journals and textbooks which are becoming specialised rather than all-embracing, and a number of societies both internationally and within individual countries.
>
> (Cooper et al. 1998, p. 3)

There are, in fact, schools and departments which are dedicated to training and research in the field of tourism; a network for communicating the results, with international associations which stimulate research and circulate results in national and international conferences; and there exist a number of research journals which are specialized rather than popular and which strictly adhere to international peer-review practices in their selection criteria.[3]

There is, however, more uncertainty when trying to answer the question as to whether tourism is a scientific discipline. Only a few years ago, John Tribe posed this very question in a well-known work (Tribe 1997) and came to a negative conclusion:

> Tourism is found not to be a discipline.
>
> (Tribe 2004, p. 48)

According to Tribe, from an epistemological point of view, tourism is only a field of study, albeit an important, popular, and widespread one.

We consider Tribe's answer the starting point, but we think that the question of asking whether tourism is a discipline is an open issue from an epistemological point of view. The fact that, in the literature, we find supporters of every possible response can be considered the proof: while Leiper argues that tourism is a discipline of science (Leiper 1981, 2000; but see also Ryan 1997), and Hoerner (2000) gives it the name tourismology, Gunn, by contrast, classifies it as a field of study (Gunn 1987). Moreover, there are also those who find it to be in an intermediate condition, awaiting developments:

> While tourism rightly constitutes a domain of study, at the moment it lacks the level of theoretical underpinning which would allow it to become a discipline.
>
> (Cooper et al. 1998, p. 3)

Where we find agreement is in the idea that studying tourism involves different sciences, but once again, the way in which this happens is controversial. Some talk of an interdisciplinary or multidisciplinary approach (Gunn 1987; Lieper 1990; Tribe 1997; Farrell and Twining-Ward 2004; Bramwell 2007; Pearce 2005; Darbellay and Stock 2011), arguing that tourism has a uniform terminology and methodology, one which is derived from the discipline of reference (Jantsch 1972; Przeclawski 1993), while others suggest an extradisciplinary or transdisciplinary approach, saying that tourism has come to evolve its own methodology, beyond the ones of the disciplines of reference and consisting in a collaboration between academic and policy-led research (Dickens 2003; Nowotny 2003).

---

[3] In the economic field, the most important journals can be considered *Annals of Tourism Research*, *Journal of Travel Research*, *Tourism Economics* and *Tourism Management*. Without being exhaustive, the number of journals related to tourism has risen from a dozen to more than 100 in less than 20 years. See Hall (2011) for a bibliometric analysis and journal ranking.

In our opinion, this confusion stems from the fact that tourism is itself too wide a term and, moreover, is one which does not have a single meaning or definition, in the same way that the human being, society, or nature do not refer to single disciplines. In fact, tourism, if correctly understood in a holistic sense, is a cross section of the society.

> [Analysis of complexity, globalization, sustainability, and interrelation in the theory of systems] are compelling reasons for there to be a more holistic approach to tourism researches. Effectively, all these factors call for inter- and trans-disciplinary research in which traditional disciplinary boundaries might be blurred.
>
> (Stabler et al. 2010, p. 437)

Starting from this statement, it can be immediately affirmed that tourism cannot be the object of a single discipline, in the same way that there is not a single discipline which studies the human being (think of biology, psychology, etc.), the society (consider sociology, political science, etc.), or the whole nature (physics, chemistry, etc.).

Therefore, we must reconsider the question of whether or not tourism is a discipline. To this end, we argue that it is useful to refer to the division of knowledge into *genus disciplines* and *species disciplines*, where the first constitute the great traditions of research to which the second belong. If, with Tribe, we exclude the possibility that tourism is a genus discipline, there remains the possibility that it might be a collection of species disciplines belonging to different genus disciplines.

Returning to the same categories which Tribe refers to (those indicated by Hirst 1965, 1974; see also Toulmin 1972; Donald 1986), we must therefore ask what characteristics a genus discipline or a species discipline must possess.

According to Hirst, a primary form of knowledge, a discipline, must have the following characteristics:

1. It must possess an interrelated set of concepts upon which the knowledge is developed (the object).
2. The concepts must assume a distinctive form of logical structure (the method).
3. The results must be proved, in accordance with an own criterion, in the face of real experience (verifiability and falsification).
4. The content cannot be further reduced, but must constitute a fundamental "building-block" of knowledge (indivisibility).

These characteristics define a genus discipline, but within one genus, many species discipline can coexist. Therefore, Hirst's same criteria can also be used to define a species discipline, although with a different approach:

(a) Criteria (2) and (4) are, so to speak, "inherited' from the genus discipline and therefore do not have to be demonstrated for the species discipline".
(b) Criteria (1) and (3) must, on the contrary, be proved at the species level, showing their own specificity in the object of study, to which corresponds a specific interpretation of the reality.

Having excluded, with Tribe, the possibility that tourism is a genus discipline, yet, we must understand, with regard to condition (b), whether there is room for one or more species disciplines: for example, what is the geography of tourism within geography, the history of tourism within history, the sociology of tourism within sociology, and so on.

1.4.3 Is Tourism Economics a Species Discipline or a Field of Study?

Letting each discipline to find its own answer, what can we say about the economics of tourism in relation to economics as a whole? Is it a species discipline or just a field of study?

First of all, we have to consider the type of relationship between economics and tourism economics. To this end, we draw inspiration from the important work of Pareto on mathematical economics (Pareto 1911). Among the many methodological problems faced in that work Pareto introduced, within the discussion about economic models and the assumptions of the economic equilibrium, an important distinction between pure economics and applied economics.

He began with two statements: (1) that in the economic fact there are a great number of constraints which derive from the observation of reality (such as, for example, customs and habits, laws, institutions, the specific nature of the product, tax regimes, unions, associations of producers, and so on); and (2) that economic models differ for the degree of approximation with which these constraints are taken into consideration.

On the basis of these premises, and concentrating on the constraints which are explicitly considered by the economic-mathematical model, Pareto proposed the following distinction:

> Applied economics must study everything; pure economics extracts from this study only the notions of a type which is useful to analyze.
>
> (Pareto 1911. *Our translation*)

In this statement, Pareto identifies with great simplicity a *fundamentum divisionis* which explains the scientific specialization of the various economic disciplines. Before doing anything else, economics, like any other form of scientific knowledge, abstracts and ignores all of the details which are irrelevant for the object of study. In the real world, however, it has to deal with more specific constraints. Pure economics is concerned with general and primary constraints of the economic fact; the study of the economic fact with more specific assumptions is the content of the various disciplines that are known as applied economics.

So, both because of the major interest in "real-world" economic phenomena and because of the more specific object of study, tourism economics undoubtedly belongs to applied economics. We can therefore affirm that tourism economics is to economics what applied economics is to pure economics. Compared to economics, tourism economics is located with a greater degree of realism nearer to a particular object of study, placing itself within a precise process of specification of assumptions, but still within the realm of economic theory. Therefore, the research carried out in the field of tourism economics is conducted through theories and stating hypotheses in models which have a different degree of abstraction compared to those in economics; moreover, research is carried out with other disciplines, such as statistics and econometrics, for the analysis of empirical observations and in the processing of data.

However, recognizing that tourism economics is the specific study of particular assumptions rather than of general models does not provide an answer to the question we started from, since specific studies can give rise to either a species discipline or a field of study of applied economics. Moreover, the applied nature of tourism economics, as compared to economics, still does not confer on it the properties of a species discipline. In so far, as part of economics, it possesses characteristics (2) and (4), that is to say a "method" applied to a "fundamental building-block of knowledge".

Then, we still have to consider whether tourism economics possesses characteristic (1), that is to say, a specific object of study, and characteristic (3), meaning that its theorems correspond to stylized facts which are specifically observable for tourism. If this were not the case, tourism economics should be seen as *a field of study in applied economics* but, should it be possible to demonstrate the autonomous characteristics with respect to the object of study and to verifiability and falsification, then we ought to speak of *species discipline in the area of applied economics*.

Let us consider, first, the object of study of tourism economics, by searching for differences with the object of study of economics itself. There are two issues to be considered, the tourism product and the tourism destination.

1.4.3.1 The Tourism Product

The tourism product is a "complex product," in the sense that is composed of a set of different goods and services which are demanded by visitors during their holiday at the destination; in a technical sense, the tourism product is a bundle of goods and services which are grouped according to the purpose of the purchase, the holiday (see Sect. 2.5). The object of study of economics is, on the other hand, generally identified as a single good or service, defined according to technological or market criteria.

The concept of the bundle of goods is not new in economics, but is normally used as a composite good, with reference to the principle of aggregation, which is useful both in microeconomics (for example, in the consumption theory and in index numbers) and in macroeconomics (for example, in the determination of the aggregate value of production, income, and price indexes). In economics, therefore, the bundle of goods is a functional tool, one of the many in the economist's toolbox, but rarely (and never systematically) an object of study in itself. In tourism economics, on the contrary, the bundle of goods *is* the object of study, since the tourism product is a composition of different goods and services, from which particular effects on demand and supply are derived.

1.4.3.2 The Tourism Destination

In economics, production takes place in firms and in sectors that produce goods and services and which are always identified by technological criteria. They are analyzed in markets in which the only reference to the other firms operating in the same market is about strategic interaction; only exceptionally they are considered as part of economic districts. In tourism economics, on the contrary, production is always attached to a "tourism destination" which is neither a firm nor an industry but represents a mix of companies (producing either goods or services), and of public and private support structures. The object of study of tourism economics, hence, is mainly the destination, not the firm.

Consequently, we feel able to assert that the concepts of the tourism product as a bundle of goods and services, and of the tourism destination as a systemic mix of firms, constitute the specific object of study of tourism economics and differ from the main objects of economics, which is the production process of a firm and the decision process of a consumer. Therefore, Hirst's first criterion, necessary to define a species discipline, is satisfied.

There still remains Hirst's third criterion to consider. We must, therefore, see whether the tourism product as a bundle of services, and the destination as a mix of firms, possess interpretive power which reveals itself through specific theorems, supported by economic models, to demonstrate some stylized facts of tourism.

1.4.3.3 The Love for Variety Theorem

With regard to the bundle of tourism goods and services, in tourism economics we can demonstrate the Love for Variety Theorem (see Sect. 4.3.2). This theorem states that a destination aims at increasing the sophistication of the tourism product because the variety has the effect of increasing the tourist's utility. Also, natural and artificial resources, often available as public goods, are arguments of the tourist's utility function. We can therefore state that the development of a tourism destination depends both on the variety of the local product offered and on the natural resources available in the destination. Moreover, the Love for Variety Theorem extended to tourism resources explains some other stylized facts of tourism: the existence of destinations which mainly develop on the basis of their natural resources and with limited local variety as well as destinations which do not have natural resources but which develop their entrepreneurial organization to produce a great variety of local products (Andergassen et al. 2012).

1.4.3.4 The Coordination Theorem

In the tourism destination, mix of many activities, a problem of coordination arises between the different economic agents involved, particularly among the private firms supplying the variety of goods and services which make up the tourism product. A holiday in the destination is not feasible unless both accommodation and complementary goods and services are available to the tourist: think of the tourist who needs accommodation, catering, transport to and within the destination, and so on. Hence, tourism in the destination may be seen as a "permit" to stay, issued by each of the various firms offering tourism services. The hypothesis of an economic good over which many agents have property rights is known as anticommon, a case of ownership fragmentation which is opposite to the common good. The Coordination Theorem (see Sect. 4.3.1) stems from the anticommon nature of the tourism product and explains two stylized facts which are important for understanding tourism: the need for a coordinating body in the destination (the Destination Management) and/or the creation of a specific firm for producing the package holiday (the tour operator).

From considering the tourism product as a bundle of goods and services and the tourism destination as a mix of firms, two theorems can hence be derived: the Love for Variety Theorem and the Coordination Theorem, the explanatory power of which demonstrates that *the economics of tourism also satisfies Hirst's third criterion.*

Then, if Hirst's first and third criteria are satisfied, it can be argued that tourism economics is a species discipline in the area of economics, its genus discipline. We can therefore put aside the hypothesis of tourism economics as simply being a field of study of applied economics.

A further confirmation of this statement is the following. In fact, since there must be a common method for genus and species disciplines, it is necessary to verify that the two theorems of Sections 1.4.3.3 and 1.4.3.4 can also be applied to economics in general. This can easily be verified, since the Love for variety theorem is an extension of the love for variety economic model (Dixit and Stiglitz 1977), and the Coordination theorem is an extension of the economic model of the anticommon (Michelman 1982; Heller 1998, 1999).

To finish, by paraphrasing Papatheodorou (2003a), we feel able to affirm that *tourism economics is an established discipline in applied economics.*

This conclusion obviously regards the economics of tourism.[4] However, the same question should be posed for the other genus disciplines studying tourism.

[4] This sharing of belonging and of disciplinary autonomy confers a reciprocal enrichment between economics and tourism economics, since the "richness" of the tourism phenomenon introduces into applied economics many non-traditional research themes, alongside with the traditional topics of microeconomics and macroeconomics. Therefore, if economics supplies tourism economics with the method and the analytical toolbox, the latter returns a stimulus to research inferred from

Since some answers might be positive and others negative, this diversity may itself contain a selection criterion: those that are found to be species disciplines are the core business of tourism studies, while those that are found to be fields of study only are ancillary studies of tourism. In this way, research into tourism must be interpreted as the logical union of different species disciplines. This conclusion allow us to reinterpret Tribe's statement which we started from: *tourism studies are a discipline, neither of the species nor of the genus type, but a convergence discipline of species disciplines belonging to different genus disciplines.*

This need of convergence means that not only economics, as stated by Stabler et al. (2010), but every discipline related to tourism studies:

> Needs to engage more with other disciplines to show its relevance and part of this must be to acknowledge and to contribute to the debate on inter- and trans-disciplinarity.
> (Stabler et al. 2010, p. 437)

1.4.4 The Central Role of Tourism Destinations

The evolution of tourism research has established the destination as a central concept within tourism economics and, in recent years, several articles have been focusing on various aspects of the destination. Nowadays, research on destinations is one of the "hot issues" in tourism studies. Although a rough indicator, the number of entries in Google Scholar allows to provide some anecdotal evidence on this point: in this search engine "tourism destination(s)" have 36,000 entries (on 16th of January, 2012) while, on the same day, "tourism firm(s)" have 2,600 entries, "tourism demand" 10,600, and "tourism market(s)" 25,500. More precise searches in specific databases might clearly lead to slightly different results, but the suggested bottom line is that research in tourism studies pivots around the organization, the management, the development, the sustainability, and, we claim, the economics of tourism destinations.

From the researcher's perspective, the destination embodies in one single concept all the specific and problematic features of tourism, such as its systemic nature, in which "space" plays a fundamental role (Leiper 1990). It is indeed in the destination that tourism supply meets tourism demand; it is in the destination that environmental and cultural resources, attractions, the hospitality industry, etc. are located; it is in the destination that tourism demand reveals itself. Therefore, the destination is the *trait d'union* between the complexity of the sector, the complementarity of the many goods and services which constitute the tourism product, and the intangibility stemming from the supply of the territory.

To study the destination from the economics perspective, we need to recall that neither micro nor macroeconomics help us understand its specific features, which

observation, so contributing to the innovation and richness of its themes: this relationship between abstraction and reality has often proved to be prolific for economics.

are somehow discussed by other approaches, such as geography, management, marketing, and organization (however, since such literature belongs to other disciplines, the economic content is often negligible). Thus, we argue that the intersection between destinations and economics is not an empty set and that something such as the economics of destinations does exist. The demonstration, which has been sketched in this section and unfolded throughout the book, is based upon the following rationale:

(a) There are some particular economic features in the tourism sector that call for a novel and independent analysis.
(b) Those economic features appear at the destination level.
(c) It is the existence of such "economics of destinations" that allows tourism economics to be defined as an independent discipline within applied economics and to elect the destination as the reference point of the tourism research, thus facilitating the convergence of genus disciplines belonging to different species disciplines.

To conclude, the strong overlapping between the economics of destinations and the economics of tourism is the main reason why we decided to entitle this book: *The Economics of Tourism Destinations*.

Part I
Introduction to the Economics of Tourism

Chapter 2
Definitions and Key Concepts

Learning Outcomes
On the completion of this chapter you will:

- Understand the key terms used in the study of the tourism sector.
- Identify the definitions officially adopted by national and international organizations.
- Understand the indicators used to measure tourism flows.
- Reflect on the role of the economics of tourism with respect to other disciplines in studying the tourism phenomenon.

2.1 Introduction

Tourism is a highly complex phenomenon and can be fully understood only by adopting a multidisciplinary approach (Chap. 1). In fact, the tourism activity has been studied by many disciplines, being economics, geography, sociology, management and history the most productive; however, this book will focus only on the analysis of the economic aspects surrounding the tourism activity. Hence, our approach should contribute to the deep understanding of tourism as an economic phenomenon, by leaving to other disciplines the task of providing a more complete picture of how tourism works.

The main goal of this chapter is to present the key terminology and indicators of tourism, their interpretation in the context of economics, with the aim of reducing, if not eliminating, any degree of ambiguity in the use of such terms. Accordingly, this book will use the standard toolbox and methodology of economics given that the Economics of Tourism can be understood as an applied

G. Candela and P. Figini, *The Economics of Tourism Destinations*,
Springer Texts in Business and Economics, DOI 10.1007/978-3-642-20874-4_2,

discipline positioned within the broad borders of the economic science (Candela and Figini 2009, see also Sect. 1.4).

The economic relevance of tourism is remarkable, the UNWTO—the United Nations World Tourism Organization (2010) estimates that tourism is roughly 9 % of the global Gross Domestic Product (GDP) and 8 % of world employment. Nevertheless, measuring the economic contribution of tourism in a national economy is not an easy task. There are statistical issues which need to be discussed, particularly related to the definition and the classification of concepts linked to both the demand and the supply side of tourism.

As a demand side example, we can consider a tourist who purchases food or meals in the destination. The purchasing activity per se is not specific of tourism, as this consumption would have also happened in the place where the tourist lives. However, it is possible that the *tourist–consumer* could modify the composition and the value of the purchase since different types of goods and different prices are available at the destination.[1] Hence, some questions arise: should we consider such variations of consumption within the study of the Economics of Tourism? And if so, how do we quantify and aggregate the data?

From the supply side, there are companies which are particularly relevant for the tourism activity although their target is not limited to the tourism sector, for example, railways companies or shopping businesses. Should we also study those companies when analyzing the tourism supply? Is it possible to unequivocally identify a comprehensive *tourism industry*?

These are only some of the key challenges for the Economics of Tourism, which will be investigated in detail in this book. To start with some definitions and key concepts, this chapter is organized as follows. In Sect. 2.2, we will provide a definition for our object, the Economics of Tourism, while the methodology of study will be discussed in Sect. 2.3. The concepts of *tourism* and *tourist* will be defined in Sect. 2.4, while Sect. 2.5 will provide a discussion on the key features of *tourism output (tourism product)*. In Sect. 2.6, we will describe the main indicators for the measurement of the tourism activity.

2.2 The Economics of Tourism

The Economics of Tourism investigates all the economic aspects derived from the activity of a tourist. In our context, the adopted approach is based on the idea of a standard type of tourist (*representative tourist*) defined as an *individual who, for*

[1] For example, tourists are more inclined to eat *fajitas* when they travel to Mexico rather than in their home country. Similarly, the personal consumption of wine increases on average when tourists locate themselves in France or in Italy.

leisure or other purposes, temporarily leaves the place of residence for being hosted in a destination, activating successive economic effects that are worth investigating.

The tourism phenomenon starts in the tourist's place of residence, at the moment when the planning of the trip and of the spending happens. Then, it becomes real with the trip toward the destination, where the tourist expects accommodation, entertainment, amenities, and *loisir*.

The French term *loisir* (leisure), which we often use to indicate a bundle of free time and recreational activities (Dewailly and Flament 1995), is appropriate to summarize the tourist's activity. Let us consider the example of a person who loves country lifestyle and, during her free time, helps a farmer in the vineyard: the same activity is working time for the farmer while it is *loisir* time for his guest. Hence, the difference between working time and leisure time is central and directly points to the economic theory of individual labor supply (see Sect. 6.2).

Once the destination is reached, the tourist may stay for a short or for a long period of time, and enjoys the tourism activities (accommodation, attractions, entertainment, etc.) that justified the choice of the destination. In this destination, the tourist will demand goods and services, spending part of her income. Once the tourism trip is over, the tourist will return to the place of residence.

Although such description of the tourism phenomenon is still incomplete and imprecise (see Sect. 2.4), it permits to identify and follow the *traces* left behind by the tourist during the trip, thus spotting a series of economic issues which are the object of study for the Economics of Tourism. These can be defined as: (a) the economic analysis of the tourism space; (b) the economic problems derived from investment in private infrastructures which compound the tourism supply in the destination (hotels, attractions, etc.), as well as public infrastructures (highways, airports, hospitals, etc.); (c) the organization of tourism markets (carriers, tour operators, travel agencies, etc.); (d) the analysis of tourism demand and tourism expenditure; (e) the multiplier effect of tourism expenditure on aggregate (regional or national) employment and income; (f) the effects on the international economy in terms of currency markets and balance of payments.

In today's world, such a description of the representative tourist, which reminds us of *Goethe*'s *Italian Journey*, no longer corresponds to the tourism phenomenon that we observe in a post-modern economy (Battilani 2001). The increase of percapita income, the increase of leisure time due to the reduction of the working hours, the evolution of the welfare state, a greater individual mobility, the transport revolution of low-cost airlines, the economic globalization, the spreading of competition and the usage of the Internet, and the heterogeneity and the plurality of the tourism experience are all factors that make more challenging the qualitative and quantitative identification of tourism.

The simple model of *departure–trip–stay* explained before for a traditional tourist is then no longer valid for the investigation of tourism in the current context.

Among the many reasons why such simple model does not reflect the complexity of the tourism activity we can highlight that:

- Nowadays, tourism does not necessarily imply staying overnight, otherwise certain small tourism destinations such as Republic of San Marino or Andorra would be underestimated. Additionally, today's free time constraints and changing tastes are some of the factors that explain the change in holiday patterns, that is, on average the tourist takes more holidays throughout the year but each one of a shorter length of stay. These changes have direct and indirect economic consequences for tourists, businesses, and destinations.
- Traveling does not necessarily imply tourism. We can find many examples of individuals traveling for non-tourism purposes (e.g., diplomatic envoys or military personnel). This issue will be discussed in detail in the definition of tourist (see Sect. 2.4.1). On the contrary, some researchers argue that tourism does not necessarily imply traveling, since one could be a tourist in the place where he lives. According to Raffestin (1986):

  > I do not mean simply strolling around, but that a person could apply on his territory a different pattern of observation; in this sense there would not be a geographical but a sociological movement, a modification in the level of perception by the tourist: the trip is not only horizontal and real, but also vertical and abstract.
  >
  > (Raffestin 1986, p. 1. *Our translation*)

  We are so used to think that taking a trip is such a necessary component of tourism that Raffestin's rationale may sound paradoxical and consequently it is necessary to give further arguments to support it either from: (a) a psychological/motivational point of view (for instance, there might be a psychological disposition to tourism—although the trip does not take place—when a person buys a guidebook or watches a documentary to know something about a certain destination), or from: (b) an economic perspective (for example, for an Italian wine producer there is not any significant difference between a bottle of his wine purchased by a German person in Berlin in an Italian restaurant or by the same person as a tourist during a holiday in Italy). To summarize, nowadays the trip needs to be interpreted in a broader sense, not only as a movement from the tourist's region of origin but also as a sociological and psychological "movement" as well, with several consequences in terms of spending analysis. However, in contrast to the above debate on the "philosophical" distinction between tourism and trip, for our purposes the trip is still the key element of the tourism phenomenon. Therefore, the statistical definition of tourism treats the tourist's physical movement in the space as the necessary feature of tourism (see Sect. 2.4.1).
- Finally, due to the increase and diversification of tourism destinations, it is no longer possible to apply an ex ante identification of tourism territories. Specifically, the tourism space is no longer defined just as a place of natural, artistic, cultural, and historical attraction but, more generally, as a "supply of territory".

As an example, the location of some of the most important historical events may become tourism destinations when tourists start visiting them.

> The data suggest that war stimulates promotional, emotional, military and political tourism, and that war-related tourism attractions are the largest single category known.
>
> (Smith 1998, p. 202)

The former location of the Twin Towers of New York becomes an important place to be visited by tourists in Manhattan; similarly, a forgotten location on the countryside can be seen as appealing and transformed in a tourism destination for farmhouse holidays. In other words, when the potential demand is transformed in effective demand any territory can become a tourism destination. Hence, in a world with high mobility, the tourism destinations are more and more difficult to identify or delimit. An example is the success of *artificial landscapes* such as water parks, amusement parks or, more in general, theme parks.

The Economics of Tourism establishes its historical roots in the Economics of Outdoor Recreation (EOR), which mainly deals with holidays and short trips to public gardens and natural parks (Clawson and Knetsch 1969; McConnell 1985, and cited references; see Sinclair and Stabler 1997, pg. 1–14, for an analysis of the historical evolution of tourism; see Moore et al. 1995, for a discussion on the relationship between tourism and leisure). Although these recreational trips do not constitute the key objects of study for modern Economics of Tourism, this field borrows from the EOR one of its key models for an introductory identification of the founding moments of the tourism experience. They are the following five:

1. The *anticipation* phase comprises the decision and planning of the recreational activity. If this phase leads to the act of purchasing, the recreational experience begins.
2. The *outward journey* is the physical movement to the place of destination. The duration of the trip can vary, the EOR distinguishes three categories of journey: (a) *user-oriented* places that are easily accessible such as gardens, playgrounds, etc.; (b) *resource-based* places that require longer trips, such as mountains, national parks, etc.; (c) *intermediate* places which are outdoor tourism destinations that can be reached for a day or a weekend. To be precise, according to the EOR the trip should be seen not only as a disutility, linked to a sacrifice of time needed to reach the destination but also as a key element of the tourism activity, characterized by its own intrinsic utility.
3. The *experience* phase, which consists of the direct fruition of the recreational activities located in the destination. This applies to typical outdoor activities such as hunting, fishing, camping, swimming, or picnicking. The experience phase also includes the minitrips to close-by sites and visits to friends and relatives living nearby.
4. The *return journey* (the inverse phase of the outward journey) is the movement from the destination to the region of origin. The itinerary of the return journey does not necessarily coincide with the outward journey, depending on whether or not a different itinerary from destination to origin (that does not involve the exact same sites and towns that have been already visited during the outward journey) exists. Finally, it is important to stress that the traveller's psychological

attitude during the return journey, which usually precedes returning to the ordinary routine, is usually quite different from the attitude during the outward journey.
5. The *memory* is the phase to recall the tourism experience, this happens when the recreational activity is totally over.

It is relevant to highlight that the five stages of the EOR notably coincide with the phases identified in the departure–trip–stay model that we explained earlier as the standard model for the Economics of Tourism. Also notice that in the EOR model the phases of anticipation and memory are fundamental also from an economic point of view. In the anticipation phase, the tourist spends time and resources deciding when, how, and where to go on holiday. In the memory phase the tourist shares the experience with other people, e.g., friends and relatives, thus possibly affecting future recreational activities. For the Economics of Tourism, *cultivating* and *sharing* the memory of a trip are central moments of the holiday since they may influence future repetitions or decisions of a new trip. Interestingly, there may also be more direct economic effects linked to the memory phase, such as the cost of printing the photos of the holiday. By explicitly exploring the economic aspects of the memory phase (for example, the importance of *word-of-mouth*, in Sect. 10.6.3) we will introduce new topics within the Economics of Tourism.

2.3 The Use of Models in the Economics of Tourism

A scientific theory provides answers to open questions and addresses the complexity of the phenomena under scrutiny by proposing models, that are interpretative patterns of the real-world complexity. To that respect, the Economics of Tourism is

Notes 2.1. The Scientific Method and the Use of Models in Economics
Scientists seek to fully understand life phenomena, and thus their investigation cannot be limited to the mere description of such phenomena but should answer to all the *why* questions regarding their happenings. The scientific method can be seen as an itinerary that provides an interpretation (that can be defined as correct) of the real world. Without entering into the epistemological debate, we present here the main steps of the scientific method in a schematic manner. The scientific method begins with (a) the initial observation of a phenomenon, follows with (b) the inductive step to establish the assumptions and hypotheses related to the phenomenon, and (c) the deductive process that allows to move from the initial hypothesis to the propositions in a logical and coherent manner, finalizing with (d) the empirical verification which permits accepting or rejecting the hypotheses employed.

This rationale used by scientists in examining phenomena is the adopted methodology by the natural and social sciences, and therefore, it is also used in Economics. In particular, Economics applies the scientific method through the use of models, which are abstract representations of reality that economists use for explaining past economic events as well as predicting future ones. In this sense, a model must be judged on the basis of internal, logical coherence, and the ability to explain economic facts, and not on its strict adherence to reality. In fact, there exists already a perfect model of the reality, which is the reality itself! But reality is so complex and full of background noise that needs to be simplified by extracting only the important concepts which are considered useful to explain a certain phenomenon. This is done with a process of abstraction that is made possible through the use of models.

not different from other social sciences and, indeed, adopts the same scientific method (Notes 2.1, see also Tribe 2011).

There are various ways of defining a model, and each discipline that studies tourism tends to adopt different approaches. In the context of Economics of Tourism, the approach followed consists of moving from the first intuitions of the tourism phenomenon—explained in the previous section, to more rigorous content. One of the simplest and most popular models used in tourism is Leiper model (1990) which defines tourism as a *system* composed by three key dimensions:

- The *tourist*. The tourist is the main element of the system and therefore its definition and classification should be provided first.
- The *space*. In Leiper model, the tourism space is divided into three geographical regions: (a) a *traveller generating region*, which is the market generating the tourism activity and where the stimulus which motivates the trip begins; (b) a *destination region* in which most of the economic impact of the tourism activity takes place; (c) the *transit routes*, generally intended as the journey through space and time that is needed to reach the destination, and technically includes all the sites that can be visited along the way.
- The *travel and tourism industry*. The travel and tourism industry can be seen as a system of entrepreneurial and organizational activities that are involved in the production of tourism services. This industry includes, for example, accommodation, transport, the firms and organizations supplying amusement and entertainment services, and products to tourists.

Leiper model presents a framework which enables the definition of tourism as a system (Fig. 2.1); this perspective allows us to understand the overall process leading to tourism from both the demand and the supply side and in which the three key elements interact with each other. Among the several advantages of adopting Leiper's model, we can remark that the model is rigorous and flexible at the same

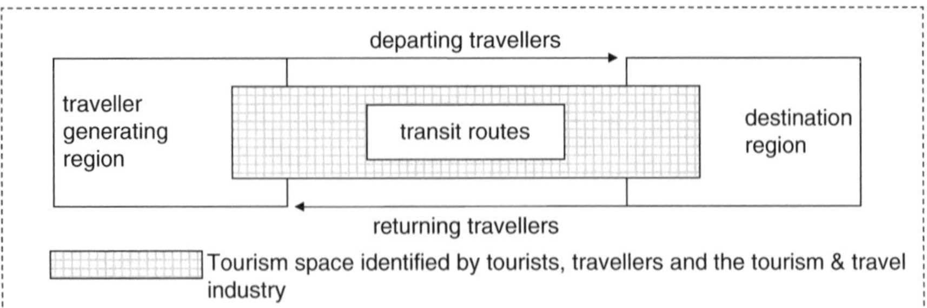

Fig. 2.1 Tourism as a system: the Leiper model

time, thus allowing us to identify, on the one hand, different types of tourism activities (e.g., from mature types of tourism, like cultural tourism, to emerging ones, like environmental tourism) and, on the other hand, any scale of travel (from day trips to intercontinental ones). Hence, this approach is helpful to understand how many elements and organizations are involved in the process of creating the tourism experience and that its structural components belong to a unique *system* where they interact with each other.

The description of tourism as a system has proved quite influential and has been further developed by the specific literature;[2] following (McIntosh et al. 1995) tourism can be defined as a *complex system* in which four key elements interact: (1) the tourist, who generates the demand for tourism experiences; (2) the businesses, which produce the demanded goods and services; (3) the political and administrative system, which affects the organization and development of tourism supply and demand in the destination; (4) the host community, including the part not directly involved in the tourism activity.

Although in this basic model everything in the system is interdependent, each of these components has to be studied in an isolated manner to gain deep understanding on the characteristics of tourism, and this book, only focusing on the economic dimensions of tourism, is not an exception. While we deal with the analysis of the main characteristics of tourism demand and tourism supply in the next chapters, the rest of the second chapter is devoted to the detailed definition of tourism and tourist, and their measurement.

[2] Leiper model has been widely used, for example, in cultural tourism (Richards 2002) or in sport tourism (Hinch and Higham 2001). For an overview, see Hall and Page, 2006. It is also recommended to keep in mind that, in addition to Leiper model, the complexity of the tourism phenomenon has also been studied from the perspectives of both the Chaos Theory and the Theory of Structural Instability (see McKercher 1999; Russell and Faulkner 1997, 1999, 2004; Faulkner 2001; Blake et al. 2003; Ritchie 2004).

2.4 Tourism and the Tourist

As a result of the difficulties exposed in the previous section, to define tourism and the tourist is certainly not an easy task. Notwithstanding, it is an essential task to accomplish from both theoretical and practical perspectives, given that the measurement of the economic effects of tourism closely depends on the chosen definition. Indeed, the problem of defining the tourist is interconnected to the problem of measuring the tourism sector itself (see Sect. 2.6).

2.4.1 *Some Definitions of Tourism and Tourist*

As definitions may vary according to whether we focus on psychological, sociological or economic aspects of tourism, it is worth pointing out that our main objective here is to identify the definition that allows measuring the extent of tourism flows in the most precise way as regards the ability to pick out the economic impact of tourism.

The first question to address is very simple: who is the tourist? Although from a general point of view we could use the definition given at the beginning of Sect. 2.2, from a statistical perspective there exist many definitions that have been used by official national statistical offices. This heterogeneity does not simply stem from the confusion of concepts but is also a direct consequence of the objective difficulty of theoretically identifying the tourism phenomenon. The coexistence of different definitions is often a problem faced by international tourism organizations, particularly in the attempt to provide a uniform theoretical content and measurement criterion. The UNWTO (United Nations World Tourism Organization) has a central role in providing the definition, terminology, and criteria related to the measurement of tourism. As a result, a series of recommendations have been adopted by the commission for statistics of the United Nations (UNSTAT) and published under the title "Recommendations on Tourism Statistics" by UNWTO and UNSTAT in 1994. Since 1995, all the data gathered by national statistical offices and then transferred to the UNWTO follow such internationally accepted criteria, and therefore it is possible to undertake cross-country comparisons.[3]

Prior to giving the UNWTO's definition of tourism, let us briefly present a "historical" evolution of the definition of tourist. These definitions appear to be more technical than conceptual since they pay special attention to the typology of tourist and the constituent elements of the tourism activity. The word "tourist" appears for the first time in English at the beginning of the nineteenth century and the first definition, in chronological terms, was given by Herman Von Schullard in 1910:

[3] To learn more about the functions, instruments, and objectives of the UNWTO, read Case Study 15.2, along with Sect. 15.5.2.

> [Tourism is] the total sum of operators, mainly of an economic nature, which directly relate to the entry, stay and movement of foreigners inside and outside a certain country, city or a region.
>
> (Gilbert 1990, p. 8)

In order to ensure that this definition is not too restrictive, the concept of "foreigner" should be understood, broadly speaking, not only as a tourist from another country but more simply as "non-native guest". The successive definition of 1937, given by the League of Nations, is indeed more precise on that issue and specifies that:

> A tourist is the individual that spends a period of time of at least 24 h in a country different than that of residence.

This definition has two key features: on the one hand, by making no reference to the motivation behind the trip, it implicitly considers tourists all individuals who travel for either leisure or business; on the other hand, those people who arrive to a destination with the objective of living there for business, work, or personal reasons are not tourists.

The motivational factor is instead the key component of the definition of "visitor" which was adopted in 1968 by the *International Union of Official Travel Organization* (which became the *World Tourism Organization* and now UNWTO):

> A visitor is defined as the person who travels to a country other than that of residence, for any reason other than paid work.

While in the definition by the League of Nations the emphasis was made in the length of stay, i.e., at least 24 h, this last definition makes an important distinction, since the word "visitor" is used. The visitor is anyone who travels, according to certain motivations. Then, we can technically call "day-tripper" or "same-day visitor" anyone who stays in the destination less than 24 h while it is technically called "tourist" anyone who stays in the destination more than 24 h (in other words, a visitor who stays overnight is a tourist).

The process of defining tourism experienced a decisive and definitive step forward when, with the joint efforts of UNWTO and UNSTAT, the definition of tourism was approved, with universal acceptance, in 1994:

> The activities of persons travelling to and staying in places outside their usual environment for less than a year, for any main purpose (leisure, business or other personal purpose) other than to be employed by a resident entity in the country or place visited.

This definition pivots around three main dimensions on which tourism has to be defined and distinguished from other forms of travel: (1) the *movement*, that is, where does the tourist travel? (2) The *time*, that is, for how long does the tourist travel? (3) The *motivation*, that is, why does the tourist travel?

(a) As regards the movement, the UNWTO defines tourism as the activity of travelling outside the usual environment of an individual: this is intended as the geographical area (though not necessarily a contiguous one) within which the person conducts his/her regular life routines. Hence, tourism does not involve commuters (e.g., students or workers) who regularly travel for their daily activities. We might be tempted to provide a negative rather than a positive definition, that is, by listing what tourism is not: any movement within the region where the person commonly lives, the daily trips due to study, work, health care, family, or shopping; any temporary or permanent change of a person's residence; any temporary or permanent movement aimed at the production of income; any movement of diplomats, military personnel, political refugees, stateless persons, and nomads. The key limitation of relying on the negative definition of tourism is that it does not provide information about the reasons that bring a person to change her routine behaviors in favor of a trip. At the same time, it is important to note that the person who, for example, decides to tour her town of residence definitely undergoes a psychological experience as a tourist (see Sect. 2.2) but without being registered as tourist. This prevents us from effectively analyzing the economic effects of such experience.

(b) As regards time, the maximum length of stay is defined, in contrast to earlier definitions, 1 year; beyond that limit the travel is not considered tourism. Interestingly, the UNWTO defines as visitor any person travelling, independently on whether or not they stay overnight in the destination. Then, *tourists* (or overnight visitors) are defined as the subset of visitors staying overnight, while the *same-day visitors* (or excursionists) do not stay overnight.

(c) As regards the motivation, the purpose of visit could range from leisure to business, from visiting friends and relatives (VFR) to culture and heritage interests, and many others (see Sect. 2.4.2). However, it is essential to understand that the UNWTO definition of tourism does not include purposes of visit related to the exercise of an activity remunerated in the visited place. This restriction correctly prevents us from qualifying migrant workers as tourists, since they travel with the goal of finding (or accepting) a job in the visited destination. On the contrary, any employee of companies not resident in the visited region, as well as self-employed persons staying for a short period of time (less than a year) to provide a service such as the installation of equipment, repair, consultancy, etc. or travellers entering in business negotiation with companies located in the destination, or looking for business opportunities (including buying and selling), or participating in trade fairs are considered (business) tourists.

We can complete the task of defining tourism by recalling some other definitions that alternatively assume a holistic approach and underline, in a more comprehensive way, all phenomena associated to tourism flows. Jafari's definition of 1977 is:

> Tourism is the study of man away from his usual habitat, the industry which responds to his needs, and the impact that both he and the industry have on the socio-cultural, economic, and physical environments.
>
> (Jafari 1977, p. 6)

whereas in 1979 the *British Tourism Society* claimed, on the basis of the definition provided by Burkart and Medlik (1974), that:

> Tourism is deemed to include any activity concerned with the temporary short-term movement of people to destinations outside the places where they normally live and work, and their activities during the stay at these destinations.

The use of a holistic definition has many limitations from a statistical point of view, but helps underline that the investigation of tourism requires an interdisciplinary approach and the participation of numerous researchers from different branches of the social sciences. For example, those aspects related to territorial and spatial features are analyzed by the Geography of Tourism; the historical evolution of tourism is of interest for the History of Tourism; the issues related to the tourism production are a topic of investigation for Management studies; instead, the Psychology and Sociology of Tourism are interested in the individual or social motivations for travelling; the transportation system and urban planning are studied by Engineering; and so on.

Hence, the holistic definition of tourism makes economics only one of the numerous research fields interested in tourism. The corollary of this view is that to correctly understand the tourism phenomenon, the Economics of Tourism should collaborate and be nourished with other disciplines as well. In other words, tourism can be metaphorically seen as a *cross section of a society*, where all the aspects of social life are involved. Lundberg et al. (1995) stress on this idea by stating that:

> Tourism [is] an umbrella concept.
>
> (Lundberg et al. 1995, p. 4)

2.4.2 *The Taxonomy of Tourism*

After providing the definition of tourism, we should now move on to its classification and wonder how many types of tourists and tourism there exist. Among the many classifications, the most important one comes from the UNWTO and UNSTAT conventions and makes reference to the three key dimensions in the definition of tourism: the type of movement, the purpose of visit, and the length of stay.

The first distinction makes reference to the tourist's trip and is simplified by the Table of Mobility (Table 2.1). This can be read by columns according to the tourist's region of origin (the tourist could come from the same country or from abroad) and it can be read by rows according to the tourist's destination (the tourist could travel to the same country or abroad). In this way, we can identify the four basic types of tourism:

1. *Domestic tourism:* activities of a resident visitor within the region of reference.
2. *Inbound tourism:* activities of a non-resident visitor within the region of reference.
3. *Outbound tourism:* activities of a resident visitor travelling to other regions of the world.

Table 2.1 The table of tourism flows

	Origin within the region	Origin outside the region
Destination within the region	1. Domestic tourism	2. Inbound tourism
Destination outside the region	3. Outbound tourism	4. Transit tourism

4. *In transit tourism:* activities of a visitor while passing by or crossing a region which is neither the region of origin nor the region of destination.

In Table 2.1 it is also possible to identify other typologies of tourism, which are often used to distinguish the different types of travellers:

5. *National tourism* is the sum of both domestic and outbound tourism, in other words, it corresponds to tourism activities by residents of the region of reference (sum of the flows 1 and 3).
6. *Internal tourism* is the sum of both domestic and inbound tourism, that is, tourism in a specific region by residents and non-residents (sum of the flows 1 and 2).
7. *International tourism* is the sum of both inbound and outbound tourism, that is, tourism that implies crossing over the borders of a region (sum of the flows 2 and 3).

As one may have noticed, the word *region* has been used in the above classification. This was done deliberately and is intended to be unspecific. In the most common specification, *region* may refer to a country, but the same classification could be used to monitor tourism of a region within a country (a state, province, or a city) or, similarly, the term *region* can also refer to an international level (for example, the European Union).

The second classification deals with the reasons why people decide to travel. What are their motivations or purposes of visit? They can be classified as:

- *Leisure purposes*. This consists of the traveller having free and leisure time at the traveller's own expense. For example, tourists going to the beach, to the mountains, or to the lakes for holidays, or visiting historical sites or art cities. Also, many tourists travel as supporters of a sport team or participant in a sport event, or simply visit family and friends who live far away.
- *Professional reasons*. These are trips where expenses are usually paid for by a company, organization, or institution. Some examples of this are: (a) trips to where a person is participating in a congress or a conference; (b) trips to where a person is meeting or working with clients or suppliers; (c) trips to where a person represents a company, organization, or institution at trade fairs.
- *Other personal reasons*. There are many other reasons for a person to travel: education and training, health and medical care, religious pilgrimages, and shopping.

The third classification distinguishes the types of visitor according to the length of stay:

1. *Excursionists* (or *same-day visitors*, or *day-trippers*): visitors who stay in the destination less than 24 h, thus not staying overnight.

2. *Tourists*: visitors who travel for more than 24 h. These types of trip imply that the visitors stay overnight in the destination, at least for one night.

A widely accepted convention also allows us to distinguish between: (a) holidays (this involves staying at least four consecutive nights in a different region from where the tourist lives); (b) short-term holidays (this involves spending one to three nights in a different region from where the tourist lives).

There exist other methods to classify tourists according to different characteristics (for further details refer to Smith 1988; Cooper et al. 2008; Wall and Mathieson 2006). Of particular interest are the classifications of tourists according to:

- *Socioeconomic variables*: age, gender, level of education, employment status, work status (full-time versus part-time), type of activity (including students and retired), the composition of the travel party (going alone, with friends, with family), the organization of the trip (with a tour operator, individually organized).
- *Characteristics of the trip*: the time of the year when the trip takes place, how far the destination is, the transportation means used.
- *Type of spending*: the different categories of expenditure associated with tourism (the cost of transportation, the cost of accommodation, the purchase of food and dining out, tickets or entrance fees, buying souvenirs, etc.).
- *Type of accommodation:* hotels, motels, hostels, campsites, bed and breakfast, rented apartments, or staying with friends or relatives.

Note that the details of these classifications should be clearly defined in order to be able to correctly gather data or for measuring purposes.

Finally, it is important to acknowledge the differences between international and domestic visitors especially in terms of classification. In the following subsection, a discussion of the main particularities of the international visitor and the domestic visitor from an economic perspective is given.

2.4.2.1 The International Tourist

As already outlined, we call *international tourist* any person who travels to a foreign country and stays a minimum of 24 h (or at least one night) and a maximum of 1 year. Consequently, we identify as distinctive features of the international tourism crossing an international border and fulfilling a minimum and maximum length of stay. With respect to the purpose of visit, it is possible to distinguish between leisure, business, health or visiting friends and family whereas the border-crossing trips motivated by paid jobs, study (such as attending college or university), or migration are not included in international tourism.

In 1963, the concept of *international visitor*, which comprises both the tourist and the day-tripper (excursionist) was introduced. In 1981 the statistical classification was completed by adding the definition of *international travellers* to the one of international visitors. International travellers include, as non-visitors,

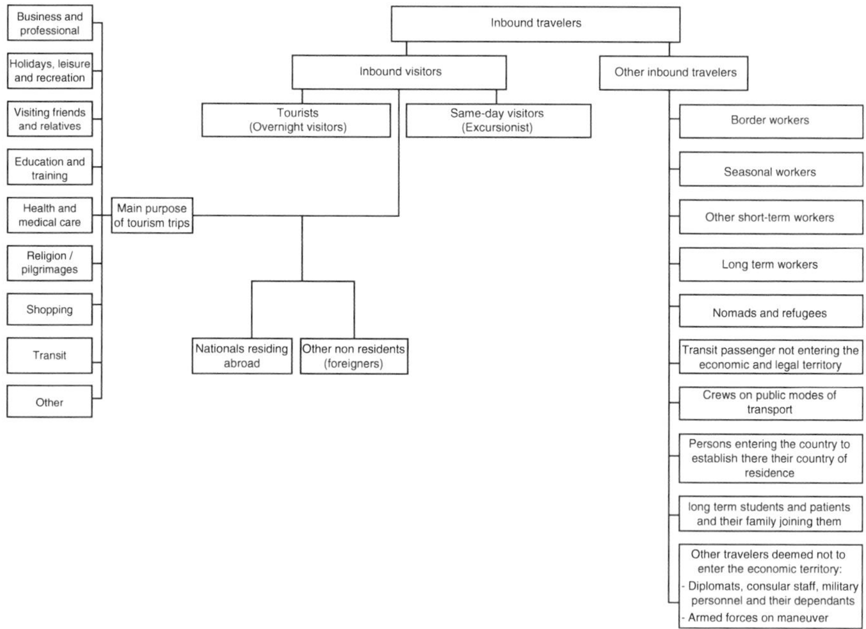

Fig. 2.2 Classification of international travellers. Source: UNWTO (2007), p. 18

international migrants (people who enter a country and stay for more than 1 year), and those who fit into any of the following groups: (a) people, along with their families, who are looking for a job in another country; (b) diplomats, members of the army, their subordinates, and their families; (c) refugees; (d) nomadic peoples; (e) people who live in one country but work in another; (f) travellers who transit in the country.

In contrast, the following groups are considered international visitors by convention: (a) the crew of ships and aircrafts; (b) business or trade travellers including technicians, but only if they lodge in the destination country for less than a year; (c) employees of international organizations such as FAO, UN, etc.; (d) people who live abroad and return to their country of origin temporarily.

The last official convention, signed in 1994, finally considered as international visitors the sum of: (a) *international tourists*, those who spend at least 24 h (or stay overnight at least for one night for the above described purposes) and less than 1 year in the country of destination; (b) *international day-trippers*, those who spend less than 24 h in the country of destination.

International day-trippers consider those *same-day* visitors who arrive and leave the country of destination on the same day; *cruise ship passengers*, but only if they stay on board overnight (otherwise they would be put in the same groups as international tourists); *crew members* (including military crew members on warships) as long as they stay on board overnight.

Figure 2.2 shows all these criteria jointly with the purposes of visit. Additionally, it also takes into account those groups of travellers who are not included in the official tourism statistics, by showing in a clear way how the tourism phenomenon is classified.

2.4.2.2 The Domestic Tourist

The study of domestic tourism had not been of particular interest until the second half of 1970s, in contrast to the attention paid to international visitors. Unlike its international counterpart, domestic tourism rarely involves language barriers, exchanging currency, or applying for a visa and, consequently, domestic tourism is far more difficult to identify and measure than international tourism. Until 1991, based on the 1981 and 1983 indications by the UNWTO, it was common procedure to apply the recommendations adopted for the international visitor to the domestic visitor as well. However, the UNWTO in 1991 indicated specific criteria and recommendations to classify and measure domestic visitors.

According to these criteria, we call *domestic visitor* a person who resides in a given country, regardless of nationality, who travels to a location within the same country (but different from the place of residence) for no longer than 6 months, for any motivation except for the case of paid job in the visited location.

Similarly to the classification of international visitors unfolded in the previous sub-section, here domestic visitors comprise: (a) *domestic tourists,* who spend at least 24 h (or at least one night), but less than 6 months in the destination; (b) *domestic excursionists (domestic day-tripper)* who spend less than 24 h in the destination.

Having outlined so far the many existing caveats in the issue of tourism definition and measurement, we can now move on to the definition of the tourism product.

2.5 The Heterogeneity and Plurality of the Tourism Product

The tourist's activity, from an economic perspective, is expressed by the demand of goods and services in the region of destination. It is precisely in the destination that the great part of the tourism activity takes place and where the economic issues of production, employment, localization, quality, etc., arise.[4]

But, how can we define the output of the tourism sector? What do tourism enterprises produce? And what are the main characteristics of the tourism product? Since the 1970s there has been an ongoing debate on how to define the tourism product which, arguably, is not as easy as to define "cars" the output of the automotive industry (on the definition of the tourism sector, see Sect. 3.2). Whereas some authors argue that the tourism output refers to the concept of (only) a service, an intangible service

[4] However, it is worth underlining that a portion of the tourist spending might take place in the region of departure before the trip.

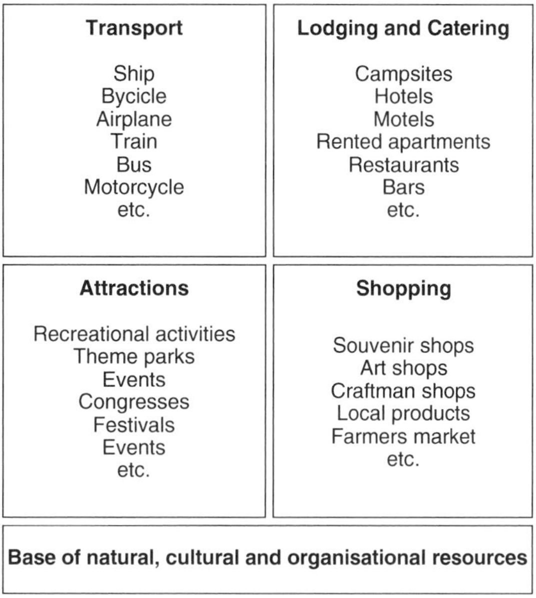

Fig. 2.3 The tourism product as a basket of goods

which the tourist enjoys while in holidays, supplied by system of enterprises and identified as tourism product (Wahab 1975), others perceive tourism output as a complex mixture of goods and services (Gilbert 1990).

In the Economics of Tourism the second perception is prevalent and, in fact, tourism product is defined as a *bundle of goods and services*:

> Tourism spending is constituted by a plurality of heterogeneous goods and services which are purchased during or for the holidays: transport, lodging, catering, support services for example in beach or skipass, leisure and entertainment and, finally, other goods purchased in the destination (shopping).
>
> (Gardini 1986, p. 5, *Our translation*)

In this textbook we define the tourism product (or tourism output) as a *basket of different goods and services demanded by the visitor during the tourism experience*. A basket which contains, in technical sense, products with the same aim, the holiday.

Figure 2.3 clearly shows this idea of basket of different products, which can be classified in to four main groups:

1. *Transport,* in any form (by road, by sea, by air);
2. *Lodging and catering*, ranging from fancy restaurants and five-star hotels to simple kiosks on the beach;
3. *Attractions,* it is in this area where a massive diversification of tourism services is present, according to the consumers' preferences, to the supply or to the innovation of products;
4. *Shopping*, which involves retailers, artisans, artists, etc.

Table 2.2 Heterogeneity and plurality in the tourism product

Type of tourist	Accommodation in hotel	Accommodation in a rented apartment	Local restaurant	Seafood restaurant	Beach services	Night club
Ulysses	1	0	0	2	1	1
Columbus	0	1	1	1	2	0

In addition, as observed in Fig. 2.3, the tourism product is always based on both natural and cultural resources which constitute the *territory*: nature, the landscape, beaches, mountains, historical monuments, the heritage, art cities, and local villages are the primary inputs of the tourism product (Briassoulis and van der Streaten 1992).

The tourism product can be described and examined according to two criteria: *heterogeneity* and *plurality*. We name by heterogeneity the list of different goods and services which compound the tourism product, and by plurality we name the diversity of the list among tourists, which ultimately defines the different types of tourism.

Let us introduce an example where Ulysses and Columbus are two people who enjoy travelling and thus both decide to spend one day on the beach, but their choices are different. To start with, only Ulysses stays in a hotel, while Columbus has rented an apartment. In addition, Ulysses has seafood both for lunch and dinner while Columbus wants to taste all local food specialties. Finally, Columbus spends the whole day on the beach while Ulysses lies on the beach only in the afternoon since he plans to spend the evening at the night club.

Ulysses' and Columbus' short holiday can be formally described in Table 2.2, which shows both the heterogeneity of goods and services included in the tourism product and summarizes the key differences between their types of holiday. In the table, the quantity of the different goods and services purchased in 1 day by each type of tourist are reported.

This representation of the tourism product can be easily generalized. The tourism product is always compounded by a list of heterogeneous products given that, on the one hand, there is not one single industry producing all the products purchased by tourists and, on the other hand, any branch of the economic activity does not produce goods and services only for tourists. Even hotels, which are often identified with the tourism sector, represent only one part of the tourists' spending and, although marginally, they can offer their services also to clients other than tourists.

Furthermore, there are so many types of tourism (business, religious, sport, mountain, cultural and heritage, sea and sand, spa, etc.) that such plurality could authorize the use of the word *tourisms*.

If we return to Fig. 2.3 it is possible to underline the fact that tourism output always makes a reference to a territory. In other words, any good or service must be referred to the consumption region which, following Leiper model (see Fig. 2.1), can be classified as *transit region* (goods and services consumed while the tourist is travelling to the destination) or *destination region* (goods and services consumed in the destination). Therefore, tourism output should be interpreted as a *sorted* list, a *basket of goods and services that are referred to different types of tourism and to different regions*. A formalization of this definition follows.

Given a generic good or service represented by x_{ij}, where $j = 1, 2, 3, \ldots, n$, is the j-th good or service and $i = 1, 2, 3, \ldots, m$, is the i-th type of tourism, the tourism output in destination r is defined as a set of goods and services x_{ij} which take a positive value if j is chosen by the i-th tourism and takes zero if j does not belong to the basket of the i-th tourism.

$$\left[x_{ij} \geqslant 0, j = 1, 2, 3, n | i; r\right]$$

For any given destination, the heterogeneity of products and the plurality of types of tourism are the two dimensions that justify the use of a matrix to identify the tourism output. In the matrix:

1. The unit of measure of the goods and services is the tourism day (henceforth referred as overnight stay).
2. The heterogeneity of the product appears in the columns. The j-th column is denoted with the vector $\mathbf{X}_j$, where $j = 1, 2, 3, \ldots, n$, being n a finite number.
3. The plurality of types of tourism appears in the rows. The i-th row is denoted with the vector $\mathbf{T}_i$, where $i = 1, 2, 3, \ldots, m$, being m a finite number. It is worth noticing that within this matrix notation, all visitors (tourists and day-trippers) are included: for day-trippers, the value of the accommodation services will take the value of zero.

Hence, the matrix of the tourism output $\mathbf{\Pi}$ can be represented as:

$$\mathbf{\Pi} = \left[x_{ij}\right] \text{with } i = 1, 2, ..., m \text{ and } j = 1, 2, ..., n \tag{2.1}$$

or, in extended form, as:

–	$\mathbf{X}_1$	$\mathbf{X}_2$	...	$\mathbf{X}_n$
$\mathbf{T}_1$	x_{11}	x_{12}	...	x_{1n}
$\mathbf{T}_2$	x_{21}	x_{22}	...	x_{2n}
...	...	...	...	...
$\mathbf{T}_m$	x_{m1}	x_{m2}	...	x_{mn}

where x_{ij} indicates the quantity of good or service j in the basket for tourism i on a tourism day. In this matrix, we find $x_{ij} = 0$ when the product j is not demanded by tourism i, and $x_{ij} > 0$ when the product j is included in the type of tourism i. For example, any museum service can be null in the case of trekking and hiking tourism, but positive in the case of cultural tourism. In the case of day-trippers, the row corresponding to this type of tourism would present zeros in those columns related to lodging, given that such type of tourism does not imply any overnight stay in the destination.

We must point out that the values taken by x_{ij} can be either integers or fractions considering that each coefficient has 1 day as reference unit. If we take the example of a cultural holiday consisting of a 4-day visit, this implies staying four nights in the region of destination, eight meals, the visit to two museums, and five guided excursions to monuments, the corresponding daily values will be: one stay at the hotel per day, two meals per day, half visit to museums per day, and 5/4 guided excursions to monuments per day. Therefore, the values to be introduced in the matrix in the row corresponding to that type of cultural tourism will be: 1 stay at a hotel, 2 meals, 0.5 museum services, and 5/4 excursions.

Tourism typologies change over time and consequently, matrix $\mathbf{\Pi}$ should indicate a reference date. In other words, the *matrix of tourism output has a historical dimension*. Therefore, we will include new rows for new types of tourism and we will eliminate rows for obsolete ones. Likewise, the diversification or change in tourism habits will be reflected in the corresponding row either adding or deleting goods and services or modifying the coefficients.

It is important to note that matrix $\mathbf{\Pi}$ strictly refers to the goods and services that constitute the tourism product and, therefore, those elements that are not part of the tourism experience are not included. Despite occasional (for instance, clothing souvenir) or important purchases (for example, handicraft) happen during the tourism trip, they do not strictly constitute characteristic elements of the tourism product and hence they do not appear in $\mathbf{\Pi}$. Although this expenditure is taken into account as an activity of the *tourist as an ordinary consumer* and appears in Fig. 2.3 in the tourism basket, thus entering into the statistics of tourism expenditure (see Sect. 2.6.3) it is conceptually important to distinguish and separate those goods and services that are characteristic elements of the tourism product (accommodation, attractions, transport), thus appearing into $\mathbf{\Pi}$, from the ordinary acts of consumption of the tourist as a consumer. To clarify, in the case of a tourist who eventually decides to purchase a book on the history of the visited destination, this purchase is not part of the tourism product of "cultural tourism" but it is an option of the tourist as a consumer. This will be further developed in Chap. 5, where the difference between the *tourist–consumer* and the *consumer–tourist* will be described in detail.

2.6 The Measurement of Tourism

We have reviewed the challenges in the definition and classification of the tourism phenomenon stemming from the diverse concepts of tourism and tourists (see Sect. 2.4) and now we turn our interest into a new task. Since tourism is fundamentally characterized by the mobility of tourists throughout the territory, either in transit or within the destination, this adds more issues in the statistical measurement of tourism, since measuring something in movement is certainly a more challenging activity.

2.6.1 On the Tracks of the Tourist

In order to measure the tourism phenomenon, it is essential to understand where the tourist "makes tracks" and to identify those moments and places when and where the tourist should be checked in order to have a complete picture of the tourism flows. For that purpose, it is important to determine which activities are strictly referring to the tourist behavior.

The common techniques to gather statistical data of the tourism phenomenon consist of market research carried out through: (a) tourism enterprise surveys; (b) accommodation surveys; (c) household surveys; and (d) frontier surveys. Each of these is, individually, insufficient to provide a complete picture of the tourism phenomenon and hence the measurement of tourism flows and expenditure should consider a mix of all of the previous surveys.

As regards international tourism, the elementary source of data to survey inbound tourism comes from the act of crossing borders (providing the number of foreign incoming tourists) and the act of demanding local currency which is recorded by financial institutions (providing foreign tourists' spending). Likewise, this method permits surveying outbound tourism. By following these tourists' tracks, it is possible to obtain a sufficiently precise estimate of the international tourism flows. The gathering of statistical techniques have to be adapted to different situations, for example, the type of borders. It is easier to obtain figures of tourists travelling by air or by sea than by road. In fact, in the latter case, tourism flows are often estimated by the data collected at hotels and other accommodation establishments.

In general, the tourists' tracks are evident when they demand accommodation to stay in the destination. However, this is not a perfect measure of tourism flows given that, for example, it does not identify day-trippers or tourists who stay in holiday homes or hosted by friends and relatives. To overcome these difficulties, there exist indirect alternative ways of following the tourists' tracks. For example, the use of proxy variables when the process of tracking down the tourist turns out imprecise, misleading or simply too slow has been suggested. In the Republic of San Marino, where the great majority of visitors are composed of excursionists coming from the nearby Adriatic coast, a measure of the number of day trippers is estimated analyzing the number of vehicles in public parking spots over a certain period of time. Alternative proxies are, for example, the change in the consumption of water and electricity or the amount and the composition of collected waste, these being suitable indicators to estimate the numbers of day-trippers or tourists who stay in holiday homes.

So far in Chap. 2, we have acknowledged that the concept of "representative tourist" should be considered obsolete, and that tourists' tracks and behaviors often blend into those of non-tourists. Two of the main pitfalls of this situation are that: (1) the task of assigning available data to specific statistics of tourism is difficult to accomplish; (2) the points of investigation on tourism phenomenon tend to widen beyond control. Given these challenges, let us investigate in the following sections how we can quantify tourism flows and estimate tourism spending.

2.6.2 The Measurement of Tourism Flows

In the previous sections of this book, we had the opportunity to understand that certain key variables are closely related to the *tourist's movements*. And, according to the table of mobility (Table 2.1), these can be distinguished according to their origin (where the tourist lives) and destination (where the tourist goes). The main statistical variables that we use to measure tourism flows are three:

1. *Arrivals* (A) defined as the number of visitors reaching the destination, regardless of the duration of their visit.
2. *Nights* (N) defined as the total number of nights that the visitors spend in the destination (also called *overnight stays*).
3. *Average length of stay* (L) defined as the average number of nights that visitors spend in the destination. This is measured by the ratio between the number of nights N and arrivals A:

$$L = \frac{N}{A} \tag{2.2}$$

If, in the period under observation for a hotel, only two tourists are accommodated, one staying for three nights and one staying for five nights, our indicators will measure: $A = 2$ (two arrivals); $N = 8$ (eight overnight stays) and $L = 4$.

Arrivals and departures are flow variables that naturally refer to a period of time (such as a month or a year) as well as referring to a destination region (such as a town, a state or a country), but could also be applied to a single hospitality unit (such as a hotel or a campsite).

It is important to remark the difficulties in measuring day trips, which is explicitly referred in the matrix of tourism output. For example, given a visitor that arrives at the destination d, $A_d > 0$, but does not stay overnight, $N_d = 0$, the average length of stay for this tourism activity is zero.

Formally:

$$\text{if } A_d > 0 \text{ and } N_d = 0 \text{ then } L_d = \frac{N_d}{A_d} = 0 \tag{2.3}$$

Alternatively, it is possible to proxy day-trip visits by assigning the value of one to their overnight stays. This implies that:

$$\text{if } A_d = N_d \text{ then } L_d = \frac{N_d}{A_d} = 1 \tag{2.4}$$

Thus, the way we quantify day-trippers will ultimately affect the statistical measure of tourism flows and depends on which convention we decide to adopt when measuring A_d and N_d. The expression (2.3), (the one accepted by the UNWTO) underestimates and expression (2.4) overestimates the correct measure of the length of stay.

Finally, we can also calculate an *index of saturation*, B, which is defined as the ratio between the number of overnight stays and the resident population in the destination, P, multiplied by the number of days of the period under scrutiny, D:

$$B = \frac{N}{DP} \tag{2.5}$$

For example, if the index is referred to a 1-year period, $D = 365$. D is introduced to increase the precision degree of this measurement since the local population stay every day in their residence region. Hence, the index of saturation measures the average daily number of tourists per resident of the destination. For example, if the value of overnight stays throughout the year is $N = 1{,}000{,}000$ and the size of the local population is $P = 5{,}000$, then we calculate this index as $B = 1{,}000{,}000/(5{,}000 \times 365) = 0.548$. The result indicates that in that destination there is an average of approximately "half of a tourist" per resident every day.

An alternative index of saturation, B', can be computed as the ratio between the overall number of arrivals and the resident population in the region of destination:

$$B' = \frac{A}{P} \tag{2.6}$$

2.6.3 The Tourism Expenditure

Tourism expenditure refers to the amount paid for the purchase of goods and services, for and during tourism trips. It includes expenditure by visitors themselves, as well as expenses that are paid for or reimbursed by others (UNWTO 2007).

The issue of the timing of tourism expenditure is relevant. Tourism is particularly characterized by a temporal dimension which extends before and after the tourism trip. For the calculation of the tourism expenditure, the UNWTO (2007) states that all services delivered before the trip and clearly related to the trip, (for example, inoculations, passport visas, medical control, travel agency services, etc.) should be included in the tourism expenditure. In addition, all goods purchased before the trip that are intended to be used on the trip (specific clothes, medicines, etc.) or brought along as gifts, should also be included.

Moreover, during a trip a typical tourist consumes food, purchases grocery and artisan items, uses public and private transport, financial, administrative, and health services, and demands a wide array of leisure products. Not all these purchases can be clearly defined as tourist ones, in fact many of them are typical of regular consumers. Once more we face the complex nature of tourism, where there is an amalgam of goods and services that can be purchased by tourists and non-tourists, making more difficult the measurement of tourism expenditure. This issue has two main consequences: (1) from a statistical point of view, the whole tourism expenditure is almost impossible to determine (unless precise tourist surveys are undertaken) since an important part of it is composed by ordinary consumption blended with the consumption of the residents; (2) from the Economics of Tourism point of view, it is useful to distinguish between the purchase of goods and services which are included in the matrix of the tourism product (the ones that, from this perspective, are worth investigating) and ordinary consumption, in which the tourist acts as a typical consumer and for which the standard theory of consumption applies.

Therefore, tourism expenditure can be classified in to:

a) *Specific spending*, which arises as a direct consequence of the trip;
b) *Ordinary spending*, which is made regardless of the trip (for example, shopping).

From the point of view of the tourist, the *real* or *effective* tourism spending is the sum between the *specific* spending and the *ordinary* spending during the trip and stay. Note that the ordinary spending can differ according to the various types of the tourist experience. Such a difference can be both qualitative (fully adapting to the habits of consumption in the destination) and quantitative (for example, the average number of meals consumed at a restaurant is generally higher during the tourist's stay than during daily life).

Another important distinction to analyze is between:

1. *Goods and services* purchased during the trip and the stay.
2. *Durable goods*, which are purchased for tourism purposes and can be used repeatedly for several years. Examples are holiday homes, boats, camping tents, camper vans, etc.

From our perspective, when we talk about *tourism expenditure* we are strictly referring to the tourists' spending of type *sub*-1 while we refer to *tourists' investment* for those purchases of durable goods of type *sub*-2 which usually allow for subsequent acts of consumption (see Sect. 5.6). Therefore, the definition of tourism expenditure provided at the beginning of this section does not include the tourists' investment in durable goods. Neither it comprises the money paid to relatives and friends, which does not represent payments for tourism goods or services.

It is important to remark that the use of the term "tourists investment" here does not correspond to the economic concept of *tourism investment* used in Economics of Tourism, or more in general in Economics, which is defined as any increase in the stock of public and private capital for tourism goals. This mainly consists of investment in tourism infrastructures (i.e., tourism ports, highways, public gardens, etc.) and in private capital (i.e., real estate investments in the hotel industry, restaurants, etc.). This change in the capital stock of tourism businesses is simply referred as investment.

We must also stress on the classification of expenditure that refers to the sources of funding:

Table 2.3 Consumption of the tourism product

Type of tourist	Accommodation in hotel	Accommodation in a rented apartment	Local restaurant	Seafood restaurant	Beach services	Night club
Ulysses	40,000	0	0	80,000	40,000	40,000
Columbus	0	60,000	60,000	60,000	120,000	0
Total	40,000	60,000	60,000	140,000	160,000	40,000

Table 2.4 Additional consumption of the tourism product

Type of tourist	Accommodation in hotel	Accommodation in a rented apartment	Local restaurant	Seafood restaurant	Beach services	Night club
Ulysses	0	0	0	0	20,000	0
Columbus	0	0	0	0	0	20,000
Total	0	0	0	0	20,000	20,000

- Spending paid by the traveller;
- Spending paid or reimboursed by firms, such as for conferences or business meetings;
- Spending paid or reimboursed by the public administration, for meetings or missions carried out by its representatives.

Finally, let us return to the difference between *tourism product* and *additional consumption*. This is something that we previously studied in Sect. 2.5, explicatively identified by the matrix of tourism product on the one hand and by the additional purchases by a tourist that behaves as an ordinary consumer on the other hand. The use of indices of arrivals, overnight stays, and expenditure will allow us to better distinguish these two components of total expenditure.

We further develop the example of Ulysses versus Columbus (which we presented in Table 2.2) and assume that the destination receives 30,000 overall tourists classified as: 20,000 Ulysses-type of tourists with an average stay of 2 days and 10,000 Columbus-type of tourists with an average stay of 6 days. Then, the overnight stay is translated into 40,000 tourists who behave according to the first row of Table 2.2 and 60,000 who behave according to the second row. The total number of overnight stays is hence 100,000. If we multiply every row of Table 2.2 by the number of stays for each type of tourist, we obtain the matrix presented in Table 2.3.

Furthermore, let us also assume that Ulysses and Columbus might consume additional goods in the destination. For example, if we suppose that half of the Ulysses-type tourists buy one unit of beach services and one third of Columbus-type tourists pay the entrance fee for a club every night, we should introduce these items in Table 2.4 to represent all consumed goods. If we vertically sum up the rows of Table 2.3 and 2.4 we obtain the total consumption by the tourists in the destination, which is shown in Table 2.5.

We can now introduce the prices for each good and service (for example, 50 € per overnight stay at a hotel, 40 € per overnight stay at rented apartment, 20 € per meal at the local restaurant, 25 € per each fish-based meal, 10 € per each unit of beach service, 30 € for each entrance fee at the club) and calculate the tourist

Table 2.5 Total consumption of the tourism product

Type of tourist	Accommodation in hotel	Accommodation in a rented apartment	Local restaurant	Seafood restaurant	Beach services	Night club
Total	40,000	60,000	60,000	140,000	180,000	60,000

Table 2.6 Total tourism expenditure

Accommodation in hotel	Accommodation in a rented apartment	Local restaurant	Seafood restaurant	Beach services	Night club	Total expenditure
2,000,000	2,400,000	1,200,000	3,500,000	1,800,000	1,800,000	12,700,000

spending of each tourist and the tourism expenditure of all tourists, which is 12,700,000 € in our example (see Table 2.6). From a supply viewpoint, 12,700,000 € also corresponds to the aggregate revenue for the tourism firms of the destination in our example.

Furthermore, we can compute the individual tourist spending in the following ways:

- *Daily spending*, or spending *per day*, S_N, as the ratio between aggregate tourism expenditure (S) and the number of nights spent at the destination:

$$S_N = \frac{S}{N} \tag{2.7}$$

- *Per capita spending*, or spending *per person*, S_A, as the ratio between tourism expenditure and the number of arrivals at the destination:

$$S_A = \frac{S}{A} \tag{2.8}$$

In our example, $S_N = 12{,}700{,}000/100{,}000 = 127$ € and $S_A = 12{,}7000{,}000/30{,}000 = 423$ €. We can also apply the same calculation for each type of tourism. In our example, the Ulysses-type tourist has a higher spending *per day* (140 €) than the Columbus-type tourist (105 €). However, the Columbus-type tourist spends more per capita (630 €) than the Ulysses-type tourist (280 €). These indicators, calculated in real examples of types of tourists, can be very useful for tourism management and planning.

2.6.4 *The Propensity to Travel*

Complementary to the study of the tourism phenomenon and the measurement of flows and expenditure from the destination (or host region) perspective, we can also focus on the population generating the tourism phenomenon. Therefore, given P as the population (i.e., number of inhabitants) in the region of origin, T as the number of tourists travelling from the region of origin (that is, T is a subset of P) indicating the individuals from the region of origin who undertake at least one trip in a given period of time, V the aggregate number of trips undertaken in a given period of time, it is then possible to calculate the *net propensity to travel* (X_N) as the percentage of tourists in the total population of the region of origin as:

$$X_N = \frac{T}{P} \tag{2.9}$$

The *gross propensity to travel* (X_G) measures instead the average number of trips per person in the general population. Formally:

$$X_G = \frac{V}{P} \tag{2.10}$$

It is worthwhile to note that, although the maximum value for X_N is one (not more than 100 % of residents can be tourists), no general upper bound can be suggested for X_G (a tourist can take any finite number of trips during a given period of time).

We can calculate the *trip frequency* (F), as the average number of tourism trips taken by the portion of the population who qualifies as tourists, by dividing (2.10) by (2.9):

$$F = \frac{X_G}{X_N} = \frac{V}{T} \tag{2.11}$$

It is evident that the richness of information obtained by crossing these data with those from the matrix of the tourism output creates a useful set of indicators which are key for managing and monitoring the tourism activity in a region. For instance, we could calculate the indicators (2.9)–(2.11) for each type of tourism.

It is interesting to note that the net and gross propensities to travel point out the number of tourism experiences (or tourism trips); however they do not provide any information regarding the length of the trip. Let us introduce now an indicator of the *total length of the trip (Z)* outside the region of origin, which measures the total stay (in terms of number of nights spent outside the region of origin) and thus it is defined as the sum of the length of stay of each single trip taken by the population:

$$Z = \sum_{k=1}^{K} z_k \tag{2.12}$$

where $k = 1, 2, \ldots, K$ and z_k represents the length of each k-th trip. We can then obtain Z_P and Z_T, which measure the average number of tourism days, respectively, for the whole population (P) and for the tourists only (T):

$$Z_P = \frac{Z}{P} \tag{2.13}$$

$$Z_T = \frac{Z}{T} \tag{2.14}$$

Finally, if we divide *Z* by the number of trips, we obtain the average length of the trip, Z_m, as:

$$Z_m = \frac{Z}{V} \tag{2.15}$$

It is important to remark that in Sects. 2.6.2 and 2.6.3 our perspective of analysis was the region of destination while now, in Sect. 2.6.4, our perspective is from the region of origin of the tourists. While in Sects. 2.6.2 and 2.6.3 we defined the length of stay in the destination as *L*, here we define the length of the trip outside the region of origin as *Z*. The two indices *L* and *Z* will be equal when the analysis implies only one region of origin and one region of destination.

Chapter Overview

- The Economics of Tourism investigates all the economic consequences derived from the activity of a tourist prior during and after the trip.
- Tourism is defined as the activities of persons travelling to, and staying in places outside their usual environment for not more than one consecutive year for leisure, business or personal purpose other than to be employed by a resident entity in the country or the place visited.
- Tourism is a complex phenomenon that requires analysis from a multidisciplinary approach.
- The tourism product (or tourism output) is a set composed by different goods and services demanded by the visitor during the holiday experience, including transport, accommodation, meals, entertainment, among other activities.
- Basic indicators for measuring the effects of tourism as an economic activity are: arrivals, overnight stays, length of stay, expenditure, composition of the tourism output (or tourism product), and propensity to travel.

Chapter 3
The Tourism Sector in the Economy

Learning Outcomes
On the completion of this chapter you will:

- Be able to discuss the various issues related to the identification and definition of the tourism sector in the economy and what are the approaches used to measure its relevance.
- Be able to evaluate the economic impact of tourism, both at a theoretical level and in the national accounting systems.

3.1 Introduction

Tourism is one of the most important and dynamic sectors in modern economies. In 2010, international tourism globally accounted for more than 900 million arrivals, generated an aggregate income of $1,000 billion, and was estimated to be the fourth greatest contributor to the aggregate world exports right after energy, chemical products, and cars (UNWTO 2011a). In addition, as stated in the previous chapter, tourism contributed with a 9 % to the global GDP (of which around 5 % as a direct contribute) and with an 8 % to world employment (UNWTO 2010).

After reviewing in Chap. 2 the various challenges in defining and measuring the tourism phenomenon, we move on and try to provide an answer to the following two questions. Given the heterogeneity nature of the tourism product, can we meaningfully identify something called "tourism industry"? How can we successfully estimate its importance within the economic structure of a country? With such purpose, the present chapter is devoted to the provision of all the necessary definitions and methodological explanations, emphasizing what is tourism and what is not in order to demarcate the borders of tourism sector.

This chapter is organized as follows. Section 3.2 will, following a supply-side approach, identify the tourism sector. We will underline how, in contrast to other industries, e.g., car industry, it is not possible to identify a *tourism industry* in

G. Candela and P. Figini, *The Economics of Tourism Destinations*, Springer Texts in Business and Economics, DOI 10.1007/978-3-642-20874-4_3,

the national accounting system.[1] Section 3.3 will, following an input-output approach, investigate how the tourism demand will help us in estimating of the economic relevance of tourism. In Sect. 3.4 we will show how national and international statistical agencies use the satellite accounting system to effectively identify and measure tourism. We will then assess the importance of tourism for both national and international economies through the presentation of some key figures (see Sect. 3.5). Overall, this chapter will help understand the strategic quantitative and qualitative role played by tourism in both local and international economies.

3.2 The Tourism Sector

The main tool to observe the quantitative elements of an economic system is the aggregate of data recordings called *national accounting*. Such data are collected to achieve an understanding of the flows linking the operational units and industries involved in the economic activities of a country. In particular, it refers to variables that are national (or domestic) according to the criteria of citizenship (or, more in general, to the criteria of belonging to a given territory). However, the standard criterion adopted by national accountants cannot be directly utilized for tourism variables, as explained next.

3.2.1 National Accounting and the Tourism Sector

Tourism does not appear in the classification scheme of industries adopted by national accounting since the standard methodology that is adopted to identify and assess the economic sectors of a country is not applicable to tourism. The standard methodology has two main steps. First, the national accounting system identifies each economic activity according to the type of goods and services produced by such activity. Second, different economic activities are aggregated in *industries* according to either the technological features of the output and the inputs being used to produce it, or the kind of processes activated, or the final destination of the goods and services produced. The criteria used in Economics to identify an industry are the following:

1. The *technological criterion*, for which an industry is a set of firms using a similar production technology. For example, according to this criterion, Renault and

[1] Although the term "tourism industry" is often referred to in textbooks, articles and reports, in a technical sense tourism in not an industry, as we will explain in this chapter. Hence, we prefer to use the term "tourism sector".

Fiat belong to the car industry because they use similar technologies for the production of metal boxes with an engine, seats, a steering wheel, etc. that are called cars. The technological criterion focuses on the features of both the production process and its outcome, with no interest in the final destination of the output.

2. The *market criterion*, which identifies an industry according to the degree of similarity between goods, which is intended as whether the consumer possibly accepts to substitute one good with another. For example, according to this criterion, Renault and Fiat belong to the same industry because, despite the car drivers' tastes, car drivers consider a car produced by Renault and a car produced by Fiat as (imperfect) substituting each other. The degree of substitutability is commonly measured by the cross-price elasticity (see Sect. 4.2.2). Hence, goods that may be apparently similar but have a low degree of substitutability belong to different industries.

Although the choice on whether to adopt the technological or the market criterion depends on the economic problem to be studied, neither one nor the other is adequate when trying to identify the tourism sector. On one hand, this depends on the impossibility for clearly identifying the contours of the tourism activity while, on the other hand, it is a natural consequence of the heterogeneity of tourism output. In particular, the technological criterion cannot be used since a holiday usually appears as a mix of goods that are deeply heterogeneous from a production point of view (for example, lodging and food services do not use similar technologies) and some of them cannot even be produced (cultural heritage and natural goods). Likewise, we are not able to adopt the market criterion. For example, given that lodging and food services are complementary items and have almost zero substitutability (if the hotel is not available, no tourists would accept to sleep in the restaurant), they should be assigned to different industries even if they are the two key elements of the tourism basket. To summarize, using these two criteria for the identification of the tourism industry would yield either unsatisfactory or counter-intuitive conclusions.

Consequently, we are tempted *to argue against the possibility of even using the concept of tourism sector or industry*, and this seems to be the reason why something called "tourism industry" fails to exist in any national accounting system. However, since the notion of sector and of industry are very useful from an analytical point of view, an important debate around whether or not tourism is a sector of an economy exists.

On one hand, given the difficulties in identifying a distinct tourism output according to the technological or to the market criteria, some authors suggest not to use such concepts for tourism. On the other hand, some authors (Wahab 1975; Lundberg 1976; McIntosh et al. 1995; Leiper 1990) are in favour of identifying an *industry of travel and tourism*, acknowledging that different firms and organizations operate in virtue of an economic bond that allows them to produce a "unitary product". For instance, let us suppose that the only possible way of going on holiday is by an all-inclusive package tour sold by a tour operator. In this extreme case, given that the tourism industry would automatically coincide with the tour operator's activities, the issue of identification would be automatically solved (see Sect. 8.2 for a discussion of the role and function of tour operators). If we accept this position, we can reasonably define the tourism sector as *the set of all tangible and intangible activities aimed at satisfying the need for holiday*.

It would then be possible to define tourism as a *synthetic industry*, compounded by the intersection of traditional industries, where the intersection is identified according to the share of the industries' output which is demanded by tourists. This approach, which is the one used to build the Tourism Satellite Accounting (TSA) system (see Sect. 3.4.1) does not exogenously identify the tourism sector(s) but, on the contrary, endogenously includes in the tourism sector those activities that satisfy tourists' needs.

The setting up of a statistical system aimed at measuring the economic impact of tourism is therefore a complex task which, however, can be tackled by two different approaches: the *supply-side* approach and the *demand-side* approach. Let us turn the attention to both of them.

3.2.2 The Supply-Side Approach

The supply-side approach was suggested for tourism by Smith (1988) and Medlik (1988) and generically considers the tourist as a purchaser of goods and services. It focuses on an ex ante definition of the tourism sector based on the structure of its supply. Smith identifies two parts of the tourism supply: one part that only supplies to tourists and another part that supplies to both tourists and non-tourists. The first part includes all those firms that would not exist without the tourism activity, for example, hotels, travel agencies, cruises, etc. The second part includes those businesses that would still exist even in the absence of tourism, for instance restaurants, taxis, local attractions, etc. (see Smith 1995).

To generalize the difficulties in identifying the different activities surrounding the tourism sector, we can attempt to define as key components of tourism those activities for which one of the following is true: (a) part of the output constitutes a significant share of the tourism product; (b) the tourism demand constitutes an important share of the supply in this activity. In the first group we find some of the typical services produced in the destination, like coffee shops and restaurants, which do not produce only for tourists but which expenditure is a significant portion of tourism output. In the second group we find, for example, amusement parks which mainly sell their services to tourists but for which tourists do not usually spend a significant share of their money.

The above-mentioned theoretical difficulties are not critical enough to prevent us from looking for a methodology to classify the economic activities that are related to tourism. Regarding this, the most immediate approach distinguishes between tourism *core services* and *complementary services*. Core services refer to the followings: (1) transportation (airlines, shipping lines, railways, car rental, etc.);

(2) lodging and catering (hotels, motels, campsites, apartments, bed and breakfast, restaurants, bars, pubs, etc.); (3) attractions (natural and cultural attractions, heritage, theme parks, entertainment, events, etc.), (4) the travel organizing sector (tour operators, travel agents, web portals, etc.); (5) the destination management (national, regional and local organizations, tourism associations, etc.). Instead, the complementary services that are used for tourism purposes in market economies are classified as either *public* (tourism schools, infrastructures, police and health services, etc.) or *private* (money change, banks, insurance, etc.).

All activities of interest for tourism can be aggregated depending on the technical features of the production, the type of processes activated or the final destination of goods and services produced. This, according to Costa and Rispoli (1992) and Cooper et al. (2008), allows the identification of a set of *tourism departments* as follows:

- *Hospitality*. This is the key department for many tourists, although not relevant for day-trippers (since they do not stay overnight in the destination). The accommodation or lodging supply consists of a wide range of different services, which usually translates into a large variety of price-quality combinations: hotels, apartments and villas to rent, hostels, mountain huts, campsites, etc.
- *Food and beverage*. This department is characterized by a wide variety of services: traditional restaurants, restaurants in hotels, buffet restaurants, fast food restaurants, pizzerias, take-away, bars, pubs, etc.
- *Transport*. Also this department is quite heterogeneous: airlines, ferries, cruise ships, river boats, trains, buses, undergrounds, car rentals, etc. This department usually supplies to a significant number of non-tourists as well as tourists.
- *Congresses and conferences*. This department targets the participants of scientific or business conferences or political congresses. The firms operating in this section are either firms of the previous three sections, or specific business such as a congress hall, a congress center, job fairs, event management organizations etc.
- *Catering*. This department operates as a supplier to the main tourism activities and includes firms selling to restaurants, hotels, transportation companies, congress centers, etc.
- *Leisure management*. It includes all private and public businesses supplying leisure services: sport complexes, ski services, organization of shows, exhibitions or concerts, swimming pool, diving classes, etc.
- *Wholesale and retail*. This includes the sale of tourism-oriented goods (from fuel to motor vehicles such as campers, buses, etc.), complementary goods and services for the trip, and handicraft products and souvenirs.
- *Financial intermediaries*. The businesses operating within this department usually deal with currency exchange, health and travel insurances, credit cards, etc.
- *Real estate sale and rental*. This includes all the firms that are involved in the sale, purchasing, and rentals (on behalf of the owners) of real estate for tourism purposes.
- *Infrastructure management*. This includes public firms (or private providers of public services) such as airports, train stations, ports, highways, etc.

- *Cultural and environmental.* It is a key department for tourism and for cultural tourism in particular. Although it mainly deals with public institutions, it also includes several private ones (think, for example, the Guggenheim museums around the world). These institutions administer, purchase, and preserve cultural heritage.
- *Trip planning and management.* This includes the tour operators, whose main activity consists of organizing package tours in connection with many of the departments listed above.
- *Travel agency.* The retailers of trips and holidays, which usually operate as brokers between the tourists and the tour operators, are included here.
- *Public goods of support to tourism.* The public institutions that specifically work for the promotion of tourism, diffusion of information, control and supervision of the tourism activity.
- *Public administration.* This department operates at two levels: national level, in terms of national security, customs administration, laws and regulations regarding transportations, etc.; regional level, in terms of public services, visa administration (when it is of pertinence of the local administrators), etc.
- *Education and training.* This department, which varies significantly from one country to another, includes all the institutions that are involved with the professional education (chefs, guides, interpreters, etc.) and the academic education (bachelor and master degrees) of individuals who are seeking a job in the tourism sector.

The above list clearly displays the fundamental problem of monitoring tourism: some activities are exclusively directed to tourists (for example, the activities implemented by tour operators), while other activities are mainly aimed at the tourists' satisfaction (for example, the activities within the food department). Finally, other activities equally meet the demand of both tourists and local residents (for example, the wholesale and retail sale division) and, because of this, they also belong to non-tourism markets. Once again, such mixture is the reason why an exogenous classification of 'tourism activities' is insufficient and the analysis of the demand becomes vital for a complete identification of the tourism sector.

3.3 The Demand-Side Approach and the Input–Output Analysis

Given the difficulties in identifying the tourism industry from the supply-side, the demand-side approach helps define the boundaries of the tourism sector by investigating tourism expenditure. By observing the tourists' spending, in fact, we will be able to indirectly determine the amount of production (and its distribution among sectors) that is actually needed to satisfy the tourism demand, by implicitly estimating its economic impact. In particular, the *Input–Output model* will allow us to understand the degree of integration between tourism and other productive sectors, and the role of tourism in the generation of income and employment in the economy.

3.3.1 The Table of Sectoral Interdependence

The monitoring of the tourism sector from a demand standpoint is solely possible through the use of the Input–Output model, introduced by the economist Wassily Leontief, also known as the Model of sectoral interdependence. Such model is used to represent all the exchanges occurring in an economic system within a given period of time. From an empirical perspective, the suitability of the model to measure tourism, from a demand-side approach, is an established consequence of its ability to measure the effects of a change in demand onto the productive structure of an economy.

In the following pages, we will review the key aspects of the Input–Output (I-O) model by discussing a numerical example. Our goal will be to underline the one-to-one correspondence between the structure of the demand and the structure of the production (and consequently employment), which is the main implication of this model. Hence, this will also allow an endogenous definition of the tourism sector, not just as a *branch of the production system* but actually as a *product of different branches*, in line with the property of heterogeneity of the tourism product outlined in Sect. 2.5.

The I–O method focuses on the economic structure of a country by recording the transactions between any given sector and the remaining sectors of the economy, and consists of a two-way table where each sector is represented as both a row and a column. The preliminary operation consists of making a partition of the economic system into sectors, whose number mainly depends on the pursued objectives, and the quantity and quality of available data. The first tables were built by Leontief in the United States and had a small dimension (10-by-10), later on the table was extended by the national statistical institutes to include up to 200 productive sectors and more. Different countries usually adopt different versions of the table, however, it is common in all tables to distinguish between two main groups of sectors: (a) the productive sectors, which include productive units (i.e., firms); (b) the final sectors, which are the consumption units (i.e., households). Final sectors are paid with income from the productive sectors, which is spent in purchasing from them final consumption goods.

In order to grasp a full understanding of both the Leontief method and the meaning of the I–O model, we discuss the numerical example presented in Table 3.1, where the partition of the economic system yields to three broad productive sectors: agriculture, manufacturing, and services. The last one includes trade, transport, restaurant services, accommodation, etc. The table relies on the following assumptions about the economic system:

Table 3.1 The I–O table: a numerical example

	Agriculture	Manufacturing	Services	Consumption	Sales, Total
Agriculture	–	20	30	50	100
Manufacturing	20	–	40	40	100
Services	10	30	–	60	100
Purchasing, total	30	50	70		300
Value added	70	50	30		150
Total income	100	100	100	150	450

1. The economy is closed, in the sense that there is no international trade with the rest of the world. This assumption avoids the difficult task of measuring the exchanges between domestic and foreign productive units.
2. The economy is stationary, which in this example implies zero net investments. This hypothesis aims at removing the difficulties related to capital changes and to technological progress.
3. The economy does not have a public sector, this hypothesis removes the difficulties related to the input of taxation and public spending into the table.
4. Finally, we assume an exogenous and stable price system; this assumption allows us to measure the flows in monetary units but, any change in monetary values will be exclusively due to variations in physical amounts of production and not to variations in prices.

It is important to remark that the first three assumptions could easily be relaxed and, in this example, they are retained exclusively for simplifying reasons.[2] An additional simplifying hypothesis of Table 3.1, consists of assuming that the three sectors of our system will have an aggregate production with identical magnitude (100 billion €).

In our example, each row of the table represents the sales of any given sector to the remaining ones: the agricultural sector sold 100 billion € worth of production, of which 20 billion was sold to the manufacturing sector, 30 billion to the services sector, and 50 billion to the household sector for final consumption. Similarly, the manufacturing sector sold 100 billion worth of production, of which 20 billion was sold to the agricultural sector, 40 billion to services, and 40 billion to final consumption. Finally, the service sector sold 100 billion worth of production, of which 10 billion was sold to the agricultural sector, 30 billion to manufacturing, and 60 billion to final consumption. The rows of Table 3.1 only display the *sales* from one sector to others, hence they do not account for the transactions occurring within a sector.

Each column of the table represents the purchases by any given sector from the remaining ones. In our example, the agricultural sector spends 20 billion € on

[2] The release of the fourth assumption is, on the contrary, more controversial and has important implications on the whole philosophy of the I–O model. Such discussion, however, goes beyond the aim of this book.

purchasing manufacturing production and 10 billion € on purchasing services. Similarly, the manufacturing sector purchases both 20 billion and 30 billion € worth of agricultural production and services, respectively. Finally, the service sector purchases both 30 billion and 40 billion € worth of agricultural production and manufacturing respectively. Again, the columns of Table 3.1 only display the purchases from one sector to others, hence they do not account for the transactions occurring within a sector.

It is important to highlight some additional aspects of the table. Firstly, note that, although each productive sector purchases goods and services from the other productive sectors of the economy, the aggregate value of sold production is greater than the value of aggregate spending. In our example, the agricultural sector sells for 100 billion € and purchases for 30 billion €, the manufacturing sector sells for 100 billion € but purchases for 50 billion €, and the service sector sells for 100 billion € but purchases for 70 billion €. This means that the production process created a value of 70 billion, 50 billion, and 30 billion € within the agricultural, manufacturing, and service sectors, respectively. We define as *value added within a given productive sector*, the difference between its aggregate revenue and its aggregate expenditure on goods and services of the remaining sectors. These amounts are shown in a row entitled *value added*. Given that each value-added measures the paid income within a sector (as wages and profits), their sum measures the *aggregate income* generated in the economy, which is 150 billion € in our example.

Secondly, what happens to such income? Under the assumptions of zero investment (stationary assumption) and no government intervention, this income is only spent for private consumption, to purchase goods and services produced by the three sectors of the economy: in our example of Table 3.1 50, 40, and 60 billion are the values in € of household spending in agricultural, manufacturing, and service goods respectively.

Note, to conclude, that the aggregate spending on purchases by the final sector (150 billion €) is equal to the aggregate value added. This observation completes the description of the productive structure of the economy as a circuit between production, income and consumption.

3.3.2 The Input–Output Model and Its Application to Tourism

The I–O model, by means of the table representing sectoral interdependence, can tackle the issue of quantification of the tourism sector according to the demand-side approach. In this way, it is possible to measure the share of total output which is demanded by tourists.

To achieve this objective, we need to identify all those expenditures that are related to tourism activities and, consistently with Sect. 2.6, we identify tourism expenditure as the sum between expenditure for the tourism output and expenditure for other tourism consumption. Let us assume that in the economy a certain amount

Table 3.2 The technical coefficients of production

	Agriculture	Manufacturing	Services
Agriculture	0	0.2	0.3
Manufacturing	0.2	0	0.4
Services	0.1	0.3	0

of the aggregate consumption is generated by the demand of tourists. For example, 10 billion € is spent for farm holidays in farms belonging to the agricultural sector, and 30 billion € is spent for purchasing accommodation, food, and transport, which are included in the service sector.

Let us proceed in this way: if, in the I-O Table 3.1, we divide each inter-sectoral purchase by the aggregate income of the sector, we identify some parameters that measure the amount of purchasing needed to produce one unit of output in the sector. These ratios can be considered as *technical coefficients of production* and, if they are constant, the implicit assumption is that the production of each good follows *constant returns to scale*.[3] For example, in Table 3.1, 1 € worth of agricultural production requires 0.2 € worth of industrial production and 0.1 € worth of services. If we run a similar calculation for the remaining productive sectors we can build Table 3.2.

In order to understand the utility of such coefficients, we may ask the following question: what ought to happen in order to satisfy the demand for rural tourism worth 10 billion € and the demand for tourism services worth 30 billion €? On the one hand, the production of the two sectors must change by the same amount. On the other hand, as a consequence, each sector must also produce the intermediate goods that are needed to produce, for example, the agricultural goods. Therefore, the agricultural sector will have to use a share of its production which is more than 10 billion €. Similarly, the demand for tourism services will spread through the entire economic system, so that the service sector will have to use a share of its production which is more than 30 billion €.

This multiplicative phenomenon occurs because the sectors appearing in Tables 3.1 and 3.2 are strictly interdependent. Therefore, in order to satisfy the rural tourism demand, agricultural production must be equal to the tourists' demand plus 0.2 times the manufacturing production and 0.3 times the production of services (first row of Table 3.2). Similarly, the aggregate output of the manufacturing sector will respectively be multiplied by 0.2 and 0.4 of the production of the agricultural and service sectors (second row of Table 3.2). Finally, the aggregate output of the service sector will have to satisfy direct tourism demand plus 0.1 times the agricultural production and 0.3 times the manufacturing production (third row of Table 3.2).

[3] Constant returns to scale imply that a proportional change of all the inputs by a given positive factor, leads to a change in the output by the same factor (i.e., if we double all the inputs, the output doubles).

Table 3.3 Output needed to satisfy tourism demand

	Agriculture	Manufacturing	Services	Consumption	Sales, total
Agriculture	–	4.3	11.7	10	26
Manufacturing	5.3	–	15.7	0	21
Services	2.6	6.4	–	30	39
Purchasing, total	7.9	10.7	27.4		86
Value added	18.1	10.3	11.6		40
Total income	26	21	39	40	126

Such relationships can be represented as a system of three equations in three variables that can be used to calculate the simultaneous levels of sectoral outputs:

$$A = 0.2\mathrm{M} + 0.3S + D_A$$

$$M = 0.2A + 0.4S \tag{3.1}$$

$$S = 0.1A + 0.3M + D_S$$

where A, M, and S respectively denote the agricultural, manufacturing, and service production that is needed to satisfy the agricultural demand for rural tourism, $D_A = 10$, and for tourism services, $D_S = 30$. The solution of the system (3.1) is $A \approx 26$; $M \approx 21$; $S \approx 39$.

If we adopt the coefficients of Table 3.2 along with the system 3.1, we can calculate the output of each sector of the economy that is needed to satisfy the tourism demand. This is done in Table 3.3, which isolates this production from the rest of the economy.

The comparison between Tables 3.3 and 3.1 is key to understand the effects that are fuelled by the tourism demand and the set of interdependence on the production side generated by this demand. In particular, such comparison allows us:

- To compute the share, q_i, of total output of the sector due to tourism consumption, being i the sector of the economy (in our example there are three sectors, $i = 1, 2, 3$). This is obtained by dividing the tourists' demand (the second last column of Table 3.3) by the aggregate production of the sector (the last column of Table 3.1).
- To compute the share, Q_i, where $i = 1, 2, 3$, of total output of the sector which is, directly or indirectly, generated by the tourism demand. This is obtained by dividing the sector output pertaining to tourism (last column of Table 3.3) by the aggregate production by the same sector (last column of Table 3.1).
- To highlight that in a system of sectoral interdependence all sectors, including those which do not appear in the vector of tourism demand, are involved in tourism. Although in our example tourists do not consume industrial goods, the manufacturing sector is indirectly producing for tourism through supplying part of its production to those farms and those enterprises that sell goods and services to tourists in the agricultural and service sectors.

Therefore, together with vector **d** = [10 0 30], which captures the tourists' final demand in the three sectors and that can also be interpreted as the quantity of goods that are directly demanded by tourists, the system of equations (3.1) allows us to determine the following: (a) a vector **q** = [0.1 0 0.3] which quantifies the shares of sectoral output that are directly due to the tourism demand; (b) a vector **Q** = [0.26 0.21 0.39] which quantifies the shares of sectoral output that are directly and indirectly due to the tourism demand.

In such terms, the Input–Output analysis that we apply to tourism clearly shows that the tourists' final demand does not require adding any new rows or any new columns to the table of sectoral interdependence. Instead, through appropriate shares, it includes all sectors that are somehow involved in the production of goods and services consumed by tourists.

We have enough evidence to argue that *tourism does not have to be seen as a separate industry within the economy but as an intricate "fabric", a system that extends over the productive industry of a country*. Moreover, the I–O model constitutes the ideal tool for identifying the systemic nature of tourism. In addition, the I–O approach allows us to identify two alternative definitions for the tourism sector: a strong one, including only the production of firms which directly "meet the tourist" (the vector **d** of our example), and a weak one which also includes the production of firms which do "not meet the tourist", but undertake transactions with tourism firms (as the last column of Table 3.3 shows, the total income generated by the tourism sector, directly and indirectly, can be expressed by a vector **t** = [26 21 39]).

We are now able to provide a more precise answer to the issue of definition of the tourism industry and to what firms or sectors are to be included. Rather than referring to the tourism and travel industry in strict and a broad sense, it seems more appropriate to refer to:

- *Tourism and travel sector*, which comprises the production by those sectors which directly sell to the tourist. Such sectors correspond to the firms that operate to satisfy the tourism demand, without considering any structural interdependence. In our example, this amounts to 10 billion € for agriculture and 30 billion € for services, which respectively correspond to 10 % of the aggregate agricultural production (q_1) and to 30 % of the aggregate service production (q_3);
- *Tourism and travel system*, which comprises the production by all sectors that direct or indirectly work to satisfy the tourism demand. The naming "system" is used to evoke both the algebraic idea behind the system (3.1) (which we use to calculate the direct and indirect productive interdependence) and the idea that the tourism product results from the simultaneous contributions of many firms often not directly involved in satisfying tourists' needs. In our example, this is shown by the aggregate amounts presented in Table 3.3, where the agricultural sector and the service sector produce 26 and 39 billion € (respectively 16 and 9 billion more than the firms which directly sell to the tourists) and the manufacturing sector, whose contribution to the tourism system amounts to

21 billion €, but which does not include any tourism firm. The sectoral shares pertaining to the tourism system are then equal to 26 % for agriculture (Q_1), to 21 % for manufacturing (Q_2), and 39 % for services (Q_3).

The example above has been presented to support our intuition that it is impossible to define a tourism industry or to identify a tourism sector in the national accounting system. Indeed, tourism relates to production activities that are dispersed across different branches of the economy. In other words, tourism is neither a sector nor a branch of the economy; it is instead a set of relationships that are "hidden underneath" the economic system in a way that is fully consistent with the existing productive interdependence.

3.3.3 The Integration Between Two Methods of Observation for Tourism

The supply-side approach observes the tourism system by monitoring the departments, i.e., the supply of an aggregate of firms, with which the tourism sector is identified. The weakness of the supply-side approach relies on the fact that it refers to an exogenous definition of tourism sector: however, we know that many of the departments listed in Sect. 3.2 offer goods and services not only to tourists but also to non-tourists. This is further clarified in Fig. 3.1, where the exogenous variables of the model are indicated in the rectangle and the endogenous variables in the ellipse.[4] The task of identifying and monitoring these departments is necessary both to measure the production referring to the tourism system in a certain period of time (usually a year) and to appreciate all the activities that are of interest for tourism.

On the contrary, the demand-side approach monitors the tourism demand and, employing an I–O model, estimates the output (or production) required to satisfy such tourism demand. The demand-side approach is able to obtain an endogenous identification of the tourism activity (Fig. 3.2), however finds serious problems in the monitoring of the tourism demand. In other words, in the previous example the value of 10 billion € of tourists' demand for agricultural goods and 30 billion € for other tourism services, that we have simply assumed, has to be properly estimated by continuously monitoring tourists' behavior. Although the demand-side approach is theoretically superior to the supply-side approach, it only performs efficiently if it is feeded by continuous and daily observations of the tourism demand, eventually broken down by type of tourism and tourist. Nevertheless, this information is difficult to obtain, very long to elaborate, and slow to update.

[4] The exogenous variables refer to factors that are not determined in the model but are necessary to obtain the solution of the model. The endogenous variables refer to factors whose values are computed by solving the model, given the values of the exogenous variables.

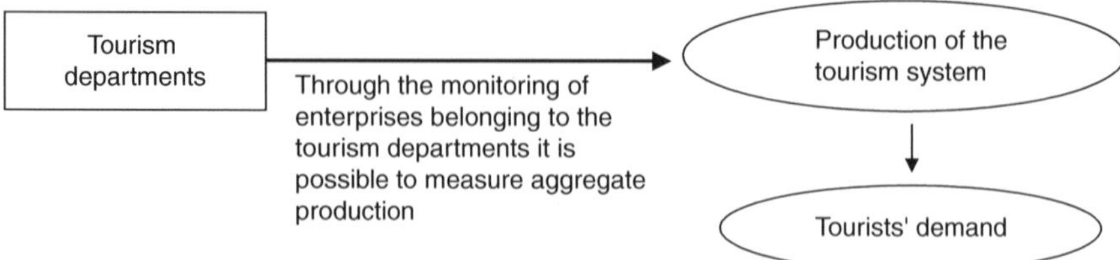

Fig. 3.1 The supply-side approach

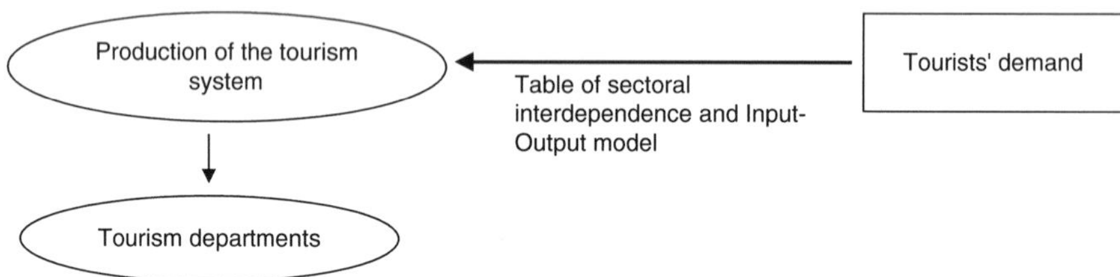

Fig. 3.2 The demand-side approach

In addition, we should mention that the table of sectoral interdependence is built through the difficult aggregation and interpretation of data that come from the information collected through questionnaires filled out by tourists (Notes 3.1). In other words, there exists a trade-off between accuracy and manageability of available information.

Notes 3.1. Surveys on Tourists' Spending Habits

Surveys on tourists' spending habits are usually submitted in public places (ports, airports, stations, beaches, museums, but also hotels and restaurants) that tourists are likely to visit, and usually consist of four sections.

The first section generally identifies the socioeconomic features of the interviewed person: age, gender, civil status, level of education, income level, employment status, type of job, place of residence, etc.

The second section generally identifies the characteristics of the tourism trip: purposes of visit, party size and composition, length of the trip, type and category of accommodation, mode of transport, booking method (e.g., own organization through internet, travel agency, through a tour operator), type of purchase (e.g., purchase of tourism services separately or within a package tour), activities undertaken during the trip. The questions about lodging are also aimed at capturing the share of tourists who stay at holiday homes or with friends and relatives, which are not recorded in the official statistics.

The third section generally investigates the spending habits and, thus, the tourist is asked to give an estimate of the overall cost of the trip and/or a daily estimate. Moreover, the person is asked to estimate the amount of money spent in the different goods and services including bars and restaurants, shopping, clubs, car rentals, taxis, museums and other cultural activities, other attractions (such as theme parks, beach services, ski pass, etc.) This is the most difficult part of the survey to answer and, since the tourist hardly manages to precisely describe the spending budget, it is possible to resort to correction methods. Two important correction methods are: (a) to add some control questions, for example the tourists are asked the number of times they have meals in restaurants and the answer is compared with the tourists' spending on meals consumed at restaurants. If these two answers are not compatible then the questionnaire may be disregarded; (b) to use an indirect estimate of the spending: for example, multiply the declared number of times the tourist goes to a restaurant by the average cost of eating at a restaurant.

The fourth section usually varies depending on the questionnaire and it reflects the main objectives of the survey (for example, the tourist could be asked to rank services based on her satisfaction). Finally, the questionnaire may end with open questions for which the tourist is asked to express spontaneous opinions and where the interviewer may add remarks such as time and place of the survey, the level of interest and understanding shown by the tourist, etc.

Obviously, in order to be able to use the collected data for estimating the importance of tourism (and for other measurement issues), it is necessary to have a representative sample of the population of tourists. How to sample a population is beyond the scope of this book and, to deepen the study of these topics, we recommend a textbook of statistics and the statistical handbooks of the UNWTO.

To conclude, it is not possible to identify an approach that is better than the other one in the observation of tourism, both present advantages and disadvantages. The theorists would prefer the demand-side approach, given that it focuses on monitoring the demand for tourism. The empiricist would adopt the supply-side approach, given that the monitoring of the supply is quicker and can rely on official data gathered by statistical offices. Regardless of the implied costs, the ideal approach would require combining the two methods in order to collect quality information in a reasonable amount of time. For example, this could be done by periodically gathering data on the demand in order to check, and possibly update, the conventions adopted to define the departments of tourism within the supply.

In recent years, the *Computable General Equilibrium* (CGE) has been proposed to measure the economic impacts of tourism in the economy. The CGE predicts, through a numerical simulation approach, the actual way the economy operates by using large systems of equations, each capturing the condition of equilibrium between demand and supply in an industry or a subindustry. The parameters of the system are estimated by using the time series of the relevant variables of interest. On the one hand, the CGE approach reduces the overestimation of the impact of tourism onto the rest of the economy, which is a critical consequence of the I–O model. On the other hand, CGE models are complex, difficult, and expensive to build, which prevents their extensive use for tourism. This is not the case though of Australia where CGE has supplanted I–O modeling, owing to widespread awareness of its flexibility in approximating real-world conditions, such as price and wage flexibility and inter-sectoral resource mobility (Dwyer et al. 2003a, 2004). For an introduction to the CGE methodology applied to tourism and a comparison between the CGE model and the Input–Output model, see Dwyer et al. (2004).

3.4 Tourism Within the National Accounting System

Nowadays there is a strong international cooperation between national statistical institutions and international economic organizations, with the goal of harmonization of the methodologies of identification, definition, and measurement of the various economic aggregates. In fact, practically all countries worldwide follow the standard statistical criteria established by the United Nations (UN), the International Monetary Fund (IMF), the Organization for Economic Co-operation and Development (OECD), and the statistical bureau of the European Union (Eurostat). Consequently, it is possible to compare economic variables across different countries and to achieve a better understanding of their differences, thus allowing a faster advance on knowledge. In the following, let us focus on the aspects of most interest for the identification of the tourism activities, following the standards set by Eurostat through the *European System of Accounts* (ESA).

Firstly, the ESA follows an exogenous definition of sectors in which the national output can be partitioned. This partition is done at different levels, following a tree structure, which has been named NACE[5] by Eurostat. A first level simply distinguishes between the *primary sector* (agriculture and mining), the *secondary sector* (manufacturing), and the *tertiary sector* (services). A second level further distinguishes *divisions* of production, i.e., in the manufacturing sector there are, among others, chemical, textile, electronic devices, etc. Within each division, it is then possible to identify *groups* and *classes* in order to provide a very detailed picture of all the economic activities of the country. In any division, a distinction between final goods (to be consumed) and capital goods (to be invested) is made. As regards tourism, in the national accounting system, any issues regarding the definition of a sector, the degree of sectoral interdependence, and the measurement of an economic activity become pivotal.

[5] NACE is the french acronym for *Nomenclature statistique des Activités économiques dans la Communauté Européenne*.

3.4.1 Final Consumption and Tourism Items

In particular, the tourism purposes for spending is important in the accounting division called "Hotel, cafés and restaurants". This is usually partitioned into two groups of extreme relevance for tourism: "Catering" and "Accommodation services", as well as three additional classes: "Gross rents", for housing spending; "Transport services", for transportation spending; "Recreational and cultural services", for spending on leisure and cultural activities. Moreover, given that the national accounts also classify the expenditure by governments and non-profit organizations as consumption, it would be natural to assign to tourism a share of the public spending on groups such as sport and recreational or cultural activities (usually consisting of subsidies to shows, festivals, etc.), education (for example, educational tours), health care (i.e., tourism by special groups of individuals, such as elderly or disabled).

3.4.2 Fixed Capital Formation and Tourism

The Eurostat system introduced a detailed classification of capital items (including both material and immaterial goods, such as software and arts) which is of great importance to tourism. As for consumption, the adopted classification is organized between categories and subcategories. From a formal perspective, tourism belongs to the category "Services" as an element of its subcategories: "Hotels and restaurants", "Transport, storage and communications", "Other community, social and personal service activities".

3.4.3 Evaluating the Tourism Production

The main difficulty consists, as already stated, in the fact that tourism can be defined as a "synthetic industrial sector", that is, it is made of a combination of output pertaining to conventional businesses belonging to several industries and whose own output is a function of the tourists' demand. Also at the level of the single production unit, the economic activity is implemented in the production of several goods and services. We can define a *primary activity*, a *secondary activity*, and *ancillary activity*. The primary activity is defined as the activity whose added value exceeds the added value of any other activity undertaken by the same unit (i.e., the lodging service is the primary activity for a hotel). The secondary activity is realized by a unit in conjunction with the primary one (i.e., the bar is a secondary activity for a hotel). Finally, the ancillary activity is not intended for an external use but just as a support for the primary and secondary activity of the firms (i.e., a coach service connecting the airport is an ancillary service for the hotel).

Moreover, for the task of measuring the tourism output we should also be able to account for *black market* and *irregular* production. For tourism, like for any other sector, the existence of non-accountable production reduces the degree of coherence and the completeness of the overall picture. As regards tourism, this problem is important both for the irregular production (i.e., lodging service sold without officially reporting the corresponding revenue in the fiscal documents to avoid paying taxes) and for the black market (i.e., tourism activities involving drugs or prostitution).

3.4.4 Tourism Balance of Trade

A specific section of the national accounts deals with the exchange of goods and services between the economy and the rest of the world. Such document is called *Balance of Payments*. The balance of payments of a country is a systematic report of all the economic transactions occurring between residents and non-residents (i.e., the rest of the world) of a given country and in a given time period. It provides an aggregate measure of all the flows of goods, services, and capital from and toward a country (for a full explanation, see Notes 3.2). Within this framework, the tourism balance of trade is defined as the difference between revenues accruing from inbound tourists visiting the country and expenditure of outbound tourists.

Notes 3.2. The Balance of Payments

The Balance of Payments (BoP) is the accounting document that records all the transactions of a country vis-à-vis the rest of the world. This includes the value of imports and exports of goods, the money lent to and borrowed from other countries, the profits and financial interests paid to and received from foreign economies, and so on.

The accounting method for the BoP is the *double-entry system*, according to which each transaction leads to two recordings of identical value but of opposite sign. Therefore, the balance of this account is always equal to zero by construction and when we talk of a deficit or a surplus of the BoP we usually refer to its balance net of the change in official reserves.

The BoP is made up of two sections (or three, in case we include also the section "Errors and Omissions" which is not relevant for our purposes): (a) current account; (b) capital account. The current account of the BoP records the non-financial transactions of a country and considers on one side the goods and services exchanged (the trade balance) and on the other side the repayments and dividends from loans and investments (factor income). The capital account of the BoP records the net change in ownership in foreign assets and include private foreign direct investments and official transactions of the central bank.

According to the recent criteria approved by the international statistical offices, the tourism balance of trade is included in the current account section of the balance of payments. It is mainly composed of transports and trips abroad.

3.4.5 Transport

In this section of the current account the international economic transactions that refer to transport services and their auxiliary activities are recorded. The individual item is classified according to the mean of transportation (air transport, sea transport, etc.), the kind of activity it leads to (cargo transportation, passenger and auxiliary services, where cargo transportation is not of interest for tourism and will be disregarded in our discussion). In the tourism balance of trade it is also recorded, among the assets, the transport services that resident companies supply to non-residents, both domestically and abroad. Similarly, the corresponding services provided by foreign vectors to domestic tourists, regardless of the location of supply, will be recorded among the liabilities. Finally, we classify under "other services" all auxiliary and support services to transport, of which taxes and fees paid to travel agencies are just two examples.

3.4.6 Trips Abroad

Under "trips abroad" we record the tourism expenditure by national travellers abroad and the revenues accruing from inbound travellers. The physical counterpart of these amounts of money is the basket of goods and services (including complementary consumption) that we identify as the tourism product (see Sect. 2.5). This does neither include the expenditure for international transport (which is recorded under "transport") nor all of the items which are explicitly accounted for in other sections of the current account (like, for instance, insurance and personal services).

3.5 The Tourism Satellite Account

Following the theoretical framework of the Input–Output model (see Sect. 3.3) to measure tourism, the *United Nations World Tourism Organization* (UNWTO) have been working in the last 20 years on redefining and harmonizing the national methods of accounting tourism activities. In particular, the UNWTO suggested the adoption of a satellite system of national accounting for tourism (the *Tourism Satellite Account*—TSA) as a way to deal with the heterogeneity problem of the tourism activity.

The satellite accounting systems are special systems that are designed to be fully coherent and integrated with the national accounting system and that allow each country to respond to the needs of certain areas of the economy.

> Satellite accounts are one way in which the System of National Accounts may be adapted to meet differing circumstances and needs. They are closely linked to the main system but are not bound to employ exactly the same concepts or restrict themselves to data expressed in monetary terms. Satellite accounts are intended for special purposes such as monitoring the community's health or the state of the environment, or tourism activities.
>
> (Eurostat 2011)

In practice, the satellite accounts integrate the national accounting system with monetary, physical, and geographical information, by mixing alternative statistical information (such as sample observation of tourists' spending) in a coherent way with national statistics. Two types of satellite accounts can be identified, according to the their relationship with the national systems: (a) accounts that allow alternative analysis; (b) accounts for special functions or objectives.

The first type tries to extend the national systems toward a better identification, classification, and evaluation of accounting aspects that are presently disregarded, and which may lead to their future incorporation into the national systems. A simple example is the satellite accounts that attempt to evaluate and embody the use of environmental resources into the economic system. The satellite accounts of the second type usually relate to specific (financial or productive) activities of the economy which are not identifiable in the national accounts, and aim to introduce elements that complement, without distorting, the national system. Tourism, intended as a complex consumption act, is the easiest example we can make of this second group.

The central problem facing accountants is the difficulty of achieving a precise identification of the area that is subject to the examination and, for the reasons we explained in the previous sections, tourism is not exception of such complexity. Indeed, we have seen that the tourism product directly and indirectly involves a wide array of industries that operate also (but not only) to satisfy tourists' needs. The TSA provides the methodology of gathering data regarding the tourists demand (such as surveying samples of the tourists' population) and then combining it with national accounting data about the supply of goods and services that are important for tourism according to the Input-Output matrix (see Sect. 3.3). For greater details on TSA, see Spurr (2006), UNTWO (2008a), Frechtling (2010), and the Case Study 3.1.

Case study 3.1. An Example of Tourism Satellite Accounts: Canada

Canada is among the countries that in recent years have closely adopted the resolutions set by the UNWTO on satellite accounts. Along with the creation of the Canadian Commission for Tourism in 1994, it was also one of the first countries that published a TSA as part of its National Accounting System. Canada's pioneering experience actually started in 1984 with the creation of a task force which, in 1989, concluded its activity with a report in favor of adopting satellite accounts for tourism, thus receiving the appreciation of the UNWTO and UNSTAT.

The first critical step toward the creation of a TSA must deal with the definition of tourism. The Canadian TSA adopted the internationally accepted definitions for tourism-related issues (see Sect. 2.4). Central to such definition of tourism is the reference to the location of residence outside which the tourism activity takes place. The criterion adopted by Canada in its TSA sets at 80 km (approximately 50 miles) as the benchmark distance so that any trip to a destination within 80 km from the location of residence would not qualify as tourism.

Data used for the compilation of TSA come from different sources. There are five sample surveys on both Canadian and non-Canadian tourists who spend their money in Canada. The collected figures are combined and compared with the data coming from household budget surveys as well as from sectoral investigations on travel agencies, tour operators, etc. in order to reach a balance between the demand and the supply of each product, i.e., both the inputs and outputs of each industry.

> One of the most important accounting identities (or constraints) found in the I–O tables is that supply must equal demand for each commodity. In other words, the sum of the expenditures on a particular commodity must equal the revenues generated from sales (taking into account exports and imports). Similarly, there is an additional constraint that each industry's total output (revenues) must equal its total inputs (costs). In practice, these identities are not satisfied as a result of limitations of the statistical system. For instance, data obtained from surveys or administrative sources provide different estimates for the same phenomenon, have different levels of quality, may contain reporting errors, and may not provide complete coverage, and so on. Ensuring that the data jointly satisfy both of these accounting identities through an iterative process referred to as the balancing of industry and commodity accounts is an integral part of compiling the I–O tables.
>
> (Statistics Canada 2007, p. 21)

The TSA allows national accountants: (a) to estimate the contribution of tourism to Canada's GDP, so as to appreciate its strategic role in the national economy (in 2002 tourism was estimated to contribute for $23.3 billion to the GDP, with a share of 2.2 %); (b) to analyze the composition of the demand which, according to Statistics Canada (2007), in Canada in 2002 was composed by 31.1 % of spending in transport, 28.6 % in accommodation, 19.3 % in food and beverage services, 9.6 % in other services for tourism such as recreation and entertainment, and 11.3 % in other consumption goods; (c) to establish the supply of each industry that is directed to satisfy the tourists' demand (for example, 92 % for travel agencies, 79 % for air transportation, 66 % for accommodation, etc.)

In conclusion, the TSA provides the Canadian statisticians and policy makers with a deep understanding of the tourism phenomenon, an estimate of its importance for the national economy, and helps define the best management practices for tourism. The Canadian experience is internationally recognized and the TSA is nowadays seen as the key accounting tool for understanding the economic impact of tourism.

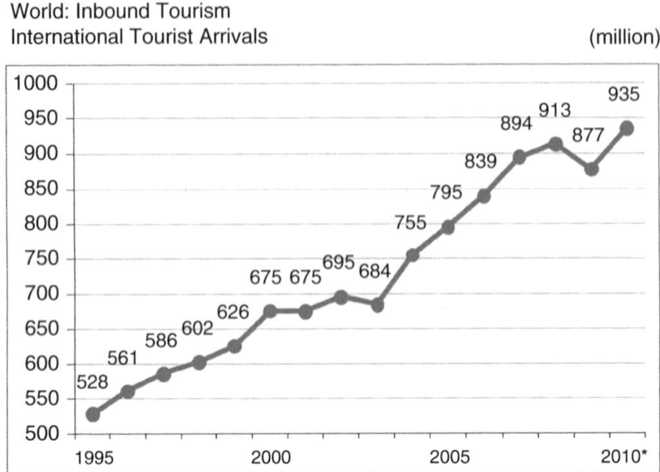

Fig. 3.3 International tourist arrivals in the world, 1995–2010. Source: UNWTO (2011a), p. 1

3.6 The Role of Tourism in Contemporary Economies

We complete the chapter with a brief recognition of the key features and dynamics of international tourism flows and their impact on both national and international economies. WTTC (2011) estimates that tourism accounts for about 9.3 % of the world's GDP and employs 235 million people worldwide.[6] Figure 3.3, which displays the recent evolution in the number of international arrivals worldwide, clearly shows that the trend of international tourism is experiencing a sustained and constant growth:[7] the number of international tourists in 1950 was 25 million, and increased up to 500 million in 1995 and in 2007, 900 million (UNWTO 2010). The average growth rate for arrivals during the 2000–2009 was 4.1 %, which is quite significant if we consider that the terrorist attacks of September 11, 2001, and the consequent geopolitical instability, the SARS epidemic infection in 2003, the recent economic

[6] The World Travel & Tourism Council (WTTC) is the global forum for business leaders in the Travel & Tourism industry. With the Chairs and Chief Executives of the foremost Travel & Tourism companies worldwide as its Members, WTTC has a unique mandate and overview on all matters related to Travel & Tourism. WTTC works to raise awareness of Travel & Tourism as one of the world's largest industries.

[7] All figures presented in this section come from two documents that are published by the UNWTO and that (on a yearly and quarterly basis) analyze the state of tourism worldwide: "Tourism Highlights" and "World Tourism Barometer". UNWTO also publishes other relevant documents that can be found on the UNWTO's website (www.unwto.org).

recession, etc., all happened in this period.[8] In Fig. 3.3 the global financial and economic crisis was reflected in the reduction of international tourist arrivals in 2009, but in 2010 there was already a strong recovery (provisional figures estimate that international arrivals were up of almost 7 % to 935 million in 2010; UNWTO 2011a). The UNWTO remarks that the vast majority of destinations worldwide posted positive figures, sufficient to offset recent losses or bring them close to a full recovery (see Notes 3.3 for a brief history of tourism evolution worldwide).

Notes 3.3. A Brief History of Tourism

The genesis of tourism can be found in various activities associated with travel and leisure in Europe in the early civilizations. We refer in particular to: the Roman spa, mainly used in cities, but which also gave life to stays in the countryside and near the sea; pilgrimages, already widespread in primitive societies but institutionalized by the great monotheistic religions; and finally the *Grand Tour* that, since the Sixteenth century allowed to recover the central role of classical civilizations of the Mediterranean in the European culture. If the term "tourist" was born in reference to the Grand Tour, it was only at the end of the Eighteenth century that tourism was recognized as a relevant economic activity and social phenomenon; in that time the consumer society came to light, with an emerging European middle class for which a clear separation between working and free time arose.

In that period the so-called modern tourism was born, with the development of the early tourism structures and tourism resorts, where the primary economic activity was precisely tourism. The United Kingdom was the first country to develop modern tourism, due to the significant economic development brought about by the industrial revolution. The first type of modern tourism, which quickly spread from England to the rest of Europe was the spa. In the mid Eighteenth century the English town of Bath recorded a strong increase in arrivals and overnight stays, thanks to the proximity with London, which made it a fashionable destination among the aristocracy and the bourgeoisie. The most important innovation introduced by the British was to transform Bath from being a spa resort into a city of entertainment and leisure, by building hospitality facilities and other recreational structures. The example of Bath was followed by other British spas (Epsom and Tunbridge Wells) and, subsequently, from the early seaside resorts.

(continued)

[8] The relationship between tourism, war, and terrorism is of great current interest for the Economics of Tourism. As an example, we recommend the special issues of the *Journal of Travel Research* (1999), of *Tourism Economics* (2000), and the works of Sonmez and Graefe (1998), Sonmez (1998), Bonham et al. (2006), Arana and Leon (2008), Thompson (2011). As regards the impact of the recent financial and economic crisis on tourism see the special issue of the *Journal of Travel Research* in 2010 (Sheldon and Dwyer 2010, for an introduction).

It was at the turn of the Eighteenth and Nineteenth centuries that, with the decline of spa tourism, the rapid development of seaside tourism, which suddenly became fashionable, took place. The evolution of the early seaside resorts followed the same pattern of Bath: Brighton became the most important resort of England mainly because it understood how to combine the attraction for the sea with the development of leisure activities for tourists. At that stage, tourists used to go to seaside resorts in summer in search of cold seas and fairly low temperatures.

In a second phase, starting in mid-Nineteenth century, southern European seaside resorts began to exploit a new trend, that of winter tourism in warmer seas than the English one. In particular, it was the French Riviera to achieve the best results in this sense, rapidly becoming a favorite resort for the élite tourism.

In a third phase, tourism entered the era of mass tourism with the success of the warm seas in summer. A preview to this phenomenon can be traced in the United States of the early Twentieth century, but it was after the Second World War that the strong economic growth and the greater possibility of spending for the growing middle class set new patterns of consumption and lifestyle. The glamour of tanning and the beach was the key factor in explaining the success of seaside tourism in Mediterranean countries, which more and more began to accommodate tourists in the summer. Other types of tourism, such as mountain tourism, joined the success of seaside tourism as a mass tourism experience. The growing proportion of the population of developed countries that joined tourism was the biggest challenge for the hospitality industry: the growing incomes, the worsening of the quality–price ratio, the escape from crowded resorts and the search for new destinations led to the development of intercontinental tourism which are benefiting countries of different regions, such as the Seychelles, the Maldives and the Caribbean Islands. These countries grew mainly investing in the development of tourism.

In the age of post-modern globalization we are living in, tourism has greatly modified its structure: the taste of consumers has changed, it is less standardized than in the era of mass tourism; new technologies have created new opportunities in the choice of the destination, in the budget constraint and in the way of organizing the trip (see Chap. 12). Finally, the great economic development of important countries such as Brazil, Russia, India, and China suggests that in the near future the developing world will become more and more an important region of origin of international tourism, not only a region of destination.

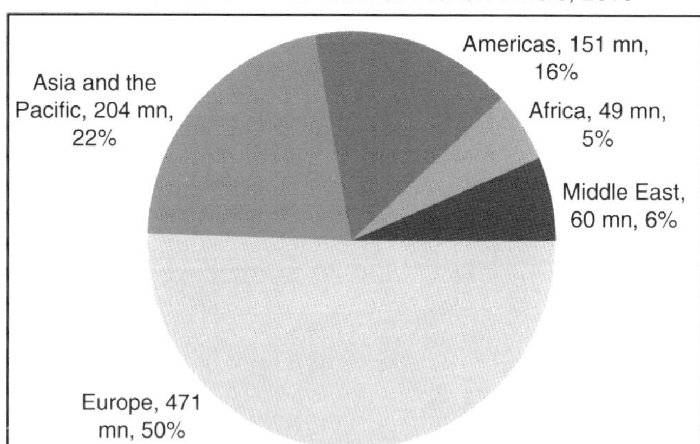

Fig. 3.4 International tourist arrivals: breakdown by region. Source: UNWTO (2011a), p. 4

A striking feature of modern international tourism, hence, is its resilience. However, recovery came at different speeds among different regions, and was primarily driven by emerging economies. Indeed, although tourism is often hurt by the occurrence of negative events, it always recuperates its "health", mainly by shifting the geographical distribution of its regional and sub-regional flows. Although Western and Southern European countries and North America still receive the highest number of international tourists, in the period 2000–2009, the number of international tourist arrivals grew by 5.7 % in Asia and the Pacific, 6.2 % in Africa and 8.8 % in Middle East but only by 1.8 % in Europe, and 1.0 % in the Americas (UNWTO 2010). In Fig. 3.4 we can observe that of the 935 million international tourists, 50 % of world inbound tourism is concentrated in Europe while 22 % is in Asia and the Pacific (UNWTO 2011a). Therefore, a second striking feature of international tourism is the changing pattern in the distribution of flows across regions.

Table 3.4 displays the allocation of the international tourism receipts across global regions which in 2009 amounted to 611 billion € ($852 billion), half of which in Europe. Table 3.4 also shows percapita spending. This is an indicator which varies significantly across regions to reflect different costs of living and average length of stay, and range from 380 € for a trip to a Central/Eastern European country to 930 € to North America and 2,210 € to Oceania.

The most visited international destinations in 2009 were France with 74.2 million arrivals (almost 10 % of the worldwide international tourism), the United States with 54.9 million, Spain with 52.2, and China with 50.9 million which recently surpassed Italy, now standing in fifth position, with 43.2 million international arrivals (Table 3.5).

Table 3.4 International tourism receipts

	International tourism receipts				US$			Euro		
	Local currencies, constant prices, change (%)			Share (%)	Receipts			Receipts		
					(Billion)		Per arrival	(Billion)		Per arrival
	07/06	08/07	09/08	2009	2008	2009	2009	2008	2009	2009
World	5.5	1.3	−5.7	100	941	852	970	640	611	690
Advanced economies[a]	4.9	1.9	−6.7	64.2	613	547	1,160	417	392	830
Emerging economies[a]	6.8	0.1	−3.8	35.8	328	305	740	223	219	530
By UNWTO regions:										
Europe	2.7	−1.2	−6.6	48.5	473.7	413.0	900	322.0	296.1	640
Northern Europe	4.0	−2.0	−2.9	7.1	70.2	60.9	1,150	47.8	43.6	820
Western Europe	2.2	−2.3	−7.2	16.9	162.2	143.7	980	110.3	103.0	710
Central/Eastern Europe	8.9	2.1	−8.2	5.6	57.8	47.4	530	39.3	34.0	380
Southern/Mediter. Eu.	0.9	−0.8	−7.0	18.9	183.5	161.1	940	124.7	115.5	670
Asia and the Pacific	10.0	4.6	−0.7	23.9	208.9	203.7	1,120	142.1	146.1	810
North-East Asia	8.3	8.4	0.7	11.8	99.9	100.3	1,020	67.9	71.9	730
South-East Asia	16.0	−1.0	−6.3	6.4	59.8	54.3	870	40.6	38.9	630
Oceania	6.4	2.9	5.2	3.9	33.7	33.5	3,080	22.9	24.0	2,210
South Asia	6.8	7.4	−0.2	1.8	15.5	15.6	1,550	10.6	11.2	1,110
Americas	6.6	4.9	−10.1	19.4	188.1	165.2	1,170	127.9	118.5	840
North America	7.6	6.9	−12.3	14.0	138.9	118.9	1,290	94.5	85.2	930
Caribbean	0.9	−3.1	−4.9	2.6	23.6	22.2	1,140	16.1	16.0	820
Central America	10.6	−1.1	−7.1	0.7	6.4	5.9	770	4.3	4.2	550
South America	6.8	2.4	−1.3	2.1	19.2	18.2	850	13.1	13.0	610
Africa	9.7	−3.5	−4.4	3.4	30.2	28.9	630	20.5	20.7	450
North Africa	7.4	−3.9	−4.3	1.2	10.8	9.9	570	7.3	7.1	410
Subsaharan Africa	10.9	−3.3	−4.4	2.2	19.4	18.9	670	13.2	13.6	480
Middle East	9.4	0.8	−0.9	4.8	39.7	41.2	780	27.0	29.5	560

Source: UNWTO (2010), p. 5

[a]Based on the classification by the International Monetary Fund (IMF), see page 147 of http://www.imf.org/external/pubs/ft/weo/2010/01/pdf/text.pdf

Table 3.5 International tourist arrivals: top ten countries in 2009

International tourist arrivals				
	Million		Change (%)	
Rank	2008	2009	08/07	09/08
1. France	79.2	74.2	−2.0	−6.3
2. United States	57.9	54.9	3.5	−5.3
3. Spain	57.2	52.2	−2.5	−8.7
4. China	53.0	50.9	−3.1	−4.1
5. Italy	42.7	43.2	−2.1	1.2
6. United Kingdom	30.1	28.0	−2.4	−7.0
7. Turkey	25.0	25.5	12.3	2.0
8. Germany	24.9	24.2	1.9	−2.7
9. Malaysia	22.1	23.6	5.1	7.2
10. Mexico	22.6	21.5	5.9	−5.2

Source: UNWTO (2010), p. 6

Table 3.6 International tourism receipts and expenditure: top ten countries in 2009

Country	International tourism receipts (billion dollars)	Country	International tourism expenditure (billion dollars)
United States	93.9	Germany	81.2
Spain	53.2	United States	73.2
France	49.4	United Kingdom	50.3
Italy	40.2	China	43.7
China	39.7	France	38.5
Germany	34.7	Italy	27.9
United Kingdom	30.1	Japan	25.1
Australia	25.6	Canada	24.2
Turkey	21.3	Russian Federation	20.8
Austria	19.4	Netherlands	20.7

Source: UNWTO (2010)

Finally, Table 3.6 shows the ranking of the top ten countries as regards international tourism receipts as well as the top ten countries as regards international tourism expenditure. The United States is the country with the greatest international receipts (93.9 billion $ in 2009) as well as the second in expenditure on international tourism right after Germany (73.2 billion $). The difference between receipts and expenditure for international tourism measures the tourism balance of trade (see Sect. 3.4): Germany and the United Kingdom display a significant deficit in this account, respectively 46.5 and 20.3 billion $. The countries with the greatest surplus are instead the United States (20.7 billion $), France (10.9 billion $) and Italy (12.3 billion $). On this last issue, a final remark is about the strategic position of tourism in contributing to the equilibrium of a country's balance of payments. For instance, Italy is a strong importer of energy and hence has a structural deficit in the energy balance of trade: thus, the surplus in the tourism balance of trade is a strategic asset which, one could say, partially pays Italy's energy bill.

Chapter Overview

- The definition, identification, and measurement of the tourism sector is a challenging task, due to the heterogeneity of goods and services included in the tourism product, thus implying that the tourism phenomenon is spread across many economic sectors and economic activities.
- The tourism sector cannot be quantified through neither the national accounting system nor the standard criteria for the identification of economic activities (the technology criterion and the market criterion).
- To measure the economic impact of tourism two approaches can be employed: a supply-side approach which implies the identification of all the departments involved in the tourism phenomenon, and a demand-side approach which implies the use of Input–Output method to identify the sector as a result of that production satisfying tourism demand.
- The Satellite Accounting System (TSA) is a specific methodology which effectively measures and quantifies the importance of tourism in the economy. The TSA consists of the combination of statistical data collected from the tourists (through surveys) and the Input–Output matrix for tourism with supply-side information that refers to all industries that are involved in relevant productions for tourism.

Chapter 4
The Economics of Tourism Destinations

Learning Outcomes
After completion of this chapter, you will be able to understand:

- The concept of tourism destination, its main features, and the reasons why its economic aspects justify a specific investigation.
- The key aspects of tourism demand, at the analytical (elasticity), theoretical (relationship between tourism demand and destination management), and empirical (forecasting methods for tourism demand) level.
- The life cycle model applied to the tourism destination and the principles for the optimal management of its evolution.

4.1 Introduction

The *tourism destination*, intended as the location of tourism structures events and services as well as the place where travelers' needs are fulfilled, is the core of the tourism system. Usually, the destination is geographically well defined, but its boundaries may often blur and evolve. According to Davidson and Maitland (1997):

> A destination is a single district, town or city, or a clearly defined and contained rural, coastal or mountain area
>
> (Davidson and Maitland 1997, p. 4)

From our perspective, this definition is too vague, since type and dimension are recalled in a very general way. According to Papatheodorou a tourism destination is:

> A geographical area of variable territorial scale, where tourism is a predominant activity both from a demand-side (i.e. tourists) and a supply-side (i.e. infrastructure and employment) perspective.
>
> (Papatheodorou 2006, p. xv)

G. Candela and P. Figini, *The Economics of Tourism Destinations*,
Springer Texts in Business and Economics, DOI 10.1007/978-3-642-20874-4_4,

Although the latter definition is much more precise, from our perspective has two main caveats: firstly, it lacks any reference with the systemic nature of tourism; secondly, tourism is not necessarily a predominant economic activity in the destination: think of medium and big size cities that are important business or cultural destinations but for which tourism only generates a tiny amount of its income. On the basis of this discussion, and by recalling the concept of tourism system previously defined (see the Leiper model in Sect. 2.3 and Fig. 2.1) it is possible to define a destination as:

> A territorial system which supplies at least one whole tourism product aimed at satisfying the complex requirements of the tourist.

From a geographical perspective, a destination can exceed the limits or borders of a city or a province and, depending on the characteristics of the territory and of the demand, the destination can be identified with a cultural district, a town, an administrative region, or with the intersection between regions or provinces; it could eventually be the whole country. Moreover, from a management perspective, the existence of tourism requires the organization of a *destination management* body to coordinate the tourism supply and its promotion, regardless of the economic importance of tourism within the local economy.

Being a physical place where the needs of the demand meet the supply, the destination concentrates just in one concept all the elements of tourism that we studied in Chaps. 2 and 3. The destination embodies all the significant elements of the tourism product: it gathers all the businesses hosting tourism, offers all the primary attractions, and aims at satisfying a relevant share of the tourism demand. The destination is the connecting element between the complexity of the tourism sector, the heterogeneity of the tourism product, and the intangible goods supplied by the territory.

In light of such criterion, the entire discipline of Economics of Tourism could be interpreted as *Economics of Destinations*. Thus, it is necessary to identify a way to distinguish those features that are really characteristic issues of the destination from those features that are specific of a single firm or general for the whole economic system. The adopted approach to understand such distinction and to select those issues that are the core of the Economics of Tourism Destinations is the following:

- The *Microeconomic level* refers to the price and quantity of the elementary goods and services included in the tourism product;
- The *Macroeconomic level* refers to the aggregate value of the goods and services demanded by tourists, in a given period of time, and in a given economic system;
- The *Intermediate-economic level* refers to the overall quantity of "tourism" (as measured by the number of overnight stays), demanded by tourists in the spatial aggregation of production called destination.

As regards the "micro" level, the Microeconomics of Tourism employs the same analytical tools of the Consumption and Production theory; thus, we refer to any microeconomics textbook for a general overview of this theory, and to the second part of this book (from Chaps. 5 to 12) for specific applications of such theory to the context of tourism. As regards the "macro" level, from Chaps. 13 to 16, a discussion of the tourism demand from a macroeconomics point of view is provided and, hence, topics such as the tourism multiplier, the relationship between tourism and International Economics, tourism and economic growth, etc. are reviewed. Finally, the present chapter focuses on the "intermediate" level by studying the most typical relationship in the Economics of Tourism: the relationship between the overall quantity of overnight stays in the destination and its determinants (own price, changes in the demand, evolution of the destination, etc.).

Within this framework, this chapter is organized in the following manner. We start by explaining basic concepts related to the destination such as tourism demand and the elasticity (see Sect. 4.2). That is followed by Sect. 4.3 with the presentation of some economic characteristics of the destination, such as the coordination issue or the problem of completing the tourism product through the search for variety. In the same section, we briefly introduce concepts such as *destination management* and *destination marketing and branding*, referring to more specialized texts of those disciplines for a deeper analysis. Sect. 4.4 discusses the strategic goals of the destination, which can be summarised as the search for maximization of tourism expenditure: reaching the target, we will see, will depend on the values assumed by the elasticity of demand. Finally, Sect. 4.5 presents a number of models aimed at describing the evolution over time of tourism demand in the destination, which is a crucial aspect to take into consideration when trying to understand the effect of tourism policy and planning at the destination level.

4.2 An Introduction to the Tourism Demand

We know that the tourism product can be defined as a basket of different goods and services that are offered at the destination level. Given the complex aggregate of heterogeneous products and the plurality of types of tourism (see Sect. 2.5), it makes no sense to refer to a generic demand for tourism. Thus, in the Economics of Tourism the concept of demand can be referred only to segments of the tourism market with significant degree of homogeneity. The identification of such segments can be achieved following two alternative criteria:

- A *territorial criterion*, according to which we refer to tourism demand in terms of a given destination, a given region, a given country, etc.;
- A *typology criterion*, according to which we refer to the demand for, i.e. beach-based tourism, cultural tourism, heritage tourism, rural tourism, etc.

In this book, we suggest the adoption of several demands for tourism, which individually depend on factors such as the territory and/or the tourist's motivation for a trip. Classification of the demand by segments does not prevent us from defining a demand function for each elementary component of the tourism product: one for accommodation services, one for museum entrances, one for beach services, etc. In a macroeconomic context, on the contrary, we can consider a unique demand for tourism by means of the aggregation of tourism expenditure, which is obtained by taking the sum of the expenditure for different goods, services, and types of tourism measured according to the price system (see Sect. 2.6.3).

To start with, we introduce the *demand function*. In Economics, the demand function is a static relationship between the desired quantity of a good and its unit price, *ceteris paribus*, i.e., all other things being equal. It is usually represented by the function:

$$q = f(p, [\ldots]), \tag{4.1}$$

where q represents the demanded quantity for a good as a function f of its unit price p, and where the symbol [. . .] indicates that all the other variables that may have an effect on q are assumed to be invariant. Such other variables are income, price of other goods, preferences, effects of fashion and advertisement, the behavior of other consumers, etc. Usually, the demand function describes an inverse relationship between price and quantity (*Law of Demand*): *ceteris paribus*, as the price of a good rises, its quantity demanded decreases, and vice versa.

4.2.1 The Demand for Different Types of Tourism at the Destination

For the Economics of Tourism, at the intermediate economic level we can identify three types of demand function.

1. The *demand for a type of tourism at the destination*, considering the number $N_{i,r}$ of overnight stays of tourism i, at destination r, as a function of its daily price $v_{i,r}$, $f_{i,r}$: $v_{i,r} \to N_{i,r}$.[1]
2. The *overall demand for a type of tourism*, which considers the number N_i of overnight stays of tourism i as a function of its average daily price v_i at different destinations. This can be written in terms of the function, F_i: $v_i \to N_i$.
3. The *overall demand for a destination*, which considers the overall number N_r of overnight stays at destination r as a function of the average daily price v_r of the different types of tourism offered at that destination. This can be expressed in terms of the function, g_r: $v_r \to N_r$.

[1] Throughout the chapter, we will use N, the number of overnight stays, as the relevant variable to identify the "quantity" of tourism demanded by tourists while, for simplicity, we will sometimes refer to as days, but the underlying assumption is that days have always to be considered as the number of nights spent at the destination. We will use v, as the unit price, that is, the price of one day of tourism.

In synthesis, the tourism phenomenon is consistent with several demand functions. Each refers to a market segment identified by types of tourism and/or destinations. If we explicitly indicate the monetary income of the tourists in the demand function and assume that each destination is specialised in the supply of only one type of tourism,[2] we can build the following demand functions:

$$N_{i,r} = f_{i,r}\left(v_{i,r}, [\ldots, M_i, M_{\text{tou}}, \ldots]\right) \text{ where } i = 1, 2, \ldots, m \text{ and } r = 1, 2, \ldots, R_i, \tag{4.2}$$

$$N_i = F_i(v_i, [\ldots, M_i, M_{\text{tou}}, \ldots]) \text{ where } i = 1, 2, \ldots, m, \tag{4.3}$$

where M_i and M_{tou} respectively indicate the amount of disposable income for tourism i and for all types of tourism at destination r. Expressions (4.2) and (4.3) can be used to understand two important aspects of the curve representing a demand function: the *movement along* the curve and the *movement of* the curve.[3] In particular, a variation in the tourism demand, measured by the number of overnight stays, that is due to a price change (i.e., by holding every other variable included in [...] as constant) leads to a movement along the demand curve. The idea of "price change" should be intended as *relative* to the price of other goods. Instead, the change in the number of overnight stays due to other variables, such as the disposable income or the share of income allocated to tourism activities, leads to a shift of the demand curve. These two alternatives are clearly displayed in Fig. 4.1, representing the function $f_{i,r}$, and where the horizontal and vertical axis are respectively assigned to the number of stays ($N_{i,r}$) and to the price ($v_{i,r}$). In particular, the reduction of the price from $v_{i,r}$ to $v'_{i,r}$ yields an increase in the number of stays from $N_{i,r}$ to $N'_{i,r}$ along a given demand curve (movement from point A to point B) consistently with the Law of Demand. Differently, an increase of M_{tou} (or of M_i) usually leads to an increase, *for any given price* v, in the number of stays from $N_{i,r}$ to $N''_{i,r}$, hence on a new demand curve (movement from point A to point C).[4]

The distinction between movements along and movements of the demand curve can be explained as follows in the tourism context:

1. A change in the tourist's number of days spent at the destination due to a variation in the price of this type of tourism in such destination, $v_{i,r}$, *ceteris*

[2] This hypothesis will be maintained throughout the chapter, and is made to simplify the economic problem of the destination by reducing case *sub* (3) into case *sub* (1).

[3] With reference to the graphical sketching of the demand function in the plane (N; v), we define as a *movement along the curve* any change of the quantity demanded N stemming from the change in price v, *ceteris paribus*. Instead, we define as *movement of the curve* any change in the quantity demanded N stemming from the change in relevant variables other than price (such as income, price of other goods, etc).

[4] See Sect. 5.3 for a detailed discussion of the demand for tourism as a function of the money available for holidays.

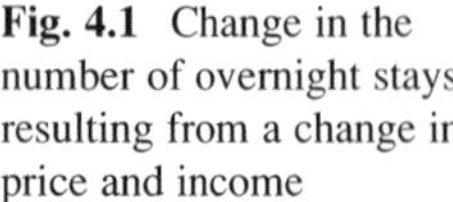

Fig. 4.1 Change in the number of overnight stays resulting from a change in price and income

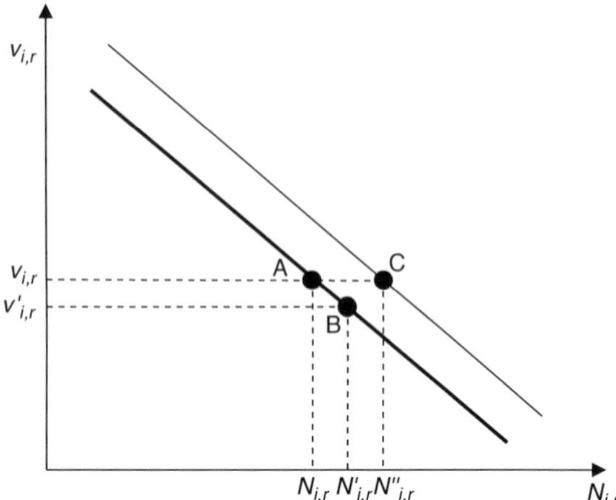

paribus (i.e., by holding constant M_i, M_{tou}, and the price of alternative holidays) can be represented by a movement along the demand curve: the corresponding change in the quantity demanded is often called *idiosyncratic effect of the destination*;

2. A change in the tourist's number of days spent at the destination due to a variation of disposable income for this type of tourism, M_i, *ceteris paribus* (i.e., by holding all the remaining variables as constant, prices included) is captured by a shift of the demand curve: this is called *idiosyncratic effect of tourism*;
3. Finally, a change in the tourist's number of days spent at the destination in response to a variation in the overall disposable money for tourism, M_{tou}, *ceteris paribus* is also captured by a shift of the demand curve. This is called *market effect.*

These effects can be clearly seen with some examples.

- Let us imagine that a destination known as Alpha specialised in beach tourism has experienced a demand contraction meaning that there has been a reduction in the tourists' number of days in such destination. How should we interpret such variation? This will depend upon the causing factors or events. In general, the idiosyncratic effect and the market effect are not mutually exclusive and often occur contemporaneously (either by addition or by compensation). Firstly, the contraction in the number of days spent by tourists in Alpha may be due to an increase in the price of tourism at the destination, for example, caused by a variation in the exchange rate in case of international tourism. *Ceteris paribus*, this implies a loss in appeal for Alpha compared to other destinations and can be explained as an idiosyncratic effect of the destination (movement along the curve). However, the contraction may be rather due to a loss of interest for beach tourism in general (idiosyncratic effect of tourism). Alternatively, it could also depend on the reduction of tourists' disposable income for tourism (because of either a decrease in the amount of disposable income, the market effect, or a drop in households' propensity to travel). Under the last assumption, the demand contraction does not depend on any change in the appeal of the destination Alpha relative to alternative destinations, but rather on a general shift in demand (movement of the curve). Note that such shift may also result from a loss of Alpha's competitiveness but for reasons other than the price (like, for example, obsolescence of the tourism structures and infrastructures, or environmental damage, or simply the fact that Alpha is no longer a fashionable or popular destination; see Sect. 4.5).

- Let us now imagine the example of an increase in tourists' number of days in the mountain tourism destination Beta, that is, an expansion of the tourism demand in Beta. Such increase may be explained by a series of alternative possibilities depending on the occurrence of either an idiosyncratic effect of the destination (a lower price, movement along the curve), or an idiosyncratic effect of winter tourism (for example, tourists find skiing a more appealing option—movement of the curve), or rather a general expansion of the tourism market (more tourists visit the destination, movement of the curve).

It is important to analytically distinguish between these different cases and understand the reasons behind an expansion or contraction of the tourism demand. In practice, such effect is observed not only through tourists' number of overnight stays but also through other indicators, e.g. the number of arrivals or accommodation occupancy rates. In any case, the correct understanding of such effects becomes essential to ensure that tourism planning and policy in a destination are effective.

4.2.2 The Elasticity of the Tourism Demand

In the study of the tourism demand, the concept of elasticity is essential. Broadly speaking, the elasticity can be defined as *the ratio between the percentage change of variable y and the percentage change of variable x, when x causes y,* as shown in (4.4).

$$\varepsilon = \left|\frac{\%\Delta y}{\%\Delta x}\right|. \tag{4.4}$$

In Economics of Tourism four types of elasticity can commonly be calculated: (a) *own-price elasticity*, which gives information on the variation in tourism demand due to changes in the price of tourism; (b) *cross-price elasticity*, which indicates variation in tourism demand due to price changes of other types of tourism or other destinations, it is sometimes referred as the competitor's position *vis-à-vis* price changes in a destination; (c) *elasticity related to available money* which explains variations in tourism demand resulting from changes in tourists' amount of money allocated to that type of tourism; and (d) *income elasticity of tourism expenditure* which differs from sub-case (c) in the variable of interest, in this case, the tourists' disposable income is the variable observed to explain changes in tourism expenditure. Given the importance of elasticity in the Economics of Tourism, in the following we present a detailed explanation on how to calculate and interpret each type of elasticity.

4.2.2.1 Own-Price Elasticity

For the calculation of the own-price elasticity (direct elasticity) we consider the general demand function (4.2), $N_{i,r} = f_{i,r}(v_{i,r})$. The elasticity of tourism demand is *the ratio between the percentage change of the quantity demanded* $N_{i,r}$ *and the percentage change of price* $v_{i,r}$ which caused it. This general definition can have two interpretations. Firstly, when dealing with a discretely valued demand curve the term *arch elasticity* should be used: this is the case where percentage changes are considered, as in (4.4). Secondly, when we take the limit for very small percentage changes of price, the concept of derivative can be used, as in expression (4.5). In this latter case, we assume a derivable demand function.

$$\varepsilon = \left| \frac{\partial N_{i,r}}{\partial v_{i,r}} \cdot \frac{v_{i,r}}{N_{i,r}} \right|. \tag{4.5}$$

Given that the tourism demand is commonly characterised as an inverse (or negative) relationship between the demanded tourism (measured by the number of nights in the destination) and the daily price of tourism (Law of Demand), that is, the derivative of the demand function is negative, it is common practice to take the elasticity in absolute value, so that its range of variation becomes $0 \leq \varepsilon < \infty$. For this reason the significant values of ε are defined with respect to the unity (note that the absolute value of the elasticity can be different for different points ($v_{i,r}$; $N_{i,r}$) along the demand curve):

- At points where $\varepsilon > 1$ the demand is called *elastic*: a given percentage variation in price leads to a greater percentage change in demand for tourism.
- At points where $\varepsilon < 1$ the demand is said to be *inelastic* (or rigid): a given percentage variation in price leads to a smaller percentage change in demand for tourism.
- Finally, if at a given point it is the case that $\varepsilon = 1$ we claim that the *elasticity is unitary* in that point. In this special situation the percentage change in the demand for tourism and the percentage change in price are of identical value.

4.2.2.2 Cross-Price Elasticity

We refer to the general demand function for tourism (4.2) explicitly in terms of the price of different types of tourism i and j at the same destination r (4.6), or of the same type of tourism i at a different destination k (4.7):

$$N_{i,r} = f_{i,r}\left(\ldots, \left[\ldots, v_{j,r}, \ldots\right]\right) \text{ where } j \neq i, \tag{4.6}$$

or:

$$N_{i,r} = f_{i,r}\left(\ldots, \left[\ldots, v_{i,k}, \ldots\right]\right) \text{ where } k \neq r \tag{4.7}$$

The coefficient of elasticity calculated with respect to the price of other types of tourism or other tourism destinations is known as *cross-price elasticity* (indirect elasticity) and is *the ratio between the percentage change of the quantity demanded $N_{i,r}$ and the percentage change of price $v_{j,r}$ of another tourism or $v_{i,k}$ of another destination*. The cross-price elasticity is also named competitors' price elasticity or substitute price elasticity. In particular, according to (4.6), this is:

$$\mu_{(i,j)r} = \frac{\partial N_{i,r}}{\partial v_{j,r}} \cdot \frac{v_{j,r}}{N_{i,r}}, \tag{4.8}$$

while, according to (4.7), it is:

$$\mu_{i(r,k)} = \frac{\partial N_{i,r}}{\partial v_{i,k}} \cdot \frac{v_{i,k}}{N_{i,r}}. \tag{4.9}$$

In the more general case of a change in the price of a different type of tourism at a different destination, i.e. the case where $N_{i,y} = f_{i,r}\,(\ldots[\ldots,v_{j,k},\ldots])$, the elasticity is:

$$\mu_{(i,j)(r,k)} = \frac{\partial N_{i,r}}{\partial v_{j,k}} \cdot \frac{v_{j,k}}{N_{i,r}}. \tag{4.10}$$

The elasticity μ presented in (4.8–4.10) is particularly interesting for some of the values it may take.

- In case $\mu_{(i,j)r} > 0$ ($\mu_{i(r,k)} > 0$) we can say that tourism i at destination r is a *substitute* for tourism j at the same destination (4.8) or that the destination r is a substitute of a different destination k for the same tourism i (4.9) because the number of overnight stays $N_{i,r}$ increases as a consequence of a raise in the price of other types of tourism or other destinations, and vice versa. As an example, consider the existing substitutability between staying at a hotel versus staying at a bed and breakfast, or between two similar sea and sand resorts, that basically offer the same type of tourism: when the price of tourism in one destination goes up, everything else being equal, tourists will partially move to the other destination.
- In case $\mu_{(i,j)r} < 0$ ($\mu_{i(r,k)} < 0$) we can say that tourism i at destination r is *complementary* to another tourism j at the same destination (4.8) or that the destination r is complementary to another destination k for the same tourism i (4.9) because the number of overnight stays $N_{i,r}$ increases as a consequence of a

drop in the price of other types of tourism or other destinations. Consider, as an example, the tourism consisting of visiting museums and the tourism consisting in attending live shows at the theatre in a cultural city. It is likely that, in the event that entrance to the museums is granted for free by the public administration, the increase in cultural tourists in the destination would imply an increase also in the number of tourists attending shows at the theatre.

- Finally, in case $\mu_{(i,j)r} = 0$ ($\mu_{i(r,k)} = 0$) the types of tourism or the destinations are said to be *independent*. For example, a change in the price of tourism in Palma de Mallorca would certainly have no effect on the number of overnight stays in Rome.

Therefore, the sign of cross-price elasticity informs us whether different types of tourism and destinations are substitutes, complements, or independent from each other. From observing instead the absolute value of cross-price elasticity, we can easily evaluate the extent of such a relation. Both elements are key analytical and policy tools for private (tour operators) and public bodies (the destination management) working in a given destination.

Finally, the concept of cross-price elasticity can also be applied to some microeconomic aspects of the tourism demand. For example, it might be interesting to measure the (likely positive) cross-price elasticity between consuming meals at traditional restaurants versus the change in price in fast food restaurants, or the (likely negative) cross-price elasticity between taking a tour of the archeological site of Pompei, Italy, rather than visiting the nearby archeological museum of Naples.

4.2.2.3 Elasticity Related to Available Money

The elasticity related to available money measures how the tourist's behavior responds to variations in the tourist's available income or in the amount of money allocated by the tourist for holiday purposes (a variable that is directly connected with available income).[5] We still consider the demand function (4.2), $N_{i,r} = f_{i,r}\ (v_{i,r},\ [\ldots, M_i,\ M_{\text{tou}}, \ldots])$, but we now only consider changes in M_{tou} or in M_i.

The elasticity related to available money can be defined as the ratio between the percentage change in tourism demand, measured by overnight stays, $N_{i,r}$, and the percentage change in the amount of money allocated to tourism, M_{tou}. Formally:

$$\rho_{i,r,M_{\text{tou}}} = \frac{\partial N_{i,r}}{\partial M_{\text{tou}}} \cdot \frac{M_{\text{tou}}}{N_{i,r}}. \tag{4.11}$$

[5] If the tourist allocates a constant share of his budget to each tourism activity, it is possible to replace available money with disposable income in the formulas of elasticity. However, this is rarely true, and it is better to keep the two aspects separated (see Sect. 4.2.2.4).

A version of such elasticity can be calculated with reference to the particular type of tourism i, and with respect to the money M_i that has been allocated to it:

$$\rho'_{i,r,M_i} = \frac{\partial N_{i,r}}{\partial M_i} \cdot \frac{M_i}{N_{i,r}}. \tag{4.12}$$

With reference to the possible values of the elasticity (4.11) and, similarly, to the possible values of (4.12), we can formulate the following statements about the sign and the size of $\rho_{i,r}$:

- If $\rho_{i,r,M_{\text{tou}}} < 0$, then the number of nights $N_{i,r}$ for tourism i at destination r decreases as the tourist's money available for holidays increases. In this case we say that tourism i at the destination r is an *inferior* tourism, because as the income allocated to tourism increases, tourism i and/or destination r become substituted for more exotic and/or higher quality destinations or types of tourism;
- If $\rho_{i,r,M_{\text{tou}}} > 0$, then tourism is said to be a *normal tourism*, because the number of nights $N_{i,r}$ increases together with the availability of money to be spent on tourism. Such situation is typical for the great majority of types of tourism and destinations, and should be studied under three additional sub-cases:
  - In case $0 < \rho_{i,r,M_{\text{tou}}} < 1$: the tourism demand is inelastic with respect to available money because the number of nights increases less than proportionally;
  - In case $\rho_{i,r,M_{\text{tou}}} > 1$: the tourism demand is elastic with respect to available money because the number of nights increases more than proportionally (this is the case for luxury destinations and types of tourism);
  - In case $\rho_{i,r,M_{\text{tou}}} = 1$: the tourism demand is unitary elastic because the number of nights increases proportionally to the available money used for tourism;
- If $\rho_{i,r,M_{\text{tou}}} = 0$, the demand is perfectly *inelastic* and the number of nights is independent on the availability of money used for tourism. This is certainly the case when the tourist's choice exclusively depends on her affection for the destination r.

The graphical representation of (4.11) in the plane (M_{tou}; $N_{i,r}$) is called *Engel curve* and is presented in Fig. 4.2. In particular, the section of Fig. 4.2a where $0 < \rho_{i,r,M_{\text{tou}}} < 1$ (continuous line) can be referred to as a normal tourism. Instead, Fig. 4.2b (continuous line) displays the case of an inferior tourism because as M_{tou} increases the number of stays decreases. Finally, Fig. 4.2c displays the case of a luxury destination, given that the number of nights in the destination grows more than proportionally than the available money for holidays, at least up to the point of inflexion (continuous line). With respect to Fig. 4.2, it is important to highlight that a destination can possibly change its nature according to different values of M_{tou}. For example, a normal destination may become inferior when tourists enjoy a level of M_{tou} beyond a given critical level and then decide to

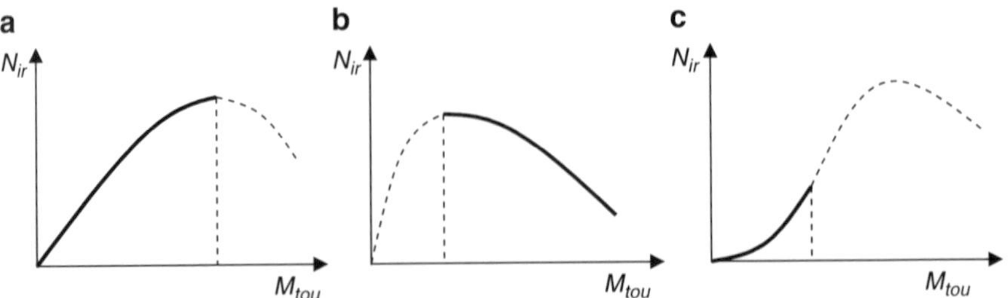

Fig. 4.2 Elasticity related to available money: three relevant cases

spend their holidays in more fashionable or expensive destinations. This implies that the above classification should not be taken too rigidly.

Once again, at the microeconomic level, this type of elasticity and the corresponding classifications may be extended to the individual tourism firms. For example, hostels and one-star hotels may easily become inferior types of accommodation when the average income of the tourists grows.

4.2.2.4 Income Elasticity of Tourism Expenditure

We complete our discussion by considering an Engel curve capturing the relationship between tourism expenditure M_{tou}, and percapita income Y:

$$M_{\text{tou}} = g(Y), \tag{4.13}$$

The income elasticity of tourism expenditure can be defined as the ratio between the percentage change in tourism expenditure and the percentage change in disposable income that generated it. Formally:

$$\rho_{\text{tou}} = \frac{\partial M_{\text{tou}}}{\partial Y} \cdot \frac{Y}{M_{\text{tou}}}. \tag{4.14}$$

Figure 4.3 shows three key aspects of the income elasticity of tourism expenditure, ρ_{tou}. In the first interval, for low values of Y, M_{tou} is zero and becomes positive only after a critical level of income, Y^{+}, is reached. In the second section, between Y^{+} and Y^{0}, the tourism expenditure increases more than proportionally to income, making tourism a luxury good. Finally, but only for levels of income higher than Y^{0}, M_{tou} increases less than proportionally and progressively moves toward the saturation of the tourist needs, here represented by the level of spending K. When K is reached no further increases in Y have an effect on tourism expenditure. In Fig. 4.3 we explicitly indicate the value of the elasticity ρ_{tou}, calculated according to (4.14) and relative to the above mentioned cases.

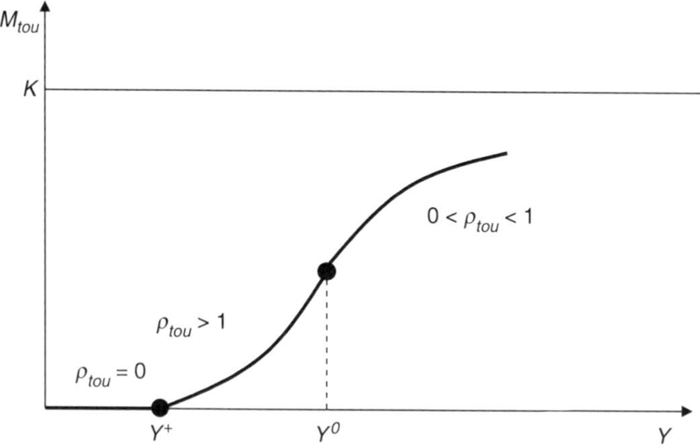

Fig. 4.3 Income elasticity of tourism expenditure

4.3 The Destination as the Core Element of the Tourism System

Given the heterogeneity and the plurality of the tourism product (see Sect. 2.5), the destinations are perceived as a *mixture* (an amalgam) of different structures, facilities, and attractions. Hence, each kind of tourism destination (mountain and beach resorts, historical and art cities, locations offering a festival, an event, amusement parks, or hosting of conferences, etc.) can be seen as a functioning mixture of cultural, economic, and environmental ingredients.

Although achieving a complete recognition and classification across such a variety is a challenging task, we can certainly identify a number of common features in all destinations, following Cooper et al. (2008):

- *All destinations are amalgams.* This implies that all their components must share the same qualitative features and have to be coordinated. For example, the elegant interiors of a luxury hotel located in a run-down area of a town are clashing elements (see Sect. 4.3.1).
- *All destinations have a value.* To become a destination a location needs to be perceived as interesting and worth a visit. Moreover, the concept of destination is naturally dynamic. In other words, the tourism mixture must adapt to the quantitative and qualitative characteristics of the tourist needs. Regarding the concept of tourism destination, the existing literature agrees on the existence of a well-defined evolutionary process (the Tourism Area Life-Cycle) characterized by several phases (see Sect. 4.5).
- *All destinations are inseparable from consumption.* A standard feature of tourism is that it is consumed where it is produced. In other words, the destinations' product is perishable, it cannot be transported, it cannot be stored and, hence, destinations suffer from tourism pressure (see Sect. 16.4). At the

same time, destinations are also sensitive to the qualitative alterations that follow the seasonal concentration of tourists or to the circumstances where many forms of tourism compete for the same resources and at the same time (see Sect. 7.5).

- *All destinations are shared with non-tourists.* The existing structures and infrastructures at the destination contemporaneously serve tourists and day trippers, residents, and workers. For example, tourism at beach resorts coexists with fishing and navigation, or any other alternative use of sea resources. Similarly, farmhouse tourism shares many features with agricultural activities. Again, trains and stations are crowded with tourists, day-trippers, and commuters. For the same reason, at some destinations the tourism phenomenon can operate as a creator of conflicts and competition between tourists and residents (see Sect. 15.3.2).

As already highlighted, the tourism destination is an amalgam, a mixture in which the following five components can be identified:

1. The *attractions*. These are all the artificial, natural, cultural, or event-related resources that fulfill the main purpose of the trip and around which the whole destination pivots. Although the resources play a fundamental role for the destination, a comprehensive analysis, and classification of the different types of resources is carried out when discussing the topic of sustainability, in Chap. 16.
2. The *amenities*. In the destination, the tourists ask for a series of services, structures and goods. It is in such differentiation (accommodation, food and beverage, shops, etc.) that the tourism supply spreads over different economic sectors.
3. The *accessibility*. With reference to a tourism destination, this is intended as the accessibility from, and to, terminals as well as the efficiency of the local mobility system. Developing and maintaining efficient networks are crucial to achieve the success of a destination, given that this may "reduce" the distance between the destination and the tourists' region of origin. Similarly, the availability of new, alternative means of transport (shuttle buses, bicycle pathways, etc.) are equally important for enjoyment of the tourism experience.
4. The *auxiliary services*. The great majority of destinations counts on the existence of a local tourism organization and a system of auxiliary services for the tourist's and/or the tourism firm's benefit (e.g., promotion, information, etc.) Such organization and system can be either public, or private, or a combination of both.
5. The *infrastructures*. The infrastructures are any type of underground or aboveground construction that is needed as a base for any activity (not only tourism-related) in the destination. These include systems and devices for the communication (Internet network, home and cell phone system, radio, television, etc.), utilities (electricity, water, etc.), and other services (hospitals, police, etc.). Considering that an infrastructure is usually supplied by the public sector, we define as *superstructure* any element supplied by the private sector that creates tourism opportunities for a given destination.

Each of the above five inputs is necessary in the destination in order to produce the tourism output. In other words, the tourism product should be seen as the multiplicative function of the five inputs listed above: the lack of at least one of the five inputs is a sufficient condition for the output not to be produced. Also, the supply of each input must be visible and accessible in the output to enter the tourist's utility function. This calls for the fundamental role that has to be played by the destination management (see Sect. 4.3):

> The type of tourist attracted to a destination will be determined by the quality and mix of attractions, superstructures and infrastructures present and, consequently, the role of planning and management of the whole tourism product at the destination is crucial for target markets to be attracted and for a satisfactory tourism experience to be achieved.
> (Cooper et al. 1998, p. 121)

To summarize, the fundamental issues that need to be addressed for a full understanding of the tourism destination from an economic point of view can be listed as follows: (a) the search for coordination in the destination, both economically and logistically; (b) the search for variety in the tourism product so that the tourist's satisfaction may increase; (c) the completion of the tourist's product by supplying those structures and infrastructures that the tourism market is unable to provide efficiently (public goods); (d) the tackling of externalities both among different types of tourism and between residents and tourists, or between current and future tourists; (e) the management and planning of the overall tourism product; (f) the identification of a target market, which is a typical topic of marketing; (g) the use of technology innovation in order to reach and maintain the competitive standard of the destination.

All these topics, with the exclusion of (c) and (d) which are classical examples of market failures calling for public intervention and which will be investigated in Chaps. 15 and 16, will be discussed in the next sub-sections. For an introduction and a review of the recent, but yet quite rich, literature on the economic issues of destinations see Candela and Figini 2010b; see also Haugland et al. 2011.

4.3.1 The Coordination of Activities in the Destination

The success of a tourism destination is only possible when a complete bundle of complementary goods and services produced by a number of independent privately owned businesses is available for tourists. During the stay, the tourist needs accommodation, transport, leisure and cultural activities, food and beverages, etc. and all these goods and services have to be supplied in a coherent and organised manner. The coordination between the different firms involved in the supply of the tourism product is therefore a common and fundamental issue in any tourism destination.

Hence, tourism in the destination can be interpreted as a "permission to stay" granted by the several firms supplying services for tourists. If just one firm does not grant permission, the tourism activity cannot take place. Let us pose a simplified example, a destination characterized by the existence of only two types of firms: hotels, which only offer lodging services but no meals, and restaurants, which supply meals but no lodging. In such a scenario, the tourist who wants to spend a holiday in the destination must purchase a certain number of services from both firms. And the tourist would not move to the destination if one of the two services is unavailable. The unavailability has to be interpreted extensively: not only the case in which the firm refuses to sell its services to the tourist, but the more general case in which the supply of services does not match the tourist's requirements. As an example, we can think of the case of a luxury hotel located in an area where only fast food restaurants are available, or the case of an expensive gourmet restaurant located where the only lodging opportunity is offered by a one-star hotel: such combinations are difficult to match with tourists' needs.

The catchy idea regarding the existence of a unique economic good, whose property is fragmented across different firms, is known as *anticommon* and is not new in Economics,[6] although the concept has not been sufficiently exploited so far. However, it finds in the Economics of Tourism a perfect application (Candela et al. 2008b; Andergassen et al. 2012; Alvarez-Albelo and Hernandez-Martin 2009; Wachsman 2006). Note that this concept is exactly the opposite of the much better known *common good*, a good which is available to everyone and without well-defined property rights (Hardin 1968, see Sect. 16.3.1).

The introduction of the idea of anticommon in the context of a tourism product can be simply formalized in the following model. Consider a destination in which there are only two firms: a hotel, offering accommodation, and a restaurant, offering meals. Tourism activity needs the purchase of one unit of accommodation services and one unit of food services per day. Let p_h and p_r be the unit (daily) price of a hotel service and the unit (daily) price of a restaurant service, respectively. In our simplified example we assume that the tourism demand function (see Sect. 4.2) $N = f(v)$ is linear and is therefore given by $N = a - v = a - p_h - p_r$, where $v = p_h + p_r$ is the unit (daily) price of tourism made of one unit of two complementary goods: accommodation and food. Note that in this case, the elasticity of demand is $\varepsilon = |v/N|$ throughout the demand function.

4.3.1.1 Case A. Uncoordinated Firms in the Destination

Firstly, we consider the general case in which both firms are privately owned businesses, whose general goal is to maximize their own profits, and no coordination exists. If, with no loss of generality, we simplify our discussion by assuming null production costs, the maximization problem of the two firms operating in the destination can be formalized as follows (Candela et al. 2008b). As regards the hotel:

$$\max \Pi_h = p_h N = p_h(a - p_h - p_r), \tag{4.15}$$

[6] Michelman (1982), Heller (1998, 1999). For an introduction to the topic, see Parisi et al. (2000, 2004).

whose first-order condition

$$\frac{\partial \Pi_h}{\partial p_h} = a - 2p_h - p_r = 0,$$

allows the calculation of the equilibrium price of one unit of hotel services as:

$$p_h = \frac{a - p_r}{2}. \tag{4.16}$$

The optimization problem for the restaurant is instead:

$$\max \Pi_r = p_r N = p_r(a - p_h - p_r), \tag{4.17}$$

whose first-order condition

$$\frac{\partial \Pi_r}{\partial p_r} = a - p_h - 2p_r = 0,$$

allows the calculation of the equilibrium price of one unit of restaurant services as:

$$p_r = \frac{a - p_h}{2}. \tag{4.18}$$

By solving the system of two equations (4.16) and (4.18) in two unknowns (p_h and p_r) we can simultaneously calculate the following equilibrium prices:

$$p_r^* = p_h^* = \frac{a}{3}. \tag{4.19}$$

Consistently, the daily price of the tourism product including one unit of hotel services (one overnight stay) and one unit of restaurant services (two meals and a breakfast) is given by:

$$v^* = p_h + p_r = \frac{2a}{3}, \tag{4.20}$$

which, according to the demand function, implies a number of stays equal to $N^* = a/3$. In equilibrium, the two firms earn the following profits:

$$\Pi_h^* = \Pi_r^* = \frac{a}{3} \cdot \frac{a}{3} = \frac{a^2}{9}. \tag{4.21}$$

4.3.1.2 Case B. Coordination Provided by an External Authority

However, we can demonstrate that this free market solution is not optimal neither for the firms nor for the tourists. To explain this, let us now assume that an authority that is external to the market coordinates the tourism product by deciding to supply a combined package of accommodation and meals. This corresponds to looking at the above decision problem from the standpoint of a centralized, profit-maximizing destination.[7] If we keep considering the same demand function, we have:

$$\max \Pi = vN = v(a - v), \tag{4.22}$$

whose first-order condition:

$$\frac{d\Pi}{dv} = a - 2v = 0,$$

leads to the equilibrium unit (daily) price of the holiday at the destination:

$$v^{**} = \frac{a}{2}, \tag{4.23}$$

and to an optimum number of stays $N^{**} = a/2$. If we compare (4.23) with (4.20), it is clear that $v^{**} < v^{*}$ while $N^{**} > N^{*}$. The obvious conclusion is that without a coordinating authority in the destination, the price tends to be too high and the number of overnight stays too low[8] while, with a central coordination, the number of tourists increases and the price drops. Coordination favors tourists; however, is there an advantage also for local firms?

Since in our example the two firms have identical costs (both equal to zero), the authority in the destination will ask firms to set identical prices $p_h^{**} = p_r^{**} = a/4$. In light of (4.15) and (4.17), it is easy to show that the authority intervention causes profits for both firms to be:

$$\Pi_h^{**} = \Pi_r^{**} = \frac{a}{4} \cdot \frac{a}{2} = \frac{a^2}{8} \tag{4.24}$$

---

[7] We remind that the assumption of null production costs implies the equivalence between profits and revenues. In this way, the assumption of profit maximization is coherent with the real-world goal of revenue maximization of the destination, that is, in other words, maximization of tourism expenditure.

[8] The issue of a fragmented supply in the destination is similar to the issue of double intermediation, which is typical for firms operating at different levels of the distribution chain. For an application of this problem to both hotels and airlines, see Wachsman (2006). For an application to the relationship between tour operators and travel agencies, see Sect. 11.5.2.

and given that $a^2/8 > a^2/9$, the profit level (4.24) is greater than (4.21). This implies that with a suggested (or imposed) central coordination provided by the destination management, both hotels and restaurants earn more profit than under the alternative scenario. The coordination of the destination, it is important to say, can theoretically be provided either by a private association of tourism firms or by a public body.

In either case, the tourism destination authority must: (a) coordinate with businesses supplying components of the tourism product; (b) compute and post the aggregate price of such product (e.g., the daily price of the holiday in the destination); (c) compute and post the price of the different services composing the tourism product. To conclude, the anticommon nature (the fragmentation of property rights) of the tourism product implies the superiority of the solution imposed by central coordination. This allows the participating businesses to earn a greater profit by supplying at the same time the tourism product to a larger number of tourists at a lower price. This win-win solution, hence, is welfare improving.

4.3.1.3 Case C. Coordination Provided by a Tour Operator

It is important to notice that the advantages of coordination do not necessarily imply the intervention of an authority that is external to the market. The coordination could equally be provided endogenously to the market by means of a tourism firm, the typical tour operator (see Sect. 8.2). The tour operator sells the overall tourism product, the package holiday, composed of the single services that the tour operator purchases from the individual firms. To undergo such task, the tour operator typically assumes an insurance role against the market risk, by paying a discounted price for the tourism services that are purchased in advance. Restaurants and hotels will rationally decide to accept the discounted price provided that the profit is higher than under the no-coordination alternative (sub-case A).[9] Therefore, the role of the tour operator is to replace the market failure due to the anticommon with a decentralized market solution (Candela et al 2008b).

To formalize, assume that the tour operator purchases services from the local restaurant and the hotel. Let $(p_j - d)$ be the price written on the corresponding contract, where p_j is the unit market price for $j = h, r$, and d is a discount which we assume identical for both businesses. The coordinating firm aims to maximize its own profit subject to the participation constraints of the restaurant and the hotel. Such constraints realize the idea that, in order for the two local firms to be willing to sign the contract, their individual profit must be higher than or equal to the profit without coordination, i.e., at least $a^2/9$ according to (4.21). The optimization problem for the tour operator is therefore:

[9] The discussion of this type of contract (free sale contract) will be presented in Chap. 11 (see also Castellani and Mussoni 2007).

$$\max_{v,d}\Pi = vN - (p_h - d)N - (p_r - d)N = (v - p_h - p_r + 2d)N \tag{4.25}$$

s.t.

$$N = a - v$$

$$(p_h - d)N \geq \frac{a^2}{9} \quad \text{(participation constraint of the hotel)}$$

$$(p_r - d)N \geq \frac{a^2}{9} \quad \text{(participation constraint of the restaurant)}$$

Let us now suppose that the tour operator offers the restaurant and the hotel the minimum profit for them to be willing to participate in the contract, that is $(p_j - d)N = a^2/9$, and that the prices are those expressed in (4.19). Then, the optimization problem for the tour operator becomes:

$$\max_{v,d}\Pi = vN - \left(\frac{a}{3} - d\right)N - \left(\frac{a}{3} - d\right)N = \left(v - \frac{2a}{3} + 2d\right)N, \tag{4.26}$$

s.t.

$$N = a - v$$

$$\left(\frac{a}{3} - d\right)N = \frac{a^2}{9} \quad \text{(participation constraint of the hotel)},$$

$$\left(\frac{a}{3} - d\right)N = \frac{a^2}{9} \quad \text{(participation constraint of the restaurant)},$$

By replacing one constraint with the other, we can calculate the following temporary expression for d:

$$d = \frac{a}{3} - \frac{\mathrm{a}^2}{9(a - v)} = d(v), \tag{4.27}$$

which we can plug into the objective function (4.26):

$$\max_{v}\Pi = v(a - v) - \frac{2a^2}{9}, \tag{4.28}$$

and whose first-order condition:

$$\frac{d\Pi}{dv} = a - 2v = 0$$

easily leads to:

$$v^{**} = a/2 \text{ and } N^{**} = a/2, \tag{4.29}$$

which are identical to the price and quantity (4.23) calculated under the assumption of coordination by the local authority.

This case however, introduces a very important difference in the allocation of profits. Indeed, if we substitute the solution (4.29) into (4.27), we obtain $d^* = a/9$ and:

$$\Pi_h = \Pi_r = \frac{a^2}{9} \text{ and } \Pi = \frac{a^2}{4} - \frac{2a^2}{9}. \tag{4.30}$$

According to (4.30), the distribution of net profit across firms will depend on the value of d. The bottom line is that the existence of a positive profit for the tour operator generates a distribution conflict, which was not present under the scenario of a local coordination authority external to the market that, being a public body or a non-profit private institution, does not seek profits. This result has very important consequences in terms of tourism policy and sheds lights on the strategic role played by the destination management, particularly in developing countries. If the destination management is ineffective, and the role of coordination is left to foreign-owned tour operators, a major share of profits generated by tourism activities will exit the country, thereby leading to little or no positive effects on the domestic economy (see Sect. 13.2 for the analysis of the income multiplier) and, possibly, negative consequences for social sustainability (see Sect. 16.3.2).

To conclude, it is possible to generalize the results presented in this subsection by stating the *Coordination Theorem*:

> Given the anticommon property of the tourism product, coordination among firms in the destination, which can either be provided by the destination management or by a tour operator, increases total profits of the tourism sector.

A corollary of such theorem considers the distributional issue:

> When coordination is provided by an external tour operator, profits of the local tourism sector are lower than in the case of coordination provided by the destination management. The type of coordination chosen in the destination is therefore not distribution neutral.

An application of the coordination theorem to the context of tourism management can be found in Buhalis and Costa (2006).

4.3.2 The Variety in the Tourism Product of the Destination

This section provides an argument in favor of the idea of product diversification, i.e. the increase of available consumption opportunities should be a target for the destination aiming to improve tourists' satisfaction. This has an effect in tourists' spending, and ultimately has an economic repercussion onto the businesses operating in the destination.

While in Sect. 4.3.1 the Coordination Theorem argues that the destination needs to create the necessary network to facilitate the access to all complementary services of the tourism product to make the tourism activity in the destination possible (in our example, the destination must offer both hotel and restaurant services), in this section the *Love for Variety Theorem* supports the idea that the destination should respond to tourists' preferences for diversification by supplying a great variety of local products. As an example, this theorem states that, in order to increase tourists' satisfaction and their willingness to spend, the destination should have both seafood restaurants and pizzerias, both a golf course and a kartdrome, etc.

We will discuss the Love for Variety Theorem by reassessing the application of the Dixit and Stiglitz (1977) model for tourism as it has been provided by Andergassen and Candela (2012). We assume that tourists have a utility function of type $U = (h^a + X^a)^{1/a}$, which exhibits a *constant elasticity of substitution* (CES) between good h and good X.[10] We assume that the utility of the tourist is defined over: (a) the number h of the overnight stays at the hotel located in the destination; (b) the quantity X of a differentiated bundle of local goods, where x_i denotes the good supplied by the i-th firm operating in the destination, $i = 1, 2, \ldots, n$ and $n \geq 1$ (we assume that each firm produces only one variety of the output, so that n is both the number of varieties and the number of active firms in the destination); (c) the amount y of non-tourism goods (general consumption). In this model, the tourism output is defined as a basket **T** which includes the number of nights at the hotel and the different varieties of local goods, $T = (h, \{x_i\})$.

In such framework, the overall tourism demand can be separated into three demand functions that pertain to the tourist: a demand for overnight stays in the destination, a demand for local tourism goods, and a demand for non-tourism goods. In particular: in (4.31) we use a CES function to express the utility from tourism consumption, i.e., by considering both h and $\{x_i\}$ $(i = 1, 2, \ldots, n)$; in (4.32) we assume a linear utility function to account for non-tourism consumption; in (4.33) we express the overall utility function using again a CES:

[10] The elasticity of substitution measures how easy is to substitute one good with the other in order to maintain the same level of utility: it is computed as the ratio of two goods to a utility function with respect to the ratio of their marginal utilities. The CES is a family of functions $U = (x^a + y^a)^{1/a}$ that has constant (but generally different from one) elasticity of substitution. The Cobb-Douglas (CD) utility function, $U = x^a y^b$, which exhibits a constant and unitary elasticity of substitution is then a special case of the more general CES utility function.

$$U_T = \left[h^\gamma + \left(\sum_{i=1}^{n} x_i^\alpha\right)^{\gamma/\alpha}\right]^{1/\gamma}, \tag{4.31}$$

$$U_Y = y, \tag{4.32}$$

$$U = \left(U_Y^\beta + U_T^\beta\right)^{1/\beta} = \left\{y^\beta + \left[h^\gamma + \left(\sum_{i=1}^{n} x_i^\alpha\right)^{\gamma/\alpha}\right]^{\beta/\gamma}\right\}^{1/\beta}, \tag{4.33}$$

where $0 < \beta < 1$ implies that the non-tourism good y and the tourism product T are gross substitutes (in particular, as $\beta \to 1$, they become perfect substitutes). $\gamma < 0$ indicates that variables h and X are gross complements (but become perfect complements as $\gamma \to -\infty$). Finally, by assuming that $0 < \alpha < 1$, and $\alpha > \beta$, we characterize gross substitutability between the local varieties. These parametric assumptions are sufficiently plausible and general to fully characterize the tourist's preferences.

Finally, we assume that the price of the non-tourism consumption is the *numeraire* of the model, thus $p_y \equiv 1$. Let p_h, p_i, and M denote the price of one night at the hotel, of one unit of good i, and the tourist's income, respectively. Then the tourist's budget constraint is:

$$y + p_h h + \sum_{i=1}^{n} p_i x_i = M. \tag{4.34}$$

Consistent with Dixit and Stiglitz model, we assume identical firms individually setting the same price (symmetry hypothesis) so that $x = x_i$ and $p = p_i$. Under this assumption, the functions (4.31)–(4.34) simplify as follows:

$$U_T = \left[h^\gamma + n^{\frac{\gamma}{\alpha}} x^\gamma\right]^{\frac{1}{\gamma}} = U_T(n), \tag{4.31a}$$

$$U_\gamma = y, \tag{4.32a}$$

$$U = \left(U_Y^\beta + U_T^\beta\right)^{\frac{1}{\beta}} = U(n), \tag{4.33a}$$

$$y + p_h h + npx = M. \tag{4.34a}$$

If we differentiate (4.31a) with respect to n we obtain:

$$\frac{\partial U_T}{\partial n} = \frac{1}{\gamma}\left[h^\gamma + n^{\frac{\gamma}{\alpha}} x^\gamma\right]^{\frac{1-\gamma}{\gamma}} \left(\gamma n^{\frac{\gamma-\alpha}{\alpha}} \frac{x^\gamma}{\alpha}\right) = \left[h^\gamma + n^{\frac{\gamma}{\alpha}} x^\gamma\right]^{\frac{1-\gamma}{\gamma}} \left(n^{\frac{\gamma-\alpha}{\alpha}} \frac{x^\gamma}{\alpha}\right) > 0, \tag{4.35}$$

thus $\partial U / \partial n > 0$. The inequality (4.35) shows that, under the general assumptions made by Andergassen and Candela (2012), the tourist's utility is positively related to the variety within the local tourism product. The effect of the increase of n in the utility function (4.31a), and the corresponding effect in the overall utility presented in (4.33a), leads to a shift of preferences toward the tourism product and a corresponding reallocation of spending within the tourist's budget constraint. *Ceteris paribus*, as a result of this change we do expect the overall demand for overnight stays to be greater in destinations that offer a product with more variety. Correspondingly, given that prices and income are assumed constant, we expect the demand for non-tourism goods to decrease.

Consistent with our findings, the *Love for Variety Theorem* (Andergassen and Candela 2012) can be stated as follows:

> The reorganization of a tourism destination toward increasing the variety of available goods and services raises the tourists' welfare and their availability to spend on tourism, so to shift income from non-tourism to tourism consumption. Regardless any possible externalities on the environment, the increased variety will likely stimulate the economic development of the destination.

It is important to note that the analytical property $x'(n) < 0$ implies that the demand for the variety produced by the i-th firm is a decreasing function of the degree of variety. This fact introduces an economic limitation (given by the production costs facing the firms operating within the destination) to the expansion of the variety of X (Andergassen and Candela 2012).

Moreover, we must take into consideration that the tourism bundle also includes natural and artificial resources as public goods (see Sect. 15.2). Hence, it is easy to understand that the development of a tourism destination depends on both the variety of the local production (the above-mentioned tourist's love for variety effect) and the resources available there (Andergassen et al. 2012). Such extended version of the Love for Variety Theorem can be used to provide a justification for the existence of both tourism destinations that primarily rely on natural resources but with a limited local variety (e.g., part of the coastal area of Sardinia or Corse) and those that count on a great variety of production but limited natural resources (e.g. the coast of Benidorm in Spain or Rimini in Italy).[11]

4.3.3 The Destination Management

Most of the economic issues presented in this chapter, from the coordination of activities to the supply of variety, to the management or the destination's life cycle phases (see Sect. 4.5), are among the main tasks of a branch of research called

[11] For an extension that integrates the theorems of Coordination and of Love for Variety into a unified model, see Andergassen et al. (2012).

Destination Management. This research field consists of a set of techniques and actions aimed to the sustainability and the rationalization of the way tourism resources are being used within the territory (D'Elia 2007).

While we redirect to more specific textbooks for a deeper analysis of such issues (Wang and Pizam 2011), in what follows we discuss the main functions pertaining to the body in charge of the Destination Management, sometimes called Destination Management Organization (DMO).

- The management of the network of firms operating in the destination; this should be done in order to make all services demanded by tourists efficiently available (*Coordination Theorem*) as well as ensure tourists' satisfaction by means of a diversified supply (*Love for Variety Theorem*). We must underline the strict connection between the Destination Management and the Site Management, the latter being a field which is specialized in the management of locations with great historical, artistic, and/or natural interest.
- The management of services (and, more in general, the territory) that are shared between tourists and residents. Tourism activities could either lead to a situation of synergy or conflict between tourists and residents; the conflict implies that tourists exceed in the consumption of resources (or territory) that are also of interest to the local population. In particular during the peak season, the DMO is in charge of managing the destination's carrying capacity, both socially and environmentally, including its potential congestion in critical nodes during certain periods (see Punzo and Usai 2007; for the analysis of the city of Rimini, Italy, see Figini et al. 2009).
- The management of the destination's competitiveness, usually based on three dimensions: (a) the pricing policy, in order to match the features of the supply with those of the demand (see Sect. 4.4); (b) the quality policy, in order to make the destination as welcoming and liveable as possible to tourists; (c) the promotion policy, from the coordination of the destination's web portal (see Sect. 4.3.5) to the management of the marketing policy, i.e. the development of a characteristic territorial brand for the destination (see Sect. 4.3.4).
- The management of the evolution and the change in the destination, responding to the different life cycle phases (see Sect. 4.5).
- The management of the territory, consisting of a set of activities such as planning the development of tourism structures or the promotion and preservation of the tourism resources.
- The management of crises. One of the main tasks of the DMO consists of facing any event that could potentially compromise the appeal, and sometimes the existence, of the destination. Such threats are classified as either: *traumatic events*, such as terrorist attacks, natural disasters, health crises, geopolitical crises; *causing events* such as local or international economic crises that can have a great impact on tourism. On the one hand, traumatic events heavily affect tourism but mainly on a short-term basis and their consequences are easily reabsorbed; on the other hand, causing events are very difficult to control when their origins are beyond the destination's competence, and their effects

are often uncertain and long lasting (for a discussion of the crisis and risk destination management see Boniface and Cooper 2009; Aktas and Gunlu 2005; Beriman 2003; Glaesser 2006; Kotler et al. 2009).

Destination Management is a recent and still evolving field of Management Science which often investigates case studies and adopts an empirical approach through which general conclusions can be inferred. For example, a typical finding is that the success of a destination's management depends upon: (a) the degree of coordination between the different administrative levels in charge of tourism management (local, regional, national tourism authorities); (b) the coordination with destination marketing (see next section); (c) the act of promoting the tourism destination through cultural and sport events or as film locations; (d) the development of an effective brand for the destination (*destination branding*).

Finally, the Destination Management's key fact argues that the success of a location essentially depends on the skills shown by the private and public bodies that are involved in the tourism supply, as well as on their ability to organize as a system and operate as a network that efficiently addresses the critical features of the territory (see Case Study 4.1).

Case Study 4.1. The Management of a Destination: the Case of Spain

Until the first half of the nineteenth century, many travelers regularly visited the cold Northern European sea shores because, at that time, great medical attention was given to the health benefits of swimming in cold water, while staying in the sun received little therapeutic attention. For this reason, the Mediterranean beach resorts were of no particular interest for international and domestic travelers.

Before the boom of beach-oriented tourism at the beginning of the twentieth century, the Iberian region between San Sebastian and Santander (the northern region between Cantabria and the Basque Country) was Spain's only tourism region. Its relevance was mainly linked to the Spanish kings and the aristocracy who preferred skipping Madrid's hot summer temperatures and spent their summer holidays in the cooler northern regions. The significant distance of this region from Madrid, which was the main source of domestic tourism demand, as well as the state of underdevelopment of the Iberian Peninsula in general, prevented the expansion of its sea resorts and attractions.

During this period, the majority of foreign visitors went on holidays to the Atlantic shores and were mainly attracted by the sea's cold temperature, while the great majority of Spanish tourists preferred spending their holidays at thermal spa resorts located in the country's interior, which were easily reachable from the main urban areas. After the Second World War, many Mediterranean countries experienced a significant increase in the number of tourists. During that time Italy, Greece, and Spain quickly became the

European symbols of "sun, sand, and sea tourism" (also known as "the SSS tourism").

In the Mediterranean context, the case of Spain resembles the case of Italy in many ways but also displays a number of key differences. For example, in Italy the development of tourism had been driven by the expansion of the domestic demand while in Spain this was mainly due to the great expansion of foreign demand that, in particular during the 1960s, worked as an engine of growth for both the tourism sector and the whole Spanish economy. Such a sudden shift in the role of tourism in Spain can be traced back to the 1959 economic policy implemented by the government of dictator Francisco Franco who, after a long period of autarchy, allowed the entrance of foreign investments in Spain and promoted international trade. That created a favorable environment for the expansion of tourism in the Iberian country, with the positive contribution of foreign tour operators helping in the creation of massive and constant inflows of tourists, mainly from Germany and the United Kingdom. In particular, the constantly growing international tourism demand and the massive flow of foreign investment are considered the responsible factor for the unexpected economic growth in regions such as the Balearic and Canary Islands, and the famous Costa del Sol. As Cortés-Jiménez (2008) demonstrates, since 1959 the huge and constant increase of international tourism meant flows of foreign currency receipts for Spain which in turn assisted in financing the industrialization process and thus the economic development of the country. Later remarkable economic events are the membership of the European Community and the introduction of the Euro.

In the last 10 years, the high rate of economic growth and the success of low-cost airlines have allowed a continuous tourism growth driven by domestic demand for SSS destinations on the Mediterranean coast and the diversification of tourism for foreign visitors.

During the last decade, Spain has also developed new kinds of urban and cultural tourism. The most noticeable example of this is offered by the city of Barcelona which has experienced enormous economic growth specifically due to the impact of tourism. The historical capital of Catalonia, and Spain's second leading city in both size and importance, is known worldwide for having exploited the typical elements of urban tourism: the *heritage*, that is the town's artistic and cultural patrimony, and the *back region*, consisting of a mixture of the traditional ingredients of the local population's daily life, and the artificial attractions for tourists' leisure and entertainment.

Thanks to the key role played by the government of the autonomous region of Catalonia, the city of Barcelona is now known for the enhancement of its unique cultural and historical heritage. Examples are: the recent restoration of the ancient port; the creation of original tourism routes for the most diverse types of tourism, such as the route targeting works of art by the great architect

(continued)

Antoni Gaudí. At the same time, Barcelona set itself up as a laboratory of architectonic and urban innovations and recently adopted a dynamic and experimental character. Some important events, such as hosting the 1992's Olympic Games and the 2004's Mediterranean Forum, are known to be the key reasons for Barcelona's distinct style.

4.3.4 Destination Marketing

As each attraction or economic activity in the destination has to set up clear and effective marketing strategies, similarly, the destination needs to define and characterize itself among the competing destinations, this is a typical object of investigation for *Destination Marketing*. According to this research field, a destination must behave identically to any firm trying to sell a product. In other words, the marketing of a destination—like that of a product—can be divided up into a series of operations including the identification of its target markets and its positioning with respect to competing destinations (Heath and Wall 1992).

A typical way to develop marketing strategies is by *destination branding* (Morgan et al. 2004), i.e., by developing a strong brand for the identification and the promotion of the territory (e.g., the brand of Spain, whose logo is inspired by the combination of colors and shapes that recall the work of well-known Spanish artists such as Mirò). The brand also helps identify the characteristic features of the types of tourism that can be experienced in the destination. The destination marketing raises economic and promotional issues:

- The *economic issue* for the destination marketing lies on its public good nature (see Sect. 15.2) and, for this reason, free-riding behaviors by the activities located in the territory may occur. Any business located in the destination may be tempted to avoid paying its share of marketing costs by claiming that such activity would not generate any advantage with respect to competing businesses. If each firm behaves similarly, the general effect would be that little or no private contribution will be given to cover the overall marketing costs, thus the destination marketing would not take place. A first way to solve this problem is by making the destination marketing directly provided by a public authority (e.g., the Tourism Minister or a Tourism department) which finances its costs through general or specific taxes raised on the tourism sector: individual businesses should be called to contribute proportionally to the benefits received from the marketing policy. An alternative solution may require the setting up of a private consortium involving all the businesses located in the destination, which take care of the destination marketing. Such an institution would be able to internalize the externalities associated to the creation of the destination brand.

- The *promotional issue* may arise when the destination marketing overlaps with the marketing of the tourism product. This, in principle, would not be a problem in case the destination is a "monoproduct" because no practical differences would exist between the destination and the type of tourism to promote. Complications may arise in the case of a "multi-tourism" destination, where the following two alternative strategies may be used: (a) to promote the destination but not the different types of tourism; (b) to implement a different strategy for each of the different types of tourism on which the destination builds.

4.3.5 Destination Web Management

In this section we introduce a topic that will be discussed in greater detail in Chap. 12. We will quickly review the effects of the *Information and Communication Technology* (ICT) both onto the destination as a whole, and on the individual business that are located in there. The ICT, in fact, can be seen as a *democratic* tool (in the sense that on the web all destinations are equally reachable) for the information, promotion, and management of activities in the destination. The main issues related to the web management of the destination can be summarized as follows.

- On the one hand, the ICT can operate as a collector for all the available tourism supply at the destination. In other words, by means of a single web portal, a potential tourist can reach all the relevant information, provided through web links, multimedia (pictures, videos, audio-guides, etc.), and detailed information on hotels, restaurants, other attractions, directions, etc. In this way, the web portal operates as a sort of virtual travel agency for the promotion of the destination acting as a public information desk for its tourism product.
- Through the web portal, the tourist should at least find the contact information for the booking center of the destination. Ultimately, one should be able to make reservations and safely pay the holidays (both package holidays and single services). Ideally, the web portal should unify the reservation system for all the structures located in the destination and being linked to the international payment systems (credit and debit cards, etc.).
- The ICT should also provide coordinated management services for tourism businesses operating in the destination. This should be done by gathering and monitoring the data regarding arrivals and overnight stays, by integrating such data with collected statistics on the number of contacts, as well as on the quantity, quality, and type of information that was seen online by tourists. This would also offer the opportunity to improve the online information by targeting the visitor's preferences and needs, and possibly prepare and implement policies aimed at achieving goals such as the smoothing of the seasonality (on this topic, see Sect. 7.5) by means of promotional policies in particular times of the year.

- The web portal of the destination must offer Internet visibility and support services, in particular for the benefit of small businesses with limited technical competences and which are usually unable to be effectively present on the net.
- Each tourism destination should be integrated with the main *Global Distribution Systems* (GDS) as well as the most popular online travel agencies (OLTA, Chap. 12) in order to be able to efficiently compete against similar destinations. A possible pitfall must be mentioned in regard to the online management of a tourism destination: the risk of excessive or incoherent information flowing through the portal, i.e., from upper levels (country, province, town) to lower levels (individual businesses), and vice versa, within the destination (Choi et al. 2007).
- Finally, the web portal could post files for downloading onto, for instance, iPads or smart phones for a deeper virtual experience while visiting the destination and/or allow forms of social networking by experienced tourists for the benefit of potential ones, i.e. by letting them post their rankings and comments on the satisfaction received while visiting the destination.

On the one hand, to be able to reach all the above goals, the destination must count on a crew of well-trained operators. In today's world, where Internet appears as the main information center and increasingly the main booking tool for tourists, a destination with a limited ICT may experience a significant loss of marketing power in relation to other competing domestic and international destinations. In other words, the ICT represents an extraordinary tool in achieving the improvement in: the competitiveness of the destination, the quality of tourism services, the satisfaction of tourists' needs, the profits earned by tourism firms. It is a key instrument for the solution of the coordination issue presented in Sect. 4.3.1. On the other hand, we must stress on the fact that as information quantity and quality increase, it becomes easier for tourists to choose their holidays based on the price of similar alternatives, resulting in shrinking market power and profit opportunities for tourism businesses and destinations.

In addition, the introduction of the ICT brings into the market products that can be thought as tourism substitutes, as long as they are able to reduce mobility and hence decrease tourism demand at the destination; this is particularly true as regards business and cultural tourism. Today's technology allows for substitutes—although imperfect—for business trips (e.g., video conferences), for cultural trips (e.g., multimedia museums) or for tourism services (e.g., audioguides) in a way that will progressively be more common over time.

To conclude our analysis, the development of ICT captures the essence of what market competition is. On the one hand, globalization of the markets and increasing returns to scale allow a destination to increase the benefits stemming from a positive reputation. On the other hand, it leaves room for the creation, the development, and the promotion of niche markets from which small destinations may greatly benefit.

4.4 The Pricing Policy of the Destination

In market economies, each individual firm aims to supply the price/quantity combination of goods and services in order to maximize net profits given the existing market structure, the tourists' demand, and the technology of production.

The destination *as a whole*, i.e. intended as a combination of different firms operating in the territory, must however forgo the goal of aggregate profit maximization for two main reasons: firstly, the destination does not have the same decision power of an individual firm; secondly, even if the destination had such power, the computation skills needed to gather and elaborate data on the production costs of hundred of individual "productive units" would simply not be available in most cases.

Therefore, the primary goal of the destination must be a non-canonical one: the maximization of the aggregate gross revenue coming from the tourism exploitation of available resources; in other words, *the goal for the destination becomes finding the combination price/overnight stays that leads to the maximisation of tourists' spending.*[12]

In the following subsections, we will discuss three situations where the goal of maximizing tourism expenditure is presented under three different assumptions: (a) tourists' decision on how long to stay in the destination is only driven by the holiday's price; (b) tourists also take into consideration the overall quality of the tourism resources of the destination; (c) tourists follow a two-stage decision process, where their decision of whether or not to travel to the destination (which ultimately affects the number of arrivals) comes before the decision on how many nights to spend in the destination (which ultimately affects the number of overnight stays). We develop these three models in the following subsections.

4.4.1 Price, Overnight Stays, and Tourism Expenditure

In the first case, tourists set the value of N (the number of overnight stays) in the destination r for the type of tourism i, solely as a function of the unit (daily) price v of the holiday.[13] Therefore, the number of stays N can be written as a function of price according to the demand function $N = f(v)$, by holding as constant all the

[12] Since tourism expenditure is proportionally related to overnight stays (and to arrivals), and being the data on the former generally less available than the latter, the working goal of the destination usually becomes the maximization of overnight stays or arrivals. Some authors, however, disagree on the adoption of tourism expenditure as a target. For a critical discussion of this topic, see Dwyer and Forsyth (2008).

[13] From now on, we will simplify our formal exposition by omitting the subscripts for the type of tourism i and for the destination r. However, it is still intended that we refer to a particular type of tourism and a given destination.

remaining relevant variables that might affect demand (see Sect. 4.2). To be able to solve the expenditure maximization problem, we first need to introduce the relationship between tourism demand and tourism expenditure as described by the following product:

$$S = vN = vf(v), \tag{4.36}$$

where S indicates the aggregate expenditure calculated by the product between v, the daily price of tourism, and N, the quantity of tourism measured by the number of overnight stays, which in itself is a function of price through the demand function.

Expression (4.36) suggests that if planning and policy makers want to study how expenditure varies with price, they must account for two different and opposite effects; firstly, a change in the daily holiday price produces a direct effect on tourists' spending and, secondly, an inverse effect on the number of overnight stays, thus indirectly affecting the demand function. For example, the rise of v, on the one hand determines an increase in the amount of daily spending for a given length of stay in the destination; on the other hand, it decreases the length of stay and hence the number of stays and the overall amount of spending associated with the holiday. In principle, the overall effect on (4.36) is ambiguous as it depends on the net difference between two opposite effects.

What is important to highlight is that the optimal price strategy, i.e. the strategy that maximizes tourism expenditure, essentially depends on the elasticity of demand (see Sect. 4.2). In order to demonstrate it, we have to identify the price associated to the highest tourism expenditure. Mathematically, we set the derivative of S with respect to v equal to zero.

$$\frac{\partial S}{\partial v} = N + v\frac{\partial N}{\partial v}. \tag{4.37}$$

The second-order condition, ensuring that the critical point is a maximum and not a minimum, is satisfied under the normal assumptions on the demand function. If we multiply and divide $v\partial N/\partial v$ by N, and keep in mind the definition of elasticity ε presented in (4.5), expression (4.37) can be rewritten as:

$$\frac{\partial S}{\partial v} = N(1 - \varepsilon). \tag{4.38}$$

Expression (4.38) shows the existing relationship between the sign of the first derivative of S and the value of ε (taken in its absolute value). We can study three alternative situations:

(a) If $\varepsilon < 1$ then $\partial S/\partial v > 0$; when the demand is inelastic the tourism expenditure is in a direct relationship with the daily holiday price; in other words, as the price rises, tourists' aggregate spending also increases, and vice versa.

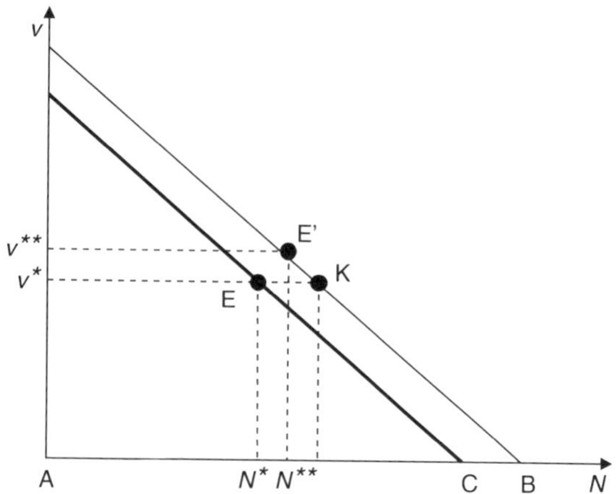

Fig. 4.4 Maximizing tourism expenditure

(b) If $\varepsilon > 1$ then $\partial S/\partial v < 0$; when the demand is elastic the tourism expenditure is in an inverse (or negative) relationship with the daily holiday price; in other words, as the price rises, tourists' aggregate spending decreases, and vice versa.
(c) If $\varepsilon = 1$ then $\partial S/\partial v = 0$; when the tourism demand has unitary elasticity the tourism expenditure does not change with the daily holiday price.

This last case is particularly interesting: a unitary elasticity corresponds to the situation of a null first derivative (4.38) which corresponds to the greatest amount of tourism expenditure in the destination, also known as *Cournot point* in the economics literature. Therefore, we can conclude that

> the destination that aims at maximising tourism expenditure must identify a daily price of the holiday for which the price/overnight stay combination is associated to a point on the demand curve where the elasticity is unitary.

Figure 4.4 shows the case of a linear demand function where the Cournot point, the price-stay combination leading to the maximum tourism expenditure, is at point $E\ (N^*, v^*)$, with an abscissa of $N^* = ½$ AC. In such a case, a price reduction would lead to an increase in expenditure when $N < N^*$, while it would lead to a decrease in expenditure when $N > N^*$.

Figure 4.4 also helps us define the best response the destination management should give in case the demand were to shift, i.e., in case one of the factors that we held constant in (4.36) was to change. For example, let us assume a destination where the current holiday price is consistent with the Cournot point E on the demand curve. If the demand were to increase (the demand curve were to shift to the right, due to a positive market effect or to a positive idiosyncratic effect of the destination or the type of tourism hosted) and the price were to remain constant, we would observe an increase in the tourism demand, thus leading to a greater number of overnight stays in the destination (from point E to point K). Expression (4.37) immediately shows that on the new price-stay combination, the elasticity would be less than unitary and the tourism expenditure no longer at its maximum. In particular, such parallel shift does neither affect the value of v nor that of $\partial N/\partial v$, but would only increase the number of stays and, given that N is at the denominator of the formula for elasticity, this would decrease the absolute value of ε. The firms operating in the destination would then optimally increase the unit price to v^{**}, so to bring the number of stays to N^{**}, which is intermediate between the values of N before and after the increase in demand. Such a price change would increase tourism expenditure until the new Cournot point is being reached at E', where the elasticity becomes unitary again. A similar rationale, *mutatis mutandis*, can be presented for the case of a negative movement to the left of the demand curve, where we could start from the Cournot point E' and eventually reach point E through a drop in price.

To conclude, we can summarize the main findings of this subsection by stating that the destination aiming at maximizing tourism expenditure must react to exogenous events which affect the demand of tourism (either market or idiosyncratic effects): the best strategy would suggest to go *where the wind blows* and follow the observed tourism demand evolution, i.e. to raise the price in response to an increase in demand, and to lower the price in response to a decrease in demand.

4.4.2 Price, Overnight Stays, and the Quality of Tourism

We now consider a tourism destination that wants to invest in the quality α of its tourism product, where quality α is assumed to depend on the degree of exploitation of a tourism resource of given amount R.

Let the ratio $q = N/R$ define the intensity of exploitation of the resource by the tourism sector. Lanza and Pigliaru (1995), Huybers and Bennet (2000), and Pintassilgo and Silva (2007) assume that the quality of tourism is in an inverse relationship with the intensity q, so that $\alpha(q)$ exhibits a negative derivative $\partial\alpha/\partial q < 0$. If, with no lack of generality, we normalize the amount of resources by setting $R = 1$, then q is identical to the number of overnight stays in the destination, $q = N$. Also, let $q_m = N^\circ$ be the maximum number of overnight stays that the resource can tolerate (that is, its carrying capacity) beyond which the exploitation of the resource becomes unsustainable (for a discussion of the concept of sustainability and carrying capacity we refer to Chap. 16).

With these premises we can define α as follows:

$$\alpha(N) = 1 - \frac{N}{q_m} \text{ with } N \leq q_m. \tag{4.39}$$

Expression (4.39) can be used as a convenient measure for the quality of a resource because it takes value $\alpha\ (N^\circ) = 0$, in case of maximum exploitation of the resource, and takes value $\alpha\ (0) = 1$ when the resource is in its natural state before being exploited by tourism. Lanza and Pigliaru make the additional assumption (adopted also by Pintassilgo and Silva) that price directly depends on the quality of tourism resources through θ (a *quality premium*, see Andergassen and Candela 2012).

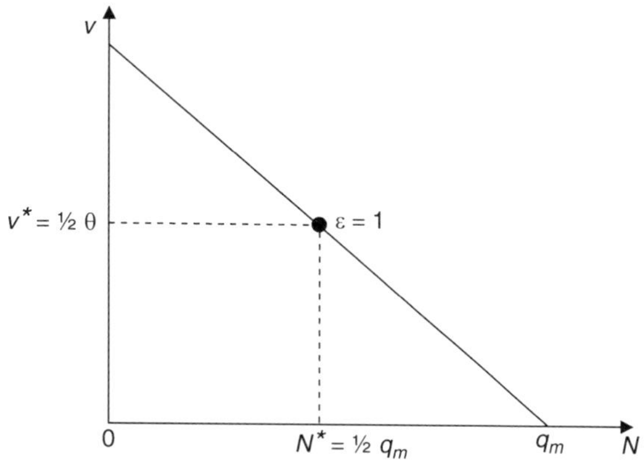

Fig. 4.5 The tourism expenditure maximization problem when taking into account the quality of tourism resources

In particular, it rises according to (4.39) as the number of overnight stays decreases, and vice versa:

$$v(N) = \theta\alpha(N) = \theta\left(1 - \frac{N}{q_m}\right) \text{ with } \theta > 0. \tag{4.40}$$

Function (4.40) is the inverse function of the tourism demand which explicitly accounts for the quality of the tourism resource. If we take (4.36) into consideration, the aggregate tourism expenditure for this case is defined as:

$$S = Nv(N) = \theta N - \frac{\theta N^2}{q_m}. \tag{4.41}$$

If the destination management is aimed at maximizing the value of S, the first order condition of (4.41) has to be satisfied as:

$$\frac{\partial S}{\partial N} = \theta - \frac{2\theta N}{q_m} = 0,$$

from which the optimal number of overnight stays is:

$$N^* = \frac{q_m}{2}, \tag{4.42}$$

and the optimal price, as determined by (4.40):

$$v^* = \frac{\theta}{2}.$$

Expression (4.42) confirms also for this case that the formal solution of the tourism expenditure maximization problem is given by the Cournot point. In particular, Fig. 4.5 clearly shows that N^* lies in the middle of segment $0q_m$. Also, expression (4.42) allows us to point out that $N^* < q_m$. In other words, if tourism has an impact on the resource and tourists positively value its quality, it is generally the case that the optimal strategy for the destination should achieve only a partial exploitation of the tourism resource.

Indeed, the fact that tourists value the quality of the resource and that the price decreases with its depletion, implies that the full exploitation of a resource is a suboptimal strategy for the destination and that the greatest revenue can only be achieved with a number of overnight stays that is lower than its maximum sustainable level. In other words, the tourism destination finds it optimal to set the price at a level higher than the price associated to N°, the maximum number of overnight stays that the resource can carry. Such a higher equilibrium price, which is still associated to the Cournot point $(N^*; v^*)$, provides a stronger force than the negative effect on aggregate expenditure due to the decrease of overnight stays.

Finally, notice that (4.42) depends on the definition given for the measure of quality, presented by (4.39). In particular, if we assume the quadratic expression adopted by Pintassilgo and Silva (2007), $\alpha = 1 - (N/q_m)^2$, the numerical solution becomes $N^* = q_m/\sqrt{3}$ which, on the one hand, is no longer associated to the Cournot point but, on the other hand, confirms the idea that a portion of the tourism resource has to remain unexploited, should tourism expenditure be maximized. Actually, the choice of a quadratic expression assigns to the share of unused resources a greater importance than its complement.

4.4.3 Price, Overnight Stays, and the Two-Tier Tourism Demand

In this section, the tourism demand is no longer simply measured by the overall number of overnight stays in the destination but is decomposed in its two components: arrivals and length of stay, which are both decided when planning the holidays. In particular, the tourist first decides whether or not to travel to (to arrive at) the destination, and then decides how long to stay there (the length of stay). Following Fabbri (1988), we will try to analyze these two arguments separately by looking at the effects on the destination's goals. We recall from Sect. 2.6.2 that the number of overnight stays can be expressed as the product of the number of arrivals and the average length of stay (the duration of the holiday d):

$$N = Ad. \tag{4.43}$$

To start with, we have to find out what are the determinants of A and d. If we assume that the tourist has already chosen the destination, and given the amount of tourist's income, the problem of the determination of the length of stay can be reduced to the standard price-quantity economic model for consumption. If the holiday "behaves" like an ordinary good, we can assume that its duration d is a decreasing function of the daily price v: *ceteris paribus,* the greater the daily price of the holiday, the less the tourist stays in the destination.[14] Accordingly,

$$d = d(v), \text{ with } \partial d/\partial v < 0, \tag{4.44}$$

which we can simplify by assuming a linear relationship:

$$d = D_1 - D_2 v \text{ with } D_1; D_2 > 0. \tag{4.45}$$

The identification of the key determinants of the arrival, the second argument of tourism demand, is more complicated. In particular, simply relying on the classical Consumer Theory becomes quite problematic in this case because, on one hand there are so many socio-economic motives behind the desire for taking holidays and, particularly, for taking a holiday in a specific destination. On the other hand, the choice of a given destination is a binary variable that only has two possible realizations: "yes" or "no".

Generally speaking, the decision of traveling to a destination is the result of considering the complex set of services that characterize the tourism product in the destination as well as its average price. In addition to these two elements, the choice is often the reflection of a so-called "accumulation effect", building on own or other tourists' preferences and on how fashionable or popular the destination is. Thus, in contrast to the study of the length of stay, we cannot rely on a unique and simple independent variable for the arrival function in the tourism demand. Therefore, we just express a generic function:

$$A = A(.), \tag{4.46}$$

where the symbol (.) means that several are the variables that should be listed within the parentheses. The economic literature on this topic (see Crouch and Ritchie 1999) seems to agree in highlighting the following: (a) the primary resources and attractions available in the destination; (b) the presence of mobility factors to ease the access to the destination, usually consisting of transport hubs and infrastructural systems; (c) the effectiveness of destination marketing, management, and planning policies; (d) the environmental status, essentially depending on the degree of exploitation of natural resources; (e) considerations on the safety, distance, and relative price of the destination; (f) the variety of local products supplied (see Sect. 4.3.2).

[14] In a more general model, the relevant variables in the determination of the holidays length should be classified as either socio-demographic variables (for example, the composition of the tourist's family), economic variables (the price of the holiday relative to other destinations or to the level of income), or market variables (when the holidays is a package tour, its duration is usually predetermined by the tour operator). For a discussion of this topic, see Alegre and Pou (2006), Alegre et al. (2011) and Pestana Barros and Pinto Machado (2010).

In what follows, we will focus our attention only on one single element: the *overcrowding and congestion of the destination*, which is an essential factor to consider when deciding to travel. Therefore, we assume the following specification for (4.46):

$$A = A(N), \tag{4.47}$$

which allows us to rewrite (4.43) as:

$$N = A(N)d(v) = f(N, v), \tag{4.48}$$

and where the number of overnight stays N can also be used as a measure for the degree of overcrowding in the destination. To be able to study (4.48) we first need to specify the analytical properties of function $A(N)$. Regarding this, we can introduce two alternative specifications:[15]

(a) Tourists are driven by a *snob effect* and they escape the crowd; in this case, the number of arrivals decreases as the degree of overcrowding increases, which implies that:

$$A' = \frac{dA}{dN} < 0. \tag{4.49}$$

(b) Tourists are driven by a *bandwagon effect* and show attraction for the crowd; in this case, the number of arrivals increases with the degree of overcrowding, which implies that:

$$A' = \frac{dA}{dN} > 0. \tag{4.50}$$

Although the hypotheses (4.49) and (4.50) are referred to the same model, they will be discussed separately since their implications and policy conclusions are different.

4.4.3.1 Case A: The Snob Effect in Tourism

Let us consider the two-tier demand function (4.48) under the assumption expressed by (4.49). We can easily discuss this case by following the graphical approach presented in Fig. 4.6, where we plot a family of curves L representing the length of stay functions in the linear version (4.45), each one associated to a given value of A.

[15] In the economic literature, the analysis of these effects in a general perspective dates back to Leibenstein (1950).

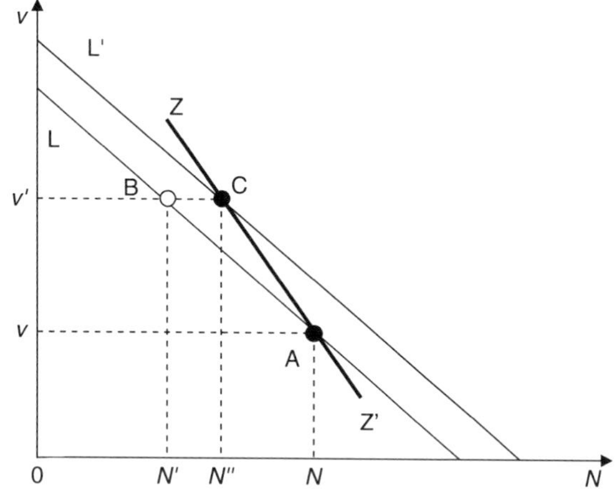

Fig. 4.6 Tourism expenditure maximization in case of tourists getting away from the crowd (snob effect)

In light of (4.49), as the overcrowding decreases, the curve L shifts up. In particular, the increase in the daily price of the holiday from v to v', leads to two effects:

1. for a given number of arrivals, the number of overnight stays decreases as a consequence of a reduction in the average length of stay; the *instantaneous price effect* consists of a movement along curve L from point A to point B, where the number of stays decreases from N to N', with $N' < N$, due to the fact that the average length of a stay has also dropped;
2. the reduction in the number of overnight stays decreases the overcrowding of the destination and, because of the snob effect caused by tourists who are getting away from the crowd, increases the number of arrivals: the holiday's length curve shifts outward from L to L' by an amount that depends on the intensity of the snob effect; this can be represented by a movement from point B to a point C, so that the number of stays increases from N' to N'', with $N'' > N'$.

If we consider the composite effect given by (1) and (2), we find that the final level of overnight stays after the rise in price will be equal to N'' which is associated to point C. Note that in our demonstration, the only *equilibria* are at points A and C, while point B is not an equilibrium point.

The mathematical envelope of points like A and C (curve ZZ') in Fig. 4.6 represents the overall two-tier tourism demand (4.48), which explicitly accounts for the "arrivals" component as an inverse function of the overcrowding (since tourists escape the crowd), and the "length of stay" component, which is an inverse function of the price. A quick examination of this curve shows that when tourists are driven by the snob effect, the net effect of the two components of the tourism demand is to *increase the degree of rigidity of the overall demand*. Indeed, it is apparent that the elasticity along ZZ' is smaller than along each element of the family of curves L from which ZZ' is obtained.

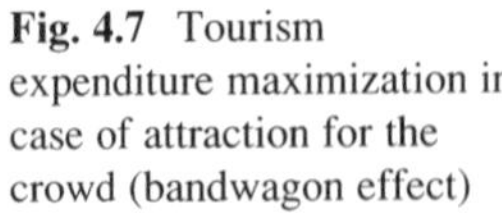

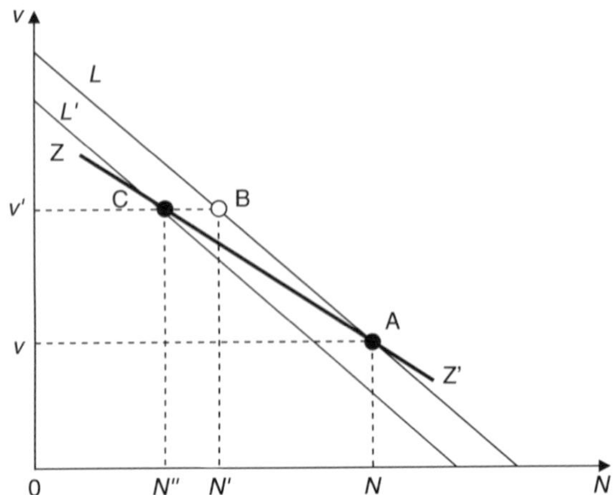

Fig. 4.7 Tourism expenditure maximization in case of attraction for the crowd (bandwagon effect)

The overall effect can be described as follows: the increase in the daily price of the holiday leads to a reduction in the length of stay at the destination and, consequently, lowers the overall number of overnight stays. This reduces the level of overcrowding and generates a wave of new arrivals by tourists who are driven by the snob effect. Therefore, the initial reduction in the number of stays is partially compensated and the tourism demand becomes less elastic.

Finally, notice that the more intense the snob effect becomes, the lower the elasticity will be. For big shifts in curve L', the demand ZZ' may even result in an upward sloping curve (when N'' lies on the right of N). This would be the case when the snob effect is so significant to offset the instantaneous decreasing effect in the average length of stay due to the price increase.

4.4.3.2 Case B: The Bandwagon Effect in Tourism

Let us again consider the two-tier demand (4.48), but under the assumption expressed by (4.50). Hence, contrary to Fig. 4.6, Fig. 4.7 shows that when the degree of overcrowding in the destination drops the curve L shifts in. In particular, the increase in the daily price of the holiday from v to v', generates two effects in Fig. 4.7:

1. For a given number of arrivals, the number of overnight stays decreases as a consequence of a reduction in the average length of stay; the *instantaneous price effect* consists of a movement along curve L from point A to point B, where the number of stays decreases from N to N', with $N' < N$, due the fact that the average length of a stay has also dropped. Notice that the instantaneous effect is then identical to the case (A) of tourists getting away from the crowd;
2. The reduction in the number of overnight stays decreases the overcrowding of the destination and, because of the *bandwagon effect* caused by tourists who are *attracted by the crowd*, this leads to a drop in the number of arrivals: the

holiday's length curve shifts inward from L to L' by an amount that depends on the intensity of the bandwagon effect; this can be represented by a movement from point B to a point C, so that the number of stays decreases from N' to N'', with $N'' < N'$.

If we consider the composite effect given by (1) and (2), we find that the final level of overnight stays following the rise in the price will be equal to N'' which is associated to point C. Note that in our demonstration, the only *equilibria* are at point A and C, while point B is not an equilibrium point.

The mathematical envelope of points like A and C (curve ZZ') in Fig. 4.7 represents the overall two-tier tourism demand (4.48), which explicitly accounts for the "arrivals" component, now a direct function of the overcrowding since tourists are being attracted by the crowd, and the "length of stay" component, which is an inverse function of the price. A quick examination of this curve shows that when tourists are driven by the bandwagon effect, the two effects sum up, and the net effect is to *increase the degree of elasticity of the overall demand.* Indeed, it is apparent that the elasticity along ZZ' is greater than along each element of the family of curves L from which ZZ' is obtained.

The overall effect can be described as follows: the increase in the daily price of the holiday leads to a reduction in the length of stay at the destination and, consequently, reduces the overall number of overnight stays. This reduces the level of overcrowding and, because of the bandwagon effect, the number of arrivals of tourists who are being attracted by the crowd. Therefore, the new contraction in the number of stays adds up to the initial one, so that the tourism demand in the destination becomes more elastic than in the previous case, with the degree of elasticity that is greater as the bandwagon effect intensifies.

By comparing the cases of tourists escaping and being attracted by the crowd, we can immediately see that each of the two alternative assumptions on the relationship between arrivals and overcrowding has a different impact on the elasticity of the two-tier tourism demand. In particular, the behavior of tourists who escape the crowd yields a lower elasticity (curve ZZ' in Fig. 4.6 is steeper) than the behavior of those who are attracted by the crowd (curve ZZ' in Fig. 4.7 is flatter).

If we link these findings both with the destination's goal of maximization of tourism expenditure and with the existing relationship between expenditure and elasticity (see Sect. 4.4.1), the reason why the daily price of a holiday is greater in exclusive destinations than it is in popular destinations becomes clear. Given that in exclusive destinations the demand tends to be more rigid, the Cournot point corresponds to a higher price and, consequently, to a relatively lower number of stays than for popular destinations, where the demand exhibits higher elasticity. This last statement leads us to the important conclusion that the causal relationship between the degree of popularity/exclusiveness of a destination and its price goes from the former to the latter, and not the other way round. In other words, *if due to any social or environmental reason, a destination is chosen by elite tourism, it will optimally set higher prices; on the contrary, a destination being chosen by "mass" tourism will optimally choose lower prices.* Therefore, a destination that is willing to modify its nature is recommended to not use price as a tool. For example, if a mass tourism destination willing to become more "exclusive" tries to increase prices, it may certainly suffer from the perverse effect of losing former tourists (less attracted by a now less popular destination) without being able to attract new ones (who do not arrive in a still relatively crowded destination).

4.5 The Evolution of the Destination

So far, our theoretical discussion on tourism destinations has been based on the implicit assumption that tourism demand manifests itself at one point in time. Therefore, we have used comparative statics in order to study the way in which either idiosyncratic or market changes affect tourism demand and the market equilibrium. In other words, the analysis was carried out independently on the way the destination could move from one situation to the other. In this section, we will introduce some dynamic considerations and discuss some models that will help us understand the evolution of the demand for tourism and destinations over time.

4.5.1 The Destination Life Cycle

The model most frequently used to analyze the evolution of tourism demand over time is known as *Tourism Area Life Cycle model* (TALC). The Life Cycle model was first introduced in economic literature with the aim of explaining the markets' dynamic for durable and comfort goods. The Life Cycle model has then found a perfect application to the case of tourism, with particular reference to the evolution of a destination over time.

The first scientists who applied the Life Cycle model to tourism had identified three stages in the life cycle of a destination: the discovery, the growth, and the decline, the last being the phase when tourists decide to abandon a destination in favor of a new one (Gilbert 1939; Christaller 1964). The most popular version of the TALC model, which was first introduced by Butler (1980), builds around six stages and has the S-shaped graphical representation of Fig. 4.8, where the relationship between time (measured on the x-axis) and the number of overnight stays at the tourism destination (measured on the y-axis) is displayed.[16]

[16] For an introduction to the TALC model we refer to Cooper (1990) or to Shaw and Williams (2004) and Butler (2006) for a more recent discussion on the link between sustainability and the TALC. See also Swann (2010) for an interesting extension of the model to take into account the effect of cycles or waves in demand.

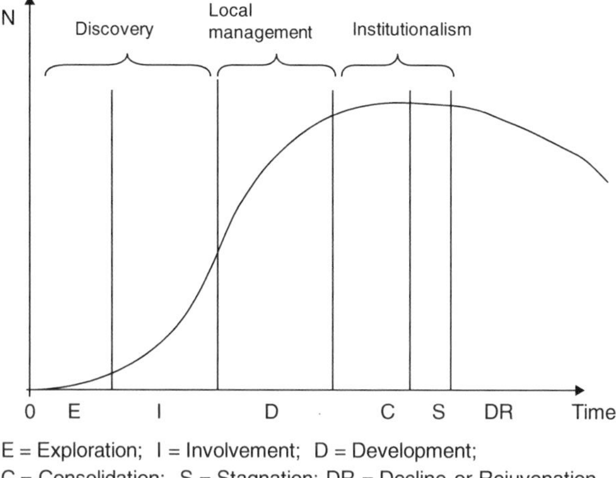

Fig. 4.8 The tourism area life cycle model

- According to Butler, the life cycle of a destination begins with the *exploration* phase by a small group of adventurous tourists, whose goal is not to visit mass holiday destinations and who tend to escape institutionalized tourism. Although at this stage the destination is normally constrained by having limited access and by the lack of tourism structures and facilities, these tourists are attracted by its natural beauty, its cultural heritage, or by the possibility of higher levels of contact and interaction with the local population. In this phase, the number of tourists remains negligible and the tourism sector is almost not existent. Consequently, there is no activity of the destination management whatsoever at this stage.
- In the *involvement* phase, the set of local activities aiming at hosting and entertaining tourists and promoting the destination is getting organized and yields a regularly increasing number of overnight stays. This is when a tourism season and a tourism market appear, i.e. when the private sector of the economy starts to invest in tourism structures. In this phase, the public sector still fails to provide any coordination service or completion of the existing tourism product with the necessary infrastructure. The organization of the destination is therefore in the hands of an uncoordinated private sector.
- In the *development* phase, the destination experiences a significant number of tourists, in particular during the peak season. The number of overnight stays rises at an increasing rate, and often exceeds the size of the local population. This is when the destination experiences a change in the tourism organization in the sense that the public sector starts playing a fundamental role in the coordination and/or the completion of the tourism product, in building infrastructures and supplying public services in order to give the destination an international appraisal. The activities of management and control serve a double purpose;

on the one hand, they contribute to the positive resolution of economic problems facing the private sector; on the other hand, they may have a role in intermediating with the tour operators. Indeed, the development of a destination often goes through a number of agreements signed with international travel agencies and tour operators, which start playing a key role in the destination. However, such a phase implicitly lays the premise of the destination decline. The overcrowding, along with the increasing size of the local population attracted by the economic opportunities provided by tourism, may significantly deteriorate the structures and facilities, endanger the quality of natural resources and diminish the overall appeal of the destination.

- In the *consolidation* (or maturity) phase we still observe an increase in the number of overnight stays, but at a decreasing rate. In this phase of full maturity the management changes, given that the tourism product can no longer be kept under the local operators' full control. The destination is now well integrated into international markets and its global role is better managed by external, often international, operators. They promote the destination by including it in their global offer and by supplying a set of services that are better suited for the needs of mass tourism (such as all-inclusive holidays with international standard quality). The destination continues to exhibit a great appeal for hotel chains and other multinational corporations as well as for many international tourists, so that it can be considered a consolidated location for tourism flows and tourism business.
- The *stagnation* phase is reached at the peak of the number of overnight stays and constitutes the stage when the destination begins losing its appeal in the eye of tourists. This is when the location mainly becomes the destination for repeat visits by conservative tourists, when the tourism operators must undertake major promotional investments in order to maintain a constant number of tourists and positive profits. This is when the destination begins to face serious environmental, social, and economic difficulties and needs to solve conflicts among different stakeholders.
- During the phase of *decline*, the tourism destination loses tourists who become progressively more attracted by other newer and more fashionable destinations. It becomes more dependant on short-term trips of tourists living nearby. At this stage, many tourism structures are obsoletes and can be devoted to alternative uses. Local operators may start planning new projects to revitalize the destination, replace the existing attractions, and *rejuvenate* the tourism product.

A synthetic representation of the key features of the demand, the supply, and the destination management along the different phases of the TALC model is presented in Table 4.1.

The TALC model received significant attention for its suitability to a range of different issues: (a) it provides a good explanation of the different phases of the life cycle of tourism areas from a historical perspective; (b) it allows to discuss the reasons for the continuous change of tourism destinations; (c) it describes the relationship between the stages and the development of the center and the suburbs

Table 4.1 A synthetic representation of the life cycle of a tourism area

Phase	Tourism flows	Features of the supply	Destination planning and control
Exploration	A few tourists	No tourism facilities	No planning and control
Involvement	Increasing tourists	Early tourism structures are born	Local but uncoordinated control
Development	Increasing tourists, at a higher rate	Investment in infrastructures and in the completion of the product	Public control through the destination management
Consolidation	Increasing tourists, at a lower rate	Internationally integrated, with multinational operators	International control
Stagnation	Peak in the number of tourists	Obsolescence and loss of competitiveness	Conflicts among different stakeholders
Decline/ Rejuvenation	Decreasing tourists	Decay of many facilities, need of restyling	Search for rejuvenation strategies

of a tourism destination; (d) it explains the rationale behind the investments undertaken by multinational tourism firms (see Sect. 14.2.2).

At the same time, the TALC model has been attracting a number of authoritative critiques regarding its interpretative effectiveness both for strategic (i.e., destination marketing) and forecasting purposes (Haywood 1986). For example, it has been observed that the S-shaped curve presented in Fig. 4.8 is highly unstable and quite sensitive to exogenous factors such as economic growth, strategies followed by local governments and by the multinational tour operators, the number of competitive destinations, etc. In addition, the curve is quite difficult to interpret if the destination hosts several types of tourism at the same time (i.e., business, leisure and cultural tourism). These issues, along with the intrinsic individual features of each destination, make the exact shape of the TALC model quite unpredictable and its duration very random. Moreover, we often perceive that some destinations seem "stuck" in a given phase of the life cycle (for example, they never pass the exploration phase), while others move from development to decline in just a matter of years.

These critiques reveal that the TALC model cannot be taken as unique for all destinations. Instead, we should think of a specific life cycle model for any destination and for any type of tourism, each with its own shape and length. In other words, the TALC model cannot be taken as a robust interpretative tool:

> [Many factors] can delay or accelerate progress through the various stages. Indeed, development can be arrested at any stage in the cycle, and only tourist developments promising considerable financial returns will mature to experience all stages of the cycle. In turn, the length of each stage, and of the cycle itself, is variable. At one extreme, instant resorts such as Cancun (Mexico) or time-share developments move almost immediately to growth; at the other extreme, well-established resorts such as Scarborough (England) have taken three centuries to move from exploration to rejuvenation.
>
> (Cooper et al. 1998, p. 114)

At the same time the TALC model stresses on the relationship between the stages of the destination evolution and the management and marketing strategies, investment and attractions which must be specifically redefined in each stage of the life cycle. For instance, in the early phases the tourism operators are required to take actions toward building their market share. Instead, during the development stage they should preserve and consolidate their market shares and oppose the pressures of new comers. Also, as the growth rate of overnight stays vanishes, the destination should not wait for the inevitable decline but implement new strategies to rejuvenate their product instead. For all these reasons, and regardless of its theoretical caveats, the TALC is a very popular model and is currently used to understand the status and future prospects for tourism destinations (see the empirical study of Almeida and Correia (2010) for Madeira or the theoretical approach of Swann (2010) for the case of tourism resorts).

Any problem related to the maturity of the tourism product or of the destination can be bypassed by undertaking a set of restyling actions (Case Study 4.2). This strategy of rejuvenation usually consists of assigning a new meaning to an old product with the purpose of prolonging the duration of the development phase or, possibly, of starting a new life cycle. The restyling of the tourism destination is in all aspects similar to the strategies adopted for any other industrial product (for example, this is what fashion does to the clothing and shoe industry) and always consists of finding a new style for the destination. The act of restyling engages local operators in two different ways.

1. Through the reorganization of the destination toward a different and new presentation of the tourism product, this is known as *organizational restyling*. This strategy has been followed by a number of seaside resorts that were going through their consolidation phase, by promoting, for example, thalassotherapy holidays, entertainment holidays, etc. Some coastal destinations in Italy and in Spain are good examples of organizational restyling.
2. The structural modification of the destination in a way that involves investments in deep aspects of the territory and not just esthetic changes. This refers to *real restyling*, which in Industrial Economics is generally associated to the idea of *process innovation*, i.e., with all those changes that affect the stock of real capital available to a firm through new flows of investment. In the special case of tourism, this may require massive restorations of the existing tourism structures to satisfy the evolving needs of the demand (i.e. a hotel restoration aimed at gaining "one more star" in the official classification) or to meet the needs of different tourism segments (i.e., the development of a congress venue in a seaside destination to attract business tourism).

It is important to add other considerations on the concept of *real restyling*. It requires both the introduction of new structures (like communication infrastructures, transportation hubs, and leisure facilities) and the restoration of existing ones. Similarly, some destinations may have natural resources not previously used that, if exploited, may extend the length of the peak season or attract new segments of tourism.

Undertaking a *real restyling* strategy requires a strong degree of cooperation between the private and the public sector. To ensure the success of such a "cycling and recycling" strategy, a tourism destination must count on a number of highly professional and forward-looking managers who invested, as early as in the development and consolidation stages, in human capital by training new generations of future entrepreneurs and managers. Lozano et al. (2008) stress on the relationship between the TALC and models of economic growth. In particular, they argue that the duration of the development stage significantly depends on the quality of private investments as well as on the public intervention aimed at controlling the environmental deterioration and the congestion of the destination, which are phenomena that are intrinsically related to the decline stage.

Case Study 4.2. The TALC Model Applied to a Mature Destination: The Case of Rimini, Italy

The case of Rimini (on the Northern Adriatic coast of Italy) is one of the most interesting to be analyzed within the framework of the TALC model. In the nineteenth century, the Rimini province was mainly an agricultural area, although there were some important urban settlements (the town of Rimini itself dates back to the Roman Empire). The "tourism adventure" of Rimini started around 1840, with the development along the huge sandy beach of the first bathing establishment, owned by the counts Baldini. The bathing establishment, however, quickly ran into financial troubles since it was offering high-quality services at high prices while Rimini was not able to attract sufficient demand by the few élite consumers of that time. In 1869 the municipality of Rimini took over the establishment and started at the same time an investment plan in recreational and leisure structures (such the Kursaal, a pre-contemporary spa and wellness center). In this early phase of *involvement* of Rimini as a tourism destination, thus, the public sector mainly replaced the private one in the planning and management of the tourism structures.

Up to the early twentieth century, though, the hospitality capacity was mainly concentrated in the city center, while the seaside did not have many hotels. To meet the need of having big hotels nearby the sea, in 1908 the Grand Hotel (which became worldwide famous thanks to the work of Federico Fellini, himself a Rimini citizen) was built by a private company (Smara) but it had been strongly backed by the Rimini mayor of the time, Ruggiero Baldini, who also put Smara in charge of the bathing establishment on the forefront beach. However, both the Grand Hotel and its bathing establishment did not reach economic success and, to avoid bankruptcy, the municipality took in charge of both activities. Indeed Rimini crossed a long and unsuccessful phase of involvement in which some errors were made (the élite tourism targeted was not providing sufficient economic returns) and in which there had been a strong local public control.

(continued)

But it was indeed at the same time (early twentieth century) that Rimini started its phase of strong tourism *development* with the success of its new-born hospitality industry which was mainly serving the middle and low segments of the market: family-run hotels, guest houses, villas, and apartments to rent became very numerous. Rimini quickly became in the 1930s one of the most famous resorts in Italy. After the Second World War the development phase reached its highest peak thanks to the Italian economic boom of the 1950s and 1960s: a plethora of small family-run hotels and guest houses quickly covered the 40 km of coast of the Rimini province (more than 1,000 hotels were registered only in the main city) and were successfully offering to the new Italian middle class family-type holidays at very low prices.

In the 1970s Rimini already entered in its phase of *consolidation* and maturity: the total number of overnight stays in Rimini and its province was over 15 million in 1972 and reached its maximum at the beginning of the 1980s, the time when Rimini was entering the *stagnation* stage, with more than 18 million overnight stays per year. The *decline* started in the summer of 1989, when a massive pollution of the Adriatic seaside due to the combination of industrial and agricultural waste and climatic conditions caused a massive drop in the number of tourists. This boosted the need of renewing the image of Rimini and restoring its tourism structures. The phase of *rejuvenation* was then planned by taking into consideration different strategies. On the one side, the main core market of beach tourism was reinforced with important investments in the area of leisure and entertainment, and Rimini quickly became a fashionable and unique resort in the Mediterranean area for youngsters looking for socialization and fun. On the other hand, diversification was searched in two directions: firstly, through the enhancement of the many cultural and environmental attractions available in the area surrounding Rimini; secondly, through important investments in the re-qualification of hotels and in the construction of congress venues which, mainly with the aim of prolonging the peak season and developing a shoulder season, were attempting to attract business tourism into the city. A major achievement in this restyling process came with the opening of the new trade fair quarter in 2001, just outside the city of Rimini, now the third trade fair pole in Italy.

This rejuvenation policy quickly showed its success: in the 1990s the overnight stays started to grow again (and since then they remained stable over 15 million per year), while arrivals steadily grew over two million per year in the 1990s and are now approaching three million. The organizational and real restyling allowed Rimini to fight and beat the decline by repositioning itself in the tourism market. A key feature of Rimini success lies on the effective and efficient coordination between the system of Rimini small and medium-size tourism businesses and the local destination management that most of the time was effectively backing the private sector requests.

After having crossed all the phases of the TALC, Rimini has now been able, after the stagnation, to find the path for a new start, based on a multiproduct tourism: (1) the traditional and family type of tourism, asking for relax and easily accessible beaches at very low prices; (2) the youngster tourism, asking for socialization and entertainment on the beach and a lively night scene; (3) the business tourism, which brings de-seasonalization and a more profitable turnover to the local firms.

4.5.2 Types of Tourists and the Evolution of the Destination

Another way of looking at the destination's evolution over time is by considering the different types of tourists who visit the destination. It is therefore possible to refer to a segmentation of the tourism market and relate it to the different phases of the evolution of the tourism product.[17] In this way, the weaknesses of the TALC model can be partially corrected by acknowledging that the different phases of the tourism destination's evolution can be described around two dimensions: time and the type of tourism hosted. We will consider two alternative classifications of tourists in the following two sub-sections.

4.5.2.1 Independent and Package Tourists and the Stages of the Destination

According to Cooper et al. (2008) tourists can be classified as:

- *Package tourists*; these people are interested in a type of tourism that meets international standards, they are usually associated to high growth rates, and often cause a restructuring of the economy of the destination, as well as several problems related to social and environmental sustainability.
- *Independent tourists*; these people easily adapt to the local environment and social structure, they are usually associated to low growth rates and often stimulate the development of structures with local ownership.

The types of tourists that a destination hosts have an influence on the destination phases. In the *discovery* stage a small number of tourists discover a new location and arrive independently, by self-organizing the holiday, without the help of tour operators. As a result, local private entrepreneurs start investing in tourism, for example to provide greater variety of products and services to satisfy tourists' needs. Hence, that is the beginning of the *local control* phase which sets the premise

[17] We will discuss the segmentation of the tourism market in Sect. 6.7.5, while the psychological and sociological determinants of the demand will be briefly referred to in Sect. 6.6.

for the creation of a destination fully equipped to attract more tourists. Subsequently, a series of initiatives through *local public management* joins the existing private entrepreneurship to improve and complete the tourism supply of the destination. The public sector contributes to the creation of new or better infrastructures that further stimulate tourism flows. The following stage is called *institutionalism*, and is when the destination mainly hosts package tourists whose needs are usually met by all-inclusive tourism packages provided by international tour operators. To take advantage from the spreading of mass tourism, the production technology for tourism services evolves toward exploiting favorable economies of scale in transportation, marketing, and hospitality.

Each phase of this three-stage model partially coincides with a phase of the TALC model, as displayed in Fig. 4.8. In particular, the stages of discovery and local control seem to coincide with the phases of exploration, involvement and development, while the stage called *institutionalism* certainly coincides with the consolidation stage.

Once again, these stages should be taken as neither mandatory nor deterministic for each destination, but as mere indications of a sequence of steps that may even be interrupted along the way. On the one hand there are destinations that supply a mature product to a group of individuals where the number of "independent" prevails over those who are interested in tourism packages (Rimini, Italy is one of the most relevant examples). On the other hand, there are destinations for which the tour operators planned to shorten the discovery stage in order to immediately jump into the development phase (some Caribbean islands are examples of this type). We can argue that the issues of those destinations which skip one or more stages of the evolutionary process must be addressed with ad hoc policies. For example, the destinations which accommodate mass tourism without offering all-inclusive packages often present quality-related issues in the hospitality industry and are not price competitive with respect to the tour operators. Similarly, the destinations that want to "skip" the discovery stage often find impossible to attract local capital and impose a great degree of stress on the local environmental and social systems.

4.5.2.2 The Psychographic Classification of Tourists and the Evolution of the Destination

In 1974, Stanley Plog was the first to present a widely accepted classification of tourists with a focus on their psychographic characteristics. The three typologies suggested by Plog are:

1. The *psychocentric* is a tourist who tends to be overly cautious during her trips, prefers secure and familiar destinations with standard quality of the facilities, where she tends to repeatedly return;
2. The *allocentric* is a tourist who puts other people at the center of her attention, tends to be very adventurous, require basic standards of the facilities, is easily

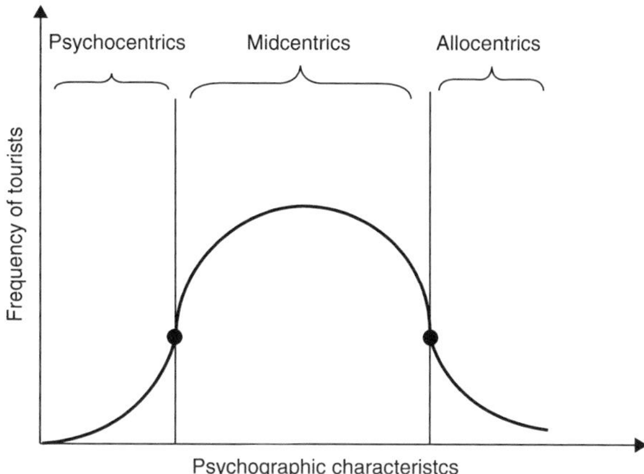

Fig. 4.9 Tourists' psychological characteristics and their frequency

prone to discovering and taking trips to new locations to which she rarely returns;

3. According to Plog, the great majority of individuals should however be qualified as *midcentric* as they fall in between these two extremes.

Plog's taxonomy received a number of critiques which either oppose the approximation that comes from using psychological characteristics as segmentation criteria or because such individual characteristics may significantly change over time depending on the trip taken (one can be at the same time psychocentric in weekend breaks and allocentric in the summer holiday) or being correlated to changing factors such as the tourist's income, profession, etc. Although Plog's classification raises a number of issues, it nevertheless operates well when applied to tourism destinations. Indeed, the evolution of destinations can be explained by following Plog's approach and by identifying the types of tourists hosted by the destination. Figure 4.9 shows the relationship between the psychographic characteristics and the frequency of tourists. Given that there are only a few psychocentrics and allocentrics and many more midcentrics, only the midcentric destinations will attract mass tourism.

According to this conceptual setup, a tourism destination may start its life cycle with the *allocentric tourism market* stage where only a small group of tourism pioneers are hosted. Immediately after, the destination will equip itself to receive more visitors and create opportunities for safer and more comfortable trips. This will set the conditions for the arrival of midcentric visitors, while the allocentrics will slowly abandon the destination in favor of new locations yet to be discovered. This corresponds to the *mass tourism market* stage.

The midcentric destinations might be able to preserve their competitive advantages and maintain their profitability and their market share. However, it might also be possible for these destinations to become excessively popular, which would push out midcentric tourists in favor of psychocentrics. This will likely lower the price of the tourism product, require the creation of more standardized package tours, and allow for the supply of no-risk and vary safe and familiar types of holidays.

Plog's taxonomy is obviously related to the ones we had previously discussed. For example, independent tourists must be found within the group of allocentric individuals. Similarly, the exploration phase in the TALC model must not focus on psychocentric individuals, which are not adventurous at all. In addition, we must stress again on the fact that the process of evolution from one stage to the other should not be taken as unavoidable, and that neither the generated income nor the level of employment in the destination should be thought as only connected to the mass-type of tourism.

As a general conclusion, we argue that each of the models presented to describe the evolution of a tourism destination is intrinsically vulnerable to exceptions and never implies a must-occur sequence of stages. The life cycle may follow a non-canonical sequence or simply skip one or more phases or be interrupted at any moment. Nevertheless, knowing the details of each stage in the evolutionary process of the demand is, as we have seen, a key factor for the definition of a competitive tourism product in the destination as well as for the identification of a sound and effective tourism policy at the destination level.

This is why we believe that the evolution of a destination should be studied in light of as many models as possible, so that the interpretative strengths of one approach can be used to compensate the weaknesses of another. Also, this may help us when a destination contemporaneously displays the features of different phases. Three interesting examples are: Rimini, Italy, which supplies its tourism services mainly to mature, midcentric, and independent individuals; Torremolinos, Spain, which receives mature, midcentric but package tourists; New Zealand, which almost exclusively attracts allocentric tourists of both types: independent and package tourists.

4.5.3 *Forecasting the Tourism Demand*

For all that has been said so far, it is straightforward to conclude that forecasting the evolution of the tourism demand is a key strategic element for the destination. Forecasts have a crucial role for the destination's formulation and implementation of appropriate medium- and long-term tourism strategies (Song and Turner 2006). The forecasts have a key role in the identification of the destination stages and for the best planning of the economic and social activities that are connected with tourism: marketing, production, financial planning, definition of private and public strategies for the short, medium, and long run. Li et al. (2005) state that:

> The developments in tourism forecasting methodologies [are] able to interpret the causes of variations of tourism demand, support policy evaluation and strategy making, and predict future trends in tourism development.
>
> (Li et al. 2005, p. 82)

The techniques that are used to forecast some key indicators of the tourism demand (e.g., number of arrivals, overnight stays, tourism expenditure) largely depend on the adopted statistic approach which, according to Var and Lee (1992) can be classified as: (a) quantitative; (b) qualitative; (c) mixed. The quantitative approach is based on the available historical time series of tourism movements and other related economic variables; the qualitative approach consists of the analysis of the opinions of privileged witnesses, experts, and stakeholders; finally, the mixed approach is characterized by the combination of the two previous approaches. While we refer to more specialized publications such as Bar-On (1989), Song and Li (2008), Morley (2000), or Song and Turner (2006) for a deeper analysis of forecasting methodologies and approaches, in what follows we briefly review their main elements, recalling that from a methodological point of view:

> Studies which have compared the accuracy of different forecasting methods have indicated that, of quantitative methods, no one technique is necessarily superior to another.
>
> (Stabler et al. 2010, p. 71)

4.5.3.1 The Quantitative Approach

The quantitative approach relies on the measures and indicators of the tourism phenomenon that we presented in Chaps. 2 and 3 and on the source of data which can derive from the National Accounting System, the administrative records of tourism firms or sample surveys that are done by filling up questionnaires. The quantitative analysis of historical data for future projections, approach that implicitly assumes that past behaviors can be used to forecast future ones, can be done in light of three alternative ways of interpreting reality: (a) *time series analysis*; (b) *structural models*; (c) *neural network models*.

The statistical analysis of a time series can be seen as a way of making a forecast with no regard to the economic theory. This can be particularly appropriate when we are interested in making short-term predictions of variables that have not yet been precisely modeled by theory, or when we do not have enough information to distinguish between explanatory variables and their consequences. The time series analysis aims at identifying the properties of past data on tourism with the objective of finding useful forecasting criteria; in particular the focus is on a single variable of which we want to identify its dynamic components such as its cyclical behavior, its seasonality, its trend, as well as its deviation from the trend.

Instead, when information about the causal relation between variables and sufficient data are available, the best approach would be to rely on structural (econometric) models which, unlike the time series analysis, are usually based on models developed by the economic theory and focus on the specification and estimation of the existing cause–effect relationship between tourism phenomenon and other economic facts. When these estimated relationships are statistically significant and appear stable enough over time, they can be used for forecasting purposes. Therefore, the goal behind structural models is to estimate the functional form linking independent and dependent variables that are related to the demand for tourism in a destination, in order to forecast future values of the variables. A structural model can consist of one (single equation approach) or more equations (multiple equations approach) and can be typically written as:

$$N_{ij} = f\left(v_{ij}; E_{ij}; Y_i; T_{ij}; D; X_j\right), \tag{4.51}$$

and where N_{ij} denotes the number of overnight stays in the destination j by tourists who are residents of region i; v_{ij} denotes the relative price of region j with respect to its competitors as measured in the currency of region i; E_{ij} is the symbol for the exchange rate between i and j; Y_i is a measure of the level of income in the region of origin;[18] T_{ij} symbolizes the transport costs between i and j;[19] D indicates one (or more) dummy variables to account for special factors; finally, X_j is vector of characteristics of destination j, often identified by the following control variables: (1) the so-called *destination loyalty*, which is linked to the reputation and the organizational structure of the destination (Alegre and Juaneda 2006); (2) destination specific resources or events, including political facts and typical fairs (Loeb 1982; Uysal and Crompton 1984; Gunadhi and Boey 1986); (3) expenditure in marketing and advertising (Divisekera and Kulendran 2006).

The multiple equation version of (4.51) has been often used to test the multistage choice model of the tourist (see Sect. 5.3). If we take the *Almost Ideal Demand System* (AIDS) model that was first introduced in literature by Deaton and Muellbauer (1980), the allocation of tourism expenditure across different destinations and alternative types of tourism can be estimated by the means of a multiple-regression system (for the application of the AIDS model to tourism, see Papatheodorou 1999; Lyssiotou 2000; Durbarry and Sinclair 2003 and Cortés-Jiménez et al. 2009). Unlike its one-equation counterpart which stresses on the tourism flows within the region of destination, the AIDS model focuses on the flows from a region of origin to several destinations. In particular, tourism expenditure in a destination is the dependent variable of each equation, while its independent variables consist of the tourism flows toward alternative destinations, the relative price of the holiday with respect to its competing alternatives, and the aggregate spending of the tourists.

Many other typologies of structural models have been recently used to estimate and forecast the tourism demand. Among the most popular ones there are the multiequation methods of: the *vector autoregressive* (VAR) model applied to study the demand for Thai tourism by Song et al. (2003) or the British demand for tourism in Mediterranean countries by De Mello and Nell (2005); the *error correction model* (ECM) used by Dritsakis (2004a) to study the German demand for

[18] The effects on tourism demand stemming from the exchange rate, the relative price and income are estimated in terms of elasticity (see Sect. 4.2.2). See Stabler et al. (2010, p. 50–55).

[19] The price of transport as a determinant of tourism demand should be treated with care and be the subject of far more theoretical and empirical investigation than has been the case to date. (Stabler et al. 2010, p. 58).

tourism in Greece. In addition, we can find single-equation models such as *the panel data model* which for example has been used to investigate the inbound tourism demand for the Canary Islands in Spain by Garín-Muñoz (2006) or the specific Canary island of Tenerife by Ledesma-Rodríguez et al. (2001); we also find the *structural time-series model* (STSM) applied by Blake et al. (2006) to examine the tourism demand in Scotland and Cortes-Jimenez and Blake (2010) to study the international tourism demand in the United Kingdom by types of tourism; and finally, the *time-varying parameter* (TVP) model employed by Song and Wong (2003) to study the inbound tourism demand for Hong Kong and Li et al. (2006) to examine outbound British tourism demand.

As regards the data used for forecasting purposes, they can be classified into: (a) cross-section data, which refer to different agents (tourists, tourism firms) or countries but measured in the same time period (for example, the international arrivals in different countries of the world in a given year); (b) time series data, when they refer to the same agent or the same aggregate, but measured in different time periods (for example, the international arrivals in a given country over a given time-span); (c) panel data, a mix of the previous two, when we deal with two-dimensional observations, one dimension for the agents or the aggregates, and the other for the time.

Finally, the neural network models have been developed in order to replicate the working mechanism of a human brain and to analyze complex systems which—like tourism—count on non-linear relationships between their variables of interest. The main advantage of this approach consists of the fact that the prior identification of a specific model is not a requirement for this type of analysis. Although neural networks are designed to self learn, in the sense that they can correct their own mistakes by the means of specifically designed learning algorithms, their main limitation consists of producing models with non-objective interpretations.

The application of neural networks in the Economics of Tourism is quite recent, as shown by publication dates of works such as those by Law (2000), Pattie and Snyder (1996), Uysal and El Roubi (1999). Although there is some disagreement on which approach should be seen as superior, all the above authors share the idea that neural network models can be seen as a successful alternative to the more popular forecasting models listed above (see also: Lim 1997; Chu 1998; Greenidge 2001; Kulendran and Witt 2001; Cheong Kon and Turner 2005; for an introductory review, see Palmer et al. 2006).

Other quantitative forecasting methods that have recently been applied to tourism are the rough set approach, the fuzzy time-series method, and the genetic algorithms. For a comprehensive survey of the recent literature, see Song and Li (2008).

4.5.3.2 The Qualitative Approach

Unlike the quantitative methods, the qualitative forecasting techniques do not require the availability of numerical observations and data banks. Instead, the reliability of the forecasts of the qualitative approach depends on the skills and the expertise of opinion leaders, researchers, and stakeholders. There are two adopted methods within the qualitative approach: the *Delphi Method* and the *Method of Scenarios*.

The Delphi Method consists of a forecasting procedure which combines the competences of a number of experts in different fields with the aim of creating a virtual discussion and agreement on the expected evolution of some key variables. In its application to tourism, this approach requires the participation of several experts from different fields, such as economists, business people, psychologists, sociologists, statisticians, etc., who may have an opinion on the long-run evolution of tourism demand. The Delphi Method consists of multiple sessions during which experts never meet in order to prevent them from influencing others' opinions and in which agreement on a final document builds up. The main weakness of this method lies on the fact that individual experts may often divert the attention toward unusual and marginal aspects of the tourism phenomenon, while distracting it from key facts or relationships that should be highlighted instead.

The Method of Scenarios is also used to achieve long-term forecasts. According to Van Doorn (1986), a scenario can be defined as one or more sequences of events that may bring a destination from its current state to desirable situations in the future. The minimal components of a scenario are: (a) the analysis of the current situation; (b) the description of the future image; (c) the identification of the evolutionary path. The Method of Scenarios may differ according to the goal we want to pursue. On one hand we have *positive scenarios*, which aim at predicting the future by assuming continuity in the present trends. On the other hand, we have *normative scenarios*, where a future goal is defined and the attempt to identify and develop new and innovative paths to reach it is pursued. Alas, the forecasting Method of Scenarios also suffers from some limitations. Among others, Van Doorn stresses on the lack of verifiability of scenarios from a quantitative perspective, the relative absence of theoretical considerations that may be needed for the accurate formulation of scenarios, and the subjective evaluation of (mainly political) variables that have a long-term impact on the tourism phenomenon.

4.5.3.3 The Mixed Approach

Different approaches may lead to different forecasts. Therefore, we may feel the need to adopt a combination of them in order to reduce the risk of errors. The mixed approach consists of combining different forecasting models with the aim of producing a unique, and likely more accurate, forecast.

> Although [the mixed approach] has been rarely applied to tourism studies, some empirical results suggest that the combined use of different methods leads to more accurate forecasts.
> (Var and Lee 1992, p. 689)

There are two possible combinations: (a) combining different quantitative methods; (b) combining qualitative and quantitative approaches. The first combination consists of calculating the weighted average of elementary forecasts (Bates and Granger 1969) according to:

$$A_{ij}(t) = k_t A_{ij}^1(t) + (1 - k_t)A_{ij}^2(t), \tag{4.52}$$

where: $A_{ij}(t)$ is the mixed forecast for period t; $A_{ij}^1(t)$ and $A_{ij}^2(t)$ are the corresponding elementary forecasts; k_t and $(1 - k_t)$ represent the weight assigned to the elementary forecasts, also depending on their reliability.

With special regard to the combination of quantitative and qualitative methods, the most popular approach consists of combining the regression method with the Delphi Method. In the first stage, a multiple regression is run in order to identify the factors affecting the tourism phenomenon. In the second stage, a pool of experts is gathered to add qualitative considerations to the quantitative findings (Uysal et al. 1985). A mix between quantitative and qualitative approaches is commonly used by the UNWTO as a forecasting tool for the publication of its quarterly report, the *Tourism Barometer*.

In light of our brief discussion, it is easy to acknowledge that the stakeholders and the policy makers operating in the destination may count on a wide range of techniques to help forecast the tourism demand and the likely evolution of the destination. Although some of these approaches became less popular over time, it is still worth mentioning them as key elements in the history of the analysis of the tourism demand. For example, the qualitative methods have become progressively more marginal, in a world where the quantitative measures and their accuracy receive the greatest attention from researchers. However, their use in all those situations where quantitative data are unreliable or become available too late is still suggested as a valid approach.

Chapter Overview

- The destination is a territorial system which supplies at least one whole tourism product aimed at satisfying the complex needs of the tourist.
- In general terms, the demand for tourism in a destination is the relationship between the number of overnight stays for a given typology of tourism and the daily price of that holiday.
- In the study of the tourism demand the concept of elasticity (the ratio between the percentage change of variable y and the percentage change of variable x, when x causes y) is essential.
- The destination management has to: solve the anticommon issue by means of coordinating the tourism firms operating in the territory, increase the variety of services included in the tourism product, deal with marketing and branding issues, etc.
- A working goal for the destination may be that of maximizing the tourists aggregate expenditure. This can be reached in the Cournot point of the demand curve, where the own-price elasticity takes a unitary value.

- The optimal price strategy to address the exogenous changes in the demand (stemming from either idiosyncratic effects or from market effects) suggests to "go where the wind blows", i.e., to raise the price when the demand increases and to lower it when the demand decreases.
- The life cycle model for the evolution of a destination exhibits a stretched S shape; the six stages characterizing this process are: exploration, involvement, development, consolidation, stagnation, and decline (or rejuvenation).
- Several forecasting techniques are applied to tourism. They can be classified into: quantitative approach, qualitative approach, mixed approach.

Part II
The Microeconomics of Tourism

Chapter 5
The Consumer Theory Applied to the Tourist

Learning Outcomes
On the completion of this chapter, you will:

- Understand the choice models that explain how the tourist decides as regards length of stay, type of holiday, and location.
- Learn the criteria followed by the tourist when choosing between purchasing a package holiday or self-organizing a holiday.
- Understand the tourists' decision process in purchasing durable goods, such as a holiday home.

5.1 Introduction

In Chap. 4, we discussed the concept of tourism demand as strictly referred to a given destination, a given type of tourism, or any combination of the two. In particular, we considered the tourism demand at the destination as the relationship between the number of overnight stays and the daily price of the holiday, and then we used it as a tool to study the economic problems facing the destination as well as to interpret its solutions in light of the planning and policy of tourism.

It is now time to examine the microeconomics behind the tourism demand, by investigating the process followed by single tourists in determining which goods and services should be purchased to satisfy their needs. In principle, the study of these topics belongs to the Consumer Theory.[1] However, their specification within the Economics of Tourism must be dealt with by using more specific models that incorporate more stringent and more realistic behavioral constraints that are often at work in tourism.

---

[1] For an introduction of the basics of Consumer Theory, refer to any microeconomics textbook. For a quick recall of the consumer's choice standard model, see Theory in Action 5.1.

G. Candela and P. Figini, *The Economics of Tourism Destinations*,
Springer Texts in Business and Economics, DOI 10.1007/978-3-642-20874-4_5,

In order to proceed in the analysis, we first recall and sort the categories of tourism spending that we have so far identified. The goods and services purchased by a tourist for the purpose of a holiday can be classified according to three groups:

1. *Goods and services included in the tourism product*: they are the basic elements of the holiday (travel, accommodation, entertainment, etc.) and appear as the components of the tourism output matrix;
2. *Goods and services pertaining to tourism consumption*: they are associated with extemporaneous and occasional purchases made during the trip, but are not directly associated with it; such spending can be classified as follows:

   a. Spending in the tourist's region of origin, during the preparation of the trip (maps, guidebooks, etc.);
   b. Spending in the destination during the holiday, like purchasing *souvenirs*;

3. *Goods pertaining to tourism investment*: they usually consist of durable items purchased by the tourist for holiday purposes.

Although being a direct consequence of the tourism phenomenon, the second of these three groups does not show any peculiar element to be brought forward: indeed, the consumption of such goods can be easily interpreted within the standard models of the Consumption Theory, and therefore will not be analyzed. We just recall that the investigation of (2b) is necessary to understand the economic (both direct and indirect) effects of tourism on the economic system of the destination (see Sect. 3.3 and the Input–Output model applied to tourism), but it does not require the development of an ad hoc model. In addition, (2a) differs from the household's regular consumption pattern merely for the motivational aspects that, however, are not easily observable and distinguishable from the rest of consumption.

Therefore, a Consumer Theory applied to the tourist behavior, for which we devote this and the following chapter, will be needed only to study type (1) spending. In addition, we will devote Sect. 5.6 to briefly explain type (3) spending, by applying the theory of consumption for durable goods.

Given its importance throughout the Microeconomics of Tourism, the distinction between *the tourist who purchases a "package" holiday* and *the tourist who self-organizes the holiday* has to be clarified. The tourist who purchases a package holiday is an individual who buys an *all-inclusive* tourism product from a tour operator or with the intermediation of a travel agency (Chap. 8). The tourist who self-organizes a holiday is an individual who *produces* the holiday by purchasing separately its different components (travel, accommodation, leisure services, etc.). Such distinction is the key to understand the choices behind any act of purchasing tourism services and inspires the three choice models for the tourist that we will discuss throughout this chapter.

This chapter is organized as follows. After recalling in Sect. 5.2 the concept of tourism as a bundle of goods and services, we will introduce in Sect. 5.3 the basic model for the analysis of the tourist as a consumer, who decides the type of tourism and the destination to visit in order to maximize her utility function subject to a set of constraints. This is the section where we will identify the key variables that drive the tourist's choice: (a) her *preferences for tourism*, formally captured by the utility function to optimize; (b) her *income* which, together with "time" (discussed in Chap. 6), represents the most binding factor for consumption; (c) the *price* of tourism, relative both to other types of tourism and destinations, and to the price of the other goods and services included in the tourist's consumption basket.

In Sect. 5.3, the tourist's choice will be discussed by identifying and separating the three logical stages of the choice process: the *how-much-to-spend* stage, the *how-to-spend* stage, and the *where-to-spend* stage. Then we will distinguish between the tourist self-organizing the holiday and the tourist buying a package holiday. Section 5.4 will study the choice on whether or not to buy package holidays produced by tour operators, while Sect. 5.5 will examine the behavior of the tourist who self-organizes the holiday by buying all the elements that transform it into a whole tourism product. Finally, in Sect. 5.6, we will briefly discuss the tourist's investment by making a direct reference to the theory of consumption of durable goods. The systematic discussion of more specific topics related to the consumer theory applied to the tourist is postponed to Chap. 6.

Theory in Action 5.1. The Optimal Choice of the Consumer

In this section, we recall the intuition and the algebra of the standard model of consumption. Each consumer, a rational individual who wants to maximize own welfare, faces the choice problem of how much to consume of several alternative goods that can be purchased on the market, given own available income. In the simplest setup, the choice is between good x, with a given price p_x, and good y, with a given price p_y.[2] The choice is aimed at maximizing the consumer's utility function U which has two arguments: the quantity of good x and the quantity of good y. The basic assumption of the model requires that both arguments are directly linked with utility, that is, higher the quantity of good x (or good y), higher the level of utility that can be reached by the consumer. However, the consumer cannot increase the quantity purchased of the two goods indefinitely since he faces a budget constraint, that is, the consumer has to choose the combination of goods to purchase given own personal income Y. This constrained optimization problem can be formally described as follows:

$$U(x, y) = U(x) + U(y)$$

$$s.t. \quad p_x x + p_y y = Y$$

(continued)

[2] In a more general setting, the good y can be thought as the basket of remaining goods that can be consumed in alternative to x, requiring an overall spending of M units of currency. If this basket of goods is considered the *numeraire*, with price $p = 1$, the choice is between good x and the rest of spending M.

Here, for simplicity, we assumed a utility function that can be separated into its two independent variables.

To solve this problem, we build the following Lagrangean function with λ as its Lagrangean multiplier:

$$L = U(x) + U(y) - \lambda\left(p_x x + p_y y - Y\right)$$

The first-order conditions of $L(x, y, \lambda)$ are

$$\frac{\partial L}{\partial x} = U'(x) - \lambda p_x = 0$$

$$\frac{\partial L}{\partial y} = U'(y) - \lambda p_y = 0$$

$$\frac{\partial L}{\partial \lambda} = p_x x + p_y y - Y = 0$$

By replacing and solving, we obtain the consumer's equilibrium condition:

$$\frac{U'(x)}{U'(y)} = \frac{p_x}{p_y} \tag{I}$$

In (I) we can recognize the consumer's equilibrium condition: the equality between the marginal rate of substitution between good x and y and the corresponding marginal rate of transformation, equal to the relative price between goods, p_x/p_y.

If the good y is considered a basket of alternative goods (see footnote 2) with spending M and price $p = 1$, the equilibrium can be written as:

$$\frac{U'(x)}{U'(M)} = p_x \tag{II}$$

5.2 Purchasing the Tourism Product

The concept of "basket of goods" is a standard tool in economic theory. The basket denotes a set of available consumption goods in which the consumer picks up the preferred quantity for each good. If we recall the definition of the tourism product as a bundle of heterogeneous goods and services (see Sect. 2.5), it is straightforward to re-interpret it as a "tourism basket" for the aims of the Economics of Tourism.

Alas, the basket is not only a tool of analysis, but also becomes the object of study for this discipline.

5.2.1 *The Tourism Basket*

Let us use again the matrix of the tourism output that we originally presented in Sect. 2.5, where each row (the vector $\mathbf{T}_i$, where $i = 1, 2, \ldots, m$) identifies a tourism basket. $\mathbf{T}_i$ is composed of a sequence of n goods and services measured on a daily basis.

$$T_i = [x_{i1}, x_{i2}, \ldots, x_{in}] \tag{5.1}$$

A tourism basket is always related to the territory in the sense that its characterization cannot be independent of the destination where the holiday takes place (Chap. 4). By using the terminology introduced in Chap. 4, we denote as $r(i)$ the destination where the typology of tourism $\mathbf{T}_i$ is present, with $r(i) = 1, 2, 3, \ldots, R_i$, where R_i stands for the number of tourism destinations offering the basket $\mathbf{T}_i$. Some types of tourism can be purchased from several competing destinations ($R_i > 1$), while other types of tourism can be experienced only in a single location, thus operating in a condition of monopoly ($R_i = 1$). Hence, each basket can be identified with a pair of elements: (a) the vector $\mathbf{T}_i$, which includes the quantity of goods and services characterizing one day of holiday type i; (b) the scalar r, identifying the destination where the holiday is available.

In economics, the concept of basket becomes central to the analysis when related to the concept of price. In particular, the price of the basket identifies the amount of money needed to purchase the goods and services belonging to it and that implies the knowledge of the unit (daily) price of each item in the r-th destination, which can be represented by the vector $\mathbf{p}_r = [p_{1,r}, p_{2,r}, \ldots, p_{n,r}]$. To take also into account international tourism, the exchange rate between the currency of the r-th destination and the currency of the tourist's region of origin, c_r, is also needed. Therefore, the daily (unit) price of the i-th tourism product in destination r, which we define as $v_{i,r}$ (remember it as "value"), is given by the monetary value to be spent on the goods and services needed for one day of such holiday:

$$v_{i,r} = c_r \left[\sum_{j=1}^{n} p_{j,r} x_{ij} \right] \tag{5.2}$$

where the exchange rate c_r allows to express the price in the currency of the tourist's country of origin. Note that (5.2) is a general expression, given that by setting

$c_r = 1$ we refer to the case of domestic tourism, while with any other value for c_r, we refer to the international tourism case.[3]

The pair ($\mathbf{T}_i$; $v_{i,r}$) gives us a complete description of the tourism product in a destination; these two variables, which we already used in Chap. 4, are of great help for analyzing models of consumption. Prior to the discussion of such models, it is important to deepen the understanding of the concept of basket by following two alternative perspectives: (a) the aggregate analysis of the tourism basket and (b) the structural analysis of the tourism basket.

5.2.2 The Aggregate Analysis of the Tourism Basket

Expression (5.2) displays the price of tourism i in the destination r, which we can use to build three alternative average prices (see Sect. 4.2.1):

1. The average price of tourism i, v_i, across different destinations of a region (for example, the average daily price of a beach-based holiday in France);
2. The average price of the different types of tourism hosted by the destination r, v_r (for example, the average price of leisure, cultural, and business tourism in a city like Paris);
3. The price of tourism, as the average price of different types of tourism offered by different destinations, v_m (or, in other words, the average price of one day of holiday in France).

The computation of these prices may involve two different aggregation techniques, called simple and weighted, which can be illustrated with reference to case (2) following the different types of tourism captured by Ulysses and Columbus and already discussed in Chap. 2. The same could be said, *mutatis mutandis*, with regard to average price of types (1) and (3).

Let us recall the tourism products presented in Table 2.3, which should now be referred as hosted by region r, and fix the prices (written in local currency) for the different services included: 50 for one overnight stay at a hotel, 40 for one overnight stay at a rented apartment, 20 for a meat-based meal, 25 for a fish-based meal, 10 for one unit of beach services, and 30 for one entrance at a club. According to these prices and to the characteristics of the tourism products outlined in Table 2.3, the

[3] This economic definition differs from the one we introduced in Chap. 2, where crossing a country's border was considered a sufficient condition to generate international tourism. Indeed, in case the tourist's country of origin shares the same currency with that of the destination (like any pair of countries in the Euro zone), we would record the trip as international tourism in the official statistics, without considering it as international tourism from a purely economic point of view. We refer to Chap. 14 for a deeper discussion of the economic distinction between domestic and international tourism, which ultimately relies on the role played by the exchange rate in the calculation of the price of tourism.

daily price of the Ulysses type of tourism is 140, while for the Columbus type is 105. How can we calculate the average daily price of a holiday at the destination r?

There are two possibilities: on the one hand, we could just take the simple average of daily prices as $v_r = (140 + 105)/2 = 122.50$. On the other hand, we could take into consideration the relative importance of each type of tourism by calculating a weighted average, where the number of stays is the chosen weight for the calculation. Let 40,000 and 60,000 be the number of stays, respectively, of Ulysses type and Columbus type of tourism (Table 2.3) at the destination r. The weighted average is $v'_r = (140 \times 40{,}000 + 105 \times 60{,}000)/100{,}000 = 119$.

In general, the two formulas do not produce the same numerical result. Also, the choice between the two possible ways of averaging out depends on the nature of the issue under investigation and the goal. Consider that, unlike the simple average, the weighted average depends on the tourism structure of the destination; therefore, the weighted average price might vary with the number of overnight stays for one type of tourism, although the prices may stay the same.

Finally, we must underline the fact that these averages are often used by tourism operators and stakeholders to analyze the degree of competition across destinations and/or types of tourism. Moreover, the choice of the best method of aggregation essentially depends on the available information and data on prices and tourism flows.

5.2.3 The Structural Analysis of the Tourism Basket

With the term *structure of a basket*, we refer to the type of relationship between the goods and services included there. As this regard, three different relationships can be outlined:

- *Substitutability*: two elements (x_{ih} and x_{ik}) belonging to basket $\mathbf{T}_i$ are said to be substitutes when one can be used to replace the other without (significantly) affecting the tourist's satisfaction. For example, a show at the *Opéra Nationale de Paris* is a substitute of a show at the *Théâtre du Châtelet* in Paris. The idea of substitutability introduces a key economic problem; any two substitutes (x_{ih} and x_{ik}) must enter the tourism basket in a combination that minimizes the amount of money spent on them, given the level of satisfaction that the tourist gains from consuming that type of tourism. This approach, which is presented in Fig. 5.1a, is dual to the problem of utility maximization subject to a given level of the consumer's income. Point E represents the optimal bundle of two goods which, under the standard assumptions for the Consumer Theory, are in a relationship of substitutability and given a level of utility represented by the indifference curve U°. As prices change, the basket structure does too. In particular, Fig. 5.1a shows that as the price of x_{ih} decreases (or the price of x_{ik} increases), the new optimal combination of the two goods becomes E': the

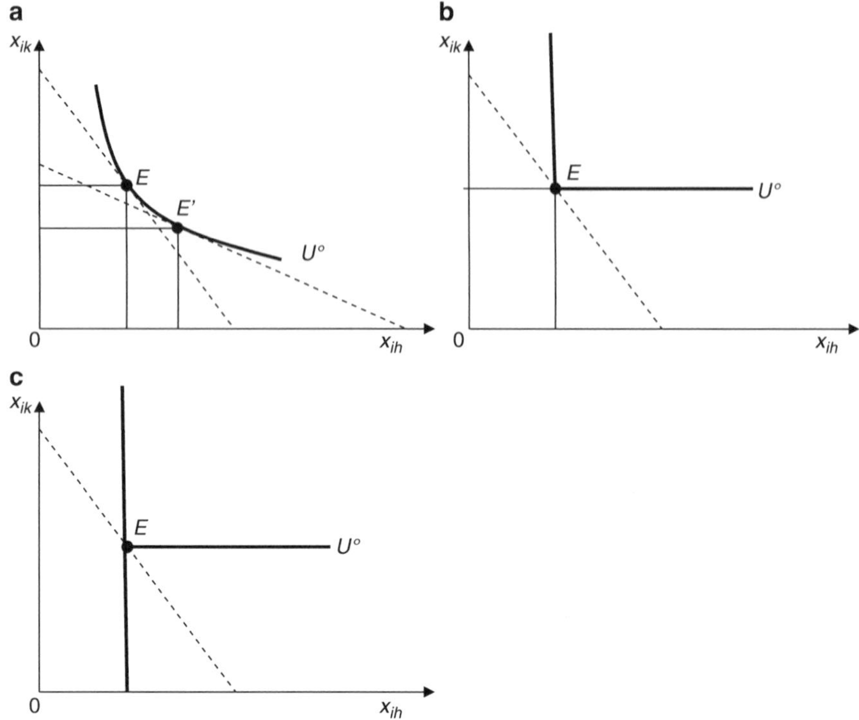

Fig. 5.1 Substitutability, complementarity, and lexicographic ordering in the tourism basket

tourist partially replaces x_{ik}, now become relatively more expensive, with more units of x_{ih}, now become relatively cheaper.

- *Complementarity*: two elements (x_{ih} and x_{ik}) are said to be complementary when they are in a given ratio within basket $\mathbf{T}_i$; for example, the number of overnight stays and the number of breakfasts that are generally consumed on a holiday. Failing to respect the complementarity between two or more goods from the supply side implies a loss of profitability (think about a hotel with no breakfast offer and another one selling one overnight stay together with two breakfasts: both are clearly not competitive for most types of tourism). The problem is displayed in Fig. 5.1b where, given the typical "L-shape" of the indifference curve for complementary goods, it is clear that relative price only has a negligible importance: most important is to provide the goods in the exact ratio.
- *Lexicographic order*: a pair of elements (x_{ih} and x_{ik}) within basket $\mathbf{T}_i$ are said to satisfy a lexicographic order when one good is always preferred over another one, regardless of the quantity. This is the case, for example, of sex tourism where the interest in the destination's cultural heritage is marginal with respect to the main motivation of the trip. This structure is called "lexicographic" because it operates like the order of words in a dictionary: A always comes before B; however, when two words begin with the same letter, the second letter

determines the ordering (AA comes before AB). Adopting a lexicographic ordering always translates into choosing the basket that includes most of the preferred item A, while any good or service of type B is additional only to complete the basket. For this reason, given the high rigidity of the demand for good x_{ih}, the price of the individual components of the tourism basket is unimportant. The problem is shown in Fig. 5.1c.

The composition of the tourism product, intended as a basket of goods and services, has important consequences on marketing and pricing strategies; for example, failing to respect the complementarity in, or the lexicographic order between goods will likely translate into pushing the supply out of market; at the same time, failing to exploit the relationships of substitutability between goods may lead to a loss of competitiveness in price. Therefore, the manager of the tour operator and the destination manager are expected to consider such properties so as to achieve the best economic result.

In conclusion, we must stress that the structure of the tourism basket unfolds a precise economic problem that has to be solved by the producer.[4] However, in all the theoretical models presented in this chapter, the implicit assumption is that the basket is always optimally identified, that is, the supply side has already solved its optimization problem: this will allow to focus on the demand side and discuss the consumption choice of the tourist.

5.3 The Choice of the Tourist as a Consumer

Along with all other goods, also tourism aims at satisfying the consumer's needs. Therefore, it competes with all the remaining goods in the allocation of personal income.

1. If we indicate with N the overall number of days spent on holiday by the tourist, with N_i the number of days spent on tourism i, with $N_{i,r}$ the number of days spent on tourism i in destination r, and, finally, with $(y_1, y_2, \ldots, y_n)$ the list of non-tourism consumption goods, the individual utility function can be generically written as:

$$U = U\big(y_1, y_2, \ldots, y_n; N; \ldots, N_i, \ldots, N_{i,r}, \ldots\big), \tag{5.3}$$

with positive first-order conditions and negative second-order conditions for each of its arguments, consistent with the standard assumption of decreasing marginal utility.

---

[4] These arguments link, for example, with the issues of coordination and variety for the destination management (see Sect. 4.3) or with the issue of double markup for the tour operator (see Sect. 11.5).

However, function $U(.)$ in its general formula (5.3) is very difficult to analyze. The Consumer Theory developed an approach to simplify the problem by imposing some restrictive, yet plausible, assumptions on the properties of goods and preferences. This makes the consumer's choice much easier to understand in theory and to deal with in practice. For example, no individual would be able to simultaneously decide all aspects of own consumption. Instead, it is more realistic to think in terms of a sequential choice between goods that were previously allocated across groups. Such simplifying and restrictive assumptions are the Aggregation Theorem, the Separability of Preferences, and the Multistage Budgeting.

The *Aggregation Theorem*, first proved by John Hicks and Wassily Leontief, argues that a set of goods which prices change at the same rate (that is, maintaining their relative prices as constant) can be dealt with as if it were a unique good. In virtue of such theorem, if we assume that this is a property of all the n non-tourism goods, then they can be treated as a unique *composite good* $M_C = p_1y_1 + p_2y_2 + \ldots + p_ny_n$, here symbolized by the amount of money M_C spent on all the goods other than tourism. The Aggregation Theorem ensures that such approach does not alter the expression of preferences and allows to focus on the choices that are of greatest interest for the Economics of Tourism, that is, the decision of the consumer as a tourist.

The *Separability of Preferences* allows another important simplification. Preferences are defined to be separable when goods can be allocated to groups such as the preference for one group can be described independently from the preferences of another group.[5] For example, when meals are being thought as belonging to a unique group with defined preferences, then the tourist may sort the preferences based on the meal's different courses and independently from the restaurant in which they are being served, or from any other good being consumed within the same group. In the opposite case, when preferences are not separable, we say that the preferences for a group are *conditional* to the way the goods within another group are being chosen. In this latter case, the preferences for the meal's courses can be different depending on whether the meal is being consumed in a steak-house or in a seafood restaurant.

In light of the Aggregation Theorem and the hypothesis of Separability of Preferences, if we assume that preferences are referred to an aggregate group of non-tourism goods versus tourism and, within tourism, groups are characterized by the different types of tourism and, within any type of tourism, groups are characterized by different destinations, the general form of the utility function (5.3) can be presented as in (5.4):

$$U = f\left[u(M_C, N), u^{\circ}(\ldots, N_i, \ldots), \hat{u}(\ldots, N_{i,r}, \ldots)\right]. \tag{5.4}$$

[5] Note that other definitions of preference separability exist. Indeed, we rely on the hypothesis of *implicit separability* which has to do with the structure of the consumer expenditure (Deaton and Muellbauer 1989).

Here, $u(.)$, $u^{\circ}(.)$, and $\hat{u}(.)$ have the usual properties of the utility functions defined over their arguments (positive first derivatives and negative second derivatives). Separability can be understood in two different ways: *weak separability* if we require that function $f(.)$ is increasing in each of the sub-utility functions u, u°, and $\hat{u}$, each one associated with a group of goods; *strong separability* if we require that the function $f(.)$ is additive, thus taking the simple form:

$$U = u(M_C, N) + u^{\circ}(\ldots, N_i, \ldots) + \hat{u}(\ldots, N_{i,r} \ldots). \tag{5.5}$$

When the hypothesis of separability is applied to all goods (and not solely to groups of goods), we say that the preferences are characterized by *independent wants*. Technically speaking, the marginal utility function of each good only depends on the amount of such good. This is the assumption that will be largely adopted to characterize the different models of consumption applied to the tourist.

Both the Aggregation Theorem (needed to build groups of consumption goods) and the assumption of separability of preferences (necessary to "break" the general problem into sub-problems) are required to simplify the consumer's decision into a *Multistage Budgeting* choice. In other words, for the consumer, it is optimal to split income into two or three decision-making stages. In the first step, the income is allocated across main groups of goods, while in the following steps, the budget assigned to each group is allocated across the goods and services belonging to that group.

In order for the Multistage Budgeting to be optimal,[6] the consumer must have all the necessary information needed to decide in each stage. This includes: (a) the exact form of the utility function characterizing the consumer's preferences; (b) the list of average prices for the groups of goods; and (c) the available budget to be spent for each group. It can be shown that when such information is available, the solution of the multistage budgeting is optimal and identical to the solution of the simultaneous one-stage choice. The advantage of the multistage budgeting is that it can be significantly easier to compute than the one-stage choice.

Let us proceed assuming that all the previous hypotheses are satisfied. In this case, the groups of goods in the function $f(.)$ can be organized in a way that the tourist can choose the optimal consumption through a three-stage budgeting decision which involves the following: (1) the budget to be allocated between tourism and non-tourism goods, (2) the budget to be allocated to each type of tourism, and (3) the budget to be allocated in each destination. This choice problem can be represented as in Fig. 5.2 through the utility tree, where we only focus on the branches that directly deal with tourism:

- The tourist first decides how to allocate personal income between the share to be spent on tourism and the share to be spent on other consumption goods

[6] It has been demonstrated that weak separability is the necessary and sufficient condition to complete (at least) a two-stage budgeting choice (Deaton and Muellbauer 1989).

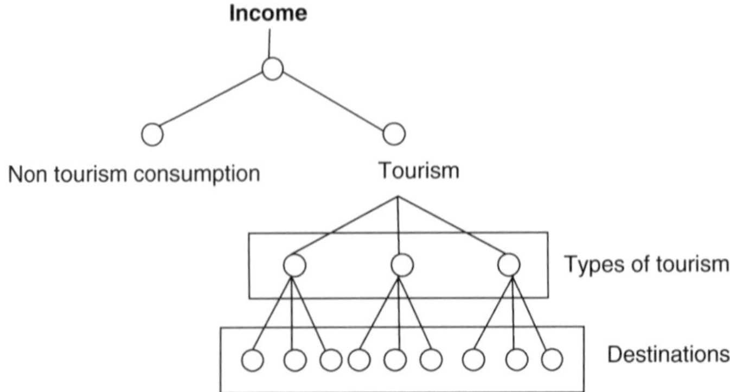

Fig. 5.2 The utility tree of the tourist's choice problem

(including the possibility of saving, when the model allows for inter-temporal choice). In other words, in the first stage, the tourist decides *how much* to spend on tourism activities.

- Then, the tourist must decide how to allocate the "tourism budget" across the different types of tourism. In other words, in the second stage, the tourist decides *how* to spend among different types of tourism.
- Finally, the tourist ought to decide *where* to spend the budget allocated to each type of tourism, by choosing the destination. In other words, in the third stage, the tourist decides *where* to spend the holiday.

Conceptually speaking, nothing prevents the tourist facing the three-stage problem on deciding to solve the *where* stage before the *how* stage. However, the sequence presented above is supported by plenty of empirical evidence on the way the tourist seems to behave in practice.[7]

5.3.1 The First Stage of the Tourist Choice

In what follows, we present the details of the tourist's three-stage choice model. We begin with the first stage, which deals with the decision of how much to spend on tourism. Consistent with Sect. 5.2.1, if we use v_m as the average price of tourism, the choice problem can be formalized as follows:

$$\begin{aligned} \max \quad & u = u(M_C, N) \\ s.t. \quad & v_m N + M_C = Y, \end{aligned} \tag{5.6}$$

[7] A significant share of tourism trips includes visits to more than one destination. A model of multi-destination tourism trips is in de Oliveira Santos et al. (2011).

where N denotes the number of days spent on holiday, M_C the money allocated by the tourist on goods and services other than tourism, and Y the overall income. The unknowns of (5.6) are the values of N and M_C.

5.3.2 The Second Stage of the Tourist Choice

We now consider the second stage, where the tourist must decide how the income allocated to tourism has to be shared across the different existing types of tourism. For the sake of simplicity, we will consider the case with only two types of tourism (for example, beach-oriented versus mountain-oriented types of tourism) which we label with $i = 1, 2$. The tourist's optimal decision comes from the solution of the following choice problem:

$$\begin{aligned} &\max \quad u^{\circ} = u^{\circ}(N_1, N_2) \\ &s.t. \quad v_1 N_1 + v_2 N_2 = M_{\text{tou}};\ N_1 + N_2 = N;\ M_{\text{tou}} = v_m N, \end{aligned} \tag{5.7}$$

where v_i, with $i = 1, 2$, is the average price for tourism i across destinations. Problem (5.7) specifies three constraints which are directly linked to the solution of the first stage: (a) the *monetary constraint,* which drives the budget allocated to the two types of tourism, $v_1N_1 + v_2N_2 = M_{\text{tou}}$; (b) the *time constraint*, according to which the overall number of days spent on holiday must be equal to the sum of the days spent for each type of tourism, $N_1 + N_2 = N$; and (c) finally, the third condition defines M_{tou} as the overall budget allocated to tourism, which is the first-stage solution. The unknowns of (5.7) are the values of the overnight stays for each type of tourism: N_1 and N_2.

5.3.3 The Third Stage of the Tourist Choice

We now move onto the third stage of the choice problem, which is about where to spend the budget allocated across different types of tourism (for example, in which destinations to spend the money allocated to beach-oriented tourism and, similarly, to mountain-oriented tourism). For simplicity, we will focus on a case where there are only two possible destinations for each type of tourism (for example, a domestic and an international destination), which we label with $r = 1, 2$ for each tourism i. The formal problem can be written as follows:

$$\begin{aligned} &\max \quad \hat{u} = \hat{u}(N_{1,1}, N_{1,2}, N_{2,1}, N_{2,2}) \\ &s.t. \quad v_{1,1}N_{1,1} + v_{1,2}N_{1,2} = M_1, \quad N_{1,1} + N_{1,2} = N_1, \quad M_1 = v_1 N_1, \\ &\qquad\ v_{2,1}N_{2,1} + v_{2,2}N_{2,2} = M_2, \quad N_{2,1} + N_{2,2} = N_2, \quad M_2 = v_2 N_2. \end{aligned} \tag{5.8}$$

Here, $v_{i,r}$ is the daily price of tourism i in the r-th destination ($i = 1, 2$ and $r = 1, 2$). Like in the second stage, among the constraints of (5.8) we have all monetary and time constraints as well as the budgets, M_1 and M_2, to be spent for each type of tourism. By solving problem (5.8), we determine the optimal number of days that the tourist wants to spend: (a) within tourism 1, in each of the two destinations, $N_{1,1}$ and $N_{1,2}$; (b) within tourism 2, in each of the two destinations, $N_{2,1}$ and $N_{2,2}$.

5.3.4 The Prices of Tourism in the Tourist Choice

At first glance, the solution of the multistage choice seems completed. Instead, it is important to underline a key aspect of the solution that so far we have deliberately omitted to discuss: the degree of accuracy of the information available at each stage of the choice problem. In fact, at each stage of the decision process as seen in formulas (5.6–5.8), the average prices v_m and v_i are taken as given, which is not logically correct. By recalling Sect. 5.2.2 and the concept of demand function, we are aware that the average price depends on individual prices and on the number of overnight stays for each type of tourism.

The appropriate formulas for calculating such average prices can be determined by adopting the *principle of consistency* to the constraints that appear in the subsequent stages of the decision process. Let us begin with the second stage of the problem by substituting in (5.7) the definition of M_{tou} for the value of N within the time constraint, and then plug the result into the monetary constraint. Thus,

$$v_1 N_1 + v_2 N_2 = v_m (N_1 + N_2), \tag{5.9}$$

from which

$$v_m = \frac{v_1 N_1 + v_2 N_2}{N_1 + N_2}. \tag{5.10}$$

Therefore, the correct value for the price of tourism appears as a weighted average of the prices of different types of tourism, by treating the number of overnight stays as weights.

We can follow the same approach when dealing with the third stage, where it can be easily seen that the prices of each type of tourism are also weighted averages of the price for that type of holiday at different destinations:

$$v_1 = \frac{v_{1,1} N_{1,1} + v_{1,2} N_{1,2}}{N_{1,1} + N_{1,2}} \text{ and } v_2 = \frac{v_{2,1} N_{2,1} + v_{2,2} N_{2,2}}{N_{2,1} + N_{2,2}}. \tag{5.11}$$

Thus, the correct definition of the average price as in (5.10 and 5.11) introduces an important complication in the solution of the multistage choice problem.

In particular: (a) v_m is taken as given when solving the first-stage problem (5.6), although this value can be calculated only after having solved the second-stage problem (5.7); (b) similarly, the average prices v_1 and v_2 are taken as given when solving the second-stage problem (5.7), although these values can be calculated only after having solved the third-stage problem (5.8).

Hence, the correct definition of the average price not only introduces a complication in the calculation, but also has a number of logical implications. On the one hand, if we take prices as weighted averages as in (5.10) and (5.11), we can no longer approach the tourist's choice problem using the multistage budgeting since one can no longer solve the optimization problem at one stage without knowing the solution for the subsequent stages. On the other hand, if simple averages rather than weighted averages were used (see Sect. 5.2.2), the solutions to (5.7) and (5.8) would not be consistent with the monetary and time constraints, thus performing as mere approximations of the optimal values with no a priori information about the size of the error being made. These observations would lead to disregarding the use of the multistage approach in favor of the standard solution of the simultaneous choice problem.

However, it can be of some interest to investigate whether, and under what conditions, there exists a family of utility functions and a sufficiently general method of solution that would let the multistage approach bypass such problems and still be considered a viable approach. In this respect, it can be demonstrated that the multistage budgeting problem can be rationally solved by using the Bellman principle of optimality through a backward induction procedure, which starts from the last stage and identifies provisional solutions that are replaced backward up to the first stage. When the definitive solution is then found in the first stage, it is possible to move to the subsequent stages and find all the optimal solutions. The Bellman procedure can be successfully used with a sufficiently general family of utility functions: the CES (see Sect. 4.3.2) of which the well-known Cobb–Douglas function is a special case.[8]

Thus, for this class of utility functions, multistage budgeting can be successfully used to disentangle the tourist's choice problem in three phases:

1. The decision on *how much* to spend for the holidays, that is, the choice of the optimal duration of holiday versus the alternative non-tourism consumption goods. In this first stage, the tourist decides the pair (N^*, M^*_{tou}).
2. The decision on *how* to spend the budget allocated to tourism, that is, the choice of the optimal allocation of holiday time and budget across the available tourism opportunities. In this second phase, the tourist decides the two pairs (N^*_1, M^*_1) and (N^*_2, M^*_2).

[8] For a full description of Bellman's principle, we refer to any textbook of dynamic programming or advanced economics. For a simple description with an application to tourism, see Candela and Figini (2010a).

3. The decision on *where* to spend the time and budget allocated for each time of tourism, that is, the choice of the optimal allocation of time and budget across the available destinations. In this third phase, the tourist decides the four pairs ($N^*_{1,1}$, $N^*_{1,2}$), ($N^*_{2,1}$, $N^*_{2,2}$), ($M^*_{1,1}$, $M^*_{1,2}$), and ($M^*_{2,1}$, $M^*_{2,2}$).

This multistage budgeting approach, under sufficiently general assumptions, is hence able to explain the number of overnight stays in a given destination based on the tourist's preferences, the tourist's income, and the price of the tourism product and of the available alternatives. Thus, it is a very useful model to be successfully applied to the analysis of the tourism destination presented in Chap. 4.

Before discussing in the following sections further models of tourist's behavior, it is necessary to highlight the characteristics of the solution to the choice problem. Under the standard assumptions of the consumer theory, it is possible to have two different types of solutions, both are represented in Fig. 5.3, with reference to the second stage of the problem. Figure 5.3 plots the budget constraint of the problem as well as the indifference curve associated with the equilibrium at $u°(N_1, N_2)$.

Figure 5.3a shows the standard case of an *internal solution*: given the budget allocated to tourism, the tourist optimally chooses a mix of different types of tourism (i.e., some days spent on the beach in seaside destinations, and other days spent trekking in mountain destinations). Instead, Fig. 5.3b shows the particular case of a corner solution, where the tourist decides in favor of a unique type of holiday (in this case, only the tourism of type 1, i.e., beach tourism). Therefore, our model sheds lights on the rationale behind choosing different ways to be on holiday.

An analogous discussion can be made, *mutatis mutandis*, with reference to the solution of the third stage, which may also lead to *corner solutions*. In particular, one of the values of $N_{i,r}$ may be zero, which means that the whole amount M_i will be spent in the other destination. Alternatively, the tourist will optimally choose a diversified holiday by traveling to different destinations.

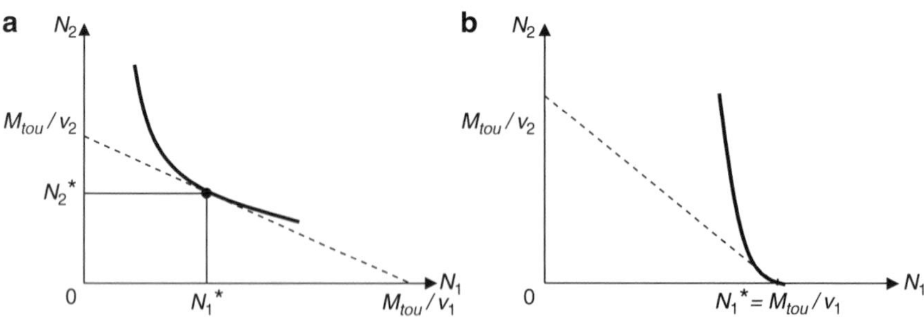

Fig. 5.3 Two alternative solutions to the second stage of the tourist's choice problem

5.4 The Purchase of a Package Holiday

In the previous section, we presented a general model to describe the tourist's choice with respect to the optimal quantity of tourism to include in the consumption basket. In particular, the number of overnight stays was the choice variable, while the daily price of the holiday was an exogenous variable of the problem. However, such a smooth setup of the problem is not realistic for many practical circumstances. For example, a tourist may be simply asked to decide whether or not to purchase a holiday, with no possibility to decide its composition, duration, and overall price. In practice, the tourist would be facing a binary choice: a "Yes, I buy the holiday" versus "No, I don't buy the holiday" type of choice. This holiday, which is very popular in real-world tourism, can be defined as package holiday, package tour, forfeit trip, or all-inclusive holiday.

The model to use for this situation is different from the one discussed in Sect. 5.3, mainly because here the tourist is not given a *continuum* of choice on the length of stay, but only offered the option of purchasing or not a given package tour. Actually, this is the typical situation that tourists encounter when purchasing a holiday from a tour operator's catalog in which the choice is whether or not to buy, for example, an all-inclusive 12-day trip to Egypt at the price of 2,000 € or an all-inclusive 17-day cruise in the Caribbean seas at the price of 3,000 €.

To model this situation, which is based on a binary decision scheme, let us consider the case of a subject who is asked to choose between "purchasing" or "not purchasing" an all-inclusive tour to a given destination, with given length and given price. In particular, were he to decide to purchase the holiday, he would pay its price and gain utility from its consumption; alternatively, were he to decide to not purchase it, he would have more money to spend on other alternative goods and services.

The model setup is then the following. The key variables are Y, the tourist's income; V, the price of the all-inclusive tour; $T = 0, 1$, the binary variable associated with the tour, taking value zero in case the tour is not purchased or one otherwise; and $U = U(Y, T)$, the tourist's utility function, with income and the tour as its arguments. Notice that V is in capital letter because it measures the whole cost of the holiday. It is straightforward, however, to divide V by the given length of the package holiday, N_H, and find the *equivalent daily price of the holiday*, $v_H = V/N_H$.

In such a model, the utility received by the tourist would be $U(Y, 0)$ in case he does not purchase the holiday or $U(Y-V, 1)$ in case he does. It is then possible to introduce the following equation:

$$U(Y - V^*, 1) = U(Y, 0), \tag{5.12}$$

that defines the implicit price V^* which, as a root of equation (5.12), makes the tourist indifferent between the two alternatives of buying or not the holiday. In Economics, V^* is usually known as the *reservation price* and measures the maximum amount of money the individual is willing to pay to buy the good. It is now

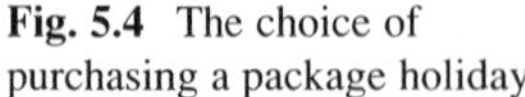

Fig. 5.4 The choice of purchasing a package holiday

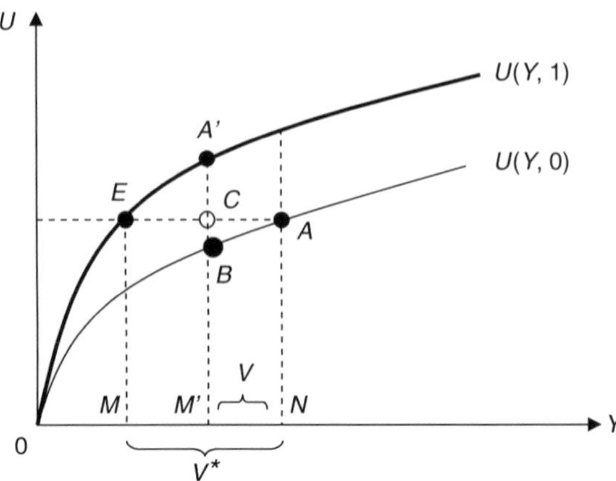

possible to motivate the choice: if the price of the holiday is lower than (or at most equal to) the reservation price, the tourist finds it convenient to (or is indifferent toward) purchasing the holiday; in the opposite case, he does not purchase it. More formally,

$$\begin{array}{lll} \text{if} & V^* \geqslant V, & \text{the holiday is purchased} \\ \text{if} & V^* < V, & \text{the holiday is not purchased.} \end{array} \tag{5.13}$$

The value of V^* depends on the functional form of the utility function and on the individual's amount of available income. Figure 5.4 displays the graphical structure of this decision by means of a standard utility function only depending on income, $U(Y, 0)$, and its vertical translation, $U(Y, 1)$, which also accounts for the purchase of the holiday.[9] Condition (5.12), associated with an initial level of income equal to $0N$, identifies a level of utility NA with respect to $U(Y, 0)$ in the case the tourist does not buy the holiday. The same level of utility NA translated to $U(Y, 1)$ identifies a point E and a segment ME.

Since by construction the tourist is indifferent from being in point A or in point E, the segment MN provides the measure of the reservation price V^*. Therefore, if the price of the all-inclusive tour is lower than or equal to MN, the tour is purchased; in case it is higher, it is not purchased. For example, if the price V of the trip is $M'N$, the tourist buys the package holiday and his overall utility rises from NA to $M'A'$.

Figure 5.4 also allows to identify the *surplus accruing from the tour* in terms of utility. It is

$$A'C = A'B - CB, \tag{5.14}$$

[9] The key assumption behind Fig. 5.4 is that the higher the income, the more enjoyable the tour is. Alternatively, we could assume a constant utility value for the holiday, a case that would only marginally change the diagram, with a parallel shift up of U in the chart, without affecting the essence of the choice problem.

where $A'B$ measures the utility accruing from the tour and CB the disutility of having to forgo income and hence alternative consumption goods due to the purchase of the holiday. Therefore, condition (5.13) may alternatively be expressed as the tour should be purchased if its price is such that $A'C \geq 0$.

5.5 The Tourist Who Self-organizes the Holiday

We will now develop the last general model for the tourist as a consumer. This will be the model for a tourist who decides to self-organize the holiday, in the sense of purchasing directly all the services that are included in the tourism product and that compose the holiday: transportation services, lodging, food services, and any other private or public service that are perceived by the tourist as appropriate or necessary.

This behavior, which is another very common one for tourists, can be interpreted in light of the *Household Production Function* (HPF) model, which is a well-known economic theory that integrates elements of the Consumer Theory with elements of the Production Theory.

The general model we adopt is the one described by Deaton and Muellbauer (1989), which is applied by McConnell (1985) to the case of self-organizing (self-producing) a holiday. From an empirical stand point, the model has been studied by Deyak and Smith (1978) and Bocksteal and McConnell (1981 and 1983). As Deaton and Muellbauer (1989) argue in favor of this model when investigating consumption, we believe that its clarity and elegance can be quite appropriate for studying the case of many tourists independently self-organizing the holiday. Indeed, the HPF model fully captures the need for some travelers—mainly day trippers, but very often tourists—to produce their own holiday by directly putting together single pieces of the holiday, as if they were tiles of a mosaic (more technically, the inputs of a production function), so as to achieve the optimal combination of income and utility.

Analytically, we must consider two alternative models each focusing on a different problem. In the first model, we will assume that tour operators do not exist and hence the "full holiday" is not available on the market (i.e., it is a non-market good), and this is what leads the tourist to self-produce it. In the second model, the tourist has to choose between self-producing or purchasing a holiday that is produced and sold by tour operators on the market (i.e., the holiday is a market good).

5.5.1 Self-organization of the Holiday

We begin by discussing the case of the holiday as a non-market good. Let us assume that the tourist has chosen a pair ($\mathbf{T}_i$; r) corresponding to the type of tourism i and destination r. However, given that such combination is not available for purchase by any tour operator, she must privately organize the holiday by searching, selecting, and purchasing each component of $\mathbf{T}_i$, an activity that is time consuming.

The standard assumption of the model is that the number of overnight stays N is a direct function of the time spent on planning it, L. We also want to account for the possibility that the destination management had spent an amount Q to ease the process of self-organizing the trip. For example, this may consist of creating an integrated web portal with all the information and the tools needed to reserve and purchase tourism services in the destination (see Sect. 4.3.5 and Chap. 12). Let the coefficient of proportionality for the relation of self-organization be $k(Q)$, with $\partial k/\partial Q > 0$. Therefore, the production function of the tourist self-organizing the holiday can be written as

$$N = k(Q)L. \tag{5.15}$$

Now, if we recall from (5.2) that v is the daily price of the holiday and if we denote with w the unit cost of time spent in producing it (as in McConnell (1985), we consider w as the unit wage, that is, the opportunity cost of time) the total cost of the self-organized holiday is

$$C = vN + wL. \tag{5.16}$$

If we plug (5.15) into (5.16), we obtain

$$C = vN + \omega(Q)N \text{ with } \omega(Q) = w/k(Q), \tag{5.17}$$

so that

$$C = [v + \omega(Q)]N = \pi N. \tag{5.18}$$

where $\pi = v + \omega$ is the *shadow price* of the self-organized holiday: the daily price when the individual services are independently purchased and assembled and when the cost of producing the holiday (in terms of foregone working time) has been taken into consideration. It is important to stress that in this model, unlike the standard case described in Sect. 5.3, the price of the holiday is endogenous and subjective, since it depends on the individual opportunity cost of time.

To fully describe the model, after having analyzed the tourist as a producer, we also need to consider the tourist as a consumer by introducing the problem of utility maximization with respect to a (modified) budget constraint. Similar to that presented in Sect. 5.3, where we used M_C to characterize non-tourism consumption, we can write the problem of utility maximization as

$$\begin{aligned} \max \quad & U(M_C, N) = U(M_C) + U(N) \\ s.t. \quad & M_C + \pi N = Y. \end{aligned} \tag{5.19}$$

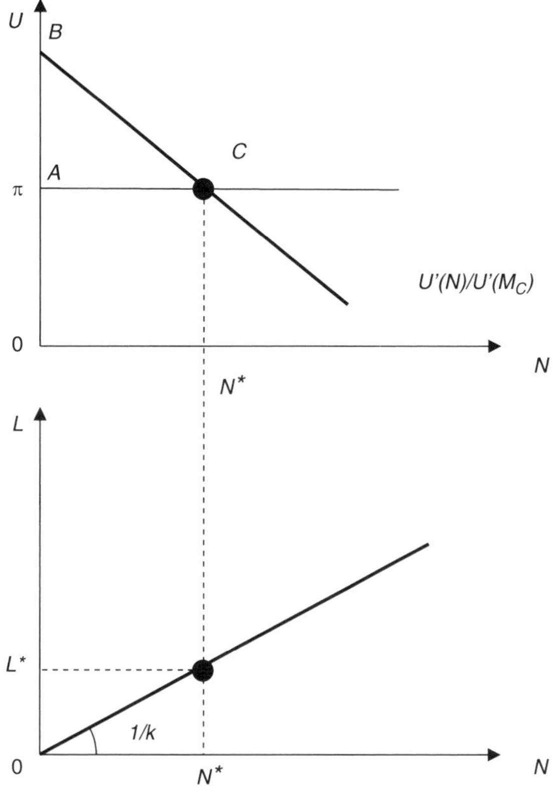

Fig. 5.5 The self-production of the holiday

Note that although the budget constraint has the same meaning of the one already presented in Sect. 5.3, it is now written in terms of the shadow price for one day of the self-organized holiday π, rather than in terms of the exogenous daily price v. The solution to (5.19), the details of which were recalled in Theory in Action 5.1, can also be applied to this case by using equation (I) and by setting $x = N$ and $p_x = \pi$. The equilibrium is identified by (5.20) where the marginal utility of the holiday $U'(N)$ is linked with the marginal utility of money $U'(M_C)$ and the shadow price of the holiday:

$$\frac{U'(N)}{U'(M_C)} = \pi. \tag{5.20}$$

Expression (5.20) allows to determine the optimal length of the holiday, N^*, and through (5.15) the amount of time L^* that the tourist should optimally spend for producing it. The solution to this problem is graphically presented in Fig. 5.5: the area ABC is the *self-producing tourist surplus*.

5.5.2 The Choice Between Self-organizing and Purchasing a Holiday

We now discuss the more advanced case where the tourist can choose between self-producing the holiday and purchasing it on the market as a package holiday produced by a tour operator and sold at the equivalent daily price $v_H(1 + m) = V/N_H$ increased by a percentage m that accounts for its intermediation by a travel agency. In light of what is expressed in the previous section, the solution associated with this choice problem is immediate, given that the tourist aims at maximizing own surplus; the choice between self-organization and purchase depends on which of the two, between the shadow price of the self-produced holiday and the market price including the cost of intermediation, is lower.

While discussing the topic of *anticommon* in the destination, in Sect. 4.3.1 we have seen that the total price paid out by the tourist who purchases lodging and meals separately is $2a/3$, which is more than the price of purchasing a joint supply of the two items, $a/2$. However, if we denote with m the markup received by the firm responsible for the sale and distribution of the package tour (for example, a travel agency, see Sect. 8.3), the condition against self-organization of a market good is

$$2a/3 \geqslant (a/2)(1 + m),$$

which implies that $m \leq 1/3$. In more general terms, the choice between producing or purchasing a holiday depends on the following conditions:

- If $\pi < v_H\,(1 + m)$, then the tourist should self-produce the holiday;
- If $\pi > v_H\,(1 + m)$, then the tourist should purchase the holiday;
- If $\pi = v_H\,(1 + m)$, then the tourist is indifferent between the two alternatives.

It is important to stress on the fact that π is generally different for different individuals; indeed, its value depends on the opportunity cost w as well as the individual's productivity displayed by the own production function. In addition, it should be kept in mind that the time spent in self-organization is usually greater for international than domestic holidays, which makes the domestic tourist more likely to self-organize (and the international tourist more likely to purchase) the holiday.

We highlight a final element of the self-organization model. What is the likely effect of an investment in information and/or organizational resources (for example, an improvement of the destination's web portal)? First, such investment is likely to increase the productivity of self-organizing a holiday. This can be addressed by assuming an increase in Q which, given that $\mathrm{d}k/\mathrm{d}Q > 0$ by assumption, implies, according to (5.17), that $\mathrm{d}\omega/\mathrm{d}Q < 0$. Thus, π decreases and N^* increases.

Therefore, any investment aimed at improving the information and the organization of resources in the destination has a positive impact on the number of overnight stays due to the general reduction in the reservation price needed to justify the self-production of the holiday. This also affects the tourist's selection strategy between purchasing and self-producing; indeed, given m, such investment shrinks the market size of the tour operators by lowering the cost and increasing the incentive of self-production.

From a more practical stand point, the self-production model yields a number of considerations. In particular, the destination that aims to stimulate independent tourism must deal with two important issues:

1. First, it must take into consideration the relationships of substitutability and complementarity between the different tourism services included in the holiday. On the one hand, the destination must be aware of the substitutes and complements that are allowed by the tourism production technique (see Sect. 5.2.3); on the other hand, it must guarantee the existence, within its own territory, of all the substitutes and complements requested by the tourist when self-organizing the holiday.
2. A second issue regards information circulation. Self-production of a holiday must rely on the existence of an adequate information system. Otherwise, the self-producing tourist will not be able to build the same holiday produced and sold by the tour operator.

5.6 The Purchase of Durable Goods

In Economics, the term *investment* is usually referred to the purchasing of real assets such as machinery, instruments, or other intermediate goods, undertaken by firms to increase their existing stock of capital. Since in the rest of the book we will extensively study such form of investment, to avoid unnecessary confusion, with the term "investment" we will denote the purchasing of capital goods by tourism firms and with the term "tourist's investment" the purchasing of durable goods by tourists, the issue we analyze in this section. The difference between these concepts is twofold: first, in the tourist's investment, the act of investing is undertaken by a consumer, not by a firm; second, it refers to final (durable) consumption goods, not to intermediate goods. Examples of tourist's investments range from holiday homes, boats, motor homes, to smaller objects such as video cameras, tents, and fishing poles. What all these goods have in common is the fact that they do not exhaust their use in a unique act of consumption but, on the contrary, can be used for several holidays, either of the same type (like holiday homes and boats) or of different type (like motor homes and video cameras).

Most of such goods are not purchased by tourists who buy all-inclusive holidays but, on the contrary, by independent tourists who intend to self-organize their own holidays. Ultimately, these durable goods can be seen as factors of production for this latter group of tourists. This is why the word "investment" can be used for such goods, although they do not directly refer to firms. It is important to stress on the fact that such concept has nothing to do with any natural characteristics of the good. For example, a holiday home purchased by a tour operator for its clients qualifies as an act of investment, while the same home purchased by a tourist will qualify as a tourist's investment. Similarly, a motor home will qualify as an investment when purchased by a rent-a-car company and as a tourist's investment when purchased by a consumer.

5.6.1 The Purchase of Durable Goods in Tourism

The demand for durable goods is somehow related to time and, hence, their economic problem can become very complex to analyze and solve. Indeed, a durable good can be described as a stock of potential and future flows of consumption services.[10] Consistent with Deaton and Muellbauer (1989), we now summarize the specific issues raised by models of durable consumption goods and developed by the economic theory.

- It is important to distinguish between *purchasing* and *consuming* durable goods. The act of purchasing refers to the stock, while consuming refers to an outflow of services that tears and wears the good beyond what would happen naturally. For example, when purchasing a holiday home (e.g., an apartment in a seaside destination), the subject modifies not only the composition of her portfolio (by converting a financial asset such as bank savings into a real asset such as the apartment) but also the availability of future acts of consumption, in the form of tourism services. The same applies for the purchasing of a motor home, with an important difference from the stand point of the effect that the flows have on the stock: in the case of a holiday home, the depreciation is usually negligible; in the case of a motor home, the depreciation is much more significant.
- Since a durable good often delivers its services over several years, a decision made today will have the effect of constraining future acts of consumption; for example, the act of purchasing a holiday home usually leads an individual to engage in spending the holidays in that destination for a significant number of years.
- Decisions regarding durable goods are heavily dependent on the set of available information: any new information could lead to an anticipation or to a delay in the purchase. For example, a geopolitical crisis in the destination could lead to the fall of real estate prices, thereby driving many property owners to delay the act of selling the house.
- The decision to purchase durable goods usually depends on the expectations on incomes and prices. For example, a drop in the interest rate (which usually triggers an increase in real estate prices at a later time) may convince tourists to anticipate the future purchase of a holiday home; similarly, the expectation of a

[10] It is worth recalling that stock variables are measured at a *point* in time, while flow variables are measured over a *period* of time.

drop in the household's income due to a rise in taxes may provide a reason to delay the purchasing of a motor home, considering that owning such a good usually leads to significant flows of spending in future periods.
- The perceived quality of durable goods is usually, but not always, affected by technological changes; for example this is a key factor to be considered by those who are willing to buy a motor home.
- Durable goods tend to stay on the market for a long time; it is usually possible to distinguish between new and used goods, and the latter is usually classified in terms of other criteria such as age and use. The market for new items operates at the same time as the market for second-hand ones (think about the real estate market) so that prices and quantities in each market may interact in ways that can be complicate to disentangle.
- The market for durable goods is often imperfect: the information is usually incomplete (this is certainly the case for holiday homes) and asymmetric (this is usually the case for second-hand motor homes), and both phenomena significantly complicate the economic analysis.
- It is important to distinguish between the new demand for durable goods and the demand justified by the need of replacing them. For example, the act of purchasing a holiday home in a destination is economically different according to whether the purchase is undertaken by a new tourist in the destination or by an "old" tourist who already owned another holiday home. The two phenomena share a similar effect on the real estate sector, but have a different impact on the total number of overnight stays in the destination.
- Transaction and legal costs associated with durable goods may be significantly high: for example, purchasing a holiday home may require a significant number of legal registrations and fees to pay.

All these issues may explain why the tourist's investment is characterized by great volatility; such demand is sensitive to fashion, to the business cycle, to the evolution of the natural environment, to sociopolitical factors, etc. For example, many destinations have experienced a phase of development characterized by strong tourists' investment in holiday homes, which quickly turned into decline as a consequence of excessive urbanization, leading the destination "out of fashion" due to sustainability problems. On the contrary, there are markets for durable goods that experience a permanent excess of demand due to the fact that producers are unable to keep up with an increasing demand (this is, for example, the case for high-quality yachts).

5.6.2 The Tourist's Investment

The centrality of the tourist's investment in the tourist budget and in his choices requires to devote part of this chapter to investigate this problem more formally.

Given the complexity of the issue under investigation, we will narrow the study to the most standard and basic models, referring to more advanced consumer theory books (such as Deaton and Muellbauer 1989; Mas-Colell et al. 1995 or Jehle and Reny 2000) for a deeper discussion. We will keep focusing on two different cases: the act of purchasing a holiday home and a motor home, which are paradigmatic for their strong differences as regards prices, depreciation, obsolescence, etc.

5.6.2.1 Case A. The Tourist's Investment in a Holiday Home

In developing an explanation of the purchase of a durable good, complications arise as a consequence of the inclusion in the model of inter-temporal preferences and budget constraints. Indeed, the decision to purchase a durable good *today* impacts *tomorrow*'s setup and choices.

The extension of the consumer's model to be used for durable goods involves the concept of *user price* instead of price. The user price of a durable good incorporates the market price plus any additional cost paid in each period of time (for example, one year) as a consequence of the ownership and the use of the good. For example, when considering a holiday home, the user price includes the yearly interests paid on the price either as an opportunity cost (in case the tourist has disinvested previous savings to purchase the holiday home) or as a direct cost (in case the holiday home is purchased through a mortgage). The user price must also include the (yearly) maintenance costs, taxes, and the difference between the original purchasing price and the actual market price of the good in case the owner intends to sell it.

A simple inter-temporal model that can be applied to this case considers a two-period span, $t = 1, 2$. The assumption is that of a consumer who has decided to spend the holidays in a given destination in both periods, by purchasing at time $t = 1$ a holiday home in the destination that can be used also in period $t = 2$. We consider a tourist who either has liquid assets to be spent on purchasing the house (foregoing an interest rate r on his financial assets), or can start a mortgage with a financial institution (at the same interest rate r). In addition, we assume that the tourist will earn certain incomes both at time 1 and 2 and that the rate of depreciation of the house is zero (which is quite realistic for real estate properties). If we impose the condition that the good must not affect the tourist's decisions beyond the second period (neither as an asset nor in terms of any related outstanding liabilities), we can define a consumption model where the market price of the house at time 1 is v_1, while the price at which the house can be sold at the end of time 2 is v_2. If, for the sake of simplicity, we assume zero maintenance costs, the user price v^* of the house can be written as

$$v^* = v_1(1 + r) - v_2 = (v_1 - v_2) + v_1 r. \tag{5.21}$$

Note that v^* is the difference between the capitalized value of the house price at time 1 and the price at time 2, and measures the change in the value of the house from period 1 and 2 after including the interest paid on the mortgage (or forgone from having used own assets that could have otherwise been invested at the same rate r). Clearly, given the house's two prices, the user price is directly related to the interest rate ($\partial v^*/\partial r > 0$). This also implies that the demand for holiday homes in a given destination must depend on r. In particular, as the interest rate increases (and v^* rise), *ceteris paribus*, we would expect a drop in the demand for holiday homes, and vice-versa.

In addition, as in any other model of consumption, the demand for holiday homes in the destination crucially depends on the personal (current and future) income, on his financial situation (in terms of stock and composition of assets and liabilities), and on his preferences.

Given that the user price essentially depends on the difference between v_1 and v_2, three alternative hypotheses can be studied:

1. If $v_1 = v_2$, that is, if the price does not change over time, then the user price of the house is uniquely determined by the interests paid on its initial price, $v_1 r$, which is either a direct payment (in the case of the mortgage), or an opportunity cost (in case the tourist invests personal assets). As stated before, when r goes up, v^* also goes up.
2. If $v_1 > v_2$, that is, if the expected selling price is lower than the current price, for example, $v_2 = v_1(1 - m)$, then the user price depends on both the interest rate and the capital loss suffered by owning the holiday home for the whole period, $v^* = v_1(r + m)$. In this case, the expectations on the future evolution of real estate prices in the tourism destination become essential in driving the purchasing decision.
3. If $v_1 < v_2$, that is, if the expected selling price is higher than the current price, for example, $v_2 = v_1(1 + n)$, then the user price is $v^* = v_1(r-n)$ and may even become negative when $n > r$. In this case, since the price is negative, the purchasing decision can be theoretically consistent with an infinite demand for holiday homes, which will only be bound by the financial constraint. In such a situation, the motive behind the purchasing would no longer be tourism, but mainly speculation.

Up to now it has been emphasized that the price of a durable good is an essential piece of information for the tourist with an interest in purchasing a holiday home, even when he intends to stay at the destination only for a portion of the year. This is due to the fact that the house enters the financial portfolio of the subject and that financial and tourism motivations mix together. As argued by Bimonte and Punzo (2007), this fact needs to be taken into serious consideration when analyzing the relationship between tourists and residents. Indeed, the evolution of a tourism destination strongly depends on whether the tourists mainly decide to stay in "rented types" of accommodation, such as hotels or apartments, or in privately owned properties. In these regards, the main differences are as follows.

- The tourism destination specialized in holiday homes is often oversized, at least during the peak season; the flip side is that the destination suffers from a capacity slack, given that houses and apartments are essentially empty and not used for a significant fraction of the year (unless the owners often travel for short breaks or weekends throughout the year). Hence, these destinations struggle to precisely define their overall carrying capacity (Chap. 16).

- The tourists who own holiday homes are often actively involved in the management of the destination and, as the local population, they are sensitive to fluctuations in real estate prices and tend to closely follow the local population's perceptions on the quality of tourism, the evolution of the destination, etc.

  For such tourists, the destination is a big condominium, whose friendly and professional guardians are the permanent residents.

  (Bimonte and Punzo 2007, p. 205. *Our translation*)

- The relationship between the local population and holiday home owners exhibits only secondary elements of conflict, since the two groups share an *implicit social pact* (Bimonte and Punzo 2007); however, a trade-off between tourists and residents may arise when the high demand for holiday homes by the former inflates real estate prices at the disadvantage of some of the latter. For example, the high demand for apartment in some Catalan coast villages such as Llançà or Cadaqués has increased the real estate prices, making it difficult for the local population to afford a house near the beach.
- Besides a limited number of exceptions, the destinations that specialize in holiday homes are characterized by the phenomenon of *tourists' proximity*, in the sense that the choice of the destination where to purchase a second home is often made by taking into consideration the time and the distance needed to reach the destination. For example, inhabitants of big metropolitan cities such as Barcelona purchase second residences in the coastline of Catalonia to spend not only the summer holidays but also short breaks and weekends throughout the year.
- A consequence of the previous point is that such tourism destinations usually suffer from remaining locked in the mono-culture that is of great interest and comfort for its owner-tourists, and this usually works against the organization of glamorous events and the adoption of marketing strategies designed to attract big numbers of tourists.
- Finally, the existing data support the intuition that the average spending of tourists staying at hotels is higher than the average spending of tourists living in holiday homes. Such a difference may significantly affect the economic development of the destination, in particular when taking into consideration the economic effects that are synthesized by the tourism multiplier (Chap. 13, see also Piga 2003).

5.6.2.2 Case B. The Tourist's Investment in a Motor Home

The analysis presented in the previous section suggests that before deciding whether a durable good should be purchased or not, the main economic element to take into consideration is its user value. With this in mind, the purchasing of a motor home displays a number of peculiarities with respect to the purchasing of a holiday home: (a) for goods such as motor homes or caravans, the sale price of the used item is usually lower than the price of a new item (except the case of particular types of luxury goods); and (b) these goods usually suffer from heavy wear and tear due to usage.

If we keep in mind these two observations, and if we maintain for the motor home the same two-period setup that we adopted for holiday homes, its user price v^+ can be written as

$$v^+ = v_1(1 + r) - v_2(1 - d) = (v_1 - v_2) + v_1 r + v_2 d, \tag{5.22}$$

where the observation *sub* (a) allows to focus only on the case where $v^+ > 0$ (i.e., we exclude zero or negative user values because generally $v_1 > v_2$), while condition *sub* (b) suggests to explicitly introduce a rate of deterioration for the good, d, which depreciates its existing stock. In other words, we assume that a fraction d of the good fades away in each period, by only leaving a fraction $(1 - d)$ of the good to future use.

Given that different tourists may display different preferences for "nomadic" holidays, we should expect that the same value v^+ is compatible with different tourists' behaviors, either in favor or against this type of tourism.

Chapter Overview

- The goods and services demanded by tourists can be classified as (a) goods and services included in the tourism product; (b) goods and services pertaining to tourism consumption; and (c) durable goods defined as tourist's investment.
- From the choice models standpoint, we must distinguish between the case of the tourist who purchases a package holiday from the case of the tourist who self-organizes it.
- The price of a tourism basket is the sum of the individual prices of each good and service included in the basket or, equivalently, it is the daily price of a holiday of a given type at a given destination.
- The goods and services included in the basket may be characterized by substitutability, complementarity, or following a lexicographic order.
- In the case of all-inclusive tours, that is, when the tourist can only decide whether or not to purchase the holiday; the choice depends on the comparison between the price of the tour and own reservation price.
- The analysis of the tourist's investment, which deals with purchasing durable goods, faces a series of complex issues such as expectations on future prices, technological obsolescence, market imperfections, and high transaction costs.
- The demand for a durable good depends on factors such as the user price, the interest rate, the depreciation rate, the tourist's preferences and financial wealth.

Chapter 6
A Close Examination of the Consumer Theory Applied to the Tourist

Learning Outcomes
After reading this chapter, you will:

- Learn advanced theoretical models that further investigate the choice problem of the tourist.
- Understand the importance of some key factors such as time, habits, and the evolution of preferences within those models.
- Know the consequences on the tourist's decision process of having incomplete information on the price and the quality of tourism services.

6.1 Introduction

This chapter is devoted to present and explain advanced models of consumption applied to the tourist's choice, which can be seen as extensions of the basic and standard models of consumption presented in Chap. 5. Particularly, four extensions of the consumer theory will be examined throughout the chapter.

First, it is important to remind that the most important constraint faced by consumers in their choices is time, which is even more binding than prices and income. Any consumption activity, from going to the cinema to having a meal at the restaurant to enjoying a holiday implies the use of time, in addition to the use of income to buy the goods. In our application to tourism, we will first consider a model where the tourism experience, like the consumption of every other good, implies the use of time in a framework in which time is a scarce resource and where, consequently, the same units of time cannot be allocated to any alternative activity. This will be done in Sect. 6.2, where the close examination of the tourist who chooses the allocation of time and income across alternative purchases will be presented.

G. Candela and P. Figini, *The Economics of Tourism Destinations*,
Springer Texts in Business and Economics, DOI 10.1007/978-3-642-20874-4_6,

Second, Sects. 6.3 and 6.4 will present a model focusing on the characteristics of the holidays: according to Lancaster (1971), consumers do not buy goods per se, but for the characteristics they embody, which are aimed at satisfying their needs:

> The tastes which are accepted as given for each individual are not preferences over collections of specific goods but deeper preferences over objectives which are to be achieved by the consumption of goods.
>
> (Lancaster 1979, p. 7)

As regards the application to tourism, among the alternative available holidays the choice depends on the features displayed by the holiday (or destination) and which, in a different mix, are associated with the tourist's desires (distance, safety, comfort, environment, entertainment, culture, etc.).

The third close-up, developed in Sects. 6.5 and 6.6, bypasses the assumption of exogenous preferences of all the previous models. The critique to the approach of exogenous preferences relies on the idea that preferences do change over time and are strongly affected by both economic and social phenomena. By assuming endogenous preferences, the attempt is to integrate the economic perspective (which usually focuses on the price and income constrains faced by the consumer) with the sociological one (that focuses on the formation of habits and preferences). Such interdisciplinary approach seems more attractive for the investigation of tourism given that, as we asserted in Chap. 2, tourism can be seen as a cross-section of the society where all the aspects of social life are involved.

Finally, it is relevant to remark that all the models presented so far rely on the key assumption that the subject has complete information about the alternative available destinations, the alternative available types of tourism, their prices, and their quality. However, considering that people usually choose a holiday without having previously been exposed to it, such assumption can be quite misleading. Indeed a tourist is usually asked to choose with *imperfect information* about the characteristics of the holiday: in particular the daily price, the quality, or possibly both are often unknown before the holiday is experienced.

Moreover, even if the tourist is fully informed about the destination's characteristics, it may be difficult to associate them with the available tourism firms. Alternatively, the tourist might not know the full range of available alternatives but may be familiar only with a subset of them. Finally, we must also account for the fact that the tourist can overcome the lack of information by imitating the behavior adopted by other subjects. All these topics will be discussed in Sect. 6.7.

6.2 The Role of Time in the Tourism Choice

Any consumption activity, including the holiday, implies the use of time. For this reason, we cannot achieve a complete understanding of the tourist's choice by neglecting the role of time in the decision process, which is closely linked to the concept of length of the holiday.

The basic distinction drawn in Economics regarding the use of time is between working and leisure time, where leisure time means any time left after working (or studying). Leisure time and working time are substitutes, in the sense that the more time is spent working, the less leisure time is available and vice versa. Modern societies do not usually allow for a discretionary use of time, in the sense that the size of each of these two components (the *annual leave*, the amount of paid holidays) is usually decided by the employer on the behalf of its employees. In what follows, we discuss two alternative hypotheses. In the first case, we will assume that the worker can freely decide the length of own holiday time: this is the case of a professional worker or a self-employed; in the second case (which is the one of employees), we will suppose that the annual leave is already written in the worker's contract (and usually decided at the national or at the firm level by the representatives of employers and employees or by the law).

In the first case, given the standard assumption of *unlimited wants*, it becomes natural to rely on the hypothesis that the duration of the holiday is equal to the time available for leisure activities. In the second case, the two time intervals may not be equal because, in addition to the time constraint, the tourist is also bound by budget constraints; in particular, were personal income not sufficient to pay a long holiday, the subject may decide to spend part of own leisure time at home. These two alternative scenarios will now be unfolded.

6.2.1 The Holiday's Length Is a Choice Variable

In the first setup, the model studies the choice between consumption and the supply of labor (which provides income to the subject and that can be allocated to consumption activities). If we use as a framework the three-stage model discussed in Sect. 5.3, we are positioned in the *first stage* where the tourist's total income, Y, is no longer treated as exogenous but as a choice variable along with the total number of overnight stays, N. In other words, the subject can decide to allocate time working, therefore earning an income Y, or in leisure activities, which will take the form of holidays of total length N.[1]

The tourist's utility depends on money M, which is the measure for aggregate consumption other than tourism, and the overall amount of overnight stays, N:

$$U(M,N). \tag{6.1}$$

The tourist allocates available time (T) between labor time (L) and holiday time (H):

$$T = L + H. \tag{6.2}$$

If we denote with w the daily wage earned by the subject and with R a rent (non-labor income), personal total income is

$$Y = wL + R. \tag{6.3}$$

[1] The allocation across alternative types of tourism and destinations will be carried out in subsequent stages of the multistage model.

By assuming that spending leisure time at home does not bring any utility while implies a loss of income due to the wage foregone while not working, the problem can simplified by setting $H = N$. Therefore, the tourist's optimization problem can be written as follows:

$$\begin{array}{ll} \max_{M,N} & U(M,N) \\ s.t. & M + v_m N = wL + R \quad \text{with} \quad L = T - N, \end{array} \tag{6.4}$$

where v_m is the average price of one day of holiday (defined in Sect. 5.2). After plugging the second constraint into the first one, we obtain

$$M + (v_m + w)N = wT + R. \tag{6.5}$$

Given v_m and w, the *full price* of one day of holiday can be defined as $v^\circ = v_m + w$, which is the sum between the *explicit* market daily price of the holiday and the *implicit* price of time (equal to the daily wage foregone while not working).[2] In addition, wN measures the opportunity cost of the time spent consuming the holiday and $Y^\circ = wT + R$ is the *full income*, the maximum income that would be earned were the available time be entirely spent working. Once again, if we assume a utility function with a separable structure, the model (6.4) can be written as

$$\begin{array}{ll} \max_{M,N} & U(M,N) = U(M) + U(N) \\ s.t. & M + v^\circ N = Y^\circ \end{array}. \tag{6.6}$$

The optimal solution to the problem can be easily found by the means of the solution method sketched in Theory in Action 5.1, where we set $x = N$, $p_x = v^\circ$, and $Y = Y^\circ$:

$$\frac{U'(N)}{U'(M)} = v^\circ = v_m + w. \tag{6.7}$$

As the demand curve AB in Fig. 6.1 clearly displays, expression (6.7) allows us to calculate the optimal values N^*, working time L^* and, through (6.2), monetary income $Y^* = wL^* + R$.

This result allows us to study how the tourist's choice is affected by changes in the wage rate. In particular, an increase in wage generates two effects. First, it lowers the marginal utility of money by making the tourist richer than before; this is

[2] Note that although the concepts of *full price* and *shadow price* (see Sect. 5.5.1) both refer to the allocation of time, they are quite different concepts: the full price accounts for the price of time spent for the consumption of the holiday, while the shadow price accounts for the price of time spent for its production. Moreover, the full price is identical for every tourist working at the wage w, while the shadow price is not borne by the tourist who purchases the package holiday from a tour operator but only by the self-organizing tourist.

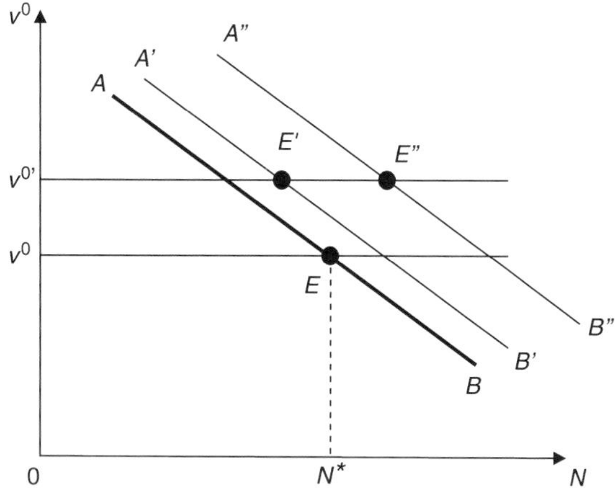

Fig. 6.1 Wealth and substitution effect in the choice model

the well-known *wealth effect*. Second, it increases the full price of the holiday, since one day spent away from work has become relatively more expensive in terms of foregone income, the so-called *substitution effect*. Figure 6.1 accounts for both effects: the wealth effect leads to a shift to the right of the *AB* curve, while the substitution effect yields an increase in the full price from v° to $v^{\circ\prime}$. Depending on whether *AB* shifts to $A'B'$ or to $A''B''$ due to the relative size of the wealth effect, an increase in the wage rate may lead to a decrease (point E') or to an increase (point E'') in the holiday time with respect to *E*.

The explanation is simple since the overall effect of an increase in wage depends on the tourist's preferences who, having become relatively richer, can afford a longer holiday but has to balance it with a relatively more expensive holiday due to the increase in the opportunity cost of leisure time. To illustrate this, let us assume a simplified version of the model in which we have two subjects with same income but different wage, like, for example, a retired person and a worker. The model predicts that the retired person will choose the longest possible holiday because the opportunity cost is lower. This is the essential reason why cruises are usually chosen by rich retired people rather than rich workers. The worker is instead more likely to spend the same amount of money on a shorter but more intense holiday, for example, by flying to an exotic destination for a short break rather than using more time on a longer holiday.

6.2.2 The Annual Leave Is Exogenously Set

We now assume that the tourist cannot freely choose between working time and leisure time, since the annual leave is "institutionally" determined by the law or by collective bargaining, and set equal to H°. To inspect this case, it can be useful to focus on the third stage of the multistage model (see Sect. 5.3.3), that is, the choice of the destination. In other words, the tourist has already chosen holiday

$\mathbf{T}_i$ and, consequently, has already allocated amount M_i to it (note that our description would not change should we consider instead the second-stage problem).

The tourist's utility depends on vector $\mathbf{T}_i$ spent in the alternative destinations $r = 1, 2, \ldots, R_i$ where the holiday of type i is possible:

$$U\left(N_{i,1}, N_{i,2}, \ldots, N_{i,R_i}\right). \tag{6.8}$$

Expression (6.8) replicates the corresponding function displayed in Sect 5.3, but now the tourist's choice appears to be constrained in two ways: first, the total amount of spending for overnight stays cannot exceed the available amount M_i; second, the tourist must fulfill the requirement that the holiday's length must not exceed the annual leave, $H°$.

Moreover, the two constraints may be satisfied as mere weak inequalities: it would be possible for the time constraint to be active so as to allow the budget constraint to be satisfied as equality, or the other way round. This implies that the tourist cannot spend more (but can spend less) than M_i, as well as that the tourist can either choose to allocate the entire time between the destinations or, alternatively, decide to spend part of the holiday at home. To summarize, the tourist's choice problem becomes

$$\begin{array}{lc} \max_N & U\left(N_{i,1}, N_{i,2}, \ldots, N_{i,R_i}\right) \\ s.t. & v_{i,1}N_{i,1} + v_{i,2}N_{i,2} + \ldots + v_{i,R_i}N_{i,R_i} \leq M_i \\ & N_{i,1} + N_{i,2} + \ldots + N_{i,R_i} \leq H°. \end{array} \tag{6.9}$$

With no lack of generality, this model can be simplified by assuming that there are only two available destinations:

$$\begin{array}{lc} \max_N & U\left(N_{i,1}, N_{i,2}\right) \\ s.t. & v_{i,1}N_{i,1} + v_{i,2}N_{i,2} \leq M_i \\ & N_{i,1} + N_{i,2} \leq H°. \end{array} \tag{6.10}$$

The unknowns of problem (6.10) are ($N_{i,1}$, $N_{i,2}$), which can be solved given the prices ($v_{i,1}$, $v_{i,2}$) and the values of M_i and $H°$.

Given the relatively small dimension of problem (6.10), only the graphical solution is provided, while the details of the analytical solution are given in Theory in Action 6.1. Figure 6.2 presents the constraints of the problem by the means of functions BB' (the budget constraint) and FF' (the time constraint). The shaded area $OFEB'$ represents the set of all bundles that satisfy both constraints and among which the tourist must choose the one that maximizes utility. The bundles within the area BEF are consistent with the budget constraint but do not comply with the time constraint, while vice versa for those within the area $B'EF'$.

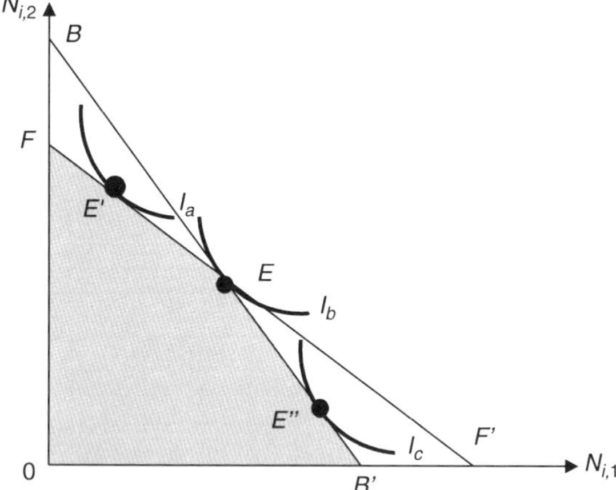

Fig. 6.2 The choice between two destinations when the length of the annual leave is exogenously set

Theory in Action 6.1. The Algebra Behind the Model with Exogenous Length of Holiday Time

The solution method for this model, which is characterized by weak inequality constraints, is based on generalized Lagrange multipliers (Theory in Action 5.1) and the corresponding Kuhn–Tucker conditions. Under the assumption of exogenous length of the holiday time, the problem to solve is

$$\begin{array}{ll} \max & U(N_{i,1}, N_{i,2}) \\ s.t. & v_{i,1}N_{i,1} + v_{i,2}N_{i,2} \leq M_i \quad \text{and} \quad N_{i,1} + N_{i,2} \leq H^{\circ}. \end{array}$$

The Lagrange function associated to the problem is

$$L = U(N_{i,1}, N_{i,2}) + \lambda_1(M_i - v_{i,1}N_{i,1} - v_{i,2}N_{i,2}) + \lambda_2(H^{\circ} - N_{i,1} - N_{i,2}).$$

Here, λ_1, $\lambda_2 \geq 0$ are the generalized Lagrange multipliers defined with respect to the two constraints. The system of first-order conditions associated to $L(.)$ are

$$\begin{aligned} \frac{\partial L}{\partial N_{i,1}} &= \frac{\partial U}{\partial N_{i,1}} - \lambda_1 v_{i,1} - \lambda_2 = 0 \\ \frac{\partial L}{\partial N_{i,2}} &= \frac{\partial U}{\partial N_{i,2}} - \lambda_1 v_{i,2} - \lambda_2 = 0 \\ \frac{\partial L}{\partial \lambda_1} &= M_i - v_{i,1}N_{i,1} - v_{i,2}N_{i,2} \geq 0 \\ \frac{\partial L}{\partial \lambda_2} &= H^{\circ} - N_{i,1} - N_{i,2} \geq 0. \end{aligned}$$

(continued)

Since this is a system of equations and inequalities, the first-order conditions must be complemented with the Kuhn–Tucker conditions to identify the active constraints:

$$\lambda_1 \left(M_i - v_{i,1}N_{i,1} - v_{i,2}N_{i,2}\right) = 0, \tag{I}$$

$$\lambda_2 \left(H^\circ - N_{i,1} - N_{i,2}\right) = 0. \tag{II}$$

To obtain the solution, we must combine a number of assumptions to identify both partial and full equilibria:

- if $\lambda_1 = 0$ and $\lambda_2 > 0$, then, in light of (II), only the time constraint is active and the solution is given by conditions

$$\partial U / \partial N_{i,1} = \partial U / \partial N_{i,2} \quad \text{and} \quad H^\circ = N_{i,1} + N_{i,2},$$

- if $\lambda_1 > 0$ and $\lambda_2 = 0$, then, in light of (I), only the budget constraint is active and the solution is given by conditions

$$\text{MRS} = \left(\partial U / \partial N_{i,1} : \partial U / \partial N_{i,2}\right) = v_{i,1}/v_{i,2} \quad \text{and} \quad M_i = v_{i,1}N_{i,1} + v_{i,2}N_{i,2},$$

- if $\lambda_1 > 0$ and $\lambda_2 > 0$, then, given (I) and (II), both constraints are active and the first-order conditions identify a system of four equations in four unknowns: the two Lagrange multipliers and the two solutions $N_{i,1}$ and $N_{i,2}$:

$$N^*_{i,1} = \left(M_i - v_{i,1}H^\circ\right) / \left(v_{i,1} - v_{i,2}\right) \quad \text{and} \quad N^*_{i,2} = H^\circ - N^*_{i,1}.$$

Note that in the last case, the solution is directly determined by the system of constraints, while the marginal utilities are equal to the Lagrange multipliers. Therefore, the multipliers λ_1 and λ_2 can be interpreted as the tourist's marginal utility associated with an increase in the money allocated to tourism, and as the tourist's marginal utility associated with an increase in the annual paid leave.

Figure 6.2 also shows three indifference curves associated with the same level of utility and derived from three different utility functions. Depending on the slope of the indifference curve, it is possible to identify three alternative equilibria.

1. If the preference set is compatible with choosing bundle E' (the map of indifference curves is generically represented by I_a), the time constraint is satisfied as an equality while the budget constraint holds as an inequality. In this case, although the tourist allocates the entire time H° across the two destinations, he is unable to spend the entire amount M_i.

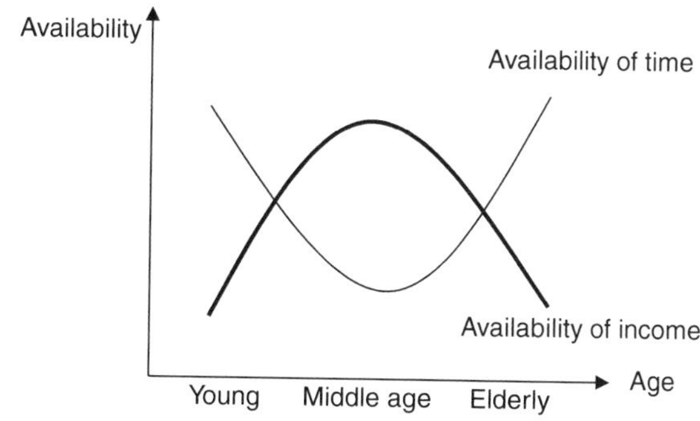

Fig. 6.3 The income-time paradox

2. If the preference set is compatible with choosing bundle E'' (the map of indifference curves is generically represented by I_c), the budget constraint is satisfied as an equality while the time constraint holds as an inequality. In this case, the tourist finds it optimal to spend all the available money, without spending the entire leisure time on holiday (and spending some leave time at home).
3. If the preference set is compatible with choosing bundle E (the map of indifference curves is generically represented by I_b), both constraints are satisfied as an equality. In this case, the tourist spends the entire amount of time and money on holiday.

In case (2), an increase in the duration of the annual leave, H°, does not increase the amount of time spent on holiday since the time constraint is not active in this case. In case (1), a decrease in the price of the holiday is unable to change the amount of time spent on holiday since the budget constraint is not active. Finally, case (3) refers to the case of *full budget*, in the sense that the tourist is neither pressured to save more than necessary nor forced to spend at home part of leisure time.

In real-world situations, where the worker's income and the annual leave are often the result of collective bargaining, the *full budget* equilibrium is an unlikely outcome. On the contrary, the life of the majority of people is characterized by the so-called *income-time paradox*, a situation that is represented in Fig. 6.3. Those people who have available time (the young and the elderly) are usually subject to a tighter budget constraint, while those people who have income (the middle-age active workers) are usually subject to a tighter time constraint.[3]

To summarize, this model allows to interpret the decisions of subjects facing two constraints. When the budget constraint is particularly binding, it is likely that the tourist will have to spend part of holiday time at home. On the contrary, when the time constraint is particularly binding, it is likely than the tourist may be forced to save a fraction of the money allocated to tourism due to the lack of leisure time.

[3] The income-time paradox is described by Edgar Lee Masters in the *Spoon River Anthology* where he writes about activities which, like tourism, are time consuming: "In youth my wings were strong and tireless//But I did not know the mountains//In age I knew the mountains//But my weary wings could not follow my vision//Genius is wisdom and youth". (Masters 1915, p. 127)

6.3 The Characteristics of the Tourism Product

In this section, we will discuss a model that was first developed by Lancaster (1971) and that is well suited for the investigation of many of the tourist's choice problems. In particular, the standard theory discussed in Sect. 5.3 does not prove to be able to explain a few key aspects of the tourist's behavior. First, the introduction of a new type of holiday (a topic that will be discussed in depth in Sect. 6.4) is inadequately explained; second, the standard theory does not seem to be able to explain practical phenomena such as the high substitutability between far-away destinations (i.e., between Rimini, Italy, and Torremolinos, Spain).

Lancaster's approach allows to focus on the intrinsic features of the holiday, which is perceived by the tourist as the input of a process that transforms it into a set of characteristics. Consistently with this interpretation, the tourist is no longer seen as purchasing a holiday per se, but actually engages in the act of purchasing a mix of characteristics that are embodied in the holiday, such as relaxation, leisure, socialization, and cultural enrichment. Different types of holiday are so because they present a different mix of such characteristics: a cruise on the Mediterranean Sea provides relaxation and cultural enrichment, while a beach-oriented holiday in a mass tourism destination mainly provides leisure and socialization.

The immediate consequence of looking at the holiday in this way is that the tourist is now seen as having preferences for the holiday's characteristics rather than for the holiday per se. In other words, according to Lancaster's approach, the tourist's decision now consists of choosing the type of tourism that produces the best combination of the desired characteristics. Regarding such characteristics, this approach relies on the following assumptions:

1. Characteristics are observable and can be objectively measured.
2. Characteristics are linear, in the sense that doubling the amount of a good leads to doubling the amount of each of its characteristics.
3. Characteristics are additive, in the sense that if one overnight stay shows one unit of the characteristic and a 100-km trip shows three units of the same characteristic, a holiday composed of a 100-km trip and one overnight stay includes four units of the characteristic.

Hypotheses (1), (2), and (3) allow the reduction of tourism in terms of its own characteristics by the means of simple proportionality relationships that we call *consumption technology*. Rather than relying on complex algebraic methods to describe this model, we may find it more practical to adopt a two-stage optimization process.

1. In the first stage, the problem is to identify the efficient choice as regards the types of tourism, where with the term "efficient" we intend a situation where it is impossible to increase the amount of one characteristic without reducing the amount of another. This stage of the problem is completely independent of the tourist's preferences.

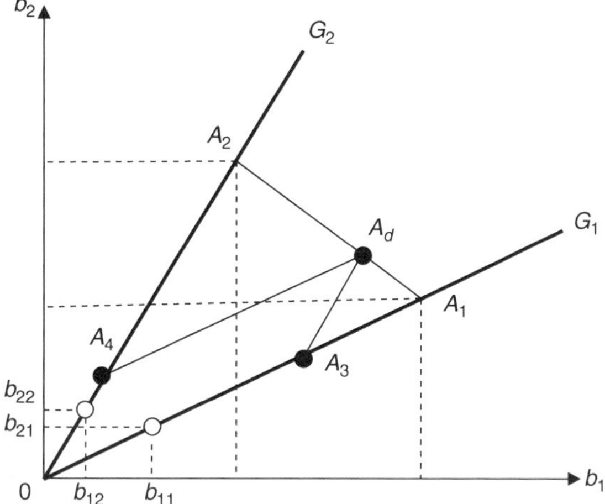

Fig. 6.4 The characteristics of the types of tourism and the overnight stays

2. In the second stage, the problem consists in choosing the optimal combination of characteristics among those qualified as efficient. In this stage, the tourist's preferences matter.

With no loss of generality, we develop the Lancaster approach for the second stage of the multistage model presented in Sect. 5.3.2, which deals with the allocation of money across alternative types of tourism.[4] We will focus on the simplest case with two characteristics, $z = 1, 2$, and two types of tourism, $n = 1, 2$.

In Fig. 6.4 the two characteristics, b_1 and b_2, of a holiday are measured on the horizontal and the vertical axis, respectively. Purchasing one day of holiday T_1 will produce b_{11} of characteristic 1 and b_{21} of characteristic 2; therefore, N_1 overnight stays lead to $b_{11}N_1$ of characteristic 1 and $b_{21}N_1$ of characteristic 2. In other words, relatively to the holiday T_1, the radius OG_1 represents the combination of the characteristics delivered by the holiday-type 1 as the number of overnight stays N_1 increases. Similarly, OG_2 represents the combination of the characteristics delivered by the holiday-type 2 as the number of overnight stays N_2 increases.

The relationship between the quantity of the characteristics and the number of overnight stays can be better appreciated with an example: let us consider the case of two types of tourism (beach-oriented versus mountain-oriented tourism) and two characteristics (comfort versus nature) which are delivered by both types of tourism in different amounts. We assume that beach-oriented tourism is characterized by a large amount of comfort and a small amount of nature, and vice versa for mountain-oriented tourism. If we take b_1 as comfort and b_2 as nature, the slope of each line in Fig. 6.4 indicates the ratio between the characteristics owned by each of the two

[4] However, no substantial change appears in case we were to investigate the choice among alternative destinations for a given type of tourism.

types of holiday; in particular, vector OG_1 is associated to beach-oriented holiday and vector OG_2 is associated to mountain-oriented holiday.

If the tourist spends the entire amount M_{tou} on holiday T_1, we assume that she would be able to purchase the combination of characteristics identified by A_1. Similarly, if the tourist spends the entire amount M_{tou} on holiday T_2, we assume that she would be able to purchase the combination of characteristics identified by A_2.[5]

Instead, should the tourist decide to allocate M_{tou} across the two holidays, she would be able to access any combination along the budget constraint A_1A_2 (to be more precise, any combination within the area OA_1A_2 is feasible, but the points that do not belong to the segment A_1A_2 are not efficient). In other words, by allocating the available budget between beach-oriented and mountain-oriented destinations, the tourist can obtain many different combinations of comfort and nature.

For a given combination A_d along A_1A_2 in Fig. 6.4, it is possible to easily identify the budget allocation that makes A_d feasible. Starting from A_d, we draw a parallel line to OG_1 until we cross OG_2 in point A_4 and we draw a parallel line to OG_2 until we cross OG_1 in point A_3. Consistently to the Parallelogram Rule for vector addition, point A_d is the sum $(A_3 + A_4)$. Therefore, if qM_{tou} is the share of budget spent on A_3 and $(1 - q)M_{tou}$ is the share of budget spent on A_4, the tourist may be able to achieve any combination of comfort and nature along A_1A_2 by allocating available money between the two types of tourism according to the values given to q.

Therefore, the slope of line A_1A_2 measures the rate of substitutability between nature and comfort when changing the share of spending from beach-oriented to mountain-oriented tourism. Each movement along the line A_1A_2 leads to an efficient combination that is consistent with both the consumption technology and the budget. In addition, the frontier A_1A_2 changes with M_{tou} and with prices v_1 and v_2. Therefore, such a frontier must be interpreted as the budget constraint for this model of tourism consumption.

We can now move to the second stage of the problem: the choice of the optimal basket subject to the constraint A_1A_2. If preferences are defined over the characteristics and have positive marginal utility, we can superimpose the map of the indifference curves to the budget constraint as in Fig. 6.5.

The optimal combination is given by point A^*, where the highest indifference curve is tangent to the set of efficient combinations A_1A_2. Finally, if we use the Parallelogram Rule, we can identify spending shares A_3^* and A_4^* which comply with the optimal choice. The tourist facing the choice between the beach-oriented and the mountain-oriented holiday will choose with A^* an intermediate combination between comfort and nature in full respect of the utility and the budget constraint. A corner solution is also admissible; for example, if the tourist chooses point A_1^*, this implies that she is more interested in comfort than nature and that only the beach-oriented holiday will be chosen, and the other way round for A_2^*.

[5] We remind that the position of A_1 and A_2 on the segments depends on M_{tou} and on the prices of the two holidays, and is the solution of the second stage of the multistage model of Sect. 5.3.

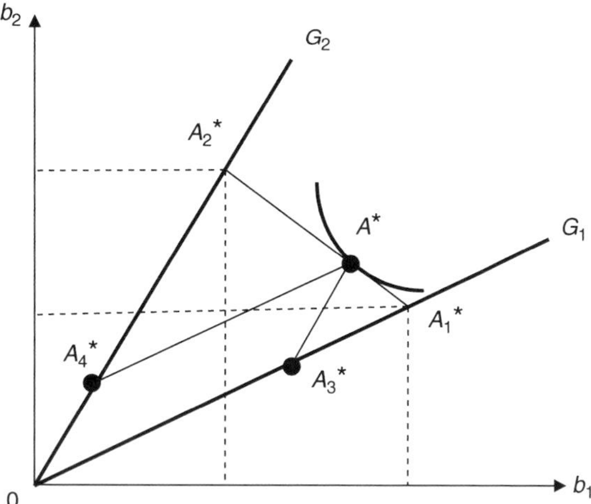

Fig. 6.5 The choice of the optimal basket

Lancaster's idea to polarize the attention on the characteristics of a good (or service) rather than on its physical quantity admits as a corollary the possibility of decomposing the price of a good in a set of prices that assigns an economic value to each of its characteristics. Such an application is known as *hedonic price model.*

In particular, the term hedonic price identifies the price of a given attribute b_z (in the above example, nature or comfort) that is implicit in the total price v_i of holiday $\mathbf{T}_i$; the *hedonic price function* describes the price of a given tourism (dependent variable) as a function of a set of characteristics (independent variables) according to

$$v_i = f(b_1, b_2, ..., b_z). \tag{6.11}$$

In expression (6.11), the partial derivative $\partial v_i / \partial b_z$ measures the effect of a variation in the z-th characteristic on the price of the i-th holiday, given the value for the remaining characteristics. If such derivative is positive (negative), the characteristic b_z is valued as an improvement (worsening) for the holiday relative to a given standard holiday. The absolute value of the partial derivative measures the change in the expected price of the holiday as we let the z-th characteristic to change, still relative to a given standard, and this lets us rank the price intensity of the individual characteristics.

It is important to underline that the observable variables of the model are the price of the holiday and the measures for its own characteristics. Instead, the hedonic prices operate as latent variables that are not observable but that can be estimated via the econometric specification of the hedonic price function which, in the standard literature, is usually assumed as additive and can be estimated either in absolute prices or in logarithms (Theory in Action 6.2). The characteristics that appear in the empirical function can be either quantitative (like the ones displayed along the axis of Fig. 6.4) or qualitative (in which case we must rely on dummy variables).

The hedonic price methodology, originally developed to correct the price indices from variations in the quality of goods, has been used to estimate the impact of characteristics of houses on their market price (Rosen 1974), and subsequently extended to other goods (such as computers, motor vehicles, and art objects), including tourism. In particular, this methodology has been used to study the package tour (Sinclair et al. 1990; Clewer et al. 1992; Taylor 1995; Aguilò et al. 2003; Haroutunian et al. 2005), ski holiday (Falk 2008), the hotel room (Espinet et al. 2003; Chen and Rothschild 2010), the apartments to rent (Salò and Garriga 2011), and the comparison between hotels and apartments (Juaneda et al. 2011).

Theory in Action 6.2. The Hedonic Price Methodology and the Choice Modeling

The hedonic price methodology is based on the estimation of a function (the hedonic price function) that can be expressed either in absolute values or in their logarithms. The characteristics included in the function can be either quantitative, b_z per $z = 1, 2, \ldots, m$ (i.e., the square meters of the hotel room), or qualitative. In particular, qualitative variables are dealt with by the means of binary dummy variables which take either value 1, in case the characteristic is present, or zero otherwise (i.e., the room has a balcony or not); thus, $d_z = 0, 1$ per $z = (m + 1), (m + 2), \ldots, Z$.

(a) *The hedonic-price function in absolute values.* The function (6.11) is assumed to be additive, so as the total price results from taking the algebraic sum of the hedonic price of each single characteristic. Let us consider an example in which we have to estimate the price of the holiday as a function of three characteristics of which two are quantitative, comfort (measured, for example, by the number of tourism firms that operate in the destination) and natural environment (by using as a proxy an index of air quality), and one qualitative characteristic: the opportunity of swimming in the sea, a characteristic owned by beach-oriented tourism but not by mountain-oriented tourism. The hedonic-price function for tourism can be written as follows:

$$v = c + \alpha_1 b_1 + \alpha_2 b_2 + \beta d. \tag{I}$$

If we define the characteristics of the beach-oriented tourism as b_{11}, b_{21}, and $d = 1$ (see Fig. 6.4), while those for the mountain-oriented tourism are b_{12}, b_{22}, and $d = 0$, the Lancaster model along with expression (I) allows us to evaluate the expected price v of the two types of tourism as

$$v_1 = c + \alpha_1 b_{11} + \alpha_2 b_{21} + \beta, \tag{IIa}$$

$$v_2 = c + \alpha_1 b_{12} + \alpha_2 b_{22}. \tag{IIb}$$

By means of expression (I), it is possible to estimate the coefficients α_i and β which capture each characteristic's contribution to the aggregate price of tourism; in other words, the coefficients α_i of (I) can be interpreted as the hedonic prices of those characteristics: α_1 for comfort, α_2 for nature, and β for swimming in the sea. It is by means of these coefficients that we can rank the various characteristics, according to their sign, intensity, and effect on the expected price.

By means of expression (I), it is also possible to evaluate the effect on the holiday price of a change in the characteristic i of tourism, by treating quantitative and qualitative variables separately. For the quantitative variables, we can calculate the partial derivative:

$$\frac{\partial v}{\partial b_z} = \alpha_z \quad z = 1, 2. \tag{III}$$

Instead, as regards the qualitative variables, we must set a standard (which may be the mountain-oriented tourism) $v^* = c + \alpha_1 b_{12} + \alpha_2 b_{22}$ to which we may think of adding the possibility of swimming in the sea, $v_3 = c + \alpha_1 b_{12} + \alpha_2 b_{22} + \beta$, therefore having

$$v_3 - v^* = \beta. \tag{IV}$$

(b) *The hedonic price function in log scale*. In this case, function (6.11) is still assumed as additive, but it is now written in terms of logarithm of prices. If we consider the same example sub (a), the hedonic price function for tourism can be written as follows:

$$\ln v = c + \alpha_1 \ln b_1 + \alpha_2 \ln b_2 + \beta d. \tag{V}$$

If we consider the same levels adopted in sub case (a) for each characteristic, expression (V) provides the estimate for beach-oriented and mountain-oriented tourism in log scale:

$$\ln v_1 = c + \alpha_1 \ln b_{11} + \alpha_2 \ln b_{21} + \beta = K \quad \text{therefore} \quad v_1 = e^K \tag{VIa}$$

$$\ln v_2 = c + \alpha_1 b_{12} + \alpha_2 \ln b_{22} = H \quad \text{therefore} \quad v_2 = e^H \tag{VIb}$$

According to (V), we can still estimate the effect on the price of a change in the characteristics of tourism; however, this must be interpreted differently than before. Regarding the quantitative characteristics, we have

$$\frac{\partial \ln v_1}{\partial \ln b_z} = \alpha_z \quad \text{with} \quad z = 1, 2. \tag{VII}$$

(continued)

Since the difference between the log values of a variable measures its growth rate, expression (VII) measures the elasticity of the price of tourism to the z-th characteristic, that is, the percentage change in the price of tourism associated to a one percent change in the given characteristic, other things being equal.

When dealing with qualitative variables, *ceteris paribus*, we must refer again to the standard $\ln v^* = c + \alpha_1 \ln b_{12} + \alpha_2 \ln b_{22}$ to which we may think of adding the possibility of swimming in the sea, $\ln v_3 = c + \alpha_1 \ln b_{12} + \alpha_2 \ln b_{22} + \beta$, therefore having

$$\ln v_3 - \ln v^* = \beta \quad \text{that is} \quad \ln\left(\frac{v_3}{v^*}\right) = \beta \quad \text{therefore} \quad e^{\beta} = \frac{v_3}{v^*}. \qquad \text{(VIII)}$$

If we subtract one unity from both sides of (VIII), we can express the price growth rate (note that for small values of x, it is the case that $e^x - 1 \approx x$):

$$\frac{v_3 - v^*}{v^*} = e^{\beta} - 1 \approx \beta \qquad \text{(IX)}$$

Expressions (VII) and (IX) are still consistent with the idea that the coefficient of a characteristic can be interpreted as the hedonic price of the characteristic, although it is now written as a percentage.

The hedonic price can be used to "price" non-market characteristics, and in the last few years, many techniques and approaches have been developed to provide the policy maker and the researcher with an evaluation of non-market goods, such as common resources, public and semipublic goods, and, more in general, the territory. Among the most-used methodologies, we recall the Contingent Valuation, the Travel Cost, and the Choice Modeling. While we refer to specific publications for an overview of the main differences among alternative methodologies, particularly between contingent valuation and choice modeling (Louviere et al. 2000, and Mazzanti 2003), we now focus on the most popular methodology used in tourism studies, the choice modeling (or choice experiments).

Choice experiments are a survey-based technique which investigates individual behavior and estimates the value of goods (or projects) by asking people to choose among scenarios which differ in the combination of alternative levels of some selected attributes (characteristics). One of the advantages of choice experiments lies in their ability to model individuals' hypothetical demand for non-market goods and to elicit individuals' willingness to pay for goods and services that may otherwise be unattainable from observing actual behaviors.

This methodology develops through three main steps: (1) identification of the basic attributes (with their levels) of the good or project to be evaluated; (2) choice experiments, in which respondents choose among alternative hypothetical scenarios characterized by different combinations of attribute levels; and (3) econometric analysis of respondents' choices, which allows to estimate the relative importance of the attributes and, if a monetary factor or a price is included as an attribute, the willingness to pay for different levels of the other attributes.

Since the holiday is a composite good, the overall utility of which depends on how the component characteristics are arranged, the choice experiments have often been applied in tourism economics to analyze tourists' preferences with respect to holiday attributes, recreational and heritage demand, attractiveness of a destination, and tourism policies, thus allowing to disentangle the willingness to pay of tourists for (hypothetical) changes in the composition of the tourism product. Among the many papers that recently used this methodology in tourism economics, see Apostolakis and Shabbar (2005), Brau et al. (2009), Crouch and Louviere (2004), Figini et al. (2009), Figini and Vici (2012a), Huybers (2005), and Huybers and Bennet (2000).

6.4 New Products and New Markets

The model based on the holiday's characteristics introduced in Sect. 6.3 is also well suited to study the evolution of the tourism market, since it can explain how new types of holiday enter or exit the market. In this regard, let us examine what happens to the equilibrium in the model when variations in the tourist's income and in the holiday's price are introduced.

If income increases (and M_{tou} will most likely increase, see Sect. 4.2.2), the efficient frontier A_1A_2 shifts away from the origin and the tourist will now be able to purchase higher amounts of both goods. If prices are unchanged, then the new budget constraint, A_3A_4, will be parallel to A_1A_2, as shown in Fig. 6.6.

However, when prices change and M_{tou} is kept constant, the slope of line A_1A_2 must change. In particular, if v_1 increases sufficiently (or v_2 lowers sufficiently), the budget constraint moves toward A_2A_5 and its slope may even become positive, for example, when reaching the position A_2A_6 in Fig. 6.6. This would be the situation where the tourist chooses only tourism $\mathbf{T}_2$ and where the comfort of the beach-oriented holiday has become so expensive that she decides to spend all the budget in the mountain-oriented holiday. In other words, when the slope of the frontier becomes positive, one type of tourism is *off market*.

We are also able to study what happens when a new tourism product $\mathbf{T}_3$ (intended as a holiday with a different combination of characteristics such as comfort and nature) enters the market: for example, a beach-oriented holiday in a destination of great natural interest. From a geometric standpoint, this corresponds to introducing a new vector OG_3, which lies in between OG_1 and OG_2. If we assume that the entire amount M_{tou} is being spent on this new product, for a given v_3, the consumer will choose point A_3 in Fig. 6.7.

Therefore, all the new combinations that are on A_1A_3 and A_3A_2 are now feasible. It can be shown that the combination A_1A_2 is no longer efficient (see Fig. 6.7) and

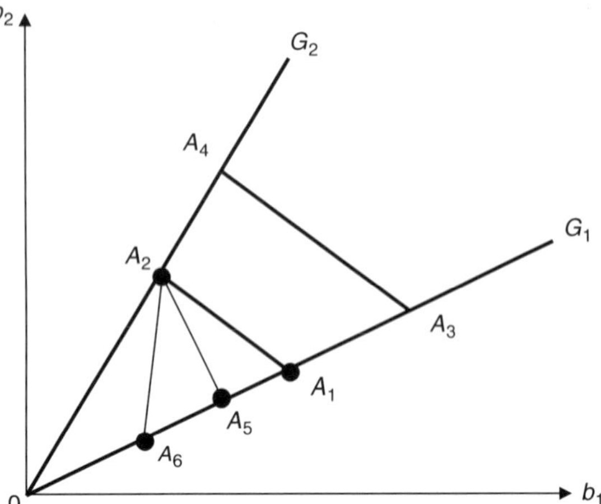

Fig. 6.6 Variations in the tourist's income and in the price of holidays

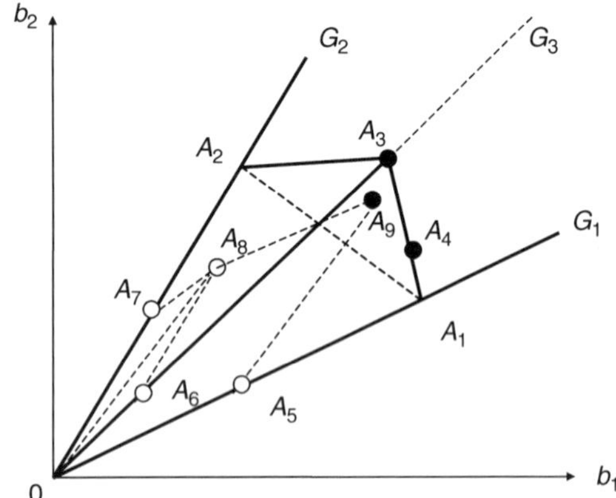

Fig. 6.7 The new holiday effectively enters the market

that combinations such as A_5, A_6, and A_7 are not efficient because they are internal to the consumption possibility frontier (this is also the case for point A_9 which can be obtained by reiterating the parallelogram rule). Regardless of the fact that the new tourism product is being purchased together with beach-oriented or with mountain-oriented holiday, the analysis of the frontier is sufficient to conclude that the new tourism has effectively entered the market.

But if the new product's price is too high, the angle of the frontier line progressively moves inward. As shown in Fig. 6.8, when the frontier becomes a convex set (see, for example, the line $A_1A_5A_2$), then the new tourism $\mathbf{T}_3$ (relative to vector OG_3) is unable to enter the market because it is dominated by the prices of tourism types $\mathbf{T}_1$ and $\mathbf{T}_2$. In particular, given that the new holiday has a combination of characteristics that the consumer is not willing to purchase at that price, sooner or later it will exit the market. For an example of a new product in the tourism market, see the case of Food and Wine Tourism (Case Study 6.1).

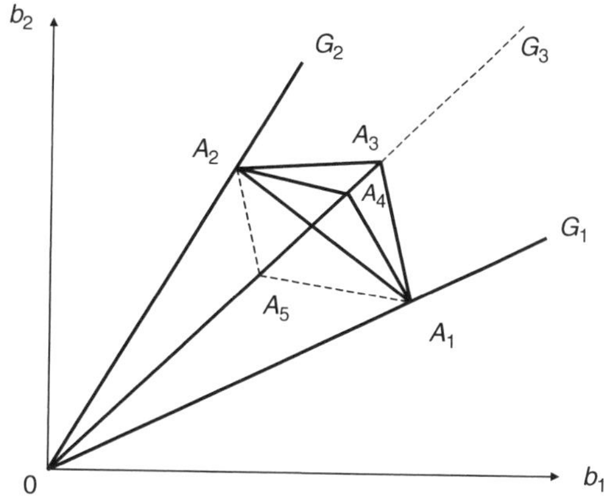

Fig. 6.8 The new holiday enters and exits the market

Case Study 6.1. New Products Enter the Market: The Case of Food and Wine Tourism

The awareness that tourism can enhance economic growth in countries, regions, and destinations where there are resources to promote is a well-established fact. The competition coming from these new tourism destinations force mature destinations to question, update, rejuvenate their strategies, or introduce new products into the tourism market.

One of the success paths developed in this sense is food and wine tourism (FWT), which allows tourists to experiment "with all five senses" the traditions and the culture of the visited territory. FWT is also able to mitigate the crowding-out effect that tourism often has on the other economic sectors of the territory (see Sect. 13.4) by enhancing and complementing sectors such as agriculture, livestock farming, and food industry. The planning and management of FWT are hence linked to historical, cultural, geographical, and economic factors. Starting from wine or food tasting, the local management of the destination can quickly promote the cultural heritage and the natural resources of the territory, by transforming it into a tourism destination.

The first examples of promotion of FWT are located in the United States, particularly in California, where many wineries opened their gates to visitors in the 1970s, as in the famous Napa Valley. Usually, the wine experience starts with a guided tour in the field, where the tourist can visit the different types of grapevine, having the possibility to taste them under the guidance of an expert. Then, the visit moves to the wine cellar, where tourists are exposed to the methods, machinery, and techniques of wine production and then brought to the tasting room, where they can taste the different wines and, obviously, buy them.

FWT has been a particularly successful strategy for a mature destination such as Italy. However, given the extreme heterogeneity of the Italian agricultural production and richness, the tourism of many other products has been promoted in addition to wine: cheese, oil, and ham are the most important

(continued)

among the many. The structure of the touring experience is the same: first, the visit to the processing units and production phases; later, the tasting of the output.

Although FWT can be the main motivation of the trip, it can rarely be the only one. FWT is successful for the whole destination if wineries and food producers are able to integrate this type of activity in a whole tourism product; hence, coordination from the destination management (either public or private in the form of a consortium of producers) or from external tour operators and travel agencies is needed to link the visit to the hospitality sector and to any other offer of cultural and leisure resources from the territory. On one hand, since food is culture, a full understanding of the product can be reached only by knowing the historical and cultural background of the territory that produces it; on the other hand, the integration with museums, natural parks, leisure activities such as a spa, and farmhouses is necessary to motivate not only a same-day trip but also a longer holiday.

As an example among the many, in the Langhe region of Piedmont (Northern Italy), many tourism itineraries have been developed starting from the famous local wine production (mainly Barolo) and linking it to the artwork of famous novelists such as Fenoglio and Pavese. Is it then possible to visit the sites described in books as *Il partigiano Johnny* or *La malora*, visit the house where the novelists were born, and, at the same time, taste wines and the truffles, and visit the museum of rural culture or the places of local religious tradition. Another important example of FWT is the one of Chianti, a region in Tuscany where the homonymous wine is produced and where the food and wine products have been successfully integrated into a holiday which encompasses the cultural and artistic heritage, the landscape, and the environment.

This brief description aims at demonstrating that the FWT has been able to enter the market because of its characteristics, some of which were new (the quest for food culture) and some others were a "better" combination of other existing types of tourism: the countryside might have the same beauty of a mountain or a beach destination; its small town and villages might be full of history, art, and culture as a cultural destination, and the accommodation in a farmhouse with a garden and a swimming pool might have the same comfort of a four-star hotel. Finally, the FWT is also useful to implement a policy of deseasonalizing, aiming at a more effective and efficient use of resources and capacity (see Sect. 7.5.4).

6.5 The Endogenous Preferences

In standard models, economists usually consider the functional form of utility as given and delegate the examination of how preferences shape and change to other disciplines such as Psychology and Sociology. However, given that economic models are often unable to interpret and forecast real-world events, many economists have shown a growing interest in the integration of economic models with those of other social and human sciences. In recent years, this led to the development of new investigative fields such as Psycho-Economics, Neuro-Economics, and Behavioral Economics, which all have brought new insights into the mechanisms of preferences formation (Bruni and Sugden 2007). By following the original work by Etzioni (1993), now we adopt a socioeconomic approach to study preferences and the way economic events may affect them. This approach, which is well suited for the Economics of Tourism, accounts for a complex relationship between economic variables and preferences: in particular, preferences determine choices with their economic consequences, but such choices and consequences have a feedback effect on the formation of preferences, which therefore have to be considered endogenously.

For example, when the price of a beach-oriented holiday temporally rises relative to that of a mountain-oriented holiday, the latter will also be purchased by some of those individuals who did not consider it as an option under the previous conditions. However, it may be the case that many tourists will decide to continue spending their holiday on the mountains even after the price ratio has returned to its original level; in other words, the price change may induce the tourist to experience a mountain-oriented holiday and to develop a "taste" for mountaineering.

This integrated approach assigns to both preferences (with factors affecting them, such as changes in values, group dynamics, leaderships, and advertisement and marketing strategies) and constraints (income and prices) the power of affecting the tourist's behavior. Then, the researcher who wants to apply the theory of endogenous preferences must investigate both elements (preferences and constraints) rather than focusing on just one (the constraint for the economist, the preferences for the sociologist). As an example, the integrated approach could provide the key for understanding the effect of changes in habits (due, for example, to the development of an environmentalist awareness or to associations that push in favor of eco-tourism) that make standard mass-tourism holidays less accepted by tourists.

Given that the model with endogenous preferences is of great interest for tourism, we now discuss some of the tourism features that can be better understood by using this interdisciplinary approach.

6.5.1 Multiplicity and Incompatibility

The standard economic models assume that preferences are not ambivalent or contradictory. Thus, given a holiday price, the tourist decides whether to purchase it or not without hesitations, while the only possibility for ambivalence is when there is indifference between alternatives. This approach is unable to explain the behavior of subjects with incompatible preferences. An example of such situation is that of a person who, before spending a night at the pub, asks a friend to forbid him to drive the car in case he gets drunk, even if he eventually asks to do otherwise. What is the actual preference of such person? Does he prefer to drive even if he is drunk, given that he asks for it? Or does he prefer not to drive, given that he had asked his friend to prevent him from doing it? Given that many of tourists' behaviors are driven by similar episodes of uncertainty and ambivalence, the standard models, which only assume *transitive* preferences, are not able to explain them.

6.5.2 Preferences are Simultaneously a Process and an Outcome

In many behaviors, not only political or economic but also directly related to tourism, subjects "act" upon their own preferences. They obtain satisfaction not just from the choice but also from taking the necessary actions to reach it. For example, for many subjects, shopping while on holiday is a source of leisure and a way to escape from a daily routine. Therefore, a model that treats shopping just as a source of spending and disutility would miss a key psychological element of this activity. Similarly, by making reference to the model discussed in Sect. 5.5, it is not necessarily the case that the tourist who self-organizes the holiday would consider the time spent planning it only in terms of the amount of income foregone while not working (opportunity cost), but rather as a source of enjoyment and a positive contribution to the pleasure of going on holiday. Under this latter assumption, the entire model of self-production would be significantly altered.

6.5.3 Preferences that Change Preferences

Many tourists display a systematic inclination toward investing resources and making efforts in order to modify their own preferences. This idea is supported by the existence of a great number of tourism and cultural activities that some people decide to undertake before (or during) their holiday in order to better define their preferences: for example, in order to improve own cultural awareness, a tourist might decide to attend a course of introduction to art history or to impose a visit to the main museums of the destination.

6.5.4 Society, Groups, Leadership, and Persuasive Advertisement

Finally, the assumption of endogenous preferences allows us to fully appreciate the way that cultural and social factors, such as opinion leaders and persuasive advertisement, effectively shape the tourist's behavior; this is an opportunity that tour operators usually exploit with the goal of orienting international tourism flows. In addition, we must emphasize the importance of fashions in the evolution of tourists' preferences as regards destinations and types of tourism.

All the above factors support the approach of endogenous preferences and suggest the idea of building a theory of consumption applied to the tourist that includes both the elements that constrain preferences and the factors that shape and change them, and where the research methodology integrates the approaches developed by Economics, Sociology, and Psychology.

As a sort of conclusion, the process of formation of preferences can be identified by focusing on the so-called *image of the holiday* (Cooper et al. 2008) and where four stages can be determined: (a) the tourist develops a vague idea about the holiday, intended as a desirable activity that is worth demanding; (b) the tourist decides when, how, and where the holiday should take place and the "image is focused"; (c) the tourist experiences the holiday so that the image gets modified and updated through the experience itself; and (d) the memories, the regrets, and the alternative possibilities are reshaped in order to define the tourist's attitude toward the past holiday as well as the choice of future ones. These four stages, which partially overlap with the phases of the Outdoor Recreation Model discussed in Chap. 2, are just the outcome of an endogenous process aimed at building personal preferences on the types of tourism or holiday.

As a general conclusion of this paragraph, it is important to remind that, apart from the necessary simplifications adopted by the economic models, the tourism experience as a whole can only be understood by adopting a holistic point of observation, where the method of investigation must be multidisciplinary.

6.6 Psychological and Sociological Aspects of Tourism Consumption

The systemic and holistic nature of tourism generated an extensive literature on the psychological and sociological motivations behind the tourist's choice for a certain type of tourism, for a particular destination, or, more generally, for taking a holiday. A key element for this decision is the tourist's capital of knowledge about tourism, which ultimately can be affected by other people's behavior (i.e., friends and relatives), persuasive forms of advertising, other sources of information (i.e., magazines, Internet sites, and social networks), etc. Hence, in addition to the economic motivations already discussed (prices, income, and time), Psychology and Sociology assert that other determinants for tourism must also be identified in order to fully understand the tourist's choice.

Among the psychological factors, the perception of risk (Sonmez and Graefe 1998), the traveler's personality, the attitude toward other people including the local population, etc., must be taken into consideration; a well-known model investigating the psychological motivations of tourism was developed by Plog

(1974) and classifies tourists according to a continuum of states ranging within two extreme poles: the *psychocentric* and the *allocentric* (the model was already described in Sect. 4.5.2).

Among the sociological factors, those of greater relevance include the cultural values of the social group which the tourists usually refer to. McIntosh et al. (1995) studied the motivations of tourism by distinguishing four categories: (a) physical reasons, aimed at providing relief to the body and/or the mind (sport, fun, leisure, and wellness); (b) cultural reasons, aimed at meeting and knowing other cultures; (c) interpersonal reasons, aimed at meeting new people, socializing, or just visiting relatives and friends; and (d) status reasons, that deal with the desire to "use" tourism as a *positional good* in order to achieve prestige and social acceptance among the referring group.

The psychosociological approach allows a deeper understanding of a number of key factors that are behind the motivations of tourism, and which may be classified into four categories that relate to either the tourist's "lifestyle" or to the tourist's "life cycle".

1. The *education*. The level of education is a key factor to determine a person's propensity to travel for tourism (and where to) and is linked to the consumer lifestyle. According to psychologists and sociologists, the education widens a person's horizons and stimulates the desire to travel. The higher the level of education, the more the tourist becomes conscious of alternative traveling opportunities and receptive to new stimulus.
2. The *mobility*. With the term "mobility," we mean both the individual's physical abilities or disabilities and the means of transportation that the tourist uses or might use. The level of mobility remarkably affects the individual's propensity to travel and consequently affects tourism.
3. The *ethnic group*, *social class,* and *gender*. Different ethnic groups, different social classes (groups or communities in which the population can be divided according to observable characteristics), and gender are all elements that affect the choice of the type of tourism, the destination, and the holiday's characteristics.
4. The *cognitive age*. This term combines the individual's age with the family status (Shih 1986). In this respect, the fundamental ages as regard tourism are as follows: (a) the childhood, during which the subject follows the family's decisions; (b) the adolescence, during which the individual has the possibility of taking holidays away from the family but in a protected environment; (c) the young single phase, when the subject travels alone or with the own circle of friends; (d) the phase of traveling with a partner but without children; (e) the phase of family holidays, when children are still babies; (f) the stage of the "empty nest," when kids are in phases (b) or (c) and take independent holidays; (g) the elderly age, with its specific needs and demands for tourism.

Other models have been recently developed around the idea of endogenous preferences. The taxonomy of behaviors that have been identified can display a great deal of relevance, in particular when referred to particular groups of tourists or to particular consumption conditions. Just to recall a few (see Apostolopoulos et al. 1996 for a deeper examination of the sociology of tourism):

- The *habits formation*. According to this model, the subject chooses the type of tourism that, within the budget constraint, involves the smallest deviation from a previously chosen holiday. This model leads to different conclusions than those obtained with the standard economic models described in this chapter and in Chap. 5, given that it relies on the sequence of choices previously made; the model is due to Machina (1987) and Pollack (1978) and builds upon the model of directional choice (Georgescu-Roegen 1936). For an application to tourism, see Agliardi (1988).
- The *return of preferences*. This hypothesis refers to the ascertainment that two or more types of holiday can alternate in the tourist's experience. The reason for this choice resides either in the fact that (a) the time and the budget constraints do not allow a simultaneous consumption of the different holidays included in the tourist's utility function; or (b) the expected consequences of the choice are not realized by the experience. In other words, the preferences at the moment of the consumption are different from those when the choice was planned, and this can lead to a change in the subsequent choice.
- The *regret*. The key idea behind the model of regret (Loomes and Sugden 1986) is that the tourist's choice implies an elaboration of the alternatives, in the sense that the tourist is not only interested in the chosen option but also in the rejected alternatives. Unlike the standard economic theory, though, the set of available options greatly matters for the choice that is being made.
- The *bandwagon effect*. It takes place when the tourist's demand depends or is a consequence of the choices made by others. This effect corresponds to an imitative behavior mainly driven by socio-cultural factors (see Sect. 4.4.3).
- The *snob effect*. It is the opposite of the bandwagon effect; hence a decrease in the tourist's demand inversely depends on the number of other tourists demanding the same holiday. The *élite* character of the holiday is what motivates the snob effect (see Sect. 4.4.3).
- The *Veblen effect*. It occurs when the preference for the holiday increases with its price. This could be the case when a holiday becomes a status symbol or when the access to its consumption is very exclusive, and tourists use the holiday as a positional good.

6.7 Information in the Tourist's Choice

All the economic models used so far in the investigation of the tourist's decision process are based on the assumption that the subject knows all the necessary information to make a "rational" choice: the set of alternative destinations and the types of holiday, together with their price and quality features. Tourists know everything and hence decide optimally. This hypothesis, although useful for a start up of the theoretical analysis, is definitely too strong to be applied to real-world behaviors and must be replaced with the hypothesis of *incomplete information*.

6.7.1 Incomplete Information in Tourism

The economic literature identifies three different forms of incomplete information in the consumer's choice. Applied to tourism, they can be listed as follows:

1. The *technological uncertainty*, which assumes that at the moment of purchasing a holiday, the tourist does not have information about its quality; the term "technological" is used because the lack of information regards the technology of production adopted by the destination or by the tourism firm from which the characteristics of the final product are derived.
2. The *market uncertainty*, which assumes that the tourist is aware of the fact that similar holidays may be sold at different prices, but those prices are unknown; the term "market" refers to the lack of information about prices in the market where the holiday is sold.
3. The *uncertainty of the alternatives*, which assumes that the tourist does not have complete information about the entire range of possible alternatives, and therefore chooses the type of holiday or the destination within a limited geographic area (spatial-local information) or within the boundaries of previous tourism experiences (time-local information); the reason for the name is because the lack of information regards the set of possibilities among which the tourist can choose.

Incomplete information may affect the tourist's behavior in two ways:

- Without the knowledge of the full set of information, the tourist may not find sufficient reasons for changing the type of holiday already chosen. This conservative attitude may hamper innovation and full competition in the market.
- A widening of the information set allows the tourist to reach a more efficient choice. As a direct consequence, the tourist is usually inclined to invest part of own resources (time and money) to search information produced by other subjects (web portals, search engines, travel agencies, guidebooks, etc.).

A last clarification is needed before the presentation of the main models dealing with incomplete information: the identification of the exact moment when the search occurs. We may distinguish two hypotheses that lead to different consequences:

- The *long-distance* search, operated by the tourist before the holiday begins, at the moment of its reservation.
- The *on-site* search, operated by the tourist after the holiday has started, at the destination.

In the next subsections, some of these aspects of information uncertainty will be analyzed through very simple models, which are direct applications of microeconomics theory to the tourism market. We will consider, in particular, the technological uncertainty and the market uncertainty: in Sect. 6.7.2, we will discuss the tourist's search for price information, while in Sect. 6.7.3 and 6.7.4 we will analyze the issue of quality uncertainty of the tourism product.[6]

6.7.2 The Price Search

When not all the relevant information is available, the tourist may find it convenient to self-produce it, in the sense of spending time and other resources in gathering the information needed. In this section, we will examine the factors that affect the decision of how much information to collect, by focusing on the search for the best price among holidays or tourism products of given quality. Although tourists are often in a situation of simultaneously searching for the best price and best quality, in order to identify the best quality/price combination, for the sake of simplicity we will examine these two searches separately: in this subsection, we assume that all the alternative holidays are of the same quality but different prices; in the next subsection, we will assume that all the alternative holidays have the same price but different quality.

As regards the price search, we introduce two simple models (Stigler 1961) describing the search process of a tourist who wants to collect information. In both cases, the tourist faces a certain price distribution for a given holiday (or tourism service), that is, the tourist knows that services of the same quality are sold at different prices, but does not know which firms currently offer the best price and the exact amount of the best price. By starting a search process, which has its specific costs (in terms of time and resources spent on it) and benefits (the outcome of a lower price), the models define the optimal amount of information that should be collected before proceeding with the purchase. In other words, the models determine the *stopping rule*, which consists of determining the optimal number of queries to be carried out for the simultaneous search, or of determining the maximum acceptable price for the sequential search.

The search process can be either simultaneous or sequential. There is *simultaneous search* when the tourist acquires a predetermined amount of information before deciding which product to buy. As an example, when deciding where to buy a certain holiday, the tourist may inquire the price at n travel agencies, and then decide to buy the best offer out of the n received. A simultaneous search operates similarly to the extraction of n ballots from a ballot box, ranking the number (that is, the price) that appears on each ballot and then choosing the ballot with the lowest number. The choice variable for the simultaneous search (its stopping rule) is the

[6] We will not study the uncertainty on the alternatives, referring to Agliardi (1988) and Nicolau (2010) for an application to tourism of the directional choice model developed by Georgescu-Roegen (1936) under the assumption of local preferences.

size n of the sample. In other words, the tourist has to decide how many queries to submit before making a choice.

There is *sequential search* when the tourist considers one product at the time and decides whether or not to buy it at that price (that is, whether or not to continue the search). For example, before deciding where to spend the night, the tourist may decide to visit one hotel after another and ask for the price (the quality of the accommodation is kept identical by assumption) and then interrupt the search when the hotel that charges a price smaller or equal to the one that the tourist is willing to pay is found. A sequential search operates similarly to the extraction (without replacement) of ballots from a ballot box one at a time. The choice variable for the sequential search (its stopping rule) is the *reservation price*, which is the maximum price that the tourist is willing to pay for the good.

A preliminary question has to be raised before describing the two models: what is the best search process to activate? Definitely, the answer depends on many factors, and it is likely the case that the same tourist prefers one search method over the other depending on the circumstances. In this section, the problem of which search method to use will not be investigated, but we acknowledge that the simultaneous search is more likely to be preferred by those tourists who can collect the information in advance; similarly, the sequential search is the preferred option when the tourist has to produce a prompt reply to the information. In particular, the tourist who is already in the destination usually finds it easier to follow a sequential search, while the tourist who books the holiday from home usually prefers a simultaneous search through web portals, travel agencies, or collecting brochures. Finally, it might also be the case that a searching mix is adopted, by following a sequence of simultaneous searches.

6.7.2.1 The Simultaneous Price Search

Let us consider the case of a tourist who has to travel to the destination and look for an overnight accommodation. Let us assume that all hotels are identical in quality, but each hotel charges a different price for the same type of room. Although the tourist does not know which hotel offers the best price (this is indeed a case of market uncertainty), the distribution of prices is known through the search process.

To keep the model as simple as possible, in what follows we discuss the case where only two prices for the same accommodation can be charged: hence, the tourist can find two types of hotels: highly efficient hotels (which we label with H) that charge 200 per night, and inefficient hotels (which we label with L—*low*) that charge 300 per night. Moreover, the tourist knows that the probability of finding a hotel of each type is equal to $q = 0.5$, that is, the number of type-H hotels is equal to the number of type-L hotels. However, given that the tourist is unable to distinguish the type of a hotel, a search starts (in this case, by visiting the different hotel websites or a search engine and simulating a reservation).

Given the assumption of simultaneous search, the tourist must calculate the benefit associated with alternative sample dimensions. Table 6.1 displays this

Table 6.1 The benefits accruing from different sample dimensions in case of simultaneous search

Number of queries	Prob. of finding only hotels of type L ($p = 300$)	Prob. of finding at least one hotel of type H ($p = 200$)	Expected price $E(p)$	Marginal benefit $B'(k)$
1	0.5	0.5	250	–
2	0.25	0.75	225	25
3	0.13	0.87	215.5	9.5
4	0.06	0.94	206.25	9.25
...	...	...	...	...
∞	0	1	200	0

calculation; the first column presents the number of queries that can be carried out together with the corresponding probabilities of finding only type-L hotels (second column) versus at least one type-H hotel (third column).

In the case of only one query, there is an identical probability $q = 0.5$ of finding either type of hotel; however, in the case of two queries (second row of the table), there are four possible outcomes: *HL*, *LH*, *HH*, and *LL*. In the first three outcomes, the tourist encounters at least one hotel of type-H and then will be offered a price equal to 200, while in the last outcome, he will be offered (and pay) a price equal to 300; in other words, when the number of queries is two, the probability of paying 200 is $q = 0.75$ (third column), while the probability of paying 300 is $1 - q = 0.25$ (second column). With three queries (third row), the possible outcomes are eight: *LLL, LLH, LHL, LHH, HLL, HLH, HHL,* and *HHH*, seven of which show at least one type-H hotel. Hence, the probability of paying 200 is $q = 0.875$, while the probability of paying 300 is $1 - q = 0.125$; similarly for the cases with more than three queries.

The expected price is defined as the weighted average of the possible prices by using probabilities as weights, $E(p) = \Sigma_i p_i q_i$, where q_i denotes the probability of paying price p_i, with $\Sigma_i q_i = 1$. In the simple case of Table 6.1, $E(p) = 200q_1 + 300(1 - q_1)$, where q_1 is the probability displayed under each assumption about the sample size and the expected price is represented in the fourth column of the table. Finally, the marginal benefit of the search, $B'(k)$, is measured as the decrease in the expected price due to a one-unit increase in the number of queries; in particular, the marginal benefit $B'(k)$ of the i-th query can be calculated as the difference between the expected price associated to $(k - 1)$ and to k surveys, $B'(k) = E(p_{k-1}) - E(p_k)$. The last column of Table 6.1 clearly shows that the marginal benefit of the search is a decreasing function of the sample size, which is a general property which does not depend on the particular assumptions of this example.

To identify the optimal sample size in terms of number of queries, the tourist must also take into consideration that searching information is expensive in terms of both out-of-pocket costs (for example, the cost of making phone calls to the hotels in order to gather price information) and opportunity costs (the cost of the time being distracted from alternative, more relaxing activities).

We assume that such cost, $C(k)$, increases with the number k of surveys, and that the first and second derivatives are $C'(k) \geq 0$ and $C''(k) \geq 0$, hence we assume that

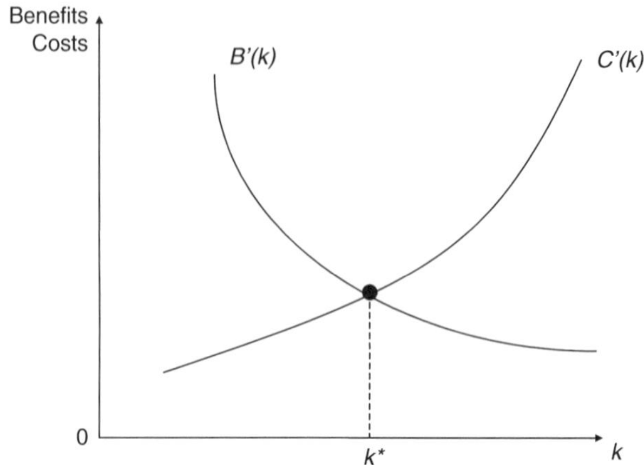

Fig. 6.9 The optimal number of queries in the simultaneous search for price

there is a *fatigue effect*. The application of the general optimization rule requires for the tourist to choose the optimal k such that the marginal benefit accruing from the k-th unit of information is equal to the marginal cost of getting it:

$$B'(k) = C'(k). \tag{6.12}$$

The solution corresponds to k^* in Fig. 6.9, where the upward sloping marginal cost curve and the downward sloping marginal benefit curve for the simultaneous search are shown. After running k^* queries, the tourist chooses the hotel with the lowest price among the k^* hotels in the sample (in the above example, since the price is a discrete variable, any hotel among those charging the lowest price will be randomly chosen). Running less than k^* queries would not be optimal because the expected benefit (i.e., the reduction in price that may occur from calling one additional hotel) would be greater than the cost that must be borne for it. Similarly, a number of queries greater than k^* would not be optimal because the marginal cost of the last query would exceed its expected benefit. Note also that the existence of a positive marginal cost is a sufficient condition for preventing the tourist from gathering all the potential information.

Obviously, the search cost varies from tourist to tourist, as it depends on preferences, income, the opportunity cost of time, and many other particular circumstances such as the tiredness due to the trip and the arrival time at the destination. Therefore, the value of k^* is not the same for all tourists: let us consider two tourists X and Y who are identical in every aspect except the marginal cost of their search, which is 9.20 for X (who can be less tired due to a shorter trip) and is 9.40 for Y (who is more tired due to a longer trip). As it can be clear by comparing these values with the marginal benefits listed in the last column of Table 6.1, for tourist X it is optimal to undergo four queries before choosing the hotel, while for Y three queries is the optimal number; this implies that for Y, the probability of rationally choosing a type-L hotel is higher than for X. Another interpretation of X and Y is that the former is a tourist booking in advance, in which case the marginal costs are generally lower than for the latter, a tourist already on-site and tired after a long trip, who will rationally pay a higher price.[7]

Up to now, we have implicitly assumed that the tourist chooses the hotel only for one night and *una tantum*. An important extension of the simultaneous search model relies on removing such restriction. Indeed, in many circumstances, a tourist chooses a hotel for more than one night or it can be the case that the tourist will be returning in the same destination. In the first case, we use the term of *multiple purchase*, which is due to a repetition of the overnight stays, while in the second case we use the term *repeat purchase*, which deals with a repetition of the visits (arrivals). Both cases introduce deviations from the model just developed, and therefore two alternative hypotheses have to be developed:

1. A unique search leading to multiple purchase; this is the case of a tourist who spends several nights in the chosen hotel.
2. A unique search leading to repeat purchase; this is the case of a tourist who decides to return to a hotel on the basis of past experience and information that was previously gathered.

The Multiple Purchases

Let us again consider the example displayed in Table 6.1, but removing the hypothesis that the tourist stays for one night only and assuming multiple purchases. In this case, the marginal benefit of the query must be considered for each of the nights spent in the hotel. This is why in Table 6.2 we modify the marginal benefit of the search, $B'(k)$, by multiplying its value times the number of overnight stays (up to three nights in the table) that the tourist wants to spend at the hotel. Clearly, the second column of Table 6.2, related to just one overnight stay, replicates the entries of the last column of Table 6.1.

As regards the marginal costs, a once-off search undergone when choosing the hotel distributes its marginal cost on each day of the tourist's stay. The optimal condition (6.12) then becomes

$$NB'(k) = C'(k).$$

The consequence of a multiple purchase is that the marginal cost of the information falls, and for the tourist becomes optimal to increase the number of queries.

[7] The advantage of the simultaneous search carried out in advance is even more evident nowadays, thanks to the meta-search engines such as Booking.com. The economic consequence of these websites is to render the marginal cost of an additional query basically equal to zero, implying that the optimal size of the search sample increases (see Chap. 12). However, in real-world searches, the problem is tremendously complicated by the quality issue, which we avoided in this simple model, by assuming the same quality for all the hotels.

Table 6.2 The marginal benefit in the simultaneous search with multiple stays

Number of queries	One overnight stay	Two overnight stays	Three overnight stays
2	25	50	75
3	9.5	19	28.5
4	9.25	18.5	27.75
...	...	...	...
∞	0	0	0

From Table 6.2, we see that a marginal cost equal to 28 implies the optimal solution of one query for a tourist spending just one night at the hotel, two queries in case of a two-night stay, and three queries in case of a three-night stay.

This extension suggests that a longer length of the holiday improves the benefits accruing from gathering information and optimally leads to a longer search activity. In other words, the tourist who intends to have a longer holiday is the one who gathers the largest amount of information, while the short-term tourist is usually the one who is willing to choose on the basis of fewer alternatives.

The Repeat Purchases

We now discuss the case of repeat purchases. If we label with Φ_t the information set owned by the tourist at time t, the return to a previously visited destination allows the tourist to exploit the search made in the past. Therefore, in the case of repeat visits, the assumption on the correlation between information gathered during the previous and the current search, that is, the correlation between Φ_{t-1} and Φ_t, becomes an essential element to take into consideration. We can highlight three cases:

- If $corr(\Phi_{t-1}; \Phi_t) = 0$, past prices are uncorrelated with current prices: in this case, the information searched by the tourist is valid only for one period, and current information is completely independent from the information coming from previous searches. In this case, the model completely overlaps with the general model of simultaneous search.
- If $corr(\Phi_{t-1}; \Phi_t) = 1$, which identifies the case of perfect correlation between current and past prices, the search at time $(t-1)$ remains valid also in period t (a positive and perfect correlation occurs when, for instance, all the hotels of the same quality operating in the destination increase the price by the same percentage). In this case, the model completely overlaps with the model of multiple purchases, and the hypothesis of repeat arrivals can be assimilated to one of repeat stays.
- Finally, if $corr(\Phi_{t-1}; \Phi_t) > 0$, the informative content of the past search may not be completely reliable; in other words, it is likely the case that the tourist may find optimal to integrate previous information with a partial new search activity in the current period, in order to update the existing set of information.

As a general conclusion, the existence of a positive correlation between prices charged by tourism firms in different periods justifies the following statement:

> A positive correlation of successive asking prices justifies the widely held view that inexperienced buyers (*tourists*) pay higher prices in a market than do experienced buyers. The former have no accumulated knowledge of asking prices, and even with an optimum amount of search they will pay higher prices on average. Since the variance of the expected minimum price decreases with additional search, the prices paid by inexperienced buyers will also have a larger variance.
>
> (Stigler 1961, p. 218–9. *Italic added*)

Therefore, the tourist who arrives for the first time at the destination does not have any past experience to count on. Given that the information set only includes current information, it is likely the case that this tourist will end up paying higher prices than the more experienced tourist.

6.7.2.2 The Sequential Price Search

We now discuss an example similar to the one presented in Sect. 6.7.2.1; however, we now assume that the tourist undergoes a sequential search, thus deciding to purchase a hotel accommodation only when the requested price is less or equal to p_r, the reservation price of the tourist. To further simplify things, we assume that prices can vary between $p_{\min}$ and $p_{\max}$ (the minimum and the maximum prices that can be charged by hotels at the destination) and that the distribution of prices is uniform. As a consequence, the price paid by the tourist will be between $p_{\min}$ and p_r. Given the assumption of uniform distribution, all prices $p_{\min} \leq p \leq p_r$ can happen with the same probability so that the tourist's expected price, $f(p_r)$, is

$$\frac{p_{\min} + p_r}{2} = f(p_r). \tag{6.13}$$

In the simple case of a non-multiple and non-repeat purchase (one arrival and one overnight stay), expression (6.13) shows a positive relationship between $f(p_r)$ and p_r in the interval $[p_{\min}, p_{\max}]$, that is, $f'(p_r) > 0$. Moreover, when $p_r \geq p_{\max}$, the tourist finds optimal to accept the first price offered; on the contrary, when $p_r < p_{\min}$, the tourist will not accept any offer.

Also in the case of sequential search, we must consider the search cost for the tourist. As in the case of simultaneous search, we assume that the costs are both out-of-pocket costs and the opportunity cost of time spent in the search; in particular, we should expect that a low reservation price increases the search time, while a higher reservation price would reduce the number of hotels that will be inquired. Therefore, the average search cost $c(p_r)$ falls as p_r increases. For the tourist, the average expected full price of one stay, $E(p)$, is then equal to the sum between the average search cost, $c(p_r)$, and the expected price, $f(p_r)$:

$$E(p) = c(p_r) + f(p_r). \tag{6.14}$$

The choice variable of the tourist is the reservation price, p_r, which will be set by the tourist so as to minimize the total expected full price of one overnight stay, that is, when $c'(p_r) + f'(p_r) = 0$, and will accept to spend the night at any hotel that offers a price $p \le p_r$.

It is straightforward to see that the sequential search model leads to conclusions similar to the ones found in the simultaneous search model. The reservation price rises (and the expected search time falls) if the marginal cost of the search increases.

Again, the optimal amount of queries depends on the size of the purchase. If the tourist demands N overnight stays (*multiple purchase*), the expected full price of the holiday becomes $E(p) = c(p_r) + Nf(p_r)$. If we compute the average full price, $E(p)/N$, it is clear that the reservation price falls when the length of the holiday increases, and the other way round. The economic explanation for such relationship goes as follows: the higher the number of nights the tourist spends in the destination, the greater the benefit from undergoing a search that lowers the expected price.

A general discussion of the simultaneous and sequential search models highlights that a behavior that appears as suboptimal within standard models with complete information could instead appear as economically rational under imperfect information and market uncertainty. According to the standard model, a tourist who purchases at a given price when it is known that there exist other hotels that offer the same service at a lower price seems irrational; however, once we acknowledge that the information might be incomplete and expensive to collect (in the sense that the tourist has to invest time and money), the model of this section defines a decision rule that does not qualify such behavior as suboptimal.

The models introduced in this section are very simple. We could make them more realistic (and more complicated) by developing several extensions (see Case Study 6.2 for a real-world example): (a) by introducing more complicated price distributions than the uniform; (b) by allowing the tourists to become more efficient as long as they carry out the search activity (for example, through the introduction of a *learning-by-searching* process that would drive to an *adaptive behavior*). A reasonable assumption in this regard would be to assume that when beginning the search, the tourist does not have a prior knowledge of the distribution of prices; however, the more the information is gathered, the better the estimation of such distribution (Phelps 1988); (c) by assuming that there is a different distribution of prices for each group of tourism firms: for example, the tourist may assume that the distribution of prices in hotel chains is different than the one of independent hotels. We decided to disregard these complications and deal directly with the other important feature of the purchase activity: the search for the quality of the tourism product and, in general, of the holiday at the destination.

Case Study 6.2. The Search for Price in the Case of a Trip to Mexico: Self-organizing or Purchasing the Holiday?

In recent years, Internet definitely brought a revolution into the travelers' habits and in the organization of the tourism sector (Chap. 12). If someone wants to self-organize a holiday, it is very easy today to browse the many specialized web portals and to look for flights, hotels, itineraries, tickets for museums, etc. Internet allows tourists to widen the range of alternatives, in terms of destinations, things to do, and prices. As we already know (see Sect. 5.5), the tourist can self-organize a holiday that is not available in the market by directly purchasing the different services; instead, when the tourism product already exists on the market, the consumer can decide on whether to purchase or self-produce it.

In practice, what is the best thing to do for the tourist? A comparative analysis of the distributive channels has been made specifically for Mexico (Nwosu 2008) by investigating the case of a 2-week holiday for two people to take place in February 2008 and that included a 1-week tour to the archeological sites of Yucatan and Chiapas and a 1-week stay at a beach-oriented destination on the Mayan coast. The experiment used the simultaneous price search method, by contacting a number of travel agencies (four), web portals (four), and by the means of two attempts of self-organization, one at the beginning and one at the end of the search process (in doing so, we could also estimate the "learning effect") and by taking into consideration the opportunity cost of the time involved with the search.

The lowest total price (3,210 €) turned out to be the one associated with the second attempt of self-production. Even if we compute the cost associated with the search time, this option remained the most convenient. To achieve this outcome, the use of Internet happened to play an essential role in purchasing the individual components of the trip, and probably the outcome would have been different without the help of such information and distributional channel.

As regards package tours sold on web portals, those with similar characteristics were particularly difficult to find. Only two packages were found, but only one could be thought as an appealing alternative to self-production, given that its price was 3,653 €, which was close enough to the 3,210 € of the self-organized holiday. As regards travel agencies, the price turned out to be significantly higher: the lowest of the alternatives (4,893 €) was the result of a 15 % price reduction granted by the tour operator. The remaining prices ranged from 5,646 to 6,983 €.

The conclusion of this experiment of price search was then in favor of self-organization. However, it must be pointed out that this conclusion should not be taken as general. First, the outcome of this case study may depend on the fact that the features of the requested holiday were pretty unconventional and possibly hard to find in the form of an all-inclusive tour package. Second, the

(continued)

level of competence when using the Internet (portals, search engines, etc.) is an essential element of the experiment. In particular, the experiment revealed a remarkable component of self-learning: at the beginning, the search produced a holiday with a price higher than 5,000 €; after having spent overall 10 h visiting web agencies and specialized search engines, it was possible to reduce the price by 40 %. Therefore, for those people with a high opportunity cost of time, or with a strong disutility associated to search, the purchase of a package holiday may remain the best choice.

It is however evident that nowadays the competition takes place on the Internet: traditional travel agencies can no longer be competitive neither in price nor in the variety to be offered to the tourists. A profitable future for these agencies, therefore, must be pursued in terms of quality, customer care, and customized service (see Sect. 8.3).

6.7.3 The Quality Search

In the previous section we assumed identical quality, different prices, and incomplete price information; in this section instead, we assume that there exist several products with identical price but different qualities, and tourists have incomplete information about the quality. Although in the real world the tourist simultaneously searches for price and quality, the formalization of the two assumptions together would remarkably complicate our formal analysis;[8] we decided instead to leave this case to more advanced literature and to focus now on the quality search process.

For tourism, the quality issue is of great importance. However, the quality analysis involves two types of problems: on one hand, it is necessary to precisely define the concept of "quality" with reference to the whole bundle of goods and services included in the matrix of the tourism product; on the other hand, one has to keep in mind that consumers may find quite difficult to evaluate the information regarding the quality of a holiday.

With reference to the latter issue, the actual possibility of evaluating the quality, we distinguish two cases: the search goods and the experience goods (Nelson 1970). The term *search good* defines a consumption good the main features of which , and quality among them, can be precisely observed and evaluated by the consumer before the purchase (an example is clothes, given that they can be tried on before purchasing); the term *experience good* defines a consumption good the main features of which, and quality among them, cannot be observed in advance and may be assessed only after the purchase and the act of consumption (examples are theater plays or restaurant meals).

The distinction between search and experience goods primarily deals with the nature of the consumption act, rather than with the technical characteristics of the good.

[8] We would have to assume that the choice variable is the tourist surplus, which inversely depends on price and directly on a quality index.

For this reason, the holiday as a whole owns the feature of an experience good because, in general, it is impossible for a tourist to assess its quality before the experience itself (and this is particularly true for the tourist who purchases the holiday from home or who visits a new destination); on the contrary, if we focus on the repeat tourist (i.e., the tourist who returns to the same destination) or to some of the factors that compose the tourism product (such as accommodation), the good may be a search good (this is particularly true for the independent tourist self-organizing the holiday while already arrived at the destination).

In light of this distinction, we have now to discuss the optimal search rule for both search goods and experience goods.

6.7.3.1 Quality Search Models in Case of Search Goods

This case is substantially similar to the case outlined in Sect. 6.7.2. The aim is to determine an optimal stopping rule which is identified by the general principle that the search should continue up to the point where the expected marginal benefit of the search equals the expected marginal cost. However, an important difference occurs: in the quality search models, benefits and costs must be measured in terms of utility and not of price. Therefore we have to modify the assumption regarding type-*H* hotels (high quality) and type-*L* hotels (low quality): we now consider that all hotels sell at the same price (equal to 200), but the different quality of service leads to a different value for the tourist's utility: $U(L) = 50$ and $U(H) = 100$ (indeed, the utility a tourist receives, given the same price, increases with the quality). We still assume the same discrete distribution of hotels, where $q = 0.5$ is the probability of finding type-*H* hotels.

Similarly to Table 6.1, Table 6.3 displays this probability as a function of the number of queries: in the case of only one query, there is the same probability $q = 0.5$ of finding either type of hotel; however, in the case of two queries (second row of the table), there are four possible outcomes: *HL*, *LH*, *HH*, and *LL*. In the first three outcomes, the tourist encounters at least one hotel of type-*H* and then will gain a utility equal to 100, while in the last outcome he will gain a utility equal to 50; in other words, when the number of queries is two, the probability of having utility equal to 100 is $q = 0.75$ (third column), while the probability of having utility equal to 50 is $1 - q = 0.25$ (second column). With three queries (third row), the possible outcomes are eight: *LLL, LLH, LHL, LHH, HLL, HLH, HHL,* and *HHH*, therefore the probability of having 100 is $q = 0.875$ (in seven of the eight cases, there is at least one type-*H* hotel), while the probability of having 50 is $1 - q = 0.125$; similarly for the cases with more than three queries as shown by Table 6.3.

The expected utility is defined as the weighted average of the possible utilities by using probabilities as weights, $E(U) = \Sigma_i U_i q_i$, where q_i denotes the probability of having utility U_i, with $\Sigma_i q_i = 1$. In the simple case of Table 6.3, $E(U) = 100q_1 + 50(1 - q_1)$, where q_1 is the probability displayed under each assumption about the sample size and the expected utility is represented in the fourth column of the table. Finally, the marginal benefit of the search, $B'(k)$, is measured as

Table 6.3 Simultaneous quality search in the case of search goods

Number of queries	Prob. of finding only type-L hotels ($U = 50$)	Prob. of finding at least one type-H hotel ($U = 100$)	Expected utility $E(U)$	Marginal benefit $B'(k)$
1	0.5	0.5	75	–
2	0.25	0.75	87.5	12.5
3	0.13	0.87	93.75	6.25
4	0.06	0.94	96.88	3.13
...	...	...	...	...
∞	0	1	100	0

the increase in the expected utility due to a one unit increase in the number of queries; in particular, the marginal benefit $B'(k)$ of the i-th query can be calculated as the difference between the expected utility associated to k and to $(k - 1)$ surveys, $B'(k) = E(U_k) - E(U_{k-1})$. The last column of Table 6.3 clearly shows that the marginal benefit of the search is a decreasing function of the sample size, which is a general property which does not depend on the particular assumptions of this example.

In general terms, if we assume continuous distributions of the quality index and if we use M_k to label the best choice within a sample of k elements, the expected utility from a search of dimension k can be indicated as $\mathrm{E}[U(M_k)]$ so that the marginal benefit for the k-th attempt will correspond to the difference between the expected utility of the best outcome out of k and out of $k - 1$ surveys:

$$B'(k) = E[U(M_k)] - E[U(M_{k-1})]. \tag{6.15}$$

As regard the marginal cost of the search, $C'(k)$, it can be defined as a function of the number of queries and, consistently with Sect. 6.7.2, we assume a positive relationship (and an upward sloping curve). The optimum condition requires the marginal cost to be equal to (6.15):

$$B'(k) = E[U(M_k)] - E[U(M_{k-1})] = C'(k). \tag{6.16}$$

Expression (6.16) allows to calculate the optimal size k^* of the quality search. In light of these simple changes, all the conclusions of Sect. 6.7.2 about the price search remain true for the case of quality search, and will not be repeated. Substantial differences rather appear when the case of experience goods is analyzed, given that the quality assessment of a whole holiday can be slow, expensive, and often impossible to achieve prior to the holiday experience itself.

6.7.3.2 Quality Search Models in Case of Experience Goods

The process of gathering information on the quality of an experience good (as the holiday, which can be quality assessed after it has taken place) requires a partially different formulation for the optimal stopping rule. Indeed, if we think of the tourist who reserves the holiday in advance, from home, it is practically impossible to carry out a full quality search by respecting the two constraints that are identified in the hypothesis of search goods seen in the previous subsection. In fact, for an experience good: (a) the tourist cannot inspect the good before purchasing it; and (b) the inspection can be carried out only during the holiday, when the purchase has already taken place. For the holiday as a whole, and particularly for the tourist who books in advance, the *information can only be acquired through experience* and such condition requires the introduction of a new model for the tourist's behavior (Nelson 1970).[9]

Let us consider the case in which the tourist has already acquired the experience of $(k - 1)$ destinations or types of tourism (the past holiday experiences), and the problem of whether to undergo an additional k-th search (i.e., the tourist decides to experiment a new type of holiday or destination) or to confirm the best choice out of the $(k - 1)$ alternatives already experienced, M_{k-1}. Like in the case of search goods, the additional information that the tourist gathers through a new experience allows to increase own information set and, therefore, the formulation of the marginal benefit of the information remains that of expression (6.15).

The case of an experience good strongly differs from that of the search good in the marginal cost of information: in this situation, the cost of gathering information (which is always the act of consuming a new holiday) depends on the effect on the utility function. The marginal cost of the k-th experience is therefore measured by the loss of utility between the act of consumption of the best brand within an already selected sample of $(k - 1)$ elements, $U(k - 1)$, and the utility of having to consume the k-th randomly selected brand estimated by the mean of the utility distribution, U°:

$$C'(k) = E[U(M_{k-1}) - U^\circ]. \tag{6.17}$$

Expression (6.17) can be interpreted as follows: the cost of a new tourism experience consists of the difference between the utility of a "safe" holiday (in the sense of a holiday that has already been experimented) and the utility of a new tourism experience. More explicitly, it consists of the utility loss arising from the "risk of spoiling the holiday time" by undergoing a new tourism experience.

As before, the optimal dimension of the search must be referred to the condition that the benefit associated to the k-th experience has to be equal to its marginal cost. After replacing (6.17) into (6.16), we get

$$E[U(M_k)] - E[U(M_{k-1})] \geqslant E[U(M_{k-1}) - U^\circ]. \tag{6.18}$$

Since it is reasonable to expect that the marginal costs for search goods (6.16) are less than the marginal costs for experience goods (6.17), it is possible to conclude that:

> We predict a larger sample size for search than for experience [goods].
>
> (Nelson 1970, p. 317–8)

[9] In this case, the tourist may consider the price as an indicator of quality, so to prefer those purchases characterized by higher price; for such estimation procedure to be rational, the assumption of a positive correlation between quality and price of a product has to be introduced.

This general conclusion has important consequences as regards tourism: first, it is expected that the tourist who reserves from home is rationally less informed than the one already on site, at the destination; second, the average level of the tourist's utility is generally lower in case of an experience good; third, the variability in utility is also higher in case of an experience good.

Finally, in a world with incomplete information, there is a large variety of behaviors among tourists. First, there are tourists mainly dealing with search goods and others who mainly deal with experience goods; second, there are tourists booking from home and others purchasing when already at the destination; third, there are tourists who simultaneously search and others who search sequentially.

All these differences generate important effects on the strategies pursued by tourism firms and destinations in terms of price transparency, supply of information, or in terms of the quality offered as well as on the market structure. In fact, the information incompleteness justifies the development of services of mediation specialized in producing information, such as traditional agencies, tourist offices, and, more recently, social networking. We will discuss again these issues in Chaps. 10 and 11; what is left to analyze at this stage is an interesting effect that directly relates to the search process when dealing with an experience good: the informational cascade.

6.7.4 The Informational Cascade

In the previous sections, we have considered the search of information by single tourists who do not interact. Now it is time to study what happens when interactions in the behavioral pattern of tourists are introduced. One of the most interesting regularities about consumption (and tourism in particular) is that consumers with incomplete information tend to observe the consumption decisions of other people and often choose to imitate them. This hypothesis, often used in the economic literature to explain financial crises, bank runs, fashions, waves of panic, investment choices, or the adoption of a new technology (Banerjee 1992; Bikhchandani et al. 1992, 1998), is well suited for the investigation of tourism. As an example, let us think of the behavior of a tourist who arrives at the destination for the first time and must decide in which restaurant to have dinner. Often, this choice is made by observing whether or not a restaurant is crowded, a behavior that implicitly assumes that tourists who are observed to dine in the restaurant have better information. This implies that the imitation of other people's behavior may operate as a solution to the issue of incomplete information. Such behavior, technically called *herd behavior*, produces an *informational cascade* that relentlessly produces, for instance, the coexistence of empty and crowded restaurants side by side in the same area of a tourism destination.

The model of informational cascades, first applied to tourism by Figini and Vici (2012b), can be described as follows: let us assume to have N tourists who, in sequential order, must choose between two restaurants located on the seaside avenue of a destination. For simplicity, let us assume that both restaurants offer the same menu at the same price and that the tourists are unable to know in advance the quality of the supplied food. In particular, we assume that although tourists know that there is a restaurant H that offers high quality meals while the restaurant L offers low quality meals, it is impossible for them to identify which is the restaurant type.

The tourists can collect information about the quality of restaurants in two ways: (a) by using previously gathered information, as guidebooks or website reviews, which only has a probability $0.5 \leq q < 1$ to be correct;[10] (b) by observing what other tourists are choosing (that is, by inferring that they have taken their decision based on some *private information* of higher quality).

In the first place, the model determines the choice of the subject who chooses first. Given that the first tourist cannot observe any other agent, she must decide only on the basis of her own private signal. For simplicity, let us assume that such signal does not carry any informative content, that is, it has an equal probability ($q = 0.5$) of being either correct or incorrect. In practice, this corresponds to assuming a random choice (for example, by tossing a coin). Also, this implies that there is a 50 % chance for this tourist to decide that the first restaurant is of type-H and to end up having dinner there.

Let observe the second tourist who, unlike the first one, can both use own information and rely on observing the first tourist's behavior. The scenarios that may occur in front of the first restaurant are the following: (a) both the tourists own a signal that the restaurant is of quality H and both dine there; (b) both tourists own a signal that the restaurant is of quality L and do not enter (i.e., they enter the second restaurant); (c) the first tourist has entered the first restaurant, but the second tourist believes this is a restaurant of quality L. This means that the second tourist owns two contrasting signals that offset each other. In this last case, it is plausible to assume that the second tourist may decide to enter the restaurant (by giving greater importance to the first tourist's choice) with probability 50 %, or not to enter (by giving greater importance to the own signal) with probability 50 %.

If we assume that the information owned by the third tourist is identical to the first two, we can easily identify the following alternatives: (a) the fact that the first two tourists are both in the first restaurant will be considered an information of greater quality than any privately owned signal (in this case, the third tourist will confirm the choice of the first two); (b) the same can be said if the first two tourists are not eating in the first restaurant (also in this case the third tourist will confirm the choice by not entering the first restaurant); (c) in case the first two agents did not agree on the choice of the restaurant, the third tourist will make her decision based on her private signal (and in this case, the fourth tourist will face an identical set of scenarios as the third one); and so on.

In cases (a) and (b), indeed, an informational cascade has started, becoming unstoppable because the observation of other people's behavior carries greater informational value than any (imperfect) private signal. When the informational

[10] However, as we saw in the previous section, it may be quite difficult to assess and judge this information in the case of experience goods.

Table 6.4 The informational cascade

Rank of the tourist who chooses	Prob. of having an informational cascade	Prob. that the cascade is correct	Prob. of not having an informational cascade
1	–	–	–
2	0.75	0.38	0.25
3	0.88	0.44	0.12
4	0.94	0.47	0.06
...	...	...	...
∞	1	0.5	0

cascade is at work, an external observer may see a crowded restaurant alongside another one that remains inexorably empty. Table 6.4 clearly, built on the assumptions of this example, shows that a very limited number of individuals are needed to generate an informational cascade.

The fundamental problem of an informational cascade is that it is not efficient, neither for the tourists nor for the firms. As regards the tourists, the fact that either restaurant can be crowded is independent on whether or not they are the restaurant of type H: in fact, since the informational cascade starts from a signal that has no informative content, there is only 50 % of probability that the informational cascade is correct, that is, the crowded restaurant is really the one of high quality (Table 6.4, third column). This critical inefficiency arises from the fact that the cascade only depends on the choices made (and on the signals owned) by the first few agents; in other words, the great majority of information owned by the tourists is not used. Indeed, if tourists were aware of the existence of the effect played by the informational cascade, they should rationally choose to eat at the empty restaurant. However, experience teaches us that this is a very difficult decision to take!

The occurrence of informational cascades is a problem also for firms. In particular, (a) it makes profit more less predictable, and the management more difficult (an informational cascade is fragile and can unexpectedly change: an empty night for a restaurant can, with the same probability, become a booked out night on the next day if new tourists, with no previous information, arrive at the destination); (b) when a firm suffers from a negative cascade, there is no remedy against it: even the release of public information in support of the quality may not have the strengths to modify it (firms are advised to act in advance so as to facilitate the development of a positive cascade: this is one of the reasons why the "happy hour" is an extremely effective strategy in this sense);[11] (c) finally, for sufficiently general specifications of the model, firms may rationally decide not to invest in increasing the quality of their product: in fact, the equilibrium determined by an informational cascade is often a pooling equilibrium (see Sect. 10.4.2),

[11] The happy hour is the commercial practice of bars and restaurants to offer discounts in particular times of the day (usually before the evening/night peak time).

in which no firm has any interest to invest in quality due to the higher volatility of the profits (Figini and Vici 2012b).

Chapter Overview

- Time is an essential variable affecting the tourist's choice process Analytically, two cases have to be distinguished: the tourist can freely decide the length of the holiday (which depends on the wealth and the substitution effects); or the length of the holiday is exogenously set by the law or by collective bargaining, as the length of the annual leave.
- An alternative approach to the investigation of the tourist's choice is due to Lancaster, and focuses on the demand for the intrinsic characteristics of the holiday. The tourist exhibits preferences for the characteristics and not for the types of tourism.
- The endogenous preferences approach studies the process of formation and change of preferences by taking into consideration a two-direction relationship between preferences and economic decisions.
- Some interdisciplinary models shed light on the sociological and psychological motivations of tourist's choice (psyco-allocentrism, education, ethnical group, and age), thus allowing to explain phenomena such as the crowding effect, the snob effect, and the Veblen effect.
- Relative to the standard model, the existence of incomplete information affects the tourist's behavior, and it is in the tourist's interest to invest resources to collect new information.
- The search for information can be simultaneous (if the tourist gathers all the information before deciding to purchase) or sequential (if the tourist considers one product at a time and decides whether to buy it or to continue the search).
- We call search goods those goods which quality can be assessed by the consumer before the purchase; we define as experience goods those goods which quality can be observed only after purchasing and using them.
- The informational cascades are phenomena where tourists consider other tourists' behavior as the relevant information driving their own choice. The informational cascades are inefficient both for tourists and for tourism firms.

Chapter 7
Production in Tourism

Learning Outcomes
On the completion of this chapter you will:

- Understand the reasons why tourism firms exist and how they can be identified and classified.
- Discuss two relevant issues related to tourism production: the seasonality of demand and the role of technology.

7.1 Introduction

With this chapter we begin to study the supply side of the tourism sector, by focusing on the economic rationale of firms supplying goods and services that are included in the matrix of the tourism product (see Sect. 2.5). By recalling that tourism can be classified and defined according to the dimensions of plurality and heterogeneity, also tourism firms are many and diverse: they range from travel agencies to tour operators, from hotels to campgrounds, from transport companies to amusement parks, to museums, etc.

The way in which the tourism sector is organized results from economic decisions regarding the production structure and its evolution over time. In fact all economic sectors, including tourism, develop around two extreme cases of organization of production: the *market*, that is, through external relationships between independent firms; the *firm*, that is, through the development of an internal organization carrying out the different tasks of production. These topics will be discussed in detail in Sects. 7.3 and 7.4.

Prior to examining the economic rationale of the different types of tourism firms (which will be done in Chaps. 8 and 9), in the present chapter some general issues related to production in tourism are introduced and discussed. Firstly, an accurate and more formal definition of tourism product, which qualifies not only in terms of technical and commodity characteristics, but also in the terms of the location, the

G. Candela and P. Figini, *The Economics of Tourism Destinations*,
Springer Texts in Business and Economics, DOI 10.1007/978-3-642-20874-4_7,

time, and the state of nature in which the product becomes available, will be presented (see Sect. 7.2). In doing so, we will then be able to distinguish among spot, future, and contingent markets. Another important classification of tourism goods and services presented in Sect. 7.2 is related with quality and, particularly, with the distinction between those goods and services for which quality can be tested before the act of purchasing (search goods) and those for which quality can be assessed only after the consumption (experience goods).

Section 7.5 presents the issue of seasonality, one of the most important characteristics of tourism activity, and which has important implication for the organization of tourism production. It is important to remark that, although seasonality is presented in this chapter with particular reference to the case of a tourism structure, its economic consequences are general and can be extended to most of tourism activities and destinations. Finally, Sect. 7.6 is devoted to shed light on the relationship between tourism and technology.

7.2 The Taxonomy of Tourism Production

Let us recall again Sect. 2.5 to highlight that the tourism product is composed by heterogeneous goods and services demanded by a plurality of tourism types. Nevertheless, the taxonomy of n goods demanded by m types of tourists is not sufficient to achieve a complete classification of all the goods and services that are of interest in the study of Tourism Economics. To this aim, the concept of *complete system of goods* is often used in Economics, where goods and services are described and classified according to the following dimensions:

(a) The physical description
(b) The location where the good becomes available to the consumer
(c) The time when the good becomes available to the consumer
(d) The State of Nature (that is, the contingent condition) in which the good becomes available to the consumer.

The State of Nature (sometimes called "state of the world") is the specific combination of values that the exogenous variables can take when the good or service is consumed. The set S of all the states of nature has the following characteristics: (a) it is *finite* in number; (b) it is *complete*, that is, it includes all the possible states of the world that can occur at the time when the holiday is spent; (c) it only has *mutually exclusive items*, that is, the occurrence of one state of nature implies the non-occurrence of the remaining states; (d) the states are not subject to the tourist's control. Among the variables composing the state of nature, both environmental variables (like rainy or sunny days or the beach and seawater quality) and health-related variables (like the flu or the "Montezuma's revenge," the typical traveler diarrhea) are included.

This characterization leads to a non-physical definition of the product, so that its primary distinction (the physical characteristics) ought to be complemented and completed with additional information regarding its availability. To better explain this, let us consider the case of an umbrella. On the one hand, this good has a well-defined physical characterization, which no producer can deviate from (with the exception, say, of color and size). On the other hand, we all know that on a rainy day, an "umbrella left at home" is quite different from an "umbrella brought with us." Therefore, a technically identical object becomes an economically different good according to the location where it stands. Also, an "umbrella available today" is a different item from an "umbrella available tomorrow": also the different time of delivery of the umbrella would determine a different economic value for this item.

Finally, an umbrella becomes a different economic good according to the contingent situation of whether it rains or not (the state of nature), thus affecting its economic value. Note for example how umbrellas are more frequently exposed in shops during rainy days, which is when they are more likely to be sold, at a higher price. An umbrella is therefore a unique commodity which has different utility and different economic value according to its location, the time of availability, as well as the state of nature. Therefore, the economic concept of good or service goes well beyond the simple idea of a physically well-defined commodity.

Such economic characterization of goods and services is key when dealing with the tourism product. We already know that the overall number of tourists must be distinguished according to the type of tourism and the destination; however such distinction is not enough to economically describe the holiday that is different (and has different value and utility for the tourist) according to the period of time and to the state of nature in which it is consumed. For example, the price of accommodation greatly differs between high and low season; similarly, the tourist's satisfaction accruing from the holiday heavily depends on the realization of the state of nature.

Taking into consideration these further dimensions exponentially increases the number of "available products," and this can be described by the notion of *complete system of goods and services*, where each good or service j that enters the tourism basket i, x_{ij}, is also identified by the destination r offering the good, the time t of consumption, and the state of nature s attached to the act of consumption: x_{ij}^{rts}. In the complete system of goods and services we would therefore have a total number of goods equal to $(N \times R \times T \times S)$, where N is the number of "physical" goods, R is the number of destinations, T the periods of time when a product can be consumed, and S the states of the world that could occur. Note however that, although the number of tourism goods and services increases significantly, such specification has no impact on the substance of the problem from an economic point of view.

This specification, on the other hand, allows us to classify the markets on the basis of the type of availability of the goods and service traded. We can distinguish:

(a) *Spot markets*, markets where goods are traded and delivered at the same time;
(b) *Forward markets*, markets where goods are traded now but delivered to future dates;
(c) *Contingency markets*, markets where the value of traded goods depend on the state of nature occurring at the time of consumption.

In Economics of Tourism, forward markets take into account the issue of intertemporal choice and are very common. These markets exist each time a tourist makes a reservation for a future date or a tour operator signs a contract for services that will be delivered in other seasons. Differently the contingency markets take into account the issue of choice under uncertainty and the insurance against risk. These markets exist each time a tourist has the possibility to cancel a reservation without paying the full price or a tour operator insures itself with allotment contracts (see Sect. 8.2.1) against a level of demand lower than expected. Such topics will be fully developed in Chap. 11.

A different taxonomy of the tourism product focuses on the issue of quality in the tourist's choice. To classify tourism according to quality raises a twofold problem:

1. On the one hand, consumers generally have limited information about the quality of the products. By recalling the distinction discussed in Sect. 6.7.3, we can define search goods those goods which quality can be assessed before the act of purchasing them, while with the term experience goods we define those goods which quality can be assessed only after the act of consumption or, with respect to tourism, after the holiday experience.
2. On the other hand, it is necessary to precisely define the concept of quality when applied to a composite good like the tourism product. It seems appropriate to qualify the holiday as a whole as an experience good since, generally, a tourist can assess its quality just at the end of the experience. Nevertheless, in the tourism product there are goods and services that can be referred to as search goods, such as the hotel accommodation for a tourist who repeats the visit in the destination or most shopping activities.

7.3 Market Relationships Versus the Organization of Firms

We now turn to investigate the organization of firms and their relationships of interdependence within the sector and on the market, in order to understand how and why the different tourism goods and services are produced, sold, and consumed. Every economic system presents crucial organizational issues, since they affect the way in which final goods and services are produced. The problems are so important that, according to Simon (1991), modern economic systems should be interpreted as organizational rather than market systems.

Using as an example the car industry, the issue under investigation pivots around the following questions: should a car producer manufacture the engine, the battery, the cockpit, etc. or should these components be supplied by other companies and then bought and assembled by the car producer? Again, should the car producer set up an internal IT department to manage the company's information system, or should consult an external specialized IT company? In other words, should the car producer rely on in-house production or outsourcing its activities?

Moving to an example related to the tourism sector, should a tour operator be also the owner of the hotels, the restaurants, the carriers, the booking center, etc.

used by tourists or should the tour operator leave these services to other independent companies from which it buys the services? Should the tour operator use the services of professionally trained staff or should it rely on market relationship with independent consultants and external firms? Again, the tour operator has to choose between in-house and outsourcing the production of a package holiday.

To provide a comprehensive and complete answer to these questions, we first have to recall that, in a market economy, the organization of production ranges between two alternative systems of production:

1. The *market*, which consists of a set of decentralized relationships between independent economic agents governed by an information mechanism called price;
2. The *authority*, which consists of transferring the "right of choice" on some decision sets from one economic agent to another, as it happens in firms. In other words, one agent confers to another the right of choosing what action to undertake on its own behalf.

The choice between the two alternative systems mainly depends on a benefit–cost analysis. Both cases build upon the existence of contracts, which are legally binding (written or oral) agreements with mutual obligations for the parties involved. Although contracts are discussed in Chap. 11, let us now focus on the economic convenience on whether to choose, in producing tourism services, market contracts rather than authority contracts. In doing so, we will also identify the reasons leading to the creation of what can be called tourism firm, that is, a firm that is organized to produce holidays and/or goods and services included in the matrix of the tourism product.

In a market economy, the firm should be intended as an organized and hierarchical structure of resources (usually classified as either capital or labor) pursuing the goal of yielding profits by producing and selling goods and services. The economic literature provides several possible explanations for the birth of a firm. The first explanation[1] is due to Adam Smith (1776), who identifies in the division of labor the reason for its existence; in fact, the enterprise is created in order to allow several workers to operate in a coordinated manner under the same roof and the same management, as it is explained in the famous example of the pin factory:

> One man draws out the wire, another straights it, a third cuts it, a fourth points it, a fifth grinds it at the top for receiving, the head; to make the head requires two or three distinct operations; to put it on is a peculiar business, to whiten the pins is another; it is even a trade by itself to put them into the paper; and the important business of making a pin is, in this manner, divided into about eighteen distinct operations, which, in some factories, are all performed by distinct hands, though in others the same man will sometimes perform two or three of them.
>
> (A. Smith 1776, Book I, Chap. 1)

[1] In addition to those listed in this section, we also recall the "New-Marxist" interpretation, which argues that a firm exists to pursue the objective of capturing surplus value by exploiting workers through a hierarchical structure, as well as the "New-Hobbesian" interpretation, which claims that a firm is created in order to compensate and control for the human tendency "to do evil."

Fig. 7.1 The firm as a *black box*

Adam Smith's argument, which focuses on the production of goods and services, has been subsequently generalized in technological and organizational terms. In this perspective, the firm is an institution within which the production factors are purchased and the production process is made by selecting, using, and organizing the available production techniques, with the aim of profit maximization. In short, the firm is similar to a "black box" in which the factors of production are the input and the final product is the output (Fig. 7.1).

Given the minor importance of technology in the tourism's black box, let us focus on its organizational elements: the creation of the final output (such as the package holiday for the tour operator) by combining overnight stays, meals, and other services is not exactly the same as producing a car by assembling its components in an assembly line. Indeed, in the case of tourism a useful interpretation is to consider the firm as a set of contracts, as a way of supporting the idea of tourism as an anticommon.[2] The approach used to tackle this phenomenon is provided by the Theory of Organizations, a field of Economics that studies the birth, the operation, and the efficiency of the organizations (Milgrom and Roberts 1992).

In the more general model, the creation of the firm is justified by the *transaction costs*, that is, the costs of stipulation, execution, and control of contracts (Coase 1937). According to this approach, when maintaining a market relationship with other independent firms is either too expensive or too complicated, i.e., it is too difficult to define a complete contract,[3] a firm gets created as a team production to overcome such informational problems (Alchian and Demsetz 1972). In these circumstances, the authority solution outperforms the market solution and the agent formerly being a supplier is hired by the newly born firm, becoming a dependent worker. The relationship between the employer and the employee is regulated by an incomplete contract, since it does not specify what the employee has to do but leaves in the hands of the employer the right of deciding the tasks and performances of the employee in each particular circumstance.

We illustrate this problem with a simple example. Let us assume an individual who wants to produce and sell package holidays. In order to fulfill such aim, the agent requires the contribution of many other agents (hotels, restaurants, promoters,

---

[2] Recalling Sect. 4.3.1, the holiday can be considered as a "permission" to stay granted by each firm offering the goods and services needed in order to stay overnight in the destination. We already demonstrated that a coordination activity can be successfully used to solve the failure in the supply of services when it involves too many property rights in the destination.

[3] We refer to Sect. 11.1 for a definition of complete and incomplete contracts.

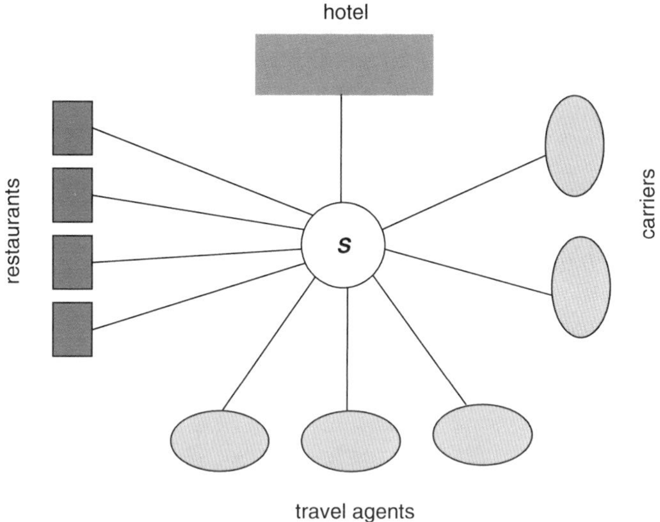

Fig. 7.2 Production as a network of contracts

etc.) which relationships are regulated by contracts. The holiday's producer can use three alternative types of contract to reach the goal of producing a tourism product:

1. *To rely on market relationships*. For this alternative, an office, a telephone, and a computer will suffice, since the subject will contact hotel and restaurant managers, travel agents, and eventually stipulate specific contracts with them. This option is shown in Fig. 7.2, where any person *S* endowed with necessary skills can perfectly undertake an activity of tourism production by completely relying on market relationships, that is, by agreeing precise performances with various providers and by paying them what is established in the contracts. From a commercial practice standpoint, the option for the market requires a number of complex, yet feasible, operations: (a) the identification of all the agents with whom to build relationships; (b) the appraisal of their professional skills; (c) the definition and the stipulation of a contract with each of them. Other difficulties may arise. For example, once the contract has been executed, it is necessary to check if the quantity and the quality of the performance corresponds to what was established, if the timing of the execution has been respected and, in case a performance does not meet the standards of the contract, it is important to verify whether this is due to a fault of the contractors or to external unrelated events.
2. *The production as a team project*. For a system of market contracts to be interpreted as a team project, the functions of coordination and control must be carried out by *S*; such a key role is necessary since the output is obtained through the combined contribution (sometimes subsequent and sometimes simultaneous) of several agents. In this particular circumstance, the only result

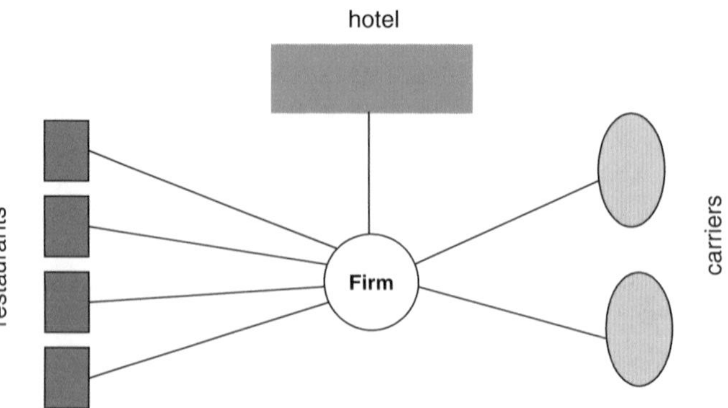

Fig. 7.3 Production as a hierarchic organization

that really matters is the aggregate output, while the individual contribution may not be directly observable, rising principal–agent problems (see Sect. 11.6). In such cases, the remuneration can only be based on aggregate performance and, in practice, such incentive scheme works pretty poorly. When this happens, a member of the team contributes to increase the aggregate value of production, but the benefits will be shared equally with all the other members. The issue of not being able to closely observe the activities of the other subjects implies that one of the agents, that can only be *S* in Fig. 7.2, arises as a team leader, thus being able to check individual performances and to allocate incentives accordingly. *S* will then have the right of gaining the residual revenue accruing from the coordination activity (as demonstrated in Sect. 4.3.1). The interpretation of the firm as a team project can explain its role as a centralized contractual structure, although the main limit is to explain it only as the tool to overcome opportunistic behaviors. Hence, this can mainly apply for small-size tourism firms engaged in the production of simple trips, while for large-size firms a more general vision is needed.

3. *The firm as a hierarchic organization.* In our example, the producer may as well decide to hire, through job contracts, the agents whose contribution is needed for the production of the tourism product (for example, the newly born firm can hire travel agents). Once these agents are hired by the firm as employees, they carry out their tasks under the employer supervision. With this solution, the number of market relationships diminishes. This arrangement is depicted in Fig. 7.3 where, with respect to Fig. 7.2, the promotion and distribution agents have been internalized and a firm for the production of holidays has been introduced. However, the same rationale can be used as regards to hotels and restaurants, eventually bringing, in the extreme case, all the relationships within the firm. In order for the firm to be an efficient solution to the production process, it is necessary that the supervision, the organization, and the coordination costs under the firm's authority be less than the transaction costs associated to the contracts stipulated through the market mechanism. This production option based on the firm implies a number of complex decisions to be taken: (a) the

firm must assume a hierarchical organization in which tasks and responsibilities are clearly defined and assigned; (b) the firm has to clearly identify the decision process to activate in unexpected conditions; (c) the firm bears the risk of production, given that the employees' wage is usually independent from the firm's revenue (except the case of incentive contracts) and the profit is residual; (d) the firm has to control the employees' activity since their income is (totally or partially) independent from their effort.

In order to identify the most convenient solution between the market and the firm, and among the different types of firm, the key issue is how to take into account both the *production costs* and the nature and the amount of the *transaction costs*. The production costs are the costs of producing a holiday, and thus include all payments derived from each existing contract (see Tremblay 1998; Wolf 2004; Lamminmaki 2007). The transaction costs are defined according to the nature of the transaction and therefore can be classified as:

(a) Ex ante transaction costs, which are the costs the agent faces when defining the features (the clauses) of the contract;
(b) Ex post transaction costs, which are the costs the agent faces after having defined the contract and during the time of its execution.

Clearly, firms arise when their costs are less than the respective costs borne through market relationships since the minimization of total costs yields, given the same revenue, the maximization of profits. In addition to justify the birth of a firm, the model of transaction costs also provides an explanation for the firm's size (and of its growth or internationalization, see Sect. 14.2). Indeed, production and transaction costs vary according to the size of the organization and the size of the market.

After having classified the transaction costs, the next step is to identify the reasons why these costs arise. We recall six causes:

1. *Information asymmetry*. The parties involved in a contract have different information sets (for an analysis of information asymmetry in air transport, see Papatheodorou and Platis 2007). The seller commonly has more complete and precise information than the buyer about the characteristics and the quality of the good being sold. For example, the restaurant owner knows exactly the quality of the ingredients used to prepare the food, while customers do not. This applies in labor relationships too: for instance, a promoter perfectly knows own professional skills and the effort put in own activity, while the tour operator does not.
2. *The specificity of the transaction*. A transaction is called "specific" when its value is higher inside than outside the relationship. For example, if a marketing and communication company develops a brand or a logo for a tourism destination (probably recalling its main attractions and features), this investment is practically worthless outside the relationship with the destination: the same logo cannot be sold to other destinations. In other words, once the investment has been carried out, the corresponding costs cannot be recovered outside the specific relationship (see Sect. 11.7.1).

3. *The duration and the frequency of the transactions.* Some transactions, like the purchase of a single charter flight, are one-off; instead, other transactions are frequently repeated and engage the same parties at regular time intervals (for example, when dealing with the weekly shipment of tourists to and from the destination). It is straightforward to think that different types of contracts would be used in the two cases.
4. *The uncertainty and the complexity of the transactions.* As we have seen in Sect. 7.2, the holiday is not a standard product but its value depends on the time of delivery, the destination, and the state of nature it may occur. This great extent of uncertainty makes the outcome of tourism contracts as more imprecise than those involving, for example, a car's sale. For example, the quantity of "skiing weeks" sold in a mountain destination strongly depends on the weather conditions, which are hardly predictable and controllable (however, see Sect. 7.6).
5. *The difficulty of measuring the performance.* When the quality of the agents' performances is difficult to assess, it becomes difficult to design an efficient mechanism of incentives for their actions.[4] Therefore, the firm may take over in order to reduce the costs of controlling their activity. For example, if the tour operator observes low sales for a particular destination, it cannot understand with certainty if this is due to a low effort in the promoter sale activity or to a low appealing of the destination itself.
6. *The network of transactions.* Although some transactions are essentially independent from each others, many others are strongly interdependent and require relevant coordination costs that are minimized if they are kept "under the same roof." For example, the success of a package holiday depends on the network of contracts with all the suppliers of services that, as pieces of a jigsaw puzzle, have to be perfectly put in place for the holiday to be successful.

To conclude this discussion, assuming that the production costs are the same under the firm and the market solution, transaction costs may change in response to the nature of the transaction and to the way in which it is organized: therefore, the rule of economic efficiency suggests the adoption of the organizational model that best operates toward the minimization of costs which, in turn, prefers the solution that reduces the transaction costs (for a more in deep analysis, see Tremblay 1998 and Wolf 2004).

7.4 Production and Sale of the Holiday

The production chain of the holiday is composed by various firms that operate to make the whole tourism product and the individual services available to final consumers, the tourists. In order to tackle the organizational issues underlined in

[4] See Sect. 11.6 for a more in-depth discussion of this issue, with reference to the relationship between tour operators and tourism firms.

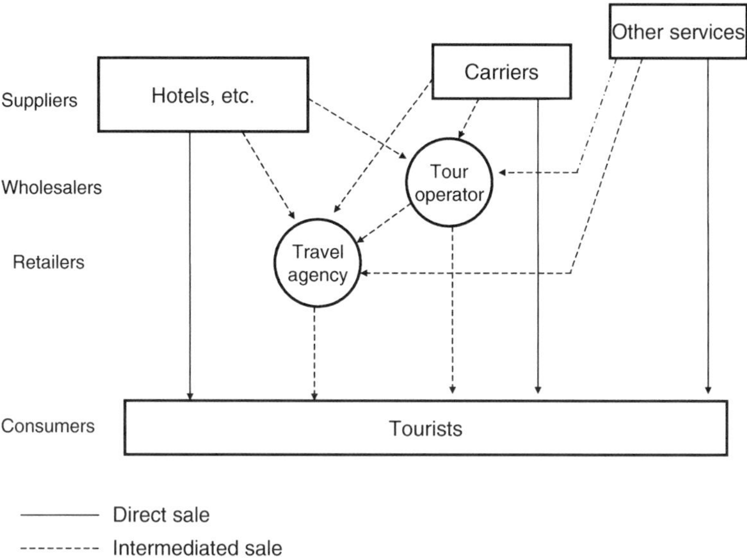

Fig. 7.4 Production and distribution of tourism services

Sect. 7.3, the commercial practice and the development path of the tourism sector have lead to a situation in which there are: (i) *tour operators*, firms specialized in the production and sale of the whole tourism product, the package holiday; (ii) *travel agencies*, firms aimed at the promotion and distribution of package holidays and at the sale of individual or assembled tourism services; (iii) suppliers of single services (hotels, attractions, carriers) that can both sell to travel agencies and tour operators and also sell directly to the tourists, thus giving birth to a complex and diversified organization of the sector, as depicted in Fig. 7.4.

In Fig. 7.4, the key role of travel agents (among which online travel agencies, web portals, and meta search engines are to be included, see Sect. 8.3.3), whose main activity is to link producers and final consumers, is explicit. In extreme synthesis it can be observed that in the organizational model of the tourism sector, the tour operators are situated at the *wholesale* level, while the travel agencies are situated at the *retail* level. However, as Fig. 7.4 clearly displays, these firms can operate either in combined or independent manner, so that the sale of the tourism product can follow various channels:

- Suppliers → tourist
- Suppliers → travel agency → tourist;
- Suppliers → tour operator → tourist;
- Suppliers → tour operator → travel agency → tourist.

In the market for holidays, even if all the other channels are effectively operating, the main distribution channel involves the tour operator and the travel agency. Indeed, tour operators sometimes directly sell to tourists and, similarly, travel agencies often engage in the production of "on demand" holidays by setting up a direct relationship with the suppliers. Finally, the distribution path from the supplier to the client is a frequently used channel, particularly with the development of ICT (see Chap. 12): we ought to recall that this is the path followed by the self-producing tourist (see Sect. 5.5).

> The principal role of intermediaries is to bring buyers and sellers together, either to create markets where they previously did not exist or to make existing markets work more efficiently and thereby expand market size. For travel and tourism, intermediation comes about through tour operators or wholesalers assembling the components of the tourist trip into a package and retailing the latter through travel agents, who deal directly with the public. However, [...] this is not the only way by which the tourist product reaches the customer.
>
> (Cooper et al. 1998, p. 247)

The existence of intermediaries in the tourism market generates benefits for firms, tourists, and destinations. Tour operators are in the position of reducing the costs of promotion by focusing on their relationships with intermediaries rather than on the direct promotion of their package holidays to tourists.

Tourists benefit from the presence of an intermediary because they can buy an all-inclusive holiday, by reducing the search costs in terms of time and money (see Sect. 6.7); in addition, they take advantage of the travel agent's professional know how.

Destinations can draw a remarkable benefit from the promotion activity implemented by international tour operators and travel agencies. However, the tour operators' goal of profit maximization is not often compatible with the goals of the destinations (see Sect. 4.3.1).

Prior to widely discuss the activity, the cost structure, and the price strategy of the producers and the retailers of holidays, it is relevant to introduce an important phenomenon attached to tourism: the seasonality of tourism demand and the economic consequences for tourism firms. The focus on seasonality will allow to focus on some general issues which apply to almost all tourism firms and destinations.

7.5 Seasonality in Tourism

Tourism is a seasonal activity, both because many types of tourism depend on the climatic conditions of the destination (e.g., the Mediterranean resorts can host sea and sun tourism only in the summer months), and because tourism mainly depends on people's free and leisure time, which is linked to the school calendar and to the availability of paid holidays at the workplace. In Economics, the concept of seasonality is defined as follows:

> Seasonality is the systematic, although not necessarily regular, intra-year movement [of a variable].
>
> (Hylleberg 1992, p. 4)

In the Economics of Tourism, the definition of seasonality closely follows: it is *the systematic variation, although not necessarily regular, in the number of overnight stays and arrivals throughout the year*, with important effects on the tourism firms (tour operators, travel agencies, hotels, carriers, and attractions) and other subjects (primarily, the destinations) that are involved in the tourism system (Butler 1994 and 2001; Candela and Castellani 2008). The seasonality, however, is not a strictly tourism phenomenon; just to give an example, the production of typical Christmas food (such as *panettone* in Northern Italy or *turrón* in Spain) faces a strong seasonal demand. Since these products have to be sold in a very short span of time, there are a number of technological and organizational issues for the Agriculture and Food sector that have to be tackled.

The seasonality of tourism flows has obvious implications for all the firms that deal with tourists: tour operators produce and sell the holidays off-season; travel agencies are forced to work overtime in preparation for, and during the holiday season; many hotels adapt to the seasonality by shutting down their business off-season; transport services follow the seasons by adapting their supply to the variable number of passengers throughout the year (e.g., less runs per day or eliminating routes off-season).

Indeed, the economic analysis of seasonality must address the following questions: how do we measure seasonality? What are the patterns and the typical profiles of seasonality? Which are the economic problems linked to seasonality? In the following subsections, we will provide some preliminary answers to such issues.

7.5.1 The Identification of Seasonality

The identification of the seasonality component of tourism flows can be done by analyzing the time series of the overnight stays, usually referred to a given destination (town, region, or nation), a typology of tourism, or both. According to the aim of the investigation, monthly, weekly, or daily data can be gathered and used.

The topic of seasonality is hence strongly related to statistical techniques adopted for time series analysis. While we refer to more specific textbooks for a proper study (e.g., see Greene 2003; Griffiths et al. 2000), in what follows we provide a descriptive outline of the various components in which tourism variables such as overnight stays or arrivals at time t, $N(t)$, can be ideally decomposed:[5]

$$N(t) = f(T, C, E, S, H, IR, U), \tag{7.1}$$

where the symbols in parentheses, respectively, denote:

- *Trend* (T): these are the systematic long-term variations in the number of stays, usually monotonic (increasing or decreasing), and imputable to general

[5] There are different statistical techniques that can be used to analyze seasonality, and the approach we follow is the "mainstream" model. However, other more sophisticated methods can be used, see for example Bar-On, 1989 and the special issue (n.1, 2007) of *Economia dei Servizi*.

phenomena such as the increase in population, the economic development, the phase of the destination's life cycle (see Sect. 4.5.1), the change in tastes, etc.

- *Cycle* (*C*): these are the short-term cyclical fluctuations in the number of stays that are determined by variations in the macroeconomic environment (such as cyclical fluctuation of income and employment, changes in inflation, exchange rates variation, etc.).
- *Periodic Events* (*E*): these are cyclical variations in the number of stays that are uncorrelated with economic indicators but can be explained by the occurrence of sport (like the Olympic Games), artistic (like the Cannes Film Festival or the Expo), and religious (like the Jubilee) events. Some of these events are related to the same destination (like the Cannes Film Festival) while some others move across destinations (like the Olympic Games).
- *Seasonality* (*S*): these are cyclical variations in the number of stays that occur every year, with statistically similar timing and intensity.
- *Holidays* (*H*): these are punctual fluctuations in the number of stays that are imputable to fixed holidays (like Christmas) or moving holidays (like Easter) as well as to "long weekends" or "bank holidays."
- *Irregular components* (*IR*): these are variations in the number of stays due to unpredictable events (like strikes, terrorist attacks, natural disasters, the lack of snow in a ski resort, etc.).
- *Residuals* (*U*): these are variations in the number of stays that cannot be explained by any of the previous factors: this is technically called "noise."

In case of daily time series it would be necessary to introduce an additional component: the *daily variation* (*D*), capturing the change of overnight stays during different days of the week as a consequence, for example, of business trips during the week and leisure and cultural trips over the weekend.

In what follows, assuming that is statistically feasible to do it, we isolate and study the seasonality component *S* only.

7.5.2 The Profiles, the Indices, and the Causes of Seasonality

It is possible to identify four main patterns of seasonality, which are presented in Fig. 7.5 by using hypothetical time series of overnight stays, normalized between 1 and 10, against the months of the year, which are conventionally indicated from 1 (January) to 12 (December): the discontinuous line that connects the vertical axis to the first month reminds us of the fact that December of a given year is in continuity with January of the following year.

Figure 7.5a displays the typical seasonal profile of a destination with only one peak season (the summer) characterized by high intensity of tourism, with an absolute peak in the number of stays in August (this is typically the case of a beach-oriented destination, e.g., coastal Northern Italy or Costa Brava in Spain). Figure 7.5b displays the typical seasonal profile of a destination that adds to the

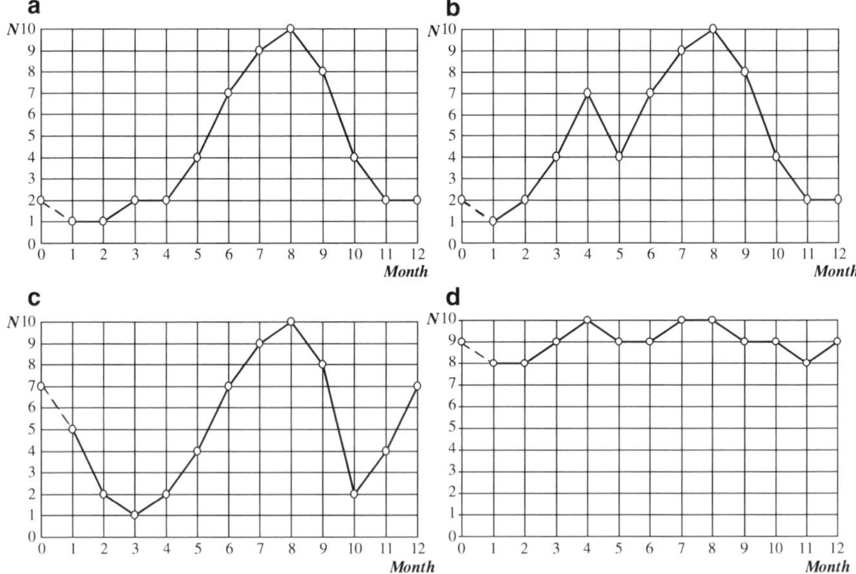

Fig. 7.5 The profiles of seasonality

peak season also a shoulder season (a minor peak that falls between the high season and low season and offers fares and rates between those of the other seasons), the Easter break in this case (this may be the case of a beach-oriented destination in Southern Italy or in Costa del Sol, Southern Spain). Figure 7.5c represents the typical seasonal profile of a destination that has a double season (the summer and the winter) with peaks in August and around Christmas and New Year's Eve holidays; the "dead" periods are limited to the months of May and October (this is typically the case of mountain resorts, like the destinations in the Alps). Finally, Fig. 7.5d represents the typical profile of a destination with no seasonality, such as the great majority of art cities and cultural destinations (cities like Florence or Paris). Indeed, there are some fluctuations in this last case too, but with much lower intensity than the other three patterns. Examples of such profiles built using real-world data are reported in Case Study 7.1 and in Case Study 7.2.

It is important to observe that *different destinations and different types of tourism are characterized by different seasonality*: ski tourism is mainly monoseasonal while mountain tourism is certainly bi-seasonal; cultural tourism does not present patterns of seasonality while wellness and spa tourism usually takes place during the middle seasons; business tourism tends to be at its lowest during summer holidays and other festivities. The diversity between the seasonal profiles of various types of tourism—as we will see in what follows—creates an interesting opportunity for destinations to target specific segments of tourism in order to increase tourism flows during low-peak seasons.

Moreover, we also observe that tourism is characterized by phenomena that might be called "micro-seasonality," that is, cyclical fluctuations across very short periods of

Case Study 7.1. Four Destinations with Different Seasonality Profiles

The monoseasonality is a typical characteristic for those beach-oriented destinations that developed during the mass-tourism phase after the second world war. Regardless of the extensive investments aimed at stretching the length of its tourism season (see Case Study 4.2) the Italian province of Rimini is still characterized by strong seasonality (Fig. 7.A), with the majority of tourists hosted during the summer season. The highest peak in the number of stays is reached during the month of August but in all the summer months, from June to September, the number of stays is more than one million. This number usually fades during the rest of the year and reaches its trough during the December–February period. If we compare the data of 2000 with those of 2008, a marginal reduction in seasonality appears, as the three indices reported at the bottom of Fig. 7.A show. As a general trend, the number of stays during the summer season seems to decrease in favor of a slightly higher number of stays during the rest of the year.

A profile of monoseasonality with a shoulder season is reported in the Italian town of Caserta, when Italian tourists hosted in hotel structures are isolated from the rest of the tourists. Such series, reported in Fig. 7.B for year 2001, displays a peak during the months of July and August, and then a

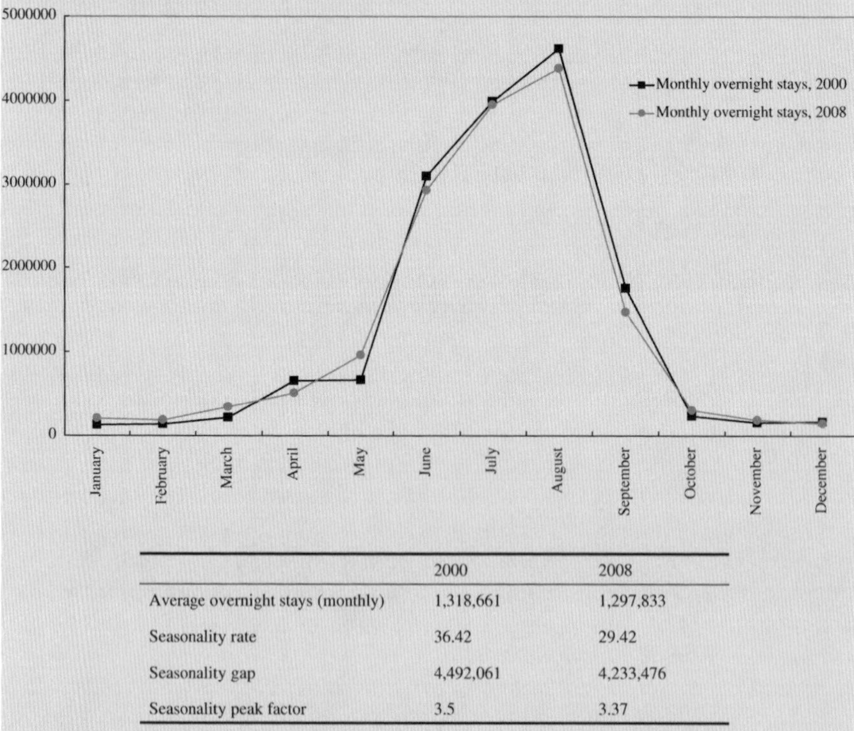

	2000	2008
Average overnight stays (monthly)	1,318,661	1,297,833
Seasonality rate	36.42	29.42
Seasonality gap	4,492,061	4,233,476
Seasonality peak factor	3.5	3.37

Fig. 7.A Profiles and indices of seasonality of the Italian province of Rimini (2000 and 2008)

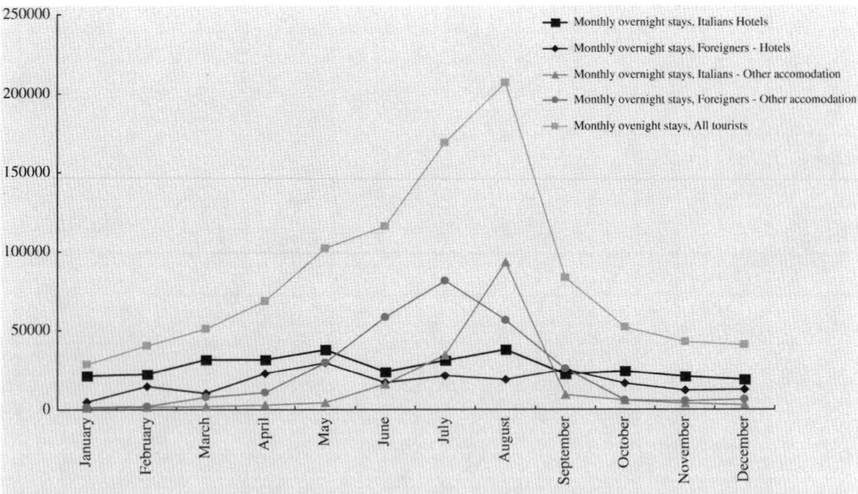

	Monthly overnight stays, Italians-Hotels	Monthly overnight stays, Foreigners–Hotels	Monthly overnight stays, Italians-Other accomodation	Monthly overnight stays, Foreigners-Other accomodation	Monthly overnight stays, All tourists
Average overnight stays (monthly)	27,156	17,233	14,795	24,297	83,481
Seasonality rate	1.97	6.36	117.2	51.55	7.19
Seasonality gap	18,653	25,233	92,376	79,813	177,845
Seasonality peak factor	1.39	1.74	6.3	3.35	2.47

Fig. 7.B Profiles and indices of seasonality of the Italian province of Caserta (2001)

second peak (of a slighter smaller size) during the spring months from March to May; if we add to this component the number of overnight stays at hotels by foreigners (which are typically important during the spring season), the spring peak becomes even more important than the summer peak. Therefore, the profile of the town of Caserta is a good example of how different types of tourism show different seasonal profiles that, at least partially, compensate.

Many mountain-oriented destinations are characterized by bi-seasonality, in the sense that they are able to attract tourists both during the winter (the skiing season) and the summer (the trekking season). Let us consider the particular case of Val di Fassa, in the Italian region of the Dolomites, where the attractions and the natural resources are appealing to those tourists who are interested in the practice of winter sports as well as to summer activities on the mountains. The data about the number of stays during 2007 (Fig. 7.C) show that the highest peaks are reached during the winter months, usually in January and February, and the summer ones, particularly in July and August, this last month being the highest peak throughout the year. This profile shows that the "dead season" is composed by 3 months: May, October and November.

(continued)

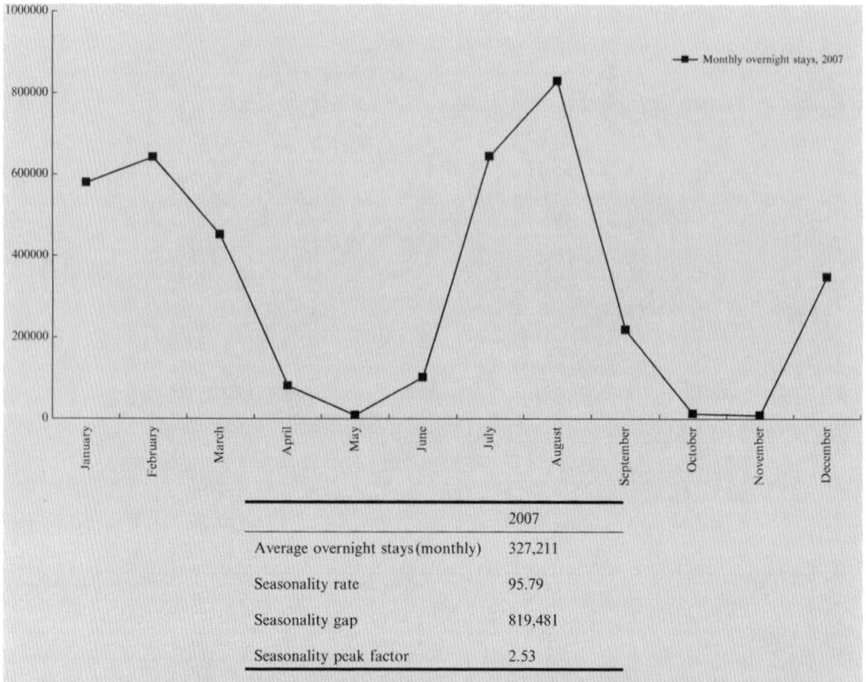

	2007
Average overnight stays (monthly)	327,211
Seasonality rate	95.79
Seasonality gap	819,481
Seasonality peak factor	2.53

Fig. 7.C Profiles and indices of seasonality of Val di Fassa (2007)

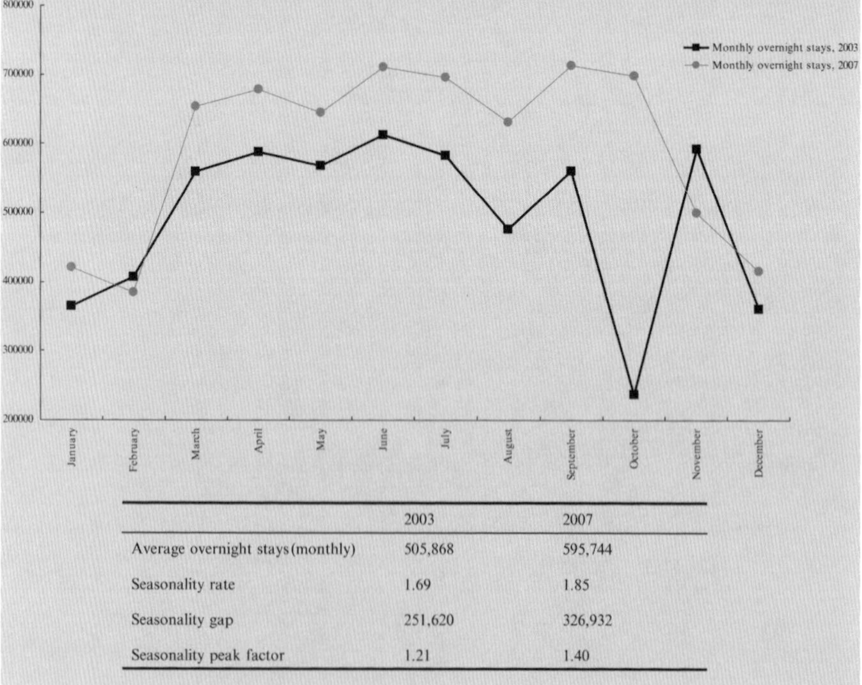

	2003	2007
Average overnight stays (monthly)	505,868	595,744
Seasonality rate	1.69	1.85
Seasonality gap	251,620	326,932
Seasonality peak factor	1.21	1.40

Fig. 7.D Profiles and indices of seasonality of the Italian town of Florence (2003 and 2007)

Finally, the absence of seasonality is typical for art cities and, more in general, for cultural destinations. Such destinations offer historical sites, churches, buildings, museums, in short the heritage, which visits are usually independent of a specific season and, for this reason, they usually display regular tourism flows throughout the year. An example of a cultural destination characterized by a constant flow of tourism is the Italian town of Florence. The available data for the years 2003 and 2007 show that the number of Italian and foreign tourists is consistently high throughout the year (Fig. 7.D). Indeed, there is not any significant difference between the maximum and the minimum number of stays, and the seasonality indices tend to be quite small, much smaller than in the previous cases. June is the month during which Florence experiences the highest number of stays, although the differences among the different months of the year are negligible.

In general, we can set as a rule of thumb that a *seasonality peak factor* with a value lower than 2 usually corresponds to destinations with low or absent seasonality; with a value between 2 and 3 corresponds to destinations characterized by some degree of seasonality; with a value greater than 3 to destinations with great seasonality. Finally, we observe that the seasonal peak factor is a more stable and reliable indicator than the seasonality rate, which is instead more subject to variations, even small, in the number of minimum stays, that represents the denominator of that index.

Case Study 7.2. Seasonality Changes Over Time in a Given Destination: The Case of Alghero (Italy)

Pulina and Cortés-Jiménez (2010) study the seasonal behavior of the tourism demand in Alghero (Sardinia, Italy) by separately analyzing domestic and inbound tourism demand. Using monthly overnight stays in Alghero, these authors plot the averages over three decades: the Eighties, the Nineties, and the period 2000–2009. This permits examining if there have been changes in the seasonal behavior of tourism demand over time (see Fig. 7.E).

Figure 7.E shows a relatively stable and monoseasonal distribution along the decades. The peak season occurs in August and the second highest in the month of July while the low season runs from October to March. This is a type of seasonality where most of the activity is concentrated in summer with the highest presence of Italian tourists in August. This is a very traditional behavior of the tourism demand which is highly influenced by the traditional school and working holidays (in many European countries, among them Italy, the traditional holiday month is August). It is also worth remarking the fact that the number of Italian tourists staying in Alghero does seem identical overtime.

(continued)

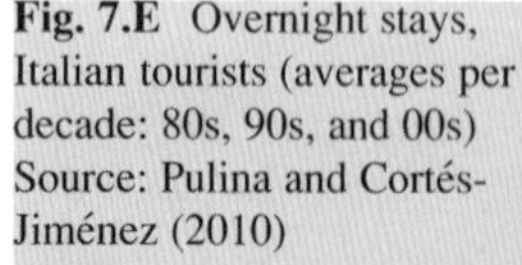

Fig. 7.E Overnight stays, Italian tourists (averages per decade: 80s, 90s, and 00s) Source: Pulina and Cortés-Jiménez (2010)

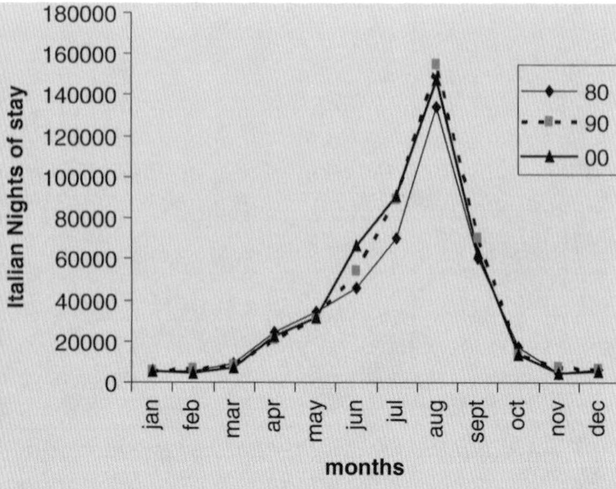

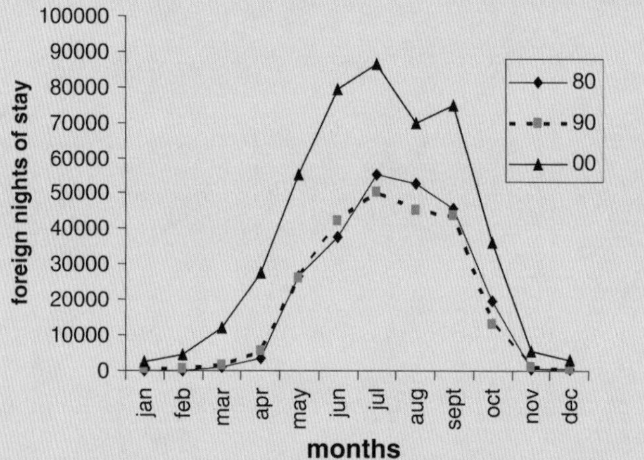

Fig. 7.F Overnight stays, foreign tourists (averages per decade: 1980s, 1990s, and 2000s) Source: Pulina and Cortés-Jiménez (2010)

The same authors replicate the analysis for inbound tourism, and the resulting seasonal pattern is different and evolving over time as it is shown in Fig. 7.F. Inbound tourism in Alghero shows a much more even distribution along the year. However, if in the first two decades (1980s and 1990s) the seasonal pattern is characterized by a relatively flatter distribution with a clearly defined high season during summer months and almost non-existent tourism activity in winter months, in the last decade bi-seasonality is present, with the first peak in July and the second peak in September though at a slightly lower level. Off-season months, that were not appealing in the past, such as March and April, show notably higher tourist flows in the last decade.

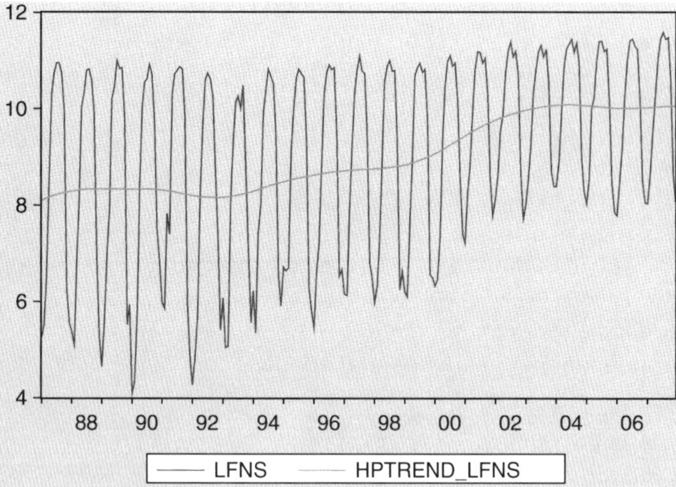

Fig. 7.G Overnight stays in Alghero, foreign Tourists, 1987M1–2007M12 Source: Pulina and Cortés-Jiménez (2010)

The investigation of foreign tourists' presence in Alghero by decades yields an interesting conclusion: the 2000s show a new tourism paradigm characterized by a significant growth of foreign tourism demand in Alghero throughout the year (and not only in the summer months), and the development of a two-peak tourism season.

Another way of observing the seasonal behavior of the tourism demand examines the monthly distribution of overnight stays in Alghero by foreigners in the period 1987M1–2007M12 (M1 stands for January, M2 for February, and so on until M12 for December). This is shown in Fig. 7.G and it seems that from 2000 onwards there is a change in the seasonality pattern. It is clearly observed that the low season (with the lowest number of overnight stays) is significantly higher, thus receiving more tourists over the year. This could be described as a process of smoothing the seasonality.

Such a change in the seasonality pattern is probably a consequence of the development of low-cost airlines. In fact, Alghero became a low-cost flight destination in June 2000 when Ryanair started flying to the local airport. With about a 2-year lag from the Ryanair arrival, several "low-cost" airline companies started flying to Alghero-Fertilia (e.g., Martinair from Amsterdam, Air One and Spanair from Barcelona, Maersk from Copenhagen, and Czech from Prague). Hence, starting from only one Ryanair route in June 2000 (from London) there has been an increase in both the number of routes and number of carriers: in June 2005 there were 19 airline routes from various European destinations offered by 17 low-cost carriers.

time. For example, hotels experience a remarkable variation in the number of stays between week days and weekends; similarly for transport companies, amusement parks, etc. With special regards to transport firms and networks (train stations, airline hubs, etc.) there exists an even more extreme version of micro-seasonality associated to the different hours of the day, given that the demand for transport services is typically concentrated in the early morning and in the evening.

A number of synthetic indicators have been suggested to measure the extent of seasonality; some of them only take into account the extremes of the distribution of stays over the period, while others are more analytical and are a function of the entire distribution. Among the first class of indices, according to Bar-On (1989), if we label with N_{max} the highest peak in overnight stays, with N_{min} the minimum number of overnight stays, and with N_{av} the average number of overnight stays, we can list:

- The seasonality rate: N_{max}/N_{min};
- The seasonality gap: $N_{max} - N_{min}$;
- The seasonality peak factor: N_{max}/N_{av}.

Among the indicators built on the entire distribution of tourism flows, the most popular ones are indices borrowed by the literature on inequality, such as the Coefficient of Variation, the Theil index, the Atkinson index, and the Gini coefficient. Some studies compare the robustness of the results by using different indices: the naïvest are obviously the indices that are exclusively based on the maximum and the minimum values, while the most commonly used—even though not perfect—is the Gini coefficient. The choice of the appropriate index obviously depends on the goals of the investigation, the costs, and the quality of available data.[6]

Regardless of the index used, the seasonality should be measured with respect to two concepts, linked to the length of the period under investigation:

1. The *intra-seasonal seasonality*, which refers to the variation in tourism flows among the months of a single season: for example, the distribution of overnight stays in a Mediterranean resort during the different months (or weeks) of the summer season. In this regard, a *de-seasonalization* policy would require to shift tourism flows from July and August to June and September.
2. The *inter-seasonal seasonality*, which refers to the variation in tourism flows between the high-peak and the low-peak season (from January through December). In this regard, a *de-seasonalization* policy would require to re-balance the existing tourism flows with other types of tourism that are characterized by different profiles, i.e., to promote business tourism in a summer destination.

Hylleberg (1992) identifies the causes of seasonality which, when applied to tourism, can be listed as follows. (a) The *natural causes* (weather conditions,

[6] For comparative studies on seasonality indices, see Wanhill (1980) and Baum and Lundtrop (2001). Works that use different indicators and seasonality methods are Marcoullier (1996), Wilton and Wirjanto (1998), Dillon (2000), Rosselló Nadal et al. (2004), and De Cantis et al. (2011).

average temperatures, hours of light, days of sun, etc.); it is important to notice that the effect of climate on tourism flows is changing: indeed, globalization offers the real opportunity to find all-year-round destinations with a summer season, and this becomes crucial for tour operators that can offer a wide array of holidays and destinations in their "holiday portfolio" in order to de-seasonalize.[7] (b) The *calendar*, for the effect of religious (Christmas, Easter, etc.) or civil festivities (national holidays, Labour Day, etc.). (c) The *institutional causes*, school holidays, or bank holidays, i.e., days in which business is closed. (d) The *social causes*, like traditions and inertial behaviors for which people take the annual paid leave always in the same period. (e) The *events*, when they are so important to motivate movements from other regions (for example, sport events, trade fairs, etc.).

Such list of causes for seasonality is effectively summarized by Butler (2001) when writing:

> Tourists travel in peak season because they want to, because they have to, or because they have been conditioned to.
>
> (Butler 2001, p. 18)

7.5.3 *The Effects of Seasonality*

There exists a broad literature on the impact of seasonality of tourism flows onto the anthropological, sociological, economic, and environmental system (among the other, see Rosselló Nadal et al. 2004; Koenig-Lewis and Bishoff 2005; Candela and Castellani 2008, and their references). Two preliminary observations are needed: firstly, the stronger the presence of mass tourism, the higher the impact of seasonality. Secondly, the destinations specialized only in a single type of tourism are the ones that are mostly stressed by the effect of seasonality. Let us now investigate the effects of tourism seasonality on the different dimensions of social life, starting with the economic effects.

7.5.3.1 The Economic Effects

We start by distinguishing between the economic effects in the long run and the economic effects in the short run.

Economic effects in the long run

All the economic effects of seasonality derive from one consideration: tourism is a service, and a service cannot be stored: it is not possible to produce and stock

[7] Moreover, also destinations are affected by climate changes (like the global warming), having the opportunity to lengthen, or being forced to shorten the tourism season, respectively in the case of beach-oriented and ski-oriented tourism (Agnew and Viner 2001).

services (like hotel rooms or air seats) in periods of low demand to sell them when the demand is higher. Therefore, the fundamental issue that has to be tackled during the planning stage of the investment is the definition of the optimal size of the firms and the infrastructures that are to be located in the destination. The size of a parking lot that the city council plans to build, the number of rooms that a hotel should have, the carrying capacity of the airplane that an airline company should purchase, etc. These are all examples of investment decisions that immobilize capital for a long period of time since, obviously, hotels or airplanes cannot expand or contract their capacity depending on the tourism season.

The relationship between size and seasonality becomes crucial for the tourism firm's investment. On one hand, if the investor builds a hotel that is big enough to face tourism flows in the peak season, it must also bear higher costs during the low season, that is, when the hotel remains substantially empty, with very low occupancy rates. On the other hand, a small hotel is possibly suited to address tourism demand in the low season but will face congestion costs and losses for not earning potential revenue during the high season. Regardless of the decision, the existence of seasonality implies *seasonality losses* for the firm. The aim of the firm in the investment stage, hence, is to identify the *optimal size of the investment* in order to minimize the seasonality losses.[8]

We illustrate the problem by analyzing the simple case of a public infrastructure, like a parking lot that must accommodate the tourists' cars (the analysis would change only formally, without substantially affecting the conclusions, if we considered the case of a private firm, like the decision on the hotel size). Without loss of generality, we assume that the destination receives a monoseasonal type of tourism, in which the number of stays during the high season, labeled as N_H, is much higher than the number of stays during the rest of the year (low season), labeled as N_L.

We also assume that the destination can only choose between a small parking lot, K_{S}, and a big parking lot, K_{B}. Again, the problem would be more complicated, without substantially affecting the conclusions, if we also allowed for intermediate sizes. The two parking systems have different average daily management costs (respectively C_S and C_B) as a function of the number of stays. As usual in economic theory, the average cost functions are U-shaped with respect to quantity, with a minimum average cost associated, respectively, for the two lots, to the exact number of stays during the low and high season. That is, the minimum average cost for the small parking lot is associated with N_L and the minimum average cost for the big parking lot is associated with N_H. For each lot, a smaller use with respect to their minimum would increase the average cost, mainly because the infrastructure would be underused; a greater use would increase the average cost mainly because of the excessive wear and tear of the structure and because of the opportunity cost (lack of earnings) deriving from not being able to satisfy the excess of demand.

---

[8] For a discussion of the seasonality losses see Sutcliffe and Sinclair (1980), Manning and Powers (1984), and William and Shaw (1991).

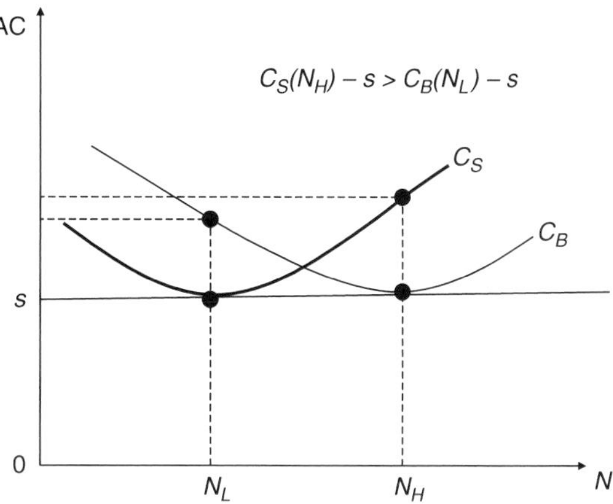

Fig. 7.6 The optimal size choice problem when there is seasonality

Moreover, we assume that the minimum average cost for the two parking lots is the same, and equal to s, so that we can write: $C_S(N_L) = C_B(N_H) = s$. This simply means that the average cost for the small system (which, for example, has 100 parking slots) is minimum when 100 cars are parked, where 100 is also the number of cars arriving at the destination during the low season; similarly, the average management cost of the big system (which, for example, has 500 parking slots) is minimum when 500 cars are parked, where 500 is the number of cars arriving at the destination during the high season. These two average costs are the same.

Finally, we assume that the high season lasts D_H days, while the low season lasts D_L days; if we normalize the length of the year to 1 we can express the number of days of each season as percentages of the whole year, $D_H + D_L = 1$. To conclude, let us assume that there is no difference between high season and the low season prices.

By taking into account all these assumptions, we can represent the optimal size choice problem as in Fig. 7.6.

Now, given the above-mentioned assumptions, which parking lot should the destination build? The big one or the small one? In this simple example, the solution may not be particularly difficult to find: firstly, we should begin with the identification of the yearly operating costs of the two systems, which is the weighted average of the average management costs during the low and the high season, with weights given by the duration of each season. Hence, for the small parking lot we have

$$sD_L + C_S(N_H)D_H = s(1 - D_H) + C_S(N_H)D_H = s + [C_S(N_H) - s]D_H, \qquad (7.2)$$

while for the big parking lot we have

$$sD_H + C_B(N_L)D_L = s(1 - D_L) + C_B(N_L)D_L = s + [C_B(N_L) - s]D_L. \qquad (7.3)$$

The choice depends on the comparison between the costs expressed by (7.2) and (7.3).

If

$$s + [C_S(N_H) - s]D_H < s + [C_B(N_L) - s]D_L,$$

that is

$$[C_S(N_H) - s]D_H < [C_B(N_L) - s]D_L,$$

then the small parking lot, K_S, is more profitable. If, instead

$$s + [C_S(N_H) - s]D_H > s + [C_B(N_L) - s]D_L,$$

that is

$$[C_S(N_H) - s]D_H > [C_B(N_L) - s]D_L,$$

then the big parking lot, K_B, is the most profitable option (this is the case shown in Fig. 7.6, where $D_H = D_L$).

In spite of the fact that the solution is not univocally defined, such model allows us to capture the fundamental variables that affect the optimal choice: (a) the *technology*, that determines the shape of the cost curves of each parking lot, and that is represented by the relative "steepness" of C_S with respect to C_B; (b) the *seasonal gap*, that is, the difference between the number of stays in the high and in the low season, N_H and N_L; (c) the *season length*, measured as a fraction of the year and represented by D_H and D_L.

On top of these three factors, if we allowed for the possibility of charging different prices in the high and the low season, the choice would also depend on: (d.1) the *price during the high season*, when the price is exogenously given (that is, it is not under the firm's direct control), which presupposes that the tourism market is highly competitive; (d.2) if we assume instead that the firm may be able to set, although not completely, the prices during the high as well as the low season, we would also generate an effect on the number of stays N_H and N_L (and likely also on D_H and D_L). With no need to further complicate our analysis, we can reasonably claim that, in this last case (d.2), the optimal size would depend on the elasticity of the demand with respect to price.

The description of the model presented in this section allows us to state two conclusions. Firstly, from an economic point of view, it is not always true that the size of the tourism structure must be referred to the seasonal peaks; the malfunctioning resulting from an undersized structure with respect to the extent of demand in the high season may be (although not always is) the rational outcome of an economic calculation. Secondly, each solution is partially inefficient: the small-size structure will be inefficient due to the impossibility to satisfy the potential demand during the peak season and to the lack of efficiency due to the overuse of the structure; the big-size structure will be inefficient due to its underuse during the low season. Therefore, regardless of the solution, *the seasonality always introduces additional management costs.*

Economic Effects in the Short Run

After the investment has been realized and the capital immobilized in the long run, the seasonality places a number of serious issues also in the short run, involving both the production side and profitability.

We first consider the production issue. If the size of capital is chosen according to the high season, it becomes impossible to store production as inventories during the low season: any service produced and unsold at a certain time (like, for example, the overnight stay at a hotel room when such room remains empty at that night) is a service for which production costs have been borne and that will never be sold, the worst situation for a firm from the economic standpoint. This is why many restaurants and hotels often reduce their activity (or even shut down) off-season, when the costs of a running business are not justifiable by the low number of tourists.

Similarly, if the size of capital is chosen according to low season, the tourism structure may be facing an excess of demand during the high peaks of the season. Although this may partially compensate the insufficient use of the structure during the low season, it often implies serious problems of overcrowding, overbooking, higher operational costs and, ultimately, a lower degree of tourist's satisfaction, with a corresponding loss in reputation (for the specific firm as well as for the entire destination).

If we consider instead the issue of profitability, we must first define and distinguish between the *rate of overall profit*, which is measured in relation to the invested capital, and the *rate of managerial profit*, which is measured in relation to the capital effectively used (see Notes 7.1). To clarify this issue, let us assume a hotel with a relatively high rate (20 %) of managerial profit, earned during the only three months of the year in which it is open. The rate of overall profit, however, is just 5 %, computed by dividing the rate of managerial profit by 4, since the hotel is open only 3 months out of 12, that is, one fourth of the year. The fact that when there is seasonality of demand the rate of capital use drastically reduces the rate of overall profit (Mathieson and Wall 1982), raises some doubts about the investment profitability. Indeed, every entrepreneur has to consider the opportunity cost of the investment, which is the return that could be earned if the capital was assigned to its best alternative use. If, for example, the available capital were to be invested in financial markets, a financial rate of return higher than 5 % would be enough to prevent the immobilization of capital in the tourism investment from being the optimal solution. The conclusion is that, when there is strong seasonality, the rate of managerial profit has to be sufficiently high in order to reach an economically convenient rate of overall profit.

In addition to reducing the profitability of the investment, the seasonality also increases its level of risk: any negative event that may hit the firm or the destination during the (short) peak season would not find any compensation during the long periods of low season. It is clear that the risk associated to the tourism activity is higher than the case in which there is not seasonality.

However, we must not forget that the seasonality also dispenses a number of positive economic effects. For example, expensive events and special attractions

Notes 7.1. The Profit Rate and the Rate of Capital Use

To introduce and measure the concepts of profit rate and of rate of capital use, we consider the example of the owner of a hotel with B beds that, hence, can host B tourists. The owner can rent the hotel for one year to a tourism entrepreneur, at the price g for each service accommodation, e.g., for each hotel bed. In such case, the amount of capital K invested by the entrepreneur is given by $K = 365gB$, that is, the annual rent paid to the owner.

The amount of productive capital, K°, can be measured instead by the rental price, that is, the value paid to the owner with respect only to the services that are actually sold: $K^{\circ} = gN$ where with N we denote the number of overnight stays in the hotel during the year.

It is now straightforward to compute the overall profit rate earned by the tourism entrepreneur as the ratio between profit π and the amount of invested capital:

$$r = \frac{\pi}{K}.$$

Such profit rate can be interpreted as the product between two ratios, which can be obtained by dividing and multiplying by the amount of productive capital, K°:

$$r = \frac{\pi}{K^{\circ}} \cdot \frac{K^{\circ}}{K} = r_m U,$$

where $r_m = \pi/K^{\circ}$ and $U = K^{\circ}/K \leq 1$. Therefore, the determinants of the overall profit rate are: (a) the rate of managerial profit, r_m (which depends on the amount of productive capital); (b) the rate of capital use U. Therefore, to keep the rate of overall profit as constant when U decreases (for example, when the season shortens), the rate of managerial profit must increase.

are usually economically sustainable only during the peak moments of a high season, when the number of interested tourists, usually only a small fraction of the total number of tourists, is beyond a given threshold and ensures that the break-even point for the event is reached. This benefits both tourists and the local population.

As we are discussing the economic effects, employment deserves a special attention. The seasonality effects on the labor market should be ascribed to the temporary inflow of workers when the seasonal demand cannot be satisfied by the supply of local workers; migrating workers are usually low skilled and/or coming from peripheral labor markets. Moreover, the seasonal opening up and shutting down of tourism businesses tend to reduce the incentives needed to boost the demand and the supply of high skilled workers, which seldom become part of the permanent team of workers. On the other hand, seasonality also generates a number of positive effects for workers. In fact, many individuals (for example, students) can easily find a temporary occupation in the tourism sector: the seasonal employment within tourism can hence constitute a good balance between unemployment and underemployment. Another example is the farmer who can increase own revenue by offering farm holidays during the peak season.

7.5.3.2 Other Effects

We now consider two non-economic effects of seasonality that are somewhat related to the economy: the environmental and the sociocultural effects.

The Environmental Effects

These effects must be referred to the negative impact on the natural environment due to the strong presence of tourists during the high season peaks and have to be analyzed in connection with the well-known problems of natural resource management and of carrying capacity (these topics will be discussed with greater details in Chap. 16). With respect to the environment, the seasonality may also display positive effects. By backing up the nature's tendency to automatically regenerate some of the resources used by tourism, the shutting down of tourism structures off-season may be the only, although necessary, alternative that allows the natural environment to recover its sustainable status.

The Sociocultural Effects

Although such impact affects both the hosting tourism destination and its visitors, the existing literature usually focuses on the negative aspects of the tourism crowding onto the local communities. The primary concern has usually to do with issues such as parking congestion, traffic jams, and all the additional costs (that are usually paid by resident through taxes) in order to maintain street cleaning and waste collection, security, and health assistance. Special attention must be paid to the correlation between tourism overcrowding and the increase in the level of (micro) criminality. At the same time, we must also consider the sociocultural positive effects of seasonality, usually resulting from the synergy existing between the needs of tourists and those of the local community (Figini et al. 2009). Many residents usually take advantage from cultural events offered during the high tourism season (which would otherwise be impossible to be organized) or from the use, off-season, of those tourism structures (such as swimming pools or tennis courts) that are built only because of the tourists' demand. Finally, during the low season, the local residents may be able to recuperate the real local traditions, which are usually just staged for the tourists' enjoyment during the high season.

In addition, from a purely sociological point of view, although a high seasonality can have deep negative implications on the family life by altering the equilibrium during the seasonal peaks (the hyper-activity during the peak season driven by the search for a decent rate of managerial profit), it may also display positive effects in the sense that it makes possible for the worker to achieve a sufficient level of income during the high season and to have time to spend with the family or to cultivate hobbies during the low seasons. In other words, seasonality is not necessarily a negative factor for everyone.

7.5.4 The Tourism Policies for Smoothing the Seasonality

A policy corollary to the previous discussion is as follows: before undertaking any policy directed to smooth the seasonality, the tourism destination (or the tourism firm) must carefully balance the positive and the negative effects of seasonality, including the costs of implementing such policy. This statement leads to two further observations.

The first one is an observation of *positive economics*. Unlike what we would say from a purely economic point of view, the optimal distribution of tourism flows does not imply the complete absence of seasonality: an optimal level of seasonality, which is different for different destinations, exists. However neither the theoretical nor the empirical economic literature has yet formalized a general modeling of optimal seasonality:

> The question of what constitutes an 'optimal' degree of seasonality for a destination is a pertinent and important one, but also one that remains largely unanswered in the present literature.
>
> (Koenig-Lewis and Bishoff 2005, p. 216)

The second one is an observation of *normative economics*. Any policy aimed at the smoothing of tourism seasonality must be designed after a careful investigation of all the positive and negative economic, environmental, and social aspects, so to make sure that the costs do not outweigh the advantages. Such investigation may rely on the Cost–Benefit Analysis (CBA) and, to evaluate the policy's environmental impact, on the Environmental Impact Assessment (EIA) (see Candela and Castellani 2008).

Finally, this analysis allows us to classify the policies for smoothing the seasonality in the following way:

1. *Policies for seasonality management*; this would be the case when, although the positive effects of seasonality may outweigh the negative ones, controlling the seasonality may still be beneficial.
2. *Policies for smoothing the tourism seasonality*; when this policy is perceived to be beneficial for the tourism destination, it can assume two forms:

(a) *Policy for the infra-seasonal readjustment*, when it aims at redistributing the number of stays within the same season. This is the only feasible policy when the demand for tourism services in the destination is concentrated during only one season (for example, for climate conditions);
(b) *Policy for the inter-seasonal readjustment*, when it aims at redistributing the number of stays throughout the different seasons of the year.

By recalling the recent literature, we will now discuss the policy tools that can be used to implement policies *subcases* (1), (2.a), and (2.b).

7.5.4.1 The Tools for Seasonality Management

Various policy tools to manage and control seasonality exist. Obviously we start mentioning the use of different price policies across seasons to redistribute demand (i.e., increasing the price when the peak season occurs and reducing the price when the low season occurs). Alternatively, there are real interventions such as the implementation of policies that can ease the mobility and diminish the congestion within the destination: all the policies that support tourists' responsible behavior belong to this type of tools. These policies can be classified into two categories: the *restraining actions* and the *organizational actions*. The *restraining actions*, which are usually enforced by laws and regulations, are designed to force tourists to undertake a behavior that shifts the congestion threshold. As an example, the visitors of the *Galleria Borghese* in Rome (Italy) are required to not exceed a 45-min visit to the painting gallery; similarly, the tourists in the coralline barriers of the Red Sea must follow a strict code of environmental safeguards, or tourists to *La Alhambra* of Granada (Spain) can visit in groups of limited size. Instead, the *organizational actions* consist of interventions designed to induce the tourists' responsible behavior without making them feel any sense of constriction (the most popular technique, which relates to the field of Marketing, consists of releasing information with the purpose of affecting the tourist decision on *when* to visit the destination; see Cooper et al. 2008).

7.5.4.2 The Policy Tools for Infra-Seasonal Readjustment

The policy of reducing the demand during the high peak is justified when the number of stays exceeds the overall carrying capacity, and this jeopardizes the sustainability of tourism in the destination. The tools that can be used may: (a) be *direct*, by imposing a quota on the number of arrivals; (b) be *indirect*, by levying a tax on each tourism stay in the peak season; (c) go from a system of linear pricing to a two-part tariff (a price policy composed of a fixed component, usually paid at the moment of the arrival, and a variable component, usually calculated as a function of the number of stays, Candela et al. 2009b) that might preserve the number of stays by reducing the number of arrivals (that is, by increasing the average length of stay).

Moreover, some destinations have deliberately implemented a de-marketing strategy in order to reduce the number of tourists in the seasonal peak. Finally, the destination may concentrate its efforts toward the organization of shows and cultural or sport events during the shoulder season (see Sect. 7.5.2) so to affect the decision of those tourists who already have decided to spend their holidays in the destination, but have not decided yet when to visit it.

Finally, if a better distribution of the tourism stays over time is not a viable option, it would be recommendable to preserve the total number of stays by trying to reallocate them in the surrounding region, by promoting marginal sites (towns or villages nearby) or creating a new urban center.

7.5.4.3 The Policy Tools for Inter-Seasonal Readjustment

After acknowledging that not all types of tourism are characterized by the same seasonality, the policies aimed at smoothing overnight stays across seasons should avoid strong dependence from a single type of tourism and should introduce into the destination an adequate *tourism mix*, i.e., supporting types of tourism with different seasonality patterns. Although such policy is not available in the same way to all the destinations, four are the strategies designed to increase the tourism demand off-season: (a) the diversification of the tourism product, by the means of investing in resources that otherwise would not be used or through the supply of alternative attractions; (b) strategies of price differentiation, usually involving low prices and discount sales during the low season; (c) the introduction of suitable infrastructures for the accommodation of tourists throughout the year (this is the case, for example, of a congress center); (d) a marketing activity aimed at informing tourists about the new opportunities, targeting those consumers who have both time and income to take holidays during any season of the year (this is the case, for example, of tourism by elderly individuals).

7.6 Tourism and Technology

Although tourism is commonly included in the list of sectors that are considered as technologically weak, the goal of this section is to show that this is often not the case. As the most striking example, tourism is the activity that, at the beginning of the XXI Century, has first taken advantage of the Information Technology (IT) revolution, both in the demand and in the supply side of the market. While in this section we just outline the main features of the relationship between tourism and technology, we refer to Chap. 12 for a more in-deep analysis.[9]

[9] A recent report on the role of technology in tourism and its growing importance is in UNWTO (2011b).

To start with, we must acknowledge that technological progress has been contributing to the advancement of the great majority of firms involved in tourism production. In fact, many investments in technology have been implemented to improve the internal and external communication systems, to reduce energy waste, to introduce new accounting systems and methodologies for the collection of the data needed for the management. Here, we do not only refer to the hotel management information systems, but also to the application of the yield management to decision methods, which usually involve the use of technical instruments of operational research and the automatic building of customer-based databases (see Sect. 9.5).[10] Also, the technological evolution of the transport systems has to be greatly acknowledged and is the essential premise for the modern mobility of tourists. Finally, also the amusement parks often use advanced levels of technology, even though its main scope is the creation of simulations.

Provided that the main tourism firms (attractions, transport, and accommodation) are so closely affected by the technological evolution, should this characteristic be extended to the tourism product in general? In other words, it still remains unclear whether the technological innovation can be thought as directly affecting the tourism destination or rather indirectly, by only affecting the firms that concur to produce it. On this regard, we can consider two examples that are related to the issue of seasonality: the definition of the optimal capital size and the problem of curbing the effects related to the weather.

Firstly, if we recall from Sect. 7.5.3 the problem of solving for the optimal size of the invested stock of capital, innovation may allow to produce a structure with intermediate size between the big and the small structures. Most likely, such intermediate structure will be over utilized to a less extent during the low season and underutilized to a less extent during the high season, leading to better economic performances.

Secondly, if we consider instead the climatic factors, it is remarkable that such conditions often affect the tourist's satisfaction, in particular for those who engage in *en plain air* tourism. As we already know from Sect. 7.2, this tourism product is called contingent good because it is contingent to the state of the world that takes place when tourism is experienced: the weather conditions, the temperature, the quantity of rain or snow, etc. Therefore, such good carries an *exogenous quality*, in the sense that its features do not entirely depend on the firms' strategy but also on events that are exogenous to its production (Candela and Cellini 1998, see also Sect. 10.3.2). We must therefore investigate whether there exist instruments that can be used for reducing uncertainty in the satisfaction of outdoor recreational activities.

The answer to this question depends on the possibility or not to smooth, among the different seasons, the level of satisfaction that a tourist receives from the purchase of a holiday with exogenous quality, that is, of a tourist who does not

[10] For a comprehensive review of studies on Internet applications to tourism and their implications on tourism management, see Buhalis and Law (2008).

have constraints, other than the weather, when choosing in which period to spend the holiday. In fact, if the tourist feels that the holiday *en plain air* returns a level of satisfaction, measured by own consumer surplus, which is similar in all the seasons of the year, one of the most important factors of seasonality disappears. To better explain this, we refer to a simplified version of the model presented by Candela and Cellini (1998), in which we focus on three fundamental variables only: R_T, the tourist surplus; p_r, the consumer reservation price, that is, the maximum price that the tourist is willing to pay for the holiday (see Sect. 5.4); v, the price the tourist effectively pays. By definition, the consumer surplus is given by the difference:

$$R_T = p_r - v. \tag{7.4}$$

If we label with U the utility received from the holiday under good weather conditions and with u the utility received under bad weather conditions ($u < U$), and with π the probability of good weather, so that $(1 - \pi)$ is the complementary probability of bad weather, we can define the tourist's reservation price as follows:

$$p_r = U\pi + u(1 - \pi) = u + \pi(U - u).$$

If, with no loss of generality, we set $u = 0$ and $U = 1$, we obtain

$$p_r = \pi. \tag{7.5}$$

Then, if we plug (7.5) into (7.4), we obtain

$$R_T = \pi - v. \tag{7.6}$$

The smoothing of seasonality of an outdoor recreational activity can be achieved by trying to reduce the variations of R_T during the various seasons of the year which are due, for any product with exogenous quality, to the probability of having good weather, π. But how can such probability be affected? The technology (and therefore the technological improvement introduced by the firms and by the destination) can allow the producer to have a greater control on the quality. On one hand, this can be done by increasing the probability of good weather conditions; on the other hand, by decreasing the degree of dissatisfaction that derives from undergoing a tourism activity during the low season. Examples of the first type are the systems for producing artificial snow (see Case Study 7.3) or stadiums with retractable roofs where outdoor sports can be practiced indoor during a day of cold rain. Examples of the second type are the gyms endowed with artificial climbing walls when the rain does not allow to climb outdoors or heaters used to increase the temperature in the outdoor terrace of a bar.

Case Study 7.3. Tourism and Technology. The Case of Artificial Snow

In the last few decades, the great majority of ski resorts have invested considerably in increasing the number of ski pistes, in building faster and safer ski-lifts and cable cars and in improving the connection between resorts. Such investments can be profitable only if an adequate and regular level of snow is guaranteed. This is why snowmaking plants have spread consistently.

The first example of snowmaking dates back to 1948, in Connecticut (U.S.), when W. Schoenknecht, manager of a ski resort, decided to transport on the ski slopes around 500 tons of ice to counteract the lack of natural snow. Such amount of ice, conveniently treated, allowed people to ski for about two weeks. Such treatment, though, happened to be very expensive, and the same Schoenknecht presented, in the following year, the first prototype of machine aimed at producing artificial snow. After many tests, such machine became operational in 1950. Since then, the technology to produce artificial snow has greatly improved and nowadays there are many specialized firms in engineering and producing snowmaking cannons and systems of artificial snow.

In Europe, artificial snow systems started in 1963, when Linde Company of Munich (Germany) sent its engineers in the U.S. to study the principles of refrigeration engineering. The following year, the German technicians proposed a solution to develop a snow cannon. Only in 1968 a patent for the production of artificial snow was registered, and in 1969 the first cannon to produce snow was operational in Europe. Other European companies followed the example of Linde and the improvement of the production standards was so important that European machines started being exported to the U.S. market with great success. In 1979, the Austrian company Hammerle purchased the patent to produce snow cannons from Linde. In 1983, Hammerle was purchased by Elektra Bregenz, that then founded Sufag to furtherly develop the production of snow cannons. This company, among others, is still active in the growing market of artificial snow and snow programming.

In the Alps, artificial snow appeared in some ski resorts in the 1970s. The main aim was to reduce the degree of uncertainty due to snow falling. There had been many winters in a row in which snow falling started very late in the winter season, in some cases even after Christmas holidays. To avoid the negative effects on arrivals and revenues in the peak period of winter tourism, artificial snow systems were implemented for programming snow on the ski slopes in order to allow skiing since the opening of the season, at the beginning of December. Nowadays, the use of snow programming systems is so widespread that natural snow might be considered as the integration of the artificial snow, not the other way round.

The use of snow programming systems is controversial with respect to the effect on the environment: environmentalists and tourism stakeholders have often different views on evaluating if and where snow cannons are appropriate, and the global warming, together with the greater variability in snow falling, deepens such conflict. Not only the negative effects of artificial snow

(continued)

on the environment, but also the economic and financial sustainability of such investment (the average investment is estimated to be 140,000 € per hectare of piste) is under discussion. On the other side, it is a fact that many winter seasons have been literally saved by the use of snow programming systems, in the absence of snow falling.

Data show that Austrian and Italian ski resorts are the destinations that use snowmaking systems most heavily. In 2004, around 40 % of ski slopes in the two countries were endowed with snow cannons. Investment in the field of snowmaking is high and the distribution of costs between the companies that manage the ski plants and slopes and the public administration changes case by case. In many resorts, the local authorities are also owners of the ski piste management (see Sect. 9.4). It is hence very difficult to understand who finally pays for the investments, since the possibilities of subsidizing are diverse not only across countries but also within a single country. For example, it is worth to highlight the case of the autonomous province of Bozen, in Northern Italy, where public subsidies aimed at financing snow programming systems cover up to 25 % of the total cost. To conclude, it is very difficult to estimate the impact of snow cannons on the price of the skipass, although the positive effect in terms of satisfaction, reduction of the risk linked to the *exogenous quality* of the ski holiday, and increase in the length of the winter season are evident.

Chapter Overview

- The tourism product is uniquely identified on the basis of its physical description, location and date of delivery, and state of nature when the product is made available.
- The tourism operator may organize production through the market, that is, through the price as the information mechanism connecting demand and supply, or through the authority, that is, by transferring the "right of choice" on some decision sets from one economic agent to another.
- The production process can be represented as a series of contracts, which are agreements that are legally binding for the parties involved.
- A firm is born as a response to high transaction costs, which may be either ex ante or ex post, and which usually depend on information issues. The economic decision on whether to start a firm or to use market relationships depends on the comparison between production and transaction costs.
- Tourism is a seasonal activity: the key factors determining the seasonality of tourism demand are natural causes (the climate), the calendar (civil and religious holidays), institutional factors (school and bank holidays), social causes (fashion, traditions), and events.
- To reduce the effects of seasonality we may undertake a number of policies for: the management and control of seasonality, for infra-seasonal smoothing, for inter-seasonal smoothing. For example, the tourism mix, the development of alternative attractions, price differentiation strategies, ad hoc marketing, spatial delocalization, and de-marketing are policies that can be implemented to these aims.

Chapter 8
The Production and the Sale of Holidays: Tour Operators and Travel Agencies

Learning Outcomes
On the completion of this chapter you will:

- Learn the difference between fixed and variable costs of production, and how the forecasting of demand is fundamental in setting the price of the package holiday.
- Be able to identify the conditions of profitability for travel agencies, both in the short and the long run.
- Understand the recent changes in the organizational structure of holidays due to the development of online travel agencies.

8.1 Introduction

After having analyzed in Chap. 7 why tourism firms arise and develop and how they are organized, and after having discussed some general topics affecting the supply side of the tourism sector (the seasonality of demand and the technology change), we now start to investigate the economic rationale of tourism firms. With the term "economic rationale" we mean the process, logically divisible into three stages, through which the tourism firm: (a) has to estimate the average costs of production; (b) in order to fix the price at which to sell its services; (c) with the aim of maximizing profits, the long-run goal of any privately owned firm.

By following a criterion that is widely accepted within the tourism literature, the discussion of these firms will unfold by separating:

(a) The firms producing and distributing "all-inclusive" holidays, respectively tour operators and travel agencies (although travel agencies usually sell individual services too). These firms will be studied throughout this chapter.
(b) The firms producing the "primary factors" of the holiday (accommodation, transport, attractions such as amusement parks, museums, historical sites, and natural reserves), which will be analyzed in Chap. 9. As we already know from

G. Candela and P. Figini, *The Economics of Tourism Destinations*,
Springer Texts in Business and Economics, DOI 10.1007/978-3-642-20874-4_8,

Chap. 7, these firms can sell to final consumers, either directly or through travel agencies, or to tour operators for the composition of their package holidays.

Given that a complete discussion of tourism firms would require a monograph for each of them (and possibly involve other fields such as Business Organization, Management, Marketing, etc.), in our book we will strictly review the economic aspects only. Although the many differences in their organization, the volume of production, the nature of services they produce, the structure of markets they compete in, tourism firms share several economic characteristics, which allow us to follow a unitary approach. We list five common characteristics:

1. The great majority of tourism firms are privately owned companies[1] that supply private goods and services. The distinction between private and public goods (see Sect. 15.2) is based on two properties that public goods present: (a) the property of *non-rivalry in consumption*, that is when the act of consumption of one subject does not diminish the amount of good available for consumption of others; (b) the property of *non-excludability in consumption*, that is when it is—technically or economically—impossible to exclude any subject from using the good. A public good presents these two properties; on the contrary, any private good presents some degree of rivalry and excludability in consumption.
2. Firms operate and compete in markets which structure departs from the theoretical ideal of perfect competition. Tourism markets can be better studied by the means of oligopoly and monopolistic competition models (see Sect. 10.2). In particular, tourism firms often adopt strategies of product differentiation (see Sect. 10.3) or price discrimination (see Sect. 9.5) in order to pursue the objective of diminishing the degree of substitutability between tourism services and, ultimately, to increase their market power (and profits).
3. The cost structure of many tourism services, as the flight, the overnight accommodation, or the package holiday, is mainly composed of fixed costs. For example, the price of a flight is almost completely determined by fixed costs (the airplane amortization schedule, the fuel cost, the salaries of the crew, the airport fees, etc.) that do not depend on the number of passengers on the flight.
4. Given that the tourism product is a pure and non-storable service (a hotel room that remains vacant for a specific night corresponds to a service of accommodation that has been produced and never purchased), the accurate forecast of the number of stays becomes fundamental for the firm to estimate the average cost of production. As a consequence, its profit heavily depends on the spread between estimated and real demand as well as on the set of decisions regarding the extent of investment, when capital gets immobilized and the optimal size of the service to be produced is decided. In order to reach the objective of minimization of the average (unit) cost, tourism firms must achieve the optimal use of their structure: in particular, the loading factor is the relevant indicator to control in this case.

[1] Public bodies (like the agencies for tourism promotion and the public infrastructures) will receive special attention in Chap. 15, when dealing with the public intervention in the tourism sector.

5. Due to reasons from 2 to 4 above (the ability to enjoy some market power, the relevance of fixed costs, the difficulty in estimating the demand), tourism firms usually set the price by using the *markup method*, which consists of increasing the estimated average cost by a percentage that accounts for the indirect costs and that allow the firm to reach the desired profit.

For the sake of clarity, we choose to undergo an in-depth discussion of the five above economic characteristics as long as the different types of firms will be analyzed: the tour operator in Sect. 8.2, the travel agency in Sect. 8.3, and the other firms in Chap. 9. Concepts such as full cost, markup, loading factor, etc. will be used several times in this and the next chapter and they will become familiar as long as the study proceeds.

8.2 The Tour Operator

The tour operator can be defined as a firm whose main activity consists of stipulating contracts, at various levels of risk, with providers of basic tourism services such as transport, accommodation, entertainment, etc., including contracts with insurance companies for the management of all the risks involved in the tourism experience. The final aim of the tour operator is to produce "package holidays" (also called "all-inclusive tours," or "package tours") that are then sold to the customers, mainly through the retailing channel represented by travel agencies.

Two main types of tour operators can be distinguished: (a) tour operators that are *outgoing specialist*s, namely the organizers of trips (often in foreign countries) for tourists located in the same region of the tour operator; (b) tour operators that are *incoming specialist*s, that is, organizers of package tours or short excursions for tourists who already have reached the destination where the tour operator is located.

Among the outgoing specialists we can distinguish between: (a) those that are *mass-tourism oriented*, offering standard products, serving many popular destinations, and working with several travel agents and countries at the same time; (b) *destination-oriented* tour operators, which primarily focus on one or more destinations within the same geographical area; (c) tour operators specialized in *special kinds of holidays*, such as adventure tourism, trekking, cycling tourism, and so on.

Among the incoming specialists we can distinguish according to the services being supplied, which can be: (a) *meeting services*, which corresponds to the set of services offered at the destination to the new tourist, for which the culture, the language, and the traditions of the destination are often unknown; (b) *accessibility services*, when the tour operator supplies tours and excursions in the destination.[2]

[2] For a deeper analysis of the management and marketing issues related to tour operators and travel agencies, see more specific textbooks such as Goeldner et al. (2005) and Holloway and Taylor (2006).

The market structure for tour operators presents two main characteristics (Stabler et al. 2010).

1. A low degree of sunk costs, leading to ease of entry and exit the market. Since capital costs are low, and it is quite easy for the tour operator to differentiate the product and find a suitable market niche, the market for package tours is very dynamic with a very high number of firms operating on the market (about 1,500 in the UK, more than 2,000 in the US) and a high rate of birth and death every year.
2. A high and rising degree of market concentration in many countries, so that an important share of the overall number of holidays is sold by a few firms: for example, the four main tour operators in the UK market (TUI, Thomas Cook, First Choice Holidays, and MyTravel) took 46 % of the air holiday licenses in 2007 (Papatheodorou 2003b). In many other European countries, the five largest operators' share of the market is over 60 % (Toulantas 2001). The rate of market concentration rose in the last few years due to the double merger of TUI with First Choice and of Thomas Cook with MyTravel.

Ease of entry and exit and high market concentration suggest that the market for tour operators has a dual structure, with the main segment, absorbing the greatest share of the market, organized as an oligopoly, and the marginal segment, with a great number of small firms operating in market niches with intense competition.

8.2.1 Functions and Activities of the Tour Operator

Since the tour operator decides the type of holiday, the destination where to offer it, the market segment to target, and the characteristics of the package tour, its role cannot be defined as mere brokerage. On the contrary, the tour operator can be assimilated to any business that, by entering raw materials (the raw services provided by hotels, carriers, etc., and the attractions available in the destination) in the production black box, produces, as the output, the holiday (see Fig. 7.1).

The package tour can be produced in two different ways.

1. The package is prepared following the request of a tourist (or of a group of tourists): in this case, the tour operator is usually referred to as tour organizer, and its activity assumes the connotation of just-in-time production. The firm offers a consulting and advising service to the tourist, usually accompanied by the selection of service providers, reservation, confirmation, and on-site assistance to the tourist.
2. The package is produced on the basis of marketing research and surveys aimed at targeting the tastes and the expectations of the travelers. Then, the tourist chooses among the many standardized products that are promoted in the tour operator's catalog.

By carrying out these two activities (activity 2 is obviously its core business), the tour operator stipulates the many contracts shown in Fig. 7.2. Among the main types of providers trading with the tour operator there are hospitality firms (hotels, residences, etc.) and carriers, including all types providing transport services to the tourists. The hospitality firms may be either independent or owned by the tour operator itself, while transport services may be supplied by well-known commercial carriers, by companies offering charter flights to the tour operator, or by carriers that are owned by the tour operator itself.

To sum up, by recalling the terminology used in Sect. 7.3, the services included in the package tour can either be provided by the market or be owned by the tour operator. In the first case, the tour operator signs contracts while, in the second case, it adopts a strategy of *vertical integration*. With the word "integration" we mean a set of formal and binding arrangements between companies, ranging from property takeover to mergers, to franchising agreements. In particular, we define as vertical integration the situation where there is property takeover between the different production units composing the supply chain. Usually each member of the supply chain produces a different good or service that, combined with the other ones, tends to satisfy the final consumer's needs. There is "forward" vertical integration when a company takes over and controls pieces of production that are closer to the final consumer: for example, when an airline starts up its own business as a tour operator in the travel industry or when a tour operator purchases a chain of travel agencies. Instead, there is "backward" vertical integration when the company takes over and controls subsidiaries that produce some of the inputs used in the supply chain: for example, when the tour operator purchases an airline company or when it creates an alliance with a multinational hotel chain.

In case the tour operator makes use of accommodation and transport services owned by others, which still remains the most common market solution, the services must be purchased well in advance in order for the holiday to be prepared and promoted. The advance with which the contracts must be stipulated identifies one of the critical issues of the tour operator's activity, since it must commit itself to buy services well in advance without knowing whether or not the package holidays will sell. This condition requires a great exposure to risk; hence, the risk allocation provided by the contracts stipulated between tour operators and tourism services suppliers becomes a key element.

The main types of contracts used by the tour operator in its transactions with providers are:

- *The allotment (or allocation) contract*. The tour operator bargains with the service provider (for example, the hotel) the availability of a given number of rooms for specific dates of the year (or even for the whole season) and the right to re-sell them to final consumers as part of the package holiday. In the allotment contract, the tour operator holds the right to return any unsold room by a deadline (usually a few days before the usage, although the *release back period* is also negotiated within the contract). From an economic point of view, the allotment is a *forward contract with an option*. In particular, the contract is a forward because the features of the service and the price are defined immediately, but the "act of consumption" is delayed to the future date in which the holiday is spent; the contract is an option in the sense that the tour operator is allowed to withdraw from the contract (and release some of the rooms that were optioned) in exchange of paying a premium (see Sect. 11.4.2).

- *The free sale contract.* This agreement, on the contrary, implies the immediate purchase of the service and the commitment to pay its value regardless of the real occupation. From an economic point of view, this is a future contract (see Sect. 11.4.1). The free sale contract allows the service suppliers to rely on a certain volume of sales, thus transferring the risk of unsold, at least partially, on the tour operator (Castellani and Mussoni 2007).
- *The contract with commission.* Compared to the previous two types of contract, this is a less demanding and risky contract for the tour operator. None of the parties involved are bounded, neither in terms of dates nor in terms of availability to provide. It is a simple contract of brokerage that works at the time of booking, which is paid against a prenegotiated commission. Given that medium- and large-sized tour operators usually sign contracts characterized by a certain volume of availability and lower prices (necessary conditions to implement their tourism catalogs), this type of contract is mainly used by small tour operators, tour organizers, and travel agencies.

Not only hotel rooms but also seats on an airplane (or on any other means of transport) can be purchased in accordance with the above types of contract. A tour operator can decide to rent an airplane for the entire season, for specific dates only, or to buy a group of seats from commercial and charter airlines. This last alternative, which is usually more expensive, tends to be considered for specific, low-demand holidays or for just-in-time tours.

By focusing on the contracts, we just illustrated the main activities of a tour operator that organizes its production by setting up market relationships with independent suppliers. Alternatively, the tour operator can internalize production through hotels and carriers that are directly or indirectly owned. In such case, the organizational form lies in the hierarchy of the vertically integrated firm. Differently from before, the economic issue of such organizational form is not related to the type of contracts to be signed, but to the reason why a process of vertical integration is economically superior. The concept of transaction costs, which was introduced in Sect. 7.3 to justify the birth of a firm, may well explain the tour operators' process of vertical integration.

Let's go back to Fig. 7.2 to explain the strategic reasons for vertical integration. Suppose that the tour operator, the firm "manufacturing" the package holiday, acknowledges that transaction costs (both ex ante and ex post) related to its contracts with hotels and carriers are too high, and that it would be cheaper to directly own the accommodation provider. When the containment of transaction costs fully offsets the increased internal costs due to process of purchasing and managing the hotel, total costs decrease and profits increase. Hence, the strategy of vertical integration is implemented.

Once the hotel has been taken over, the tour operator faces a similar problem with other suppliers, such as carriers. Once again, if the reduction of transaction costs is sufficiently high, it may decide to undergo a further process of integration, this time taking over the carrier company. This process leads to the expansion of the tour operator's size and to the reduction of market transactions. When this process continues and involves operational and production units in different countries, the tour operator becomes a multinational company (see Sect. 14.2.2).

In addition to the advantages earned through the reduction of transaction costs, a process of vertical integration may also ensure some benefits in terms of production costs. These benefits may take various forms and can be listed in: (a) *economies of scope* achieved through the connection with complementary activities: the economies of scope are reductions in the average cost that the production of a good may allow in terms of the production of another good, when they are both produced within the same firm; (b) *economies of scale* achieved by increasing the size of the firm: the economies of scale are reductions in the average cost as the quantity produced increases; (c) reduction in markup costs following the exclusion of intermediaries from the production process (see Sect. 11.5.1); (d) greater control in the availability and the reliability of the services; (e) consolidation of the market position and growth of market power.

Another strategic choice for the tour operator's activity is the decision about *horizontal integration*, the process of merger or acquisition between two or more firms, mainly implemented to gain from economies of scale and to strengthen the market position. The process of horizontal integration can raise the issue of market concentration and hence the need for efficient regulation and control by the Competition Authority (Papatheodorou 2006), together with the issue of market entry and exit (Evans and Stabler 1995).

8.2.2 The Organization of the Tour Operator and Its Operational Process

The study of the operational process of the tour operator, here intended as the complex of operations that must be fulfilled and coordinated before the holiday goes on the market, is of great importance. The delicacy of this issue stems from the fact that these activities must be carried out within precise periods of time, well before the holiday season. In fact, the planning of the new tourism season can last many months, and more than one year may pass from the preliminary stage of defining the idea of a package tour and the first tourists' departures. The ability to correctly forecast the market demand is indeed crucial. In the case of short holidays or weekend breaks, with a lower volume of sales, this planning stage may be shorter but still significant to justify a dynamic programming of the tourism activities.

The stages of the operational process of a tour operator can be described following Cooper et al. (2008, Chap. 12).

- *Market Research*. The main outcome of this preliminary stage consists of estimating the overall market size as well as the size and the trend of the potential demand for the types of holiday or destinations under scrutiny. In this stage, the selection of the destinations to be included in the catalog takes place.

- *Capacity planning*. The forecasts that have been produced during the previous stage are now used: to plan the capacity to be exchanged with the suppliers through allotment and/or free sale contracts; to identify the precise features of the holidays (hotels or resorts where to accommodate the tourists, the length of the holiday, the airports of departure and arrival, etc.).
- *Financial assessment*. In this stage, the tour operator sets the price of the holiday, some months in advance with respect to the beginning of the tourism season. This anticipation obviously implies a number of financial issues, such as the decision on which currency to use for accounting purchases and sales, with the related problem of price and exchange rate adjustments (see Sect. 14.4). Indeed, the tour operator is exposed to the risk of unexpected movements in the exchange rate, of an increase in the price of oil, airport fees, taxes levied on tourists, etc., which can affect its overall profits.
- *Marketing*. Package tours are then promoted through the catalog (which can also be online) that usually includes: (a) visual representations that recall the image of the holiday and of the destination; (b) a written text describing the main features of the destination and of the holiday; (c) a table summing up all the relevant information such as price, departures dates, the length of stay, departure points, the list of all the services that are included as well as the optional services that may be added to the package. The editing of the catalog usually begins several months before the date of its publication, with an analysis of its layout and of the communication and promotion strategy to be undertaken. Once the catalog has been printed out, the tour operator must plan the way it will be distributed to the travel agencies and other means (for a discussion of the web marketing and the publication of catalogs on the web, see Chap. 12).
- *Administration*. This stage aims to identify the personnel required to manage the project. Because of the seasonality of holidays, only a proportion of the work-force will be composed by employees, while the majority of the activities will be carried out by temporary workers.
- *Tour management*. This is the final moment of the tour operator's planning, which consists in the holiday experience. Often, these tours require a tour manager with the function of receiving and guiding the group, as well as solving small and big problems that tourists experience during their stay.
- *Control*. To build and enforce its reputation, the tour operator must rely on an efficient system of control that is able to prevent and to prosecute the contractual wrongdoing of the service suppliers and, at the same time, to possibly reimburse those tourists who were victims of such misbehavior. After the holiday, the tour operator must then run a set of checking activities based on the praises, suggestions, or complaints of the tourists. This audit can be arranged as the so-called: (a) *police patrol activity*, through which the tour operator runs random checks on the quality of the services composing the package tour, with the double goal of punishing ex post the providers who failed to respect the contracts and of discouraging ex ante similar behaviors; (b) *fire-alarm activity*,

where the tour operator establishes a compliance procedure that allows the tourists to directly raise the attention of the tour operator on inefficiencies and breaches of contract occurred during the tour. Both activities have strengths and weaknesses, and they have to be used jointly to be more effective.

All the above listed activities, naturally, contribute to the costs borne by the tour operator and, hence, they have to be correctly estimated before fixing the price of the tourism product.

8.2.3 The Cost Structure and the Price of the Package Tour

In this section, we analyze the cost structure faced by the tour operator when producing the package holiday. The analysis of production costs is a fundamental step in the correct management of the tour operator activity; in fact, once the costs have been estimated, the tour operator computes the price to be printed in the catalog, a price that aims at profit maximization. As we have already mentioned, the price can be modified only as a result of specific events, such as a large variation in the exchange rate, and only if the brochure clearly mentions this opportunity. From a theoretical point of view we say that the prices set in the tour operators' brochure are "rigid," given that changing them is difficult and involves significant *menu costs* (which are the costs related to changing a price after it has been published in a printed form, just like the price posted in a restaurant menu). The consequence of such condition is that an error in the estimates of the production costs can lead to "wrong" prices, prices that do not allow to reach the management's goal and that are difficult to change once the tourism season has started. The decision on price setting undertaken in uncertainty conditions is exactly the economic problem faced by the tour operator, a problem that will be unfolded in the rest of this section.

Let us focus on a particular holiday of type i in the destination r, for which the tour operator has to set the price to be posted on the catalog and/or on the web site. To correctly fix the price, the tour operator has to estimate the costs. The first stage in the analysis of the tour operator's costs consists of identifying the *direct management (or running) costs* (which will be denoted by the symbol DC), that is, those costs that are exclusively attributable to the specific holiday under investigation. In general, direct costs are: (a) costs of the accommodation (hotel, resort, or other accommodation); (b) costs of the carrier that operates the connection to (and from) the destination, as well as any transfer within the tourism area; (c) costs of in-site support services, including the costs for tourists' hosting and guidance; (d) costs of any meals included in the program; (e) tolls, airport and port fees, tips, and other similar costs.

Within this category of costs it is worth distinguishing between fixed costs and variable costs. *Direct fixed costs* (DFC) are the costs faced by the tour operator regardless of the number of the participants to the tour (e.g., the costs of a free sale contract for hotel accommodation, the cost of renting a charter flight, or the cost of hiring a tour guide). The incidence of direct fixed costs on the individual traveler depends on the total number of tourists who purchase the holiday.[3] The tour operator must produce a forecast, that we denote with $E(N)$, of the number N of tourists who are expected to purchase the tour, a forecast that is directly linked to the *load factor* of the services included in the holiday. The *Direct Fixed Unit Cost* (DFUC) is then computed as the ratio of the direct fixed costs and the expected number of tourists:

$$\text{DFUC} = \frac{\text{DFC}}{E(N)}.$$

With the term *Direct Variable Costs* (DVC) we define instead the costs that vary directly with the number of participants, such as the cost of meals, insurance, or admission to museums. Since the amount of DVC increases with the number of tourists who purchase the package tour, their direct reference to the unit cost is particularly easy and can be done without having to rely on any hypothesis about the load factor. Therefore, if we let DVUC denote the *Direct Variable Unit Cost* of holiday i at destination r, we have by definition:

$$\text{DVC} = \text{DVUC} \times N.$$

Once the direct fixed and variable costs are computed, the *Direct Unit Cost* (DUC), that is the cost of the holiday per participant, can be computed as follows:

$$\text{DUC} = \frac{\text{DFC}}{E(N)} + \text{DVUC}. \tag{8.1}$$

Once the DUC has been determined we can proceed with the determination of the package tour price, p, by using the well-known *full cost model* for non-perfectly competitive markets, which requires adding a percentage (known as markup) on the direct unit cost. If we denote with m the percentage of markup,[4] the price of holiday i in the destination r posted on the catalog is

$$p = \text{DUC}(1 + m). \tag{8.2}$$

This is the price that, after being published in the brochure, will be kept fixed throughout the season. It is important to notice that the markup is not the actual gain

[3] This observation provides a sufficient reason for the adoption of a price discrimination policy as a function of the time of departure. On one hand, this allows to impute to the tourists departing in the peak season some of the costs that are not paid by those who go on holiday off season (see Sect. 9.5); on the other hand, this policy allows to use the price in order to smooth the seasonality of the tourism flows (see Sect. 7.3).

[4] The markup can be the same for all types of holidays produced by the tour operator or different depending on the type i of tourism for each destination r.

accruing from each participant. In fact, the per-tourist actual gain depends on: (a) the accuracy of the forecast $E(N)$ that has been used for the determination of (8.1); (b) the extent of *indirect costs* (IC) borne by the tour operator. The *indirect costs* (IC) account for all the expenditures that relate to tour operator's general activity and that are not directly attributable to the individual package tour. Typical costs within this category are those for the administration, marketing and promotion staff, general expenses, bills and rents, machinery depreciation, etc. The tour operator has to allocate a share of these indirect costs to each package tour.

Regarding the first point, if we denote with m_r the real markup after selling the package tour at the price given by (8.2), it can be easily verified that:

- if $E(N) = N$, i.e., if the markup was based on a correct sale forecast, then $m = m_r$;
- if $E(N) < N$, i.e., if the estimate was too low, then the DUC is lower ex post due to the allocation of the same amount of fixed costs over a larger number of tourists; since the real markup ends up being higher than expected, $m < m_r$, the situation is not optimal for the tour operator, since it can be argued that the price was set at a level too low;
- if $E(N) > N$, i.e., the estimate was too optimistic, then the DUC is higher ex post due to the allocation of the same amount of fixed costs over a smaller number of tourists; in this case the real markup is lower than expected, $m > m_r$, the situation is not optimal for the tour operator, since it can be argued that the price was set at a level too high and the real markup might be too low to allow the tour operator to reach a profit.

Putting together accurate forecasts is therefore important both for setting a competitive market price and for getting the target profit on the package holiday under scrutiny; this is particularly true when the holiday implies significant fixed costs. In this regard, it is important to highlight that the contracts signed by the tour operator with its suppliers differ according to the distinction between fixed and variable costs. For example, if the contracts used to buy accommodation in a hotel are free sale contracts, the underlying costs are essentially fixed costs because they are borne regardless of the number of sold package tours (in this case we say that the tour operator follows a *full-costing* strategy); instead, if the contracts are allotment contracts (or even contracts with commission), the underlying costs are, at least partially, variable costs as they are subject to confirmation on the basis of actual sales (in this case we say that the tour operator follows a *direct-costing* strategy). Therefore, the choice of the type of contract may provide the tour operator with a strategic tool to control the nature of its costs. Then, in the presence of high uncertainty of demand, the tour operator might prefer to stipulate allotment contracts (that are less risky although a bit more expensive) to prevent that an error in the forecasting stage will negatively affect the economic result; on the contrary, if there is little uncertainty about demand, the tour operator may prefer to stipulate free sale contracts because they tend to be less expensive although a bit more risky (see Sect. 11.4 for a discussion on the price differences between allotment and free sale contracts).

Although the markup is linked with the tour operator's profit, it does not coincide with it. In fact, the profit is obtained only after the deduction of all the indirect costs of production from the markup charged on the holiday. The tour operator's profit, π_{TO}, can then be determined by adding the revenues accruing from all types i of holiday in all destinations r and subsequently subtracting the direct and indirect costs:

$$\pi_{TO} = \sum_i \sum_r p_{i,r} N_{i,r} - \sum_i \sum_r \mathrm{DC}_{i,r} - \mathrm{IC}. \tag{8.3}$$

The economic analysis of the tour operator has to be completed with a model that is able to explain the magnitude of the markup that can be charged, given that so far we implicitly referred to m as purely exogenous. The economic theory affirms that the level of markup is endogenously determined by the degree of market power enjoyed by the firm. The smaller the number of market competitors and the higher the differentiation of the product, the higher the firm's market power and, consequently, the higher the markup charged on direct unit costs (see Theory in action 8.1).

Theory in Action 8.1. The MarkUp and the Price Elasticity

In a perfectly competitive market, firms are price takers and are subject to the market price that in equilibrium is equal to their marginal cost. Because they are facing a perfectly elastic demand, such firms have no other strategy but to decide the quantity to be produced and earn the "normal" zero profit.[5]

In imperfect markets, however, firms are price makers and are able to earn a positive profit by adding a percentage of markup to the cost of production when setting the price. The value of markup depends on the market structure, which is generally synthesized by the term "monopoly degree" or "market power."

To understand how firms with market power can use this opportunity when setting the price p of a good or a service, let us consider the case of a monopolist whose demand function is $Q = D(p)$ where Q denotes the quantity produced. Let $C(Q)$ be the total cost of production. Under these conditions, the monopolist's profit will be given by

$$\pi = pQ - C(Q) = pD(p) - C[D(p)].$$

[5] In perfect competition it is said that firms do not make any profit. This means that firms do not earn extra profits over the standard remuneration of capital which, in economic terms, is already computed in the costs. In other words, if the equilibrium interest rate on the financial market is 5 %, a tourism firm operating in a perfectly competitive market remunerates the capital invested with an interest rate of 5 %; since in the standard economic model the interests are computed as costs, no profit remains to the management after the interests have been paid back to the capital owners.

Since the firm will fix the price in order to maximize profits, and assuming that the demand function and the cost function are both differentiable, the profit-maximization condition will be

$$\frac{\mathrm{d}\pi}{\mathrm{d}p} = D(p) + pD'(p) - C_Q D'(p) = 0,$$

from which it is easy to get

$$p - C_Q = -\frac{D(p)}{D'(p)}, \tag{I}$$

where C_Q denotes the marginal cost of production. If we divide both sides by p, on the right-hand side of (I) we obtain (the absolute value of) the reciprocal of the price elasticity for the demand function $D(p)$, so that the above condition (I) can be written as

$$\frac{p - C_Q}{p} = \frac{1}{\varepsilon}. \tag{II}$$

This result has general validity and indicates, for example, that for the firm operating in perfect competition (for which ε, the price elasticity, is infinite, thus $1/\varepsilon = 0$) the price must be equal to its marginal cost C_Q. On the contrary, for the firm with market power (and a downward sloping demand curve), there is the possibility to set the price higher than the marginal cost. The term $(p - C_Q)/p$ of (II) is called the *Lerner Index*, which is named after the economist who first introduced it in the literature.

If we assume that the production technology shows constant returns to scale (at least for a firm operating under normal conditions relative to its potential), we can state that the marginal cost is equal to the variable unit cost VUC. Therefore, the expression (II) can be rewritten as

$$p = \frac{\mathrm{VUC}}{\left(1 - \frac{1}{\varepsilon}\right)} = \mathrm{VUC}(1 + m) \text{ with } m = \frac{1}{\varepsilon - 1}.$$

The price is then set by increasing the average variable cost by a markup m which value is linked to the price elasticity of demand. This is the *full cost pricing rule* which, in its simplest version, requires the firm with market power to set the price on the basis of the average cost, thus increasing it by a percentage (which is precisely called markup) that inversely depends on the price elasticity of demand.

Therefore, the price elasticity embodies all the conditions that define the monopoly degree and is closely linked to the specific market structure where

(continued)

the firm operates, namely, (a) the number of competitors and their pricing policy; (b) the firm's market share; (c) the existence of substitutes for the good or service supplied, and the degree of product differentiation in the market.

If we denote with MP a measure of the monopoly degree (the firm's market power), we can conclude that

$$m = F(\mathrm{MP}), \text{ with } F' > 0. \tag{8.4}$$

This conclusion, which is well known in economic theory, is however not sufficient to fully explain the tour operator's behavior, because in the tourism market the tour operator also suffers from the competition of the self-organizing tourists. In Sect. 5.5, we already saw that the tourist always compares the option of self-organizing the holiday by independently buying the different services included in the tourism product (transport, accommodation, etc.) with that of purchasing a package holiday. If we denote with z the shadow price of a self-organized holiday similar to the package tour being sold by the tour operator, the condition that the tour operator must comply with is that the market price of the holiday be not higher than the cost of self-organizing the holiday:

$$p \leq z \tag{8.5}$$

Thus, if we replace (8.5) with (8.2), we obtain

$$\mathrm{DUC}(1 + m) \leq z, \tag{8.6}$$

which leads to

$$m \leq \frac{z - \mathrm{DUC}}{\mathrm{DUC}}. \tag{8.7}$$

Expression (8.7) identifies the condition for the existence of the tour operator in the tourism market. The condition $m > 0$ requires that $z > \mathrm{DUC}$, i.e., that the tour operator owns an absolute advantage relative to the cost of self producing the holiday. This advantage can be explained in terms of professional skills, in terms of bargaining power in the purchase of services, as well as in terms of power of coordination (see also Sect. 4.3.1):

> Coordination of the several goods and services of the tourist product are what Milgrom and Roberts (1992) call 'design attributes', in which small failures in coordination are very costly. Thus, one of the main roles of intermediaries is to enhance and facilitate tight coordination, thus reducing the costs of broken coordination that would likely arise in a direct market exchange between the tourist and final sellers.
>
> (Calveras and Orfila 2007, p. 5)

If condition (8.7) is satisfied, then the tour operator has a potential market for its tours, but the markup must still comply with both condition (8.4), imposed by market competition, and condition (8.7), imposed by the competition with self-organizing tourists. In other words, m will be set as the minimum between the values indicated by the two conditions:

$$m = \min\left[F(\mathrm{MP}); \frac{z - \mathrm{DUC}}{\mathrm{DUC}}\right]. \tag{8.8}$$

Therefore, solution (8.8) completes the determination of the price for the package tour, unfolded through the full cost pricing strategy (8.2).

Finally, two additional remarks on the pricing strategy of the package holiday are needed. From Sect. 5.5.1 we know that the shadow price of the holiday directly depends, as an opportunity cost, on the tourist's income (the higher the income, the higher the shadow price) and inversely on the ease with which the destination management releases information, thus rendering the self-organization of the holiday more widely accessible (the more the information, the lower the shadow price). Therefore, if the binding constraint in formula (8.8) is the one coming from the competition of self-organizing tourists, the tour operator's markup, as well as its level of profits, will depend on the following conditions: (a) it will be higher for tour operators that work with those segments that sell to high-income tourists; (b) it will be lower for tour operators that work in a destination that facilitates independent search by the tourists.

In short, when setting the market price of a package holiday, the tour operator suffers from the competition of other operators, of self-organizing tourists, and also from the potential competition of the destination, when it facilitates the release of information and thus promoting the self-production of the holiday.

8.2.4 The Tour Operator's Pricing Strategy

As already stated throughout the book, tourism services have the following important characteristics: (a) they are absolutely "perishable" because they cannot be stored and subsequently sold in a more favorable time: what remains unsold is definitely lost from an economic point of view; (b) they are subject to a volatile demand, with strong seasonal and cyclical components, for the reasons stated in Sect. 7.5.

As these characteristics may negatively affect its economic performance, the tour operator needs to implement any strategy aimed at reducing the risk of economic loss in presence of such uncertainty. The marketing and pricing strategies are therefore very important; not only these involve the way in which the brochure is prepared and promoted (with clarity, transparency, and style) but also the different pricing strategies that can be applied when selling the holiday. By anticipating some of the aspects that will be treated more organically in Sect. 9.5, we here discuss the following strategies:

- The *early booking*. When presenting expression (8.1) we highlighted that the precision of the forecast is essential for the calculation of the DUC. To ease the control of such estimate, the tour operator may undertake marketing, advertising, and early sale campaigns based on special discounts to stimulate the advanced booking. By anticipating as much as possible the comparison between actual sales and forecast ones, it is possible to take early actions if sales do not meet the targets. In particular, if there is insufficient demand for a particular destination included in the catalog, the tour operator may be able to take action to avoid losses, for example, by renegotiating the contracts with the suppliers of tourism services, or by transferring the existing contracts to other intermediaries, or by canceling the destination from the set of available holidays. To stimulate the early booking, the holiday is usually offered with a consistent discount on the market price. However, the tour operator often keeps the right: (a) to cancel the contract and refund the customers if the sales are below a minimum threshold; (b) to modify the contract, by combining two or more tours or by changing the characteristics of the accommodation; (c) to adjust the price, in order to respond to an increase in actual costs, as in presence of currency appreciation (Chap. 14), or changes in transport fares or local taxes. The typical contract stipulated for the early booking requires that the change in the price should be communicated to customers well in advance to let them decide whether or not to confirm the purchase. Since price increases are usually unwelcome by customers, the contract might include a clause that explicitly forbids surcharges or that indicates a maximum limit for the price increase. Alternatively, the tour operator may stipulate an insurance contract to hedge against such financial risks (see Sect. 11.3). On the other hand, the tour operator must protect itself against the possibility of cancelations. For this reason, for example, many early booking contracts exclude any reimbursement or limit it very heavily when the cancelation time is close to the departure.
- The *dynamic pricing*. When more sophisticated statistical models and management tools become available to tour operators to make forecasts and to monitor reservations more precisely, and when the printed catalog loses importance relative to the web, it is possible to reformulate prices even on a daily basis and make them fully available to travel agencies and to final customers. Then, travel agencies can promptly advertise the holiday by highlighting the price change with respect to what is printed in the catalog. As we will soon see, this policy is not exactly a last-minute price, but a more general reservation management policy: by the means of dynamic pricing, the holiday's price continuously changes, depending on the evolution of reservations. There is no standard formula or precise algorithm for applying this pricing strategy, in the sense that the tour operator often tries to find the best strategy by rule of thumb or by a tit-for-tat strategy (see Sect. 9.5).
- The *last-minute pricing*. The tour operator's pricing policy may require a last-minute sale at a price much lower than the official market price. By running last-minute sales the tour operator aims at recovering some of the costs already incurred by signing free sale contracts with hotels and carriers. However, this

strategy may lead to problems in the dynamics of bookings. Indeed, if tourists are aware of the possibility of last-minute discounts they most likely be encouraged to postpone the booking, a behavior that certainly contrasts with the need for the tour operators to monitor with certainty and in advance its sales.

- The *low cost*. The practice of low cost, that was originally established as a sale condition for air transport (see Sect. 9.3), recently became a more general strategy followed by any type of tourism firm, including tour operators. The supply of low-cost holidays requires a particular attention to the structure of production costs. Their reduction, a necessary condition for the supply not to imply an economic loss, can be achieved following three alternative paths: (a) a real reduction in costs, which affects the features of the product, offered with *no frills*, that is, without accessory or optional services, which may be purchased by paying an extra price; (b) the marketing path, according to which the low-cost supply must be supported by strong advertising and promotion strategies aiming at sufficiently high volume of sales that enable significant economies of scale, since the low-cost strategy reduces the per-customer earning. This path, hence, is obviously not suited for tour operators operating in small market niches or segments; (c) the organizational path, which tries to modify the supply chain by eliminating (or reducing) the intermediaries and by making a full use of Internet tools and direct selling to tourists. The low-cost strategy should not be confused with policies based on special discounts (early booking, see above) or clearance sales (see below), given that the former is the outcome of specially designed packages, usually advertised and promoted through special low-cost catalogs, which are printed at the beginning of the season and constantly supplied.
- The *clearance sale*. Very close to the last-minute strategy, this strategy is more easily interpreted as a sale because the price can be reduced down to the point where it is below the average cost. Because the service is perishable, to sell it off at a low price is anyway better than not selling it at all (provided that the price is at least above the marginal cost, see Sect. 8.3.2), and this motivates the offer when it is almost certain that no other customer will buy the service at the normal price.
- The *discount*. To support sales, the tour operator often offers a discount, which can either be in percentage terms or as a fixed amount. Discounts usually differ according to tours and destinations, and this allows the company to encourage tourism activity during certain periods of the year and at those destinations where the number of reservations is below the threshold of profitability. In order to avoid the risk of spoiling the market, however, discounts are not offered during the peak season. Many discounts are offered with the clause of "subject to availability," which consists of offering only a limited quantity of products at the discounted price. Such clause obviously requires a great deal of transparency on the behalf of the tour operator, in order not to raise concerns or doubts about its inability to comply with the announced conditions.

- The *roulette formula*. According to this policy, the visitor chooses the destination and reserves the hotel category at a price that is lower than the market price posted on the catalog, but the tourist agrees in not knowing, sometimes until the day of arrival at the destination, in which tourism structure will be hosted. This strategy allows the tour operator to manage with a great deal of flexibility the (free sale) contracts signed with hotels, by also providing a tool to deal with overbooking (see Sect. 9.5). In exchange with a low price, the tourist accepts the risk to end up in a hotel with fewer services (for example, without the swimming pool) or distant from the beach; however, the customer may as well be upgraded and enjoy accommodation in a structure of higher quality, if there are unsold services. This is a relatively old travel policy, as it first appeared in the 1970s, but together with the last-minute strategy is back in vogue.
- *Confidential price*. In addition to these pricing policies, tour operators can also sign private agreements with some intermediaries or with certain clients (i.e., an event management or a big company) with which they relate more frequently; such practice, which can include discounts or other favorable conditions, is commonly called "confidential price."

Each of the tour operator's several pricing strategies is justified both by the fact that the package holiday is not a storable good and by the need to conclude contracts in advance. The variety of prices offered through the different strategies often reaches a point that the price posted in the catalog may be absent or just taken as a mere reference point because, in practice, it is continuously changed by the tour operator and communicated, via e-mail or Internet, to travel agencies, which update them in the shop window or on their web site.

8.3 The Travel Agency

Along the holiday's supply chain, the travel agency operates as the traditional intermediary and retailer that directly deals with final customers. In other words, the travel agency is the link between the tour operator and the tourist.

Similarly to the tour operating market, also the market for intermediaries is characterized by ease of entry and exit, high number of agents, and a sharp polarization between the extremely large and the very small. In this matter, an important difference between the US and the European market exists. In the US, with around 40,000 travel agents, the great majority of them are single based agents (one third of which, thanks to the development of the Internet, are home-based agents). In Europe instead, the great majority of the 80,000 travel agents are multiple branches, often linked (through direct ownership or license agreements) to the big tour operators.

As done in the previous section, we will first discuss the functions and the activities of the travel agency, and then we will focus on its economic rationale, that pivots around the determination of the conditions of profitability. Finally, we will stress on some aspects related to the development of online travel agencies.

8.3.1 Functions and Activities of the Travel Agency

The primary function of the travel agency is to sell travel services to business and leisure tourists. From an economic stand point (the terminology is borrowed from commercial practice), the travel agency operates as "agent" of many "principals," where the principal may be a tour operator, a hotel, a transport company, etc. Therefore, the travel agency sells package tours produced by tour operators and basic services produced by other tourism firms. A travel agency may also offer ancillary services to the tourist, such as travel insurance or visa services.

The travel agent's activity is therefore extremely broad and includes: (a) the intermediation in the sale of the tour operators' holidays; (b) the organization of specific trips (through the search and subsequent sale of a bouquet of tourism services), according to the tourist's request; (c) the booking and sale of single tourism services, such as air and train tickets as well as hotel and other accommodation; (d) the sale of tickets for special events; (e) the provision of travel and health insurance to protect against the risks associated with tourism activity.

According to which of the above services is the most important, travel agencies can be classified into three categories.

1. Agencies mainly dealing with all-inclusive holidays. Such agencies can be further distinguished in *incoming* versus *outgoing* agencies; incoming agencies are located in the destination and mainly work with incoming tourists and with external tour operators; outgoing travel agencies are located in the region of origin of tourism flows and mainly work with potential tourists.
2. Agencies mainly operating toward the accommodation of large groups.
3. Agencies mainly working with medium and large firms to meet the travel requests of managers and employees. Such activity falls into the category of *business tourism* and *incentive tours*.[6]

The travel agency is the subject that accomplishes the most delicate stage in the production and distribution chain of the package holiday: the relationship with the tourist. In this relationship, on the one hand, there are the clients (the potential tourists) with their own preferences and their difficulties in finding reliable information and in choosing the right package; on the other hand, there is the travel agency with its own professional experience (often resulting from years of formation and practice), which provides information to the customers and help them evaluate the different packages supplied by the tour operators. Within the wide range of services offered by the travel agency, it is sufficient here to discuss three of its activities.

[6] The business tourism can be classified as: (1) trips organized to meet customers or suppliers in order to sign contracts, to develop business plans, or for technical assistance; (2) trips organized to attend trade fairs; (3) trips organized to attend conferences, conventions, or business meetings. Incentive tours, instead, consist of trips purchased by a company to reward managers or promoters for their accomplishments or to strengthen their sense of belonging to the company.

1. *The sale of package tours*. For the travel agency, the sale of all-inclusive tours is an important, and often vital, activity. This is the case not only because of their impact on the firm's income but also because the sale of package holidays determines its public image. The agency's reward is a commission that is usually determined as a percentage of the market price of the package holiday. Often, the contracts between tour operators and travel agencies are of incentive type (see Sect. 11.6), in the sense that they start at a basic rate which increases progressively as further sales targets are achieved (these commercial agreements are technically called "over commission").
2. *The sale of tickets*. The right to sell tickets of any kind is not automatically linked to the possession of an authorization to operate as travel agency, but it is subject to the authorization of the carrier, which depends on the fulfillment of particular requirements: for example, an agency willing to sell air tickets on a global scale must obtain a IATA (International Air Transport Association) license, which is released only having passed a careful investigation on the qualifications and the experience of the agency. Such requirements may be in terms of: (a) the training and refreshing of the agency's employees; (b) the hardware and the software used, such as the computer reservation systems; (c) the agency's location; (d) the guarantee of solvency. Again, the agency's commission is usually determined as a percentage of the tickets' price.
3. *The booking of services*. Within the list of travel agency's activities the booking of single services is very important. A great part of the agency's activity is devoted to booking services such as hotel accommodation or air transports for the benefit of business or leisure tourists. The booking of tourism services is based on the availability of information related to tourism destinations, hotel chains, carriers, events, etc. Usually, the travel agency gathers public and private information, detailed maps, suggestions about the routes to explore and the local attractions or events to attend, the complete and reliable list of hotels, restaurants, and shopping centers, in short, all the pieces of information that may be used to build a "library for the tourist." To this aim, the direct experience of the agent remains the key operational asset: it often happens that the travel agent personally experiences the tour or the holiday, in particular when the tour operator allows the travel agent to freely test the package before selling it to the general public.

With such professional activity, the travel agency achieves a comparative advantage in the production of information with respect to the potential tourist. In other words, and using the terminology of Sect. 6.7, the cost of information search for the agency is lower than the cost for the tourist: such gap provides the reason for the existence on the market of the travel agency as an intermediary in the reservation and sale of services.

This conclusion can easily be demonstrated by referring again to Table 6.1. When discussing the search for the optimal level of information, in Sect. 6.7.2 we assumed two tourists with different costs of information production: tourist A had an absolute advantage and a per-search cost of information equal to 9.20, while tourist B had a higher cost, equal to 9.40 per-search. It is straightforward to rename tourist A as the travel agency while the tourist B can be thought of as its client. Under such conditions, the travel agent can rationally undertake four surveys and end up purchasing an overnight stay at an expected price of 206.25. The tourist B, however, has the convenience of carrying out only three surveys so that the expected price will be 215.50 (see Table 6.1). The difference between these two prices allows a market exchange to occur and justifies the travel agency to exist. In particular, if A is a travel agency, it does not act for itself, but retrieves the information with the goal of selling the service to B at a price $206.25 < p < 215.50$. Such price happens to be beneficial for both the travel agency, which owns a profit equal to (p - 206.25), and the tourist, who is able to save a sum equal to (215.50 - p) by buying the service through the agency rather than independently.

Finally, as part of this process of information gathering and distribution, the agency uses its experience, skills, and reputation to ensure the credibility of information and the quality of proposed services. Therefore, the agency's charge is not only justified as an information provider but also as a reputation provider (see Sect. 10.4.3).

8.3.2 The Profitability of the Travel Agency

As previously said, the profitability of the travel agency depends on the remuneration that it receives from the sale of tourism services, and this usually consists of a commission paid by tour operators, hotels, carriers, insurance companies, and so on. Such commission is commonly calculated as a percentage of the service's price. The amount of the commission varies according to the type of the contract and also reflects the travel agency's bargaining power.

Recently, it has become a common practice for tourism firms to sell their services to travel agents at a net price, enabling the agency to set the final market price at its own discretion. This is particularly relevant for online travel agencies and when the agency operates more or less as a kind of tour organizer. In such cases, the remuneration may consist of a markup charged on the net price of the services. Such markup must comply with all the constraints already analyzed when discussing the tour operator's activity: on the one hand, the markup is a function of the agency's market power; on the other hand, the agency must consider the shadow price of the tourist self-producing the holiday. For example, recalling the case of the previous section, we have: $206.25\ (1 + m_{\mathrm{TA}}) < 215.50$ from which, with a simple calculation, it can be easily verified that $m_{\mathrm{TA}} < 4.48\ \%$.

In all the remaining cases, the agency's income comes from a commission which remunerates its activity as intermediary. So, if we denote with p the average price of services, with Q the number of sold services, and with g the commission paid to the travel agency in percentage terms, its net revenue NR (net of the payment to be

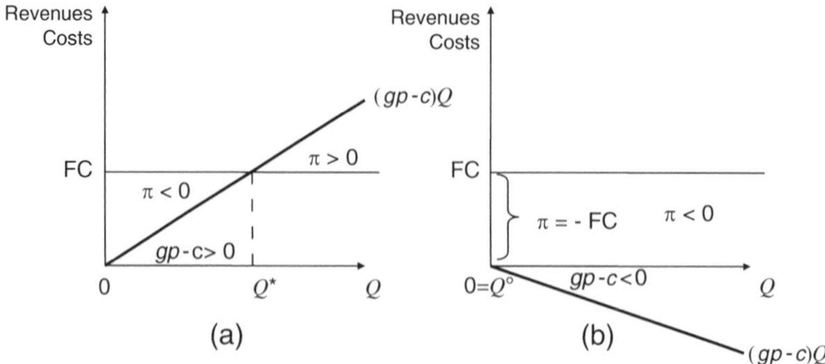

Fig. 8.1 The conditions of profitability of the travel agency

made to the providers) is: NR $= gpQ$. Such revenue will be used to cover the agency's variable costs (VC) and fixed costs (FC), so to leave a profit, π_{TA}:

$$\pi_{\mathrm{TA}} = gpQ - \mathrm{VC} - \mathrm{FC}. \tag{8.9}$$

Since, by definition, the variable costs depend on the quantity of services, and assuming that they grow linearly according to a factor c, we have VC $= cQ$. If we plug this relation into (8.9) we get

$$\pi_{\mathrm{TA}} = (gp - c)Q - \mathrm{FC}. \tag{8.10}$$

Equation (8.10) is represented in Fig. 8.1a as the difference between two curves, one rising from the origin, $(gp - c)Q$, and the other as a constant equal to the fixed costs FC. In order to guarantee a positive profit to the travel agency, the following two economic conditions have to be identified.

1. *The condition of existence on the market*, $(gp > c)$. Such condition claims that the commission for the service sold by the travel agency must be strictly greater than its unit production cost.[7] It can be easily verified that if $gp < c$, i.e., if the curve in bold is downward sloping, as in Fig. 8.1b, any increase in production would lead to an additional loss equal to the difference between the two variables. In this case, the optimal solution for the agency would be to exit the market: with such decision the agency would minimize its loss, which would only amount to fixed costs ($\pi_{\mathrm{TA}} = -\mathrm{FC}$). If instead, as shown in Fig. 8.1a, the curve in bold is upward sloping, the agency would have an incentive to stay in business, even when it does not reach a positive profit. Then, the condition $(gp > c)$ is a sufficient condition to ensure a loss reduction as sales increase.

[7] Since the agent's revenue is given by the commission, which usually remains unchanged for long periods of time, the policy of monitoring and controlling the variable costs is the best available tool for the agency to reach its own target in terms of profit.

To sum up, the agency remains on the market, even without earning a profit, when it has already made investments (which require fixed costs to be borne, regardless of sale) and when ($gp > c$). In this case, any increase in the quantity of sold services reduces the loss up to the point in which the profit becomes positive.

2. *The break-even point condition*, ($Q \geq Q^*$). From Fig. 8.1a it is clear that, despite ($gp > c$), when ($Q < Q^*$) the agency's net revenue does not cover the fixed costs and the economic activity leads to a loss. Therefore, a positive profit appears only when the level of sales is greater than Q^*. Quantity Q^* in Fig. 8.1a is called *break-even point* and identifies the minimum level of activity that the agency must reach in order to gain a profit. This is a necessary long-term condition for the agency's economic sustainability in the market[8]; indeed, given that by definition we have zero fixed costs in the long run, a negative profit would not be economically sustainable. Then, if ($Q < Q^*$) the agency would only survive in the market in the short run presented sub case (1), which is when the agency is stuck in the market due to the presence of fixed costs. It is also easy to verify that the break-even point strongly depends on the level of fixed costs facing the agency. Given the difficulties in increasing the revenue, the travel agency must pay attention to control its (fixed) cost.

To conclude, if ($gp < c$), the agency will exit the market even in the short run since the loss increases with sales; if ($gp > c$) and ($Q < Q^*$), the agency stays on the market only in the short term, in order to reduce the loss stemming from the existence of fixed costs; finally, if ($gp > c$) and ($Q > Q^*$) the agency stays on the market also in the long run because it earns a positive profit. It is important to highlight that the difference between the condition of profitability in the short and in the long term, here analyzed for the case of a travel agency, is a conclusion that holds for any (tourism and not-tourism) firm and that is primarily stemming from the existence of fixed costs.

In general, since the travel agency has low fixed costs and relatively low entry costs, the retail tourism market can be considered a contestable market.[9] This means that to enter and exit the sector, a firm must not bear any sunk cost. The firm only needs a shop with an appropriate show window, a broadband connection, and to sign contracts with tour operators and other service providers. It is, however, important to notice the location of travel agencies: one can often observe a bimodal distribution of shops between the town center and its periphery, in a market structure that is difficult to interpret.

[8] In microeconomics the "short run" is defined as the period of time in which there are fixed costs, while the "long run" is the period of time that is long enough to not imply any fixed cost.

[9] A market is contestable if firms can freely enter and exit the market without bearing any additional cost (Baumol et al. 1982).

8.3.3 Online Travel Agencies and Web Tourists

The web, firstly through the evolution of the *Computer Reservation Systems* and then with the development of the Internet, has radically changed (and in many ways made more difficult) the work of the travel agency. However, its main activity as an intermediary between the tourism supplier and the tourists is still key, even in the Internet era. While the role of Information and Communication Technology will be discussed at length in Chap. 12, here we only want to highlight how the Internet actually created new opportunities for tourism businesses that use the Internet for their intermediary and retailing activity: these are the so-called *Online Travel Agencies* (OLTA).

The OLTAs are web portals, characterized by a virtual location (an Internet address), offering a wide array of services to the web tourists, those customers who mainly use the Internet to self-organize their holiday. Except for their virtual location, OLTAs are basically travel agencies, which use the web as the channel to inform and sell services to the tourists. Hence, they take full advantage of the opportunities of *infomediation* (online intermediation).

Firstly, most of them help the tourists with the web search and with the booking of accommodation, flight, train, car rental, tickets for shows and events, up to the booking of all-inclusive packages. Some agencies also help the tourist search for discounted trips or compare similar offers by selecting the cheapest one. Such online agencies are called *search engines* or *meta engines*, because they scan the Web in looking for the best rates for a given destination, a particular type of holiday, or a route. On the one hand, such service is not offered for free and the price can be a bit higher than the price offered through the direct search (e.g., through the airline company website) due to the commission or the markup charged by the OLTA; on the other hand, due to their strong bargaining power and the economies of scale they can enjoy, the impact on the price might be minimal if not negligible for the tourist.[10] Sometimes these OLTAs are able to semiautomatically build package tours on their owns, thus acting as online tour operators. Finally, on line travel agencies and web portals may provide further information, such as travel guides, maps, or comments and reviews posted by previous tourists.

The online travel agencies differ in terms of the "size" of their web site (measured both by number of hits and by the number of available services), and regarding the degree of integration with other (small, medium, or giant) firms operating in the tourism sector. From this point of view, OLTAs can be classified as either big or small. The big agencies are often final terminals of the global giants that produce tourism brokerage: the Global Distribution System operators (see Chap. 12) or some large multinational tour operators (Chap. 14). Many large tour operators often prefer not to directly engage on the web: when they decide to be on the Internet, they usually prefer to create a different brand or to rely on the services supplied by external providers.

[10] It has to be added that for the tourist it is probably better to have all the relevant information (with the comparison of all the prices) summarized in one single page rather than bearing the higher costs of separate searches on the single airlines' web sites.

Besides big agencies, that obviously have market power and the ability to sell at competitive prices, also small agencies (often home based and composed by one or few workers) that are specialized in specific types of trips, or in particular destinations can be found on the Internet. The online service offered by small agencies not only benefits the customers who are in search of specific information and look for a personal contact, but also allows small- and medium-sized tourism firms to be on the Internet. In fact, without this type of brokerage, small firms may be marginalized due to their lack of technical skills that the presence on the Web does certainly require, and they might otherwise rely solely on the destination web management (see Sect. 4.3.5).

A special case of OLTA, finally, is represented by agencies offering credit to consumers and other financial services to assist the purchase of holidays, and sell last-second holidays to very bargaining prices, sometimes by the means of online auctions (see Notes 12.1), which are specifically designed for customers who almost have their luggage ready. Somehow, these agencies are able to manage the clearance sale of tour operators (see Sect. 8.2.4).

To conclude, with the development of OLTAs in recent years, the retail and brokerage market for tourism services can now be distinguished in three groups (Ioannides and Petridou-Daugthrey 2006): (a) real travel agencies that only have a physical and geographical location; (b) real travel agencies that also have a virtual location on the web; (c) virtual travel agencies that are only located on the web. This leads to two conclusions that should be highlighted.

Firstly, the OLTA can be seen as the contemporary evolution of the traditional travel agency, not as its substitute. For this reason, the economic rationale of an online agency should not be seen as *qualitatively* different from that of a traditional agency, and can be analyzed according to the framework presented in Sect. 8.3.2. The difference with the traditional agency is rather *quantitative*. What is different in the OLTA is the ability to search and to manage the information (and thus the percentage of markup that can be charged), the cost structure (and thus the relative importance of fixed and variable costs), the market power against the suppliers of services (and thus the value of the commission that the OLTA receives).

Secondly, in the age of Internet, a real travel agency can survive only if it is able to identify a market niche, so to exploit comparative advantages; however, an increasing integration with the web is always necessary.

Chapter Overview

- The tour operator is a firm that stipulates contracts, at different levels of risk, with tourism service providers, with the aim of building "all-inclusive" package tours which are then sold to tourists mainly through travel agencies
- The tour operator produces package tours by either purchasing services provided by independent firms or through a strategy of vertical integration. In the first case

the tour operator signs contracts, mainly "allotment" and "free sale" contracts, with its suppliers: in the second case, it acquires full control of all the other stages of the production chain.

- In determining the unit cost of a package holiday, the tour operator must distinguish between direct (fixed and variable) and indirect costs. The direct costs depend on the load factor of the tourism structures, which must be estimated by the tour operator by adding a stochastic component to the cost.
- The tour operator's profit depends on the accuracy of the estimates on the number of tourists, on the markup charged on direct costs, and on the importance of the indirect costs (which are the costs related to the general organization, administration, and structure of the tour operator).
- The travel agency is the traditional point of contact between tourists and the providers of tourism services. It deals with selling package tours, organizing trips on request, collecting and distributing information to the tourist, selling travel and health insurance, issuing air and train tickets, and booking accommodation services.
- An important activity for the travel agency is that of information searching, which sets it in a position of comparative advantage relative to the tourist, because of the lower search costs it bears.
- The profitability of the travel agency depends on the relationship between the price of the service, usually set by the supplier, and the commission paid to the agency. To stay on the market, such commission must be greater than the variable unit cost, but to ensure a positive profit it must also cover the fixed unit cost, so to exceed the break-even point.
- Online travel agencies (also known as OLTAs) share with traditional travel agencies the structure of their economic problem. In the Internet age, a traditional travel agency must specialize in market niches and aim for a stronger presence on the Web.

Chapter 9
The Supply of Tourism Services: Hospitality, Transport, Attractions

Learning Outcomes.
After the reading of this chapter you will understand:

- The economic relevance of finding the optimal load factor for hospitality and transport firms.
- How the intervention of the public sector and the issue of coordination are central to the provision of tourism attractions.
- What are the strategies of yield management and how they are implemented by tourism firms.

9.1 Introduction

In this chapter, where we continue from Chap. 8 the investigation of the different types of tourism firms, we study the companies that supply tourism services included in the matrix of the tourism product. These services are also included in the package holiday produced by the tour operator: the hospitality firms supply accommodation services of different variety and quality (see Sect. 9.2); transport firms supply different types of travel (see Sect. 9.3); and museums, amusement parks, and other firms supply leisure or cultural attractions (see Sect. 9.4).[1]

We will end the chapter (see Sect. 9.5) with a focus on the management strategy that can be applied by both these firms and the ones analyzed in the previous

[1] Lundberg et al. (1995) include restaurants, bars, and other catering services in the list of tourism companies. Since restaurants also serve non-tourist customers, these authors call "tourism restaurants" those that mainly serve customers who live at least 50 miles away from the business. Because this classification seems too rough and little operational, we decided to not explicitly consider restaurants in our investigation, even if they provide an important contribution to the composition of the tourism product.

G. Candela and P. Figini, *The Economics of Tourism Destinations*,
Springer Texts in Business and Economics, DOI 10.1007/978-3-642-20874-4_9,

chapter. Such strategy, which is known as yield management (or revenue management), needs the understanding of the basic models of tourism firms and of their price setting decisions. Therefore, a specific analysis can be only carried out at the end of these two chapters.

The firms providing tourism services are gathered by the fact of being located in the destination, either totally (hospitality firms and attractions) or partially (transport companies). It is therefore necessary to emphasize that a comprehensive study of their economic problems cannot be separated from considerations related to the process of organization, management, and coordination of the destination (Chap. 4). Moreover, as we already know, such coordination may also occur during the building up of the package holiday by the tour operator (see Sect. 8.2) and within the contractual agreements stipulated by these companies (Chap. 11).

9.2 The Hospitality Sector

We will first provide an introduction to the hospitality sector by classifying the different types of hospitality firms, and then, we will analyze their economic problem and conclude with the overview of some specific issues.

9.2.1 The Hospitality Sector and the Tourism System

Within the tourism product, the activity of providing accommodation services to tourists has a fundamental role because, except for the case of day trippers, visitors need a place where to rest during their trip or to stay once they arrive at the destination. The failure of the hospitality sector implies the failure of the destination as a whole. Hospitality firms are characterized by a strong dualism:

> It is important to highlight that the hotel accommodation sector is characterized by a notable dualism observed in size (large-small), ownership (chain-independent), structure (oligopoly-monopolistic competition), quality (high-low) and location (center-periphery).
>
> (Stabler et al. 2010, p. 170)

Therefore, hospitality firms can be classified according to different parameters:

- *Size*, with structures ranging from the Bed&Breakfast with a very limited number of rooms, to big hotels with the capacity of accommodating hundreds of tourists;
- *Quality*, ranging from the solely supply of the essential, yet functional, service of accommodation, to the most opulent and luxurious hotel, offering many other complementary services such as conference venues, spa, swimming pool, etc.
- *Property*, ranging from the family-run hotel to large international chains.

The internationally adopted classification of accommodation facilities primarily distinguishes between hotels (and similar accommodation establishments) and other collective accommodation establishments. The former are further classified according to their category (internationally, the most commonly used classification scheme ranks hotels from one to five stars), while the latter include facilities such as campsites, self-catering accommodation, hostels, farmhouses, apartments for rent, B&B.

Hotels are also important suppliers of complementary services, restaurant and bar services in first place, but also leisure, sport and wellness facilities, business services and conference venues, up to shopping and tour organizing management. Obviously, by providing these services in an integrated manner, the hotel represents a direct source of competition for other tourism firms, often with a competitive advantage stemming from the privileged contact with the tourist (for example, hotels that offer bikes to their guests affect the bike rental market).

Exceptionally, the accommodation establishment can be considered an attraction in itself, and not just a complementary service to the other attractions of the destination. For example, think of a Spa Hotel, in which the firm offers to its customers both the services of accommodation and wellness needed for that type of holiday. In this case, when the hotel can be considered the destination in itself, the firm's profit stems not only from the sale of the hotel room, which may be a service of less importance, but rather from the management of wellness services such as massages, medical tests, and beauty treatments, thus becoming similar to firms providing tourism attractions (see Sect. 9.4).

From the organizational perspective, the hospitality firms can be classified as (Cooper et al. 2008):

- Organizations with complete or partial accommodation services, such as hotels, motels, guesthouses, B&B, and farmhouses.
- Self-catering organizations, such as (a) the apartments or rooms for rent; (b) timeshare properties, which consist of the ownership of a house that is only limited to certain periods of the year; (c) villas and cottages; (d) youth hostels, mainly used by young travelers due to their low prices and basic supply of services (though in recent years some hostels increased the quality of their structures); (e) campsites and bungalows.
- Supporting structures for the benefit of tourists who travel with caravan homes or motor homes, carrying their own accommodation with them.
- Accommodation inside a means of transport, such as (a) cruise ships which are, by definition, traveling hotels; (b) ferries: those that offer accommodation services on longer routes have very similar characteristics to the cruise ships; (c) trains: by providing accommodation and leisure services, some trains have become similar to cruising organizations (i.e., the Orient Express in Europe, the Singapore-Bangkok in Asia); (d) some airlines, particularly in the intercontinental first-class segment.
- Other forms of accommodation, such as (a) lodging in a health care facility: some hospitals located in tourism destinations provide services other than those

that strictly relate to the health care; in particular, some hospitals offer high-quality services to their patients' relatives and friends; also, some long-term care homes are run by hotel companies and so become hybrids between luxury hotels and nursing homes; (b) the overnight stay of guests at their relatives' or friends' homes; this form of tourism (Visiting Friends and Relatives—VFR) is very popular in some countries, in particular for domestic tourism where many visitors stay in a family environment. This phenomenon does not have to be underestimated since, although not displaying any demand for the accommodation sector in the matrix of the tourism product, it may be nevertheless important for the demand of other tourism services in the destination.

Hotels are without any doubt the most important and visible segment of the tourism sector within destinations. In most of the world hotels are managed by local and independent enterprises, but in recent years global competition has driven to a process of horizontal integration through mergers and acquisitions, thus leading to the development of international hotel chains. There are three main models of ownership and management of the hotel:

- The hotel chain may directly own and manage the single hotel facility.
- The hotel management can be undertaken through a contract of franchising (Case Study 9.1), either at the individual level or as a master franchising agreement.
- Finally the hotel management can be on the behalf of an independent owner.

Case Study 9.1. International Hotel Chains: The Case of Best Western

The story of Best Western began in the United States in 1946, founded by M.K. Guertin and based on the idea that collaboration between operators in the hotel sector could generate large profits. The group, named because most of the associates were located in the western United States, was born as a consortium of approximately 50 hotels. Since then, the chain's brand rapidly spread to other continents, arriving in Europe in 1978. Best Western International is currently one of the largest hotel chains in the world; it deals with the marketing, reservations, and operational support for over 4,000 member hotels which are independent in ownership and management, and which host every night about 400,000 customers in eighty countries around the world. The independent property of Best Western's hotels, which is its greatest strength, stems from a business model designed to give each owner the maximum flexibility in meeting the needs of its specific demand.

As an example, Italy is one of the countries in which the Best Western group is massively active. In 1982 Best Western begun its activity with Best Western Italia as part of Best Western International Holding and with just eleven hotels. Since then, new memberships have grown rapidly: in 1985 it gathered 42 hotels (with an availability of about 4,000 rooms) which grew to 62 in 1988 and 76 in 1992. The 100-member goal was reached in 1997, and as of today, Best Western Italia gathers 170 hotels with approximately 12,000 rooms in 120 Italian destinations.

The success of international chains such as Best Western lies on the idea that holding the membership to a group may be the best strategy to meet the demand of an increasingly international and complex demand. The ability to adhere to a high and internationally recognized standard, while maintaining the characteristic environment of the local destination where the hotel is located, is generally appreciated by many hotel owners and tourists.

9.2.2 Costs and Prices of Hospitality Firms

In what follows, we use the word "hotel" for simplicity, to encompass all the different types of suppliers that operate in the hospitality sector. Hence, the word has to be understood in a broad sense, so as to include any type of accommodation firm ranging from family-run B&B to big hotels; from small independent companies that operate a single structure in a specific destination to international chains that control several production units operating in different destinations. As done for the other types of firms operating in the tourism sector, in this chapter we only deal with the main economic issue faced by the hotel, the estimation of the costs, and the definition of the optimal price for the accommodation service, within the economic perspective of profit maximization.[2]

We start by identifying the production costs for the hospitality service. Like for any other firm, also the hotel faces two main types of cost: fixed costs and variable costs.

1. The fixed costs are costs that do not vary with the number of bed places (rooms) being used; consequently, the unit (average) fixed cost depends on the total number of services sold, that is, on the occupancy rate of the hotel. When the occupancy rate increases, fixed costs are spread over a larger number of services, thus diminishing the unit cost when there are many tourists and, vice versa increasing it when there are many empty rooms. Among the fixed costs we list the staff payroll, the lease of the building and the equipment (either as out-of-pocket expenditure or as an opportunity cost), advertising costs, insurance premiums, etc.
2. The variable costs are costs that change according to the number of services used, which can be measured by the number of overnight stays in the hotel. Among the variable costs we list the purchase of food for the restaurant and the

[2] We refer to the literature on hotel management for the investigation of specific management issues (see for example Hayes and Ninemeier 2006, Rutherford and O'Fallon 2006).

bar, water, heating and electricity bills, the costs of laundering and ironing services, the commissions paid to travel agencies, etc.

With reference to the costs, it is important to highlight that the degree of utilization of the accommodation capacity (the occupancy rate) is of strategic importance for the hotel, mainly because the fixed costs are the largest share of total production costs. The discussion on the measurement and the analysis of the occupancy rate is postponed to Sect. 9.2.3; in what follows we will focus instead on the analysis of production costs and the definition of the price for the accommodation service.

If we denote with FC the amount of fixed costs, with VC the amount of variable costs, with N_{H} the number of overnight stays in the hotel, and with c the unit variable cost for providing the accommodation service, then total costs TC are as follows:

$$\mathrm{TC} = \mathrm{FC} + \mathrm{VC} \text{ with } \mathrm{VC} = cN_{\mathrm{H}}. \tag{9.1}$$

If we divide by the number of overnight stays, we get the unit (average) cost, UC, of the accommodation service:[3]

$$\mathrm{UC} = \frac{\mathrm{FC}}{N_{\mathrm{H}}} + c. \tag{9.2}$$

Once the unit cost is defined, the economic literature suggests several methods for the determination of the price (Kotler et al. 2009). In what follows we present the two most popular methods, the full-cost method and the target profit method, both requiring the existence of some degree of market power for the hotel, which is the same as assuming that the firm is, at least partially, price maker.

9.2.2.1 The Full Cost

According to the full-cost model, the price of the hospitality service is set with reference to the average variable cost, c. In particular, the hotel sets a markup as a percentage of c in order to cover the fixed costs and to gain a profit. If we denote with m the markup, the price can be determined by this simple formula:

$$p = c(1 + m) = c + mc. \tag{9.3}$$

According to the commercial practice, the setting of the hotel's markup aims at reaching at least a minimum return to the investment by applying a few rules of

[3] The marginal cost of production is given instead by the change in costs due to a one-unit increase in the number of stays. In our case, with constant returns we have $\mathrm{dTC}/\mathrm{d}N_{\mathrm{H}} = \mathrm{dVC}/\mathrm{d}N_{\mathrm{H}} = c$.

thumb (Shaw 1992). Among the most popular approaches there are: (a) the Hubbart formula, which starts from the target rate of profit to be reached and then goes backward to the optimal price and hence to the markup needed to reach that profit; (b) the "dollar-per-thousand rule", which indicates that for each additional $1,000 that are invested in a room the price should go up of $1 (Lundberg et al. 1995). In other words, if the amount of investment in the hotel is such that the cost of each room is $50,000, the price for the room service should be around $50.

According to (9.3) and to the overnight stays N_{H}, the hotel total revenue TR can be written as

$$\mathrm{TR} = pN_{\mathrm{H}} = cN_{\mathrm{H}}(1+m) = \mathrm{VC}(1+m).$$

By subtracting total costs TC from total revenue TR, the profit is easily obtained:

$$\pi = \mathrm{TR} - \mathrm{TC}. \tag{9.4}$$

9.2.2.2 The Target Profit

This approach pivots around the capital invested in the hotel, that can be measured both in terms of financial value, K, and in terms of the number of available services, the number of bed places, N.

With reference to K, we need to define: (a) the estimated payback time, measured in number of years, n; (b) the target profit of the investment, the rate r. Then, the overall profit is

$$\pi = \frac{K}{n} + rK.$$

By defining the average occupancy rate as q, with $0 \leq q \leq 1$ (see Sect. 9.2.3), the number of overnight stays in the hotel can be written as $N_{\mathrm{H}} = qN$. The equation for profit π, which is considered the target, can hence be written as

$$\pi = pN_{\mathrm{H}} - \mathrm{TC} = pN_{\mathrm{H}} - \mathrm{FC} - cN_{\mathrm{H}}$$

from which by substitution we obtain

$$\frac{K}{n} + rK = pqN - \mathrm{FC} - cqN.$$

If we solve this equation for p we get the price for the accommodation service determined on the basis of the profit target:

$$p = \frac{\left(\frac{K}{n} + rK + \mathrm{FC}\right)}{qN} + c. \tag{9.5}$$

Although apparently similar, the two methods of price setting are substantially different because the expression (9.3) for the full-cost method is based on flow variables only (the average variable cost and the markup), while the expression (9.5) for the target profit method also considers stock variables such as the value of the invested capital, the physical size of the hospitality structure, and the average occupancy rate.[4]

While formulas (9.3) and (9.5) are very helpful to grasp the basics of the price setting rule for the hotel, they are not sufficient to fully understand it. In fact, hotels may implement different policies as regards the posted price, ranging from simple to more complex:

- *The policy of fixed prices*, according to which the rooms are offered at the same price, that will change only seasonally or as a consequence of extraordinary events. Chronologically, this was the first price policy implemented by the hospitality sector, and is still popular in many small businesses.
- *The price varies according to quality*, according to which there is a range of different prices for rooms with different characteristics. For example, larger rooms with a terrace or with a Jacuzzi are sold at higher prices. From the economic perspective, this is the case of vertical differentiation (see Sect. 10.3).
- *The price varies according to the demand*, so that, given the room's characteristics, prices do not change to reflect different costs but to respond to the characteristics of different market segments (with particular reference to the price elasticity of demand). From the economic perspective, this is a strategy of price discrimination (see Sect. 9.5).
- *The non-linear pricing*, so that prices vary according to the quantity purchased. In this case, the hotel sets a price that decreases with the number of overnight stays, thus applying a discount on the quantity. In analytical terms, this is another strategy of price discrimination in which the price is a function of the length of stay of the guest, $p(N_{\mathrm{H}})$, and decreases with an increase in N_{H}. Such a pricing policy, which is designed to increase the average stay in the structure, is sometimes adopted by those hotels that offer a discounted price on Sunday night to those guests who book for Friday and Saturday nights.

When deciding their supply policy, hotels usually choose the posted price within a price range that reflects the degree of heterogeneity among their customers; for

[4] Although the calculations of (9.3) and (9.5) have been presented in terms of overnight stays (per person or per bed place), they can be similarly computed "per room", according to the commercial practice in use.

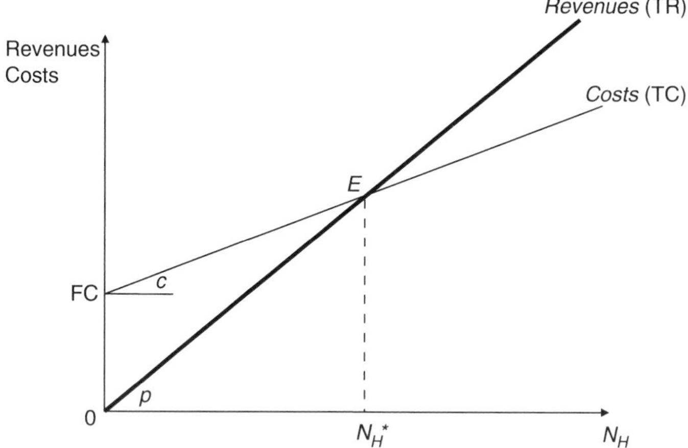

Fig. 9.1 Costs, revenues and profits for the hotel

example the hotel may set both a minimum and a maximum price for the low season and a (higher) minimum and a maximum price for the peak season. Even the use of customized price discounts should be interpreted as a further tool to implement the strategy of price discrimination, often adopted under the stimulus of competition. A popular example of special price is the one offered for weekend breaks in cultural cities, especially during the low season.

To sum up all the previous cases, we can state that the posted price is set within a range between a minimum and maximum value: $p_{\min} \leq p \leq p_{\max}$. The maximum price (the upper end of the price range) is usually called rack rate, and is quite similar to the list price of industrial companies. On the other end, the minimum price is the one usually bargained with tour operators for accommodation services to be included in package tours.

To keep things simple, the hotel's pricing policy can be reduced to a single price, the price p of expression (9.3), that can be hence interpreted as the average, weighted by the number of stays, of the different prices charged by the hotel. In this way it is possible to represent the two components of (9.4), TR and TC, in Fig. 9.1 and to identify the profit as their difference. From the diagram it is easy to conclude that if $N_{\mathrm{H}} < N_{\mathrm{H}}^*$ the hotel faces a loss since TC > TR, and if $N_{\mathrm{H}} > N_{\mathrm{H}}^*$ the hotel gets a profit instead, since TC < TR. Then, point N_{H}^* identifies the number of stays associated with the perfect equality between costs and revenues, the so-called break-even point, in which profits are nil.

Figure 9.1 is well known in the business and management literature because it well summarizes the issue of managerial control. This is also true for the hospitality sector, since the point N_{H}^* encompasses all the main issues related to the cost-benefit analysis for the tourism firm: the average price, p, which determines the slope of TR, the unit variable cost, c, which determines the slope of TC, and the fixed cost curve, FC, which determines the intercept on the y-axis of the line TC.

It is clear that Fig. 9.1 identifies the break-even point *ex post*, and leaves aside the determination of the optimal price according to the forecast of demand in different periods of the year and in accordance with the segmentation of demand. In other words, the model should be extended to embody the expectations on tourists' demand. Once more, this aspect highlights the importance of demand forecasting as a key issue for the optimal solution of the economic problem facing any tourism firm (see Sect. 4.5.3).

Another important issue to be analyzed is to provide an endogenous determination of the markup or the target profit, which are exogenous in this model. Leaving aside a more comprehensive analysis, we simply provide an intuitive answer by relying on the concept of monopoly degree, which can be measured in relation to two key elements:

1. The *direct competition*, which is the competition stemming from the presence of other hotels operating in the same segment and in the same destination; for example, four-star hotels located in the same city compete against each other for the same customers; similarly, small family-run hotels compete against each other for another segment of customers in the same destination, and so on. In short, the direct competition is between firms providing services that are close substitutes to each other.
2. The *indirect competition*, which is the competition stemming from the presence of other forms of accommodation; indeed, a four-star hotel with special offers is often an alternative to a three-star hotel, and such is a self-catering accommodation or, in the extreme case, excursionism is often an alternative. This type of competition is often affected by the change in tourists' preferences.

9.2.3 The Hotels' Management Barometers

In Sect. 9.2.2 we highlighted that N_{H}^{*} and p are two key variables for the hotel's management. On the one hand, the break-even point identifies the degree of utilization of the hotel below which the business gets a loss; on the other hand, the average price identifies the customer mix that helps determining the degree of profitability. We define as "barometers" those practical indicators that help control such management variables. In this section we introduce two of the key barometers of hotel management: the occupancy rate and the average daily rate.[5]

[5] Other useful indicators for the hotel management are the breakdown of variable costs (such as the share of labor costs on total cost, the share of spending for drinks on the total cost for the breakfast, etc.) and the ratio between liquid and financial assets.

9.2.3.1 The Occupancy Rate

The occupancy rate is a typical indicator for the hotel management. This index is the ratio between real and potential production computed over a given period of time. Potential output is measured by the number of accommodation services (the number of bed places), N, times the length of the period under scrutiny. Real output is given by the number of accommodation services that are actually sold in the same period, N_{H}. Then, the Occupancy Rate (OR) can be calculated in two different ways:

1. The generic occupancy rate, OR_{g}:

$$\mathrm{OR}_{\mathrm{g}} = \frac{N_{\mathrm{H}}}{365N} \tag{9.6}$$

2. The specific occupancy rate, OR_{s}, typically calculated for the hotels that operate seasonally and are open only for a number D of days:

$$\mathrm{OR}_{\mathrm{S}} = \frac{N_{\mathrm{H}}}{DN} \tag{9.7}$$

The two indexes can be easily related to each other, since

$$\mathrm{OR}_{\mathrm{g}} = \mathrm{OR}_{\mathrm{S}}U, \text{ with } U = \frac{D}{365}. \tag{9.8}$$

In expression (9.8), U defines the rate of seasonal use of the hospitality structure, i.e., the portion of the year in which the hotel is open and does business; the two indexes are the same if the hotel is open all year, since in such case $U = 1$.

With reference to the analysis carried out in Sect. 9.2.2, we highlight the importance of using indicators OR to monitor the economic performance of the hotel, both because the occupancy rate is linked to the unit fixed costs and because it provides a good proxy for the break-even point. Indexes (9.6) and (9.7) are obviously static management indicators, but can easily be translated into dynamic indexes when they are collected in terms of time series by taking observations over a period of time that is long enough to identify the trend, the cycle, and the seasonality of each index (see Sect. 7.5). From the analysis of such time series, the management might identify stimuli for the improvement of the occupancy rate.

9.2.3.2 The Average Daily Rate

This barometer for the hotel management aims at monitoring the price rather than the quantity (which is the case for the OR indexes). The Average Daily Rate (ADR)

Table 9.1 Prices, overnight stays and average daily rate when there are two types of tourism

Market mix	Overnight stays	Daily price	Revenue
Individual travelers	7,500	100	750,000
Organized groups	4,500	70	315,000
Total	12,000		1,065,000
ADR		88.75	

is calculated by dividing the total revenue out of the number of overnight stays in the hotel:

$$\mathrm{ADR} = \frac{\mathrm{TR}}{N_{\mathrm{H}}}. \tag{9.9}$$

It can easily be verified that expression (9.9) is nothing more than the average price p; however, the practical calculation of the ADR can be carried out by building a table that analyzes the different ways in which the rooms can be rented, that is, the market mix.

Table 9.1 describes the example of a hotel with 150 bed places, opening 100 days per year and setting two different prices: a price of 100 for individual travelers and a discounted price of 70 for organized groups (i.e., sold through tour operators). In the 100 days of opening the total number of overnight stays is 12,000, of which 4,500 is for groups organized by tour operators. In such example, the ADR can be computed as ADR $=$ 1,065,000/12,000 $=$ 88.75. From the data included in the table we can also compute the occupancy rate. The specific occupancy rate for the 100-day period of opening is $\mathrm{OR_s} = 12{,}000/(100 \times 150) = 12{,}000/15{,}000 = 0.8$. The general occupancy rate computed for the whole year is $\mathrm{OR_g} = 12{,}000/(365 \times 150) = 12{,}000/54{,}750 = 0.22$.

There are many factors affecting the ADR; some are general, and one is specific. We begin by recalling the general factors, which refer to the destination's characteristics: (a) the general economic conditions; for example, it is more likely for hotels to grant discounts in times of economic crisis and then reducing them in periods of bonanza or in response to investment in the destination's infrastructure that makes the destination more appealing for tourists; (b) the political conditions; for example the easiness of traveling or circulating in the country, conditions of potential danger, crime, terrorism, and turmoil, which are often offset by the hotels with special price reductions; (c) the environmental conditions; in particular, the environmental decay is one of the reasons why hotels most commonly engage in price discounts.

Other factors refer to more peculiar conditions: (d) the particular features of the destination; for example, seashore hotels rarely implement price reductions; a cultural destination rarely offers discounts, contrary to what happens in a business destination or in a transit city, and so on; (e) the type of the hotel, for example whether or not it belongs to a chain, whether it is located in the city center or in the outskirts.

The specific factor relates the ADR with the hotel's market mix, which is the specific distribution of customers hosted by the hotel. Tables 9.2 and 9.3 display the

Table 9.2 A first variation in the hotel's market mix

Market mix	Overnight stays	Daily price	Revenue
Individual travelers	2,250	100	225,000
Business travelers	4,500	85	382,500
Trade fair and expos	3,000	70	210,000
Congresses	1,500	75	112,500
Special discounts	750	50	37,500
Total	12,000		967,500
ADR		80.63	

Table 9.3 A second variation in the hotel's market mix

Market mix	Overnight stays	Daily price	Revenue
Individual travelers	1,500	100	150,000
Reservations	4,500	85	382,500
Tour operators	3,750	70	262,500
Congresses	1,500	75	112,500
Special discounts	750	50	37,500
Total	12,000		945,000
ADR		78.75	

Table 9.4 A comparison between two hotels

Indicator	Hotel A	Hotel B
Bed places	500	500
Occupancy rate ($\times 100$)	70	90
Average Daily Rate	90	70

same hotel of Table 9.1, that is, a hotel with 150 bed places and with a total of 12,000 overnight stays, but with a different market mix. The different customer mix is a sufficient condition to explain the different average price: the ADR is 80.63 in the case of Table 9.2, while it is only 78.75 in the case of Table 9.3. Note that the different average prices of the two tables stem from the different number of stays for each type of tourism, which are the weights used to calculate the ADR.

In the commercial practice these indexes are kept monitored, but their interpretation is by no means easy because too many factors affect their values. In fact, Table 9.4 compares two opposite situations, where one hotel has a better OR (Hotel B), while the other has a better ADR (Hotel A). Clearly, both hotels have the same daily revenue (=31,500); however, little can be concluded about their relative profitability, since the cost structure is probably different in the two cases.

Just like the barometer that measures the air pressure is a useful device that must be accompanied by a meteorological theory in order to help us predict the weather, the OR and the ADR indexes are useful barometers for the check up of the business operations which must be reconnected to the general management and competition framework to achieve a comprehensive evaluation of costs and prices. In fact, where the marketing strategy implies market segmentation, with the price varying as a function of demand, the profit level depends not only on the degree of competition in the market and on the structure of production costs but also, as we saw in the example presented in Tables 9.2 and 9.3, on the market mix.

The OR and the ADR are the most important, but not the only barometers for the hotel's management. Among the others, Murthy and Dev (1992) proposed the Yield per Room (YPR) indicator well known in the business literature as revPAR (revenue per available room). The YPR can be obtained dividing the total revenue by the number of available rooms (or, as in our case, the numbers of bed places) over the period under scrutiny. In the example of Table 9.2, YPR $= 967{,}000/(100 \times 150) = 64.47$, while in the example of Table 9.3 YPR $= 945{,}000/(100 \times 150) = 63$.

9.3 The Transport Sector

The transport sector shares with the hospitality sector many economic and management issues: in both sectors the estimation of the average cost and the price setting policy heavily depend on the strong relevance of fixed costs; both sectors operate in oligopolistic market structures; finally, they both use complex pricing strategies, so that the theory of the single price represents an abstraction that is difficult to defend in practice. For all these reasons, we will quickly overview the topics related to the transport firms by making use of notions that we have already presented in Sect. 9.2. On the other hand, we will devote to the revenue management and to the pricing strategy a specific in-depth discussion in Sect. 9.4. The most important difference with the hospitality sector resides in the average size of the transport company (and therefore on the amount of investment that is required to start a business), which is definitely very high particularly for companies operating in the air, rail, and cruise sector.

9.3.1 Transport and Tourism

Since tourism involves a movement from the location of residence, the transport system plays a key role in the organization and composition of the tourism product:

> The most spectacular site, the most impressive monument become tourism attractions in the moment they are accessible.
>
> (Dewailly and Flament 1995, p. 177. *Our translation*)

The accessibility of a tourism area depends on the transport network. Accessibility is technically defined as the area of influence exerted on the territory by a transport terminal (airport, train station, port, etc.), where the terminal is the structure through which one enters or exists a transport network. The area of influence obviously depends on the means of transport; for example the area of influence of an airport is high, given that the high speed of air transport allows tourists to reach the destination even when they are at medium or long distances; the area of influence of a train station is, for the opposite reason, much more limited. The degree of accessibility of a destination is then measured by the type and number of terminals and with respect to the surface of the territory (the so-called access density).

The link between transport and tourism is more complex than just the simple causal relationship between the development of the transport system and the evolution of the destination. Indeed, there is a continuous feedback from tourism to transport. For example, if on the one hand the development of the destination requires the constant improvement of roads, car parks, railways, ports, and airports, on the other hand it is also true that the construction of scenic routes or the restoration of railway lines that were previously abandoned can lead to the development of new tourism products.

> Tourism is about being elsewhere and, in consequence, the relationship between transportation and tourism development has traditionally been regarded as 'chicken and egg'. Adequate transportation infrastructure and access to generating markets is one of the most important prerequisites for the development of any destination. [...] On the other hand, tourism demand has stimulated the rapid development of transportation. As millions of tourists expect to be transported safely, quickly and comfortably to their destinations at a reasonable cost.
>
> (Cooper et al. 1998, p. 270)

The link between the two phenomena is not limited to these examples; indeed, and this happens for almost all means of transport, their interdependence becomes a relationship of integration when the transport is itself a type of tourism.

> Increasingly, as transport is viewed as part of leisure, the journey is at least as important as the destination itself. For some categories of visitor, the trip is therefore seen as an attraction in its own right and certainly part of the tourist experience.
>
> (Cooper et al. 1998, p. 271)

Some examples of transport which have become an attractive product in itself are: (a) rail travels, such as the Palace on Wheels in India, the Orient Express, and the Eastern & Oriental Express; (b) air travels, such as flights on vintage Concorde airplanes; (c) marine products such as cruises in general, but particularly the theme cruises and day trips by ferry to the Baltic Sea or across the Channel.[6]

Even though the whole history of tourism is inextricably linked to the evolution of the transport system, for our purposes the transport firm is just another tourist-oriented firm that we must deal with (for an in-depth discussion on the transport sector, see O'Connor 2000; Wensveen 2007). However, before turning to the economic analysis of this type of firm, let us begin with an overview of the different transport means that can enter the tourism product, either as part of a package tour or as self-organized tourism.

---

[6] We define as theme cruises those cruises offering a set of activities to be carried on board or at ports around a theme that usually characterizes the entire trip: for example, culture (art, folklore, and language courses), entertainment (music, dance, film and theater), fashion (with fashion shows on board).

9.3.1.1 Transport by Waterway

With reference to tourist transport by waterways we can distinguish between: (a) ocean transport lines; (b) cruises; (c) short-distance travel by sea (ferries); (d) services on domestic waterway routes; (e) private recreational crafts.

Although historically important, ocean travel suffered a substantial decline in the contemporary era, partially due to the high managerial costs and the competition by air transport. Such competition forced shipping companies to greatly increase the comfort of their service (by installing onboard entertainment facilities such as casino, sports facilities, shops, etc.), increase the cruising speed, and increase the size of the ship so that today's ocean trips resemble more and more cruises. Nowadays, the sea trips are still available on a purely seasonal basis, mainly aimed at tourists with special needs and with a lot of free time.

Despite the ups and downs of periods of boom and crises, the cruises represent the most important case of integration between maritime transport and tourism. Cruises "become" tourism both because of the many short stops that the cruise makes in the ports it touches and because of the intense onboard organization of leisure activities for travelers, so that the cruise can be seen itself as a destination. Rarely studied yet, cruises share common characteristics with the transport and the hospitality sectors (Dowling 2006; Papatheodorou 2006; Mintel 2007). Moreover, many cruises are sold by tour operators in combination with air transport to allow tourists to reach remote areas where the navigation is not possible, or with the provision of bus services required to transfer from one port to another.

Ferries, which usually operate over short distances, owe their development to the increase in the use of private cars. A characteristic that makes sea transport able to compete with the air transport is that tourists can carry their vehicles with them and drive them in the destination. With the term "ferries" we identify both means of slow transport that allow high loads, and also high-speed hydrofoils and hovercrafts, with limited cargo capabilities.

The inland waterways (rivers, lakes, channels) are also important to allow tourists to arrive at destination and some river transports take on the characteristics of cruises.

9.3.1.2 Rail Transport

The rail transport has marked the historical development of tourism since the first railways were built to connect some large cities to nearby beaches. Recently, rail transport has undergone further engineering, economic, and organizational development (see Henscher and Brewer 2001; White 2008), combining great comfort with high speed (examples are the TGV in France, the AVE in Spain, and the Frecciarossa in Italy), thus offering a transport service to medium-haul distances (national and international) which is competitive with air transport. Compared to air transport, rail transport offers the possibility of walking in the craft, delivers enjoyable landscapes, is more environmentally friendly, and counts on stations that are generally located in the city center, shortening the movements within the destination. Finally, the train allows, but only in some cases, the transport of private cars. In the case of rail transport, the integration between transport and tourism recently became more important not only because some railway lines were reactivated to take a form of over-land cruising, but also because cumulative and special fares have been especially designed for tourism purposes.

9.3.1.3 Bus Transport

Bus transports are very popular in some regions for two main reasons: (a) low costs; (b) the possibility of "door-to-door" transport. With regard to tourists, this form of transport is also important over the short and medium distance (transfers from hotels to airports or seaports, guided tours to the cities or surrounding areas, weekend trips organized by tour operators, organizations, or groups). Over long distances, the bus is competitive with the train only up to a maximum distance, since the bus has less comfort, becomes technically slower, and suffers more from congestion problems than the train.

9.3.1.4 Air Transport

Thanks to technological and managerial innovations, air travel has become the most popular form of transport for international tourism flows. Air traveling is particularly attractive for its high speed and for the long distance that can be covered (connecting any two destinations in the world requires at most 24 h). In the presence of geographical isolation, which is the case of remote islands or other inaccessible places, air transport is usually the only travel mode, and often the only reasonably fast. The airplane is not necessarily the most expensive means of transport, as it allows economies of speed, which reduces the complementary expenditure during the trip, this being particularly important for business tourism. Air transport has four basic categories: (a) scheduled services; (b) charters; (c) low-cost flights; (d) air taxis.

The scheduled services are based on established national and international routes, subject to public licensing schemes, organized through official timetables and operated regardless of their load factor. To avoid the risk of flying with aircrafts that are too empty, airlines have recently started the commercial practice of code-sharing, according to which two or more airlines plan the connection between two airports at the same time and use only one aircraft until reaching the full capacity, and use a second aircraft only in periods when the demand is high.

The charter flights are specifically organized by specialized airlines and according to specific contracts. In this market segment there are air-brokers which operate as intermediaries between the air company and the demand for flights. Charters flights satisfy a demand to specific destinations in specific dates, and are usually demanded by tour operators for the transport of their package tourists. To facilitate the tourist's needs, seat-only flights, which are not combined with other types of service, can also be offered. The advantage of charter flights compared to the scheduled ones is in the higher load factor; as we see in the next section, this explains the significant difference in the average cost.

Low-cost flights initially begun in North America and in the 1990s quickly spread across the European region. Ryanair (see Case Study 9.2) is the best example of how social and economic changes, when properly exploited, can create a company that in just a few years has revolutionized the competition in the market, now being one of the world's leaders. In recent years, low-cost airlines represented a real competitor for charter flights and then for scheduled flights, so that they both had to change their sales and pricing policy, marketing tools, and industrial strategies. Even the tourism destinations are faced with this new mode of air transport, so that a great deal of attention that was placed before on domestic carriers and charter companies has now shifted to the policy of low-cost connections.

Case Study 9.2. Low-Cost Companies: The Case of Ryanair

The case of Ryanair is the typical example of how social and economic changes, if well exploited, can create in just a few years new market leaders and revolutionize the structure of competition as well as marketing strategies. In fifteen years, the development of Internet and the policy of deregulation in the European airline market allowed Ryanair to become one of the largest airlines in the world. In 1985 the newly formed Irish company made its first steps by trying to break the Air Lingus/British Airways duopoly on the London–Dublin route. In that year the company was granted the license to operate on that route and started its challenge by aiming at prices lower than those offered by the two competitors. Ryanair started using an aircraft with 46 seats and the round-trip price was 99 pounds, less than half the fare offered by the other two companies.

Since 1990, the Ryanair's marketing strategy has been based on the concept of low price/no frills, and the number of passengers who choose this airline is constantly increasing. In May 1991, the company's base in London was moved to the less important (and less expensive) Stanstead airport. In 1994, the number of passengers climbed to 1.66 million, while in 1995 the company overtook British Airways and Aer Lingus on the Dublin–London route in terms of number of passengers. In 1997, the European Union fully deregulated the airline market, so to allow companies such as Ryanair (that in the meantime had become the leader on the Anglo-Irish market) to compete on routes within the EU. In 1998, Ryanair began its flights to the new European destinations of Malmoe, Saint Etienne, and Carcassonne, and to the Italian towns of Venice, Pisa, and Rimini. During the same year, its number of passengers rose to 4.63 million.

In 2000 Ryanair launched its new flight reservation website which in just three months scored 50,000 reservations. In 2002, Ryanair counted on 41 planes to transport more than 11 million passengers and by making profits by over 150 million € and revenues by 620 million €. In 2004, it added 24 new Boeing 737–800 so to reach a total of 60 aircrafts, while the number of passengers rose to 24.64 million with 2,288 employees. New major bases were opened in Rome–Ciampino and in the area of Barcelona–Girona. Nowadyas, Ryanair transports more than 70 million passengers, counts more than 7,000 employees, and has a revenue of 3,000 million €, with more than 300 million € of profit.

Ryanair's success lies in the reduction of production costs (personnel, internal organization, commissions to travel agents, services during the flight, choice of more decentralized airports), so that this company currently counts on the highest number of passengers per employee. Much of its success is also due to the use of ICT; indeed, today approximately 98 % of bookings are made online at Ryanair's web site, which is one of the most visited travel sites worldwide. On this site, the tourist can also avail of special offers and promotional discounts that allow to travel, in some cases, by paying only the airport fees, as well as other related discounted services (for example car rental or hotel booking). Ryanair has recently decided to diversify its market strategy by offering various services (e.g., international phone calling cards, insurance and financial services), always with the aim of offering the best available rates. The internet site has recently evolved into a full-blown online travel agency and virtual tour operator and uses the most effective selling techniques: daily pricing, discounts, promotional offers, price discrimination, bundling and bulking strategies, etc.

The success of Ryanair is important not only as a business model, but also for the implications for the tourism system. It is now common, in Europe, to talk about the "Ryanair tourist", a tourist who decides where to spend short holidays and weekend breaks according to where Ryanair flies to, and when special discounts are offered. The ability of the destination management in attracting Ryanair and other low-cost companies is therefore an effective tool in affecting the distribution of tourism flows; for example, at the end of 2009 Ryanair invested on Bologna, Italy, as one of its major airports in Southern Europe, with routes connecting to 30 other European cities. In 2010 the number of overnight stays in Bologna grew by a stunning 10 % (+17.2 % for foreigners). Hence, it is plausible that destination managements, local tourism firms, and airports all over Europe would be available to implicitly subsidize low-cost companies in exchange of the decision of selecting the local airport as a base for their routes. This opens interesting consequences in terms of competition and antitrust policies.

The success of this new way of traveling by air truly caused a shopping revolution, thus driving to serious economic problems (Zenelis and Papatheodorou 2008; Iatrou and Oretti 2007) and safety issues (Papatheodorou and Platis 2007).

The emergence of low-cost was also made possible by the marketing strategy based on the idea of low fares/no frills, so that the company does not provide by default any complementary service in the cabin, such as food or drinks, which are only served against the payment of an extra price. These companies also standardize their operations of maintenance, often by selecting a unique aircraft model and manufacturer and by choosing small airports with which they reach special agreements in regard to operation costs and airport fees. Finally, they have also introduced innovative marketing strategies, such as the massive use of the Internet (Chap. 12) and different pricing strategies (see Sect. 9.5 and Vila and Corcoles 2011).

Finally, the air taxi meets the typical requirements of business tourism over medium distances (800–1,000 km) and mainly involves small aircraft to reach airports located near the main industrial and financial centers.

The development of air transport has important implications in terms of organization and localization of airports and hubs, driving to key decisions for airlines and destinations, and consequences for travelers, with straightforward consequences for the structure and performance of the whole tourism sector (Field and Pilling 2003; Papatheodorou 2003b; Graham 2008).

9.3.1.5 Private Road Transport

The private road transport is dominated by the car which is an almost-perfect means of transport to ensure door-to-door flexibility and to allow the opportunity of enjoying the landscape during the trip or that of stopping when and where the tourist likes. Freedom and flexibility of movement are the main features that justify the use of private transport by the self-organized tourist. Tour operators often try to offer in the all-inclusive trip the flexibility and freedom of private transport by including in their packages car rental services that are available at destination. In the same way, commercial agreements between airlines and car rental companies allow the tourists to avail of a bulk discount when they buy the two services together, in the so-called fly and drive option.

Less popular forms of private transport are characterized by the use of motor homes, motorcycles and bicycles; however, the latter can often be integrated with the car or the train.

In the history of tourism the pioneering role for transport was certainly played by the train, which often resulted in a strong tourism development of the destinations served by efficient train stations. The next era was characterized by the car, which brought a revolution not only in people's social and economic life but also in their way of going on holiday. Thanks to cars, tourism development reached destinations not served by railways and spread more widely in large areas. Finally, we are in the era of air transport, which has meant that any destination in the world can easily be reached by tourists. The key for the historical and geographical interpretation of such evolution must still be found in the progressive reduction in the time and the cost required to travel a certain distance.

The choice of the mode of transport to be used in the trip can be best understood by using the Lancaster model (see Sect. 6.3). In fact, although in principle all means of transport ensure the same service, each one differs from the others in its characteristics, some of which may be relevant for the tourist's choice: (a) the speed, that is, the distance covered in the unit of time, (b) the comfort; (c) the safety; (d) the easiness of accessing the destination; (e) the range of complementary services offered. The preference for these characteristics obviously depends on the type of tourist, so that the chosen transport will be the result of the careful comparison between the subjective utility stemming from the combination of such features and the transport price. And since tourists do not attach the same utility to time and income, such differences allow to understand why there are tourists for each means of transport.

Another key feature for the transport business is the issue of market regulation or deregulation by public authorities (Doganis 2005; Mathisen and Solvoll 2007; Papatheodorou 2008; Zenelis and Papatheodorou 2008; Arvanitis and Zenelis 2008). Usually, reasons of public utility and the need for coordination between various forms of transport are arguments in favor of the introduction of tight regulation; however, since regulation biases competition and leads to some degree of monopoly power (with consequent disadvantage for consumers), there are arguments in favor of deregulation.

> The arguments for and against regulation are many, but basically in the short term, customers benefit from increased competition and efficiency through lower fares; but in the long term, they may suffer disadvantages from the lack of an organised and reliable schedule of services as competitors go out of business.
>
> (Cooper et al. 1998, p. 283)

In the United States, the Airline Deregulation Act of 1978 determined the "open-sky" policy as an extreme example of deregulation. The European countries were more reluctant to choose a complete form of deregulation; this was however achieved, albeit more gradually, through the adoption of three different packages of measures: (a) the first package, which came into force in 1987, opened for the first time to non-national airlines the ability to cover international routes; (b) the second package in 1990 allowed for more flexible pricing policies and expanded the ability to have multiple airlines from the same country operating on the same route; (c) the third package in 1992 consolidated the principle of free market and freedom of pricing and, after it came into full force in 1997, granted to any licensed carrier an access to all routes, including the domestic routes of a foreign country.

In this discussion about (de)regulation we can ultimately recognize all the arguments pertaining to one of the most important (and still debating) issues of economic policy: the choice between a free or a regulated market. It is therefore natural that the issue of deregulation in the transport sector has its supporters and its opponents. We refer to Motta (2004) for a general discussion of competition policy and market regulation, and to Gil Molto and Piga (2007) for the analysis of the effects of the air transport market liberalization in Europe.

9.3.2 The Price of Transport

Like companies in other sectors, also transport firms base their pricing policy on the computation of the average production cost on top of which they apply a markup. The average cost crucially depends on the load factor of the vector being employed, be it an aircraft, a ship, a bus, or a train; indeed, since the carrier's product consists of a pure service that cannot be stored, the strict rule applies that each free seat corresponds to a service that has been produced (and paid for) but has gone unsold (exactly as in the case of accommodation services). For this reason, the carrier must operate a continuous monitoring of its load factor L which, similarly to the hotel's occupancy rate, is

$$L = \frac{P}{N}, \tag{9.10}$$

where P denotes the number of passengers and N the number of available seats. Although the centrality of the load factor to the economic problem of the transport firm was first recognized by airlines, its relevance extends to other transport companies. The load factor ranges from zero to one, but, for certain types of transport (i.e., urban buses, local trains), it can easily be greater than one.

When the load factor is close to one, it commonly indicates excessive wear and tear or deterioration of the vector and a decline in the quality of the service provided. On the other hand, when the load factor is too low, it commonly indicates the rise in the cost per passenger and an inefficient management. It is then obvious that each carrier should identify its optimal load factor to achieve (above which the carrier should increase the number or the size of the vectors) and the break-even load factor, that is, the load factor below which the firm gets an economic loss.

Also for transport companies the average cost UC (for example the cost of providing a "seat" on a flight connecting two cities) can be described by the following formula, which is the adaptation to the case of transport of the expression that we have seen when dealing with the tour operator (see Sect. 8.2):

$$\mathrm{UC} = \frac{\mathrm{FC}}{P} + \mathrm{VUC} = a\frac{\mathrm{FC}}{(a-1)LN} + \mathrm{VUC} \tag{9.11}$$

with

$$\frac{\partial \mathrm{UC}}{\partial \mathrm{FC}} > 0, \quad \frac{\partial \mathrm{UC}}{\partial L} < 0 \quad \frac{\partial \mathrm{UC}}{\partial \mathrm{VUC}} = 1$$

and where a indicates the number of flights (the denominator is reduced by one unit to account for a flight, the first of the season, with no passengers), FC is the fixed cost for each flight (the aircraft's lease or depreciation charge, fuel, crew members, parking fees, taxes, freight, etc.), and VUC are the variable unit costs that are to be incurred for each passenger (mainly airport fees), while P, L, and N are the variables already defined for (9.10).

If we leave aside the value of a (in the case of repeated flights its effect is almost irrelevant since $\lim_{a\to\infty} a/(a-1) = 1$) and if we consider N a mere technical parameter for the size of the aircraft,[7] the unit cost (9.11) directly depends on the fixed cost of the flight and on the variable costs, and inversely depends on the load factor: this last relationship explains the cost difference (and hence the price difference) between scheduled and charter flights: the load factor of the latter is usually higher than the former. The ability to reach high load factors is often due to the higher flexibility of the low-cost carrier that can easily switch aircrafts across different routes in order to accommodate the demand. In technical terms, the optimal load factor can also be reached by changing N, the denominator of (9.10), and not only its numerator, the number of passengers.

As we already know, the price set by the transport company builds upon applying a markup to the unit cost (9.11). The difference between the price and the unit cost must then be used to cover indirect transport costs (marketing, administrative, and other general costs, etc.) so that only the residual represents the company's profit. Once again, the markup reflects the monopoly power gained by the carrier on that route as well as the characteristics (comfort, safety, speed, etc.) of the provided service.

It is sometimes the case, especially when the carrier operates within a duopoly or oligopoly regime, that the company might try to increase its market power by eliminating one or more competitors that serve the same route. The weapon to be used is a drop in the price of the service. But, if the competitors resist and respond with the same aggressive behavior, a war of prices might start, with the price falling even below the average cost with no apparent floor. Each company, in fact, hopes to make up in the future for current losses when, after the rivals have exited the market, set a higher markup as a consequence of the newly earned status of monopolist. The following commentary, made by Cavour during a public speech at the Italian parliament in 1853, presents a paradoxical case:

> ...of a two stagecoaches that, pushed by competition, kept reducing the price up to the point that one of the two transported for free, and then the other one announced that would have offered breakfast to their passengers.
>
> (Cavour 1939, p. 312. *Our translation*)

In other cases the price strategy may be not so aggressive, so that companies stop reducing the price when they have reached a balanced budget.

The price setting strategy applied by transport companies is much more complex than it might appear by the simple application of the full-cost method. In fact, the carriers' monopolistic power can be used to implement a number of price

[7] To be more precise, the size of the aircraft to be used is not exogenously given, but is a very important strategic decision that the firm has to take. To keep things simple we assume that the firm has already chosen in a previous stage of the decision process the size N of the vector.

discrimination policies which are aimed at increasing profits. It is a well known fact that transport companies often sell the same or very similar services at different prices rather than fixing a single price for the service: this is what happens when an airline sells tickets in business class and economy class at different fares; or when the same company sells a round-trip ticket at a price lower than the sum of the prices of two one-way tickets; or when the price varies depending on the time of booking. As we have already mentioned, such pricing strategies are so essential for the solution of the economic problem facing a tourism business that we will devote Sect. 9.5 to an introductory discussion of this topic.

Finally, we must highlight that changes in the load factor can generate either "virtuous" or "vicious" cycles between the cost of the transport service and the life cycle of the destination. As an example of a virtuous cycle we may think of the discovering of a destination that leads to the growth of the load factor for the airline that serves it (since the share of empty seats on scheduled flights decreases). Following the reduction of the unit cost in (9.11) it is possible to decrease the air fare, thus leading to a reduction in the overall price of the holiday in the destination and to a likely increase in the demand. This yields a further increase in the load factor of the air service and leads to an additional cost reduction, and so on. On the other hand, we can easily describe an example of vicious cycle, when the decline of the tourism destination offering a mature product negatively affects the carrier's load factor.

9.4 The Tourism Attractions

Tourists choose a certain destination because of its attractions that can generally be defined as "things to see and things to do". Our discussion of the tourism attractions will be divided into two parts: in the first part we will classify the different types of attractions, while in the second part we will analyze the economic problem for the firm managing a generic attraction.

9.4.1 The Classification of Attractions

We propose two different classifications. Firstly, the tourism attractions can be divided into: site-specific attractions and events.

- The site-specific attractions are those that are closely related to the geographical location and are part of the "variety" that characterizes the tourism destination (see Sect. 4.3.2). Sometimes the tourist identifies the destination with its attractions (e.g., the Pisa Tower), while some other times the destination is itself the attraction (e.g., Disneyland).

- Events can be cultural or sport events with the ability to attract visitors. Unlike site-specific attractions, what matters here is the timing rather than the location, since events can be staged anywhere. An event can also be staged to complement site-specific attractions; for example the representation of a classical tragedy in the Greek Theater of Taormina (Sicily, Italy) can be viewed as the complementary event offered by a site-specific attraction. Such complementarity is very important for the effect in reducing the seasonality of tourism (see Sect. 7.5.4).

According to a different classification, the attractions can be

- Natural attractions, which are always site-specific and are identified in the so-called destination's "gifts of nature": landscape, climate, waterfalls, natural parks, forests, etc.
- Human-made attractions that can be site-specific or events, and are primarily identified with the cultural heritage (monuments, museums, archaeological sites, etc.) and the live performances (concerts, festivals, etc.) respectively. This class also includes artificial attractions such as theme parks (Legoland in Billund, Denmark) or other amusement parks (Tivoli Gardens in Copenhagen, Denmark).

The distinction between natural and human-made attractions is not always clear-cut. Indeed, many natural attractions require considerable infrastructure in order to become accessible to tourists; this is certainly the case for many natural parks, waterfalls, mountain-climbing routes, and so on. In this section we will not deal with natural attractions, since this topic would inevitably lead to the issue of compatibility between environmental preservation and tourism exploitation, which will be dealt with in Chap. 16, when studying the relationship between tourism and the environment. As regards the events, we refer to the broad literature on the management and evaluation of cultural events (Candela and Scorcu 2004; Bowdin et al. 2010) and sport events (Mallen and Adams 2008), while in the remaining part of the section we only focus on site-specific human-made attractions.

There is considerable heterogeneity among these attractions. With respect to the principle of excludability from benefits (see Sect. 15.2), the attractions can be private goods (such as private homes open to the public and museums) or public goods (such as squares, churches, etc.). As regards the ownership, they may be owned by a public body, either the State or a local authority, or privately owned.

Even if in practice there is a wide array of different attractions, with no loss of accuracy we will limit the study to privately owned firms that manage an attraction for which a specific investment has been undertaken and that produces services characterized by excludability. In particular, we refer to a typical firm that sells to visitors a set of human-made leisure and entertainment attractions (such as amusement parks, sport facilities, ski areas, spa and wellness centers, theaters). Such firms are subject to the market rules, are oriented to profit, and are sometimes able to attract thousands of visitors per day, often being among the most important economic activities of the destination. These firms' typical economic problem is however logically similar to that of all other tourism businesses: definition of the cost structure and pricing strategy.

9.4.2 Prices and Costs in Tourism Attractions

The striking feature of the attraction's cost structure is the great share of fixed costs if compared to the variable costs: in particular, the initial investment required to create the artificial attraction and the subsequent investments needed to develop, upgrade, and maintain it are huge. Such trait provides some interesting implications:

1. Attractions normally need to operate with a very large number of visitors, so to reduce the incidence of fixed costs: their break-even point is high.
2. The massive amount of capital required to start the investment is usually raised by borrowing or by the means of specific joint ventures.
3. The local government may contribute to the payment of some of the costs required to start the project; such public help may take the form of matching grants, loans, shareholding, provision of natural benefits such as land, infrastructure, transport, or any of their combination.

The fixed costs of attractions have the economic nature of sunk costs (see Sect. 8.3.2), so that the market is non-contestable and attraction management firms often operate as monopolists. If we denote with N the number of visitors of the attraction (the total number of admissions), the profit π, which is the difference between total revenue TR and total cost of production TC, both depending on the number of visitors, is

$$\pi = \mathrm{TR}(N) - \mathrm{TC}(N).$$

The maximum profit is determined by the first-order condition:

$$\frac{\mathrm{d}\pi}{\mathrm{d}N} = \frac{\mathrm{dTR}(N)}{\mathrm{d}N} - \frac{\mathrm{dTC}(N)}{\mathrm{d}N} = 0,$$

which provides the usual condition of equality between marginal revenue MR and marginal cost MC as in (9.12):

$$\frac{\mathrm{dTR}(N)}{\mathrm{d}N} = \frac{\mathrm{dTC}(N)}{\mathrm{d}N}, \text{ that is, } \mathrm{MR} = \mathrm{MC}. \tag{9.12}$$

The equilibrium condition for the firm is shown in Fig. 9.2: condition (9.12) is satisfied in point E, the abscissa of which represents the optimal size of the attraction, while the price is determined along the demand function, where $p^* \geq \mathrm{MC}$.

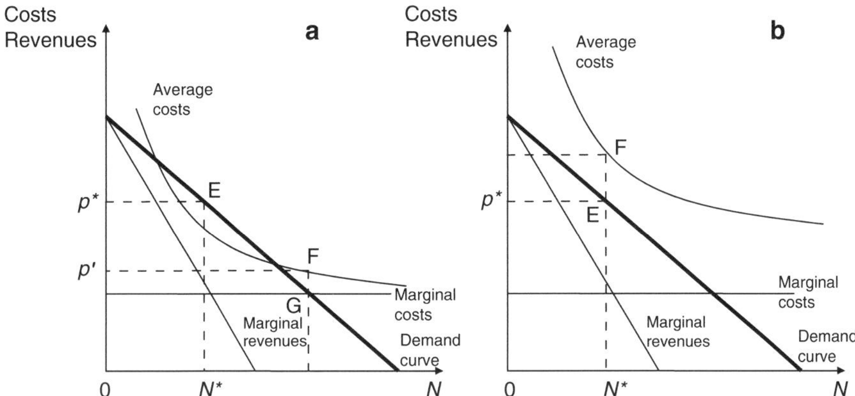

Fig. 9.2 The market equilibrium when the attraction is a monopoly

However, the careful reading of Fig. 9.2 shows that, when the fixed costs are relevant, the price cannot rely on the marginal cost only. In fact, the solution (9.12) does not guarantee that the profit is positive: this would be the case only when the average revenue (the price) is higher than the average cost (as in Fig. 9.2a). Otherwise, when the average cost UC is higher than the price (which is the case shown in Fig. 9.2b) the solution (9.12) would lead to a negative profit and the firm would be facing a loss (equal to the segment EF for each unit produced). In this case, the permanence of the firm on the market can only be guaranteed by an external intervention, which usually takes the form of the subsidy. The subsidy can either be provided by the government, aiming at preserving and enhancing the cultural heritage of the attraction, or by the destination management or by the tour operator, aiming at completing the tourism product (see Sect. 4.3.1) and meeting the tourist's love for variety (see Sect. 4.3.2).

In both cases, the unit subsidy would be equal to $(\mathrm{UC} - p^*)$, corresponding to the segment EF in Fig. 9.2b. In the first case, the subsidy would be financed through taxes while in the second case it would be ensured by the positive effect on the total number of overnight stays in the destination, with great benefits for the other firms in terms of profits. If this is the case, the coordination carried out by the tour operator or by the destination management would imply a redistribution among the tourism sector, with some firms (mainly the hospitality firms) subsidizing the attraction in order to cover its loss. Moreover, the attraction may decide, in accordance with the destination, to set a price close to the marginal cost (as an example, see price p' in Fig. 9.2a) and agree to be systematically at loss if this would sufficiently contribute to the total revenue of the destination. Once again, the per-visitor loss would be financed by a subsidy equal to $(\mathrm{UC} - p')$, which is equal to the segment GF in Fig. 9.2a.

It is easy to verify that the price set by the firm strongly depends on the price elasticity of demand (Theory in Action 9.1); clearly the monopolist would prefer to face a rigid demand, which is certainly the case for many attractions characterized by a unique cultural or historical interest, thus constituting the main, if not the sole, purpose of the trip. On the contrary, when the attraction is an accessory service in the tourist product, its demand may be highly elastic.

As for many other tourism firms, also the attraction usually implements a complex pricing strategy, going well beyond the single price policy of (9.12). Let us here recall that:

- If the attraction has a strong seasonal demand, the firm may decide to set a higher price in the peak season and a low price off season in order to attract more tourists.
- The firm may seek to gain customer loyalty by offering a number of additional benefits that can take the form of membership cards, free access to the whole structure after a certain number of visits, other types of discount, privileged access in peak times, etc.
- Rather than setting a single price for the park or for its individual rides, the firm may choose to set a two-part tariff (see Sect. 15.4.3) where the price consists of a fixed component, independent of the number of services being used, and a variable component that is proportional to the quantity of purchased services. As an example of two-part tariff we can think of the entry fee paid to access an amusement park and a separate ticket charged to ride a specific attraction. Such policy is usually designed to encourage longer visits; indeed, using six attractions within a single visit would cost much less than enjoying the same six attractions with two visits (Candela et al. 2009b).

Finally, an important issue for the attraction management comes from having to limit congestion on days characterized by a very large number of visitors. From a purely theoretical point of view this is a problem of micro-seasonality, and the management can implement any policy aimed at reducing seasonality (see Sect. 7.5.4). Alternatively, the management may decide to regulate the flow of visitors during peak days so to improve the perceived quality of provided service: (a) reducing the traffic congestion through an efficient management of parking lots; (b) managing the flow of tourists within the site by providing an internal transport service; (c) managing the queues at the attractions so that the waiting is done within an amusing environment (with various forms of entertainment) and where the tourists are kept informed on the queuing time.

9.5 The Yield Management

In the previous sections, as well as in Chap. 8, we discussed a number of factors that complicate the management of a tourism firms. These factors can be summarized as follows: (a) the provided services cannot be stored and are immediately perishable; (b) there exist many segments in the tourism market, each characterized by a different price elasticity and different preferences for complementary services;

(c) the share of fixed costs over total production costs is usually very high, which makes the planning stage much more uncertain and risky; (d) there is high variability of demand over time, for reasons related to seasonality, the timing of paid leave from work, the existence of trends and economic cycles; (e) the mechanism of reservation and booking of services, which take place well in advance, has timings and characteristics that are different among segments.

In order to address all these issues, the so-called yield (or revenue) management has been developed in recent years, consisting of a set of techniques aimed at maximizing revenues through the pursuit of the optimal occupancy rate (which may either refer to accommodation for the hotel, seats for the airline, package holidays for the tour operator) and of the optimal structure of prices, subject to the conditions of demand.

As the Fordism defines the organization of production in terms of hiring the "right" man for the "right" job, the post-Fordism defines the organization of sales, the yield management, as follows:

> Yield Management is a method which can help a firm to sell the right inventory unit to the right type of customer, at the right time and for the right price.
>
> (Kimes 2000, p. 3)

More precisely, the yield management can be defined as follows:

> An integrated set of business processes that brings together people and systems with the goal of understanding the market, anticipating customer behavior at the micromarket level and responding quickly to exploit opportunities.
>
> (Cross 1997, p. 52)

Practically, the yield management helps the manager of a tourism firm in fulfilling important strategic choices: (a) to decide whether or not to overbook, so to hedge against the risk of no-shows, but at the same time exposing the business to the risk of receiving a number of customers larger than the available services; (b) to decide whether or not to sell immediately at a discounted price, thus anticipating a certain income but incurring in the risk of foregoing sales that may occur in the future at higher prices; (c) on the contrary, to decide whether or not to put on sale services at high prices at times when there are more requests for services at lower prices, so by incurring in the risk of unsold production; (d) to determine the right combination of complementary services to offer and the vector of prices for various types of tourists who demand the service.

The yield management strategies can be grouped and classified as follows:

- Price discrimination policies that require setting different prices according to the specific characteristics of the market segments and based on the complementary services that might be offered.
- Booking management policies, addressing the issue that arises because different types of tourists (each with a different willingness to pay) demand the service at different times during the booking period (for example, leisure tourists usually buy the trip well before business tourists).

- Policies of upgrading or downgrading the provided service, which is the case when the company is able to easily switch between the different varieties and qualities of the additional services it offers; if services offered to the consumer are of higher quality than what is originally requested, there is upgrading, while if they are of lower quality there is downgrading. In the event of unavailability of the requested service, when are the consumers to be available to change to a higher or lower category, we talk about buy-up or buy-down, respectively.
- Dynamic pricing policies, a form of price discrimination over time, with which firms can change prices every day, as the booking period goes by, according to the conditions of demand.

Before discussing these strategies in detail, some general observations may be useful to introduce the topic. The yield management, which is particularly relevant for the tourism sector, can be implemented in any sector that operates in the presence of fixed capacity, perishable services, purchases that occur over a period of time through an advance-reservation system, and strong volatility in demand. The first application of yield management in the tourism sector is a consequence of the 1978 Deregulation Act of the airline sector in the United States, which forced many businesses to introduce new competition strategies, ranging from selling at discounted prices to the use of different booking and purchasing techniques. The accurate management of the fixed capacity pursued by the yield management can bring great benefits to tourism companies; for example, it has been estimated that American Airlines obtained an yearly extra profit of $500 million while the Marriott Hotel chain earned an yearly extra profit of more than $100 million as a result of implementing revenue management (Boyd 1998).

Moreover, despite the theoretical possibility to separately describe and analyze the different strategies of yield management listed above, in the business practice they are often used together (Case Study 9.3): on the one hand, this increases the probability of finding the optimal mix of actions that maximizes revenues; on the other hand, it greatly complicates the economic tractability of the issue, since their effects are mixed. For some realistic yet complex configurations the theoretical conditions of optimality have not been defined yet by the literature. In such cases, the implemented business solutions may be satisfactory but cannot be defined as optimal, and are usually based on the management experience as well as on the increased computation power of management software. Nowadays, the information technology allows for the control of a huge volume of data and for the definition of complex alternative scenarios that, however, we will not analyze in detail, referring to the specific literature (for a formal investigation of yield management in economic terms see Shy 2008; for the application to tourism, see Candela and Figini 2005, Chap. 4; for the specific revenue management literature see, among others, Talluri and Van Ryzin 2005; Ingold et al. 2000).

9.5.1 The Price Discrimination

As previously mentioned, the price setting strategy (especially for, but not limited to, transport businesses) is more complex than might appear from the simple application of the full-cost principle. Indeed, the existence of monopoly power may justify a policy of price discrimination, thus introducing a range of different prices for similar (sometimes identical) services. In doing so, firms are able to increase their degree of monopoly and the amount of total profits they earn. To price discriminate, three conditions must hold: (a) the firm has to be able to identify different market segments and each segment has to be independent of one another and can be treated separately; (b) each segment must display a different price elasticity of demand, i.e., a different sensitivity to price changes; (c) any arbitrage activity must be excluded, in the sense that it should not be possible for tourists (or for intermediaries) to purchase the service in a market segment and then resell it at a different price in another segment.

A simple and common example can explain the issue of price discrimination. Let us assume that an airline offers an identical flight service to both business travelers *B* and leisure tourists *T* and that, as it is usually the case, the leisure demand is more elastic than the demand by business travelers. To be more precise, in reality, the assumption of identical service does not hold, as any policy of price discrimination is almost always implemented together with a policy of product differentiation (see Sect. 10.3). In our case, business travelers would enjoy a better onboard service (larger seats, higher-quality lunch, free newspapers) and, more importantly, often have the option of changing, even at the last moment, their return date. From the theoretical point of view, however, what matters for price discrimination is that the different complementary services offered do not cause any relevant increase in the cost borne by the firm.

If the airline were to choose the same price for all its customers, it may be unable to sell all the available seats. Therefore, it could think of increasing total revenue by raising the load factor, and this may be achieved by reducing the price. However, a price reduction will certainly decrease the share of revenue earned from business travelers, while the same strategy may increase the share of revenue generated by the group of leisure tourists (for the relationship between price elasticity of demand and total expenditure, see Sect. 4.4.1). Therefore, the price reduction would be recommended only for leisure tourists.

In order to apply different prices to the different groups of customers, the company must be able to accurately determine the class to which each customer belongs, and then prevent the tourist from doing arbitrage, i.e., from purchasing a ticket at a reduced price in the leisure segment and then sell it to a business traveler at a higher price. The airlines usually overcome these difficulties by setting a lower rate for people who stay over on Saturday (hardly a business traveler), by issuing nominative tickets, and by linking the access to complementary services to the possession of a particular type of ticket. With price discrimination and impossibility of arbitrage, the firm can treat each of the two segments as independent markets and then aim for the maximum profit in each market, solving for the usual condition of equality between the marginal cost and the marginal revenue. This will translate in choosing two optimal prices p_T and p_B at which the flight service is offered respectively to tourists and business travelers. Given the relationship between the price elasticity (in absolute value) of the two segments of demand ($\varepsilon_T > \varepsilon_B$), it is straightforward to get that $p_T < p_B$ (see the graphical representation in Fig. 9.3 and, for a formal demonstration of this result, Theory in Action 9.1).

Theory in Action 9.1. The Model of Third-Degree Price Discrimination
Let us assume that there are two groups of travelers: leisure tourists T and business travelers B, the inverse demand functions of which are represented respectively by

$$p_T = p_T(Q_T), \quad p_B = p_B(Q_B), \tag{I}$$

where Q_T and Q_B are the quantity of seats respectively demanded by leisure and business travelers and p_T and p_B are the respective prices. Let us assume that the service is homogeneous and that the cost function of the airline is

$$\text{TC} = C(Q_T + Q_B) = C(Q), \tag{II}$$

where $Q = Q_T + Q_B$. The profit function, which has to be maximized in Q_T and Q_B by the airline, is therefore

$$\pi = \text{TR} - \text{TC} = p_T(Q_T) \times Q_T + p_B(Q_B) \times Q_B - C(Q).$$

By knowing that

$$\text{MR}_T = \frac{\partial \text{TR}}{\partial Q_T} = \frac{\partial [p_T(Q_T) \times Q_T]}{\partial Q_T} = \left(\frac{\partial p_T}{\partial Q_T}\right) \times Q_T + p_T \tag{III}$$

and recalling that price elasticity can be written as

$$\varepsilon_T = \left(\frac{\partial Q_T}{\partial p_T}\right)\left(\frac{p_T}{Q_T}\right),$$

which is

$$\frac{p_T}{\varepsilon_T} = \left(\frac{\partial p_T}{\partial Q_T}\right) Q_T. \tag{IV}$$

By replacing equation (IV) into equation (III) we get

$$MR_T = \left(\frac{p_T}{\varepsilon_T} + p_T\right) = p_T\left(1 + \frac{1}{\varepsilon_T}\right) = p_T\left(1 - \frac{1}{|\varepsilon_T|}\right). \quad \text{(V)}$$

If we maximize π with respect to Q_T the usual condition of optimality for a monopolistic firm, the equality between marginal revenues and marginal costs, MR = MC, can be written using equation (V):

$$p_T\left(1 - \frac{1}{|\varepsilon_T|}\right) = MC. \quad \text{(VI)}$$

In the same way, the same procedure can be repeated for the business segment, leading to condition (VII):

$$p_B\left(1 - \frac{1}{|\varepsilon_B|}\right) = MC. \quad \text{(VII)}$$

Since MC is the same in (VI) and (VII), the condition of profit maximization for a monopolistic firm applying a price discrimination policy is

$$p_T\left(1 - \frac{1}{|\varepsilon_T|}\right) = MC = p_B\left(1 - \frac{1}{|\varepsilon_B|}\right), \quad \text{(VIII)}$$

from which we get that the higher price (and the lower quantity) is set in the market with the lower price elasticity (assumed to be the business segment). Such result is represented in Fig. 9.3, where the part (a) depicts the equilibrium in the business segment and the part (b) represents the equilibrium in the leisure segment.

Finally, note that if the elasticity is the same in the two segments (that is tantamount to say that there is no segmentation in the market), $\varepsilon_T = \varepsilon_B$, prices are also the same, $p_T = p_B$, and we return to the general result of optimality in a monopoly without price discrimination, where the service is then sold at a single price.

Obviously, the airline sets a lower price for a group of customers only if the demand for that group is relatively elastic, while it sets a higher price if the demand is relatively inelastic. It is relevant to highlight that this strategy is implemented because profits can be increased and that firms set different fares because the increased profit from those who enjoy a lower price more than compensate the reduction in profit stemming from those customers who end up paying a higher price.

The pricing policy just described is known as third-degree price discrimination, and occurs when different groups of tourists pay different prices. By analogy, this strategy also encompasses the strategy of pricing according to season. In fact, the

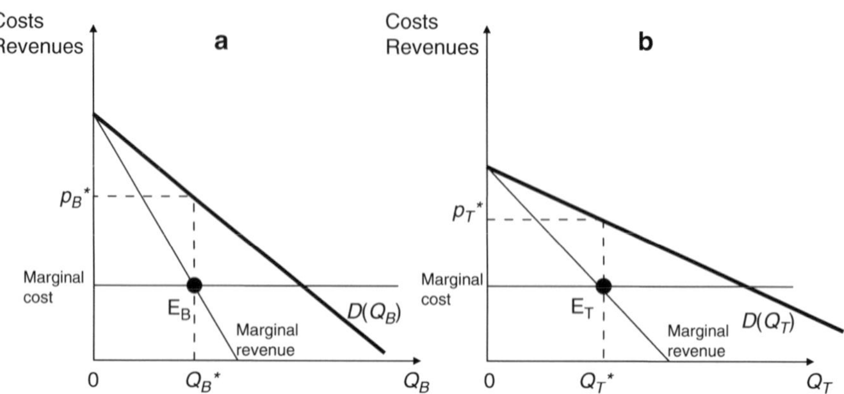

Fig. 9.3 The market equilibrium with third-degree price discrimination

practice of applying lower fares in the low season and higher fares in the peak season can be viewed as a policy that discriminates against those who have an inelastic demand and are forced to travel during the high season (perhaps because of institutional constraints, such as the time of school holidays or social constraints, such as religious festivities).

Even the "low-cost" pricing strategy, which we discussed in Sects. 8.2.4 and 9.3, can be interpreted, even if only partially, as an example of price discrimination. In such case, the same service provided is the basic flight from one city to another, and the offering of a low price becomes possible thanks to the waiver of all the frills associated with the trip. The low cost is bought by tourists who have a high price elasticity and who are not particularly interested in receiving, say, a glass of orange juice or a newspaper while on board.

Similarly, discounts can also be interpreted as price discrimination, given that they tend to attract those segments of the demand that are particularly sensitive to price changes. The policy of discounts may also pursue other marketing objectives and, when offered in the imminence of the trip, it must be primarily interpreted as a last-minute policy (see Sect. 9.5.4).

The second-degree price discrimination is instead the case when the unit price decreases with the increase in the quantity purchased, so that the price is not linear in quantity. Examples of this strategy are the round-trip ticket which has a price lower than buying two separate one-way tickets, or the weekly ski pass in which the seventh day of skiing is free. In practice, the second- and the third-degree price discrimination are usually offered in combination, so to increase the array of pricing policies that a company can offer, and which make it complicated for tourists to compare different prices.

Very similar to the second-degree discrimination are other practices such as frequent-flyer programs, which give additional benefits (in terms of discounted fares, free trips, or complementary services) to those customers purchasing a great number of services from the same company. Also the *two-part tariff* (see Sect. 9.4.2 and Sect. 15.4.3) is a type of pricing policy in which the unit price decreases with quantity.

The second- and the third-degree price discrimination policies are just an approximation of the first-degree price discrimination (also called perfect discrimination) that is almost impossible to implement in practice. This policy would require the firm to charge a price per unit sold equal to the maximum price (also known as reservation price) that each tourist would be willing to pay for that quantity. As an example, we may think of a tourist in a foreign country where the taximeter is not in use, and where the driver charges a price after trying to figure out the maximum price that the tourist is willing to pay. Again, the evolution of information technology and management techniques are now allowing the testing of sales mechanisms that closely approach the first-degree discrimination. For example, an online auction with a sale price that drops by a few Euros every X minutes encourages the tourists to buy the service when the price reaches their willingness to pay, under the uncertainty that the service may become unavailable if, in the meantime while waiting for further reductions, it gets purchased by someone else.

9.5.2 *The Booking Management*

With the solution of the third-degree price discrimination model, the firm is able to segment the market, that is, to decide how much to allocate of its product between each segment, Q_B and Q_T, given the characteristics of the demand and given the optimum price, p_B and p_T, which were previously defined.

In the real-world implementation, a further issue of complexity comes from the fact that the whole demand is not revealed simultaneously, but the different classes of tourists (business and leisure travelers) usually reveal their demand at different times during the booking period. Technically, they have a different *booking lead time*; in particular, tourists normally buy the service well before business travelers. Then, given that Q_B and Q_T are just expected sales, which automatically brings a degree of uncertainty into the framework. Were the firm to accept the early reservation made by a leisure tourist at the low price, it might then be unable to offer the service to customers who reveal their demand later on during the booking period and who are willing to pay a higher fare. If services are sold out at the low price, the firm forgoes a potential source of extra revenue. On the other hand, should the firm reject the sale at the low price in expectation of a future sale at the high price, it would expose to the risk that the service remains unsold. Therefore:

> At the heart of the airline revenue management lies the seat inventory control problem. This problem concerns the allocation of the finite seat inventory to the demand that occurs over time before the flight is scheduled to depart. The objective is to find the right combination of passengers on the flights such as revenues are maximized. The optimal allocation of the seat inventory then has to be translated into a booking control policy, which determines

> whether or not to accept a booking request when it arrives. It is possible that at a certain point in time it is more profitable to reject a booking request in order to be able to accept a booking request of another passenger at a later point in time.
>
> (Pak and Piersma, 2002, p. 2)

Based on past sales and on the analysis of time series data, this technique is applied to identify the minimum and maximum share of services for each segment, so to monitor the actual booking curve and check it on a daily basis with respect to the thresholds. This sales technique helps identify the number of rooms for a hotel (or the seats for an aircraft) to be allocated in each segment. It has been pointed out (Laws 2000) that such optimization technique is attractive for facilities that have large sales volumes and high turnover. However, even the medium-size companies may benefit from it, while small family-run businesses may find it unnecessary. There is a number of technological devices that can help in the booking management (sometimes called seat inventory in airlines' management): in particular, there is management software that operates in connection with the management systems of reservations over the Internet (Chap. 12).

Moreover, the techniques used to manage the reservations distinguish between the partial approach (single leg) and the network approach (multiple legs). According to the partial approach, each service is separately optimized, while the network approach aims at the optimization for the whole range of services. For example, undertaking the partial approach for an airline requires to account for reservations one route at the time, while the network approach would be appropriate if the booking is connected to other reservations made on different routes, even intercontinental, so to bring additional revenue to the company. For the hotel, the partial approach requires to account for reservations one night at the time, while the network approach would also consider the length of stay.

Finally, the booking management techniques can be classified in static and dynamic. With static techniques the firm decides the policy of reservations (i.e., the share of services offered at various prices) at a given time, usually before the opening of the booking period, based on past sales, past requests, and the forecast of the demand in the future. With dynamic techniques, the policy of reservation changes over time during the booking period as a result of a continuous monitoring of the actual demand. In other words, the relative share of each segment may change during the booking period by allowing the reservation in a class of service even when it is already full. The dynamic techniques can be used only if the structure is flexible, i.e., it can either accommodate customers belonging to different classes. Instead, it cannot be applied when the structure is rigid. An example of a flexible structure is a short-distance flight on a route where the difference between switching from the business class to the economy class comes from the terms written on the ticket (e.g., the possibility of changing the date without paying an extra fee) and not on the offered services (e.g., a larger seat). In this case, as usually happens, the size of the business class can be changed simply by moving forward or backward the curtain that divides the aircraft in two parts. On the contrary, an example of a rigid structure is instead the service offered on an intercontinental flight, where the service that identifies the business class requires larger and more comfortable seats.

9.5.3 The Overbooking

Closely related to the policy of booking management, the extensive deregulation in the air travel market has prompted many firms to undergo the overbooking; this consists of accepting a number of reservations that exceed the number of available services. It is important to stress on the fact that the overbooking is not a management mistake (although it may be in some cases), but is a rational strategy implemented by the company against the risk of having unsold services (empty seats or rooms) as a consequence of late cancelations, no-shows, or early or delayed departures. However, in doing so, the company is exposed to another risk that is associated with the event that all the booked guests actually show up and that the firm "goes on overbooking". In such case, the firm has to bear additional costs related to: (a) the loss of reputation (see Sect. 10.4.3); (b) the monetary compensation to be offered (according to the laws and the standards) to the tourist or, alternatively, the cost of offering an alternative service with the same or higher level of quality; (c) the opportunity cost related to customer dissatisfaction. The definition of the optimal overbooking strategy is not an easy task, since the firm has to compare the different costs involved in the two alternatives (risk of having empty seats vs. risk of going on overbooking) in a framework of uncertainty.

This practice, which was originally started by air transport companies, has recently been applied to the hotel sector and to many other types of tourism services: car rentals, ferries and cruises, tour operators. The core of the problem is to always try to fill the aircraft (or the hotel) with the optimal number of passengers or guests, usually with no empty seats (or empty rooms). The overbooking can be seen as a last resort policy of service upgrading or downgrading, which is usually the case when companies can easily change the level and the number of additional services being offered. If the alternative solution for the consumers is of higher quality than the service originally requested, we talk about upgrading (this is the case when the leisure tourist is upgraded to the business class due to overbooking). If the alternative solution is of lower quality we talk about downgrading (this is the case when the tourist is left on the ground because the aircraft is full).

Since tourism structures can almost always be defined as semirigid in the sense that they easily allow for the upgrading but not for the downgrading, when the company goes on overbooking, firstly it has to check whether there is still availability of higher class services; in case of no availability, the solution may turn out to be that of an extreme downgrading, which translates in leaving the passenger on the ground (against a monetary compensation).

To decrease the real cost (compensation to the tourists) and figurative cost (the loss of reputation), airlines might experiment with more efficient solutions for the overbooking problem, by leaving the passenger with a voluntary choice. The mechanism would simulate an upward auction: in the waiting room, the company announces the overbooking and offers a sum of money as compensation. The offer is increased up to the point where the number of tourists who accept compensation is identical to the size of overbooking.

In Sect. 8.2, we have already seen the roulette formula, that can be interpreted in the light of overbooking; this policy consists of offering the tourist the opportunity of choosing the destination and the type of hotel at a discounted price compared to the posted price. However, the tourist does not know the exact structure in which he or she will be accommodated. In this way, the tour operator is able to flexibly manage the contracts with hotels and the real sale by freely move tourists from one structure to another in order to solve overbooking problems.

9.5.4 The Dynamic Pricing

A final category of the revenue management normally used by tourism companies is the price discrimination based on the time of booking, which applies when the price changes as the reservation period goes by. Such strategy, which was already mentioned in Sect. 8.2 under the name of dynamic pricing, can be implemented by the means of increasingly sophisticated statistical models and managerial software that help the firm control for any difference between real and expected reservations. This allows the firm to predict in advance how many seats (or rooms) might remain empty and accordingly respond with an immediate change in price.

Nowadays, the dynamic pricing is mainly implemented by transport companies which advertise their fare on the Web site or through specialized online travel agencies, but is also used for hotel accommodation (Ropero 2011) and for the sale of tickets for events and shows (Schwartz et al. 2012). It can take the form of first-minute pricing, if the low price is available right at the opening of the booking period, or of last-minute (or last second) pricing if the low price is available only at the end (sometimes a few hours before) of the sale period.

In the first-minute booking (or advance booking, see Sect. 8.2) the incentive is to anticipate the reservation of those customers who are very sensitive to price changes. The discount allows the firm to monitor the sales more effectively and to take prompt action in case the booking is not in line with the cost coverage. In some cases, the advance booking allows the company the right to change its offer, for example by combining services (e.g., flying with another carrier) or by applying surcharges based on the increase in costs undergone between the booking time and the provision of the service (e.g., exchange rate adjustments, changes in fuel price, change in local taxes, etc.). On the other hand, and for the same reason, the company protects itself against customer cancelations; indeed, the sale contracts usually provide for flexible reimbursement, so that the refunded price decreases as the departure date approaches, up to excluding any reimbursement when the cancelation occurs too close to departure.

The last-minute booking allows the company to cover, at least partially, the costs incurred for providing seats in the aircraft or rooms in the hotel and that still result available in the imminence of provision. However, should the last-minute policy be applied systematically, a number of economic disadvantages would also arise for the firm. In fact, the tourist could become aware of the possibility of last-minute discounts and would be encouraged in booking late, which is the behavior opposite to what is needed to effectively monitor sales over the booking period and to maximize revenue. Therefore, the optimal strategy for the firm would be to rely on first-minute booking to anticipate with certainty the revenue from those tourists who have a low reservation price and to use the last-minute booking exceptionally, only for those situations where the load factor is very low. In other words, the firm should avoid the risk of "spoiling" the tourist with a frequent provision of this policy.

In some cases, the last-minute booking can take the form of explicit final sales, the so-called clearance sale. Since the service cannot be stored, to sell off at a low price is always better than to not sell at all (as long as the price remains above the marginal cost, see Sect. 8.3.2), which is justified when the firm is sure that no other customer will show up.

Finally, it should be noted that the yield management is not only a model of micromanagement, but also involves a number of systemic aspects. Firstly, because the yield management is applied in large companies, mainly multinational corporations with complex organizational systems, it allows a better coordination between different locations or between different types of products. Secondly, the yield management leads to coordination problems between the various firms operating in the destination when, for example, part of the demand that is not satisfied because of overbooking shifts to other competing companies. Finally, the yield management can be an interesting strategy to be implemented by the destination management: for example, with a centralized reservation system allowing the tourist office to monitor the booking in the various structures and to optimally allocate the reservation flows.

Case Study 9.3. The Yield Management in Tourism: An Experiment on the Paris-New York Route

The implementation of yield management in the business practice allows us to unfold interesting aspects of management that fall outside the theoretical analysis. Pasqualoni (2008) carried out an experiment by monitoring the fare of a flight between Paris (Charles de Gaulle or Orly airports) and New York (JFK or Newark airports), leaving on a Friday of June and returning after ten days, on the Monday, which typically defines a period attributable to tourists. The survey began a month before the departure date. The examined airlines were those that at the time served the Paris—New York route: American Airlines, Delta Airlines, Continental Airlines, Air France, and Avion (a low-cost airline which only served the Orly—Newark Airport route).

(continued)

The next step was to check the classes of service that these companies offered. Air France and American Airlines offered three classes: economy, business, and first class. Delta and Continental only offered the economy and business class. Avion, which counted on cockpits that are not organized to be divided into classes of service, offered a flat rate only for the business class. It must be pointed out that almost all airlines applied the same set of rules and restrictions for the economy class which, having the lowest fare, counted on a very limited flexibility, especially with regard to changes and cancelation policy. Business fares offered instead a higher degree of flexibility, since this class of customers is usually time sensitive and so agrees to pay high fares for not being subject to restrictive conditions. Surprisingly enough, however, Continental Airlines and Avion charged an additional cost (approximately 150–300 €) to allow changes in the departure or return date for the business class. Finally, the first-class fares had the best conditions for what concerns both ticket flexibility and the quality of onboard service.

With regard to prices, the trend for the economy class was very similar across all companies: the price was around 600 € which, besides some oscillations due to periodic adjustments, remained pretty stable up to one week before the departure, when all firms increased their prices up to about three times. Interestingly, about 3 weeks before the departure, Delta Airlines and Air France almost simultaneously changed their prices, but the first airlines did it upward (an increase of 150 €), while the second airline did it downward (by 50 €). The next day, the movements happened to be reversed: Delta Airlines lowered its price while Air France increased it. Then, on the third day the two companies returned selling at almost the same price. These movements might be interpreted as either strategic interaction or as signs of collusion.

As regards the business class, Delta Airlines kept a fare of approximately 4,000 € until two weeks before the departure, when the price went up to 7,000 €. A similar strategy was followed by Air France, which during the same period raised its fare by 1,500 €. Quite different was the policy followed by Continental Airlines, which started with a very high price, 6,700 €, but a few days before departure (and after several days when no seats were available) offered a lower business class fare. Such behavior probably revealed the existence of some canceled reservation that induced the airline to pursue a last-minute policy. Avion, finally, began with a very low business class fare, approximately 1,000 €, and increased it by "only" 300 € during the last days before departure.

The first-class fares were the highest, hovering a bit under 10,000 € and varying very little between the two companies that offered this service; Air France and American Airlines. In both cases the first-class seats were still available at time of departure: in fact they represent a very small segment of the market, which sale is a secure source of extra profit, and where a seat for a passenger willing to spend that huge amount of money must always be available.

(continued)

This survey clearly revealed the implementation of third-degree price discrimination policies, of the booking management while, except in one case, last-minute strategies seemed not to be applied. What was impossible to determine from this experiment was the number of available seats, whether they were just a few, the most likely scenario, or many. By not having actually completed the reservation, the survey was also unable to establish whether such availability of seats was real or would have led to overbooking.

Finally, it is also important to notice that many travelers, especially in the business class, are typically subject to the marketing strategies implemented by the airline through its specific frequent flying program, which tends to offer additional benefits to the traveler.

Chapter Overview

- To set the price, the hotel usually applies the full-cost or the target profit method, which can be accompanied by more detailed policies of price discrimination and product differentiation of the provided service.
- The generic (specific) occupancy rate is given by the ratio between the number of overnight stays and the number of available bed places multiplied by the number of days in a year (number of days in which the hotel is open). The average daily rate is calculated as the ratio between total revenue and the number of overnight stays, and depends on the market mix hosted by the hotel.
- The choice of the means of transport depends on the combination of characteristics such as speed, comfort, safety, distance, and the range of complementary services being offered.
- Also within the transport sector, every available seat at the time of departure qualifies as a service produced (and which costs have been borne) but unsold. For this reason, the load factor (i.e., the ratio between the number of carried passengers and the number of available seats) qualifies as a very important economic and management indicator.
- Tourism attractions are typically characterized by a relevant share of fixed costs over variable costs; this is due to the initial investments needed to make the attraction available and the subsequent investments necessary to keep it upgraded and to improve it.
- The yield (revenue) management is an integrated system of business techniques helping the company in the conduct of specific strategic choices, such as the decision of how to manage reservations, whether or not to apply the overbooking or other forms of service upgrading or downgrading, whether or not to implement price discrimination, and whether or not to use daily pricing strategies, such as advance booking or last-minute discounts.

Chapter 10
The Tourism Markets

Learning Outcomes

After reading this chapter you will understand:

- The most relevant market regimes and their application to the sectors in which tourism firms compete.
- The content and the consequences of strategies aimed at product differentiation and at taking advantage of information asymmetries.
- The importance of signaling, reputation, advertising, and word of mouth as strategies to deal with information asymmetries.

10.1 Introduction

As stated many times before, the tourism product is a set of heterogeneous and complementary services, supplied by firms that either directly serve the tourists or indirectly satisfy their demand. In other words, a whole tourism demand does not exist (see Sect. 4.2) and the tourism sector should be interpreted as a set of interconnected markets. Each tourism market can be seen as an abstract configuration in which demand and supply meet and in which an equilibrium in terms of quantity produced and price is set. The nature of this equilibrium, its efficiency, and its stability over time heavily depend on the diverse characteristics of the many existing real-world configurations.

The economic theory used to focus the analysis on three of these features: the market structure; the conduct of firms; and their performance as a result of conduct within a market structure. The so-called Structure–Conduct–Performance (SCP) approach, born as the evolution of the analysis of imperfect markets, became an important reference for the Industrial Organization and widely used, up to the 1980s, to describe markets which are led astray from the benchmark of perfect competition. In this regard, the SCP approach has both a descriptive content, allowing researchers to understand the reasons why markets are not competitive,

G. Candela and P. Figini, *The Economics of Tourism Destinations*, Springer Texts in Business and Economics, DOI 10.1007/978-3-642-20874-4_10,

and a normative content, since it allows to identify instruments of control and corrections for market inefficiencies.

The simple anecdotal evidence and a recall of the theory studied so far clarify that the SCP is inadequate to describe the complexity of tourism markets; however this methodology can be used to identify (as done by Stabler et al. 2010) the key variables to explain the organization of tourism supply:

1. The number and size of firms operating in the market, which in tourism can be measured, together with standard indexes, through the number of rooms (or bed places) for hotels, the number of passengers per kilometer for transport companies, etc.
2. The degree of market concentration and the existence of entry/exit barriers that can be proxied by the Gini index, the Lerner index, and the return on sales (ROS).
3. The existence of economies or diseconomies of scale and economies of scope, which typically apply in the sectors of transport, tour operators, travel agencies.
4. The existence of capital indivisibility, fixed capacity, and associated fixed operational costs, the latter being the great divide among tourism firms, where some (such as hotels or airlines) have a relevant share of their budget composed by fixed costs, whereby in some others (such as travel agencies) fixed costs are negligible.
5. Tourism firms are often price maker (or price quoter) so that price discrimination, product differentiation, and leadership policies are often important strategies for tourism firms so that yield management is a key factor of success.
6. Vertical and horizontal integration between firms is often observed in tourism.

Most of these elements will be unfolded in this chapter, always being consistent with the general approach of the book, where tourism is seen as a set of heterogeneous and complementary services and in which specific markets coexist. Such a diversity requires the use of a wide array of different models and approaches to interpret the complexity of the tourism phenomenon. The four key dimensions to analyze are the degree of strategic interaction between firms operating in the same market, the differentiation strategy implemented by firms, the characteristic of the goods (as either search or experience goods), and the type of information asymmetry existing in the market.

Consistently with this approach, in Sect. 10.2 we will review the main models describing the different theoretical market structures. The policy of product differentiation will be analyzed in Sect. 10.3, by distinguishing the case of vertical differentiation, which essentially deals with different qualities, from the case of horizontal differentiation, which rather deals with different varieties. The case of asymmetric information will be discussed in detail in Sect. 10.4. First, we will introduce the idea that information asymmetry can lead to market failure; then, we will analyze two of the strategies that are commonly implemented to reveal private information: signaling and reputation.[1] The relevance of asymmetric information

[1] We will also refer to Sect. 11.6 for the analysis of other types of information asymmetries as well as of the proposed solution.

for the market equilibrium also depends on the nature (mostly of experience good) of the tourism service: such aspect, as well as the differences with search goods, will be studied in Sect. 10.5. Finally, in Sect. 10.6 we will investigate the effects of advertising and of an alternative mechanism of information retrieval, the word of mouth occurring between friends and/or acquaintances, on quality and price.

10.2 The Structure of Tourism Markets

According to economic theory, the demand and the supply may meet in different market configurations technically called market regimes or market structures. The standard Microeconomics textbooks, to which we refer for a more detailed study, usually consider four basic market structures: (a) perfect competition, under which no economic agent (neither consumer nor firm) is able to affect the market price; (b) monopoly, a market in which there is only one producer who can fully set the price of the good; (c) monopolistic competition, in which firms implement a product differentiation strategy to gain market power; (d) oligopoly, under which a limited number of firms operate in the market and strategically interact with each other.

In all these models, the common hypothesis regards the behavior of the economic agents: they are always assumed to be *economically rational*. This means that, based on the information in their possession and their binding constraints, economic agents always try to maximize their objective function, represented by utility for the consumer and by profit for the firm. The four models mentioned earlier are different for a number of additional assumptions; let us unfold them.

10.2.1 Perfect Competition

In the model of perfect competition, a very large number of agents (firms and consumers) operate. Each agent has the complete set of relevant information needed in order to maximize own objective function (assumption of perfect information), given the constraints provided by the budget or by the technology. In addition, each agent decides independently in the sense that the agent's choice is not affected by the behavior of other agents (assumption of no strategic interaction). Finally, goods are assumed to be homogeneous: there is no difference between goods offered by the several market competitors.

In this situation, if it were to exist a firm A that can produce the good at a slightly lower price than the market price, fully informed consumers will direct their demand toward its product. On the other hand, the competitors can imitate firm A's production technology (as the technology is also common knowledge) and in turn lower the price of their good in order not to be excluded from the market. The process would then lead to a competitive equilibrium in which all firms sell at the price p_C (which is both the average and the marginal revenue for the firm) equal to the marginal and average cost of production. Therefore, in equilibrium firms are price taker, i.e., they are not able to change or to affect the market price. In fact, by setting an even lower price than p_C they would sell below the cost of production and suffer a loss; by setting a price higher than p_C they would turn away the demand, toward their competitors.

Although unrealistic, the model of perfect competition is a fundamental theoretical tool for two reasons. From a positive perspective it is the simplest model, around which all the other theoretical models pivot, i.e., they can be developed by relaxing some of the fundamental assumptions we mentioned earlier. From a normative perspective, the model of perfect competition plays the role of an important benchmark with which to compare other market regimes. In fact, the first theorem of Welfare Economics, which summarizes the model's main findings, emphasizes that the competitive market is Pareto efficient, which means that is no longer possible to increase the welfare of an agent without causing a loss in some other agent's welfare. Given that Economics studies the problem of choice made under scarcity of resources, the competitive market solves this problem efficiently: it is therefore the "best" solution to the economic problem. In addition, the attainment of efficiency is especially beneficial to consumers: in fact (Theory in Action 10.1), under perfect competition, the exchanged quantity and the market price are, respectively, the maximum and the minimum possible; on the contrary, since the price is equal to the marginal and the average cost of production, perfect competition brings firms to earning zero profits (net of what companies normally pay as a return on capital).

Theory in Action 10.1. A Comparison Between Perfect Competition and Monopoly Equilibria

Consider a market with linear demand function:

$$p = a - bQ, \tag{I}$$

where p is price and Q the quantity of the good. The individual supply function can be represented by a linear and increasing cost function, $\mathrm{TC} = cQ$, where the marginal cost, MC, is constant and equal to the parameter c. The economic goal for the firm, independent of the market regime in which it operates, is profit maximization, where profit is defined as the difference between total revenues, TR, and total cost, TC:

$$\pi = \mathrm{TR} - \mathrm{TC} = pQ - cQ. \tag{II}$$

The maximum profit is identified by the first-order condition, $\mathrm{d}\pi/\mathrm{d}Q = 0$, i.e., when the marginal revenue, MR, equals the marginal cost MC. The solution, however, differs according to the market structure.

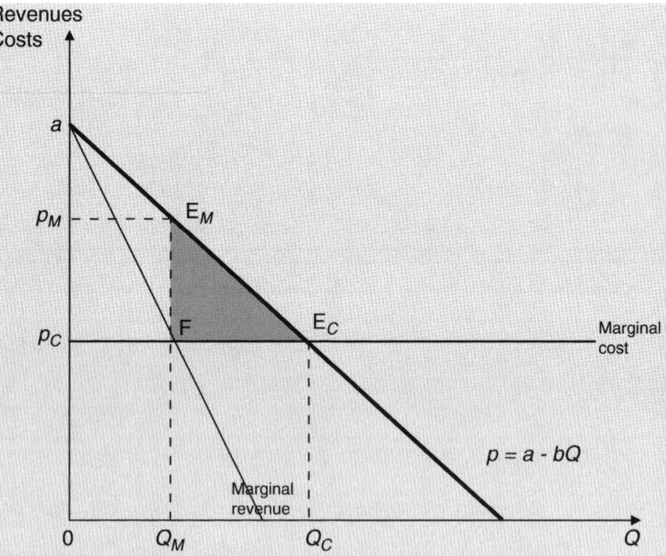

Fig. 10.A Market equilibrium under perfect competition and monopoly

Perfect Competition

Under perfect competition the price is set by the market (the firm is price taker) and we indicate it with p_C. Therefore, the first-order condition (II) simply becomes $p_C = c$. By replacing this condition in (I) we get the total amount, Q_C , produced in the market:

$$Q_C = \frac{a-c}{b}. \qquad \text{(III)}$$

The solution of equilibrium under perfect competition (Q_C, p_C) is represented by point E_C in Fig. 10.A.

Monopoly

The monopolistic company is not price taker and, since it is the only supplier on the market, must face the whole market demand represented in (I). The solution for the profit maximization problem can be obtained by substituting (I) in (II), thus leading to

$$\pi = (a - bQ)\,Q - cQ = aQ - bQ^2 - cQ.$$

(continued)

By solving the first-order condition of the profit function with respect to Q, $d\pi/dQ = 0$, we get the condition of equality between marginal revenue and marginal cost, which determines the quantity produced and exchanged under monopoly:

$$Q_M = \frac{a-c}{2b}. \quad \text{(IV)}$$

By replacing (IV) in (I) we also get the monopolistic price:

$$p_M = \frac{a+c}{2}.$$

The solution of equilibrium under monopoly (Q_M, p_M) is represented by point E_M in Fig. 10.A.

From the comparison between (III) and (IV) it is easy to state that $Q_C > Q_M$, while for $a > c$ (a necessary condition for the existence of the market, indeed if $a < c$ the firm would inevitably get a loss) we have $p_C < p_M$. To summarize, under the monopoly regime, the market trades at a higher price and at a lower quantity, thus leading to a loss for consumers.

However, Fig. 10.A allows to state an even more powerful conclusion: the monopoly produces a total loss to the society as a whole. In fact, under perfect competition, the social welfare arising from the market (which is the sum of profits and the consumers surplus) corresponds to the area aE_Cp_C. Instead, under monopoly, the consumer surplus is reduced and is equal to the area aE_Mp_M, while profits increase and are equal to the area $p_ME_MFp_C$. Social welfare under monopoly is therefore equal to the area aE_MFp_C with a decrease compared to the case of perfect competition, that is the so-called deadweight loss of welfare and is represented by the shaded area E_ME_CF in Fig. 10.A.

These few lines are sufficient to explain why in market economies antitrust laws and competition authorities are needed; such laws and institutions should have the goal to keep the markets in conditions of efficiency, thus defending the consumers against the tools used by companies to increase their profit. Indeed, since under perfect competition firms cannot earn any (extra) profit, they have all the incentives to make market conditions less competitive. This, among other things, leads to the frequent process of mergers and acquisitions of firms aiming at decreasing the degree of market competitiveness. By doing so, however, not only they harm the consumers but also reduce the overall efficiency of the market (Theory in Action 10.1).

The standard textbooks of Microeconomics usually warn that the regime of perfect competition is a limit case in the price-formation mechanism, a regime that finds full application in a few markets only, primarily the financial ones. In particular, in the case of tourism, the hypothesis of perfect competition seems hard to defend. Only a few markets, in which the absence of entry barriers to potential competitors leads to contestable markets, seem to match the operating assumptions of perfect competition. However, the Internet revolution of the last few years and the consequent improvement in the size and accuracy of information available to the public are bringing many tourism markets closer to the theoretical assumption of perfect competition (Chap. 12).

10.2.2 Monopoly

From the firm perspective, the target of profit maximization would require to operate under monopoly regime, a market in which there is only one supplier. If this is the case, the firm can satisfy the whole demand for the good and use the price as a strategic tool to increase profits. Hence, the company is said to be price maker, or characterized by market power, given that it can choose the optimal price–quantity combination that maximizes own profits.

Compared to perfect competition, under the monopoly regime the firm's profit is higher and this works to the detriment of both consumers' well-being (well below the level reached under perfect competition) and of the overall market efficiency: the monopoly regime causes a welfare loss for the economy as a whole, the so-called deadweight loss due to the monopoly. The comparison between the equilibria of perfect competition and monopoly can also highlight the distributional conflict between consumers and producers: the former prefer to buy goods produced under perfect competition while firms seek to use any tool at their disposal to gain monopoly power and drive the market away from competition.

In the real-world economy, the monopoly is not a rare occurrence, even in tourism as it is the typical market structure of attractions, such as natural parks, amusement parks, and museums where the firm manages a unique tourism resource.

10.2.3 Monopolistic Competition

One of the strategies that firms can implement in order to gain market power is product differentiation. In the real world, any product is characterized, to a greater or lesser extent, by a certain degree of differentiation; for example, no hotel is identical to another; even a beach always has some characteristics that make it unique in the eyes of the tourists. In part, the differentiation may also stem from the existence of information asymmetries, so that not all the firms have access to the same technology (or at the same cost), with the result that in equilibrium firms tend to produce similar but not identical goods. Finally, companies may use different techniques (design, technology, complementary accessories, marketing and branding policies) in order to differentiate their product and make it unique to the eyes of the customers (and, therefore, not perfectly substitutable with the goods supplied by other competitors).

The monopolistic competition can hence be defined as a market regime in which firms produce differentiated goods, i.e., goods that are only partial substitutes to each other. The name of this market structure is derived from the simultaneous presence of some features of competition (firms compete primarily on the same market and thus are in competition with each other) and monopoly (thanks to product differentiation, companies are able to sell their products in market niches, thus gaining monopoly power).

Since this market structure is a hybrid of the previous two regimes, it displays an equilibrium that is intermediate in terms of prices and welfare. In the short term, firms are able to get extra profits, though not as high as under monopoly. In the long term, however, the equilibrium is at the point where the price is equal to the average cost, thereby implying zero extra profits for the firms. It is important to highlight that the equality between the price and the average cost is set at a level above the minimum average cost and the price exceeds marginal cost. Hence, consumers purchase the good at a higher price than under perfect competition. It must be added that the welfare comparison is more difficult in this case than in the case of monopoly: in fact, being the product a differentiated good, the higher price is partially compensated by a more precise match of consumers' preferences, so to lead to greater satisfaction (measured in terms of their utility).

In the tourism sector, as well as in many other economic sectors, product differentiation is an important reality, suggesting the presence of some kind of monopolistic power by tourism firms. The segmentation of demand for tourism and the deep differences in the quality and in the variety of tourism services lead to the insurgence of markets where producers are not price takers and have some degree of monopoly power, although not being monopolists. In addition, the model for monopolistic competition seems well suited to capture the existing competition between tourism destinations. For example, within the market for Alpine tourism, the French mountain resorts are in competition with other destinations located in Switzerland, Austria, and Italy, although the degree of substitutability is not perfect due to the fact that their tourism products are significantly different in terms of characteristics of the mountains, the sightseeing, the length and the difficulty of trekking and climbing routes, the organization and provision of ski pistes, etc.

Moreover, in many tourism destinations (e.g., the Costa del Sol or a cultural city like Paris), the hospitality market in which a multitude of hotels offer a differentiated accommodation service can be well represented by the model of monopolistic competition. Even travel agencies, usually many and strategically located in the territory, offer personalized services in a market which characteristics are very close to the monopolistic competition regime.

10.2.4 Oligopoly

Under oligopoly regime a few companies operate and strategically interact with each other in the market. It is the strategic interaction, and not the limited number of firms, that economically characterizes the oligopoly. With the term strategic interaction we refer to the non-existence of an optimal strategy for the company, regardless of what the competitors do. On the contrary, the best strategy in terms of price to set and quantity to produce depends on what the competitors choose and is technically identified by a reaction function identifying how the firm optimally responds to the strategy chosen by other companies. In Economics, the oligopoly models differ depending on the type of market interaction being assumed. The basic models are as follows[2]: the Cournot's model, where firms compete and interact on the quantity to be produced; the Bertrand's model, where firms compete and interact on the price to set[3]; the Stackelberg's model, where there is a market leader setting its strategy first, then followed by a second company, called follower; the collusion model, in which the strategic interaction leads to the creation of a cartel where the participating firms act as a monopolist and gain (and share) the monopoly profit.

The oligopoly is the market structure that well describes the transport sector and the tour operating sector. Such markets usually develop as oligopolies over time, when the increase in size of firms is better suited for supplying mass tourism products and for facing the international tourism flows: the constant growth of tourism demand, the seasonality, the search for profit maximization, the possibility to gain economies of scale and scope,[4] all lead to various forms of businesses integration (also at international level, see Chap. 14), thus bringing the market from competition to oligopoly and, in some cases, to monopoly. At the same time, such dynamic trend towards a greater market concentration is counteracted by the introduction of liberalization policies and antitrust authorities which aim at bringing the markets to the theoretical benchmark of perfect competition. In this regard, it is paradigmatic to analyze the effects that liberalization is having on the air-transport market, both in terms of changes in the business strategy and in terms of consumer welfare (Gil Molto and Piga 2007).

10.2.5 Strategies of Integration Between Firms

The process of integration can take the following three forms:

1. *Vertical integration*, when the firm owns its upstream suppliers (along the supply chain, backward integration), its downstream buyers (in the direction of the tourists, forward integration), or both (balanced integration). This is the case, for example, of an airline that integrates with a hotel chain and/or with a tour operator, or of a tour operator that integrates with a travel agency.

---

[2] For a deeper discussion of these models, we refer to any textbook of Microeconomics.

[3] Bertrand's model shows that two competing firms are enough to bring the market to the perfect competition equilibrium, thereby highlighting that is not the number of firms that determines the degree of competition in the market, but the type of existing strategic interaction.

[4] The economies of scale are related to firm size and occur when the average production costs decrease as the quantity produced increases; the economies of scope are related to the occurrence of manufacturing integration and allow the firm to use common inputs for the production of more goods in one or more markets at decreasing costs.

2. *Horizontal integration*, when the firm is being taken over by, or merged with, another firm operating in the same sector. This is the case of some hotels that integrate to create a hotel chain, or of airlines that integrate to improve their average load factors.
3. *Diagonal integration*, the process through which a firm joins another firm that is not part of the same production line but operates in a related field. For example, there is diagonal integration when a tour operator joins a software company.

Integration can be undertaken either through direct investment (mergers, takeovers, or company buyouts) or through forms of contractual agreements. The most common forms of direct investment are:

- The *merger* (or consolidation), when two companies *A* and *B* combine together to form the new company *C*; very often the two original firms cease to exist while maintaining their brands for a limited period of time;
- The *acquisition* (or takeover), when the company *A* is purchased and absorbed in all its functions by the company *B*, which continues to exist on the market under its own brand.

The most common contractual agreements are as follows:

- The *joint venture*, a business agreement (a partnership) between companies (for example, a temporary consortium of firms) aimed at implementing a specific project and which ceases with this project's completion.
- The *franchising*, a contractual agreement where a firm (the franchisor) grants the use of its business model (including the name, the brand, the management, and marketing strategies) to another party (the franchisee) in exchange of a payment; many hotel chains manage their brand by the means of franchising agreements.
- The *leasing*, a contract used by private agents (the lessee) to obtain the use of durable goods and fixed assets (machinery, plants, equipment, vehicles, etc.) without having to buy them directly but in exchange of periodic payments to the owner (the lessor). In practice, the entrepreneur relies on an outside leasing company, which retains the ownership of the good; many transport companies currently use leased carriers, in part because of the lower production costs to bear and in part to earn a greater flexibility in the management of the demand for tourism which, as we know, is quite volatile and seasonal.
- The *management contract*, an arrangement under which the operational control of the firm is outsourced to a separate firm which performs the necessary managerial functions in return for a payment. This allows the transferring of organizational and technological knowledge as well as the signing of contracts for technical assistance and staff training. In exchange, this contract usually requires an initial lump sum payment and a commission proportional to the managed services.

For all the reasons stated so far, the hypothesis of a price-taker firm is not appropriate when dealing with the tourism sector. Indeed, the existence of market imperfections gives the operators the power to act (at least partially) as price makers. In such case, the most convincing and general price formation rule is the *full cost principle*, already discussed in Chaps. 8 and 9 when analyzing the process of price setting for tourism firms.

10.3 The Differentiation of the Tourism Product

The hypothesis of market imperfection implies that firms not only compete in price but also in product differentiation. As already stated, product differentiation is the condition where goods are only partial substitutes one to each other and meet, in different ways, needs of identical nature. There is product differentiation depending on the combination of two factors: (a) subjective factors, due to the fact that each consumer has personal and idiosyncratic preferences, when asked to select the exact good's features; (b) strategic factors, according to which the firm adapts to the variety of consumers' tastes by differentiating its production from that of the other firms in the same sector, thus making it somewhat unique. Before studying the economic effect of differentiation we must recall that economic theory distinguishes between two different concepts of differentiation.

1. *Horizontal differentiation*, when the products are different in the combination of their characteristics: they can have more of some features and less of others. Hence, horizontal differentiation stems from the variety of consumer preferences: goods are not ranked in the same way by all consumers, as are cars of different colors or preferences with respect to fish or meat in the meal. The spatial differentiation is a specific type of horizontal differentiation, as it considers as "different" the products that are identical in every respect but the location where they are purchased.
2. *Vertical differentiation*, when the products are different in the extent of their characteristics: while a product has more of all the features, another product has less of all the features. Hence, the vertical differentiation stems from the quality of the goods which, regardless of price, are ranked in the same way by all consumers, as luxury cars with more optional accessories or hotels that have rooms with balcony, jacuzzi, air conditioning, wi-fi, etc. are preferred by all consumers.

The difference between these two concepts can be understood by using the Lancaster's model of characteristics (see Sect. 6.3). Indeed, if we recall the composition of Fig. 6.4, we may think of representing in a similar graph different tourism products (e.g., different hospitality services) according to two relevant characteristics of hotels: the quality of food of their restaurants and the comfort of the rooms, respectively, measured on the vertical and horizontal axis.

In Fig. 10.1, the two products x_3 and x_4 are vertically differentiated, since the quantity of the two characteristics is larger in one (x_3) rather than in the other (x_4) product. Should the price be the same, consumers would only demand the good with the best quality, x_3; therefore, the existence of vertical differentiation in the market

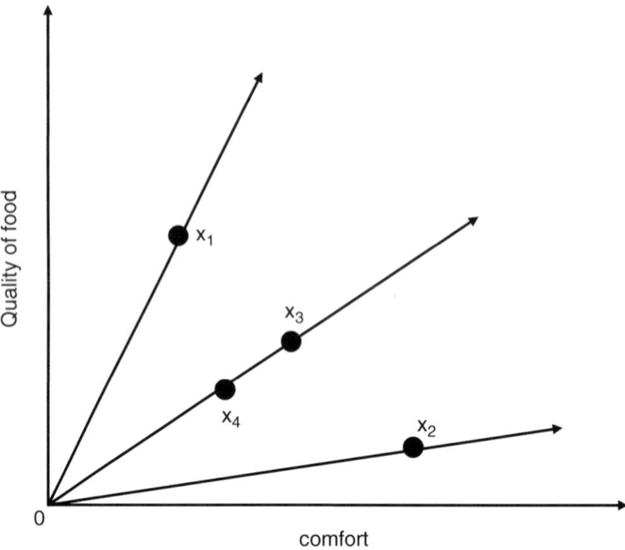

Fig. 10.1 Horizontal and vertical differentiation

can only be justified by the price difference, in the sense that the price of x_4 has to be strictly lower than that of x_3 (because of the lower cost borne by the company to produce a low quality good). The typical example of two vertically differentiated products in tourism could be the accommodation in a luxury hotel versus a budget hotel.

The two goods x_1 and x_2 in Fig. 10.1 are horizontally differentiated; in fact, none of them has a larger quantity of both characteristics than the other (the two goods are lying along different vectors). When two goods are horizontally differentiated they are characterized by a different variety and it is therefore impossible to establish a ranking of goods that applies to all consumers. When the horizontally differentiated products have the same price, consumers can be divided into three groups: consumers who prefer x_1, those who prefer x_2, and those who are indifferent. The obvious example of two horizontally differentiated tourism products can be the case of two hotels of the same category, one with a good restaurant but no sea-view rooms versus a hotel with sea-view rooms but with a mediocre restaurant.

The horizontal differentiation usually stems from the heterogeneity of consumer preferences which, in turns, allows for the existence of a variety of tourism products even when all consumers have the same income and all goods have the same price. In the case of vertical differentiation, instead, the emphasis is on quality: all consumers have the same preferences over the goods, and the existence of vertically differentiated products must stem from differences in the consumers' ability to pay. Even if all consumers prefer the good with higher quality, some of them cannot afford to buy them. In other words, only the rich tourists can pay the higher price associated with the high-quality product.

Although in the real-world tourism products differ both in variety and in quality, it is theoretically possible to separately study these two issues. And this is what will be done in the next subsections.

10.3.1 The Quality in the Tourism Product

The market characterized by products of different quality (vertical differentiation) is studied in the literature through models in which firms face a sequence of three strategic choices (Gabszewicz and Thisse 1979, 1980; Shaked and Sutton 1982, 1983). In the first stage, the firm decides whether or not to enter the market; in the second stage it decides the quality of the supplied product; in the third stage it sets the price at which the good is sold. The three-stage process enables us to fully grasp the different degree of reversibility that is implicit in each of these decisions: prices can be easily changed, while changes in the quality of the supply require an investment to gather information and in advertising; finally, the decision to enter the market must precede, both logically and temporally, the choice of what specific quality to offer. The solution of such sequence of decisions can be determined via a backward-induction process, which begins with the last stage and moves back to the first stage. Therefore, the solution firstly sets the price (*ceteris paribus* for the number of competing firms and the quality of products), then sets the quality of the product, and finally deals with the firm's decision whether or not entering the market.

The model of vertical differentiation can be synthetically summarized as follows: even when there is a large number of competitors that can potentially enter the market, the equilibrium under vertical differentiation allows (under sufficiently general assumptions) only a limited number of producers. This result is known in the literature as finiteness property and states that there is an upper limit in the number of firms (and in the quality of their products) that can coexist in equilibrium for a market of any size.

To illustrate this result in a simple manner let us refer to the last stage of the firm's choice, the price-setting stage. Let us consider a number of firms that produce, for the sake of simplicity at no costs (i.e., with zero fixed costs and zero variable costs), tourism products characterized by different quality but referring to the same package tour. Each trip of quality k, with $k = 1, 2, \ldots, n$, is characterized by an increasing quality according to the value of k and is produced by the k-th tour operator at the price p_k. We then admit the existence of a continuum of tourists with identical tastes but different incomes, Y; such income is distributed across agents according to a uniform density function in the interval $a \leq Y \leq b$, where a and b (both positive) indicate, respectively, the lowest and the highest income of tourists who demand this kind of trip.

The last-stage solution can be better understood by using the model presented in Sect. 5.4, where the only difference is that now the variable representing the trip is no longer a binary variable [0, 1], but must be expressed in the range of the different

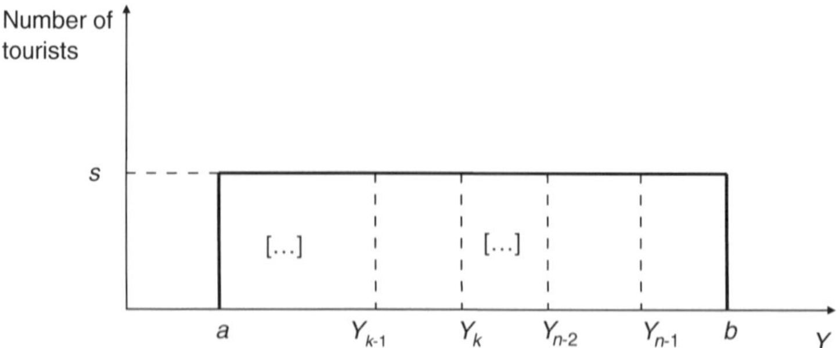

Fig. 10.2 Market segmentation with respect to the quality of the tourism product and tourists' income

quality. Thus, if $U(Y, 0)$ is the utility of those who do not purchase the package tour, the utility of the tourist buying a tourism product of generic quality k is $U(Y - p_k, k)$.

If we assume that the products are ranked in ascending order of quality, we can define, by the means of an equation similar to (5.12), the condition of indifference between purchasing the quality $(k - 1)$ tour at the price p_{k-1} and the quality k tour at the price p_k:

$$U(Y - p_k, k) = U(Y - p_{k-1}, k - 1). \tag{10.1}$$

Equation (10.1) defines, for each price p_k and quality k, the critical level of income Y_{k-1}, indicating that tourists with higher income strictly prefer the high-quality tour, k, while tourists with lower income strictly prefer the low-quality tour $(k - 1)$. Indeed, for the latter tourists the tour of quality k is relatively too expensive and they prefer to spend income in other goods.

By repeating (10.1) for each of the n qualities, one can allocate tourists to observe, for each vector of prices, the market share of each package tour. With reference to the different values of k, a virtual market segmentation with respect to the quality of the tourism product demanded by consumers as a function of the different classes of income can be drawn: all consumers do prefer the higher rather than the lower quality, but not everyone can afford paying its price. Such segmentation is represented on the horizontal axis of Fig. 10.2, whereas to understand the value on the vertical axis we must recall that there are s consumers for each level of income. Therefore the total number of tourists is $s(b - a)$ while those demanding each level-k quality are $s(Y_k - Y_{k-1})$. For example, the potential demand for the tour of highest quality, n, is given by $s(b - Y_{n-1})$, while the potential demand for the tour of quality $(n - 1)$ is given by $s(Y_{n-1} - Y_{n-2})$, and so on.

For each of the n tours of specific quality it is now possible to describe the demand function. This function depends not only on quality and price, but also on the price charged by the tour operators producing tours of different quality; it is therefore necessary to explicitly introduce an assumption on the price set by the

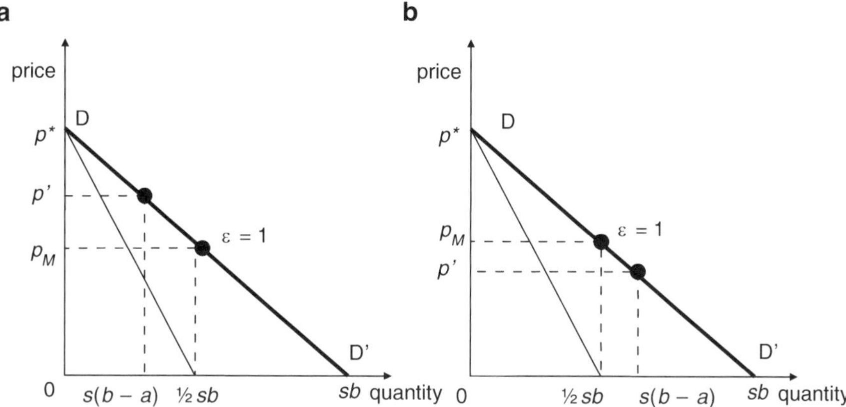

Fig. 10.3 The equilibrium for the firm producing the good with quality n

competitors. The simplest hypothesis is that the price is constant and equal to zero (since costs are zero, this assumption is economically viable).

We therefore start by considering the demand for the product of highest quality, the one of quality n, assuming that lower quality products are supplied for free, at zero price. If we assume that the demand function is linear, we just need two points to draw it. It is then sufficient to consider the reservation price for the quality-n product, both for the richest as well as for the poorest tourist.

- The tourist with highest income, b, has a reservation price p^* for purchasing the highest quality tour n rather than its immediately lower quality alternative, $(n - 1)$, at zero price; such price is determined by the following condition:

$$U(b - p^*, n) = U(b, n - 1). \tag{10.2}$$

  In Fig. 10.3, p^* is the vertical intercept of the demand for the highest quality tour (for a price higher than p^* the demand would vanish, since not even the richest tourist can purchase it).
- The tourist with the lowest income, a, has a reservation price $p' < p^*$ for the same level of quality. Such reservation price is determined as

$$U(a - p', n) = U(a, n - 1). \tag{10.3}$$

In Fig. 10.3, p' is another point in the demand function for the tour operator that offers the highest quality tour, i.e., the price that is needed to satisfy all consumers. The second point along the demand function is then $(s(b - a), p')$. At price p', the demand for the quality-n tour absorbs the entire market potential $s(b - a)$, and the tour operator who sets such price can cover the whole market with the highest-quality product.

By combining the two points determined by (10.2) and (10.3), we get the linear demand for the tourism product of quality n. Then, Fig. 10.3 represents the demand function DD' for the tour operator that produces the highest quality package tour, assuming that the price of its nearest competitor is zero, $p_{n-1} = 0$. The tourists with income progressively lower than b are willing to pay prices progressively lower to purchase the quality n rather than quality $(n - 1)$, so the demand for the tour n increases as the price decreases until it reaches the level p'. If this trip was to be offered free of charge, that is $p_n = 0$, all tourists would be able to purchase such good, even those without income; indeed the intercept of the demand function on the horizontal axis is sb.

By recalling again the assumption of zero cost, we know that the equilibrium for the monopolist coincides with the Cournot point (the point in which the price elasticity is equal to one, as discussed in Sect. 4.4.1); the first-order condition of maximum profit for the monopolist (each firm is monopolist in each quality segment) would lead to a level of production equal to ½ sb, with a price equal to $p_n = p_{\mathrm{M}}$.

We are now able to determine the optimal price for the tour operator selling the quality-n product. The alternatives for the firm are two: (a) to cover the whole market with the best tour, by setting the price p'; (b) to offer the quantity of maximum profit for the monopolist, selling at price p_{M}. Obviously, for the same cost, the optimal solution will be identified by the maximum between these two prices, $\max[p', p_{\mathrm{M}}]$ or, in terms of sold quantity, the firm's equilibrium is the minimum between these two quantities, $\min[s(b - a); ½\, sb]$. We must therefore discuss the following two conditions:

1. If $(b - a) < (1/2)b$, or $2a > b$, then the tour operator offers the product of quality n at the price p' and covers the entire market (this is the case presented in Fig. 10.3a);
2. If $(b - a) > (1/2)b$, or $2a < b$, then the tour operator offers the product of quality n at the price p_{M} without covering the whole demand (this is the case of Fig. 10.3b). The firm selling a product of lower quality, $(n - 1)$, then covers the market share characterized by lower income tourists.

Thus, the existence of inequality in consumers' income, $(a - b)$, justifies the existence of two different qualities of the tourism product in the market. To generalize our conclusion, we must proceed in the sequence of quality by asking under what conditions there is room for other tour operators and other qualities, by replicating the solution method we just discussed. Shaked and Sutton (1982, 1983) have shown that two producers only are able to cover the whole demand if $4a > b$; on the contrary, if $4a < b$ a new tour operator, supplying a lower quality tour, can enter the market, and so on. However, the process comes to an end, with a limited number of firms offering products of different quality in the market, and hence making positive profits.

If we remove the assumption of zero production costs, the result is only partially modified: the finiteness result gets confirmed only if the difference in quality implies fixed and variable costs that are identical across all firms, or when any positive change in the variable costs is a negligible function of increasing quality. Shaked and Sutton (1983) define as natural oligopoly any market for which the finiteness principle holds.

The solutions presented in Fig. 10.3 are derived from the assumption that $p_{n-1} = 0$. Such simplification can be relaxed by proposing an identical method of solution also in the segment of quality $(n - 1)$: in this case, the optimal strategy for each tour operator depends, in every stage of the solution, from the choice made by the other firms. The model is then configured as a three-stage game. The tree of the game takes the following form: (a) in the first node, the firm chooses whether or not to enter the market, as a function of the number of entrants; (b) if the firm has entered, in the second node it chooses the quality of the product as a function of the firms that have entered; (c) in the third node, the tour operator sets the price based on the quality chosen by the other firms during the second stage of the game. If, as we have already established, the solution of the game is implemented "backwards," starting from node (c) we can move back to the first stage and determine an equilibrium that is confirmed at each subgame. This can be defined as perfect equilibrium in the Selten sense (Selten 1975).

Before concluding, we would like to highlight an important consequence of this model: the equilibrium in the market ultimately depends on the parameters of the income distribution. Indeed:

- if $1 < b/a < 2$, the market offers a single quality;
- if $2 < b/a < 4$ the market offers two qualities;
- if $b/a > 4$ in the market there is room for at least three qualities, etc.

Since b/a is, in short, an index of income inequality for the tourists who demand the product (i.e., is the ratio between the maximum and the minimum income of a uniform distribution), it is immediate to conclude that as income inequality decreases, the tourism market concentrates on the tours of higher quality, which is a process in which lower quality firms gradually lose market share, until they completely exit the market.

This conclusion is essential to explain that the process of economic development, which results in income growth, leads to a progressive decline in the market share of one-star or two-star hotels (cheaper, but offering a service of lower quality) to the advantage of those of higher quality. The analytical content of this model indicates that the leveling up at the top of the tourists' purchasing power leads to a market loss suffered by those types of tourism characterized by a lower quality. It is not necessarily true, however, that this process of upward adjustment is also a social optimum (Garcia and Tugores 2006).

10.3.2 Tourism as a Good with Exogenous Quality

The quality of tourism products analyzed in Sect. 10.3.1 depends on the firm's strategy: if the firm has chosen to offer a tourism product of higher quality, by positioning itself in the high price market segment, it must be willing to bear the higher cost of production. Then, it can be said that the quality is endogenously defined by the firm itself.

However, when dealing with tourism, another concept of quality that is not under the direct control of the firm becomes important. In fact, when organizing a holiday, tourists hope that factors such as the bad weather, the occurrence of strikes at museums, or other mishaps will not spoil the holiday. The same expectation is expressed by the tourism firms, which can only hope for good conditions to hold, even though they can in some way ensure the tourists against external events that can lower the quality of the holiday: for example, an insurance against bad weather is possible by the means of discounts or partial refunds. Contrary to what has been studied in the previous section, when the quality of the tourism experience depends on events that are not under the control of the tourism firm, the quality is usually referred to as exogenous (Candela and Cellini 1998, Candela and Figini 2005).

The exogenous quality is neither set by the tourism firm nor linked to the production costs. Indeed, it owns an important effect on the level of the tourist's satisfaction, thereby being an interesting object of analysis for the Economics of Tourism. Let us refer to the tourist's choice presented in Sect. 5.4 and recalled in Sect. 10.3.1, by changing the binary variable V which represents the tour and by taking into consideration that the tourist's satisfaction now depends on a contingent state of nature. By assuming the existence of two possible events, one negative (bad weather) and the other positive (good weather), we have the following set of alternatives for the tourist:

$$V = \left[0, V^{\circ}, V'\right],$$

where the alternatives are that: (a) the tour is not purchased, $V = 0$; (b) the tour is purchased and meets the negative event: $V = V^{\circ}$; (c) the tour is purchased and meets the positive event: $V = V'$. We denote with q the probability of the positive event, and with $(1 - q)$ the probability of the negative event. The obvious consequence of such assumption is that $U(Y - p, V^{\circ}) < U(Y - p, V')$, where p is the price paid for the tour. Since the price is usually paid in advance through the reservation system, it cannot take into account the effect that external events have on the quality of the journey. Then, the tourist must modify the expression (5.12) of its reservation price by taking into account the probability of the different events:

$$U(Y - p^{*}, V')q + U(Y - p^{*}, V^{\circ})(1 - q) = U(Y, 0). \tag{10.4}$$

Once again, the tourist decides by comparing own reservation price, $p^{*}(Y|q)$, which value now also depends on the probability q, with the price set by the tour operator.

To illustrate this choice, let us consider the numerical example of a tourist who must decide whether or not to go on holiday, and whose decision does not only depend on the holiday's characteristics, which are perfectly known by the tourist, but also on climatic conditions, i.e., the external event. The two possible states of

Table 10.1 The tourist's choice when the good has exogenous quality

	Good weather	Bad weather
The tourist goes on holiday	90	30
The tourist does not go on holiday	40	40

nature are rainy or sunny, while the two possible actions are to buy or to not buy the holiday, that is, to stay at home and engage in alternative consumption activities. Table 10.1 shows the utility, measured in monetary units, attached to the four different combinations stemming from the individual decision and the state of nature.

With sunny weather, the tourists would get higher utility from taking the holiday (90), while with rainy weather the utility would only be 30 (so that the tourist would prefer to spend the same amount of money in alternative goods that could provide greater utility, equal to 40). Suppose that the tourist assigns a probability $q = 1/2$ to the event of bad weather and an equal probability to the event of good weather. Hence, the expected utility stemming from purchasing the holiday would be 60 ($=0.5 \times 90 + 0.5 \times 30$), while the action of staying at home would provide a certain utility of 40. So the tourist's surplus, supposedly neutral to risk, would be 20 ($=60 - 40$), and the holiday would be purchased.

The solution clearly depends on the probability of the events. Let us now change the setting of the above example in the following way:

- If the probability of good weather is $q = 2/3$, the exogenous quality of the holiday would be higher and would give an expected utility equal to $70(=2/3 \times 90 + 1/3 \times 30)$, while the utility associated to not buying the holiday is unchanged; in this case, the expected surplus would be 30 ($=70 - 40$).
- If the probability of good weather is only $q = 1/3$, the exogenous quality of the holiday would be lower and would give an expected utility equal to 50 ($=1/3 \times 90 + 2/3 \times 30$), while the utility associated to not buying is unchanged; in this case the expected surplus would only be 10 ($=50 - 40$).

Our example allows us to conclude that the higher the probability of bad events (that worsen the tourist's experience) the lower the reservation price. Thus, the higher the probability of bad events (bad weather, natural disasters, social turmoils) the lower the price that has to be set by the tourism firms and vice versa.

This model can be used to explain one of the reasons why off-season holidays or winter breaks (when bad weather conditions are more likely to occur) are offered at lower prices than the corresponding holidays during the peak or the summer season. Moreover, since tourists set the probability of good or bad weather relying on external information, it can be argued that weather forecast can have an effect on the expected utility and then on the tourist's choice. In this regard, an interesting application is in Zirulia (2011). Moreover, the exposure of tourism operators to weather uncertainty might give rise to the use of insurance contract in the form of "weather derivatives" (Bank and Wiesner 2011 and see Sect. 11.3).

Exogenous quality is not the only explanation for the seasonal price differentials as other reasons also play a role (for example, policies for smoothing seasonality). However, the notion of exogenous quality can provide an additional explanation for this tourism phenomenon.

10.3.3 The Variety in the Tourism Product

As demonstrated in Sect. 4.3.2 (the Love for Variety Theorem) the tourist is willing to count on a wide variety of tourism goods and services within the holiday. However, the wider the variety, the higher the costs of production and therefore the price. To investigate the trade-off between variety and production costs, we will now rely on the famous Hotelling's model (1929) of spatial differentiation by drawing an analogy between the characteristics of a product and the location of the firm.

Let us describe the market for a tourism product that has, relative to a particular characteristic *X*, different varieties x_i, $i = 1, 2, .., n$, and let us further assume that each firm can only offer one specific variety, different from the varieties supplied by the other $(n - 1)$ firms. Within the tourism market, therefore, there is horizontal differentiation. On the demand side, every tourist owns an individual preference for that characteristic. Such market can be represented in Fig. 10.4a: the varieties x_i of characteristic *X* can be considered as points of the segment *HK*, the point *H* corresponds to the variety x_h, the point *K* to the variety x_k, and the points between *H* and *K* correspond to intermediate varieties. Each firm chooses to offer a given variety by placing itself at a given point along this "variety space," the *HK* segment; in such terms, the choice of the variety to produce in Hotelling's model obviously becomes the choice of the location, along a linear space, where to open the business. The tourists' preferences can be represented in a similar way, so that every single tourist can be located at a precise point along the *HK* segment.

It should be noted that, if there is only a finite number of varieties x_i, it is extremely unlikely that tourists will be able to buy their ideal variety. When buying the good, then, tourists must both pay the price for x_i and bear an implicit cost due to the dissatisfaction stemming from the inability to exactly receive their best variety. Such cost is greater the farther the variety produced by the *i*-th firm from the desired one, along the segment *HK*.

If we measure the costs borne by the tourists along the vertical axis of Fig. 10.4, we can then measure the total cost for the tourist located in *E* who buys the variety x_d produced by a firm located in *D*. By assuming that the firm located in *D* sets a price equal to the vertical segment *CD*, we must then add to this value the cost borne by the tourist located in *E* to switch from own ideal product to that produced by the firm. Evidently, such dissatisfaction cost depends on distance *ED* and can be interpreted in full analogy with the transport cost from *E* to *D* in the Hotelling's original model.

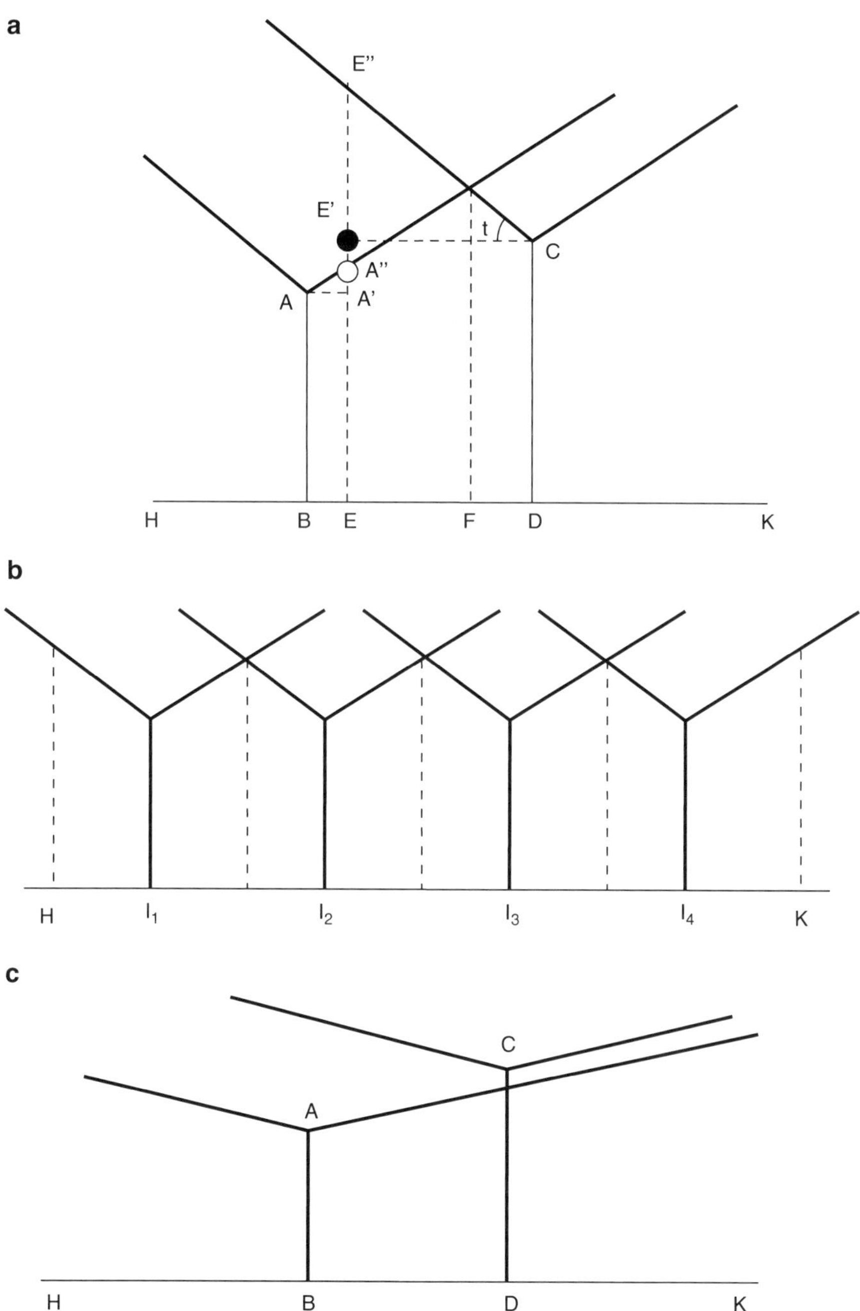

Fig. 10.4 The equilibrium in the model of horizontal differentiation

If we denote with t the dissatisfaction cost per unit of distance[5] the total dissatisfaction cost for the tourist located in E who buys the variety located in D is equal to td, where $d = D - E$. If we keep measuring the costs on the vertical axis, it is convenient to geometrically represent t with the slope, relative to the horizontal plane, of the line (or ray) whose origin is in point C. In fact, it is easy to see how the segment CE'' $(= tCE')$ along this ray represents the dissatisfaction cost, and then EE'' $(=EE' + E'E'')$ is the total cost borne by the tourist in E who purchases the variety x_d located in D. It is then clear that the tourist located in E chooses to purchase the variety x_b supplied by firm B, whose total cost EA'' $(= EA' + A'A'')$ is less than what would be borne by buying the good x_d from the firm located in D.

Once we understand how to calculate real and figurative costs (respectively, the price paid and the cost due to dissatisfaction borne by the tourist) it is easy to move to the following problem, namely to identify the location of the tourist who is indifferent between alternative varieties. Let us consider two companies B and D on the segment HK of Fig. 10.4a and, to make the problem more general, let us assume that their prices are not the same: in particular, BA is the price of B and DC the price of D, with $DC > BA$. Tourists are indifferent between the two goods if they bear the same total cost: it is then easy to draw two rays from points A and C with slope t so to identify the location of the indifferent tourist: it is clear that is located at point F. Note that the indifferent tourist is not necessarily equidistant from B and D; in our case, she is closer to D, since this firm sells at a higher price. It is obvious that when the two firms set the same price, the indifferent tourist would be equidistant, that is, at ½DB.

The identification of the indifferent tourist allows us to determine the market share of both firms: subject to the difference in prices, the tourists located along the segment HF will buy the good from B, while the tourists located along FK will buy the good from D.

If the number of firms is higher than two, Fig. 10.4a may be generalized in Fig. 10.4b and the market HK is divided into the shares of each firm, identified by the location of those tourists who are indifferent to the varieties offered by the neighboring companies.

It is important to stress on the relevance of the dissatisfaction cost. Indeed, with a simple alteration of Fig. 10.4a, it is easy to show that a reduction in the dissatisfaction cost can be depicted through a flattering of the slope of the line. Such reduction leads to a movement towards the standardization of the tourists' tastes and implies the intensification of price competition between firms, with the consequence of favoring the company that sells the variety at a lower price, so to widen its market share.[6] For very low dissatisfaction cost, it is possible that firms with higher prices

[5] The analogy between this model and Hotelling's model is now clear: t is the unit transport cost.

[6] Only if the two prices are the same, $AB = CD$, a change in the cost t neither affects the tourists nor the companies' market shares.

may be driven out of business, which is the case for firm *D* in Fig. 10.4c. In other words, the model leads to the conditions of perfect competition, where a single variety of the good is sold at the lowest price.

The model of horizontal differentiation shows that when tourism firms are faced with tourists who appreciate the variety of goods or services included in the tourism product, they tend to create their own market niche and gain an extra profit. The problem, however, must take into account the entry decisions by potential competitors. In fact, as long as the process of differentiation generates extra profits, a potential competitor may find convenient to enter the market by selecting an intermediate variety to produce (for example along the segment *BD* of Fig. 10.4a). Such process of sequential entry stops when profits are reduced to zero.

The key conclusion for the variety model is that, in the short run, the tourism market tends to be characterized by a finite number of firms each one specialized in the production of a particular differentiated good, serving a niche market and making positive profits.[7] In the long run, the competition of potential producers may lead to a growing number of firms operating in the market, thus resulting in the reduction or even the elimination of economic profits.

Also, the incumbents may try to defend their market shares by implementing strategies to halt the process of sequential entry of potential competitors before the zero profit equilibrium is reached: they do so through *product proliferation*. This expression indicates the phenomenon whereby one firm produces not just one variety of good, but a number of differentiated products. In other words, the firm does not locate in one point of the segment (as the theoretical model presented here predicts) but chooses multiple locations.[8]

Then, the model of horizontal differentiation explains why there exist tour operators that produce comfortable holidays and tour operators that produce adventurous holidays. Moreover, the proliferation principle explains why the same tour operator may include in its catalog both comfortable and adventurous holidays, so to prevent the entry of potential competitors. In fact, the incumbent tour operators

---

[7] In 1929, Hotelling believed to have shown that the companies had an incentive to move away from the extreme points *H* and *K* and get closer, side by side, to the mid-point (1/2) *HK*. In other words, he claimed the so-called principle of minimum differentiation of the product according to which firms tend to offer standardized products in equilibrium (i.e., products that are indifferent in the eyes of the consumer). Only 50 years later, D'Aspremont et al. (1979) have shown that Hotelling's conclusion contains an error related to the hypothesis of linearity in the transport costs; indeed, they claimed the opposite principle called principle of maximum differentiation of the product, indicating that the firm increases its profit as it approaches the extreme points of the segment, that is, the more it departs from the rival's location. The Hotelling's principle is not general enough as it stands valid only in particular cases. It has also been shown (Lambertini 1994) that under certain assumptions firms can increase the number of varieties well beyond those desired by consumers.

[8] This observation was first introduced by Schmalensee (1978) as regards the U.S. industry for breakfast cereals (corn flakes and the like); by discussing the antitrust laws, he noticed that just six companies produced eighty different brands. In practice, this sector adapted to the market's evolution and to the qualitative and quantitative growth of the demand, not by allowing the entry of new firms, but by increasing the number of varieties produced by the incumbent businesses.

count on a competitive advantage over potential competitors due to private information, higher reputation, and the ability to exploit economies of scale and of scope.

10.4 The Information Asymmetry in the Tourism Market

Analyzing the issue of quality and variety raises the problem of what information tourists have over alternative consumption activities. In Sect. 6.7 we discussed the case of the tourist with incomplete information; we now want to raise a different issue, the one called asymmetric information. The information is asymmetric when the parties involved in the market transaction do not have the same set of information: an agent has some private information that is relevant to the exchange and that the other party does not have.

As a typical example, the person who sells a used car certainly knows the state of the vehicle better than the prospective buyer; in this case the seller is said to have a private information on the quality of the car. The individual who buys health insurance certainly knows her health status better than the insurance agent; in this case, on the contrary, is the buyer to have a private information.

There are two types of asymmetric information.

1. The first type, known as *moral hazard*, requires that the parties have identical ex ante information, that is, before the exchange takes place, about every relevant aspect of the underlying contract, while the information asymmetry occurs ex post, that is, once the contract has been signed. This may happen in two ways: (a) if one party is able to perform actions that are not observable by the other party, we are facing a situation called *hidden action*; (b) if one party, after signing the contract, owns detailed information that the other party cannot access, we are in the presence of the so-called *hidden information*. An example of hidden action is the contractor of an insurance policy that undergoes reckless actions after signing the contract, which the insurer cannot control. An example of hidden information is the relationship between the owner of a company and its finance manager, who takes decisions based on conditions about which the owner is not informed.
2. The second type, known as *adverse selection*, requires that the asymmetry occurs when one party has ex ante private information, i.e., before signing the contract. For example, an insurance company faces adverse selection problems when offers a life insurance to a customer without knowing his true health condition; a firm faces the same problem when selling goods to another company without knowing the close-to-bankruptcy condition of the latter.

In models of moral hazard, the primary economic concern for the uninformed agent is to provide an incentive for the other party to act in the former's interest or to be able to control the counterpart's behavior. In models of adverse selection, the primary economic concern is to provide an incentive for the informed party to reveal it or to implements mechanisms to get as much information as possible.

While to the problems raised by moral hazard (and hidden action, in particular) we will devote the last few sections of Chap. 11, in this section we study the model of adverse selection by asking what are the consequences of the existence of ex ante information asymmetry on the market equilibrium.

10.4.1 Adverse Selection and the Decline of the Destination

When there is information asymmetry the theory highlights two reasons for the failure of the market mechanism:

1. The market price badly selects the product's quality, by leading to its progressive decay; this is somewhat referred to the Gresham's Law (the famous statement that in the money market "bad money drives out good money") for the commodity markets, according to which the product of low quality pushes out of the market the product of high quality.
2. An equilibrium price at which the quantity demanded equals the quantity supplied may not exist. Along with point (1), this leads to the extreme conclusion that the market may disappear even when the exchange, in the absence of private information, would be beneficial for both parties. This is the conclusion of a famous article written by Akerlof (1970) concerning the used-car market, where the key argument is that the cars on sale are mainly lemons (i.e., of bad quality).

To apply Akerlof's model to tourism, as well as highlighting its major conclusions, let us consider the example of the accommodation sector, where there are hotels of various quality. We recall the example presented in Sect. 6.7.3 by considering two types of hotels: type L hotels (low-quality hotels) and type H hotels (high-quality hotels).

Let us assume that managers of hotels L set the price of their rooms at 100, while managers of hotels H set the price at 200. From the demand side, we assume that tourists who prefer the low-quality hotels L are willing to pay up to 120, while tourists looking for hotels H are willing to pay up to 240. Should the quality of the hotel be known to everyone, then the market would perfectly work and overnight stays would be sold both in hotels L (at a price ranging between 100 and 120) and hotels H (at a price ranging between 200 and 240), to the mutual satisfaction of both hotels and tourists.

In a more realistic setup, let us now see what happens if only hotel managers know the quality of their hotel while tourists cannot observe it (e.g., because they book from home, without having access to information on the quality). In such case there is asymmetric information on the quality of the service. Suppose that tourists assume that there is an equal probability to meet any type of hotels. Then, the average price that a tourist would pay in this uncertain market condition is equal to 180 ($=120 \times 0.5 + 240 \times 0.5$), which is the average price of the hotels of different quality weighted by the probability of meeting each type of hotel.

The problem is that such price is attractive only to the managers of hotels L, since the minimum price required by managers of hotels H is 200. On the other hand, if the tourists were to know such consequence of information asymmetry, they would be sure that at the price of 180 only rooms of L-type hotels are offered, thus not be willing to pay the price of 180, since they know that the price of such hotels should be between 100 and 120. If the price was included in this range, only rooms in type L hotels would be on the market and tourists would be sure to only meet low quality hotels; in other words, type H hotels would not be on the market, despite that the willingness to pay of tourists for high-quality hotels (equal to 240) is higher than the evaluation of hotel managers (equal to 200).

Our simple example shows that, under conditions of asymmetric information, the market badly selects the quality of products and services, and can be pushed to the ultimate consequence that tourists stay away from a destination that presents a large variability and uncertainty about the quality of its accommodation sector. It is then easy to see that, for certain characteristics of the market, there might be the possibility that supply and demand do never meet, meaning that the market is so disturbed by the existence of information asymmetry that it may stop working properly.

Although the above example is very specific, tourism is in general characterized by the presence of asymmetric information in many services composing the tourism product. We may think of the quality of an all-inclusive tour, of the accommodation in a resort, of a rented car, of an item purchased while shopping and that, after having left the destination, it can no longer be replaced if it proves to be bad. Since this market failure translates into the quality deterioration of the tourism supply (which can lead to the destination decline), the problem may be so severe to induce the tour operators and the destination managements to undertake specific strategies aimed at reducing those information asymmetries that are at the roots of such market failure.

Such strategies differ based on whether the party that owns the informational advantage discloses it to the counterpart or, conversely, the less informed party extracts the information from its counterpart.

In the first case there are generally two paths: *signaling* and *reputation*. For example, a worker who is well aware of her skills certainly faces the problem of how to report her professional quality to potential employers, as this may impact on the working condition and salary; also employers would be pleased to get high-quality information that allows them to identify a candidate of great value. The role played by the CV (the *curriculum vitae*) during the hiring process is exactly to disclose this piece of private information. Similarly, the managers of type H hotels may want the potential customers to be aware of the qualitative characteristics of their hotels and also the tourists would be delighted to receive such information: the star-based classification system adopted for hotels is a mechanism through which the quality is revealed by signaling.

Therefore, there exists a win–win opportunity for buyers and sellers, providing an incentive to fully share the relevant information before the act of purchasing. However, it has to be highlighted that the interest for revealing private information is only for high-quality economic operators. Indeed, those that offer low quality products may have an incentive to creating confusion among the consumers, since the occurrence of information asymmetry in this model is the only reason that justifies their survival in the market. Hence, the main problem related to signaling strategies is that their effectiveness depends on the degree of credibility of the revealed information. The reputation is then the mechanism by which the credibility of the message can be guaranteed, at least in long run. In the tourism market, for example, the membership of the hotel to a renowned international hotel chain operates as a credible signal of adherence to quality standards.

In the second case, when is the less informed party that takes the initiative of extracting private information from the counterpart, the economic solution takes the form of the *selection* mechanism. In the example of the potential employee, interviews and selection tests are the mechanism by which the prospective employer seeks, through specific questions, to understand the quality of the candidate who, according to her responses, discloses her ability and skills. An example of such behavior in tourism may be found in the case of a tourist who is willing to pay a higher price for a contract that she may decide to unilaterally terminate if the quality standard is not met. It is clear how such contract naturally attracts the high-quality hotel but discourages those who, knowing that they offer low-quality services, may prefer a certain amount of money that is unrelated to the quality of the provided service. In both cases, however, the selection involves a cost that must be borne by the non-informed party.

Let us now turn in detail to describe these market mechanisms.

10.4.2 Tourism Markets with Signaling

In the presence of signaling, the firm with private information on the quality of own production emits signals which, if properly interpreted by the tourist, reveal the information. This signaling model was first introduced in the literature by Spence (1974) to study the relationship between the level of education and the labor market.

In this section, we apply Spence's model to the accommodation sector by recalling the example of the previous section, with hotels of two categories (low and high), and by introducing a particular assumption on the emission cost of the signal. In this regard, the essential hypothesis is that the signal should be less expensive to emit for high quality hotels (type H) than for low quality hotels (type L). For example, let us suppose that type H hotels pay for each unit of signal half of the price paid by those of low quality. Then, by indicating with s a quantitative (and continuous) measure for the signal, the cost for the type L hotel will have a one-to-one proportion to the signal, s, while the cost of the type H hotel will be equal to $s/2$.

The model pivots around the identification of a number of conditional evaluations that allow the firm to be credible in the eyes of its customers. Let us suppose that tourists consider that if the signal is less than s^*, the hotel is certainly of type L, while if the signal is equal to or larger than s^*, the hotel is certainly of type H. Given these assumptions and after recalling the values of the previous subsection, we can state that the tourist is willing to pay up to 120 for hotels signaling $s < s^*$, and up to 240 for those signaling $s \geq s^*$.

Let us see how hotels respond to such tourists' attitude. First, we consider the choice of hotels in terms of intensity of the signal to emit. If the hotel decides to not emit the signal, the optimal decision would be $s = 0$, since all values $0 < s < s^*$ are more expensive but are ineffective, since they do not affect the tourists' assessment. If the hotel decides to emit the signal, the optimal decision would be $s = s^*$, since it is sufficient to convince the tourist; then, any other value $s > s^*$ is unnecessarily expensive, thus inefficient.

Given that the viable alternatives are $s = 0$ and $s = s^*$, let us now determine which hotels find convenient not to signal ($s = 0$) and which find advantageous to signal ($s = s^*$). To solve this problem, we need to formulate another hypothesis, this time on the hotel's expected price; suppose that competition leads hotels to take into consideration their minimum prices, 100 for type *L* hotels and 200 for type *H* hotels.

Then type *L* hotels find convenient to be perceived as type *H* hotels, so to obtain a potential benefit up to 100 (= 200 − 100) only if $s^* < 100$, while they decide to not invest in the signal if $s^* > 100$. On the other hand, the type *H* hotels are characterized by a lower cost, $s^*/2$, for an identical benefit equal to 100, so they do not invest when $s^* > 200$, while they invest if $s^* \leq 200$. Then, to be credible, the signal implies that only high-quality hotels should find convenient to emit the signal: so, the best hotels take the effort of revealing their actual quality to tourists only if the separating signal falls within the range of significance, that is, if $100 < s^* \leq 200$. In such case, the tourists evaluate the signal as credible, and this characteristic gives this equilibrium the name of *separating equilibrium*.

To understand why this condition does not always hold, it is important to note that if $s^* \leq 100$, both hotels would find it profitable to choose $s = s^*$ and they would be indistinguishable in the eyes of tourist. Such situation is called *pooling equilibrium*. While the separating equilibrium is able to efficiently segment the market for accommodation by distinguishing type *H* hotels and type *L* hotels through the emitted signal, the pooling equilibrium reproduces a condition of uncertainty, in which the uninformed tourists are not willing to pay more than 180 (see Sect. 10.4.1), so holding the conditions for the market failure. We must stress that in this model the effectiveness of the signal is not linked to its ability to improve the quality of the service; in fact, the hotels eventually invest in the signal not to improve the hotel's quality but to inform the tourists about their supposed quality.

This model allows some interesting observations on the properties that signals must have to perform their role as separating equilibria. In fact, the concept of signal has been used to explain a wide range of phenomena, for example: the use of advertising for a new product which features are unknown to the customer (the experience good, see Sect. 6.7.3), the certifications of quality, the warranty, the price refunding schemes are all signals of quality. Signaling affects many of the tourism markets, and quality-based classifications of firms may be applied to many tourism subsectors, although such classification is mainly used in regard to the hospitality sector.

Hotels are assigned to different categories, mainly depending on the type of structure and offered services. The international classification system relies on the number of stars that are assigned to each structure, dividing hotels in five classes, from one to five stars. However, the star-based system does not automatically solve the problem of signaling the quality of service in a credible way to uninformed consumer (i.e., the emission cost of one additional star can be too low, thus leading to a pooling equilibrium). If this is the case it becomes necessary to avoid such market failure through public intervention; thereby the classification of hotels is usually regulated by the law, under the national (or of another local authority's) supervision, and after a system of control and monitoring of the quality requirements. In an international context, however, laws and regulations are not fully comparable across countries, nor do all countries, carry reliable controls.

> "Quality and quality assessment are rooted in the culture and context of the country in which they are located. As a result, a five-star or deluxe hotel in South East Asia will be significantly different from a property which purports equivalence in Turkey or the UK."
> (Cooper et al. 1998, p. 327)

A system of classification and control could also be put in place by business associations for the benefit of their members, thus replicating a "command and control" system and avoiding the external intervention of the public sector. However, such solution greatly refers to mechanisms of reputation (see Sect. 10.4.3) rather than signaling. To rely on an automatic solution for the signaling problem would be a desirable condition both for the hospitality and for many other tourism activities. Such market solution, as Clerides et al. (2008) clearly argue, can then be guaranteed by tour operators, which are able to provide a more accurate twinning between price and quality.

10.4.3 The Reputation in Tourism Markets

Put in a nutshell, the reputation of the firm consists of the quality assessed by tourists on the basis of the information and the experience built in the past. Ultimately, the reputation is a form of capital which accumulates over time through investment in quality and which may depreciate following bad investments (loss of reputation). Although a firm with good reputation does not have any legal commitment to keep the same level of quality also in the future, it can be easily demonstrated that the high-quality level is a credible commitment when certain conditions are met. In such cases, tourists can count on the same degree of certainty about the quality of the product that they would get if they were in possession of a contract forcing the firm to provide that same quality.

The simplest model of reputation (Shapiro 1984) suggests that the firm's reputation at time t, R_t, is equal to the quality q, supplied in the previous period, $t - 1$. The hypothesis behind such simplification is that the tourists have a one-period memory (however, we can interpret $t - 1$ as simply the past):

$$R_t = q_{t-1}. \tag{10.5}$$

The model explains the economic conditions under which a *reputational equilibrium* exists and holds; in other words, the model unfolds the reason why tourism firms keep the same level of quality for their services over time, so to satisfy the tourists' expectations, even if they may be able to choose more advantageous opportunities for production.

We describe the model by acknowledging that endogenous quality is expensive, so that the average production cost (and hence the price) of the tourism product increases with the level of its quality q, $C(q)$ with $C' > 0$. Conversely, we know that tourists are willing to pay higher price for higher quality. For simplicity, we introduce a minimum level of quality, $q^{\bullet}$; such level may be the effect of a law that introduces the minimum standard requirement or simply be due to the fact that tourists have a minimum set of information and are generally unwilling to purchase a service when it is below a certain threshold. Finally, let us assume that the firm has built over time a reputation level R^{+} corresponding to the quality q^{+}, higher than the minimum $q^{\bullet}$. Obviously, under the hypothesis of endogenous quality, $C(q^{+}) > C(q^{\bullet})$.

In order to reach the reputation equilibrium, two conditions must hold:

1. The condition of quality stability, which is a short-term requirement; it states that a firm offering a quality level q^{+} at price $p(q^{+})$ should be discouraged from suddenly lowering the quality to save on costs and gain the short-term extra profit (which will disappear as soon as the tourists realize the drop in quality and refuse to pay a price that is become too high for the new quality);
2. The condition of free entrance, which is a long-term requirement; it states that the formation of extra profits related to quality will be eliminated by the entry of new firms in the market.

Having said that, let us examine the consequences of these two requirements on the tourism firm. The first condition might suggest the possibility of an opportunistic behavior for the firm, thus reducing the quality to gain short-term profits equal to $[p(q^{+}) - C(q^{\bullet})]$ and then exit the market. To counteract this opportunity, the firm must find it more convenient to stay in the market and earn the current profit $[p(q^{+}) - C(q^{+})]$ also in the future, supposedly infinite for simplicity. If the discount rate is r, the present value of such long-run profits is given by $[p(q^{+}) - C(q^{+})]/r$. The condition of quality stability can therefore be written as

$$p(q^{+}) - C(q^{+}) + \frac{p(q^{+}) - C(q^{+})}{r} \geq p(q^{+}) - C(q^{\bullet}), \tag{10.6}$$

which is

$$p(q^{+}) \geq C(q^{+}) + r[C(q^{+}) - C(q^{\bullet})]. \tag{10.7}$$

We now consider the second condition, the condition of free entrance in the market. This condition requires that, in order not to give rise to extra profits, firms are free to enter the market up to the point where the individual profit, calculated over its entire existence according to (10.6), is the minimum required by the reputation equilibrium. That is, a condition in which the firm offering the quality $q^+ > q^\bullet$ has an advantage in indefinitely keeping this quality, thus building a reputation, $R^+ = q^+$, but without earning extra profits. The long-term reputation equilibrium of the model is then given by (10.7) which is satisfied as a strict equality:

$$p(q^+) = C(q^+) + r[C(q^+) - C(q^\bullet)].$$

This second condition introduces an interesting result, $p(q^+) > C(q^+)$: in order to prevent the quality deterioration, in the reputation equilibrium the price must be higher than the average cost. In fact, if we let $q^+ = q^\bullet$ we get that $p(q^\bullet) = C(q^\bullet)$. This equality means that no profit for the minimum level of quality is gained, which is easily understandable since there is no need for any investment in reputation in order to sell at the minimum level of quality. Finally, note that the quality premium $r[C(q^+) - C(q^\bullet)]$ depends on the discount rate, so that r becomes a sort of indicator of the severity of the existing information asymmetry. In fact, a great value of r is associated with a situation of infrequent sales, for which tourists slowly transmit to other customers the perceived quality of their experience. Given that such communication difficulty makes opportunistic behaviors more attractive for the company, a higher premium on cost is needed to maintain the reputation equilibrium. It can be easily understood that the development of new web portals and social networks (such as booking.com or tripadvisor.com) has the effect of decreasing r, thus reducing at the same time the quality premium paid by the tourist and decreasing the benefits for firms stemming from opportunistic behaviors (Case Study 10.1).

Case Study 10.1. Social Networks, Word of Mouth, and Reputation

Many tourists organize their holidays on the Internet, mostly by looking for last-minute special offers but also for collecting information on destinations and tourism structures. This explains the great success of social networks specialized in tourism as well as blogs, photo and video sharing sites, etc, which work as electronic word of mouth (sometimes called "word of mouse," see Bronner and de Hoog (2011) for a recent inquiry). The best known site for sharing information on the quality of hotels, services, and destinations as a whole is perhaps TripAdvisor, which is now available also on smartphones. The site offers a number of services for the tourists who want to self-organize their holidays, including a search engine where to enter the desired destination and dates. Then, the site displays the list of hotels with price and availability ranked on the basis of the evaluation of tourists who have previously stayed overnight. For big destinations, such as London or Paris, one can better delimit the search by selecting specific areas; a similar search can be done for flights, restaurants, and other tourism services. Another very

(continued)

popular site that allows to compare prices of hotels, write and read comments, and show photos is Booking.com.

As a reaction to the increasing role played by social networks and meta-search engines, the hotels' web sites are evolving their style by keeping an eye via *software spidering*, which analyzes the contents of a network or a database in a methodical yet automated manner to spot comments, and by being present on important social networks, such as Facebook. There are also a number of sites that advise, comment, and review travels throughout several destinations, complete with highway information, fuel expenses, restaurants, and places to visit along the way; some of these sites are very popular because they are fully integrated with maps and GPS systems, such as ViaMichelin and Maps.Google. Alternatively, the tourist may refer to more institutional sites such as www.visitbritain.com (United Kingdom), www.franceguide.com (France), and www.spain.info (Spain).

Many tourists seem to rely on charts for ranking the best beaches or the best hotels worldwide, which many popular newspapers and magazines (The New York Times, The Guardian, the Traveler, etc.) constantly publish on their web sites. In particular, Traveler offers charts for each type of holiday, beaches, hotels, including the list, for example, of the top ten Italian restaurants or the top thirty villas in Corsica.

This list of web sites and information services available on the Internet could continue. However, the quick evolution of the Internet, the social networks, and the mobile devices, together with the high speed of service innovation in this field renders this list almost useless. One could more easily be up to date by searching in Google some key words such as "Travel" and "Comments" and "Sharing" or similar words and browse what is available. What is important to remind, to conclude this Case Study, is that all these sites ultimately extend the concept of word of mouth from an activity only occurring among friends to an activity involving the entire community of travelers worldwide, without essentially changing its essential nature of tool aimed at reducing information asymmetry, at punishing opportunistic behaviors, at building reputational capital and, to summarize, at improving the level of competition in the market.

Since the reputation can be seen as a form of capital for the tourism firm, in Fig. 10.5 we show the trend in profits over the company's life span, by taking into account the free entry condition (zero total profits) and the fact that the company is able to gain only when (by offering high-quality services over the long run) it can collect the corresponding premium. Therefore, in the early period the profit is negative, and this is precisely the stage when the investment to build reputation is undertaken.

If we denote with p_e the price that a new firm can set when entering the market and replicating the existing quality q^+, we can easily observe that p_e should be equal

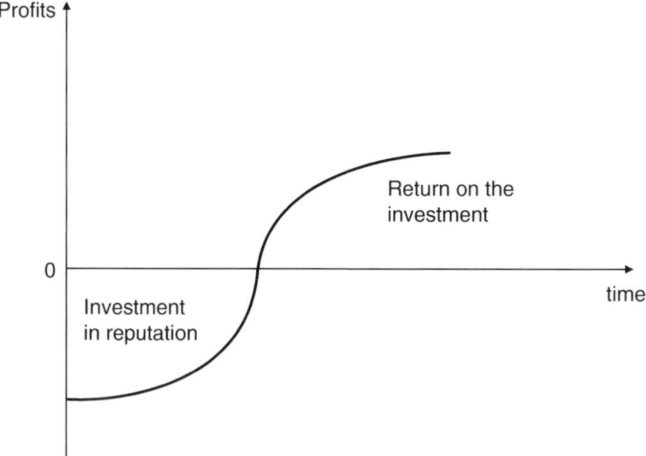

Fig. 10.5 The relationship between investment in reputation and profits

to $C(q^{\bullet})$. In fact, consumers with no previous information can only evaluate the quality of the new company as being equal to $q^{\bullet}$, thus accepting the minimum level of reputation, $R^{\bullet} \equiv q^{\bullet}$, since they do not avail of any information that can let them decide otherwise. This fact determines a loss for the new firm equal to $[p_e - C(q^+)] = [C(q^{\bullet}) - C(q^+)]$ which exactly corresponds to the cost of investment in reputation. Due to the simplification (10.5), the activity of investment in the model spans over one period only, but in practice, the investment in reputational capital may require a longer period of time.

We complete our discussion by noting that the above results have been reached by assuming that the firm life span is infinite. If we assume instead that the company has a finite life span of n periods, expression (10.6) must be reformulated as

$$[p(q^+) - C(q^+)] + \sum_{i=1}^{n} [p(q^+) - C(q^+)](1+r)^{-i} \geq p(q^+) - C(q^{\bullet}). \qquad (10.8)$$

It is immediate to observe that (10.8) does not only depend on r, but also on n. By decreasing the firm's life span, the probability that the condition of quality stability holds becomes increasingly more unlikely. Indeed, for $n = 1$ such condition never holds, and the company finds convenient to deceive the uninformed consumer. Then, given that the reputation incentive does not hold for firms planning their market activity over a short period of time, it will be beneficial for tourists to stay away from apparently attractive holidays advertised by tour operators and travel agencies which are born, die and possibly change their offer very frequently.

10.5 Search and Experience Goods in the Tourism Market

The type of information imperfection on the quality of the goods introduced in Sect. 10.4 can be usefully framed in a classification that was born in relation to industrial goods but that also turned out to be useful for the tourism product. Such classification distinguishes between:

1. *Search goods*, goods and services the quality of which can be recognized before the act of purchasing and consumption (for example, a soft drink, a newspaper, a package of biscuits);
2. *Experience goods*, goods and services the quality of which can be recognized only after the purchase, during the use or the act of consumption (for example, a restaurant meal, a holiday);
3. *Credence goods*, goods and services the quality of which cannot be perfectly recognized even after the purchase or the use (for example, a medical care, a legal advice, or the quality of a university course).

While we think that credence goods are not important for tourism and were reported only for reasons of completeness, the relevance of search and experience goods for tourism has already been highlighted in Sect. 6.7 while discussing the behavior of tourists at the destination and of tourists at distance, respectively. We now deepen the relationship between these two types of good and the asymmetry of information.

10.5.1 The Product's Quality in Models of Search and Experience Goods

In Sect. 6.7 (which we recommend reading prior to this section) we demonstrated that the activity of information searching is beneficial for tourists; in addition, we identified the optimal stopping rule in the search for quality in both types of tourism product, search and experience goods. In the same section, we also distinguished between type L hotels and type H hotels, both setting the price equal to 200 but with a different utility associated to the quality of accommodation, amounting to 50 and 100 for type L and type H hotels, respectively (see Sect. 6.7.3). Note that such assumption did not imply the existence of any vertical differentiation in the product, since the different qualities were not sold at different prices to meet the different purchasing powers of tourists, but were only justified by the opportunistic behavior of the hotels' management, as a consequence of incomplete information.

In this section, we investigate the consequences of this setup in terms of product differentiation and market structure. Table 10.2 presents a calculation similar to that presented in Table 6.1 as regards the probability of the best choice, for $k = 1, 2, 3, 4, \ldots, \infty$, with the difference that now the results of the search for quality are evaluated in terms of expected utility. The probability of finding a hotel of any type

Table 10.2 The probability of finding a high-quality hotel as a function of the number of searches

Number of searches, k	Hotels L $U = 50$	Hotels H $U = 100$	Expected utility $E(U)$	Marginal benefit $B'(k)$	Marginal cost $C'(k)$
1	0.5	0.5	75	–	2.08
2	0.25	0.75	87.5	12.5	4.17
3	0.13	0.87	93.75	6.25	6.25
4	0.06	0.94	96.87	3.12	8.33
...	...	...	...	...	...
∞	0	1	100	0	∞

Table 10.3 Expected number of overnight stays in hotels of different quality as a function of the number of searches

Number of searches, k	Number of overnight stays, Hotels L	Number of overnight stays, Hotels H
1	5,000	5,000
2	2,500	7,500
3	1,250	8,750
4	625	9,375
...	...	...
∞	0	10,000

is identical: 50 %. As we already know, the expected utility is the average of two levels of utility, 50 and 100 respectively, weighted by the probability of finding respectively all hotels of type L and at least one hotel of type H as a function of the number of searches (columns 2 and 3 of Table 10.2). The marginal benefit is equal to the difference between succeeding values written in the fourth column.

The optimal number of searches carried out by the tourists obviously depends on their search cost, and this aspect explains the crucial difference between the assumption of search and experience good. In the case of a search good, if we assume that the marginal search cost is given by $C'(k) = 2.08\ k$ (sixth column of Table 10.2), condition (6.15) of Sect. 6.7.3 indicates that for these tourists is rational to run three searches before choosing where to stay. In particular, the fourth search leads to a marginal cost that is higher than the expected marginal benefit, $B'(4) = 3{,}12 < 8{,}33 = C'(4)$, which makes it not beneficial for the tourists.

We now assume that the tourism destination hosts 10,000 arrivals per day. If, for the sake of simplicity, all tourists are the same (i.e., they have the same marginal search cost), they will distribute among the different hotels with the same probabilities shown in Table 10.2. This allows us to derive Table 10.3, which displays the distribution of 10,000 arrivals in high- and low-quality hotels, still as a function of the number of performed searches.

Table 10.3 is important since it shows that the market share of low-quality hotels tends to drop as the number of searches carried out by tourists increases and as the marginal cost of information decreases. At the limit, as tourists gather complete information (as $k \rightarrow \infty$), type L hotels disappear from the market. The opportunistic behavior of hotels, which leads to quality deterioration, is then based on the assumption of incomplete information and on the high cost of retrieving information on the quality.

In the case of experience good, the tourists must experience the holiday to get to know its quality, and this usually entails higher marginal search costs (see Sect. 6.7.3). All things being equal, therefore, the optimal number of searches for the experience goods will be lower than that for the search goods. The numbers in Table 10.3 allow us to reach an immediate conclusion: with respect to search goods, the nature of experience goods justifies a greater market share for low-quality tourism services.

The opportunistic behavior in terms of quality was here referred to the hospitality sector. However, similar conditions hold in the market for all-inclusive tours, shows, tourist-oriented markets, etc. Our findings, therefore, are far more general than the example we have shown in this section.

10.5.2 The Price in Search Models

To conclude the discussion on search models, we also have to consider the case of goods and services of identical quality but offered at different prices, thus recalling the content of Sect. 6.7.2. The issue of opportunistic behavior on price is now related to the consequences in terms of market structure: the model reaches similar conclusions to those of opportunistic behavior on quality that we presented in Sect. 10.5.1, but also allows for some interesting additional remarks.

Table 6.1 of Sect. 6.7.2 lists all the relevant variables for the problem of the uninformed tourist, and we start from there by investigating the implication on the market structure of a situation in which type L and type H hotels set a price equal to 300 and to 200, respectively, for the supply of the same accommodation service. Let us assume that the destination hosts 10,000 arrivals per day. Once again, the probabilities presented in Table 6.1 (and which are identical, by construction, to those of Table 10.2) allow to write the distribution of tourists between the two types of accommodation businesses in Table 10.4.

Compared to the previous tables, Table 10.4 also displays the total revenue for each type of hotel; moreover, in the last column the average price of the overnight stay in the destination, calculated as the average of prices weighted by the number of stays in hotels respectively asking for the "right price" and acting opportunistically is reported. A careful reading of Table 10.4 allows to draw the following conclusions about the market structure in conditions of incomplete information from the tourist's side:

- Only complete information guarantees the validity of the so-called *Jevons's law* (this law, which specifically refers to the case of perfect competition, states that there only exists a single price in the market for the same good), but this is only an extreme case for the optimal behavior of the uninformed tourist.

Table 10.4 The distribution of tourists in hotels of same quality but different price

Number of searches, k	Number of overnight stays, Hotels H	Number of overnight stays, Hotels L	Revenue, Hotels H	Revenue, Hotels L	Average price of accommodation in the destination
1	5,000	5,000	1,000,000	1,500,000	250
2	7,500	2,500	1,500,000	750,000	225
3	8,750	1,250	1,750,000	375,000	212.5
4	9,375	625	1,875,000	187,500	206.25
...	...	...	...	...	...
∞	10,000	0	2,000,000	0	200

- The incompleteness of information justifies the persistence on the market of hotels of same quality but different prices.
- Hotels willing to charge a high price find convenient to make the search for information a costly activity, since the smaller the tourist's search, the greater the profit stemming from their opportunistic behavior.
- The average price of accommodation goes down as the number of searches carried out by the tourists increases.

This last observation leads to an interesting corollary. In Sect. 6.7.2 we identified the optimal number of searches in the case of repeat stays and we observed that, since the marginal benefit is weighted by the number of stays in Table 6.2, the tourists who stay longer increase the number of queries. Then, the higher the length of stay, the more effort tourists devote to the search activity, and the lower the average price for accommodation in the destination. Thus, we can conclude by stating an interesting result for the accommodation sector in the tourism destination: the higher the average length of stay, the lower its daily price; the lower the average length of stay, the higher its daily price.

Moreover, if the tourism destination is subject to a drop in the length of stay, it is exposed to the risk of a rising average price; this happens not because real prices do increase (in fact prices remain unchanged in our example, respectively at 200 and 300 per night), but only because the share of opportunistic hotels increases. Then, our model indicates that the "hit and run" tourism enhances the opportunistic behavior of the hotels (Candela et al. 2003, Candela and Figini 2005). Such situation may create a vicious cycle for the destination: the reduction in the average length of stay increases the average price of the holiday, which leads to a further reduction in the length of stay. Similarly, for the case of a virtuous cycle that increases the average length of stay.

10.6 The Role of Advertising in Tourism

Corporate communication plays such an important role in the functioning of tourism markets that also the Economics of Tourism must focus on such topic. The firms' decision of spending in advertising stems from two main reasons:

1. The company may decide to provide information to uninformed tourists.
2. The company may engage in advertising to implement vertical or horizontal differentiation. Sometimes, advertising is not just a consequence of product differentiation but also coincides with it: advertising makes two otherwise identical goods look different in the eyes of consumers.

These two reasons are easily understandable. On one hand, when firms are aware of the tourists' difficulty in matching price with quality, they may find convenient to bear the cost of advertising as a way to disclose useful information and thereby partially limiting the effort undertaken by potential customers to search for information. On the other hand, the firms willing to differentiate their product from that of competitors must calculate the benefits and costs of advertising. Put in these terms, advertising is intended to ease the tourist's choice, by allowing them to select the preferred quality, to monitor prices, and to be informed about new tourism products.

A more comprehensive interpretation of the role of advertising must also consider other, and more controversial, elements. A difficult, yet important, topic concerns the real capability of advertising to affect and change the consumers' tastes. This question certainly applies to tourism as well, at the point that we can legitimately wonder whether some destinations are desirable for their natural, cultural, or historical attractions or rather because they are widely advertised. One thing is that customers browse through the Internet to learn about tourism opportunities and alternatives, and another is to believe that their tastes may get altered by advertising. This second opportunity would offer tour operators and online travel agencies the great power of governance of international tourism flows.

Economics does not provide a clear answer to this question, nor perhaps ever will. It is a fact that communication and advertising have always played a key role in determining what customers desire, and for this reason the relationship between advertising and preferences will not be further investigated (see Sect. 6.5 for a discussion of the mechanism of endogenous formation of preferences). On the contrary, in what follows we will discuss the role of advertising in the tourism market. In particular, we will study the role of advertising in markets for search goods and in markets for experience goods; such distinction is crucial to clarify the customer's opportunity to control the content of the advertisement prior to the act of purchasing the good.

10.6.1 The Advertisement in the Market for Search Goods

In the market for search goods, tourists are able to check the truthfulness of advertisement before buying a product, and for this type of goods firms are often forced to accurately describe the characteristics of their product. Therefore, the role of advertising is immediate: to convey information. In such case, advertising is able (at least partially) to eliminate information asymmetry and allow for greater market efficiency:

> "Advertising is, among other things, a method of providing potential buyers with knowledge of the identity of sellers. It is clearly an immensely powerful instrument for the elimination of ignorance."
>
> (Stigler 1961, p. 220)

To illustrate this concept, we recall from Sect. 10.5.1 the example of 10,000 tourists who, after arriving at the destination without prior knowledge on the quality of hotels, undertake a search activity. Table 10.3 described the distribution of tourists as a function of the number of searches carried out, subject to the condition that they do not have any prior information. However, what happens if some of these tourists have been reached by advertisement?

Let us suppose that one unit of advertisement a issued by type H hotels (for example, a banner posted on the destination portal) is used to inform on the quality of the accommodation service. We also assume that such advertisement has reached a proportion c of all tourists; these individuals can now reliably choose their hotel without having to spend time and effort in any search activity. Instead, the remaining 10,000(1 − c) tourists have to go through the search activity already described. If we assume that their optimal number of searches k is 2 (see Table 10.3), 7,500(1 − c) tourists will end up in type H hotels, while 2,500(1 − c) will end up staying in type L hotels. Given the price, the introduction of advertisement alters the distribution of tourists between high-quality and low-quality hotels: type L hotels, that in the absence of advertising would receive 2,500 tourists, now host 2,500(1 − c) tourists; instead, type H hotels, that would otherwise host 7,500 tourists, now host [10,000 c + 7,500 (1 − c)] = 7,500 + 2,500 c. Therefore, advertising increases the demand for high-quality hotels and their share of the market.

The final effect obviously depends on the amount of advertisement a, on the effectiveness of the advertising message, which is indicated by the parameter c, and on its cost which can be denoted with w. By recalling that the price of accommodation is 200, the profit for type H hotels (for simplicity, we disregard additional considerations on production costs) can be written as follows:

$$\pi = 200(7{,}500 + 2{,}500\,c) - wa. \tag{10.9}$$

This calculation assumes an additional hypothesis on the effectiveness of the advertising message c: if we suppose that the effectiveness is an increasing function of the amount of advertising, but at a decreasing rate, we can write:

$$c = F(a) \text{ with } F'(a) > 0 \text{ and } F''(a) < 0. \tag{10.10}$$

The first-order condition of (10.9) with respect to a is

$$\frac{\partial \pi}{\partial a} = 500{,}000\,F'(a) - w = 0,$$

where

$$F'(a) = \frac{w}{500,000}.$$

This condition can be used to determine a^* and, consequently, wa^*, which is the amount of spending on advertisement that leads to the highest profit. The condition is easy to read: if we consider that the term $w/500{,}000$ is the ratio between the cost of advertisement and the measure of its potential market ($500{,}000 = 200 \times 2{,}500$) we can state that advertising is implemented by high-quality hotels only up to the point where its marginal effectiveness equals this ratio. The optimal amount of advertising is then inversely related to its cost and directly related to the potential market revenue. We can also state that the expenditure in advertising is directly related to the price of the stay and inversely to the intensity of the search.

Let us now consider the role played by advertisement in the search for price, not anymore for quality. We still consider the example of Table 10.4, which refers to 10,000 tourists and we investigate what would happen if they were all reached by an advertisement issued by the type *H* hotels and informing that their price is 200. The effect of such message is clearly described by Stigler as follows:

> "The effect of advertising prices, then, is equivalent to that of the introduction of a very large amount of search by a large portion of the potential buyers."
>
> (Stigler 1961, p. 224)

Therefore, the advertisement of prices acts on the market as it were increasing the number of searches carried out by customers. Table 10.4 shows the immediate effect of such change: it raises the revenue of those hotels offering the best price and helps eliminate hotels that have an opportunistic price behavior; finally, by increasing the market share of competitive price hotels, leads to a reduction in the average price of accommodation at the destination. In particular, our conclusion seems to contradict, at least for search goods, the common idea that "advertisement increases the price." For situations where the tourists are dealing with search goods (see Sect. 6.7.3), the advertisement helps the customer identify the opportunistic firms and to moderate prices.

10.6.2 The Advertisement in the Market for Experience Goods

When facing experience goods, consumers may exert a weaker control over the truthfulness of advertisement, differently from search goods. The only credible threat that tourists who book in advance can use against the firms is that of not repeating the purchase if the service is poorer than expected (however, see the word-of-mouth effect, Sect. 10.6.3). Hence, any advertisement aimed at showing the quality of accommodation is virtually useless: in the absence of a direct verification, that is, before the consumption, any message on the quality of the product does not have any validity to the eyes of consumers.

Under such conditions, an advertising campaign may be lacking a clear message about the product; if the content of advertising is not credible, the company may decide not to release any information about the quality. Notwithstanding, Nelson (1974) argued that the advertisement may still be useful and beneficial for potential customers. With regards to the content of the advertisement, Nelson refers to: (a) direct information, which is the specific content of the message, the statement; (b) indirect information, which is the message actually conveyed by the advertisement, regardless of its content. The idea is that in the market for search goods the statement prevails, while in the market for experience goods the indirect information plays a key role. Nelson's thesis, then, is that the amount of advertising expenditure has the role of signal (see Sect. 10.4.2): consumers are aware that firms of higher quality have a greater incentive in investing resources in advertisement relative to firms of lower quality; hence, customers will look for quality among those firms that spend more on advertising, regardless of the specific content of the message.

Following Nelson's rationale, the mechanism that enables advertisement expenditure to act as a credible signal and hence as a separating equilibrium in tourism is the repeat visit, that is, the fact that the good (or service) is sold more than once to the same customer. If this did not happen, that is, if the tourist was to visit only once (which is often the case for "exotic" holidays) nothing would protect her against the possibility of false advertising, beside the word-of-mouth mechanism that we will discuss in detail in Sect. 10.6.3.

Kihlstrom and Riordan (1984) argue that advertising may also be beneficial in the case of not repeat visits, but only if the variable costs of firms supplying the high quality are lower than those of the firms supplying the low quality. Such finding may explain some advertising behaviors that are observed in the real world, such as major forms of advertising occurring in markets where consumption is hardly repeated (e.g., cars) or the case of established and well-known companies which continue to invest in advertisement (e.g., soft drinks).

Provided that the role of advertising is different in the market for search goods than it is in the market for experience goods, when comparing the role of advertising under these two market assumptions, Nelson emphasizes that:

> Our results support the hypothesis that producers of experience goods advertise more than producers of search goods. This result is important because it in turn supports our fundamental behavioral proposition: that advertising of experience qualities increases sales through the reputability of the seller, while advertising of search qualities increases sales by providing the consumer with 'hard' information about the seller's products.
>
> (Nelson 1974, p. 740)

Finally, let us recall that the advertising expenditure can be justified even as a strategy for building a barrier to the entry of new producers, so to increase the loyalty of consumers, the degree of monopoly, and therefore profits. This issue was made clear by Kaldor (1950):

> Advertising is a method of differentiating, in the eyes of the consumer, the products of one firm from those of its competitors; it is a method, therefore, of reducing the scope and effectiveness of price-competition by attaching a strong element of 'goodwill' to each firm.
>
> (Kaldor 1950, p. 14)

On the other hand, it can be argued that new brands are the ones investing more on advertisement and that advertising campaigns can be the vehicle to enter the market for new operators that have the economic resources to build their own reputation on advertisement.

10.6.3 Advertisement, Reputation, Word of Mouth

The process of information retrieval on the quality of services is considered an important issue for the Economics of Tourism, given that the holiday is mainly an experience good. To further investigate this issue we have to make two important considerations:

1. The advertising is not the only channel through which firms build their reputation;
2. The tourists avail of different sources of information, mainly comments and reviews of previous holiday experiences by friends and relatives, and observation of other tourists' behaviors (see Sect. 6.7.4).

These issues have been tackled in the economic literature in two models. The first model (Schmalensee 1978) attempts to formalize the process of reputation building on quality through advertisement undertaken by the firm; the second model (von Ungern-Sternberg and von Weizsäcker 1985), studies the effects of an alternative channel of information, the word of mouth between consumers. These models have then been applied to tourism by Delbono and Ecchia (1988).

10.6.3.1 Quality and Reputation

Schmalensee studies the effect of advertising the quality of an experience good on the market shares of firms, each one offering a single product. Let us consider, for example, a market composed by N tour operators and L tourists, each one purchasing one holiday per unit of time, as typically happens for long summer holidays. Holidays differ for their quality, q, but all have the same price. Let us assume that the representative tourist buys in period t a holiday from tour operator k. After the holiday experience there are two possible cases: z is the probability that the tourist is satisfied by k and that repeats the experience in period $(t + 1)$; $(1 - z)$ is the probability that the tourist decides to change holiday at time $(t + 1)$.

The number of repeat purchases is directly affected by the quality of the holidays offered by tour operators and by advertisement, proxied by the number of advertising messages. The models suggests that, given the initial distribution of tourists among different tour operators, there exists a single long-run equilibrium for the market shares of the firms, s_n^*, with $n = 1, 2, 3, \ldots, N$ and where the share positively depends on advertisement a_n and the quality of the product q_n.

Which of the two investments (in advertising or in quality) should be used by the firm to increase its market share is a matter of economic rationale, since both instruments are effective but are also costly. There are situations where the average cost responds sharply to the improvement in quality or where advertisement is very effective, such that:

> The lowest-quality brands have the largest shares, and the market is clearly not responding appropriately to buyers' desire for quality.
>
> (Schmalensee 1978, p. 493)

Such condition of market failure is named "perverse" by Schmalensee. This conclusion is based on the assumption that tourists have a one period memory and that, consequently, tourists are affected by advertising more than quality. In fact, if the number of purchases is very low (as it is the case for summer holidays), low-quality brands can attract new tourists with high advertising expenditure since, in case of dissatisfaction by tourists, the reputational price to be paid by firms is limited. On the contrary, if the purchase is repeated many times, reputation can become more relevant.

10.6.3.2 The Word of Mouth

In the process of reputation formation, there is an important channel of transmission of information among tourists: the word of mouth, that is, the process through which personal experiences are communicated and commented to friends and relatives, and so on. Von Ungern-Sternberg and von Weizsäcker (1985) study the effect of word of mouth on sales and quality, considering it as an endogenous kind of advertisement, not paid by internal resources of the firm.

Let us assume that an uninformed tourist chooses randomly the holiday. After the experience (at the end of the first period), she can evaluate her experience and communicate it to other potential tourists. The informational set of the tourist then becomes wider, since it now includes direct and indirect evaluations and she can improve the evaluation of different holidays over time. The solution for the model allows to reach two conclusions. The first conclusion is that:

> With a functioning goodwill mechanism one cannot say that imperfect consumer information will lead to the market undersupplying quality.
>
> (von Ungern-Sternberg and von Weizsäcker 1985, p. 538)

However, the equilibrium price is higher than the marginal cost and the tourist, due to the presence of incomplete information, pays a price that is higher than the competitive price. Then:

> In the presence of the goodwill mechanism, the market failure does not, however, take the form of low quality, but of excessively high prices (that is, prices above marginal costs).
>
> (von Ungern-Sternberg and von Weizsäcker 1985, p. 539)

According to this model, the word of mouth allows a mechanism of quality selection which partially fixes the market failure stemming from information asymmetry; hence, it is a mechanism alternative to reputation, although also in this case the higher price is a consequence of imperfect information. For each firm, the equilibrium is to select the optimal combination of price and quality: in fact, a higher quality improves the reputation, but also a low price provides an incentive to tourists to positively evaluate the holiday or the destination. This model has also an important empirical relevance, since it is a well-known empirical fact that tourists choose holidays or destinations because satisfied by previous holidays or because advised by friends or relatives.

Chapter Overview

- The relevant market regimes in the tourism sector are: monopoly (for example, the market for attractions), oligopoly (for example, the market for air transport), and monopolistic competition (for example, the competition between destinations). Firms often strategically interact and also try to increase their monopoly power by integrating, vertically or horizontally.
- There is horizontal differentiation when goods are not ranked in the same way by consumers and, given the same price, the choice is driven by personal tastes. There is vertical differentiation when goods are ranked in the same way by consumer and the choice is driven by price (higher for the good of higher quality) and consumer's income.
- There is information asymmetry in the market when the agents involved in the exchange do not share the same information set; in particular, a party owns private information that the other party does not have. The main economic problem with information asymmetry is to encourage the party who owns the information to reveal it or, alternatively, to find effective tools for the uninformed agent to get as much information as possible.
- To achieve a separating equilibrium when there is signaling, the production cost of the signal should be inversely related to the quality. Otherwise, a pooling equilibrium arises.
- A firm's reputation is given by the current quality of the product as evaluated by tourists on the basis of quality observed in the past. To build reputational capital, the conditions of quality stability and of free entry in the long run must hold.
- When there are search goods, the opportunistic behavior of firms (which ultimately leads to quality deterioration) is based on the assumption of incomplete information and on the high costs of information retrieval that are borne by tourists. When there are experience goods, the search for information is more costly and this justifies the presence of a higher share of low-quality firms in the market.
- With search goods, the advertising message mainly emits an informational content, thus reducing the costs associated to information asymmetry and reducing the degree of opportunistic behavior of firms. With experience goods, advertising cannot be informative in itself, but operates as a signal.

Chapter 11
The Contracts in the Tourism Markets

Learning Outcomes
After reading this chapter, you will understand:

- The basic models of the Theory of Contracts and their application to tourism.
- The contractual inefficiencies stemming from information incompleteness and asymmetry.
- The contracts and the business practices that have been introduced to reduce these inefficiencies.

11.1 Introduction

After having studied the economic problem of tourism firms (Chaps. 8 and 9) as well as their strategic choice in terms of product differentiation, mechanisms of signaling, reputation, advertising, etc. (Chap. 10), in this chapter we will address a number of issues arising from the transactions between firms operating in different markets. In fact, the existence of uncertainty about the future, information asymmetry, and the subsequent opportunistic behavior, the specific features of investment projects, all require the arrangement of tailor-made contracts between firms aimed at bringing back efficiency in the transaction.

The concept of contract is key to this topic: in fact, every transaction carried out in a market economy is regulated by a contract between the involved parties (seller and buyer) that must indicate: (a) the economic content of the transaction; (b) the definition of the way in which the transaction is carried out; (c) the commitments undertaken by the parties. Each contract is characterized by two dimensions: the *economic dimension*, which specifies the object of the transaction as well as the economic relationship between the buyer and the seller, and the *legal dimension* which specifies the obligations (commitments about payments and actions) and the way in which these obligations adapt to the external conditions. A contract may either qualify as implicit or explicit.

G. Candela and P. Figini, *The Economics of Tourism Destinations*, Springer Texts in Business and Economics, DOI 10.1007/978-3-642-20874-4_11,

- An *implicit contract* is an agreement that the parties consider as binding even if it is not legally effective; as an example of implicit contract we could think of a tacit agreement between two tour operators which decide one to specialize in tours to Africa and the other in tours to Latin America in order to avoid competition. Naturally, implicit contracts are not contested in court, are not backed by documents, and may not even be supported by a verbal agreement, as they rely on mechanisms other than the legal ones, such as the existence of a mutual benefit.
- An *explicit contract* is instead a legal agreement which may either take the form of a written contract or the most simple form of an informal verbal contract.

Moreover, contracts may be either complete or incomplete.

- A *complete contract* is able to precisely specify: (a) all future consequences arising from its execution; (b) the actions and payments that each party must perform in each of the possible circumstances; (c) the penalties to apply in case of infringement of the agreement.
- An *incomplete contract* is a contract for which such specification is impossible, usually because it is impossible either to predict or describe the whole set of circumstances that may arise during the contractual relationship or to agree on the actions to be taken in every possible scenario.

While we refer to the specific literature for an in-depth analysis of the several economic models of the Theory of Contracts (for example, Milgrom and Roberts 1992), before studying their application to tourism, we first identify the key elements defining the contract.

- *The nature of the transaction*. We already know (see Sect. 7.2) that goods and services can be exchanged within: (a) spot markets; (b) forward markets; (c) contingent markets. If we apply the same classification to the contracts, we can define as spot contract the agreement for the exchange of goods or services of immediate availability and sold at the current market price. Such contract is relevant for tourism: for example, the contract signed by the tourist who directly buys accommodation at the hotel reception, after agreeing to pay the price, is a spot contract. Even the purchase of an ice cream in a creamery is technically a spot contract. These contracts are not flexible, in the sense that they forgo the costs associated with the detailed description of all the possible circumstances that can arise and leave little room for ex post uncertainty. Given that, in practice, such contracts may be efficient only for situations characterized by quick and frequent transactions (so that a change in the external circumstances during the contract is a rare event), we will not investigate them. For more complex transactions that span over long periods of time and/or characterized by significant changes of external circumstances, more sophisticated contracts, such as the contingent contract and the forward contract, are usually required. These types of contract will be discussed in Sects. 11.3 and 11.4.
- *The content and the distribution of information*. Contracts differ depending on the extent of available information and its distribution between the parties. Firstly, it

is essential to know whether or not the standard quality of the exchanged product is known and if external events (with known probability) may intervene to affect its value. Secondly, it is necessary to verify whether or not the information is publicly available, that is, if agents share the same information set.

The basic model of perfect competition implies that the information is complete and symmetrical, thus allowing the stipulation of complete contracts.[1] If, as it is usually the case for real-world transactions, we assume incomplete or asymmetric information, we have to consider the possibility for the contracting parties to behave opportunistically, i.e., to undergo changes in their actions that exploit, to their own advantage, special circumstances that were not anticipated by the contract or that take advantage from private information. The most extreme case of opportunistic behavior is the non-compliance of the contractual terms. The theory of incomplete contracts precisely investigates these situations, the economic consequences and the solutions that can be introduced.

In the remainder of the chapter we will see how different types of contract can provide an efficient solution to many of the economic problems that we already know from previous chapters. We will start by recalling, in Sect. 11.2, some elements of the Theory of Contracts, both complete and incomplete.

We know that many of the decisions taken by companies are carried out under uncertainty, in the sense that the achievement of their objective depends on the occurrence of a contingent state of nature. In Sect. 11.3 we will then study the contingent contract that can optimally tackle the problems related to uncertainty. An important application of the problem of choice under uncertainty is the one involving the early purchase of accommodation services by the tour operator, well before knowing the future extent of tourism demand: Sect. 11.4 will address this issue through the study of the types of contract that are commonly used in this situation: the free sale contract and the allotment contract.

In Sect. 11.5 we will then summarize the main aspects of the contracts relating tour operators, travel agencies, and other providers of tourism services: selection contracts, contracts with price ceiling, exclusive contracts, full-line contracts. In Sect. 11.7 we will instead analyze the relationship between tourism firms and the destination authority, in which the promotion of cooperation between the parties is essential for the attainment of efficiency. Finally, in Sect. 11.6 we will see the contractual solution for the issue of postcontractual opportunistic behavior, introduced in Chap. 10 as moral hazard. In fact, if we think about the relationship between a tour operator and a travel agency, we clearly understand the importance of designing contracts that stimulate the maximum effort in promotion and sales by the travel agent under all the possible environmental conditions.

[1] The complete contract usually refers to an outside structure, the organizational and legal institutions, to regulate the cases of non-compliance by a party or any other special situations that may occur. Such an external reference can either be implicit or explicitly specified in the contract.

11.2 An Introduction to the Economic Theory of Contracts

The economic theory of contracts starts by distinguishing between complete and incomplete contracts.

11.2.1 The Economic Theory of Complete Contracts

Since the complete contract specifies actions and payments by all counterparts in any possible circumstances, the only economic problem facing the agents is to gain the maximum share of benefit given the overall benefit stemming from the transaction. However, in conditions of efficiency, any increase in the surplus of one party implies a decrease in the surplus of the other party: thus, complete contracts can deal with uncertainty but not with the distributional conflict arising from the market. With respect to this issue, the economic theory can only state that the distribution of benefits depends on the market power of the parties. Although the competition among potential contracting parties can limit this power, in the business practice it is often relevant.

Then, the economic theory of contracts suggests that parties should find an agreement in terms of actions and payments in order to maximize the overall gain stemming from the market transaction, and then bargain the individual surpluses. Otherwise, the efficiency of the exchange might be reduced.

In the real world it is almost impossible to stipulate complete contracts, for many reasons: firstly, the complete contract must predict all the possible states of nature that can occur during the execution of the contract, but the external environment always provides unexpected events. Secondly, even the best contractual consultant has a limited rationality, and not all the possible events to be considered by the complete contract can be defined. Then, the complete contract is either technically impossible, since not everything can be expected, or economically not viable, since it is too expensive to predict and deal with any possible state of nature. To conclude, the hypothesis of completeness is an interesting theoretical benchmark, but in the practice all the contracts, to a certain extent, suffer from incompleteness.

11.2.2 The Economic Theory of Incomplete Contracts

If the contract is incomplete, there exists the possibility for the parties to behave opportunistically, that is, to exploit private information in their possession or to modify their actions in order to take advantage from a situation that cannot be controlled by the contract. It is easy to understand how information asymmetry might be the source of opportunistic behavior: a particular type of information asymmetry, the one where the seller has private information on the quality of the good has already been studied (see Sect. 10.4, the case of adverse selection, when the asymmetry generates forms of ex ante opportunism), while in here we refer to the ex post opportunism. As already stated, a limit case of opportunistic behavior is the non-compliance of the contract.

The fear that one of the parties might have opportunistic behavior can have devastating effects on the market transaction. In particular, we highlight two joint aspects:

1. The contractual agreement can be ineffective, since the opportunistic behavior cannot be excluded.
2. The contractual agreement can be inefficient, since a win-win market transaction might be halted, leading to a market failure.

The problem for incomplete contracts is therefore to overcome these problems, thus limiting the opportunistic behaviors of agents by introducing in the contract elements of correction for individual behaviors. The economic theory of contracts then explores the mechanisms that can be introduced in the contract in order to make it efficient. In particular, we can identify some typologies that will be applied to tourism in the remaining of the chapter.

- *Incentive contracts.* Since it is impossible to predict every behavior of the parties, the contract can link the payment to the result. However, if the result is affected by a stochastic component, it might be the case that the simple observation of the result is an incoherent signal for the agent's effort: for example, the agent can exert the maximum effort in the promotion and sales activity but, independently from own will, the result might be below the target. In this scenario, the party might find advantageous not to exert the maximum effort, thus reducing the expected outcome of the transaction. To convince the agent to bear the risk due to the stochastic event, it is necessary to include in the contract a payment higher than the one in conditions of certainty. This premium for the risk provides the incentive for the agent to exert the maximum effort in the contract. This contract, known in Economics as the principal–agent model, aims at finding an efficient equilibrium between two contrasting forces: (a) the inclusion of the incentive, in order to induce the agent to exert the maximum effort (the incentive constraint); (b) the restraint of the risk premium, in order not to provide excessive rents to the agent (participation constraint).
- *Selection contracts.* When an agent looks for a contractual counterpart with given characteristics, the lack of complete information might lead to the wrong choice, with negative effects on the efficiency of the transaction. One of the agents might propose a range of different contracts to the other party, with different clauses, in order to attain a separating equilibrium. In this way, the contract selected by the counterpart automatically reveals its type. This kind of contract is much used in practice: in life insurance, where it is very difficult for the insurer to know the true health condition of the insured; in finance, where the bank hardly knows the financial conditions of the firm or the risk involved in an investment project; in labor, where the employer does not know the skills and the ability of the potential worker. This contract allows the uninformed party to use a first-move advantage in order to extract the private information from the other party.

- *Contracts to deal with specific investments*. These are contracts dealing with situations in which there are sunk costs, should the project not be completed or the contract not be complied. Specific investments are a very complex problem. Not only participants to the project can diminish their effort when there is lack of control or an inefficient system of penalties, but each party can "blackmail" the other party if the latter has already implemented its share of the project. To avoid this opportunistic behavior, that would bring a market failure, it is possible to find contractual solutions of commitment to "tie the hands" of the party that does not bear the costs at the initial stage of the project. Finally, some long-term clauses can be introduced in the contract, in order to assign to the party that bear the costs of the specific investment legal rights on the final result of the project.
- *Joint venture contracts*. In some case, the tourism project requires the cooperation of two or more participants, each one implementing complementary actions. Such contracts, called joint ventures, need to identify an efficient system of incentives to guarantee the overall outcome of the project, since this is the result of the joint effort of the participants: if one party fails, the project ceases to be profitable. Then, in this type of contract, the relevant issue is to define a system of reciprocal incentives. The optimal incentive should provide to both parties a sufficient remuneration to induce them to complete the project with the maximum effort. However, this is not an easy task, since it can be demonstrated that a fair division of the outcome does not guarantee the maximum effort. A mechanism based on reputation can be the solution, where the party not complying with the contract will be punished in future agreements that also involve third parties, should the information be shared at no costs. In such case, the expected future loss might be higher than the immediate opportunistic profit and the reputation would play the optimal incentive.

We can conclude this brief survey of incomplete contracts by making some observations:

- The economic theory of contracts is an important proof for the assumption of limited rationality in economics; in fact, incomplete contracts are the evidence of all the constraints that impede economic agents to behave according to the hypothesis of perfect rationality, usually considered by the standard economic models.
- The economic theory of contracts relates to the efficient allocation of decision rights. In fact, when a contract is incomplete, it is important to decide who owns the right to take action and how, should an unexpected event or a breach in the contract occurs. In this respect, the contract might present clauses indicating either internal or external solutions. The internal solution gives the decision right to one of the parties involved in the transaction. The external solution gives the right to decide about the controversy to a third party.
- Finally, the economic theory of contracts modifies the way in which the firm can be interpreted. In fact, the firm can be considered as a system of contracts, signed between the shareholders and the Chief Executive Officer (CEO), between the CEO and the managers, between managers and directors, and so on, to the

employees. All these contracts are incomplete since they are affected by similar problems of information asymmetry and opportunistic behavior that usually affect independent parties signing contracts of sale and purchase. Having said that, one of the main targets of the firm is to decide whether (and how) to organize the production through an internal team of dependent employees or through external consultancy activities: this is the object of study for the Theory of Organization (see Sect. 7.3 for a further deepening on this last point).

11.3 The Insurance Contract in Tourism

A contingent contract (i.e., an insurance contract) typically deals with the problem of uncertainty, a typical condition which arises when time elapses between the stipulation of the contract and its execution. Before dealing with the theory of insurance contracts in tourism, it is necessary to recall the key elements of the choice theory under conditions of uncertainty.

11.3.1 Choice Under Uncertainty

Under uncertainty conditions, individuals choose among alternative actions that are evaluated in accordance to the states of nature in which they may occur. The interaction between actions and states of nature gives rise to an economic outcome which is technically called payoff. Even though the states of nature are usually a continuum of events, for simplicity we consider here a simple case of discrete events.

Let us suppose two alternative decisions, A_1 and A_2, that can be taken by the agent and two possible states of nature, S_1 and S_2, consistently with the payoff matrix displayed in Table 11.1. The actions to choose are indicated in the rows of the table while the states of nature are indicated in the columns. The outcome of the interaction between actions and states of nature is displayed in table's cells and referred to as X_{ij}, with $i, j = 1, 2$.

In Economics, the predominant approach to study the problem of choice under uncertainty is known as expected utility theory. This model assumes that the economic agent knows the probabilities associated to the alternative states of nature and that the consequence of actions is always evaluated in terms of their impact on the individual utility. Such assumptions can be included in Table 11.1, by adding a final row with the probability associated to each of the states of nature (q_1 and q_2, with $q_1 + q_2 = 1$) and a final column that calculates the expected utility of each action, respectively, $U_1 = U(X_{11})q_1 + U(X_{12})q_2$ and $U_2 = U(X_{21})q_1 + U(X_{22})q_2$. This allows to rank decisions in terms of expected utility and to identify the action leading to the highest level of utility.

In any case, the choice of the action to be taken depends on the functional form of $U(.)$, representing the individual attitude towards risk displayed by the agent

Table 11.1 The payoff matrix

	S_1	S_2	Utility
A_1	X_{11}	X_{12}	U_1
A_2	X_{21}	X_{22}	U_2
Probability	q_1	$q_2 = 1 - q_1$	

facing alternatives choices with different levels of risk. In general terms, one can define three possible attitudes when a risky and a risk-free action are compared:

1. *Risk aversion*: when the expected utility of the risky action is identical to the utility of a certainty action, the subject chooses the certainty action.
2. *Risk propensity*: when the expected utility of the risky action is identical to the utility of a certainty action, the subject chooses the risky action.
3. *Risk neutrality*: when the expected utility of the risky action is identical to the utility of a certainty action, the subject is indifferent between the certainty and the risky actions.

To better understand such distinction, let us assume that a tourist had bought for 1,000 € a lottery ticket that entitles him to win either a short holiday of length X_S or a long holiday of length X_L, and where the probability attached to each alternative is $q_i = 0.5$, where $i = S, L$. Figure 11.1 displays the length of stay on the horizontal axis and the corresponding utility associated to holidays of different length on the vertical axis. It is easy to check that the utility increases with the length of stay, but less than proportionally: the utility function is then increasing and concave, i.e., $U'(X) > 0$ and $U''(X) < 0$. Such form for the utility function represents a risk-averse individual; let us try to understand why.

We start by using Fig. 11.1 to determine the utility associated to the uncertain outcome. If the probability of X_S were one (and so the probability of X_L were zero), the tourist would be enjoying a level of utility equal to $U(X_S)$; instead, if the probability of X_L were one (and that of X_S were zero), the tourist would be enjoying a level of utility equal to $U(X_L)$. All intermediate combinations of these two situations, i.e., associated with a probability between zero and one, give rise to levels of utility located along the segment *AB*. In our example, since the probability of the short stay (and consequently of the long one) is 0.5, the expected utility from participating in the lottery is located at the midpoint $C(AC = CB)$, thus identifying the intermediate length X_{LOT} with an associated expected utility $U(C) = 0.5\ U(X_S) + 0.5\ U(X_L)$.

This calculation allows us to determine the value of the certainty equivalent: it can be calculated by finding the value on the utility function which corresponds to a level of satisfaction equivalent to that received from participating to the lottery. In Fig. 11.1, the certainty equivalent, X_{CE}, is determined by the condition $U(C) = U(X_{CE})$. By construction, it is now clear that the tourist is indifferent between paying 1,000 € for a holiday with length of stay X_{CE} and participating to the lottery; since $X_{CE} < X_{LOT}$, it is easy to conclude that the tourist is risk-averse because, for the same price, she accepts a shorter holiday in order not to face uncertainty, although the expected length to stay of the lottery is longer. The segment $X_{CE}X_{LOT}$ measures the length of stay that the tourist is willing to give up

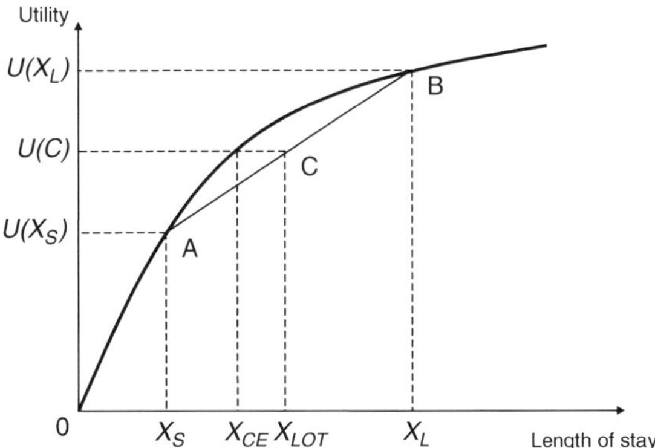

Fig. 11.1 The choice problem under uncertainty

in order to avoid uncertainty. Such segment is known as *risk premium* and it is easy to verify that its size depends on the curvature of the utility function.

We can now easily understand the alternative scenarios of risk propensity and risk neutrality. With a convex utility function ($U'' > 0$), the segment *AB* would lay above the utility function and it would be straightforward to verify that $X_{\mathrm{CE}} > X_{\mathrm{LOT}}$, meaning that the tourist would only accept a holiday of length higher than the expected length of stay of the lottery in order to give up the opportunity earned by participating to the lottery. In this case the agent is defined risk-lover. Finally, the case of a linear utility function identifies the preferences of a risk-neutral agent, for which $X_{\mathrm{CE}} = X_{\mathrm{LOT}}$.

Note that under the assumption of risk aversion, the insurance premium is positive (i.e., the agent is willing to give up a few days of holiday in order to hedge against the risk), while in the case of risk propensity the premium is negative (i.e., the agent is willing to pay to take the risk), and under the assumption of risk neutrality the premium is zero (because the two alternatives are considered as equivalent).

Finally, it is important to note that the assumption of risk aversion or propensity also depends on the amount of money at stake: it is normal to assume that with small amounts, agents are generally more prone to be risk lovers (almost all individuals purchase a lottery ticket when it only costs a few Euros, but almost nobody is willing to gamble the house!) so that the utility function generally takes a logistic form, convex at low levels of income and concave afterwards.

Now that we have introduced the key variables associated to the choice under uncertainty (the expected utility and the risk premium), we can move on to analyzing the contracts to deal with risk and uncertainty.

11.3.2 Contingent Contracts: Insurance in the Context of Tourism

Whenever there is a case of uncertainty within an economic relationship, it may be convenient to stipulate a contingent contract, that is, a contract which performance depends on the expected realization of a future state of nature. The systematic ability to stipulate contracts of such type leads to the creation of the insurance market, where individuals and companies with different propensity towards risk can improve their utility by exchanging goods in conditions of certainty with risk.

In fact, in the insurance market risk-averse individuals forgo economic uncertainty in favor of certainty by signing an insurance contract and upon the payment of a price, which is technically called *premium*. The insurance company, which is by definition risk neutral, "buys" the risk associated to the uncertain event from its customers, guaranteeing a financial coverage in case the adverse event does occur. By allowing for the possibility of exchanging risk, the insurance market helps the economic system to reach the conditions of perfect competition, with its efficient outcome. In theory, if the insurance market were able to work for all individuals and for all the possible states of nature, the presence of uncertainty would not represent a limit to the conditions of market efficiency.

In this section we focus on the insurance market when it comes to tourism. Of course, this market is available to all tourism firms willing to transfer risk, which is an inherent feature of their business activity: for example, a tour operator might want to insure against any damage to the real estate property it owns; similarly, a bathing establishment on the beach can insure against the damage suffered from a tornado or a storm, and so on. With regards to these insurance activities, however, the tourism firm does not behave differently from other types of firm, and there is no reason to further recall them.

Instead, a peculiar feature of the tourism sector is the possibility for the tourist to sign a contingent contract in order to transfer to other agents the risk associated to the holiday. Again, we do not refer here to the technical risk related to personal security during transport (especially if done with private means) or luggage security: once again, in these cases there is nothing new to add to the standard insurance contracts, except that their purchase is justified by the tourism activity. Instead, we refer to the economic risk related to the satisfaction stemming from the holiday, when this is bought in advance. The discussion is divided into two parts.

11.3.2.1 The Fixed Contract

Consider a risk-averse tourist who, with available income of 3,500, decides to buy a package holiday from a travel agency for the price of 1,000. Since there is the possibility that the tourist will get sick or that some other negative event may prevent her from departing, the price paid at the time of booking might be lost. Let the probability of occurrence of an event that prevents the departure be $q_1 = 0.01$, while the probability that nothing will happen be $q_2 = 0.99$.

The tourist is then confronted with the risk associated to two contingent scenarios: (a) the holiday does not take place and, since the price has already been paid, she would suffer a net loss of income equal to 1,000, the price paid; (b) the holiday takes place and she receives the associated benefit which, by having purchased it, is certainly valued at least 1,000. We can hence state that the second scenario leaves her income at least unchanged. The problem can be summarized by the following data:

$$Y_1 = 3,500 - 1,000 = 2,500,\ q_1 = 0.01; \quad Y_2 = 3,500,\ q_2 = 0.99. \tag{11.1}$$

The income structure expressed by (11.1) is that of a stochastic income: the tourist has a 0.01 probability of losing 1,000 (i.e., of being left with a total income, Y, equal to 2,500) and a 0.99 probability of having a full income of 3,500, including the value of the purchased holiday. An insurance company might offer a contract hedging against the economic loss due to the occurrence of the negative event that prevents her from departing in exchange of the payment of a premium P. The economic problem for the tourist is then to decide whether or not to accept the insurance contract. Since the premium is paid in any case, even if the adverse event does not occur, the structure of the tourist's income under the insurance contract then becomes

$$Y_1 = 2,500 + 1,000 - P,\ q_1 = 0.01; \quad Y_2 = 3,500 - P,\ q_2 = 0.99. \tag{11.2}$$

Given that (11.2) corresponds to a certainty income equal to (3,500 – P), the tourist must then decide whether or not to purchase the insurance contract by comparing the expected utility of the stochastic income (11.1) with the utility of certainty income (11.2), and choosing the one associated with the highest utility. So there are two possibilities:

1. If $U(3{,}500 - P) > U(2{,}500)q_1 + U(3{,}500)q_2$, then the tourist buys the insurance contract.
2. If $U(3{,}500 - P) < U(2{,}500)q_1 + U(3{,}500)q_2$, then the tourist does not buy the insurance contract.

Among other things, the solution depends on the value of P; we can then identify a value P_F for which there is strict equality between the two alternatives: $U(3{,}500 - P_F) = U(2{,}500)q_1 + U(3{,}500)q_2$. P_F plays the role of reservation price (see Sect. 5.4) and is called *fair premium*, i.e., the premium for which the tourist is indifferent between the two alternatives. Therefore, the purchase of the insurance contract depends on the comparison between the premium and the fair premium which in turn, after recalling Sect. 11.3.1, depends on the concavity of the utility function (i.e., on the tourist's risk aversion). Other things being equal, the higher the premium, the lower the probability of purchasing the insurance policy.

11.3.2.2 The Flexible Contract

In what follows, we assume that the insurance company offers the tourist a more sophisticated contract, by providing a flexible refund of amount K, with $0 < K \leq 1{,}000$, against the payment of a premium proportional to the amount being insured, $P = aK$, and where a is a parameter. With the flexible contract, the structure of the tourist's income is as follows:

$$Y_1 = 2,500 + K - aK,\ q_1 = 0.01; \quad Y_2 = 3,500 - aK,\ q_2 = 0.99. \qquad (11.3)$$

The comparison between (11.1) and (11.3) clearly shows that with a flexible insurance contract the tourist might decide to have a partial insurance by paying a proportional premium in exchange of the possibility of having [2,500 + (1 − a)K] in the occurrence of the negative event. Such problem is more general than the case of the fixed contract, and does not only require a "yes *versus* no" choice, but also needs to determine the extent of the optimal amount to insure, which is defined in terms of the expected utility, U_Y, of the income structure (11.3):

$$U_Y = U(Y_1)q_1 + U(Y_2)q_2 = U(2,500 + K - aK)q_1 + U(3,500 - aK)q_2. \quad (11.4)$$

Then, the tourist should determine the value K^* that maximizes (11.4) by taking into account the premium that explicitly appears in the budget constraint. This ultimately determines the optimal flexible insurance policy (K^*; $P^* = aK^*$) which allows the tourist to hedge against the risk (the damage stemming from being unable to take the holiday). It is straightforward to see that the insured amount K^* is inversely related to the parameter a, so that the flexibility of the insurance contract brings back to the economic notion of the demand function: $K^* = f(a)$.

When a flexible contract with fair premium is being proposed (in the flexible contract, the fair premium corresponds to the probability of the risk associated to the event, $a = q_1 = 0.01$), the risk-averse tourist always chooses to fully insure, given that the optimal insured amount perfectly overlaps with the price of the holiday. In our example, the fair premium is $P_F = 10(= 0.01 \times 1{,}000)$.

To summarize, the fixed contract only allows to fill the gap between the levels of income associated to the two states of nature. In exchange of a fixed premium and by offering the tourist a certainty equivalent the tourist decides to insure as long as the premium is less than the fair premium P_F. The flexible contract allows the tourist to choose the optimal combination of premium and quantity to be insured; it provides the tourist with a "budget line" along which to choose the preferred structure of income uncertainty. Only in the event of a fair contract, i.e., when the premium is equal to the probability of the unfavorable event, the tourist chooses the certainty income structure, while in all other cases the best choice would involve a partial degree of uncertainty.

In practice, to insure against the economic risk stemming from the holiday (i.e., the risk associated to the price to pay in advance), both types of insurance policy can be offered, as well as many of their intermediate combinations. It is often possible to access a policy with a franchise, that is, a reduction of the premium in exchange for not covering a given percentage of the damage. In addition, flexible contracts are often provided with discrete, not continuous, alternatives, this solution being justified by the existence of costs of enforcement that would become excessive if too many combinations of premiums and payments were to be allowed.

Finally, it is necessary to observe that the possibility of buying an insurance contract in order to hedge against any stochastic event that may generate uncertainty during the trip allows the (risk-averse) tourists to increase their utility. If the possibility of a contingent contract were missing, this would represent a case of market failure for risk-averse tourists. In the business practice, tour operators and travel agencies provide, especially through specialized insurance companies, different types of insurance policies to tourists, with reimbursements when the holiday cannot be taken by the tourist or even when the holiday is ruined by adverse weather conditions.

11.4 The Contracts Regulating the Transactions Between Tourism Firms

The uncertainty not only surrounds the relationship between tourism firms and tourists but also the transaction of tourism services between firms. As the most obvious example, consider the tour operator that usually buys tourism services (transport, accommodation, etc.) in great advance, many months before the "use" of the services. These purchases are then subject to a great extent of uncertainty about the future tourism demand. The contracts regulating these transactions are called forward (or future) contracts.

A contract usually includes an action (the service to be delivered or the good to be produced) and a payment (its price). The markets in which the delivery of the good or service is contemporaneous to the definition of its price are called spot markets. The identification of the spot market is given by the contemporaneity between the transaction and the definition of price, not between transaction and payment. In fact, the payment can take place joint with the delivery or deferred, in this case giving rise to a credit. The forward (future) contract is instead a contract to exchange a specified service or good for a price agreed today, at time t, with delivery occurring at a specified future time $(t + k)$, the delivery date. In the forward contract, differently from the spot contract, there is no contemporaneity between the definition of the price and the exchange. Similarly to the spot contract, also in the forward contract the time of the payment is irrelevant as it can take place at time t, if the forward contract is anticipated, or at time $(t + k)$, if the forward contract is pure.

Forward contracts are very frequent in tourism: through the reservation system tourists agree "today" the price of tourism services (for example, accommodation and transport) to be delivered "tomorrow"; similarly, tour operators stipulate forward contracts with providers of tourism services to avail of their services in future dates. In the next subsections, we will study these contracts which can be distinguished in "free sale" contracts and "allotment" contracts, according to the different distribution of the risk associated to the future configurations of demand (see Sect. 8.2.1).

11.4.1 *The Forward Contract: The Free Sale Contract*

The time factor plays a crucial role in the forward contract, in two respects:

1. As time elapses, the evaluation of goods and services usually changes.
2. In the time interval $[k = (t + k) - t]$ some external events may occur, thus modifying the market conditions of demand and supply and affecting the price.

To discuss these contracts, we set two alternative assumptions: that the firms operate in conditions of certainty, an extreme situation that allows us to focus on the effect (1); or that the agents are able to hedge against the risk associated with future changes in the market conditions, in which case both effects (1) and (2) occur simultaneously.

11.4.1.1 Forward Contracts Under Certainty

With this contract the tour operator buys at time t accommodation services that will be available at time $(t + k)$, by committing to pay the price agreed at t independently on the price that will be in force at $(t + k)$. With this contract, then, we can identify two distinct markets:

1. The forward market at time t, when the tourism services to deliver at the time $(t + k)$ are purchased at the price $p_{t,t+k}$.
2. The spot market at time $(t + k)$, when tourism services will be bought, delivered and the price $p_{t+k,t+k}$ agreed upon.

The economic problem here is the relationship between the prices set in the two markets. To investigate such issue, we must distinguish between two essential hypotheses.

- The price of the forward contract is paid by the tour operator at time $(t + k)$; in this case, it must be true that $p_{t,t+k} = p_{t+k,t+k}$. In fact, in conditions of certainty and in the absence of risk, when markets are competitive a difference between these two prices would lead to arbitrage, ultimately leading to level them out, i.e., any price difference would be rapidly cleared by the competition among the operators. A gap in the two prices might persist only in the presence of some management costs such as the case, for example, where the early sale allows the manager to save some marketing costs.
- The price of the forward contract is paid by the tour operator at time t; in this case we must take into account the "cost" of time. In fact, during the time elapsing between t and $(t + k)$, the cashed amount of money $p_{t,t+k}$ generates an interest. If r is the interest rate prevailing in the financial market, under the rule of competition it is

$$p_{t,t+k}(1+r)^k = p_{t+k,t+k} \quad \text{which is} \quad p_{t,t+k} = p_{t+k,t+k}(1+r)^{-k}, \tag{11.5}$$

given that any other difference will be absorbed by arbitrage and competition. We can conclude that with an anticipated payment, the forward price of equilibrium is equal to the present value of the spot price prevailing at the delivery date.

Although the presence of advertisement and marketing costs surely introduces an additional element of difference between the two prices, the introduction of uncertainty about the future is the real complication of this simple model.

11.4.1.2 Forward Contracts Under Uncertainty

The time introduces disruptive elements in the analysis of forward contracts. To begin with, simply assume that future events are expected. For example, the occurrence of a conflict in a tourism destination can lead to an expected increase in the demand of competitors. At time t, prior to the information on the conflict, in one of these other destinations two prices coexist: in the forward market, $p_{t,t+k} = 100$, and in the spot market at time t, $p_{t,t} = 105$. The difference of 5 is equivalent to a 5 % interest rate (the rate prevailing on financial markets) paid for the (unit) period k.

The new information on the outbreak of the conflict in the other country allows to predict that the spot price for the destination at time $(t + k)$ will increase: $p_{t+k,t+k} = 108 > p_{t,t} = 105$. In response to this information, the tour operator buys in the forward market at the existing price, since by paying 100 in advance (on which an interest of 5 will be considered) it can safely earn a difference equal to 3 when selling at 108 on the spot market at time $(t + k)$. However, by doing so, the demand for forward contracts at time t increases, thus increasing the price $p_{t,t+k}$. A new equilibrium, in which speculative transactions will cease when (11.5) will be satisfied, is determined for $p_{t,t+k} = 102.8$ $(= 108/1.05)$. Based on this simple example we can thus conclude that the forward price plays a signaling role in the expected movement of the spot price.

More often, however, the future is not as predictable as it was assumed in this example. For such reason, the economic agents have personal expectations about the probability of future events to occur. The tour operator buying at time t a free sale contract with delivery time at $(t + k)$ hedges against the risk of having to accept an unexpected higher price in case it were to operate in the spot market at time $(t + k)$. Although the forward contract sets the price in advance, it exposes the firms to the risk of unexpected shifts in demand that may occur in the time interval between the stipulation of the contract and the service delivery. Therefore, the hotel facing the forward contract offered by tour operator at a price $p_{t,t+k} = p^*$ must decide whether to accept it or not, and in the case of acceptance, it must decide the number of services for which to sign it (Castellani and Mussoni 2007).

Hence, the key issue to analyze for the hotel is to set the optimal number of rooms to sell to the tour operator and we do so by applying the mean-variance model. With no loss of generality, let us assume that the hotel is able to assess the spot price in $(t + k)$ as a stochastic variable, $p_{t+k,t+k} = V$, with known density function, mean equal to $E(V) = p^\circ$, and variance equal to $\mathrm{var}(V) = v$. Suppose that the hotel avails of N rooms, which can be either sold to the tour operator through a forward contract, N_F, or sold on the spot market, N_S. If we let $X = N_F/N$ be the share of rooms sold on the forward market at the price $p*$, and $Y = 1 - X = N_S/N$ the share of rooms sold on the spot market $(t + k)$ at the unknown price V, the hotel's choice obviously pivots around to the value of X.

The crucial aspect of such problem is that the average price p_M is also a stochastic variable:

$$p_M = Xp^* + (1 - X)V, \tag{11.6}$$

the mean and variance of which, by applying the properties of the mean and variance operators, are conditional to the value taken by X:

$$E(p_M|X) = Xp^* + (1 - X)E(V) = Xp^* + p^\circ - Xp^\circ = p^\circ - (p^\circ - p^*)X, \tag{11.7}$$

$$\mathrm{var}(p_M|X) = \mathrm{var}[Xp^* + (1 - X)V] = (1 - X)^2\mathrm{var}(V) = (1 - X)^2 v. \tag{11.8}$$

For the extreme cases, expressions (11.7) and (11.8) become easy to read: if the hotel sells its full availability to the tour operator, then $X = 1$ and so $E(p_M \mid 1) = p*$ and $\mathrm{var}(p_M \mid 1) = 0$, i.e., a forward contract covering the full capacity is associated to a certain price. On the other hand, if the hotel does not accept the forward contract, then $X = 0$ and so $E(p_M \mid 0) = p^\circ$ and $\mathrm{var}(p_M \mid 0) = v$, i.e., the hotel fully accepts the market risk. In all intermediate cases, the expected price and the variance will depend on the decision about X: it is reasonable to assume that $p* < p^\circ$, and it is easy to verify that the average price (11.7) and its variance (11.8) will decrease as the share of accommodation sold through forward contracts increases.

We conclude with two observations: the forward contract under conditions of uncertainty allows the hotel to diversify its customer portfolio in order to determine the optimal combination of performance and risk. In addition, by signing a free sale contract, the tour operator is able to provide an insurance for the risk-averse hotel management, so it becomes reasonable to assume that in equilibrium $p* < p^\circ$. If we denote with $d > 0$ the difference between these two prices:

$$d = p^\circ - p^*, \tag{11.9}$$

where d represents the premium that the hotel accepts to pay to the tour operator to hedge against the risk of future events negatively affecting the price.

Finally, if we refer to the role of tour operators that we already underlined in Sect. 4.4.1, and in particular in formula (4.11), we can easily understand that the difference d of (11.9) is exactly what allows the tour operator to play the coordination function that solves, via the market, the anticommon problem in the tourism destination.

11.4.2 Forward Contracts with Option: The Allotment

In the previous section we anticipated that, in addition to the free sale contract, the tour operator may agree to stipulate with the hotel another type of contract dealing with accommodation availability, the allotment contract. Generally speaking, this contract allows the tour operator to buy a number of overnight stays at a future date but at the price agreed today, by reserving the right to release or confirm the rooms within a deadline (usually called release date). Therefore, the allotment is a forward contract with an option.

The option is a contract whereby one of the parties, against the payment of a price, gains the right but not the obligation to engage in a transaction, while the other party is obliged to fulfill the transaction. At the release date, the option holder shall inform the other party whether or not he intends to enforce such right. However, the price of the option has to be paid in any circumstance. If the option can be enforced by the buyer (the tour operator in our case), the contract is known as *call option*. If the option can be enforced by the seller (the hotel in our case) the contract is known as *put option*.[2]

Let us consider an example. Suppose that the tour operator signs a contract with a hotel in the tourism destination A for a given number of rooms, say 1,000, to be included in one of the package holidays of its catalog. Let the price for each room be 20 while the profit for the tour operator be 15 for every tourist who buys the trip, which corresponds to a total expected profit of 15,000. Assume that, after having signed the contract, the tour operator becomes aware of the fact that the inclusion of the alternative destination B in the catalog would be preferable, since this would bring higher profits equal, for example, to 25 per room. This would lead to a total profit equal to 25,000. Efficiency would require the tour operator to change its deal to meet the new market conditions but, if the contract signed with the hotel in destination A is a free sale contract, the firm will be forced to execute it and pay the agreed price. Hence, its net profit in case of switching to destination B would only be equal to $5{,}000 = 25{,}000 - 20{,}000$, lower than the case in which it would stick with destination A.

The allotment contract allows for an alternative solution to such situation. For example, the agreement between the tour operator and the hotel in A may include the following option: the operator pays 5 for the right to reserve each room and eventually pays the full price of 20 to confirm it at a given deadline. With such an arrangement, the tour operator is able to adjust its portfolio on the release date. In particular, since the difference in profits arising from opportunity B is equal to 10 $(= 25 - 15)$ per tourist, the tour operator finds convenient to pay 5 to the hotel (the option price) for not fulfilling the contract. The net profit from opportunity B would then be 20,000 $(= 25{,}000 - 5 \times 1{,}000)$, which is still higher than the profit

[2] The buyer (seller) can exert the right to buy (sell) or not at a specific date in the so-called European call (put) option or within a deadline in the so-called American call (put) option.

associated to the opportunity A, 15,000. A similar rationale suggests that it would not be profitable to abandon the contract A if the difference in per-tourist profit generated by opportunity B were not higher than the option price.

The option may indeed represent an interesting, although costly, opportunity for the tour operator that can be exploited when there is strong uncertainty about the future demand and then a high probability that part of the rooms booked by the tour operator remains unsold. Since the option allows to transfer the risk of unsold production from the tour operator to the hotel, it is obvious to expect that the price p of accommodation paid for the allotment contract would be higher than the price for the same service in the free sale contract, being the difference a sort of insurance premium against the risk of unsold production: $p^* < p < p^\circ$. Then, in analogy with (11.9), the difference $p^\circ - p = z$ can be interpreted as the price of the option and the margin earned by the tour operator is obviously lower, equal to $(d - z)$. The allotment contract is therefore beneficial to those who believe that the market is subject to strong variations, while must be dismissed by those who believe that the market is relatively stable. Ultimately, it can be affirmed that the option is not a bet on the future price, as the forward contract is, but a bet on the market stability.

11.5 The Contracts Between Tour Operators, Travel Agencies, and Service Providers

In the two previous sections, we have studied one of the causes leading to incomplete contracts: the incompleteness of information. We have seen that the resulting economic problems can be managed by stipulating proper forward, option, and contingent contracts. In this section we will analyze some other contractual solutions that enable tour operators to address a wide range of economic problems stemming from their relationship with travel agencies and service providers. These latter firms, in fact, may undertake behaviors that clash with the tour operator's goal of profit maximization.

11.5.1 Contracts to Deal with the Double Markup: The Minimum Quota and the Price Ceiling

The contracts designed to deal with the double markup are justified by the need to regulate the relationship between firms operating at different stages of the production chain, and where each stage is characterized by non-competitive markets. This is obviously the situation for a tour operator and a travel agency: the first produces a tourism product, the all-inclusive package holiday, which is then sold to the travel agency, which sell it in turn to tourists. In case there is monopoly power (and this is very likely to happen in markets where the product is highly differentiated, as in tourism, see Sect. 10.3) the formation of the retail price by the means of the markup method tends to produce an inefficient outcome for the tour operator, which then finds the incentive to vertically integrate with the agency or to adopt specific contractual arrangements such as the retail price ceiling or the minimum quota of sales. In what follows we explain the rationale of these contracts.

Intuitively, if the holiday produced by the tour operator is sold to the travel agency, the latter has the power of setting a retail price that also includes its own profit. Following the full-cost method, the travel agency applies a markup on the cost at which the holiday is bought from the tour operator, while the tour operator (with monopoly power in its market) already included its own markup in such cost. In practice, the final price includes a double markup, since the travel agency's one gets calculated on a basis that already includes the markup of the tour operator.

We can better understand this problem by simply assuming that the unit variable cost of production of the package holiday is constant and equal to C_{TO}. The price at which the holiday is sold by the tour operator to the travel agency is then

$$p_{\mathrm{TO}} = C_{\mathrm{TO}}(1 + m_{\mathrm{TO}}). \tag{11.10}$$

Moreover, if we assume for the sake of simplicity that there are no costs of production for the travel agency, its markup is simply computed on the price p_{TO}:

$$p_{\mathrm{TA}} = p_{\mathrm{TO}}(1 + m_{\mathrm{TA}}) = C_{\mathrm{TO}}(1 + m_{\mathrm{TO}})(1 + m_{\mathrm{TA}}), \tag{11.11}$$

which becomes equal to $p_{\mathrm{TA}} = C_{\mathrm{TO}}(1 + m)^2$ if, for simplicity, $m_{\mathrm{TO}} = m_{\mathrm{TA}} = m$. In this way, it is clear that the retail price gets overcharged, thus leading to a suboptimal equilibrium both for tourists (paying a price that is too high) and for the tour operator (suffering a potential cut in sales and profits).

To demonstrate that this is a suboptimal equilibrium we may wonder what would be the equilibrium if there were vertical integration, that is, if the tour operator merged with the travel agency. In this case, the tour operator should set the price of the holiday by simply adding to the production costs C_{TO} both the markup for the production and the markup for the retail activity. Such price would then be

$$p^* = C_{\mathrm{TO}}(1 + m_{\mathrm{TO}} + m_{\mathrm{TA}}), \tag{11.12}$$

which, under the simplest assumption $m_{\mathrm{TO}} = m_{\mathrm{TA}} = m$, becomes

$$p^* = C_{\mathrm{TO}}(1 + 2m). \tag{11.13}$$

From the comparison of (11.13) with (11.11) it is straightforward to check that $p^* < p_{\mathrm{TA}}$. Therefore, with vertical integration the price would be lower and, given the law of demand, the quantity sold will be greater. Not only this would entail a higher consumer surplus, but also a higher profit for the tour operator. In other words, the condition of double monopoly in the production chain imposes, through the double markup, a damage to the market and to the tour operator in particular.

The tour operator can effectively respond to the double mark up problem in several ways. As we just mentioned, one solution would be to vertically integrate (see Sect. 7.3). But there exist alternative contractual solutions which may prevent the travel agency to damage the tour operator. In what follows, we mention two of such contracts.

1. A contract through which the tour operator imposes the agency to sell at least a minimum amount of products: to fulfill the contract, the agency has to set the price lower than (11.11) and, if the tour operator knows the demand function, $p = p(Q)$, it would require the amount Q^* corresponding to the price p^* of (11.13).
2. A contract with a price ceiling p^*. With imposing a retail price not higher than p^* the tour operator pays the travel agency with a commission g proportional to the price, computed in order to allow the tour operator to gain its target markup m_{TO}. Since the agency's revenue, given (11.10) and (11.12), is

$$gp^* = p^* - p_{\mathrm{TO}} = C_{\mathrm{TO}} m_{\mathrm{TA}}, \qquad (11.14)$$

the commission has to be fixed by the contract at $g^* = (C_{\mathrm{TO}} m_{\mathrm{TA}})/p^*$, which is equivalent to a markup equal to

$$m_{\mathrm{TA}} = \frac{g^* p^*}{C_{\mathrm{TO}}}.$$

The second solution, which consists in setting the value of g^*, is the most commonly used in the business practice, where the tour operator prefers to specify the commission on the retail price rather than the markup, because the latter would require the tour operator to reveal its production costs to the travel agency. To sum up, in order to prevent the price from including a double markup, the tour operator offers the travel agency a contract with a price ceiling p^* (on which the travel agency can eventually offer a discount) posted on the catalog of the tour operator and a commission g^* to remunerate the retailing activity of the travel agency.

Should the travel agency bear retailing costs, the price ceiling set by the tour operator should take them into consideration when computing the retail price. The rationale described earlier does not change, although the computation of the retail price is not so simple anymore: the price would be

$$p_{\mathrm{TA}} = C_{\mathrm{TO}}(1 + m_{\mathrm{TO}}) + C_{\mathrm{TA}}(1 + m_{\mathrm{TA}}). \qquad (11.15)$$

If, as in the previous case, we impose that the two markups are equal, the retail price will be equal to $p_{\mathrm{TA}} = (C_{\mathrm{TO}} + C_{\mathrm{TA}})(1 + m)$. To be efficiently applied, this solution requires the tour operator to monitor the costs of the travel agency.

Ultimately, the contracts that the tour operator stipulates with the travel agency aim at solving the problem of distribution of the extra profits generated by their monopolistic positions, when the travel agency undertakes a pricing policy that hurts the tour operators' profit. Such contractual arrangements, which certainly impose vertical constraints to the market, usually intervene when the market structure is inefficient because the producer does not directly sell to the final consumer.

11.5.2 The Exclusive Contracts

Given that the travel agency is the point of contact between the service providers and the tourists, tour operators have an interest in signing exclusive contracts with travel agencies. This practice, which is generally known as "exclusive agency agreement" is a restrictive contract allowing the tour operator to bind the agent in not making similar deals with other competing tour operators. Such contracts have the effect of increasing the monopoly degree of the tour operator, with a direct impact on its profit. By signing this contract, the travel agency accepts to not sell similar products of other tour operators.

We now develop a simple yet precise example for understanding the mechanism behind the exclusive contract, thus underlying its effect on the service suppliers, the tourists, and market competition. Suppose that the market for a given tourism destination is currently monopolized by the tour operator TO, which offers its package holiday through a travel agency TA, also a monopolist on the local retail market. Let the production cost of the holiday borne by TO be $C_{\mathrm{TO}} = 500$, on which the agency charges a markup of $m_{\mathrm{TA}} = 0.2$ (i.e., equal to 100 in absolute value). Moreover, let the markup applied by TO be $m_{\mathrm{TO}} = 1$. Also assume that TO sets the final price of the holiday through the full-cost principle in order to avoid the double markup problem (see Sect. 11.5.1): $p = C_{\mathrm{TO}}(1 + m_{\mathrm{TA}} + m_{\mathrm{TO}})$. Then, the price is equal to 1,100 (= 500 (1 + 0.2 + 1)).

We also assume that a new tour operator, E, might enter the market and compete with TO both in the supply of the product and to access the retail market through the only existing travel agency. The cost structure (and hence the level of efficiency) of this potential competitor is unknown to both TO and TA and cannot be observed by them. It may be more or less efficient than TO and hence it could potentially be able to produce the same package holiday either at a lower or higher cost than TO. We assume that TO and TA do know the probability that E is more or less efficient than TO:

1. $C_{E_1} = 250$ with probability 0.5
2. $C_{E_2} = 750$ with probability 0.5

That is, if E is of type 1, its production costs are equal to 250, and such higher efficiency would enable it to offer the travel agency a higher commission, for example, 0.8, while if E is of type 2, its production costs are equal to 750, and such lower efficiency would only allow it to offer the agency the same commission paid by TO, that is 0.2 (if the commission is lower, the agency would not sell the product of E). Finally, we assume that the travel agency's average customer has a reservation price equal to 1,100, above which the holiday will not be bought.

Given that each tour operator sets the retail price based on the full-cost principle, it is immediate to get that, given an identical markup for the tour operators, $m_E = 1$, the type 2 tour operator would not be able to enter the market because the minimum price of its holiday is equal to 1,650 (= 750 (1 + 0.2 + 1)). On the contrary, the type 1 tour operator can successfully enter the market by offering the travel agency a higher commission (0.8) and by setting a lower price, for example equal to 700 (= 250 (1 + 0.8 + 1)).

Under such conditions, the market price of the holiday will be dictated by TO when the competitor is inefficient, $p^* = 1{,}100$, or by E when it is more efficient, $p^* = 700$. Because the occurrence of each type of E is characterized by the same probability 0.5, and since TO will sell its holiday only in the first case, which has probability equal to 0.5, we can calculate its expected profit as

$$E(\pi_{\text{TO}}) = 0.5[(p - C_{\text{TO}} m_{\text{TA}}) - C_{\text{TO}}] = 0.5[(1,100 - 100) - 500] = 250.$$

The travel agency's expected profit depends on its decision to sell either the holiday of TO or of E, by choosing ex post to offer one of the two catalogs, in case E decides to enter the market:

$$E(\pi_{\text{TA}}) = 0.5(C_{\text{TO}} m_{\text{TA}}) + 0.5(C_E m_{\text{TA}}) = 100 \times 0.5 + 200 \times 0.5 = 150.$$

Since the expected profit is greater than what the agency would earn under the presence of TO only, $(150 > 100)$, it is clear that the existence of a potential competitor is detrimental to TO, which expected profit is accordingly reduced $(250 < 500)$, and favorable to TA, which expected profit is increased. To prevent the entry of E, TO may seek to restrict TA's choice by imposing a contractual agreement providing a penalty G to the agency, should it decide to sell the holiday of E after having signed the contract with TO. However, the contract ($m_{\text{TA}} = 0.2$; $G > 0$) will never be accepted by TA, since for any positive value of the penalty the travel agent's expected profit is certainly less than the expected profit in case it can freely decide for the best deal:

$$E(\pi_{\text{TA}}) = 100 \times 0.5 + (200 - G)0.5 = 150 - G/2 < 150.$$

To offset the inclusion of the penalty, TO must then propose a contract that offers a higher commission ($m_{\text{TA}} > 0.2$; $G > 0$) so that the ex ante expected profit is not lower than the ex ante profit without such contractual clause:

$$\begin{aligned} E(\pi_{\text{TA}}) &= 0.5(C_{\text{TO}} m_{\text{TA}}) + 0.5(C_E m_{\text{TA}} - G) \\ &= 0.5 \times 500 m_{\text{TA}} - 0.5(200 - G) \geq 150. \end{aligned}$$

Such inequality is satisfied by the following condition:

$$G \leq 500 m_{\text{TA}} - 100 \quad \text{then} \quad G > 0 \quad \text{if and only if} \quad m_{\text{TA}} > 0.2.$$

To be accepted by TA, the contract proposed by TO must provide a combination of an over-commission of not less than 0.2 and a penalty not more than 500 to be paid by the agency should it sell the holiday of E. Such contract, which is intended to prevent the entry of E and is technically called exclusive contract, is accepted by TA before knowing E's conditions since TA's expected profit cannot be less than under the alternative provided by E. Here we avoid discussing the stability of the exclusive contract, as the issue of non-compliance by the agency remains an open problem.

The problem may be further complicated by the fact that the introduction of the penalty G modifies the probability of entry of the tour operator E of type 1. However, despite a more complicated calculation of the participation constraint, the rationale of the exclusivity agreement would not be modified. We can thus conclude that the tour operator already operating in the market may defend its monopoly power over the menace of potential competitors through an exclusive contract, but in doing so it has to share with the travel agency a part of its own markup. Thus, only the perspective of maintaining a position of monopoly in the long run can justify the choice for the tour operator to bear the cost of excluding a competitor from the market.

In the business practice, the exclusive contract can take different and more sophisticated forms than the one indicated in this section. For example, the penalty may be just implicit, included in a contract that "locks" the agency within an exclusive relationship with its supplier (lock-in effect). For example, we know that when customers contact the travel agency, their needs may extend well beyond the simple purchase of standard all-inclusive packages, for they may require some changes in the features of the holiday, or additional ancillary services that can be especially granted by the tour operator to the agency. In addition, the tour operator may offer the agency additional contractual benefits, such as joint marketing activity, the use of proprietary software, or sharing the cost of recruiting and training personnel for the agency.

The solution of binding the travel agency through a lock-in effect has a number of advantages *versus* the simple inclusion of a contract penalty. In fact, it may be difficult for the tour operator to find out whether the agency does or does not respect the exclusive agreement (which necessarily involves monitoring costs). With the lock-in effect the penalty is hidden within a relational contract and operates as an automatic fee on the costs borne by the agent, should it decide to select another tour operator. In practice, the exclusive contract implements an alternative form of vertical integration to the point that the relationship which comes into existence between the locked-in agency and the tour operator is usually referred to as vertical collaboration.

Of course, exclusive and relational contracts raise the issue of competition protection. In fact, there is no denying that such contracts and practices reduce competition and generate economic inefficiency. In our example, the tour operator that could sell the trip at a price of 700 is kept out from the market, thus impeding that the tourist earns a consumer surplus equal to 400 (= 1,100 − 700). Therefore, the legality of such agreements closely depends on the enforcement of antitrust laws and competition authorities in the legal system. Usually, local laws prohibit (except in special cases) the explicit clauses of exclusivity, by monitoring those situations in which exclusivity is sought by stimulating particular behaviors that are implicitly embodied in a relational contract.

11.5.3 The Full-Line Contract

The tour operator usually offers a wide range of holidays in its catalog, both as a strategy of portfolio diversification to reduce the risk associated with business activity (see Sect. 14.2.1) and to meet the diversity of tourists' preferences (see Sect. 10.3). In the business practice, diversification may occur: (a) by making use of different brands, each specialized in a particular market segment; (b) by issuing various catalogs under the same brand. In both cases, the economic problem for the tour operator (and sometimes even for the big international hotel chain) is to stimulate the sale of its entire product line.

The travel agency, in fact, may not to be interested in exerting effort to advertise holidays or destinations which, although included in the catalog for the reasons recalled earlier, have a low probability of sale. To induce the agency to sell the entire range of products, the tour operator may then decide to propose special agreements, usually known as full-line contracts. An example may help understand the rationale of these contracts and how they operate in practice.

A tour operator may decide to produce two similar holidays at the same cost, one to Fiji Islands (F) and the other to Canary Islands (C), to include them in the same catalog, and want to force the travel agency to promote both. The contract in use may set the price at which the tour operator sells the holiday to the travel agency, C_F and C_C respectively, and assume that the agency is free to set the final market price (then, no price ceiling applies to this example). For simplicity, we assume that the agency does not incur in any additional cost when promoting the tour operator's catalog. Finally, suppose that the local market only serves two types of consumers: type A tourists, who have a reservation price equal to $p_F^A = 1,000$ for the holiday to Fiji Islands and equal to $p_C^A = 800$ for the holiday to Canary Islands, and type B tourists, who have a reservation price equal to $p_F^B = 800$ for the holiday to Fiji Islands and $p_C^B = 1,000$ for holiday to Canary Islands.

Should the tour operator propose the contract ($C_F = 1{,}000$, $C_C = 1{,}000$), the travel agency might sell the holiday F to tourists A and the holiday C to tourists B. In such case, while the tour operator's revenue would be equal to 2,000, the agency would make no profit since it is forced to sell at the acquisition price by the constraints expressed by the tourists' reservation prices. Therefore, the travel agency may legitimately decide to lower its level of effort by not promoting the tour operator's production: the travel agency would not worsen its budget, while the tour operator would lose the whole revenue. The contractual agreement has then to be changed, for example to ($C_F = 1{,}000$, $C_C = 800$). However, in this case the travel agency could sell F to type A tourists for 1,000 and C to type B tourists for 1,000, but it would earn the same profit equal to 200 that it would earn by just selling C. In other words, this agreement would not provide an efficient full-line incentive.

To avoid such situation, the tour operator must seek to offer a full-line contract that gives the agency the incentive to fully promote the entire catalog. The contract ($C_F = 800$, $C_C = 800$) would still allow the agency to sell F to type A tourist for 1,000 and C to type B tourists for 1,000, but providing the agency with a profit equal to 400. The tour operator, on the other hand, would see its catalog fully promoted and sold. This last contract would be an efficient agreement in the sense that the tour operator reaches its target to provide the travel agency with a fair incentive to sell its full line. With this contract, the tour operator earns 1,600, which is not as great as it might potentially earn without incentive (1,600 < 2,000), but significantly higher than the case where the agent chooses to offer only one trip (1,600 > 1,000). Ultimately, the full-line contract may be classified as an incentive contract (see Sect. 11.6), allowing the tour operator to earn an intermediate and certain profit (rather than a maximum but uncertain one) because it is not linked to any discretionary decision taken by the travel agency.

11.5.4 Selection Contracts with Hospitality Firms

In Sect. 11.4 we have studied that hotels, by stipulating free sale or allotment contracts, supply accommodation services to tour operators. With the aim of diversifying its catalog, the tour operator should be able to distinguish the hotels on the basis of the price and the quality of its tourism services (facilities, service staff, etc.), thus signing contracts both with budget hotels with unskilled staff in the low-quality segment of package holidays and with luxury hotels run by professional staff in the high-quality segment.

On one hand, it is reasonable to assume that the quality of the hotel may be observable, once the tour operator receives the feedback from tourists; on the other hand, contracts with the hotels must be stipulated well before the holiday takes place. So it may well be the case that the tour operator who does not have knowledge of its suppliers' reputation (or has not received other credible signals about the quality, see Sects. 10.4.2 and 10.4.3) will be unable to distinguish what segment a hotel belongs to. In such circumstances, the tour operator may decide to undertake a selection strategy by proposing a range of different contracts designed to give the hotels an incentive to reveal their type, by letting them choose the most appropriate agreement among the available ones.

For a better understanding of the issue under scrutiny, we assume that hotels are characterized by different average costs, which are a function of quality. Quality is measured through a continuous index q, with average q^*. In particular, high-quality hotels face relatively higher average costs, $C_H(q)$ when they use professional staff to produce low-quality tourism services, $q < q^*$, while low-quality hotels face relatively higher average costs, $C_L(q)$ when they use unskilled staff to deliver high-quality services, $q > q^*$. Therefore, with regards to average-quality service q^* we have that $C_H(q^*) = C_L(q^*)$. Such cost functions, which realistically approximate the cost functions of hotels of different quality, are shown in Fig. 11.2.

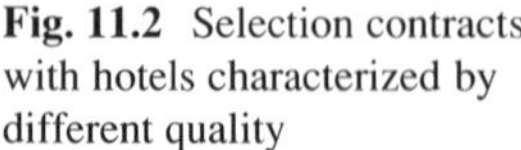

Fig. 11.2 Selection contracts with hotels characterized by different quality

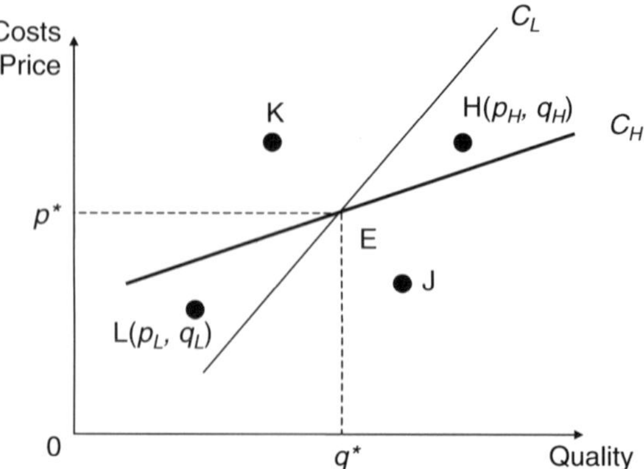

Given that the contract proposed by the tour operator must set both the quality content and the price, each contract can be identified by a specific point (q, p) in Fig. 11.2. The contracts located in the section below both curves, such as at point J, are inefficient because they do not satisfy the participation constraint and are not convenient for any type of hotels: $p < C_i(q)$ for $i = H, L$. The contracts located in the section above both curves, such as at point K, are inefficient because they are not cost-effective for the tour operator, $p > C_i(q)$ for $i = H, L$. Then, contracts of type J and K will not be stipulated.

In order to achieve a selection strategy, the range of different contracts that can be provided by the tour operator is then composed by the contract H and the contract L, respectively, characterized by the combinations (p_H, q_H) and (p_L, q_L) in Fig. 11.2. Then, the hotel with professional staff will reveal its type by accepting contract H, while the hotel with non-professional staff will reveal its type by choosing contract L. It is important to stress that such revelation will be perfectly credible given that the budget hotel would have no economic benefit from accepting the contract characterized by conditions (p_H, q_H), since $p_H < C_L(q)$. The same can be said, on the other hand, with regards to the high-quality hotel, which has no economic benefit from accepting the contract L. In other words, the two contracts H and L are able to segment the tourism market by achieving a separating equilibrium (see Sect. 10.4.2), and the tour operator can safely include in the high-level section of its catalog a hotel that accepts the contract H and in the low-level section a hotel that accepts the contract L.

Instead, should the tour operator offer a unique contract $E(p^*, q^*)$, it would inevitably achieve a pooling equilibrium, given that both hotels would optimally choose to accept the contract. Since by assumption the tour operator does not know the hotel type, it may happen that a hotel with unprofessional staff will be included in the high-quality section of its catalog and vice versa, for low-quality hotels.

By solving another problem of information asymmetry, also the selection contract introduces a cost for the tour operator; in fact, in order for the selection of high-quality hotels to work properly, it is essential that $p_H > p^*$; in other words, only a more generous contract in terms of price offered by the tour operator can credibly reveal the type of the service provider.

11.5.5 The Product Club

Tourism destinations, tour operators, hospitality firms, and other tourism businesses can decide to contractually join a so-called product club, in which a common brand guarantees the tourist to avail of services of a given quality. Once the contractual form (temporary business association, consortium, etc.) and the obligations linked to the club membership have been decided, the agreement must provide a standard depending on the firm's quality and characteristics, with specific indication for the facilities (equipment, spaces, etc.) and set a minimal required level of service. Examples of such associations are those destinations that are inspired by historical events, such as the *Via Francigena* or the *Camino de Santiago*, or the tour operators who adhere to the principles of responsible tourism, as well as the hospitality firms branded as a family hotel, bike hotels, etc.

11.5.5.1 The Creation of the Club

Such associative contracts are voluntarily signed by independent companies and can arise either under a public or a private initiative. In the case of public initiative, additional money or in-kind incentives may be provided to facilitate the aggregation and the coordination between firms. In the case of private initiative, the club may be voluntarily formed when firms evaluate that the benefit of joining the club and developing a common brand exceeds the costs of updating their structure to the required quality standard. The membership is usually cost-effective in terms of purchasing, marketing, communication, etc. and the brand often creates more visibility to the structure.

To understand the economic problem of product clubs in tourism, let us proceed with an example (we refer to Cuccia and Santagata 2004, for a deeper discussion). We assume that in the destination there are two hotels to which the local government, after having assessed the existence of a profit opportunity, suggests the creation of a club (e.g., the "Art Hotel" club) based on a given standard.

The first problem is to assess the degree of quality standard the firm is required to perform in order to accept the contract. Obviously, if the two firms already provide the same quality, there is no problem. However, a more interesting question is whether a difference in the quality level may be compatible with their simultaneous presence in the same club. Suppose that A offers services of higher quality, while B offers services of lower quality. We now must indicate a payoff structure subject to different hypotheses, by assuming that each firm decides independently the membership to the club (i.e., without knowing the choice taken by the other firm). We assume that entering the club will be worth 100 of additional profit and, if both firms subscribe, the profit must take into account an externality, which is positive for firm B, because it gets the benefit of being in a club with the high-quality company, and is negative for firm A, for the opposite reason.

We start by assuming the interesting case of a high value for the externality generated by the coexistence of the two firms in the same club, for example 200, which suggests the existence of a significant gap in the quality they individually offer. We now quantify the payoff associated to the different choices made by the two hotels under the above assumptions.

1. From A's perspective: (a) if A joins the club but B does not, its additional profit will be 100; (b) if also B joins the club, A's profit will drop to -100 (= 100 − 200) due to the negative externality associated to a perceived lower quality; (c) if A does not join there is no extra profit or extra loss generated: A's additional profit is zero.
2. From B's perspective: (a) if B joins the club but A does not, its additional profit will be 100; (b) if also A joins the club, B will benefit from the higher reputation of the club and its profit will increase of 300 (= 100 + 200) due to the positive externality; (c) if B does not join, there is no extra profit or extra loss generated: B's additional profit is zero.

The game's payoff is represented in Table 11.2, where in each cell the first number is the additional profit of A and the second number is the additional profit of B. It is then straightforward to verify that the dominant strategy for B is to join the club, whatever A does, because: $300 > 0$ and $100 > 0$. As a consequence, we can immediately eliminate the last column of the table from the possible results of A. Since in case of B joining the club the best strategy for A is to not join (as 0 is better than -100), this example suggests that a club will not be able to include the two firms of the destination, since A does not accept. A "complete" club would be a viable option only after the low-quality firm B decides to invest in quality improvements, possibly also with the assistance provided by the local government (Gandolfi 2008).

As an alternative scenario, suppose instead that the externality due to the coexistence of the two companies is now very low and equal to 50; this is tantamount to assume a low gap in their qualities. We quantify the payoffs in Table 11.3.

1. From A's perspective: (a) if A joins the club and B does not, its profit will be 100, as in the case above; (b) if B also joins the club, its profit will diminish to 50 (= 100 − 50) due to the negative externality; (c) if A does not join there is no additional profit for an identical reason to that explained earlier.
2. From B's perspective: (a) if B joins the club and A does not, its profit will be 100; (b) if also A joins the club, B will benefit from the higher reputation of the club and its profit will become 150 (= 100 + 50) due to the positive externality; (c) finally, if B does not join, there is no additional profit, for the same reason explained earlier.

From the analysis of Table 11.3 it is then straightforward to verify that the dominant strategy for B is still to join the club, whatever A does, because: $150 > 0$ and $50 > 0$. As before, we can eliminate the last column of the table from the possible results of A and then compare the remaining two alternatives. Unlike in the previous case, however, A chooses to join because $50 > 0$, and the club gets created with the membership of both firms.

Table 11.2 The product club when the firms have a high gap in quality

	Firm B	
Firm A	Join	Do not join
Join	−100; 300	100; 0
Do not join	0; 100	0; 0

Table 11.3 The product club when the firms have a low gap in quality

	Firm B	
Firm A	Join	Do not join
Join	50; 150	100; 0
Do not join	0; 100	0; 0

The conclusion stemming from these two simple yet realistic examples is that the firms agree to participate in the same product club although they do not have the same quality standard; to achieve joint membership it is then sufficient that the dispersion in terms of quality is below a given threshold.

11.5.5.2 The Club's Stability

The creation of the club does not necessarily imply its stability over time. In fact, given that these contracts imply freedom of membership, as the firms voluntarily decide to join the club they are also free to exit. It is then time to discuss whether or not the product club shows instability, due to the existence, for example, of potential opportunistic behaviors by the participating companies. In fact, after joining the club, a firm characterized by a short-term economic horizon might decide to decrease the quality of the service (together with its production costs) with the objective of making higher profits in the short term. Of course, if all firms have such opportunistic behavior, the effect will be to "water down" the qualitative content of the brand (see Sect. 11.7.2). In order to avoid these behaviors, the club may explicitly provide contractual penalties for those companies that are found not to voluntarily meet their contractual obligations. This type of analysis inevitably brings us to the Game Theory approach, with specific reference to repeated games and, in particular, to the Folk Theorem (Cuccia and Santagata 2004).

In order to avoid these theoretical complications, we will prove our statement by simply considering the example of a product club that is already in place, the one named "Art Hotel," and including five hospitality firms which quality, as in the example of Table 11.3, are very similar. We suppose that their quality can be measured according to an index of quality q_i, which respectively takes the values of (10; 11; 12; 13; 14). The quality of the club transmitted to the tourist can then be summarized by the average quality $q_{\mathrm{m}} = 12$, with a guaranteed flexibility of plus or minus two allowed by the contract: $q_{\mathrm{club}} = 12 \pm 2$. Let us also suppose that the club may experience permanent shocks in the production and in the organization of the participating companies which may alter the club's quality.

In case of symmetric shock, for example determined by a multiplicative factor equal to 0.5 that affects all businesses at the same time, the quality of their services will be cut by half to (5; 5.5; 6; 6.5; 7). In this case, the tourists will still perceive the Art Hotel as a club, although of lower quality than before, $q_{\mathrm{m}} = 6 \pm 2$, which will keep it alive but place it at the lower end of the cultural tourism market. In other words, the associative contract is a stable agreement in this case.

If the shock is asymmetric and specifically affects one firm, it would show its effects in different ways. For example, if we assume that the negative shock only hits the lowest quality firm, the quality structure of the club becomes (5; 11; 12; 13; 14). The average quality decreases to $q_{\mathrm{m}} = 11$, and over time the quality of the club will be perceived by the tourist as $q_{\mathrm{club}} = 11 \pm 2$. In such case, if the lowest quality firm is not expelled by the club, the highest quality firm (the one with a quality of 14) will no longer find convenient to stay in the club and will pull out from the contract. Such process of voluntary exit occurs when the shock lowers the club's collective reputation relative to the reputation of one single company, and can have the consequence of further decreasing the quality. In fact, the remaining four members of the club have now quality (5; 11; 12; 13) and the average quality becomes $q_{\mathrm{club}} = 10.25 \pm 2$. In this situation, and for the same reason, the company with quality 13 will no longer find beneficial to belong to the club, and exits. Such process would continue until the firm with quality 11 does also exit the contract. At that point, the whole Art Hotel brand will disappear from the market.

On the contrary, if the asymmetric shock allows a significant improvement in the quality of a firm's service, for example by a multiplicative factor of 1.5 applied to the highest quality firm, this hotel will no longer identify itself with the club's standard and will decide to exit. This process of voluntary exit is usually referred to as higher bound exit and occurs when a firm reaches a level of reputation that is too high in relation to the club's quality. In this way, the Art Hotel club will only include four members (10, 11, 12, 13) which, although it communicates the tourists a lower average quality than before, $q_{\mathrm{club}} = 11.5 \pm 2$, is still a stable club in its new composition.

Therefore, in the case of asymmetric shocks, the problems set out with these two examples are: (a) the intrinsic instability of product clubs; (b) the difficulty in maintaining the target level of quality.

The solutions to these problems must be different depending on the motivation behind the exit of the highest quality firm. In the example of higher bound exit, to maintain a club with all the five members it is necessary that all firms take advantage of the positive asymmetric shock and bear the cost of the investment that is needed to increase their own level of quality. However, it is seldom the case that such a behavior can be prescribed by the club, so it may be necessary to renegotiate the contract or that the destination management offers a subsidy to support the local firms in their investment.

Instead, in the first case above, it may be necessary to stop the "exit process" of high-quality firms by including a contract clause that provides the expulsion of the companies that are no longer able to fulfill the minimum requirements set by the club (lower bound exit). For this purpose, the clause must provide for an obligation to carry out periodic quality checks, which can be either internal or external to the club. Such activity, which can be implemented through policy patrol or fire alarm control (see Sect. 8.2.2), in the business practice usually relies on the so-called *mystery guest*, a person in charge of checking the quality of the service by pretending to be a regular customer. Of course, the monitoring costs must be borne by the product club, either through the destination management if the club is of public initiative or through a private structure if the club is of private initiative. The contract for the product club must then include provisions to help finance the necessary organizational facilities for the promotion and the control of the club itself.

11.6 Information Asymmetry in Incomplete Contracts: The Incentive Contracts

Some of the examples we discussed in this chapter can be traced back to precontractual forms of opportunism, the adverse selection. In this section we will focus instead on the moral hazard problem, which is a postcontractual form of opportunism. This is caused by the fact that some actions may lack observability, in particular when a party (supplier, customer, employee, or market agent) is characterized by objectives that do not completely overlap with those of the other party involved in the contract and by the fact that the first party's behavior cannot be easily verified, so that it may be tempted to turn the execution of the contract to its own full advantage. This party may then find advantageous to perform inefficient (yet inexpensive) actions or to bias the information in its possession. The problem of moral hazard has two basic connotations: (a) the hidden action, that is, to take actions that cannot be completely observed, and (b) the hidden information, that is, the opportunity to not reveal information to the other party.

It is worth recalling that the term "moral hazard" has been first used in the insurance industry to indicate the tendency of the insured agent to act less carefully that it otherwise would: in particular, the insurance contract can induce people to be less careful when adopting precautions to prevent or contain a damage. However, the moral hazard has proved to be a much more general issue and may arise in every circumstance where the economic agents do not fully bear the consequences of their actions or decisions. Such occurrence is extremely common both within organizations and within markets: for example, consider the case of professional services (lawyers, physicians, etc.) or lease contracts (owners are usually more careful in preserving the real-estate property than renters). Moreover, the opportunistic behavior tends to affect the organization of the firm in many respects: for example in the relationship between the employee and the employer or between the manager and the shareholders.

The economic theory tackles the problem of moral hazard mainly through the principal–agent model. This term is used with reference to a contract under which a party (the agent) acts on the behalf of the other party (the principal) with the objective of promoting the interest of the principal. The moral hazard problem, then, arises when the agent and the principal have different objectives and the latter cannot easily observe whether or not the action taken by the former effectively promotes the principal's objective.

The moral hazard arises when three conditions hold.

1. There must be a potential conflict of interest between individuals. In fact, individual interests are not always conflicting, or conflicts do not always cover all dimensions of the transaction.
2. There must be reasons to justify the mutual advantage stemming from the transaction, but the agreement must also leave room for the conflict of objectives provided subpoint 1.
3. There must be information asymmetry, for which it is difficult to ascertain whether the terms of the contract are fully complied with. In other words, the direct observation of the actions and the verification of the information must be particularly difficult.

The simultaneous occurrence of the three conditions implies a market failure: since complete contracts cannot be enforced, the market does not attain efficiency. This raises the issue of finding alternative solutions or new contractual forms to deal with moral hazard.

The first remedy is directly suggested by condition (3), and consists of increasing the resources devoted to audits and inspections, but this solution is not always viable and is often not cost-effective. Alternatively, under some circumstances it is possible to ask for the payment of a deposit to guarantee the provision of the service. The deposit consists of a sum which will be retained (or required) in the event that an inappropriate behavior is discovered. On the one hand, the payment of a deposit may represent a very effective means to create the desired incentive, but it may display the side effect that its enforcement can result in long-lasting and expensive legal suits. Finally, as an extreme solution, the moral hazard may be solved by replacing the agent, although it is easy to understand that this may not always be possible and, in some cases, it may be an expensive solution.

In the majority of cases, the solution to the moral hazard problem might stem from the existing relationship between the observation of the outcomes and the behavior of the agent, in order to provide appropriate contractual incentives to reward the effort. For example, if it were impossible to directly monitor the effort and the care exerted by the seller when dealing with its customers, it would still be reasonable to control its activity by monitoring the amount of sales and the rate of change over time. In fact, if there were a fully deterministic relationship between the effort and the amount of sales, a payment based on revenue would be a perfect substitute for a remuneration system based on the effort exerted and on degree of customer care.

Unfortunately, a perfect correspondence between latent actions and observed outcomes is rare in practice. More often, the individual behavior only partially determines the outcome, as it is impossible to isolate the impact of other external factors, which are not under the agent's control. Therefore, a remuneration system focused on the amount of sales exposes the agent's income to fluctuations due to random and uncontrollable factors. However, since most people are risk averse and the incentive contract exposes the agent to a higher level of risk, it becomes necessary for the principal to pay the agent a remuneration that on average is higher, in order to make the latter be willing to accept the risk. Finally, from the principal's perspective, the higher remuneration to be paid represents a cost. The design of an efficient incentive contract must then balance the higher performance for the principal with the higher costs borne to remunerate the higher level of risk borne by the agent.

Principal–agent problems are common in the tourism sector where, as already been stated, the information asymmetries are quite strong, both on the demand and on the supply side, with particular reference to two typical relationships. The first one is the relationship between the tour operator and the travel agency, while the second one is the relationship between the travel agency (or the tour operator) and the hotel (or other service providers).

Tour operators regulate their relationship with travel agencies mainly through the market, and contractual arrangements arise from the mutual convenience to cooperate, since both firms gain from increasing sales and the number of customers. However, there is a potential conflict of interest because the cost borne by the tour operator for the execution of the contract only depends on the commission paid to the agency, while the costs borne by the agency depend on the intensity of marketing efforts aimed at promoting the tour operator's catalog. Moreover, there is the practical impossibility for the tour operator to check the effort exerted by the travel agency: the simple observation of the amount of sales cannot be taken as a good proxy since sales also depend on many other factors and unpredictable events. What the tour operator cannot observe, then, is the intensity of sale effort undertaken by the agency, which may take the form of postcontractual opportunism classifiable as a "hidden action."

Similarly, tour operators (and travel agencies) usually sign contracts with the hospitality firms to avail of their services for own customers. These contracts also stem from the mutual advantage of cooperation between tourism firms, but the quality of accommodation services (on which the degree of tourists' satisfaction is mainly based) depends on the cost of investment in quality borne by the hotel. Since the hotel may conceal from the tour operator its private information on customer satisfaction, the specific form of postcontractual opportunism for this contract can be classified as "hidden information."

There are many solutions to this issue. For example, in the case of hidden information, an attempt can be made to increase the effectiveness of the agency's (or the tour operator's) control activity, by introducing more competition between sources of information. The travel agency may seek to obtain information on the quality of the accommodation service by directly submitting questionnaires to the customers. Moreover, the mystery guest can work quite well (see Sect. 11.5.5). An extreme solution to overcome the problem is to replace the agent with the principal itself: in this case the tour operator would directly manage its own travel agency or tourism facility, by so undergoing vertical integration (see Sect. 10.2).

If these solutions are technically impossible to implement or are not cost-effective, the incentive contract remains the only viable option. We will devote Sect. 11.6.1 to the analysis of the contents and the effect of such contract, by limiting our discussion to the typical case of the relationship between the tour operator and the travel agency. The other cases can easily be sorted out by analogy.

11.6.1 The Principal–Agent Model

We analyze the principal–agent model by discussing the relationship between a tour operator and a travel agency. The latter can affect the amount of sales by increasing its own level of commitment, care, and effort when promoting the tour operator's catalog on the retail market, but sales also depend on many other factors that are not under the agency control, such as the business cycle, international geo-political crises, fads and fashions affecting the demand and, last but not least, climate conditions. By only looking at sales, the tour operator (who cannot afford to spend its entire time by monitoring the agency effort) cannot establish whether a given outcome is due to the skills and effort of the agency or to other external environmental factors. Instead, the tour operator must come up with an incentive rule in the contract to enforce (under different environmental conditions) the agency's effort and care, with the goal of ensuring itself (the principal) the best result. In other words, the contract should allow the tour operator to optimally manage the double problem of information uncertainty (on the external conditions of demand) and information asymmetry (on the agency's effort).

We address this problem by using the following example. We assume that the travel agency's revenue depends both on the level of own effort and on external environmental conditions. For simplicity we assume that four possible external events can occur and that each state of nature (1, 2, 3, and 4) has the same probability of occurrence ($q_i = 0.25$, for $i = 1, 2, 3, 4$). Moreover, the agent can decide to exert two different levels of effort (action), high and low, respectively A_H and A_L. Table 11.4 shows that the agency's revenue stems from the combination of the state of nature that may occur and the level of effort exerted. To start with, we suppose that there is a favorable event (say, state 1) where, thanks to the positive phase of the economic cycle, sales reach the high value of 50,000 regardless of the agency's effort. Moreover, we assume that there are two states of the world where the economic crisis (state 2) or the outbreak of a conflict in the tourism destination (state 4) negatively affect the sales, which only reach the value of 25,000. Finally, there is a state of the world (state 3) where, under ordinary demand conditions, the degree of commitment and effort of the agency affects the sales: if the agency's effort is high, A_H, the sales reach 50,000, while if the effort is low, A_L, the sales are only 25,000.

Table 11.4 allows an immediate comment: on average, the agency's effort is profitable, since the expected value of sales increases with it (on the last column of Table 11.4, 37,500 > 31,250). However, the sales distribution is related to the

Table 11.4 The revenue structure of the travel agency in the principal–agent model

	1	2	3	4	Expected value
A_H	50,000	25,000	50,000	25,000	37,500
A_L	50,000	25,000	25,000	25,000	31,250

intensity of the agency's effort and the amount of revenue remains a stochastic variable: for example, by simply observing that sales can either be 25,000 or 50,000, the tour operator is unable to tell which action has been taken by the agency. And since by assumption the tour operator cannot directly observe neither the state of nature nor the agency's effort, it cannot distinguish the case in which the agency is good (or bad) from that in which it is just lucky (or unlucky).

The tour operator's problem, then, is to find a contractual structure ensuring at the same time the highest profit for itself conditionally to provide the correct incentive to induce the best effort for the agency. In other words, the agency that is extremely diligent yet unsuccessful (in states 2 and 4) should not be penalized and the agency that is lucky (state of nature 1) should not be rewarded. In order to formalize the problem, we assume that the travel agency is risk-averse and its preferences are represented by a utility function that positively depends on its remuneration, W, and negatively depends on the level of effort being exerted (which implies a cost borne by the agent):

$$U(W, A) = \sqrt{W} - A, \quad \text{with} \quad A = A_H, A_L \tag{11.16}$$

Assume also that the index measuring the effort can take the following two values: $A_H = 20$ and $A_L = 5$. Given the level of income, hence, the agency would always benefit from exerting the low effort A_L, as this guarantees a higher level of utility. It is also assumed that the agency has the ability to stipulate contracts with other competing tour operators so that the best of these opportunities will offer a level of utility equal to 120, $U^\circ = 120$. This constitutes the participation constraint for the agency.

We also assume that the tour operator (the principal in our model) is risk-neutral: its utility function solely depends on the amount of profit obtained from sales. If we abstract from all other costs, the tour operator's profit is the difference between the sales revenue X (which may take the values of 25,000 or 50,000) and the remuneration W that the tour operator pays to the agent:

$$\pi_{\text{TO}} = (X - W). \tag{11.17}$$

Then the tour operator's problem is to maximize π_{TO}, and this can be done by: (a) encouraging the agency to exert the maximum level of effort, because this maximizes the value if X in (11.17); (b) minimizing the remuneration of the agency, as this strategy decreases W in (11.17). Since it is in the tour operator's interest to stipulate the contract with the agency but, at the same time, the contract requires the agency to choose the costly action (high effort), there are two constraints that must hold:

1. The contract must allow the expected utility for the agent to be at least equal to the best alternative on the market U° (this condition is called the "participation constraint")
2. The contract must be designed to induce the agent to choose the effort A_H, because this is what the principal finds beneficial (such condition is known as "relative incentives constraint")

The problem can be solved by treating as unknowns the remuneration to be paid by the tour operator to the agent when sales are respectively 50,000, W_{50}, and the remuneration to be paid when sales are 25,000, W_{25}, and where $E(.)$ represents the expected utility derived from sales in the two cases:

$$\begin{aligned} &\max \pi_{\mathrm{TO}} = (X - W) \\ &\text{s.t.}\, E(U(W), A_H) \geq 120 \\ &E(U(W), A_H) > E(U(W), A_L) \end{aligned} \quad . \tag{11.18}$$

To fully understand the problem under imperfect information, which we have just introduced, we start by discussing the extreme case of perfect information, where the agency's effort is directly observable.

11.6.1.1 The Agency's Action Is Directly Observable (Perfect Information)

In the extreme case where there is no information uncertainty, the state of the world would be observable by both parties. Then, by comparing the information about the state of the world with the data on sales, the tour operator would precisely know the degree of effort exerted by the agency. Hence, the tour operator can force the agency to undertake the behavior that maximizes its own profit. In this case, it can easily be verified that is always in the tour operator's interest to induce the agency to exert the effort A_H, so that W is solely determined by the minimum value of the participation constraint:

$$\sqrt{W} - 20 = 120$$

from which the solution is

$$W = 19{,}600. \tag{11.19}$$

Thus, the risk is entirely borne by the tour operator, but such solution is efficient because the tour operator is assumed to be risk-neutral. In fact, the expected profit would be

$$E(\pi_{\mathrm{TO}}) = 37{,}500 - 19{,}600 = 17{,}900. \tag{11.20}$$

11.6.1.2 The Agency's Action Is Not Directly Observable (Imperfect Information)

In this case, the agency's effort is not directly observable. To solve this problem, we must first calculate the travel agency's expected utility for both levels of effort, by taking (11.16) for the different remunerations and weigh them by the probabilities presented in Table 11.4.

$$\begin{array}{ll}\text{If } A = A_H, & \text{we have } E(U(W), A_H) = 0.5(W_{50})^{0.5} + 0.5(W_{25})^{0.5} - 20 \\ \text{If } A = A_L, & \text{we have } E(U(W), A_L) = 0.25(W_{50})^{0.5} + 0.75(W_{25})^{0.5} - 5.\end{array} \quad (11.21)$$

Then, the tour operator must solve the standard maximization model (11.18), which can be rewritten so as to minimize the expected compensation to be paid to the agency for inducing the effort A_H and where the probabilities used to calculate the expected payment are those presented in the first row of Table 11.4:

$$\begin{array}{l}\min[0.5(W_{50}) + 0.5(W_{25})] \\ \text{s.t. } E(U(W), A_H) \geq 120 \\ E(U(W), A_H) > E(U(W), A_L)\end{array}.$$

The two conditions are, respectively, the participation constraint and the relative incentive constraint. By substituting the first constraint into the second and using (11.21), we can solve the problem thus finding:

$$W_{50} = 28,900; \quad W_{25} = 12,100. \quad (11.22)$$

Such a contract allows the tour operator to solve the incentive problem, since it offers the travel agency a payment that makes convenient to exert the maximum effort. At the same time, according to (11.22), the tour operator expected profit is

$$E(\pi_{\text{TO}}) = 0.5(50,000 - 28,900) + 0.5(25,000 - 12,100) = 17,000. \quad (11.23)$$

It should be noted that, in the case characterized by imperfect information, the solution without incentive would not be optimal. In fact, with a fixed payment that is independent of the amount of sales, the agency would minimize its sales effort, as this would maximize (11.16). Then, if we rewrite the problem for the case $A = A_L$, the value of W can be determined by only calculating the minimum value for the participation condition:

$$\sqrt{W} - 5 = 120$$

from which the solution is

$$W = 15,625. \quad (11.24)$$

However, it is straightforward to show that such strategy is not optimal for the tour operator, since its expected profit is

$$E(\pi_{\text{TO}}) = 31,250 - 15,625 = 15,625. \tag{11.25}$$

If we compare the profit of these various cases we can make a couple of interesting and useful remarks. Firstly, by comparing the profits calculated in (11.20), (11.23), and (11.25), we see that the condition of perfect information would be the first best for the tour operator, since the expected profit would be equal to 17,900. Under imperfect information, the contract without incentives would be the worst outcome, allowing the tour operator to earn an expected profit of only 15,625. Then, to improve from such a third best, the tour operator is forced to introduce an incentive contract, under which the expected profit is equal to 17,000, definitely a second best for the tour operator.

Secondly, under information asymmetry with incentive contract, the tour operator earns on average 900 (= 17,900 − 17,000) less than under perfect information. Such a difference corresponds to what the principal must transfer to the agent in order to compensate for the higher effort to be exerted, and therefore represents the risk premium paid to the agency to bear the risk associated with A_H. In fact, with such contract, the travel agency's income not only depends on the external environmental conditions but also on the effort. Even in this case, the general principle that "information has a cost" holds: were the tour operator able to set up a monitoring system of the agency's effort that employs resources at a cost lower than 900, it would be profitable to implement it; however, if the monitoring system becomes too expensive, it would be better to stipulate an incentive contract.

Thirdly, note that, despite the simplicity of our example, the structure of this incentive contract is exactly what is used in the business practice, where it can be configured as a contract with a progressive commission on sales. In the above example, the contract would set a 57.8 % commission rate (= 28,900/50,000) if sales are 50,000, and a 48.4 % commission rate (= 12,100/25,000) if sales are 25,000. The difference between the two commissions automatically solves the moral hazard problem with respect to the perfect information condition, under which it is sufficient for the tour operator to set a 52.3 % commission rate (= 19,600/37,500), which is intermediate between the other two rates.

11.6.2 From the Contract to the Organization

A mutually beneficial agreement is a necessary precondition for a contract that aims at dealing with a market relationship. However, in this section we have seen that the postcontractual opportunism and the existence of private information can make very difficult the agreement to be reached. The same issue can also be seen from the perspective of transaction costs, which are always incurred when trying to reach any mutually acceptable agreement (see Sect. 7.3). Incomplete contracts impose transaction costs even in the absence of any strategic behavior by the parties: it takes time and commitment to figure out and list all the possible events that can occur, to determine the actions to be carried out in each circumstance, to distinguish between costs and benefits, to ensure (also by relying on external authorities) the effective enforcement of a commitment, and, finally, to deal with inefficiencies stemming from the need to hedge against the inherent risks of an incomplete contract. In the presence of private information, there are other costs that may be relevant, up to the point of preventing the achievement of the agreement or of significantly delaying its implementation, even if there are mutual gains that can be achieved through the transaction.

In the previous subsection, we discussed the possibility of providing contractual arrangements that can be efficient, at least in the "relative sense," even though this often leads to great transaction costs. Under some particular conditions, such costs may be avoided by bringing the transaction under the control of just one firm. In other words, the inefficiencies of the tourism market may disappear if tourism firms vertically integrate: in this case, there would be no need to define a contract to deal with the market transaction, there would no longer be issues associated to the imperfect ability to bind, and the noise associated to the existence of private information would disappear. We have already discussed this solution in Sect. 7.3, when studying the birth of a tourism firm; we will discuss again about the same topic in Sect. 14.2.2, when focusing on multinational companies. Such a solution, however, inevitably creates other difficulties: for example, even if a tour operator chooses to directly handle the hospitality sector, it may be the case that it does not have the time and/or expertise to manage a hotel. In that case, it may decide to hire a management team and, again for reasons of time or expertise, it may not be able to judge the quality of their performance. And this situation would re-introduce the problem of postcontractual opportunism of the management team, who might not work as hard as the tour operator would be willing to. To summarize, both possibilities, contract or organization, albeit in different forms, may show similar problems of information asymmetry and opportunistic behavior.

11.7 The Contracts with the Tourism Destination

We end this chapter by discussing a few problems (and their contractual solutions) which mainly concern the relationship between the tour operator and the tourism destination.

11.7.1 Specific Investments and Long-Term Contracts

Tourism firms and the destination management organization might need to sign contracts in order to develop a specific tourism product or a new tourism attraction, both cases where large investments are usually needed. An interesting case of incomplete contract is the so-called specific investment (Klein et al. 1978). An investment is specific if its value is greater within the relationship between the contracting parties rather than in any external context. In other words, once the investment has been undertaken, its cost cannot be fully recovered outside the contract. The specificity of an investment is indeed measured by the percentage of its cost that is sunk if the project is not completed. As an example, the facilities and the infrastructures of a seaside resort cannot be moved outside the tourism destination in which they were originally built. The main economic problem arising with a specific investment is that much of its success depends on the parties' conduct, and the possibility of opportunistic behavior may endanger the profitability of the investment.

In this section, we consider the case involving a specific investment undertaken by the tour operator in a site made available by the destination. We will determine the optimal contractual form, the long-term contract, to be signed by the tour operator and the managers, either public or private, of the tourism destination. Let us assume that the destination is characterized by a natural attraction, a beautiful beach that is suitable for the development of a seaside resort which might be included in the tour operator's catalog. To do so, the tour operator must undertake some specific investments in the destination, for example to provide a fully equipped beach and accommodation structures. An investment of this kind is totally specific, since there is no way to eventually use it elsewhere. However, once the investment is made, it is supposed to generate an income that must be somehow shared between the two parties: the tour operator (providing the facilities) and the destination (providing the territory).

To begin with, we consider that the parties rely on a normal contract according to which the local authorities agree to make the land available for the project and the tour operator agrees to undertake the investment. The simplest hypothesis is that total income generated by the investment is shared in two equal parts. Let, for example, the total investment be equal to 10,000 and the overall present value of the total income generated in the future equal to 18,000. Should the contract provide a fifty–fifty division of total revenue, the parties would receive the following payment:

- The tourism destination would receive an income equal to: $R_{\mathrm{D}} = 18{,}000/2 = 9{,}000$.
- The tour operator would receive an income equal to: $R_{\mathrm{TO}} = 18{,}000/2 - 10{,}000 = -1{,}000$.

Obviously, under such conditions, the investment will not be implemented, since the tour operator's profit turns out to be negative. This translates into the missed opportunity of a mutually profitable project, since the overall income, net of the investment cost, is positive: $8{,}000 = 18{,}000 - 10{,}000$. It is therefore in the local authority's interests to think about a different contract for the tour operator.

The investment's goal can be achieved by signing a long-term contract, i.e., a contract that includes the explicit indication of the price at which the resource to be used has been granted. In our specific case, the long-term contract would include as clauses: (a) the specification of the price p^* at which the tour operator purchases the right to use the beach; (b) the tour operator's commitment to build the resort. In our case, the long-term contract would determine the price p^* to be paid for the right to use the beach when the net revenue (and not the total revenue) is shared:

- The tourism destination would receive an income equal to $R_D = p^*$ for granting the permission to use the beach.
- The tour operator would receive an income equal to $R_{TO} = 18{,}000 - 10{,}000 - p^*$.

Under the fifty–fifty condition, which can be written as $R_D = R_{TO}$ and hence $p^* = 18{,}000 - 10{,}000 - p^*$, the solution is $p^* = 4{,}000$. In our simple example, this amount represents the profit for the tour operator that undertakes the investment and the rent for the destination providing the area where to develop the resort.

It is important to keep in mind that other arrangements are also possible and sometimes it is difficult for the parties to agree on long-term contracts, since there are many transaction costs to be borne for their stipulation. The typical costs that tend to increase with the length of the agreement are: (a) the possibility that the identity of the contracting parties may change over time, for example if the tour operator is purchased by another company or if the local government politically changes; (b) the definition of the time horizon in which the price remains fixed (to overcome this difficulty, the long-term contract may contain a readjustment clause for p^*, which automatically adjusts to changes, for example, in the consumer price index); (c) the possibility that in the long term new and better opportunities may arise, and either party may feel locked in the agreement.

11.7.2 The Contract for Joint Investments

Two investments are said to be joint if their maximum profitability is reached when they are undertaken together, while losing most of their value when they are undertaken separately. A typical example of joint investment is the tourism exploitation of an island that requires the construction of an airport by the local authority and of a resort by the tour operator. Differently from the case discussed in Sect. 11.7.1, in this case both parties have to undertake investments.

To shed light on the economic problem arising from joint investments we use an example. For the sake of simplicity, we assume that both parties commit to a high quality investment which cost is denoted as C_{TO} for the tour operator and C_D for the destination, and such that $C_{TO} = C_D = 2{,}000$. Such high-quality investment would correspond to meeting the international standards for the tourism resort, by part of the tour operator, and to ensuring the possibility that big aircrafts of international airlines can land in the airport, by part of the destination management. The total revenue accruing from the project is assumed to be 6,000, with a revenue for each of the operators equal to 3,000 and, hence, an individual profit equal to 1,000 $(= 3{,}000 - 2{,}000)$. The payoffs of the two parties are represented in Table 11.5, where the first number in each cell indicates the profit for the destination, while the second number indicates the profit for the tour operator. When both high-quality

Table 11.5 The pay-off matrix in the case of joint investments

	Tour operator	
Destination management	Low-quality services	High-quality services
Low-quality services	0; 0	1,500; −500
High-quality services	−500; 1,500	1,000; 1,000

investments are undertaken, the payoff is represented in the bottom-right cell of the table.

Since the investment profitability depends on costly actions that are undertaken after the contract is signed, we have to allow for the possibility of ex post opportunism by the parties. This could be the case, for example, when either parties decide to build a low-quality structure or infrastructure rather than the supposed high-quality one. As an alternative to their contractual behavior, we therefore assume that each party may undertake the opportunistic action to offer a low-quality service. The low-quality investment costs, respectively C'_{D} and C'_{TO}, can be normalized to zero for simplicity (for example, the destination does not build the new airport but continues to use the existing yet insufficient airport, and the tour operator uses the existing poor-quality facilities). In such case, however, international tourists will not buy the holiday and the total revenue (and profit of both agents) will be zero. The payoff for this case is represented in the top-left cell of the table.

Moreover, we can assume that the opportunistic behavior is taken by only one contractor. For example, the tour operator may decide to complete the high-quality resort while the local authority decides not to build the new airport. Hence, $C_{\mathrm{TO}} = 2{,}000; C'_{\mathrm{D}} = 0$ and we can realistically assume that only a small proportion of tourists (the more adventurous ones) would decide to buy the holiday, so to generate a total revenue, say, equal to 3,000. This case is represented in the top-right cell of Table 11.5: the profit for the tour operator is $\pi_{\mathrm{TO}} = -500$ (= 3,000/2 − 2,000), while the profit for the destination is $\pi_{\mathrm{D}} = 1{,}500$ (= 3,000/2 − 0).

Finally, in the symmetric case, the tour operator does not undertake any investment while the local authority decides to build the new airport: in this case $C'_{\mathrm{TO}} = 0$; $C_{\mathrm{D}} = 2{,}000$. Again, we assume that only a share of potential tourists will buy the holiday, and that the total revenue would be equal to 3,000. In this last case, which is represented in the bottom-left cell of Table 11.5, the profit for the tour operator and for the destination are, respectively, $\pi_{\mathrm{TO}} = 1{,}500$ (= 3,000/2 − 0) and $\pi_{\mathrm{D}} = -500$ (= 3,000/2 − 2,000).

Table 11.5 displays the typical payoff structure of the prisoner's dilemma, the most famous strategic game, where only a mutual high-quality investment choice can provide the best outcome and where the occurrence of opportunistic behavior is expressed in the fact that if one party does not fulfill its commitment, but the other does, the one who cheats (by avoiding to bear some costs) will retain a higher profit.

Clearly, if the parties could fully commit to their actions they would certainly agree on the high-quality investment, as it represents the combination that generates the best outcome for each of the parties (it is the Pareto-efficient equilibrium). But what if such commitment is not binding? After the contract is signed, the destination management might feel the strategic convenience to deliver a low-quality airport service, given that such action would bring the highest profit whatever is the action taken by the other party.[3] In the same way, the tour operator might feel the strategic convenience to provide a low-quality hospitality service, whatever is the action taken by the destination management. Thus, both players have the dominant strategy to behave opportunistically, by offering a low-quality service. Hence, the combination of opportunistic behaviors would lead to a zero profit for both, namely an outcome that none of the ex ante contracting parties would have agreed upon.

This is the standard conclusion for the prisoner's dilemma, according to which the resulting Nash equilibrium from this game is inefficient. However, the rationale of this game leads to a further conclusion: since the parties who plan joint investments are not obliged to sign the contract and, if the parties are able to predict the perverse outcome of the opportunistic behavior, they could conclude that such threat may completely offset the incentive to invest and no agreement may take place.

In the presence of joint investments, it is therefore necessary to agree on different contractual forms. A possible solution may require that the same party, for example the multinational tour operator, is responsible to implement both investments, by then paying a price for purchasing (or renting) the land needed to build the resort and the airport. Such solution would fall within the range of the long-term contract that we discussed in Sect. 11.7.1. However, such a solution is not always feasible and another possibility may require the parties to be committed by non-contractual means (but still in the interests of both) which, to be credible, give rise to additional costs.

Finally, we recall that one of the key elements of these contractual agreements deals with the reputation of not behaving opportunistically, a reputation that each party might have built in the past (see Sect. 10.4.3). Such reputation, however, usually depends on the frequency of the agreements over time, their time horizon, and their mutual profitability. The incentives to build and keep a high level of reputation are stronger the more frequent and more profitable are the transactions.

Chapter Overview

- Different types of contracts can efficiently solve problems of choice under uncertainty, information asymmetry, opportunistic behavior, and all those occurrences that generate contractual incompleteness. Uncertainty and information asymmetry are crucial aspects of incomplete contracts since they might lead to pre- and postcontractual opportunistic behaviors.

[3] In case of delivering low-quality services, the profit for the destination would be zero (which is better than −500) if the tour operator delivers low-quality services and 1,500 (which is better than 1,000) if the tour operator delivers high-quality services.

- The individual choice under uncertainty conditions depends on the probability assigned to the occurrence of stochastic events and on the individual propensity, neutrality, or aversion to risk. To hedge against the risk, fixed and flexible insurance contracts can be stipulated by tourism firms and by tourists.
- The forward contract is stipulated at time t, when the price is agreed upon, for the delivery of a good or service at time $t + k$. The forward contract is pure if the price is paid at $t + k$; it is anticipated if the price is paid at time t. The reservation of a tourism service is a forward contract.
- Tour operators can stipulate free sale contracts (in which they perform an insurance function with respect to risk-averse service providers) or allotment contracts (in which they can avail of the option, at a later date, to release or to confirm the booked services) with firms providing tourism services.
- Contracts with price ceilings, exclusive contracts, full-line contracts, selection contracts, product clubs, incentive contracts are all contracts that efficiently deal with market failures stemming from opportunistic behaviors of the parties.
- Two investments are defined joint investments if their efficiency is maximum when undertaken together, while losing much of their profitability when implemented separately; this condition leads to the "prisoner's dilemma," and solutions might be long-term contracts, binding commitments, or reputation.

Chapter 12
The Information and Communication Technology and the Tourism Sector

Learning Outcomes
After reading this chapter, you will understand:

- The key features and peculiarities of the so-called bit economy.
- The impact of information and communication technology on the organization of tourism markets, firms, destinations, and tourists.

12.1 Introduction

As every other aspect of everyday life and socioeconomic relationships, also tourism is crossed, and sometimes deeply affected, by the evolution of a complex system of phenomena that in the common language can be defined as Internet Revolution, New Economy, Information Technology (IT), Information and Communication Technology (ICT), etc. Without entering in specific topics pertaining to the Economics of Information or to the Science & Technology debate, in this chapter we will simply try to understand if and how the economic problem and rationale of tourism firms, tourists, and destinations are affected by what certainly is a momentous change in the organization of our society:

> Some observers have gone so far as to put the Information Revolution on a par with the Industrial Revolution. Just as the Industrial Revolution transformed the way goods were produced, distributed and consumed, the Information Revolution is transforming the way information is produced, distributed and consumed.
>
> (Varian 1996, p. 590)

The ICT has a relevant impact in financial and accounting management, in marketing, in the organization of firms, in public administration, and in the decision process of consumers. All this modifies the way in which economic institutions (firms, markets, households) interact. Such changes are also of concern for the tourism sector which, indeed, always had a preferential relationship with the new

G. Candela and P. Figini, *The Economics of Tourism Destinations*, Springer Texts in Business and Economics, DOI 10.1007/978-3-642-20874-4_12,

technologies: consider, for example, the importance of the Computer Reservation System (CRS, it will be discussed below) for the travel industry. The CRS dates back to the 1950s and its use is widespread in the 1970s and the 1980s, well before the Internet revolution.

In this chapter, we will focus on two specific aspects: the first one is to check whether or not the ICT has modified the economic rationale of economic agents (firms and households), that is, the way in which they take decisions and interact on the market; the second aspect is to check the impact of ICT on the organization and strategies of tourism firms, tourists, and destinations.

The fundamental conclusion, which is worth to anticipate, is that ICT does not alter the main paradigms of Economics. As Varian (1996) clearly reminds us, Economics deals with economic agents and their behavior; whether they deal with goods, services, or "information bits" is not relevant for the economic theory. Except a few marginal adjustments due to the particular features of the information good, the same rationale that Economics uses to explain the production, distribution, and consumption of generic goods can be applied to study how information is produced and distributed. As an example, the cost-effectiveness of ICT can be considered as the outcome of any other innovation process and then tackled by the same models that explain the investment of firms in research and development. Coherently with this perspective, this chapter is full of cross-references to other chapters, to highlight how and where the ICT affects the functioning of the tourism sector and the behavior of firms and tourists.

In the previous chapters we highlighted many times the importance of information for tourism, both for the nature of experience good of many tourism services and for the additional costs that firms and tourists have to bear due to the asymmetry and uncertainty of information. We have not dealt yet, if not marginally, with information as the object of the market transaction, with its own production costs and distribution channels, which mainly go through a network. In Sect. 12.2 we will then touch upon the key aspects of the Economics of Information, a branch of the Economics that studies the production, distribution, and consumption of information, as well as its market structure. In Sect. 12.3, we will analyze more specific aspects of the relationship between ICT and tourism, by distinguishing the impact that the Information Revolution is having on tourists, firms, and destinations, and by focusing on the consequences for both the package tourism and the self-organized tourism.

12.2 The Economic Impact of Internet

As already stated in the introduction to this chapter, the Information Revolution does not upset the way in which economists approach the object of their study: the paradigm of economic rationality for the agents holds, regardless of their being consumers, producers, or the public sector. However, the rise of Internet is not neutral to the economic thinking, since this type of technological progress has been allowing to increase the amount of information being produced and consumed, bringing down its price at the same time. Then, the information appears as an important argument both in the production function and in the utility function, becoming a relevant theoretical factor and an object of transaction in the market.

To start with, let us describe what the ICT is. Firstly, we have to distinguish between: (a) ICT infrastructures, mainly the network used to transfer information and that is composed of hardware (cables, servers, aerials, etc.) and software (protocols and standards allowing the communication between the different network nodes); (b) ICT services and applications that account for a more efficient and user friendly backup and transfer of information (databases, search engines, Internet browsers, Content Management Systems, mobile phones applications, etc.); (c) information *tout court*, the content that is transferred through the network.

A key feature of ICT is then the network, which might be understood as a *third way*, alternative to the market and the firm, to undertake economic and social relations. To properly work, the network needs a high degree of coordination and cooperation between the subjects that compose it (the nodes, or hubs) but, in general terms, one can affirm that the economic system and the economic theory hold against the assault of the "new economy," in the sense that, as Varian et al. (2004) state, the key concepts and tools of analysis of Economics are not modified by the Internet revolution.

> Some scholars affirm the need of having a new Economics to understand the bit economy. I am indeed skeptic. The old economic theory – at least its toolbox – still works very well. Many effects generated by the new information economy can be interpreted within the framework of the old industrial economy – to understand the new we then know where to look at.
>
> (Varian et al. 2004, p. 13)

However, Varian himself affirms that the ICT has been producing many interesting changes in the way economists think and in the topics discussed by Economics. In particular, phenomena that were marginal in the old economy have become important, while previously fundamental issues have been relegated to the margin. In particular, the development of information networks has been changing both the internal organization of firms (through a process of decentralization of many decisions and the more widespread use of cooperation strategies, which are relatively more efficient in a network environment) and the market structure. It can be useful, then, to reshuffle the economic tools on the shelf by sorting them in a different way (Maggioni and Merzoni 2002).

We will proceed in this way. Firstly, we will focus on the relevant economic effects of ICT on markets, firms, and consumers; secondly we will discuss upon their relevance with respect to the economic theory. Then, in Sect. 12.3, we will apply this discussion to the tourism markets.

12.2.1 Information and Communication Technology, New Strategies, and Market Effects

The relevant economic aspects linked to the development of ICT can be classified as follows.

1. *Internet as a combinatorial innovation*. Varian interprets the ICT boom of the 1990s and the 2000s as a phenomenon of combinatorial innovation, that is, an innovation based on a few simple component technologies that can be combined and recombined in so many different ways to produce (or self-produce) a very high number of new products. Since the concept of combinatorial innovation is not new in Economics (Schumpeter 1934; Weitzman 1998), the Internet boom is just the recognition as more frequent of a property that, in the past, was a characteristic of big innovations only.
2. The *redefinition of property rights*. The definition of the property rights becomes a critical issue for "digital goods," that is, goods and services that can be transferred as digital files. The economic theory justifies the existence of laws on royalties and patents as economic incentives to remunerate the activity of investment in research, development, and creativity. Notwithstanding, the diffusion of digital goods has been generating many and new issues of protection of property rights. On the one hand, the strengthening in the definition of property rights of the last few years is going along with an increasing difficulty in the enforcement of the laws and in the protection of such rights, in an age when so many digital goods can easily be transferred over the net (perhaps, even this book). On the other hand, new forms of definition and protection of property rights are being introduced, as the copyleft, a form of licensing in which the author grants to everyone the permission to copy, distribute, or modify the product, only requiring that any resulting copies or adaptations are also bound by the same licensing agreement, that is, they have to be freely available to the public. In this case, the software becomes open source and the traditional limitations of the copyright are strongly limited, if not eliminated.[1] The open source products are another example of the combinatorial innovation subpoint (1), whereas a public good such as the information is able to be efficiently produced by the private sector (the community of developers) regardless of the characteristics of non-excludibility and non-rivalry of the good itself (see Sect. 15.2).

[1] The contrast between *copyleft* and *copyright* pivots around a pun on the double meaning of left and right, where politically the word "right" is associated to a more individualistic and free-oriented economic ideology and the word "left" is instead associated with a more heterodox and communitarian vision of the economic relationships. On these topics, a very interesting literature is flourishing and many scholars affirm that, contrarily to what Varian affirms, these forms of economic experimentation can bring a revolution into the fundamental paradigm of the economic action (Figini 2008).

3. The *structure of production costs*. Low fixed costs and increasing marginal costs are the normal structure of production costs for the manufacturing firms, while the ICT firm has a different cost structure: high fixed costs and very low marginal costs, basically equal to zero. A software, a song, or an e-book can be very expensive to design, create, produce, and promote, but the additional copy to be distributed can only cost a few cents of a Euro.
4. *Economies of scale*. The cost structure described subpoint (3) has important effects on the market regime, because of the strong existing economies of scale, and on the ownership structure. When decreasing average costs of production exist, it is natural to expect a process of market concentration in the hands of a few firms, just one at the limit. Consequently, the ICT sector is more subject to natural monopoly than the manufacturing sector. However, we already know (see Sect. 10.2) that the monopoly is inefficient for the society as a whole and for the consumers in particular, and the economic policy has come out with many tools to reduce the costs associated to this market failure (for example, antitrust laws, the abatement of entry barriers, the introduction of competition in granting the production license, etc.). Moreover, in the ICT sector many other possibilities arise to combat the monopoly inefficiencies, such as (a) the offer of complementary products, which can be an incentive for the firm to set a low price (point 11 below); (b) the open source, with which a community of "prosumers" (economic agents that are producers and consumers at the same time) reallocates the extra profit deriving from the position of monopoly to the benefit of the whole society.
5. *Product differentiation and price discrimination*. The ICT allows a very precise and detailed observation of the consumer preferences and behavior, thus providing new tools to strategic marketing. At the limit, the ICT allows the market of one, in the sense that services, products, and also prices can be personalized (dynamic packaging). In other words, the Internet allows to implement a strategy that in Economics previously constituted a theoretical hypothesis only: the first-degree price discrimination (see Sect. 9.5.1).
6. The *bundling*. With this term we define the policy of offering two or more products together for one price. This opportunity, which in standard economics is considered a type of price discrimination and a barrier to entry, in the new economy has become a very common sales strategy because of the high level of integration between products and the very low marginal costs borne by adding another product to the package (point 3 above).
7. The *switching costs* and the *lock-in effect*. When one buys a new car, it is relatively simple to get used to drive it. When one buys a new software, the time and the resources invested to learn and properly use it can be burdensome. Very often, other complementary software has to be changed, and sometimes the hardware too, because of technical incompatibilities. When discussing the firm, a change in the software system can imply important organizational changes and relevant switching costs that can be so high to tie the firm within specific contracts with its suppliers (lock-in effect). This phenomenon works as

demand stabilizer for the ICT firm: it is then a strategy aimed at reducing price elasticity and increasing the monopoly power.

8. The *search for information*. An interesting effect of the Internet is the abatement of costs related to the search for information: within many markets, nowadays, the consumers can access detailed and precise information on the product and the prospective seller before the purchase and 24-h a day. As already stated when discussing about the search goods, the reduction of search costs has been boosting supply-side strategies where firms frequently change the price, with very small and continuous adjustments (dynamic pricing, see Sect. 9.5), and where strategies of bundling and product differentiation aim at making the price comparison much more difficult for the consumer.
9. The *network externality*. This particular type of economies of scale from the demand side is typical for networks. In general, there is network externality if the individual demand depends on the amount of aggregate demand (see also Sect. 12.2.2). The typical example are video calls (e.g., Skype), the e-mail, the social networks (e.g., Facebook). There are two types of network externality: (a) direct externality, if it refers to the same good, as in the case of video calls; (b) indirect externality, if it refers to complementary goods, as in the case of blu-ray readers and blu-ray discs.
10. The *race for the standard*. To properly work, networks need efficient connections that go along with the standardization of software and hardware. Market leaders sometimes prefer not to standardize, although they also might find it convenient to coordinate with competitors and to identify a common standard: in fact, their sales depend both on their market share and on the market size. Therefore, if the adoption of a common standard increases the market size, also market leaders might have an interest in developing and adopting it. The identification of the standard (and the difficulties in coordination) can be explained by economic theory with game theory and reached in three different ways: (a) through a commercial war to impose the standard; (b) through a coordination and cooperation process to select the standard; (c) through the emergence of the standard from market competition and consumers' choice.
11. The *emergence of e-commerce*. With the evolution of ICT, transactions are increasingly mediated by computers: e-mediation, e-commerce, online auctions, shopbots (search engines comparing the prices) are now common tools used by consumers and producers.
12. The *productivity slowdown*. The early observations on the effect of computers on productivity were highlighting a slowdown effect (Solow 1987):

> You can see the computer age everywhere but in the productivity statistics.
>
> (Solow 1987, p. 36)

A few years later, a rise in productivity was finally observed:

> In the US the productivity slowdown – which started in the 1970s and lasted up to the mid 1990s – gave room to a prolonged period of economic growth [. . .] to assume that a change in the permanent growth rate of the economy might have happened.
>
> (Daveri 2002, p. 15)

Many reasons can explain the lag between the time of ICT innovation and the positive effect on productivity: the time period needed to search for and to develop the right template to apply; the necessity of re-organizing the firm and workers' duties due to mismanagement and skill-biases, phenomena of hysteresis in the intra- and inter-diffusion of information innovation, etc.

13. The *death of distance*. The ICT, and Internet in particular, have reduced the cost and the time needed to cover a given distance and, in particular for digital goods, have brought the economic activity to be mainly independent from the geographical location. However, the relationship between geography and ICT is much more complex, and the reduction in communication costs cannot write off the heterogeneity of resources. The study of this relationship has taken two roads: (a) the theory of the New Economic Geography that, starting with Krugman (1990), introduces new explicit hypotheses as regards the clustering and the diffusion of economic activities in the territory (see Sect. 14.3.3); (b) the analysis of the industrial districts which, following the ICT development, can refocus their role in the economic system.

Characteristics 1–13, as already underlined, imply relevant changes in the way economic agents behave and markets organize. The most important changes for the consumers can be summoned as follows: (a) the reduction of the time and the cost needed to get information; (b) the increase in the possibility of matching own preferences with products that become highly customized; (c) the possibility of directly contributing to the process of production and distribution of information through social networking, with important implications on the behavior of firms.

As regards firms, changes due to ICT cross all five forces identified by the Porter model (1980):

> The Internet is changing the industry structure by altering barriers to entry, minimising switching costs, revolutionising distribution channels, facilitating price transparency and competition, while enhancing production efficiency.
>
> (Buhalis and Law 2008, p. 617)

The ICT gives the firm the possibility of (a) reducing the costs, thus allowing to jump some of the intermediation stages, to reduce the cost of the personnel and to organize sales and production more efficiently; (b) more easily implementing strategies of yield management (see Sect. 9.5), thanks to a more efficient monitoring of the market demand and supply; (c) implementing more strategies of product differentiation and market segmentation, thus allowing the firm both to regain the monopoly degree lost as a consequence of the stronger competitiveness brought about by the ICT and to meet the consumers' demand through customization; (d) improving the postsale assistance, in order to increase efficiency and the loyalty of consumers.

As regards the market structure, the ICT allows the development of the e-commerce, transactions that take place on the electronic market. The electronic market is a virtual space where demand and supply meet. In the e-market, the low degree of information asymmetry and the low transaction costs increase the efficiency of the exchange. To identify the e-commerce, it is sufficient that the transaction is online, while the payment can either be online (for example, by paying with credit card) or offline (with bank deposit or cash, at the delivery); it is not e-commerce, on the contrary, the simple payment with credit or debit card. The delivery can either be online, for goods and services that can be digitally transferred (through the download of a file), or offline, through the standard channels of the distribution (sending a CD by mail).

Goods that more easily can be sold online are goods with a high informative content (software, multimedia products, data, various services).[2] Standard commodities have to be physically delivered and discount a high transport cost; then, e-commerce more often involves expensive goods, for which the transport cost is relatively low compared to the price. Finally, the evolution of ICT is also allowing the development of non-traditional sale mechanisms, such as the online auction (Fuchs et al. 2011 and Notes 12.1).

Notes 12.1. Online Auctions

The first online auctions started in 1995 with the site Onsale, then purchased by Yahoo! and AuctionWeb, then renamed eBay, now representing the world leader in this market. The differences with respect to traditional auctions are many (Candela and Scorcu 2004): (a) due to the size of the global market and the low cost of organization and participation, any kind of good can be put on sale in online auctions; (b) contrary to live auctions, online auctions do not last a bunch of seconds but several days, even weeks, allowing the implementation of new strategies for both the seller and the bidders; (c) in online auctions there is no physical perception of the object and the other bidders are unknown: it is then difficult to build a trusted relationship with the seller so that highly valued objects are underrepresented in online auctions; (d) online auctions allow for a better matching between sellers and buyers, obtained at very low costs thanks to the organization of powerful sites and search engines; (e) in online auctions, it is possible to gather much more information on past transactions, on the reputation of the bidders and of the sellers, and on the goods already sold.

[2] The easy and cost-effective management of databases is certainly one of the most impressive, but also more controversial fields of development of the Internet revolution. In fact, parallel to the constitution of databases on goods and services, which allow an easy comparison of price and quality, there is an increasing demand, by part of firms, for information on consumers' characteristics and tastes. Many entrepreneurial activities are recently born to search, collect, analyze, and sell information relative to the behavior and the preferences of consumers, individually or clustered. Moreover, many popular services and social networks impose their members to accept to provide their personal data to third parties. Such information is sometimes transferred in a hidden and automatic way, through the tracking of Internet browsing (for example, through cookies or spyware) or recalling the previous purchases of registered customers. On one hand, such tracking can be useful for both firms and customers, if the aim is to meet the customer preferences through a more customized service. On the other hand, the improper use of these databases can have serious implications in terms of personal privacy, limitation of individual rights, and might constitute a menace to personal freedom and a non-democratic mechanism of political control.

The main types of online auctions can be classified as follows:

- *English (ascending) auction*, where the bidders bid up and the good will go to the highest bidder; this model is the most common on the Internet as in live auctions, with the important difference that being impossible (up to now) to set the end of the online auction with the typical knockdown of the hammer, online auctions have a predetermined length and the time of the conclusion is known in advance; it is well known (Roth and Ockenfels 2000) that in this way the bidders have the advantage of hiding their offer up to the last second and this strategy, on average, leads to lower hammer prices. However, ways to adjust this negative effect for the sellers exist: for example, the overtime and the proxy bidding.
- *Dutch (descending) auction*, seldom used on the Internet as in traditional auctions; in Dutch auctions there is a starting price that goes down up to the moment when a bidder accepts the price.
- *Double auction*, where there is a bidirectional mechanism and where both the sellers and the bidders actively participate, getting to set the equilibrium price.
- *Reverse auction*, where the prospective buyer posts the maximum price he is willing to pay, and the sellers bid down to the best offer; this last mechanism is particularly important for business-to-business relationships, public procurement, and finds many applications in the tourism sector.

As for any other topic linked to ICT, even for online auctions the speed of changing is very quick; the present developments are: (a) the implementation of specialized portals that are joint efforts with traditional auction houses, guaranteeing the level of reputation needed for the online sale of high-value objects, such as art objects; (b) the implementation of live auctions, exactly working as traditional auctions and where also the Internet can be used to collect the bids. In this last case, the limitation is only technical, but one can reasonably assume that these problems will be overcome in the near future.

12.2.2 A Brief Outline of the Economic Theory of Information

What are the characteristics shared by goods and services with a high content of information? In the introduction to this chapter, we affirmed that a *bit* is not different from any other good. However, there are some specific characteristics that the informational goods share and that are of interest for the economic analysis. Let us briefly recall them.

- *Network externality*. To be efficiently distributed, the information needs a network, which is generally characterized by the existence of a positive externality, the network externality (see Sect. 12.2.1, point 9). In fact, the consumers' utility stemming from the participation to the network depends on the number of connected users, up to the congestion limit. Such externality is caused by many factors: (a) as the number of users increases, the average cost of production diminishes because the fixed costs can be spread on a higher number of units; (b) the increase in the market size allows new complementary products to be introduced; (c) the activities of customer assistance and postsale service become more effective. Because of network externality, there is a minimal number of users (the so-called critical mass) below which the market is trapped in a vicious circle where the low number of users is associated to high price and low quality. When the critical mass is reached, the network effect convinces new users to connect, thus bringing about a reduction in prices and an increase in demand.[3] The network externality can turn from positive to negative when the congestion limit is reached (bringing down the quality of the service) and when there is too much available information, becoming very difficult to manage it (this is the reason why search engines such as Google are essentials in correctly retrieving and selecting information). In economic terms, the network externality implies that the individual utility stemming from the good distributed through the network depends on the number of users demanding the good. On aggregate, the market demand function shows a first section that is positively sloping and, only in a second section, the slope becomes negative, as in the demand function of ordinary goods (Fig. 12.A, for the theoretical analysis of this property, see Theory in Action 12.1).

Theory in Action 12.1. The Market Equilibrium When There Is Network Externality

When there is network externality, the level of welfare stemming from the market directly depends on the size of the community of users, N_{tot}. Such relationship can be formalized by a utility function in which the reservation price of the consumer, p_r is weighted by the number of users N connected to the network:

$$U = Np_r - p \tag{I}$$

and where p is the price for connecting the network. Clearly, U increases with N and decreases with p. The optimal size for the network is set by the marginal consumer, the one for which the marginal utility is equal to the price of connection, $U' = p$. For this consumer it is indifferent whether or not to subscribe to the network:

$$Np_r^m = p, \tag{II}$$

where $p_r{}^m$ is the reservation price of the marginal consumer.

[3] For example, it is straightforward that the utility stemming from purchasing a phone depends on the number of people who can be called: the more the phone is used, the lower the price and the higher the convenience of accessing the phone network.

Given (I), all the consumers with a reservation price higher than p_r^m choose to connect; the number N is therefore given by $N = N_{tot} - p_r^m$ and hence $p_r^m = N_{tot} - N$ which, replaced into (II), allows to get the aggregate demand function:

$$p = N(N_{tot} - N) = NN_{tot} - N^2. \tag{III}$$

Demand function (III) is non-monotonic and describes an inverted U with respect to N. In fact, for low values of N, the reservation price increases with N, since the existence of network externality gives more value to the connection. But this is true up to a threshold point, above which phenomena of negative externality such as congestion make the demand function decreasing in N.

If there is a downward sloping supply function because of the assumption of economies of scale, which are typical for the ICT (points 3 and 4 of Sect. 12.2.1), there can be multiple equilibria in the market, although with different stability: in general terms, the demand function can cross the supply function in two points, as shown in Fig. 12.A.

In such case, three equilibria are possible: H is unstable, while equilibria in points 0 and S are stable. Then, H represents the critical mass N_1 below which the market does not exist, since it converges to the stable equilibrium in point 0 where there are no demand and supply. An ICT product has to overtake the critical mass N_1 to establish in the market with success, otherwise it will be eliminated (nevertheless, the history of technological progress is plenty of innovations that have not been able to succeed because they lacked the minimal network size). Above N_1 the market booms, up to converging to the new equilibrium S, where the size of the network is equal to N_2.

The existence of network externality and economies of scale contribute to the formation of a monopoly (point 4 of Sect. 12.2.1), since the minimum threshold is a well-known type of barrier to entry. Moreover, the critical mass contributes to the enforcement of policies of price discrimination (point 5) and to the lock-in effect (point 7).

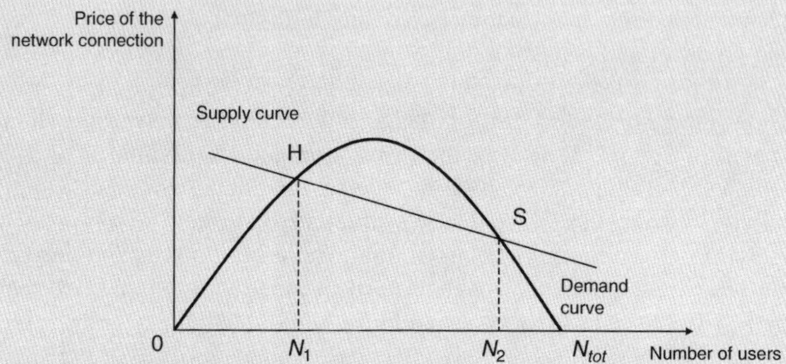

Fig. 12.A The market equilibrium when there are economies of scale and network externality

- *Barriers to entry and contestable markets*. The relative complexity of products with high content of information often locks the consumer in a long-term relationship with the provider of information services (see Sect. 12.2.1, point 7), since the change from one service to another can imply high switching costs. Some of these costs have to be understood as structural barriers (for example, consider the high switching costs that a computer user has to bear for switching from Windows to Linux), but others are just strategic barriers that firms use to lock the user within its system (for example, consider the strategy of free access to the Internet initially offered by an Internet provider that becomes a paid access after a given period).
- *New forms of intermediation*. An interesting effect is experienced by the users who connect to the Internet is related to the huge amount of available information. For the user, too much information means no information at all, without the implementation of an effective activity of comparison and selection, which is a time-costly activity. Hence, joint with the enormous production of information, the Internet Revolution has being providing the user with efficient tools and methods for selecting and retreiving useful information: search engines help the consumer to filter the information on the Internet; providers of data management, data mining, and statistical analysis help the firm in interpreting the Internet tracking of users.
- The *experience good*. Finally, information goods are basically experience goods: in fact, if the information were already known by the consumer, there would not be the need for searching and purchasing it. Hence, it is purchased only when it is not known in advance. These characteristics lead to relevant supply-side strategies: firms often offer some information for free in order to increase the user's loyalty or as an investment in reputation.

The above-mentioned characteristics of the "information bit" also affect the supply side of the market, thus leading to new marketing and organizational strategies aimed at increasing the efficiency of the production process.

Firstly, the more intensive use of communication and information networks within the firm changes its organizational model. The firm becomes less hierarchical and more "horizontal" both in the organization of the production chain and in the relationship with the customers, giving birth to a bidirectional exchange between producer and consumer.

Secondly, the cost structure of information (see Sect. 12.2.1, point 3) implies that the supply function for the firm producing information is downward sloping, as represented in Fig. 12.A. Hence, the production and distribution of information allow us to exploit huge economies of scale, so that the minimum efficient size is indefinitely big, resulting in a market structure that goes towards the natural monopoly. As a consequence, being the marginal cost of production very close to zero, the intervention of the lawmaker is needed, aimed at promoting laws to protect the property rights and to impede unauthorized reproduction but, at the same time, the public intervention has to avoid the development of too strong monopoly powers.

Given these characteristics of the demand and the supply for informational goods, markets are often structured as oligopolies (usually with a leader) or as monopolistic competition. To be more precise, the introduction of ICT brings a general increase in price competition and a reduction in profits in the short term. In the medium- and long-term, however, the firms are able to increase back profits through:

- *Strategies of product differentiation*, to counteract the economies of scale by creating new market segments or niches. In the bit economy, the product differentiation can take the form of: (a) strategies of variety proliferation (see Sect. 10.3.3); (b) strategies of mass customization to meet individual preferences and extract consumer surplus; (c) strategies of two-part tariff, composed by a fixed fee to access the network, and a variable part proportional to the number of services used (see Sect. 15.4.3); (d) strategies of bundling and selling together different products (see Sect. 12.2.1, point 6).
- *Strategies for imposing the standard*; to efficiently work, networks need internationally recognized standards (see Sect. 12.2.1, point 10): the lack of a standard impedes the efficient market development, limiting the introduction of complementary products. Hence, a temporary process of competition for the standard arises in each network, leading to a long-run equilibrium of natural monopoly.
- *Strategies of mergers and acquisitions* to increase the market share and to gain from economies of scale and network externality.
- *Strategies of price discrimination* and *revenue management* (see Sect. 9.5).

12.3 The Impact of Internet on the Tourism Sector

All the technological, organizational, and strategic innovations, as well as their impact on the market structure recalled in the previous section affect the firms belonging to the new economy, only indirectly touching upon the tourism sector. Other issues, which will be discussed in this section, are more directly affecting tourism firms and destinations.

We start by recalling from Sect. 7.6 that technology and tourism are strongly interrelated and that technology has an important role in tourism production (Nijkamp et al. 2010): tourism is certainly one of the most important economic sectors of experimentation and innovation for ICT, and tourism firms investing in technological innovation have been able to successfully redefine their organizational structure and the production chain of tourism. There are many reasons linking tourism and innovation, as recalled by Werther and Klein (1999): (a) the nature of tourism as experience good, the existence of strong information asymmetry, the high costs of information search, the plurality and heterogeneity of the tourism product, its perishability, all emphasize the importance of developing efficient systems of production and exchange of information; (b) tourism is passing through a period of structural change, where tourists demand products of higher quality, more personalized ones and tourism demand becomes more elastic to price.

Under a purely technological profile, the tourism sector has come across, in the last 40 years, four waves of technological innovation: the introduction of the Computer Reservation System (CRS) in the 1970s, the Global Distribution System (GDS, see Sect. 12.3.3) in the 1980s, the Internet Revolution since the second half of the 1990s (Sheldon 2006), and the so-called Web 2.0 since the second half of the 2000s. As a result, the structure of the tourism sector is profoundly changing:

> Hitherto, the travel distribution role has been performed by traditional outgoing travel agents, tour operators and incoming travel agencies. They were supported by computer reservation systems, global distribution systems (GDSs) or tour operators' videotext systems (or leisure travel networks). These traditional electronic tourism intermediaries [have been outpaced by] new eMediaries [...] a wide range of organisations including suppliers (e.g., airlines, hotels, etc.) selling direct on the Internet by allowing users to directly access their reservation systems; web-based travel agents; Internet portals and auction sites. [...] As a result, traditional eMediaries must re-engineer their business processes in order to survive and remain competitive.
>
> (Buhalis and Licata 2002, p. 207)

If the ICT impacts on the tourism market by mainly affecting the distribution and intermediation channel, then, it has to be analyzed in relation to two different but related segments: the package tourism, based on the role of tour operators and travel agencies, and the independent tourism, where tourists self-organize their holiday. Given the existing differences between these two segments, the ICT generally has two impacts on tourism: (a) within each segment, by modifying the way in which information is searched and gathered and services are purchased, thus affecting the tourists' choice and the firms' strategies; (b) across the segments, leading to a process of disintermediation, redefinition of the role of traditional travel agencies and tour operators, and higher mobility of tourists among the segments. Keeping in mind this difference, we analyze in the next subsections the most important effects that ICT has on tourists, firms, and destinations, respectively.

12.3.1 Information and Communication Technology and the Tourist

The effects of ICT on the tourists can be classified into three types (Buhalis and Law 2008).

1. *Reduction in time and cost needed to retrieve information.* This effect unfolds in the higher speed of collecting and comparing the existing alternative holidays directly on the website of the On Line Travel Agency (OLTA, see Sect. 8.3.3) or of a specific search engine, resulting in higher efficiency for the tourist.

2. *Reduction of the information asymmetry*. The search engines for low fares, the official sites of the destinations, the several websites used to collect and organize comments and feedback of previous tourists are all instruments that reduce the information asymmetry and promote the mechanisms of reputation building (for example, if the structure is highly rated in the web portal managed by an independent operator), signaling (for example, through the posting on the hotel's site of pictures and the prices) and selection (for example, through search engines allowing to identify the airline with the lowest price on a given route and day). The increase in the consumer surplus also goes through the widening of the range of alternative available options; through the Internet, the tourist can also access the offer of far away destinations and small firms, traditionally difficult to know. Such opportunity, however, can lead to an increase in the cost of information if the number of firms available on the Internet is too high or if the information is too chaotic. To this aim, the fundamental role played by increasingly sophisticated search engines has to be highlighted (Case Study 12.1, see also Fernandez-Barcala et al. 2010).

Case Study 12.1. Tourism Portals and Social Networks for the Tourist of 2012

Nowadays, the tourist who is willing to self-organize a holiday or just gather information through the Internet is overwhelmed by the amount of available sites and pages dedicated to travel and tourism. By googling the word "travel" the search returns almost four billion pages (they were 70 million in 2003 and 1 billion in 2009). However, the internal algorithm, the user's location, and the business model of Google allow to return, in the first page, the main search engines (OLTA, see Sect. 8.3.3) that the prospective tourist can consult and through which the holiday can be self-organized.

All the OLTAs work thanks to business agreements or partnerships with the existing GDS (see Sect. 12.3.3 and Notes 12.2) that are behind the search engines in a more or less anonymous way (for example, Travelocity.com and their partner sites, including Lastminute.com are powered by Sabre).

All the main OLTAs (Travelocity, Travelprice, Lastminute, Expedia, Opodo, etc.) are very similar in how they are organized and how they look to the Internet user. In the home page, all the possible options of search are presented: flights, hotels, car rental, cruises, special offers, last minute. Usually, it is possible to rank the returns according to the price (from the cheapest to the most expensive) or further restricting the search, for more precise entries. Many sites offer more: when a destination is chosen, the site focuses on the tourism offer of this region by becoming a real guide book, with pictures and videos, maps, news and events, weather conditions, exchange rate converter, etc.

Obviously, these sites can be the starting point for choosing the destination and organizing the transport and the accommodation if big accommodation

(continued)

structures and hotel chains are chosen but, to obtain more detailed information, the tourist should also browse the destination website. Google can still be the starting point: by digiting the name of a destination, the DMS addresses usually appear (see Sect. 12.3.4), although the tourist also has to be careful because many fake (or private) websites might pop up, with biased, commercial, or inaccurate information. The DMS is the official site of tourism promotion, showing at the same time many of the same services (search for the best price, online reservations, etc.) that the big eMediaries offer at the global level. The recent evolution of the ICT is developing interesting synergies with some special services, such as Google.Maps (to provide maps integrated with the geo-localization of attractions, hotels, restaurants, etc.), the podcast section (to download the audio guides for the visit), or some new services of augmented reality, such as the indication of what services are nearby and exactly where.

A third category is composed of specialized sites, aimed at tourists looking for specific types of holiday (for example, country houses, trekking, adventurous tourism). These sites are very often managed by private associations or single individuals who voluntarily spend their time in trying to organize all the relevant information and, for this reason, they are often incomplete and not constantly updated. However, institutional and professional websites in which the information is presented in a professional manner are nowadays flourishing also in these niche markets.

Finally, there is a growing number of websites, such as Priceline, that allow the tourists to define the details of the trip and the maximum price they want to spend; the search engine, guaranteed by the communication of the credit card details, then starts an automatic reverse auction (Notes 12.1) to check whether or not there is a company willing to sell the requested service for a price equal to or lower than the posted one and, within 60 s, the tourist gets the answer. If the offer is found, the service is automatically purchased.

Moreover, web users can complete their own informational set through the many existing social networks such as Facebook, blogs, video-sharing sites, etc., already discussed in Case Study 10.1 (see also Xiang and Gretzel 2010; Zehrer et al. 2011). It is now common for many tourism firms and DMS to open a Facebook or a Twitter profile to communicate with their followers, to publish news and special offers, and to build a special relationship with a privileged group of customers as a new form of marketing.

In 2012, many of the above-mentioned sites or services are also available on mobile devices such as smartphones, through very intuitive and easy to use applications. Such devices also have the advantage of being always connected, either through 3G or wi-fi networks, integrated with geo-localization systems such as the GPS, updated with personnel information and tastes, and can act as a perfectly flexible and mobile tourist guide.

3. *Greater possibility of building highly personalized products*. The Internet allows the tourist to easily select the most preferred combination of services, thus transforming the self-organization of the holiday as a more price competitive option with respect to the purchase of a package holiday. It also allows tour operators to introduce strategies of "just in time" production, built on the specific needs of individual tourists, hence being able to extract a greater share of the consumer surplus.
4. *Development of the e-word-of-mouth*. Nowadays, the tourist can directly contribute to the production and the distribution of information through the social networks (e.g., Facebook), forums, sites that list and rank tourism structures on the basis of tourists' comments (e.g., Trip Advisor, Booking.com). The very strong empowerment of the mechanism of word of mouth (see Sect. 10.6.3) following the development of ICT, in particular with the so-called web 2.0, has also important behavioral consequences for the firm, which reputation goes public and is less biased by own marketing strategies, with positive effects for the consumer in terms of price and quality competition.

The tourist can access the relevant information in different alternative and complementary ways:

- Through the web site of the tourism firm (airlines, tour operators, hotels, tourism attractions), where the offer conditions are published and accessible to everyone. Firms can also use pictures, videos, live web-cams, etc., to give a more precise idea of the quality, although cheating on the real quality of the service is always possible.
- Through specific search engines (OLTAs, deeply integrated with GDS, see Sect. 12.3.3, individual web sites and e-commerce intermediaries). In this way, the tourist is able to quickly compare the variety and the quality of alternative offers for the destination or for the chosen type of tourism (for example, through the web site of an association of green tourism or farm houses). These independent sites comparatively analyze the offer, working as *e-mediaries* and aiming at helping the tourist to extract the relevant information and find the best offer.
- Through the web portal of the tourism destination, where the territory and the tourism offer are presented in a systematic and organized way, thus allowing the tourist to choose and directly book and pay the selected structure or attraction. In this way, the web management of the destination becomes a key factor of competitiveness for the destination itself and of intra-destination coordination (see Sects. 4.3.5 and 12.3.3).
- Finally, the tourist can access independent sites, blogs, and forums administered by other tourists, to read comments, reviews, and tips; to watch pictures or videos; to ask specific questions; and to get to know the level of satisfaction of previous tourism experiences.

Finally, it is worthwhile to recall once again that, as Varian et al. (2004) affirm, these innovations do not change the underlying paradigms and models with which the economic theory looks at the tourist behavior: all the mechanisms and instruments described in this subsection simply change the cost of search for information (the function $C(k)$ in Sect. 6.7.2), the type of search used (it is nowadays easier to use the simultaneous rather than the sequential search, see Sect. 6.7.2), the parameters driving the tourist's choice between the package holiday or the self-organized holiday (see Sects. 5.4 and 5.5), and the effectiveness and efficiency of the word-of-mouth mechanism (see Sect. 10.6.3). All these topics were already introduced and studied in other parts of the book, well before addressing the impact of ICT on tourism in this chapter.

12.3.2 Information and Communication Technology and the Tourism Firm

From the discussion carried out in this chapter, it might be realistic to conclude that the market power of tourism firms is reduced by the development of ICT. Notwithstanding, the same ICT can also be a factor of competitiveness for the tourism firm in many respect.

- *Cost reduction and market segmentation*. The OLTA is able to produce the requested information at a cost well below the cost of self-producing the same information, but the generalized reduction in prices does not necessarily imply a reduction in the profitability. The easiness of accessing information, for example, has stimulated the reaction of firms mainly through strategies of variety proliferation and product customization.
- *More efficient integration with the policies of revenue management*. The ICT allows to improve the management of the occupancy rate for the hotel and of the load factor for the transport firms; through the continuous monitoring of reservations and the development of specific software and computation power, the implementation of more efficient strategies such as online auctions, last minute sales, daily pricing, price discrimination strategies become easier (see Sect. 9.5, see also McKinsey 2007).
- *New marketing tools*. Tour operators, airlines, hotels, and travel agencies can use Internet as another tool of marketing, promotion, and sale, using innovative ways to sell tourism services, such as online auctions (Notes 12.1). For example, English auctions (ending when the seller accepts the highest bid among a group of potential buyers) or reverse auctions (ending when the buyer accepts the lowest offer among a group of potential sellers) can be experimented.
- *Strategies of integration*. The strong economies of scale at work in ICT favor both vertical and horizontal integration policies; the existence of strong interconnections between ICT providers, firms specialized in yield management techniques and tourism firms also favor diagonal integration (see Sect. 7.3).

Although all the tourism firms are now on the Internet, there are important differences in terms of relevance and expectations that firms assign to the Web and in the definition of their business strategy. In this respect, it is useful to have three criteria of classification:

1. As regards the *business strategy*, particularly with respect to marketing, it is possible to identify four different key players: (a) big multinational companies, aiming at a dominant position in the market mainly through strategies of price competitiveness; (b) firms positioning in the segment of high-quality services; (c) firms positioning as web portals, thus providing a wide range of services, not necessarily limited to tourism; (d) firms specialized in market niches or in particular and special types of offer, they are very often medium and small size firms, usually opening a two-way channel of communication with tourists as regards their holiday experiences.
2. As regards the *business model*, it is possible to rank five alternative models for the activities provided on the Web: (a) Information Provider, if the site is mainly of information and communication, without any complexity in the updating of data and in the relationship with users; (b) Electronic Booking Service, if together with the services subpoint (a) options for direct reservation through the Internet are provided; (c) Electronic Travel Agent, if the customer can complete the whole transaction online, including the payment of the service by credit card; (d) Electronic Marketplace, if the site offers a full integration between different services, allowing for many customization options and aiming at the customer loyalty through an efficient postsale assistance; (e) Flexible Comparison Shopping Services, if the site offers many search options, price comparison, independent quality comparison, etc., thus helping the tourists in their choice in terms of quality and price.
3. Finally, as regards the *organizational model*, it is possible to identify three different actors: (a) producers of tourism services, such as hotel chains, car rentals, airlines; (b) traditional producers and retailers of package holidays (tour operators, travel agencies); (c) intermediation businesses (e-mediaries) explicitly born to be on the Internet. This last type of business is the main innovation in the sector; they are mainly entrepreneurial projects linked to the new economy and that saw the online sale of tourism services as a new and profitable business activity. In some cases, these e-mediaries are joint investments with traditional travel agencies or tour operator, and they always need an agreement with the GDS operating in the database management.

We can conclude by affirming that the evolution of the Internet is changing the organization of the market. While, on one hand, the web is another tool in the hand of traditional tourism firms to strengthen the existing relationship with customers, on the other hand, there has been a vast growth of businesses working as e-mediaries, particularly in e-commerce, thus providing new possibilities to access the tourism product, new business opportunities, and changing the structure of tourism markets.

Finally and before moving to the analysis of tourism destinations, one of the key issues to be analyzed when discussing about the relationship between tourism and the ICT is the one of disintermediation. We will now briefly discuss the topic by addressing two separate but interconnected questions. Firstly, has the process of disintermediation really taken place? Secondly, how is the process of intermediation organized in the Internet era?

12.3.3 The GDS, the OLTA, and the Disintermediation

In the 1970s, the first ICT products (the Computer Reservation System—CRS, and subsequently the Global Distribution System—GDS) allowed the tour operators, the service providers, and the travel agencies to connect their offer in a global network. Those systems, technologically very sophisticated for the time being, quickly became the most common tool used to purchase tourism services and package holidays all over the world, through the intermediation activity of the travel agencies. Together with its capabilities, the GDS was also showing some limitations: (a) the high cost for the service, thus negatively affecting the price for the final consumer; (b) the characteristics of the networks, closed and based on proprietary systems; (c) the high costs for small and medium size firms to be included in the system; (d) the complexity of the operative system and the language used, implying that the systems could be used only by trained professional personnel.

The development of the Internet perfectly adapted to the tourism sector and the Web quickly became a user-friendly interface that allowed the GDS to effectively interact with the final tourist. In just a few years the tourism market has completely changed: the GDS have integrated with the business management and yield management software, with the OLTA (of which they constitute the underlying search engine) and with tourism service providers (Notes 12.2, see also Sigala 2004; Buhalis 2006).

Notes 12.2. The GDS and Their Integration with the OLTA

The Global Distribution Systems (GDS), born as evolution of the previous Computer Reservation Systems (CRS) of the 1960s, are the main electronic interface in the tourism market and key players in the recent process of development of the tourism sector. Born as partnership between airlines, the GDS are huge databases, allowing the computer management of an enormous database of tourism services and aiming at managing the firm's resources and at improving the access to the information by part of partners or firms operating along the production chain. As any other information network, also the GDS have high fixed costs and relatively low running costs. The race to the leadership and the need to take advantage from economies of scale brought about a strong concentration in the global market, recently dominated by four global GDS: Sabre, Amadeus, Galileo, and Worldspan (these two last platforms recently merged in the same company, Travelport).

Together with the access to the platform and to the database, the GDS usually offer to their clients complementary products such as instruction courses and financial help for the employees working on the database, so that is possible to lock the agency into a relational contract and increase the switching costs (see Sect. 11.2). In this way, having borne high setup and training costs for the personnel, a travel agency would seldom change the GDS after having chosen one (lock-in effect, see Sect. 12.2.1, point 7).

With the development of the Internet, the GDS have become the core of the OLTAs (the web portals that offer reservation and information on holidays, trips, and destinations). The OLTAs are the main competitors of traditional travel agencies and the largest menace to their survival. All the search engines and reservation systems available on the Internet and known by the tourists (for example, Expedia, Travelocity, Lastminute, Opodo, etc.) are based on the GDS, of which they constitute the backbone, both in the informational content and in the management system. They offer different and integrated services such as air tickets, car rental, hotel reservations, all inclusive trips, and the organization of downright holiday packages just in time.

The integration of the GDS with the Internet through the OLTA has also affected the market structure, pushing phenomena of vertical integration and modification of the retailing sector. Yet, some critical features have to be underlined. The most important is related to the participation of airline companies in the GDS ownership or management: it is evident that airlines with strong market power can affect the way in which the information is provided, at the disadvantage of competitors, which can be relegated in the following pages on the screen. This can be harmful for market competition. For example, in 1984 the American Civil Aeronautics Board approved the first regulation on the GDS, establishing that all the airlines had to be visualized in the same manner, in order to avoid that the GDS owned by American Airlines, Sabre, could use the so-called bias listing (to list the available flights according to the flight code). In such way American Airlines (which code is *AA*) was always listed as the first company, leading to a higher number of reservations: it has been estimated that American Airlines had got, through Sabre, an extra revenue of about 40 %.

As regards the issue of disintermediation, the ICT development of the last few years does not suggest a unique answer. In some cases, the Internet has pushed for disintermediation. For example, tourists willing to spend a holiday in a given destination can quickly compare the price and quality of hotels on a search engine and then move on the chosen hotel's web site where all the options of reservation and payment are available. However, a balancing between the different channels used to sell the tourism services has to be reached, to avoid problems of compatibility of the incentives (for travel agencies and OLTAs, see Sect. 11.6.1), of competition between retailers and incoherence in the offer (if the same product is found on sale for two prices at the same time is a bad signal for the customer). For example, a tour operator has to avoid direct competition with travel agencies which is still the most popular channel of sales for package holidays. The same rationale applies for the airline company or for the hotel.[4] However, in some particular cases, the online strategy could be aimed at saving on the retailing costs, and then functional to the breaking up of the relationship with the travel agencies (for example, see the case of Ryanair, Case Study 9.2).

In other cases, the Internet has pushed for a change in the model of intermediation and retailing. In fact, only a small share of tourists directly book on the web sites of hotel chains and airlines; the majority of them book through OLTAs and it can be affirmed that the evolution of ICT is leading the OLTAs to be the winning business model for intermediation. As already recalled (see Sect. 8.3.3), the OLTA is an integrated travel portal where it is possible to: (a) directly access the single tourism services; (b) find special deals and last minute offers; (c) know the most important attractions and events for the selected destination; (d) use specific search engines, built on the traditional GDS (Notes 12.2) where the tourist can compare prices and fares, choose own preferred option, book it and pay for it.

Hence, more than the death of the travel agency, the ICT has brought about a deep transformation of the agency itself, not anymore simple retailer of the tourism services, but real tour organizer, information searcher, and e-commerce site, thus becoming the key element of the so-called e-tourism. Due to the high volumes of sales and the strong economies of scales, the OLTA is able to sell tourism services at a lower price than the traditional agency, with positive effects for the final tourist although being able to keep being profitable even if its mark up is reduced to a few Euros per transaction.

Up to now, hence, the process of disintermediation is only partial and is more a synonymous of death of the traditional travel agency rather than death of intermediation. However, in the present phase, the competition between traditional and electronic agencies pivots around reciprocal strengths and weaknesses. For the traditional agency, the most important weakness is certainly in price competition; the strength is the possibility to provide value-added services, tips and hints based on past experience and individual care to the customer. In general terms, any electronic intermediation is linked to the nature of the good or service to be transacted: the simpler the good (in terms of variety and information needed to purchase) the stronger the push for disintermediation. Applying this principle to tourism, it is easy to understand that the e-commerce is winning for the purchase of some elementary items such as air tickets, hotel rooms in a well-known destination, or last minute package holidays, while the traditional agency will survive for longer time for more complex products such as specific trips or far away destinations. In the latter cases, the reputation, the skills, and the trust of the traditional agency offer

---

[4] In the US, the effect of such situation has been unfolded when some airlines (KLM, Delta Airlines, North-West Airlines, United Airlines, and American Airlines) cut the commission rates to travel agencies from 8 to 5 % at the beginning of 1999, being the direct sale through the Internet more convenient particularly for business travelers. Such decision had a strong impact on the retailing sector, since more than 1,800 travel agencies closed down by the end of 1999.

a more precise guarantee about the quality of the services, the integration between the various products, and the compliance of the contractual clauses.

Finally, let us do not forget that the habits (most tourists love to rely on a well known and trusted agent) and issues linked to the security of e-commerce and the Internet use of the credit card lead many tourists to search for the relevant information on the Internet and then buy the product in the nearby agency.

What is evident, in our opinion, is that the ICT development has polarized the retailing market. On one hand, the globalization of the economy and the existence of strong economies of scale allow a few global competitors to survive on the global market and to build a strong reputation; on the other hand, there is room for the development of market niches in which small and medium size agents, including the traditional travel agency are able to survive, if they go in the direction of offering very specialized and customized products.

> Success will probably depend on the ability of organisations to target the most appropriate niches and to form partnerships that enhance, fulfil the need of the marketplace, image and increase market share.
>
> (Buhalis and Licata 2002, p. 219)

12.3.4 Information and Communication Technology and the Tourism Destination

To conclude this chapter, we analyze the effects of ICT on the tourism destinations.

- Firstly, the destination has to work out a web portal that run as collector and manager of the many local offers, in such a way that all the relevant information for the prospective tourist is sorted and organized in a rational way. The site should also provide links and information (pictures, maps, audio guides, videos, prices) about the whole destination, in order to allow the building up of a complete holiday experience in there; in other words, the site has to work as virtual promotion office for the destination (see Sect. 4.3.5).
- The ICT can also help the building up of an effective coordination and management center for the local tourism system, thus allowing an efficient monitoring activity of the numbers of arrivals and overnight stays in order to optimize the organization of special events (for example with the aim of smoothing seasonality, see Sect. 7.5), to implement policies aimed at decongestioning and promoting the destination, thus balancing the impact of tourism on the local territory and the needs of the host population.
- The web portal of the destination is particularly useful for those firms that, due to their small size and lack of skills, are not able to autonomously manage their strategy for the Internet. In this way, small size firms can benefit from the use of new technologies without bearing the full cost of implementing a complex website, using the destination website to promote, coordinate, and sell their products and services. This is particularly true for the hospitality sector where,

although all the hotels are on the web, their only presence is not sufficient. To be effective, the web strategy has to avoid that the information is seldom updated and has to include systems of e-booking and e-commerce, together with a strategy of Internet marketing. The small firms often lack the human and financial resources needed to promote an effective web site, and the destination web management can help overcome such limit.

- Finally, the destination web portal has to be integrated with the GDS and the OLTA, in order to be visible in the most important travel and tourism portals and search engines worldwide.

The destination web management is particularly important for responding to the needs of the self-organized tourism. As we already know (see Sect. 5.5), the self-organizing tourist usually chooses medium and small size hotels and, in the pre-Internet era, the tourist used other channels for searching information: the direct visit to the destination that was often generating forms of day-tripping off-season; traditional ways of contact (phone, mail, fax, either calling directly the hotel, or asking the information office); getting information through word of mouth or through advertising. With the Internet, the self-organizing tourist can avail of a place where the whole information on the tourism offer is located and easily available, rationally presented in a complete way.

Without an efficient web management, the destination would loose control of its territory with respect to organized tourism, managed by big multinational tour operators, and would loose competitiveness against other similar destinations. Then, the opportunities provided by the ICT, particularly to the small and medium size firms, have to be evaluated in terms of cooperation strategies within the destination, where the tourism sector of the destination cooperates to develop a common project of online commerce and promotion. As shown by some pioneering projects implemented in Northern Europe in the 1990s, rather than simply publishing online their offer, it is strategically important for small enterprises to provide the tourist with a uniform and simple key to access all the relevant information and to plan the holiday in the destination, thus guaranteeing both completeness and transparency of data and the easiness to use the system (Buhalis et al. 2006).

In a few years, many projects of development of destination websites (at the country, regional, or town level) aimed at self-organizing tourists have been implemented. Such systems, called Destination Management Systems (DMS) (Pollock 1998; O'Connor and Frew 2001), can be defined as locally integrated information systems, aimed at centrally collecting all the relevant information as regards tourism attractions and services, in order to promote and sell them through the website.

The DMS is a technological and organizational structure, where there must be, at the same time: a reserved access section (Intranet) for local operators, through which they are allowed to upload and update in real time the data related to their offer (this is the site's database); an open access section (the Internet website) where tourists are presented with all the relevant information on the destination, and booking and e-commerce services can be accessed. Nowadays, the DMS strongly differ as regards their web architecture and the quality of available services, signaling different web marketing strategies. In some cases, the destination only offers elementary information, such as the description of the site, a few maps, and the list of hotels and tourism attractions, with their phone numbers and e-mails for further contacts. This is evidently the starting point of a strategic presence on the web, only justified by the lack of technical skills and by the budget constraint. Such a website does not need advanced management skills and can be easily outsourced, since it is simply implemented through the website realization and in its (infrequent) updates (for example, on a seasonal basis, twice a year).

The next level is to realize a real web portal for the destination, with a systematic and complete gathering of all the relevant information. This task introduces many organizational problems, since the website has to contain, coordinate, and update a much higher volume of information. Finally, the ultimate level for a DMS includes the availability of online booking and sale services (directly, or linking to the structure's website), integrated with accessibility information (related to the airports and airlines websites).

The future of the DMS goes through: (a) an increasing integration with mobile devices (GPS systems, tablets, smartphones; (b) the provision of virtual guide books with interactive services (audioguides, videos, maps) to be directly uploaded on the tourist's device and personalization services on the basis of the exact position of the tourist and its characteristics.

The organizational and technical issues that the DMS has to solve involve both the database and the graphical interface of the website. To set up the database it is necessary: (a) to stipulate contracts with the local firms in order to regulate the access to the DMS; (b) to define the technical and content standards for the management of the information uploaded on the system; (c) to define how to classify the information in order to create coherent and organized sections in the website; (d) to define the role of the database administrator and the frequency of the updates; (e) to identify the technical and security procedures for the electronic transactions and for the privacy of the data. As regards the website architecture, it is necessary that the graphical interface is functional, aesthetically appealing, easy to use in its basic functions (information search, reservation, payment), and capable to manage a two-way communication channel with users.

It is straightforward to understand that these issues imply problems that are not only of technological nature but also involve the entrepreneurs' culture and their attitude to cooperate, the ability to manage medium- and long-term projects in an integrated manner, and the availability to re-think the manner in which services are offered on the market. To properly work, the DMS can be effective only if a structure of coordination exists at the destination level and the DMS can indeed be the starting motivation for developing such a coordination activity needed to overcome the anticommon problem (see Sect. 4.3.1) and to promote the destination's competitiveness. Then, not only the DMS is an instrument of territorial marketing but also of economic management of the destination, prerequisite to aiming at a Pareto-efficient solution for all the firms involved in the tourism product.

The DMS can be organized around two alternative models: either a light structure, substantially self-managed by the operators, by their association, or by the Destination Management Organization (DMO), or the creation of an external structure specialized in the web management, with dedicated human and technical skills and resources. In the latter case, the financing of the (relevant) investment can be based on fees and royalties paid by the participating firms, and the local government can intervene with the provision of a subsidy. Other forms of financing can be found, such as sponsors or banners. The choice of the coordination model depends on a plurality of factors, including the managerial culture of the destination.

The development of ICT, finally, can also lead to the development of (imperfect) substitute products for tourism, meaning a reduction in the demand for tourism, with particular reference to business tourism (videoconferences) and cultural tourism (multimedia museums). It is plausible that these services are also of interest for the management of DMS, thus becoming increasingly more important in the future (Nijkamp et al. 2010).

Chapter Overview

- Although the ICT has been modifying the management, the marketing, the organization of firms and the public administration, the decision of households and, ultimately, the very same structure of markets, the economic analysis of the information market is not qualitatively different from the analysis of markets for other goods and services.
- The information good has some peculiarity: it is distributed through networks, it is affected by relevant externality, it is subject to strong economies of scale, users have high switching costs, new intermediaries are needed, information has nature of experience good, the cost structure has high fixed costs and low marginal costs of production.
- The impact of ICT on the tourist mainly goes through the reduction in the cost of gathering information, the reduction in the asymmetry of information, the widening of the set of available choices, the higher chance of product customization, the higher chance of contributing to the improvement of the product through e-word of mouth, blogs, forums, and social networks.
- The impact of ICT on the tourism firm mainly goes through reduction in costs, better management of the load factor, of policies of yield management and of daily pricing, introduction of new marketing tools to segment the market and to find a better level of integration.
- The ICT mainly affects the role and the importance of the traditional travel agency, both because firms providing tourism services can directly meet the tourist online and because of the strong development of GDS and their full integration in OLTAs and in search engines.
- The evolution of ICT is also pushing the tourism destinations to organize their web portals. Together with being fundamental instruments of coordination, the DMS are as more important as the share of small and medium firms operating in the destination is high and as self-organized tourism is important.

Part III
The Macroeconomics of Tourism

Chapter 13
Tourism, Development, and Growth

Learning Outcomes
By completing this chapter you will understand:

- The macroeconomic principles that link tourism expenditure to production and income in the economy.
- The main theoretical and empirical findings of the debate on the relationship between tourism specialization and economic growth and development.
- The key role of tourism as engine of local development.

13.1 Introduction

The evidence that in many countries tourism constitutes a fundamental engine of local and national development is unquestionable, and in recent years it gave birth to a flourishing scientific production. These aspects can be studied using standard tools of macroeconomic theory, such as the income multiplier, models of exogenous and endogenous growth, and models of regional development applied to the tourism case.

Clearly the macroeconomic impact of tourism and of its dynamics is very complex; in this chapter, therefore, we will only provide the fundamental theoretical aspects necessary to understand the relationship between tourism and the evolution of the destination's economy, leaving the in-depth analysis to more advanced texts and to the cited bibliography.

In particular, Sect. 13.2 will analyze the impact that tourism has on the economy's short-run equilibrium, studying how the demand of tourism, being an autonomous component of aggregate demand, affects, through the multiplier, income and employment levels in the local economy. Tourism also produces a feedback effect, from income growth to the evolution of tourism demand, that we will be able to highlight a number of times.

G. Candela and P. Figini, *The Economics of Tourism Destinations*,
Springer Texts in Business and Economics, DOI 10.1007/978-3-642-20874-4_13,

In the long run, tourism can be a key factor in enhancing economic growth and development: many regions have attained economic development thanks to their ability to manage the local resources and to promote the tourism sector. The models that can help understand the impact of tourism on development will be analyzed in Sect. 13.3, while the approach of endogenous growth will be unfolded in Sect. 13.5.

Finally, tourism can also have a negative impact on other sectors of the economy when, for example, it competes for the use of capital and other factors of production. This displacement effect, known in the literature as "crowding out," will be discussed in Sect. 13.4. Lastly, in Sect. 13.6, the concept of local tourism system will be touched upon.

13.2 The Tourism Expenditure Multiplier

The effects of tourism expenditure on a region's income and employment were one of the early topics covered by economists of tourism, both from a theoretical and empirical perspective. The approach used by these economists was an application of the Keynesian multiplier, which we will now briefly discuss by distinguishing between the aggregate and the disaggregate analysis and between the multiplier and the super-multiplier.

13.2.1 The Tourism Multiplier: Aggregate Analysis

The expression *multiplier model* generally refers to a mathematical function relating economic variables, where an increase in the exogenous (independent) variable normally produces a more than proportional increase in the endogenous (dependent) variable.[1]

The model that has particular relevance to tourism economics is the Keynesian multiplier (Keynes 1936). This model analyzes the circular flow of money in a given economic system and underlines the effect of increases in exogenous expenditure, that does not depend on the circulation of national income, such as the one caused by public spending, exports, etc. According to John Maynard Keynes, each change in an exogenous component of aggregate demand will stimulate the

[1] Between two variables X and Y there exists a multiplicative relationship if they are linked by a proportional or transposed proportional function such as $Y = mX + n$, with $n \geq 0$, so that $\mathrm{d}Y/\mathrm{d}X = m$. Applications of the multiplier model are the employment multiplier (Kahn 1931), linking the overall increase in employment to the employment generated by an additional investment, and the income multiplier (Keynes 1936), linking the overall increase in national income to a new investment. Such models are so fundamental that they are discussed in any macroeconomics textbook, which we refer to for a general introduction.

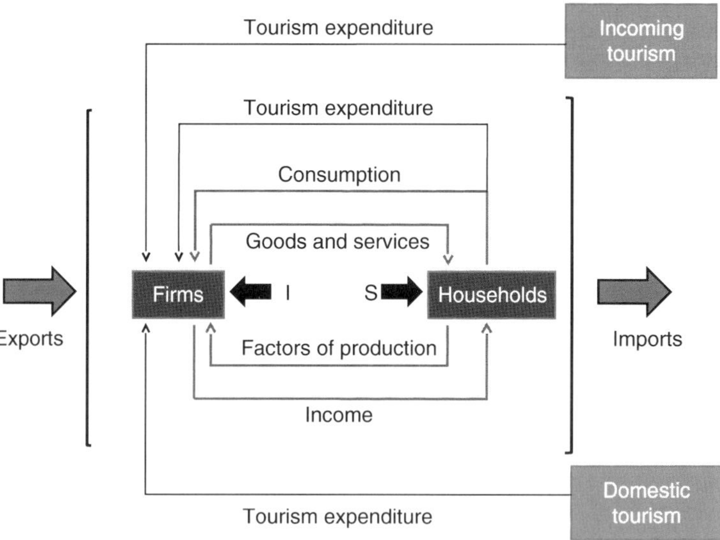

Fig. 13.1 The circular flow of income in a tourism destination

economy by a value that is greater than the initial amount, since the initial expenditure will circulate many times, thereby causing a final multiplier effect on national income.

The multiplier model can be better understood by looking at the flowchart shown in Fig. 13.1, which summarizes the functioning of the whole economy and draws particular attention to the interaction between the two aggregate economic agents of the private sector: the households and the firms. In the chart, the role of the public sector is left out, excluding the effects of both taxes and public spending for the sake of simplicity (the role of the public sector will be studied in Chap. 15).

To explain Fig. 13.1, we start without considering tourism expenditure. Households appear on the right-hand side of the chart; they posses the factors of production (capital and labor) which they transfer to firms (on the left-hand side of the chart) for production purposes; in exchange, households receive an income (wages and profits, bottom part of the chart) which is used to buy consumption goods and services C (top part of the chart) from firms, goods produced using as inputs the same factors of production that firms received from households.

There exists, therefore, a real circular flow of goods and factors of production between households and firms that moves clockwise in Fig. 13.1, and a monetary flow that moves counterclockwise. Obviously each exchange of goods for money takes place within a market: the market for goods is on the top part of the chart and the market for factors of production is on the bottom part of the chart.

By norm, households spend less than their total income, saving a portion of it (S on the right-hand side of the chart). The savings obviously cause a reduction in the demand faced by firms and partially interrupt the circular flow. Firms, however, also demand money to undertake investments (I on the left-hand side of the chart);

therefore another form of demand is generated in the private sector, in addition to that of consumption goods generated by households. Also S and I are exchanged within a market: the capital (financial) market.

The rest of the world, represented by a generic agent located outside the diagram of Fig. 13.1, also intervenes in this circular flow. In fact, in an economy open to international trade, households can spend on goods produced and sold by foreign firms, and these goods are known as imports (Z, the arrow on the right-hand side of the chart), but also domestic firms receive demand from foreign households and firms, and this demand is called exports (X, the arrow on the left-hand side of the chart).

This circular flow is in equilibrium if the sum of final production (Y, income) generated by domestic firms and the production imported from outside (Z) is equal to the overall demand facing domestic firms, which is the sum of demand generated by firms themselves for investment purposes (I), by foreign demand (X) and by households for consumption purposes (C).

By applying this circular flow model, we now introduce tourism into Fig. 13.1. By doing so, we can no longer use an abstract territorial dimension, which at the macroeconomic level is normally identified with the country, but it is necessary to provide a more precise spatial dimension. Obviously, the standard geographical unit in tourism economics is the destination, which can coincide with the country, but also with a larger region or a smaller area within the country. The parentheses in Fig. 13.1 thus take care of this point: the territory enclosed by the two large round parentheses (the destination) can, in general, host tourists from abroad (foreign tourists, at the top part of the chart), from other regions of the country (domestic tourists, at the bottom part of the chart) but even tourists from the destination itself. As one can see in the diagram, the whole tourism expenditure is directed to the firms located in the destination. However, tourism expenditure from local households comes from income generated in the circular flow, mixing with general consumption and is thus left out from the analysis. On the contrary, tourism expenditure of domestic tourists, G_1, and of foreign tourists, G_2, are net additions to the demand facing the destination's firms and are therefore relevant for our purposes.

The approach used by tourism economists is to consider tourism expenditure as an increase in the money supply which, coming from income generated outside the destination, can be treated as exogenous. Tourism expenditure, therefore, produces a direct effect on the income of the destination, which constitutes an immediate advantage for firms that operate in the territory (for example, hotels, restaurants, shops, travel agencies, service stations). Since a portion of the additional income brought into the destination and earned by firms is then transferred to the destination's households in the form of income (for example, wages to workers, profits to capital owners, rents to home and land owners) and to the government in the form of taxes, residents' income is converted into further spending in consumption goods. Hence, we can add to the initial expenditure by tourists that of the local population, generating an amplifying effect on local income that is well explained by the concept of a multiplicative function.

13.2.2 The Model of the Tourism Multiplier

To formally translate the complex relationship embedded in Fig. 13.1 we have to begin with the condition of aggregate equilibrium in the market for goods, assuming fixed prices. This relationship considers that production equals aggregate demand if the market is in equilibrium and can be written as in (13.1) (leaving out for the moment the role of the public sector: taxes and public spending):

$$Z + Y = C + I + X. \tag{13.1}$$

In (13.1), all the components of demand that are not dependent on income are called *autonomous*, while the components which depend on national income Y, such as consumption and imports, are called *endogenous*. As usual in the literature, we assume that these endogenous components of demand are linear functions of income:

- $Z = Z_0 + zY$, where $0 \leq z \leq 1$ is the marginal propensity to import, while Z_0 is the autonomous component of imports
- $C = C_0 + cY$, where $0 \leq c \leq 1$ is the marginal propensity to consume, while C_0 is the autonomous component of consumption

Our first task, therefore, is to highlight in (13.1) tourism expenditure as a component of demand. Expenditure of incoming tourists can be represented by G (Guests' expenditure) and is an additional component of aggregate demand. It clearly constitutes an autonomous component since it is not generated within the destination itself but stems from external visitors (as already mentioned in Sect. 3.4.4, the expenditure of incoming tourists constitutes, like exports, a credit entry in the balance of payments). G can be disaggregated between G_1 (if it is generated from domestic visitors) and G_2 (if it is generated from foreign visitors).

To complete the model, the expenditure made by the local population abroad, that is outgoing tourism, has also to be included. Outgoing tourism expenditure constitutes instead a part of consumption that exits the circular flow of income of Fig. 13.1; therefore it has to be subtracted from aggregate demand. We indicate this component as H (Hosts' expenditure), in part autonomous (the trips that the local population would take independently of income) and in part endogenous:

- $H = H_0 + hY$, where $0 \leq h \leq 1$ is the marginal propensity to spend abroad, while H_0 is the autonomous part of this expenditure.

With these specifications, (13.1) becomes

$$Z + Y = (C - H) + I + (X + G_2), \quad \text{where} \quad C = (C_0 + G_1) + cY.$$

By replacing in this equation the respective functions we obtain

$$Z + Y = [(C_0 + G_1 + cY) - (H_0 + hY)] + I + (X + G_2). \tag{13.2}$$

Keeping in mind that guests, both national and foreign, can cover a portion of their holiday cost by purchasing goods from their country of origin,[2] we need to add two coefficients g_1 and g_2 to deduct this cost from the overall tourism expenditure. Equation (13.2) then becomes

$$Z + Y = [(C_0 + (1 - g_1)G_1 + cY) - (H_0 + hY)] + I + [X + (1 - g_2)G_2],$$

$$Z + Y = (C_0 + cY) - (H_0 + hY) + I + X + (1 - g_2)G_2 + (1 - g_1)G_1.$$

Rewriting $G_1 + G_2 = G$ and $g = g_1G_1/\mathrm{G} + g_2G_2/\mathrm{G}$ we obtain

$$Z + Y = C_0 + cY - H_0 - hY + I + X + (1 - g)G. \tag{13.3}$$

Equation (13.3) is an equation in which income is unknown and the usual exogenous variables appear: investment, exports, and (aggregate) tourism expenditure. Since this is a first-degree equation, the solution for income can be easily obtained, recalling that $\mathrm{Z} = \mathrm{Z}_0 + zY$ and assuming that $1 - (c - h) + z > 0$.

$$Y = \frac{1}{1 - (c - h) + z}[C_0 - H_0 - Z_0 + I + X + (1 - g)G]. \tag{13.4}$$

The first-order condition of solution (13.4) with respect to tourism expenditure defines the *tourism multiplier of income*, in other words, the final effect on regional income made by an infinitely small increase in tourism expenditure:

$$\frac{\partial Y}{\partial G} = \frac{(1 - g)}{1 - (c - h) + z},$$

which can also be written as

$$\partial Y = k\partial G \quad \text{with} \quad k = \frac{(1 - g)}{1 - (c - h) + z}, \tag{13.5}$$

where k is indeed the tourism multiplier.

Equation (13.5) shows the final increase in income due to tourism expenditure; in fact, referring to the economy of a specific geographical area, expenditure by tourists from other regions (domestic or foreign) can be considered as a positive autonomous component of aggregate demand that produces additional income (exactly as exports

[2] For example, because the tourist sustained these costs before leaving the home country, or because the domestic firm directly imported goods to satisfy the tourist's demand; the first case could be that of a French tourist that brings *Perrier* mineral water from France to Italy, the second case could be that of an Italian hotel that does not serve Italian mineral water but rather prefers to serve *Perrier* to their guests.

or investment) through the multiplier k. If we assume that there is not full employment of resources, in particular labor (this assumption is fundamental in the Keynesian theory of the multiplier), an increase in tourism expenditure leads to an expansion in production, employment, and income in the destination.[3]

To conclude, let us show the combined short-run effect produced by all the components of tourism on the destination's income, by using (13.5) and recalling that the multiplier k is an increasing function of the propensity to consume (since c appears with negative sign at the denominator). As already explained, tourism expenditure differs among its various parts, meaning that expenditure of incoming tourists (foreign and domestic) has different effects than expenditure of local tourists. We have already determined that incoming tourism expenditure can be treated as an autonomous component of aggregate demand while the effect of local tourism is discussed below.

Tourism expenditure by households of the destination has obviously to be considered endogenous demand, since it depends on available income. If the tourism activity is an additional reason for spending, a change can occur either in the level of households consumption while leaving their propensity to consume (and therefore household savings) unchanged, or it can be a reason for an increase in c, thus reducing savings (for example, following the Love for Variety Theorem, Sect. 4.3.2). In this latter case, local tourism is characterized by $\partial k/\partial c > 0$, thus leading to an increase in income of (13.5). It is straightforward that the positive effect of the multiplier is generated if the increase in c is not matched by an equal increase in h; in other words, the larger propensity to spend for tourism must not translate solely in an increase of the households' propensity to travel abroad, since the multiplier in (13.5) depends on the difference $(c - h)$.

Therefore, all tourism types produce short-run positive effects on the destination's income, although through different channels: local tourism affects the multiplier, while incoming tourism (foreign and domestic) affects the multiplicand. In addition, incoming tourism, only if coming from foreign countries, has also positive effects on the balance of payments (Chap. 14).

The exact value of the multiplier can vary from one situation to the other because, as we have seen, it depends on the characteristics of the destination's economy, its social structure, and the types of tourism it hosts. Table 13.1 presents values of the multiplier for selected countries. It has to be highlighted that such cross-country comparisons must be handled with care, since the studies might have been conducted at different times or using different methodologies (Cooper et al. 2008). In addition, although the value of a destination's tourism multiplier is seldom subject to significant variation and appears to be quite stable over time, it is nevertheless reasonable to expect that the overall impact will increase as the country's economy develops.

---

[3] It is important to recall that the tourism destination being referred to can be the entire country (in this case, the autonomous component of domestic tourism G_1 does not exist), but also an internal area of any dimension, from a town to a broader region.

Table 13.1 The tourism multiplier of income in selected destinations

Region	Tourism multiplier	Region	Tourism multiplier
United Kingdom	1.73	Malta	0.68
Ireland	1.72	Gibraltar	0.66
Sri Lanka	1.59	Iceland	0.64
Jamaica	1.27	Barbados	0.60
Egypt	1.23	Virgin Islands	0.58
Dominican Rep.	1.20	Palau	0.51
Seychelles	1.03	Victoria, Canada	0.50
Hong Kong	0.87	Carlisle, UK	0.44
Philippines	0.82	Edinburgh, UK	0.35
Bahamas	0.79	East Anglia, UK	0.34

Source: Cooper et al. (1998), p. 141–142

Finally, the analysis of the multiplier's values allows for some classification on how tourism connects to the destination's economy. We can, in fact, observe three intervals in the value of k that can be of relevance (from Table 13.1 the value of the tourism multiplier ranges from a maximum of 1.73 to a minimum of 0.34).

1. If $k \geq 1$, which applies when $(h + z + g) \leq c < 1$, then one unit of additional tourism expenditure produces more than one unit of income in the destination; in this case tourism can be considered as a *development factor*.
2. If $0 < k < 1$, which applies when $0 < c < (h + z + g)$, then one unit of additional tourism expenditure produces less than one unit of income in the destination; in this case tourism can be considered as a *parasitic factor*. This is the case, for example, of the type of tourism promoted by multinational tour operators in many parts of the world: they contribute to the development of the host region but, since these activities mainly use services and goods imported from tourists' home countries, the impact on local income is relatively modest.
3. If $k = 0$, which is verified when $g = 1$, then one unit of additional tourism expenditure does not produce any income in the host region, since in this case tourism remains completely detached from the local economic activity; in such case we can say that the resort where the tourists are hosted is a *tourism enclave*, where tourism expenditure is not linked to any local business. This is more or less the case of the many tourism resorts built by German operators for German tourists only (such in the Canary or the Balearic islands) or the similar resorts developed in many tourism areas of the Pacific where Japanese tourists arrive (with Japanese flights), stay in Japanese hotels and buy only products that come from their home country.

The multiplier that we have presented so far is a static model and is not able to say anything about the period of time necessary for the multiplier to unfold its effects nor about the manner in which the transition to the new income of equilibrium will take place. In addition, the impact of tourism expenditure also depends on the time of the year in which it takes place: the tourism multiplier, therefore, is also sensitive to the seasonality of tourism (Baretje and Defert 1968). The answer to these questions requires a more in-depth analysis and more complex dynamic models, which are beyond the scope of this book.

13.2.3 The Model of the Tourism Super-multiplier

There is, however, another aspect of tourism demand that deserves further investigation: it is possible that tourism expenditure drives residents to invest in new businesses, in the expansion of existing businesses, or in the development of new structures and infrastructures for hospitality and other tourism-related activities. Therefore, it is reasonable to assume that investment, which appears as an exogenous variable in (13.1) and thereafter, is rather a function of the local population's income. We assume, for simplicity, this function to be linear:

$$I = I_0 + iY, \tag{13.6}$$

where i is the marginal propensity to invest. The assumption of linearity between investment and income is sufficient to discuss the short-run impact of tourism expenditure on the regional economy through the investment channel.[4]

Replacing (13.6) into (13.3), and solving for income, while treating exports and tourism expenditure as exogenous variables, we obtain assuming that $1 - (c - h) - i + z > 0$

$$Y = \frac{1}{1 - (c - h) - i + z}[C_0 - H_0 - Z_0 + I_0 + X + (1 - g)G]. \tag{13.7}$$

The first-order condition of (13.7) with respect to G is

$$\frac{\partial Y}{\partial G} = \frac{(1 - g)}{1 - (c - h) - i + z} \tag{13.8}$$

or

$$\partial Y = k' \partial G,$$

where

$$k' = \frac{(1 - g)}{[1 - (c - h) - i + z]}.$$

[4] In this framework we assume, for the sake of simplicity, that income can be affected by changes in tourism expenditure only. If it were not so, the investment function would be more complicated, having to capture both the impact of tourism and of other components of expenditure on income, but without significant changes in the main results of the model.

Since k' is the multiplier that also takes into account the effect of tourism expenditure on investment, and since it is easy to demonstrate that $k' > k$, it can be defined as the *tourism super-multiplier of income*. Hence, while the tourism multiplier describes the effect that tourism expenditure has on the economy of the destination, where income is only spent in consumption goods, the tourism super-multiplier describes the effect that tourism expenditure has on the economy of the destination where income is spent both in consumption and investment goods. It is easy to see that $k' > 1$ for a set that is larger than before, in other words, when $(h + z + g) - i < c < 1$; therefore there is a greater chance of defining tourism as a factor of development through the analysis of the tourism super-multiplier. Nevertheless, for a tourism enclave both the multiplier and the tourism super-multiplier are equal to zero.

The tourism multiplier and super-multiplier can take different values, leading to consequences that are explained through the use of an example. Let us assume that a developing destination receives new tourists so that expenditure for tourism and consumption goods increases by 100, $\Delta G = 100$; we also assume that 10 % of this expenditure is for goods that are produced abroad, $g = 0.1$. Tourism expenditure immediately transfers into income for the destination's households, but suppose that these households are mostly made up of landowners that spend such additional income in consumption goods (40 %, $c = 0.4$), for international trips (30 %, $h = 0.3$), and for luxury imports (20 %, $z = 0.2$). By applying (13.5) it is easy to obtain the value of the tourism multiplier for such economy: $k = 0.82$. From here, it is straightforward to obtain the total effect on income of the additional tourism expenditure, $\Delta Y = 82$. In this situation it can be concluded that tourism plays a parasitic role in the destination.

Let us now suppose instead that the additional tourism expenditure is transferred into new income for businessmen and workers, and that these two social groups have a different consumption pattern than that of landowners: for example, they do not go on international trips, $h = 0$, but rather invest, $i = 0.3$, while we assume that imports are again equal to 20 % of income, $z = 0.2$. By applying (13.7) it is easy to obtain the value of the tourism super-multiplier for such economy, $k' = 1.8$. From here, it is straightforward to determine the total effect on income of the additional tourism expenditure, $\Delta Y = 180$. We can conclude that the different expenditure behavior of local agents now allows tourism to be a factor of development. Nevertheless, had tourists directed all their expenditure to internal consumption, $g = 0$, tourism would have been very close to being a factor of development also in the *rentier* economy, $k = 0.91$. However, it would have increased the super-multiplier in the "economically active" country to a level of $k' = 2$.

In conclusion, this example underlines that the values of k and k' depend on both the behavior of guests (therefore on the value of the parameter g) and on the behavior of hosts (therefore on their propensity to consume c, which has a positive effect on the multiplier and the super-multiplier, and on their propensity to invest i, which has a positive effect on the super-multiplier).

The income multiplier is not the only multiplier that can be calculated for the aggregate analysis of the effects of tourism. Other multipliers that are commonly

Table 13.2 The multiplier of production and of employment in selected destinations

Region	(a) Multiplier of production	Region	(b) Multiplier of employment
Turkey	2.34	Jamaica	4.61
Grand County, US	1.98	Mauritius	3.76
Edinburgh, UK	1.51	Bermuda	3.02
Barbados	1.41	Malta	1.99
Gwynedd, UK	1.16	Western Samoa	1.96

Source: Cooper et al. (1998), p. 144

considered are: (a) the production multiplier, which measures the effect of tourism expenditure on production, rather than income; (b) the employment multiplier, which measures the effect that tourism expenditure has on the destination's level of employment.

Table 13.2 column (a) presents the multiplier of production for a number of selected tourism destinations. As it can be observed, the multiplier lies between 1.16 for a region of Wales to 2.34 for Turkey. It is however obvious that, by construction, the multiplier of production is usually greater than the multiplier of income.

Table 13.2 column (b) presents instead the multiplier of employment for a number of selected tourism destinations; the multipliers have been standardized to take into account the use of different measures of working time used in the various destinations. The table shows that, for example, in Jamaica for each new full-time employee in the tourism sector, more than four full-time jobs are created in the economy; however, as one can see, not all the economies have such high multipliers: if firms employ excess labor or labor with a productivity level close to zero (as is commonly the case in developing economies) it is possible that the increase in tourism expenditure will have very limited effects on employment.

13.2.4 The Tourism Expenditure Multiplier: Disaggregated Analysis

The analysis of the multiplier highlights the positive economic effects generated by tourism in terms of income and employment. However, one might have an interest in separating the effect of tourism expenditure (and of its composition) among the different economic sectors of the destination, in order to identify linkages, leakages, and crowding-out effects.

To do this, we need to undertake a disaggregated analysis of the tourism multiplier and the Input–Output (I–O) model, studied in Sect. 3.3.2, can be a useful starting point to determine the values of the tourism multipliers disaggregated by economic sector.

Since the multiplier is defined by the relationship between two incremental changes, $\Delta Y/\Delta G$, it refers to the unit value of autonomous tourism expenditure. Therefore a disaggregated analysis of the sectoral multipliers can be obtained from system (3.1) under the assumption that one unit value of tourism expenditure is directed to each productive sector: agriculture A, manufacturing M, and services S.

$$
\begin{aligned}
A &= 0.2M + 0.3S + 1 \\
M &= 0.2A + 0.4S + 1\,. \\
S &= 0.1A + 0.3M + 1
\end{aligned}
\tag{13.9}
$$

The solution of the system of equations (13.9) leads to the following values, which constitute the direct and indirect production necessary to sustain one unit of demand in each sector:

$$A \approx 1.81; \quad M \approx 0.87; \quad S \approx 1.71.$$

These values represent the *sectoral tourism multipliers, direct and indirect, of production.*

The system of equations (13.9) does not account for local household expenditure (*open input–output model*). If we want to account for such induced effect on consumption due to the additional income stemming from tourism expenditure (*closed input–output model*), we must first modify the technical coefficients of the transactions matrix adding the coefficients of consumption for local households. If we assume that the incomes V_a, V_m, and V_s of Table 3.1 are expressed as a percentage of production [0.7; 0.5; 0.3], and that these incomes are spent 50 % in consumption, distributed uniformly in the two sectors other than the one where the agents earn their incomes, we obtain the augmented coefficients of sectoral consumption.

If we indicate with d_i, where $i = A, M, S$, the endogenous local expenditure in line with the assumptions indicated earlier, the system becomes

$$
\begin{aligned}
d_A &= 0.5V_m + 0.5V_s \\
d_M &= 0.5V_a + 0.5V_s \\
d_S &= 0.5V_a + 0.5V_m,
\end{aligned}
$$

where $V_a = 0.7A$, $V_m = 0.5M$, $V_s = 0.3S$, and by substitution we obtain

$$
\begin{aligned}
d_A &= 0.25M + 0.15S \\
d_M &= 0.35A + 0.15S \\
d_S &= 0.35A + 0.25M.
\end{aligned}
$$

By augmenting the demand for these values into system (13.9), we obtain a new model that also takes into account the consumption of local households generated by the additional income earned as a consequence of a unit increase in tourism expenditure:

$$
\begin{aligned}
A &= 0.20M + 0.30S + 0.25M + 0.15S + 1 \\
M &= 0.20A + 0.40S + 0.35A + 0.15S + 1 \\
S &= 0.10A + 0.30M + 0.35A + 0.25M + 1
\end{aligned}
$$

and therefore

$$\begin{aligned} A &= 0.45M + 0.45S + 1 \\ M &= 0.55A + 0.55S + 1\,. \\ S &= 0.45A + 0.55M + 1 \end{aligned} \tag{13.10}$$

By solving the system (13.10), the following values, which constitute the direct, indirect, and induced production needed to sustain one unit of demand in each sector, are obtained:

$$A \approx 4.57; \quad M \approx 10.14; \quad S \approx 7.63.$$

These values represent the *sectoral tourism multipliers, direct, indirect and induced, of production.* The multipliers of system (13.10) are larger than those of system (13.9); in fact they take into account, in addition to sectoral linkages, the effect of induced consumption by the local population.

The disaggregated model of the tourism multiplier allows to emphasize that the benefits a destination receives from tourism are greater the higher the level of interdependence between tourism firms and the rest of the economy. In fact only a strong integration from the supply side allows tourism expenditure to spread its effects to the rest of the economy, from agriculture to manufacturing and to services, and also provides incentives for the diversification of the production structure in the destination and for the creation of new activities.

The destinations that are characterized by a relatively developed local economy experiment a consistent positive impact of tourism, due to the high level of sectoral linkages in their economic structure, while destinations poorly diversified and with little interdependence between sectors risk to undertake a process of tourism development that is not effective in the creation of income and wealth (UNWTO 2003). Therefore, from the perspective of the destination's management, the creation of linkages between tourism firms and the other sectors can be a good planning tool for sustaining and enhancing local development.

The I–O models are able to take into account the direct, indirect, and induced effects generated by a change in tourism expenditure; however, the assumptions on which they are based may lead to biased estimates (Dwyer et al. 2003b): (a) the *ceteris paribus* assumption, for which the components of the aggregate demand (other than tourism expenditure) are initially taken as given and not endogenously computed in the model; in other words it is not possible to take account of contemporary exogenous shocks in different sectors; (b) prices are taken as given and are not modified by the change in demand, which is tantamount to assume that the aggregate supply curve is perfectly elastic and that substitution effects between goods or factors of production are not at work. These caveats are the main reasons why I–O models, after having been used in the 1970s and in the 1980s, have now been replaced by Computable General Equilibrium (CGE) models.

General equilibrium theory aims to explain the behaviour of demand, supply and prices in the context of the aggregate economy where a multitude of markets exist for both goods and services and factors of production. General equilibrium theory is regarded as part of microeconomics based on detailed description of the adjustment process to the new

> equilibrium. On the other hand, the latter are built in such a way as to embed explicitly the transitional process in the numerical solution.
>
> (Stabler et al. 2010, p. 214–215)

CGE models are composed of a system of many equations, describing the condition of equilibrium between demand and supply in each market. In the standard set-up, CGE models endogenously determine the demand (price and quantity) of final components of demand, while factors of production are exogenously given (following the neoclassical assumption of full employment). In their most sophisticated applications, CGE include many dozens (if not hundreds) of equations. In tourism studies, CGE models have been extensively applied to analyze the disaggregated impact of tourism on the economy, starting with Copeland (1991). Among the many works, see in particular Dwyer et al. (2003a, b, 2004), Blake et al. (2006a, b), Li et al. (2010).

13.3 Tourism and Regional Development

It is easy to understand why the link between tourism flows and regional development is one of the hot issues in Tourism Economics, and also why it has been looked at from several points of view. Tourism geographers are primarily interested in the spatial alterations caused by the development of a tourism site and the subsequent consolidation of the various organizations that take care of the hospitality and of other leisure services in the destination; economic historians are interested in the reconstruction of the events that have led to the rise and the development of the tourism destination; applied economists examine, mainly through real-world case studies, how, and in what extent, tourism development leads to economic growth.

The historical, geographical, and economic aspects should be considered together to highlight the complexity of the existing relationship between tourism and development; however, in this context we are forced to make some simplifications and to limit ourselves to dealing with the topic exclusively from an economic theory perspective. We are aware of the shortcomings of approaching this complex problem in such a partial way, but we think that simple abstract models, once again, can indeed contribute to draw the attention on some stylized facts that are useful in interpreting the most important aspects of economic development related to tourism.

To do so, we will use a theoretical approach that extends the model of the multiplier presented in Sect. 13.2, adding a dynamic factor (i.e., explicitly considering the passing of time) and focusing on the long run rather than the short-run effects of tourism. Since the method of analysis is different, also the results will be partially different. In the short-run analysis carried out in the previous section, the basic assumption is that prices and the endowment of production factors (labor and capital) are given in quantity; therefore, the object of study is to optimize the employment rate of factors; in the long-run analysis, on the contrary, labor and capital follow dynamic growth paths. Therefore, the object of study becomes the identification of the optimal growth rate of production and income, that is, the growth rate that attains the full employment of production factors over time.

Before continuing, it is necessary to recall an important distinction for the economic literature between *development theory* and *growth theory*. With the term development theory one studies the evolution of an economy by concentrating on the *structural transformations* that mark its passage from the initial take-off phase to the consolidation of the country with high levels of per capita income. With the term growth theory, on the other hand, one studies the evolution of an economy that grows in size without undergoing structural changes. In other words, a growth model is defined as a dynamic model that studies an economy in which all the relevant variables grow at their equilibrium rate, leaving their relationship unchanged.

Following this distinction, in Sect. 13.3.1 we will consider the relationship between tourism and development from a development theory point of view, indicating the main phases that mark the evolution of an underdeveloped region that becomes a tourism destination; in Sect. 13.3.2 we will instead consider the relationship between tourism and development from the growth theory perspective, that is, of a region that is already a tourism destination, and that does not undergo structural changes.

13.3.1 The Phases of Tourism Development in a Regional Economy

To highlight the transformation that an economy undergoes from the arrival of the early tourism flows to its eventual economic take-off, we propose a model that identifies four phases (and three transformations). Such dynamic model proposes a temporal link between the multiplier and the super-multiplier.

1. *The phase of tourists arrival*. When compared to industrial goods, which can be consumed in places other than where they are produced, tourism has the peculiarity of being consumed, for the most part, in the place where it is produced. The first phase of tourism development of a region must be, therefore, marked by the arrival of early tourism flows, firstly by a small group of adventurous tourists, and later by a stable and growing flow of tourists (for an analogy with the life cycle of the destination, see Sect. 4.5.1).
2. *The phase of tourism consumption*. In the initial phase of development, tourism destinations are essentially consumption areas in which incomes earned elsewhere are transferred, following the tourists from their region of origin to the destination. In fact, tourism flows immediately bring a redistribution of purchasing power from the origin to the destination region. Through the multiplier described in Sect. 13.2, this transfer generates an autonomous demand that has a positive impact on local production and income: incomes earned by workers

and capital owners of the tourism sector are in turn spent on consumption goods; in this way regional production is stimulated not only by the goods and services demanded by tourists, but also by the additional consumption of the local population. Recalling the assumption underlying the multiplier and stated in (13.5), if tourism is a factor of development, the income transferred by tourists in phase one increases local income and the overall effect on income and employment in this phase depends, at the regional level, on the total demand of tourists and on the residents' propensity to consume. If we refer to the sectoral tourism multiplier (see Sect. 13.2.4), the direct, indirect, and induced effects of consumption by guests and by residents determine, through the linkages of the regional production system, also the sectoral distribution of gains in income, employment, and production.

3. *The phase of tourism take-off*. The consumption phase, started with the presence of stable flows of tourism, justifies the shift to the take-off phase, in which a whole production structure is developed, with the scope of producing goods and services for the tourism sector. The consumption phase is therefore followed by the investment phase, in which the tourism sector takes off, through the rise and development of those businesses and activities that will directly and indirectly aim to satisfy the demand of tourists. In this phase, additional income generated by tourism in the destination exceeds a certain threshold and, in addition to consumption, the local population begins undertaking investments. Through the concept of super-multiplier, the positive effect of tourism expenditure on the regional economy expands. In addition, with the take-off phase, the local industrial structure reaches a level of diversification and completeness that allows the destination to be independent from imports in the satisfaction of tourists' demand. Since the marginal propensity to import plays a negative role in the super-multiplier (see (13.8), where z appears in the denominator with a positive sign), the region's independence in the production for tourists makes the expansion effect due to tourism demand even stronger. With the take-off phase, therefore, tourism becomes an independent and non-occasional activity. The shift from the consumption phase to the tourism take-off phase marks for the destination the end of simply being a hospitality-based region and the beginning of a true specialization in the tourism sector, with the region becoming able to independently offer the whole tourism product. The production structure becomes more sophisticated but, in the end, it continues to be a *tourism-based monoculture*: the other economic sectors, in fact, remain indirectly dependent on tourists' demand.
4. *The detachment phase*. In this last phase the regional development continues and the destination loses its characteristic of tourism-based monoculture. The region becomes sufficiently rich to sustain investment in productive activities away from the tourism sector. Manufacturing firms and firms in the services sector are created and become independent from the needs of tourism. Many firms which received the impetus from the tourism take-off phase are now able to extend their activity outside the local market and away from the production for tourists. With the detachment phase, regional development does not forget its tourism

origins, but emancipates from it: the regional economy assumes the structure of an economy where tourism firms and industrial firms, some of which work with the tourism sector while some others are completely independent, are integrated. In this phase, the competition for the management of real resources (environment, territory, etc.) and the financial resources begins between tourism and other businesses.

The transition of the regional economy through all the four phases is not a mechanical law; the process of economic development can stop anywhere. For the model to be complete, it is then necessary to indicate the reasons that can halt the economy's transition from a phase to the following. For example, the phase of tourists arrival might not flow into the successive phase of tourism consumption when the great part of the tourism product is directly obtained from the tourists' home countries or, more in general, from outside the destination. In this case, which characterizes a tourism enclave (see Sect. 13.2.2), regional development is blocked in the first phase. Also, the phases do not necessarily follow in a mechanic way, and jumps can be observed. For example, due to a precise government intervention in terms of industrial policy, a region can directly move from the tourism consumption phase to the detachment phase.

In addition, even when the region moves from the tourists arrival phase to that of consumption, the shift to the subsequent take-off phase is not automatic. In fact, if local households do not start investing with the increase of their disposable income (by borrowing the terminology of classical economics, this happens if local agents act as *rentier* rather than entrepreneurs), the local production structure might never be able to independently supply the bundle of goods and services required to satisfy tourism demand.

The destination can be stuck in the consumption phase (and does not reach the take-off phase) when at least one of the three following conditions is true.

1. The tourism multiplier is so low that local incomes do not reach the threshold level beyond which households start saving, thus not allowing new investments to take place.
2. Although local incomes might exceed this threshold, in the destination there might not be sufficient entrepreneurial skills and know-how needed to set up a competitive offer to tourists; similarly, the financial market might not be sufficiently developed to back up the entrepreneurs' projects.
3. Finally, when a relevant share of the direct and indirect production necessary for tourism is imported from other regions, the tourism multiplier shows its effects by increasing the production, employment, and income levels of regions external to the destination.

Finally, also the shift from the take-off to the detachment phase can be problematic. In fact, to reach the detachment phase it is necessary that: (a) the local population owns important entrepreneurial skills; (b) the capital circuit is complete, that is, tourism has to play, with respect to the manufacturing sector, the role of *primary accumulation of capital* that the agricultural sector had usually done

(Varni and Negri Zamagni 1992). If either of the two conditions fails, the regional economy stops in a stage of tourism-based monoculture, without being able to spillover to other sectors and create development. The idea that the process of gradual shifting from one phase to the following is neither necessary nor automatic explains why in the real world there exist, and persist, tourism destinations that are quite different: regions that appear different because they are undergoing different phases in their evolution, or regions that appear different because they are stuck in different phases of their evolution.

13.3.2 Tourism in Growth Models

In the previous section we have focused on the development phases of a tourism region, while now the economic problem of a destination that has potentially reached the detachment phase (in which both the tourism and the manufacturing sectors are potential paths of development) will be unfolded and addressed. From this perspective, the models presented in this section deal with economic growth and expand the concept of macroeconomic equilibrium from the short run to the long run. In the history of economic thought, the first growth model presented is known by the name of the scholars that introduced it in the literature: the *Harrod–Domar model*.

Although the dynamic problem under investigation is quite complex, growth models look at the long-run equilibrium in a very simplified way: basic models such as Harrod–Domar's model consider an economy in which only one good is produced. Along this rationale, for example, we assume that in the economy only corn, which can be used both as a consumption good (for eating) or as an investment good (for seeding),[5] exists. The amount of corn that is consumed disappears from the production process, while the amount of corn that is seeded remains in the system as investment: it constitutes the capital that is used to produce larger amounts of corn in the future.

We denote with Y_t the quantity of corn harvested during period t; this variable also represents the income level of this simple one-good economy. In each period, a share of this income is consumed and a share is saved: if one abstracts from the autonomous component of consumption, as is common in long-run growth models, $C_0 = 0$, the part that is consumed by the population is $C_t = cY_t$. By definition $Y_t - C_t = (1 - c)Y_t = sY_t$ is the part that is saved. As we already know, c is called average (marginal) propensity to consume and therefore s is the corresponding

[5] This assumption is more realistic than it might seem at first glance: it means, in fact, concentrating on the *real* aspects of the economy, the quantity produced, while abstracting from the *monetary* aspects, the prices. This abstraction from the monetary aspects is typical of all contemporary growth theory and implies that all the complications caused by inflation are not taken into account since monetary variables, according to the standard theory, do not have permanent effect on the economy.

average (marginal) propensity to save. The quantity of seeds available for the productive system, due to past investment, constitutes the stock of capital K_t; therefore, investment in period t is the observed increase in capital, $I_t = K_{t+1} - K_t$.

Given this set up, the Harrod–Domar model is composed of two fundamental equations. The first equation assumes that in each period t the production and the demand of corn are in equilibrium:

$$Y_t = C_t + I_t, \quad \text{that is} \quad Y_t = cY_t + I_t. \tag{13.11}$$

The second equation considers instead the relationship between the increase in the capital stock and the increase in production (i.e., between seeded corn and harvested corn):

$$I_t = K_{t+1} - K_t = v(Y_{t+1} - Y_t), \tag{13.12}$$

where, defining $\pi = \frac{1}{v}$ as the marginal productivity of capital, we have

$$1/v = \pi = (Y_{t+1} - Y_t)/(K_{t+1} - K_t).$$

Since investment I_t appears both in (13.11) and in (13.12), we can replace the latter into the former, obtaining

$$Y_t - cY_t = v(Y_{t+1} - Y_t), \quad \text{that is} \quad sY_t = v(Y_{t+1} - Y_t). \tag{13.13}$$

This condition allows to define the equilibrium growth rate of income, which is known, using the terminology of Harrod–Domar, as the *warranted growth rate*:

$$\gamma_a = \frac{s}{v} = s\pi \quad \text{with} \quad \gamma_a = \frac{Y_{t+1} - Y_t}{Y_t}. \tag{13.14}$$

This equation, which constitutes the fundamental result of the Harrod–Domar model, affirms that in the dynamic equilibrium the growth rate of income, γ_a, must be equal to the product of the propensity to save, s, and the productivity of capital, π. If this condition is satisfied, the initial equilibrium between production and demand of corn will be maintained also in the long run: households will be able to consume what they demand and firms will be satisfied with their investment decisions. This property of the model is derived from the fact that, in the long run, investment has a dual effect on the economy: (a) on the demand side, it appears as a component of aggregate demand, (13.11); (b) on the supply side, it increases the capital stock, (13.12).[6] The dynamic problem emerges from the fact that in

[6] In the analysis of Sect. 13.2 the effect (b) was not considered, thus only focusing on the role of investment in the short run, as a component of aggregate demand.

(a) investment has an effect on the level of income, and in (b) investment has an effect on the change in the income level.

Moving to analyze the labor market, the economy must also guarantee full employment in the population, N_t. If at t there is full employment and if we denote with h_t the productivity of labor at time t, then:

$$y_t = N_t h_t, \tag{13.15}$$

where y_t is the full employment income. In order for the initial equilibrium to be steady over time, it is necessary that the growth rates of population, n, of technological progress λ and of income γ satisfy the following equality (due to the property of derivation of logarithms with respect to time):

$$\gamma = n + \lambda. \tag{13.16}$$

The growth rate of income γ in (13.16) is called the *natural growth rate* and is determined by the sum of population growth and technological progress.

In order for the economy to grow over time at its full employment level, condition (13.16), and with equilibrium between demand and supply of corn, condition (13.12), it is necessary that the natural growth rate be equal to the warranted growth rate:

$$\gamma_a = s\pi = n + \lambda = \gamma. \tag{13.17}$$

Equation (13.17) is a parametric identity, since it does not present any unknown variable. Therefore, the Harrod–Domar model reaches the equilibrium "by chance," while in general the economy might show either unemployment (if $\gamma > \gamma_a$) or inflation (if $\gamma < \gamma_a$): there is no endogenous variable allowing for a dynamic adjustment in the model. In this situation, the possible solutions presented in the literature are the *Kaldor model* (which belongs to the post-Keynesian school) and the *Solow model* (which belongs to the neoclassical school).

13.3.2.1 The Kaldor Model

The Kaldor model (1957) focuses on the distribution of total income between profits Π and wages W, and assumes that the propensity to save of the two groups are different: the propensity to save of profit earners (capitalists), s_c is assumed to be larger than the propensity to save of wage earners (workers), s_w. Therefore, total savings S is determined by the following equation:

$$S = s_c\Pi + s_w W \quad \text{where} \quad s = \frac{S}{Y} = \frac{s_c\Pi}{Y} + \frac{s_w W}{Y} \quad \text{with} \quad s_c > s_w.$$

Using Q_c and Q_w, respectively, to indicate the share (quota) of income accruing to the capitalists and to the workers, therefore $Q_c + Q_w = 1$, we can write

$$s = s_c Q_c + s_w Q_w = s_c Q_c + s_w(1 - Q_c) = (s_c - s_w)Q_c + s_w. \tag{13.18}$$

Replacing (13.18) into (13.17), we obtain the share of profits that maintains the growth rate in equilibrium:

$$Q_c = \frac{\gamma - \pi s_w}{(s_c - s_w)\pi}. \tag{13.19}$$

In the Kaldor model the production technology, measured by the productivity of capital, is assumed to be constant, that is, production uses only one technique with constant coefficients among factors. Therefore, the equilibrium of employment without inflation is warranted by a specific functional distribution of income between capitalists and workers.

13.3.2.2 The Solow Model

The Solow model (1956) assumes instead that the production technology has variable coefficients. It also introduces a production function of the Cobb–Douglas type, with constant returns to scale: $Y = AK^{\alpha}L^{1-\alpha}$, where K is capital, L is labor, and A is technical coefficient. In this model, the marginal productivity of capital is hence determined by

$$\pi = \frac{\partial Y}{\partial K} = A\alpha K^{\alpha-1}L^{1-\alpha} = A\alpha\left(\frac{K}{L}\right)^{\alpha-1} = A\alpha k^{\alpha-1}, \tag{13.20}$$

where the ratio $k = K/L$ measures the capital intensity of the production process and where the more technologically advanced the production system, the more capital is available for each worker.

Substituting (13.20) into (13.17), we obtain the capital intensity that allows to maintain equilibrium in the growth rate:

$$k = \left(\frac{\gamma}{sA\alpha}\right)^{\frac{1}{\alpha-1}}. \tag{13.21}$$

In the Solow model, hence, the equilibrium of full employment without inflation is guaranteed by the adoption of a production technology with a certain capital endowment for each worker.

13.3.3 Adding Tourism to Growth Models

After having recalled in Sect. 13.2.2 the equilibrium conditions of an economy specialized in the production of one generic good (we used the example of corn, but the model can be applied to any real economy), let us assume now that there is another economy, the same in every respect to the previous one except that this second one also receives a systematic flow of tourists. Therefore, it is necessary that a share of production in this "mixed economy" be directed to tourism consumption. Using the same terminology of Sect. 13.2, we indicate tourism demand in the economy as $(1 - g)G$. By introducing a series of simplifying assumptions (the economy does not import or export, $X = Z = 0$; the local population does not travel abroad, $H = 0$; there is no autonomous consumption, $C_0 = 0$), the equilibrium condition between production and demand recalled in (13.2) becomes

$$Y_t = C_t + I_t + (1 - g)G_t \tag{13.22}$$

Note that (13.22) reproduces the short-run equilibrium condition (13.2) but, since we are looking for the growth equilibrium of a mixed industrial and tourism economy that does not undergo structural transformations, we must assume that the share of tourism consumption in income remains constant, which is equivalent to adding another condition:

$$(1 - g)\frac{G_t}{Y_t} = q, \forall t, \quad \text{with} \quad 0 \leq q < 1. \tag{13.23}$$

The only thing left to solve, therefore, is the dynamic equilibrium of this mixed economy. With condition (13.23) and the indication of the consumption function, the Harrod–Domar model becomes

$$\begin{aligned} I_t &= v(Y_{t+1} - Y_t) \\ Y_t &= C_t + I_t + (1 - g)G_t \\ C_t &= cY_t. \end{aligned} \tag{13.24}$$

Substituting the third equation of (13.24) into the second one, solving for I_t, and replacing the result into the first equation, we obtain

$$sY_t - (1 - g)G_t = v(Y_{t+1} - Y_t), \tag{13.25}$$

and dividing both sides by Y_t, we find the warranted growth rate γ_T of the mixed (industrial and tourism) economy:

$$\gamma_T = \frac{s - q}{v} = (s - q)\pi, \tag{13.26}$$

where, by condition (13.23), the ratio $q = (1 - g)G/Y$ is assumed to be constant, with $s > q$.

The comparative dynamics with the specialized economy allows us to remark that $(s - q)\pi < s\pi$, therefore $\gamma_T < \gamma_a$. The effect of tourism on the host economy is that of lowering the warranted growth rate of income: in the long run, tourism consumption has a crowding-out effect on investment undertaken by local firms, leading to a lower warranted growth rate of income (we recall that this is the growth rate necessary to maintain the dynamic equilibrium between production and demand). It is also easy to demonstrate that tourism consumption would not lower the warranted growth rate of income only if residents reduced their consumption to make room for consumption by tourists; in this case, the consumption function would become $C_t = cY_t - (1 - g)G_t$ that, when replaced into (13.24), would reproduce (13.13), thus leading to the warranted growth rate γ_a.

To complete the analysis, also the equilibrium condition of full employment has to be considered. In such economy this condition requires the equality between (13.26) and (13.16), $\gamma_T = \gamma$. The latter growth rate is not affected by tourism and remains unchanged since it is plausible to assume that tourism does not have effects on the demographic and technological parameters:[7]

$$\gamma_T = (s - q)\pi = n + \lambda = \gamma. \tag{13.27}$$

Let us move now to the application of Kaldor's solution to this mixed economy. This can be done by considering a system of equations with (13.27) and (13.18). The solution would be

$$Q_c = \frac{q}{s_c - s_w} + \frac{\gamma - \pi s_w}{(s_c - s_w)\pi}. \tag{13.28}$$

The first-order condition of (13.28) with respect to q shows the equilibrium effect of opening up the destination to tourists on the functional distribution of income. Since in the Kaldor model:

$$\frac{\partial Q_c}{\partial q} = \frac{1}{s_c - s_w} > 0,$$

the destination with a higher share of tourism in the economy has a higher quota of profits and a lower quota of wages in the national income.

[7] However, one could consider sociological reasons for which the contact between tourists and the local population could modify the demographic pattern in the destination, in terms of birth, mortality, and migration. In the same way, it might be that the arrival of tourists and of multinational tour operators could drive a change in the production technology and, consequently, in the rate of technological progress.

Finally, by applying the Solow's solution to this mixed economy, we must consider the system of equations with (13.20) and (13.27). The solution would be

$$k = \left[\frac{\gamma}{(s-q)A\alpha}\right]^{\frac{1}{\alpha-1}}. \tag{13.29}$$

Hence, given the sign of the derivative, according to the Solow model applied to the mixed economy, the destination's share of tourism changes the capital intensity of the production technology.

In addition, in the mixed economy with tourism there is another possible condition of equilibrium apart from the ones indicated in the Kaldor and Solow models: given the values of s and π in (13.27), the share of tourism in the economy could be considered a strategic policy instrument for the destination government. This means that, in the destination, the goal of maintaining over time the equilibrium of full employment would not only depend on the economy's ability to modify, via a redistribution of income, the propensity to save, or, via technological progress, the productivity, but also on the ability to manage tourism flows and on the relative size of the tourism sector in the economy. From (13.27) we can directly obtain the value of q that achieves the full employment equilibrium:

$$q* = s - \frac{\gamma}{\pi}. \tag{13.30}$$

The mixed economy with tourism, therefore, *has an extra degree of freedom* with respect to a fully specialized economy. This is important if s and π in (13.30) appear as parameters and are not under the government's control; in this case, the dynamic equilibrium of full employment can be achieved in the mixed economy only by the correct sizing of the tourism sector. Moreover, for the (13.23), the assumption that q^* is constant requires that the growth rate of tourism consumption, $b = (G_{t+1} - G_t)/G_t$, be equal to the natural growth rate of income:

$$b = \gamma.$$

Hence, in order to maintain the level of full employment over time, tourism expenditure (which is assumed to be proportional to overnight stays) must also grow at the natural growth rate of income.

We have to recall, moreover, that both results of the depressive effect of tourism on the warranted growth rate and the possibility to use tourism as a further instrument to reach full employment apply only if the tourism sector is not an enclave (see Sect. 13.2.1). In fact, if a tourism enclave appears, the condition $g = 1$ is sufficient to maintain the equilibrium (13.14), and tourism does not affects the warranted growth rate of income; in such case, the only variables that might affect the long-run equilibrium are the propensity to save and the technological progress. This result is twin to the fact that the enclave does not have any effect on employment and income in the short run either.

The discussion of the tourism enclave would become more complicated should the model also take into account the usage of the destination's resources. The enclave can, in fact, subtract local resources from alternative uses in the other sectors of the economy, for example, transforming a natural bay into a tourism port (marina) rather than into a commercial port. In this case the enclave can produce a crowding-out effect on alternative investment opportunities, without bringing a positive effect on the conditions of full employment neither in the short nor in the long run. This crowding-out effect is discussed further in Sect. 13.4.

13.4 The Crowding-Out Effect of Tourism

An explicit assumption of the extension of the Harrod–Domar model to a mixed economy (see Sect. 13.3.3) is that the quota of tourism in the economy is constant over time. However, under the hypothesis of scarcity of resources, tourism development can be competing with the growth of other sectors of the economy. When an economic activity limits another economic activity, in economics, it is said that a *crowding-out effect* is at work; the term is borrowed from macroeconomic models of aggregate demand, when a type of expenditure, typically public spending, causes a reduction in another component of demand, typically private investment, in a way that the effectiveness of an expansive fiscal policy results strongly limited or, in the extreme case, nil.

By applying this concept to the tourism activity in the destination, three forms of crowding out of other economic activities can be listed.

1. *The crowding out of other tourism businesses*. This can take place when the development of a tourism project is undertaken to the detriment of existing tourism businesses.
2. *The crowding out of local activities*. This can take place when the development of a tourism project produces negative effects on the living conditions and on the availability of income for the local population. This phenomenon is most evident in weak communities and in less developed countries.
3. *The crowding out of non-tourism businesses*. This can take place when, due to the scarcity of resources, the development of a tourism project uses (totally or partially) a resource that consequently cannot be used in other production processes. In fact, investment in the tourism sector competes for the use of scarce resources with alternative investments in other sectors. The crowding out can unfold in the credit market (*financial crowding out*) or in the use of real resources (*real crowding out*), such as land. This phenomenon has been formally studied by Prud'homme (1985).

The three forms of crowding out each have different economic implications. Case (1) consists of the normal market competition where new tourism projects succeed at the detriment of those that have proven to be less profitable or not able to satisfy tourism demand. Therefore, the crowding out among tourism businesses enters in the evolutionary dynamics of the market, in the normal competition between firms that are created and those that are destroyed, thereby affirming also in the tourism sector, the competitive principle of "creative destruction":

> This process of Creative Destruction is the essential fact about capitalism. It is what capitalism consists in and what every capitalist concern has got to live in.
>
> (Schumpeter 1975, orig. pub. 1942, p. 82)

In case (2), the crowding out is instead the sign of a distributive failure in the market (Stabler et al. 2010) because it is the market that poorly chooses between profit and the survival of those activities that are physically and culturally necessary for the population. This failure is obviously a pathology of the market which, as all other market failures, requires government intervention to defend local communities from tourists and from a process of socially unsustainable development (see Sect. 16.3).

> Each type of tourist expenditure is associated with different distributional repercussions and although the aggregate welfare gains may be significant, there may be adverse effects on particular individuals and groups, notably those who do not own land used in the service sector... If the probable costs and benefits, both economic and non-economic, of different types of tourism were made explicit, a choice between them could be made in the context not only of their estimated income and employment generation but also of their wider social and distributional consequences.
>
> (Stabler et al. 2010, p. 208–209)

In case (3), however, a choice between alternative investments must take place. To depict the whole picture of the impact of tourism on the development of the destination, gains and losses have hence to be taken into account, by applying the concept of opportunity cost, which is necessary when a resource can be used in alternative projects. This last case of crowding out shows elements of economic strategy, where the goal is to evaluate whether a region should proceed towards an industrial development rather than of directing land and other resources to tourism. In other words, an increase in the growth rate of income due to tourism specialization might not be the optimal solution for the regional economy, should alternative uses of resources bring an even higher growth rate.

13.4.1 The Optimal Use of Scarce Resources When There Is Crowding-Out Effect

If a community produces both manufacturing and tourism goods, its national product, Y, is the sum of the value added of manufacturing and tourism sectors. Thus, indicating with $Q_M(R)$ the manufacturing product (quantity) and with $Q_T(R)$ the tourism product both as functions of the usage of the same resource $R \leq \overset{\circ}{R}$, and denoting with p_M the price of manufacturing goods and with p_T the price of the tourism product, the national product can then be written as follows:

$$Y = p_M Q_M(R) + p_T Q_T(R^\circ - R), \tag{13.31}$$

in which it is assumed that the resource is fully exploited by these two activities. Dividing (13.31) by p_M the value of the national product measured in terms of manufacturing products (the real value), Y_r, is obtained:

$$Y_r = \frac{Y}{p_M} = Q_M(R) + \tau Q_T(R^\circ - R), \tag{13.32}$$

where $\tau = p_T/p_M$ is the relative price between tourism products and industrial products (i.e., the number of manufacturing goods the economy has to give up in order to produce one unit more of tourism product).

Since R is an upper bounded resource, the economic condition of its optimal exploitation is obtained through the first-order condition of (13.32):

$$\frac{dY_r}{dR} = Q'_M(R) - \tau Q'_T(R) = 0 \quad \text{or} \quad Q'_M(R) = \tau Q'_T(R). \tag{13.33}$$

This condition is discussed in Fig. 13.2, where the marginal product of the resource in the manufacturing sector, $Q'_M(R)$, is shown with the thin line and measured on the left vertical axis and the marginal product of the resource in the tourism sector in terms of manufactured goods, $\tau Q'_T(R)$, is shown with the thick line and measured on the right vertical axis; since the available resource is entirely distributed between the two activities, the length of the abscissa is obviously R°.

Condition (13.33) is satisfied at the intersection of the two curves (point E in Fig. 13.2a), which abscissa determines the amount of resource used in the manufacturing sector (the segment $0E$) and the amount of resource used in the tourism sector (the segment ER°).

The optimal choice for the tourism destination is now unfolded: it depends on the resource's productivity in the two alternative sectors (in other words, by its degree of efficiency as an industrial input or as tourism resource), but also on the terms of trade τ between the two goods. Then, a movement of τ in favor of the tourism product can justify, *ceteris paribus*, a shift of the region towards the tourism sector, as shown by a comparison between points E and E' in Fig. 13.2a. As an extreme case, the value of τ can become so in favor of tourism that the destination finds it convenient to completely exploit the resource as a tourism input, giving up manufacturing production and fully specializing in tourism. This equilibrium (which technically is a *corner solution*) is shown in Fig. 13.2b.

This crowding out model is obviously static; it then remains to tackle whether this solution solves the destination's choice problem also in the long run, in a dynamic perspective. The solution to this problem requires the use of an endogenous growth model.

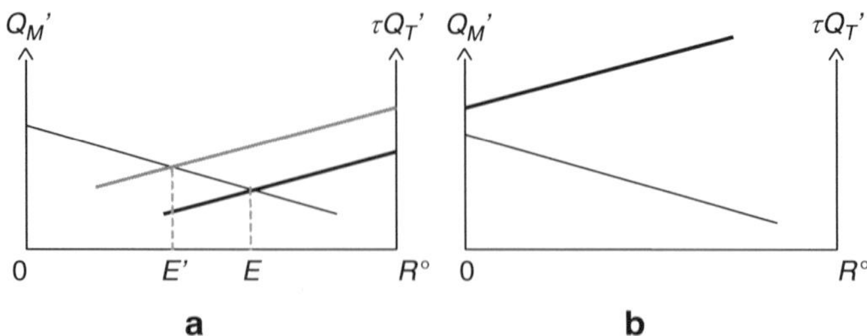

Fig. 13.2 The optimal use of scarce resources when there is crowding out effect

13.5 Tourism Specialization in an Endogenous Growth Model

In Sect. 13.3.2 we saw, using the basics of the Harrod–Domar model, that an economy specialized in manufacturing goods and a mixed economy with both a manufacturing and a tourism sector grow in equilibrium at the same exogenous rate, provided that the share of tourism in the economy is constant. Nevertheless, as Robert Solow (1956) affirms, from an intellectual perspective, to have an exogenous growth rate can be unsatisfactory.

In fact the long-run growth rate is such an important characteristic of an economy that it is not adequate to assume that it is exogenous (for example, that it is determined by demographic factors or by the rate of technological progress), particularly if our goal is to explain the evolution of the economy. The *endogenous growth models* try to overcome this limit by explaining, through the rationale of the model, the relationships that determine the growth rate of the economy.

In the literature, three methods have been developed in the last 20 years to tackle the problem of the exogenous growth rate: (a) by introducing the concept of human capital and allowing endogenous accumulation of it, through education and learning; (b) by introducing research and development activities into the model; (c) by abandoning one or more assumptions of the exogenous growth theory such as that of decreasing returns to scale of capital. The model we will refer to in this section is an extension of Lucas (1988), which introduced the concept of human capital in the literature. The human capital approach is particularly relevant for Tourism Economics because of the specific research on growth and tourism specialization that unfolded in recent years (see, for example, the special issue of *Tourism Economics*, 2007, n. 4).

The Lucas model is an optimal growth model in which the path taken by the economy over time is the consequence of individuals' decisions in terms of how to optimally allocate time between work and education. Without going into the details of the model, for our purpose it is sufficient to recall one of the main equations of the model, that for which labor productivity grows in function of the level of current human capital h, according to a parameter λ due to a form of learning which can be traced back to the theory of learning by doing by Kenneth J. Arrow. In linear form, such relationship can be written as

$$\frac{\mathrm{d}h}{\mathrm{d}t} = \lambda h_t, \tag{13.34}$$

where h_t can be interpreted as the average productivity of labor at time t. Dividing both sides by h_t, it is straightforward to find that the growth rate of productivity is equal to λ.

If we use (13.34) to compare labor productivity in the manufacturing and tourism, it is adequate to assume that the intensity of learning by doing is stronger in manufacturing than in tourism, so that labor productivity is higher in the manufacturing sector,[8] that is,

$$\lambda_M > \lambda_T, \tag{13.35}$$

where the subscript indicates the manufacturing (M) and the tourism (T) sectors. The key question is: does this difference in productivity imply a lower growth rate of the tourism specialized economy?

13.5.1 The Endogenous Growth Rate of a Tourism Destination

Starting from (13.35), Lanza and Pigliaru (1995) analyzed two fully specialized economies (one in manufacturing products M and the other in tourism products T) asking whether the tourism economy is inevitably associated with a lower growth rate than the manufacturing economy.

To answer this question it is necessary to consider the price of both manufacturing, p_M, and tourism, p_T, products, and the labor endowment L in the two economies. In particular, Lanza and Pigliaru consider the terms of trade, now defined as a function of time, $\tau(t) = p_T(t)/p_M(t)$, and, to avoid complications linked to the size of the economy, they assume that $L_M = L_T = 1$; in other words they compare two economies of equal size, normalized to one. Lanza and Pigliaru are therefore able to determine the equilibrium growth rates of both economies, applying (13.34).

Production in the manufacturing economy Q_M is assumed to be described by a production function with constant returns to scale:

$$Q_M = h_M L_M, \tag{13.36}$$

where h_M is the average labor productivity in the sector. If we assume that economy M has full employment, and recalling that labor has been normalized to one, (13.36) becomes

[8] Although in other parts of the book (see Sect. 7.6 and Chap. 12) we argue that also tourism can be a technological-intensive activity.

$$Q_M = h_M. \tag{13.37}$$

Equation (13.34) applied to this economy becomes

$$\frac{\mathrm{d}h_M}{\mathrm{d}t} = \lambda_M h_M = \lambda_M Q_M, \tag{13.38}$$

where, dividing both sides by h_M, we obtain the growth rate of productivity in the manufacturing sector:

$$h'_M = \frac{\frac{dh_M}{dt}}{h_M} = \lambda_M. \tag{13.39}$$

By considering the price of the manufacturing good as a *numeraire*, $p_M = 1$, the total income of economy M becomes equal to its manufacturing product

$$Y_M = Q_M.$$

Therefore, the growth rate of income is identically equal to the growth rate of the manufacturing product:

$$\gamma_M = (\mathrm{d}Y_M/\mathrm{d}t)/Y_M = (\mathrm{d}Q_M/\mathrm{d}t)/Q_M.$$

Moreover, (13.37) shows that the growth rate of the manufacturing product is equal to the growth rate of labor productivity h'_M, thus indicating that in the manufacturing economy income grows according to the following endogenous growth rate:

$$\gamma_M = \lambda_M. \tag{13.40}$$

Let us now move to the tourism economy. Also in this case tourism production Q_T is assumed to be described by a production function with constant returns to scale:

$$Q_T = h_T L_T, \tag{13.41}$$

where h_T is the average labor productivity in the sector. If we assume that economy T has, as in economy M, full employment, and recalling that labor has been normalized to one, (13.41) becomes

$$Q_T = h_T. \tag{13.42}$$

Equation (13.34) applied to this economy becomes

$$\frac{dh_T}{dt} = \lambda_T h_T = \lambda_T Q_T,$$

where, dividing both sides by h_T, we obtain the growth rate of productivity in the tourism sector:

$$h'_T = \frac{\frac{dh_T}{dt}}{h_T} = \lambda_T \tag{13.43}$$

Recalling that the relative price of the tourism product is equal to $\tau(t)$, the total income of economy T becomes equal to its tourism product expressed in terms of manufacturing goods:

$$Y_T = \tau Q_T = \tau h_T, \tag{13.44}$$

and therefore, in this case, the growth rate of income is

$$\gamma_T = (dY_T/dt)/dY_T = (d\tau/dt)/d\tau + (dh_T/dt)/h_T, \tag{13.45}$$

that is, to the sum of the growth rate of labor productivity in tourism (which, according to (13.42), is the growth rate of the tourism product) and the growth rate of the terms of trade. We can conclude that in the tourism economy income grows according to the following endogenous growth rate:

$$\gamma_T = \tau' + \lambda_T, \tag{13.46}$$

where τ' indicates the rate of change in the relative price between tourism and manufacturing goods.

To assess the relative performance of the tourism and the manufacturing economy we must compare (13.46) with (13.40)

$$\gamma_T > \gamma_M \quad \text{if} \quad \tau' + \lambda_T > \lambda_M \quad \text{so if} \quad \tau' > \lambda_M - \lambda_T. \tag{13.47}$$

Hence, the main conclusion of the model of Lanza and Pigliaru is that *the tourism economy can grow at a higher rate than the manufacturing economy if the terms of trade's increase more than compensates the technological gap between the two economies* (as we assumed that technological progress is higher in the manufacturing sector).

> Serious doubts about the relative performance of tourism specialization stem from the widespread belief that high growth rates are associated with the manufacturing sector, due to its better ability to generate innovation. However, this is just one of the factors at play, that we can define 'relative productivity effect'. When we compare the growth rates of two alternative specializations (tourism and manufacturing, in our case) we also have to take into account the trend of the prices of the two goods (that we can define 'relative price effect'). [...] The key point is the algebraic sum between these two effects (relative

productivity *vs.* relative price). Should the relative price of tourism decrease, tourism specialization would certainly be the less convenient. Having said that, it is easy to observe that the relative price of tourism usually increases.

(Pigliaru 2002, p. 20, *Our translation*)

To definitely conclude whether or not condition (13.47) is satisfied we need a theory of international prices for both the tourism and the manufacturing product. Lanza and Pigliaru (1995), using CES utility functions, conclude that the change in the terms of trade, τ', not only depends on the technological gap between the two sectors, but also on a parameter that measures consumers' preferences between manufacturing and tourism products. In particular, when the elasticity of substitution between these two goods is lower than one, that is to say, when the two goods are not close substitutes to each other, the model allows to conclude that an economy specialized in tourism could attain a higher growth rate of income.

A corollary of this result develops with regularity: the countries specialized in tourism tend to be small in size. Candela and Cellini (1997) demonstrate that the smaller the economy, the easier the terms of trade offsetting the technology gap: therefore, the smaller the country, the smaller the opportunity cost of specialization in tourism.

Subsequently, Lanza and Pigliaru (2000) extend their previous model by considering the endowment of natural resources in the destination. By recalling the rationale of Sect. 13.4.1, we then introduce the rate of exploitation U of a resource R of given dimension R°:

$$U = \frac{R}{R^\circ}. \tag{13.48}$$

The production function of the tourism sector, again assuming an economy of size L normalized to one as in (13.42), then explicitly assumes a multiplicative function between the labor productivity and the rate of exploitation of the resource, becoming

$$Q_T = h_T U, \tag{13.49}$$

where according to (13.34) $\mathrm{d}h_T/\mathrm{d}t = \lambda_T Q_T = \lambda_T h_T U$. The growth rate of productivity in the tourism sector when a resource is exploited in the production process then becomes

$$(\mathrm{d}h_T/\mathrm{d}t)/h_T = \lambda_T U. \tag{13.50}$$

Recalling (13.44) and (13.45), the growth rate of income is

$$\gamma_T - \tau' = (\mathrm{d}Q_T/\mathrm{d}t)/Q_T = (\mathrm{d}h_T/\mathrm{d}t)/h_T + (\mathrm{d}U/\mathrm{d}t)/U, \tag{13.51}$$

where $(\mathrm{d}U/\mathrm{d}t)/U = u'$ represents the growth rate of exploitation of the resource, which cannot stay constant over time since the resource is upper bounded, $U \leq 1$.

The optimization problem now is related to a destination that has to fully specialize either in manufacturing, which production function is still expressed by (13.37), $Q_M = h_M$, since the resource is not used in the industrial process, or in tourism that exploits resource R according to (13.49), $Q_T = h_T U$. If we keep the assumption of technological gap in favor of the manufacturing sector, $\lambda_M > \lambda_T$, we can write the growth rates of the two economies as follows:

$$\gamma_M = \lambda_M; \quad \gamma_T - \tau' = \lambda_T U + u'. \tag{13.52}$$

The condition of relative performance (13.45) now becomes

$$\gamma_T > \gamma_M \text{ if and only if } \tau' + \lambda_T U + u' > \lambda_M \text{ then if } \tau' > \lambda_M - \lambda_T U - u'. \tag{13.53}$$

In this extension of the model (Lanza and Pigliaru 2000), the tourism-specializing country takes advantage of the role played by natural resources: *even when the increase in the terms of trade does not balance the technological gap, the rate of exploitation of tourism resources can increase sufficiently to correct the technological gap and enhance growth.* However, this is a temporary condition. If the rate of exploitation keeps increasing over time, sooner or later, in a period $t = t^*$ the whole resource will be exploited, then $U^* = 1$ and $u' = 0$, and condition (13.53) would reduce to condition (13.47). Therefore, this last result suggests potential problems of sustainability of the growth process in the long run, issue on which we will come back in Chap. 16.[9] Recent contributions to the long-run sustainability of the development process are Cerina (2007), Giannoni and Maupertuis (2007), and Lozano et al. (2008).

This theoretical strand of literature has also given birth to empirical analysis aimed at assessing whether countries specialized in tourism attain higher than average growth rates. For example, Brau et al. (2007) show that the growth rate of tourism-specializing countries is greater than the growth rate of other groups of countries, thereby supporting the conclusion of Lanza and Pigliaru models. Using a sample of 143 countries observed during the 1980–2003 period they also reinforce the findings of Candela and Cellini (1997) by demonstrating that small countries specialized in tourism grow faster (with an average growth rate of 2.5 % in the period under consideration) than the other subgroups considered in their analysis (OECD countries, oil producers, less-developed countries, small countries), so showing that tourism specialization appears to be an independent and important determinant of economic growth for small countries in particular. Sequeira and Macas Nunes (2008) use different econometric techniques to show that tourism is a

---

[9] The implicit assumption of this model is that the resource cannot be regenerated. To be more precise, one should distinguish between renewable and not renewable resources. However, this would not qualitatively change the result (13.52): the long-run path of economic growth would be unsustainable if the rate of exploitation of the (renewable) resource is greater than its natural rate of regeneration (see Sect. 16.3).

Table 13.3 Real per capita GDP growth in 1990–2005 and 1980–2005

Country group	Real per capita GDP growth 1990–2005 (%)	No. countries	Real per capita GDP growth 1980–2005 (%)	No. countries
SC	2.21	23	1.60	19
STC > 0.10	1.88	11	2.26	7
STC > 0.20	1.59	6	2.41	5
STC < 0.10	2.52	12	1.22	12
All	1.61	150	1.14	122

Notes: SC (small country) indicates a country with a population of less than 1 million; STC (small tourism country) indicates a small country for which the index of tourism specialization (computed as the ratio between tourism expenditure by foreign tourists and gross domestic product) is greater than 10 % and 20 %, respectively
Source: Figini and Vici (2010), p. 797

positive determinant of economic growth, both in a broad sample and in a sample of poor countries. Differently from Brau et al, however, they do not find that tourism is more relevant in small countries than in the general sample.

Contrary to these two works, Figini and Vici (2010) use updated and improved data to find that there is not any significant independent relationship between tourism specialization and economic growth: in other words, there is not any significant difference between the average growth rate of tourism specialized countries and the other groups of countries. However, this result should not be surprising at the light of the theory: indeed, the Lanza and Pigliaru model shows the conditions under which a tourism-based growth process can flourish, despite a lower than average rate of technological progress within the sector. The empirical evidence of Figini and Vici simply shows that, on average, a tourism-based country does not grow differently from any other type of country, consistently with the theory of opportunity costs.

However, a second important result of Figini and Vici (2010) has to be highlighted: the average growth rate of countries specialized in tourism dramatically changes if we compare the 1980s and the 1990s. As Table 13.3 presents, small countries specialized in tourism attained higher than average growth rates in the 1980s but lower than average rates in the 1990s. This disappointing result could be interpreted at the light of Lanza and Pigliaru (2000) and (13.52): the high growth rates in the 1980s might have stemmed from the increasing rate of exploitation of natural resources, thus leading to a deterioration of the long-run sustainability conditions, where the "long run" began in the 1990s.

In this context, it is also important to cite a relevant strand of literature which, through time series analysis, test the tourism-led (export-led) growth (TLG) and the tourism-capital import growth (TKIG) hypotheses, that is, it attempts to explain whether tourism can be the engine of growth for specific countries and "how much" of growth can be explained by tourism.

According to TLG hypothesis, international tourism would contribute, as any other export, to income growth by enhancing efficiency through competition between local and international firms and by facilitating the exploitation of economies of scale in local firms. According to TKIG hypothesis (Nowak et al.

2007), tourism brings in foreign currency which can be used to import capital goods in order to produce goods and services, thus leading in turn to economic growth: in other words, TKIG hypothesis works through the super-multiplier (see Sect. 13.2.3) by triggering the phases of take-off and detachment described in Sect. 13.3.1.

Empirical results depend on the case studies (Case Study 13.1). Balaguer and Cantavella-Jordà (2002), Dritsakis (2004a), Durbarry (2004), Gunduz and Hatemi (2005), and Kim et al. (2006) analyze the impact of tourism on economic growth in Spain, Mauritius, Greece, Turkey, and Taiwan, respectively, and all conclude that there is a robust, positive relationship at play between the two variables: increase in tourism demand leads to economic growth. Conversely, Oh (2005) and Katircioglu (2009) do not find any long-run equilibrium relationship between tourism and economic expansion in Korea and Turkey, respectively. Finally, Cortés-Jiménez (2008) reports that domestic tourism is found to be a relevant factor of growth in Spain, whereas incoming tourism seems to be more important for economic growth in Italy. The general conclusion of this literature is that there is a strong diversification of growth experiences, and that beyond general theoretical models, each country and each destination has specific social–economic characteristics and follows a specific development path.

Case Study 13.1. Tourism Specialization and Economic Growth: The Case of the Maldives

The tourism history of the Maldives has frequently been compared with that of the Seychelles. Both are small archipelagos that have been able to make tourism a true *engine of growth* for their economies, achieving what larger countries in the developing world have not been able to do. In the Seychelles the integration of tourists and local population has been the key to its success, in the Maldives, on the other hand, the choice was to develop a tourism enclave, thus limiting the contacts between residents and tourists. Such pattern of development has, in part, reduced the economic impact of tourism and has made the accumulation of *know-how* by the local business more difficult.

The archipelago of the Maldives comprises 1,190 islands in the Indian Ocean and a population of roughly 200,000 inhabitants; from 1965 it is a sovereign country, after having been for roughly 80 years under the protectorate of the United Kingdom. Its economy has always been linked to the sea, and the transport and fishing sectors have always played a central role in the economic structure of the country. Still a relatively poor country, the Maldives made the first steps in tourism in the 1970s, with the development of the first beach *resort*; in this phase, the financial costs associated with the investment in tourism were mainly covered by the public sector. From 1978 on, investments made by European tour operators, mostly German and Italian, became more relevant; that is how a system was developed, in which the technical and financial assistance was coming from foreign firms while the local government played a role of coordination and control for the

(continued)

quality standards of the services offered. The commitment of the government in developing the infrastructure needed for tourism was important; in 1981 the international airport of Male was built in order to allow for the direct arrival of charter flights from Europe; two other minor airports were built in more recent times in some atolls, for solely tourism purposes. Some of the smaller uninhabited islands were chosen to allow for investors to transform them into beach resorts and holiday villages, while among the inhabited islands, only the capital, Male, was equipped with hotels and other hospitality structures.

The choice was therefore that of developing the tourism sector on the principle of separation between residents and tourists. In this way the social costs attached to tourism were substantially reduced and the spreading of negative behaviors like prostitution, drug consumption, or the degradation of the local social fabric were, in part, avoided. On the other hand, a negative effect was due to the limited access of the local population to the structures and infrastructures developed for tourists and, hence, to a limited multiplier effect. The great part of investments, the modern communications network, and the many infrastructures built for the tourism facilities were not fully accessible to the population nor even used by firms operating in other sectors.

Tourism development in the Maldives is therefore controversial; if the country has registered, over the years, a strong increase in tourism flows (international arrivals increased from 158,000 in 1990 to 467,000 in 2000, and up to 656,000 in 2009), the pace of economic growth has also been important: per-capita income increased from US$998 in 1990 to 2,293 in 2000, and up to 4,714 in 2010. The development strategy based on tourism enclaves, on the other hand, could make one think that the economic development could have been even bigger had the country chosen to better integrate the tourism sector with the rest of the economy.

In the last decade, tourism flows have not increased at a constant rate, also due to some external negative shocks. In 2002, due to unstable geopolitical situation following the 9-11 terrorist attacks, and in 2005, due to the destructive earthquake and tsunami of December 2004, important reductions in the number of arrivals and in overnight stays were registered (international arrivals reduced from 617,000 in 2004 to 395,000 in 2005). After the tsunami, international aid arrived from many international associations and organizations, and the government reacted with quickness and efficiency in the face of the crisis, financing projects that were directed to certain economic sectors and strongly contributed to the reconstruction of the country.

13.6 Local Development and Tourism Districts

In political economy, the tendency of firms to locate in the same area or region is well known. The first economist to systematically deal with this issue was Alfred Marshall. According to Marshall (1920) three distinct reasons can be identified to justify the tendency of firms to locate in the same region, thereby forming clusters or, in Marshall's terminology *industrial districts*:[10]

1. *The unification of the labor market*. The labor market that develops around an industrial district benefits both workers, in particular those with high skills or particular know-how, and firms. Marshall says:

   > Employers are apt to resort to any place where they are likely to find a good choice of workers with the special skill which they require; while men seeking employment naturally go to places where there are many employers who need such skill as theirs and where therefore it is likely to find a good market. The owner of an isolated factory, even if he has access to a plentiful supply of general labour, is often put to great shifts for want of some special skilled labour.
   >
   > (Marshall 1920, p. 159)

   This is also true for tourism firms. In a unified labor market, a restaurant is able to replace more easily a pizza maker who suddenly quits the job during the peak season; a travel agency can more easily find a full-time employee during unexpected peaks in business, etc.
2. *The supply of intermediate goods or raw materials*. An industrial district allows for an easier provision of specific inputs. Marshall says:

   > And presently subsidiary trades grow up in the neighbourhood, supplying it with implements and materials, organizing its traffic, and in many ways conducing to the economy of its material.
   >
   > (Marshall 1920, p. 160)

   This is also true for tourism firms. Think of the possibilities a hotel owner has of finding an electrician during an emergency when the air conditioning system fails; or a tour operator that needs to update the hardware and the software, etc.
3. *Knowledge spillovers*. Finally, in an industrial district the information circulates much easier than over longer distances, generating technological and organizational spillovers. Marshall says:

   > if one man starts a new idea, it is taken up by others and combined with suggestions of their own; and thus it becomes the source of further new ideas.
   >
   > (Marshall 1920, p. 160)

   This is especially true for tourism firms, where new ideas and new products are often of organizational nature.

Therefore, there exist advantages derived from a common location also for tourism firms. But for tourism there is something more, and a fourth argument needs to be added to the Marshallian ones.

---

[10] On industrial districts and systemic areas, see the scientific publications of Becattini and in particular Becattini (1987, 2000, 2004); see also Bagella and Becchetti (2000).

4. Since the tourism product is heterogeneous and plural (see Sect. 2.5), and since tourists' satisfaction is greater if they can easily move through a whole variety of tourism goods and services (see Sect. 4.3.2), a tourism destination finds in the concentration of different goods and services and in their variety the possibility of offering a whole, organized, tourism product to the tourist.

The local development is often linked to specialization patterns and to specific paths that, with the prevalence of one of more of the above factors, can be described by the concept of district. An example might help. The *Black Country* (Manchester, UK) is a well-defined area in the English West Midlands, that at the end of 1800 became the most industrialized region of the UK thanks to the South Staffordshire mines: foundries, furnaces, coal and steel companies that produced a level of pollution previously unseen in the history of the world, which is where the region gets its name. The *Black Country* is a classic example of local development that began as an *industrial district* for the Marshallian externalities recalled earlier, but died when the production technology that characterized it became obsolete. Over time, however, the region reinvented itself as a *cultural district*, revaluing the local heritage as a model of industrial archeology. Through the development of hospitality structures and the coordination of diversified tourism goods and services, it now offers a tourism product organized on its industrial heritage: with the arrival of the tourists the *Black Country* becomes a tourism destination, transforming itself into a *tourism district*.

This example allows to identify the main features of the different types of district that can be of interest for local development: industrial, cultural, and tourism districts.

- *Industrial districts* arise from Marshallian externalities; the creation of an industrial district is an endogenous and automatic market phenomenon that stops only if there are congestion problems (negative externalities that replace positive externalities).
- *Cultural districts* arise from the local cultural (and artistic) idiosyncratic nature of the territory. The cultural district is a model of local development that identifies and gives value to a cultural good within the territory. Santagata (2005) identifies the genesis of the cultural district in a specific culture belonging to the social groups, the institutions, or even to the natural resources (land, climate, water, accessibility) of a region, and treats time and space as its constructive elements:

> The idiosyncratic nature makes culture an atypical good for the market economy, which usually analyzes generic goods, that exist without time and space.
>
> (Santagata 2005, p. 143. *Our translation*)

  Frequently, the cultural district promotes a territorial brand, which becomes a common good for the territory; the local government must therefore guarantee the value of its cultural heritage in order to avoid the *tragedy of the commons* (see Sect. 15.2).

- *Tourism districts* arise from a diversified tourism product, because the variety of products and services increases tourist satisfaction (the Love for Variety Theorem, see Sect. 4.3.2); however, in tourism districts, firms can also take advantage of the Marshallian externalities, as in the industrial districts. The tourism district is therefore a model of local development that solves the problem of coordination and completion of the tourism product that have already been discussed in Chap. 4.

With local development, the districts tend to evolve and their primary characteristics tend to blend. The industrial district can assume cultural features (*Industrial Cultural District*) when the product is a local idiosyncratic type, like textile products, fashion, ceramics, jewelry, design. The cultural district can also take advantage of external economies if, for example, the cultural district has features of complexity (films, shows, etc.), in which the externalities can play a significant role. The tourism district can sometimes coexist with a local industry (*Evolved Tourism District,* Sacco and Ferilli 2006) or can assume a cultural feature for the destination that decides to invest in cultural tourism. Santagata (2005) defines four cultural tourism districts: the *Industrial Cultural District*, the *Institutional Cultural District* (if public intervention plays a key role), the *Museum Cultural District*, and the *Metropolitan Cultural District*.

This pattern of evolution leads Porter (1998) to identify three phases of local economic development, called: (a) factor driven, by a particular preexisting local (real or cultural) resource; (b) investment driven, when the path followed by the district is driven by new investments; (c) innovation driven, when the district reinvents itself and becomes mature in function of the innovations introduced. In this last phase the evolution leads the district to transform itself into something else, a different or more evolved district configuration.

In this dynamic process it is also necessary to identify the role of the local government, which can be a role of action or inaction. According to Cuccia and Santagata (2004) the public intervention can follow two methods of control: *top-down*, in which the authority is part of the district, and *bottom-up*, in which this intervention is not necessary in the constitutional phase (since the district is created as the result of widespread economic incentives). In the latter case the public authority could still actively intervene in the organizational phase, providing an institutional framework to the district.

In the case in which a cultural district is created around a cultural brand or the tourism district is created as a product club, the brand and the club must assume the technical role of signal. This implies a selection process for admission and (continuous) control of the quality of the local product. If the procedure of control is inefficient, an exit mechanism could start (see Sect. 11.5.5), risking to jeopardize the club's survival.[11]

[11] For an in-depth analysis of the economic issues concerning districts and local tourism systems, see Candela and Figini (2005), Chap. 11, and Candela et al. (2008b).

Chapter Overview

- Tourism expenditure is an autonomous component of aggregate demand that can be explained by the concept of Keynesian multiplier. If the tourism multiplier is larger than one, tourism can be considered as a development factor, if it is less than one, tourism is a parasitic factor, and if it is zero, tourism constitutes an enclave in the local economy.
- The tourism super-multiplier describes an additional effect of tourism expenditure on the regional economy, in which income of residents can be spent on both consumption and investment goods. The super-multiplier is greater than the corresponding multiplier and makes it easier to consider tourism as a development factor.
- A simple model that describes the development of a tourism destination identifies the following phases: arrival of tourists, tourism consumption, take-off, and detachment.
- According to the Harrod–Domar model, the growth rate of income must be equal to the product of the propensity to save and the productivity of capital to maintain the economy in its dynamic equilibrium. The Harrod–Domar model, using the approaches of Kaldor and Solow, allows for the study of the effect of tourism flows on the functional distribution of income and on the production technology.
- A mixed economy characterized by manufacturing and tourism enjoys more degrees of freedom than a fully specialized economy: maintaining the full employment equilibrium over time not only depends on the ability to modify the propensity to save or the productivity of capital, but also on the relative size of the tourism sector within the local economy.
- In models of endogenous growth, the growth rate attained by a tourism destination depends on the rate of technological progress of the different sectors and on the terms of trade between the goods produced. The application of the Lucas model to two economies, one specialized in manufacturing and the other in tourism, cannot exclude that the tourism economy grows at a faster pace than the manufacturing economy, if the dynamics of the terms of trade between tourism and manufacturing goods more than compensates for the assumption of technological gap between the two sectors.
- According to the Marshallian theory of industrial districts, there are three reasons to justify the tendency of firms to locate in clusters: the unification of the job market, the supply of intermediate goods and raw materials, and the knowledge spillovers, to which a fourth reason, specifically relevant to tourism, can be added: the possibility to offer coordination and variety in the tourism product.

Chapter 14
International Tourism: Real and Monetary Flows

Learning Outcomes
By the end of the chapter you will understand:

- The key concepts of international tourism, such as the exchange rate, the multinational company, the balance of payments.
- The main factors driving international tourism flows and the localization of firms in tourism destinations.
- The effects of a change in the exchange rate on tourism flows and on firms' behavior.

14.1 Introduction

In Chap. 2 we classified tourism flows in international (incoming and outgoing) and domestic tourism. While in statistical terms international tourism was identified by the movement from one country to another for tourism purposes, in this chapter we will highlight that the relevant economic fact linked to international tourism is not the crossing of a border, but the presence (and the fluctuation) of the exchange rate between the home country's and the destination's currencies. Hence, from an economic perspective, we are faced with international tourism when tourists (and more generally market operators) are subject to the currency exchange, with all the risks involved with its variation over time.

Indeed, the uncertainty connected to the future movement of the exchange rates introduces another strategic variable in the choice made by tourists and firms. The tourists have to consider the explicit and implicit costs of exchanging their money in one or more foreign currencies. These costs are also borne by firms, with their choice fundamentally consisting of either taking on the risk of unpredicted fluctuations in the exchange rate (which can be favorable, and therefore a source

G. Candela and P. Figini, *The Economics of Tourism Destinations*,
Springer Texts in Business and Economics, DOI 10.1007/978-3-642-20874-4_14,

of revenue, but also unfavorable and potentially leading to an economic loss) or in insuring against this risk with the instruments developed by the financial markets.

Moreover, the process of globalization and the increasing international dimension of tourism have consequences on the structure of tourism markets and on the strategies of its operators: at present, international tourism markets are mainly oligopoly markets in which a great share of economic power is in the hands of multinational companies: airlines, tour operators, hospitality firms, Global Distribution Systems, etc., with strong implications for local firms.

In this chapter we will deal with all these topics. In Sect. 14.2 we will start by studying the main features of international tourism, analyzing the changes in the market structure and in the strategies of the operators that want to compete in the international market. We will underline the role played by multinational firms in tourism and touch on the topic of globalization and how it is changing international tourism flows.

Following the standard theory of International Economics, we will separate the topics that belong to the real side of the economy from those that belong to the monetary side. The topics of real economy will be introduced in Sect. 14.3, by discussing some of the models that in the economic literature have been proposed to explain international trade (and therefore also tourism flows). The topics of monetary economy will be discussed in Sect. 14.4, by focusing on the key element of this chapter, the exchange rate. In the last paragraph, we will analyze the different exchange rate systems, how they work, the different types of financial instruments developed to protect against future variations of the exchange rate, and by looking at the consequences on the behavior of firms, tourists, and destinations.

14.2 Domestic and International Markets

The distinction between domestic and international tourism markets is not simple to determine. In fact, the usual separation made in economics, which defines an international market as a market characterized by barriers in the trade of production factors and goods, is ill suited for tourism, where the high mobility of tourists and the services offered is a fundamental characteristic of the phenomenon. Nor can we think of using distinctions based on geographic, administrative, or political borders.

> The 4500 km covered by a New York resident to spend a holiday in Santa Barbara (CA) are not enough to consider the trip as international tourism, differently from a resident in Lille (France) who travels 80 km to stay in Ostende (Belgium). It is even more curious to notice that the US continental citizens who travel to the Hawaii are considered international tourists, although they do not leave the US territory, while it is not true for trips from the Hawaii to the continental US.
>
> (Dewailly and Flament 1995, p. 50. *Our translation*)

The price of tourism as introduced in Sect. 5.2.1 (Eq. 5.2) allows instead for a sufficiently precise distinction between domestic and international markets in economic terms. If in the price $v_{i,r}$ the exchange rate c_r is variable, then tourism belongs to the international market; if in the price $v_{i,r}$ the exchange rate does not appear ($c_r \equiv 1$), or only plays a parametric role (c_r = institutionally fixed), that is, if the two countries use the same currency or if there is a fixed exchange rate (the two currencies are pegged together), then tourism belongs to the domestic market.

According to this definition, tourism between the UK and Germany should be considered an international market, while tourism between France and Spain should be considered a domestic market in economic terms. Not only this distinction allows to go beyond the political (based on the borders between countries) and geographic definitions (based on distance), but also to adapt to the evolving international situation, such as the introduction of the Euro as a common currency in most countries of the European Union. Accordingly, all the tourism flows between countries belonging to the Euro area should not be considered, from an economic point of view, international flows, although for statistical and political purposes they are recorded as international tourism.

Due to the increased mobility and tourism becoming a mass phenomenon in the late decades of the twentieth century, international tourism is one of the main topics in the study of tourism. These international flows can affect the economic growth of countries (see Sect. 13.5) and their balance of payments, thereby having both real and financial consequences.

Nevertheless, before dealing with the macroeconomic issues of international tourism, we need to identify the international market operators and study their behaviors and strategies.

14.2.1 International Tourism Operators

In the international tourism market the following operators are usually at work: (a) international transport companies, prevalently airlines; (b) international tour operators; (c) international hotel chains. Since all these firms can take the organizational structure of the multinational, in the following subsections we will see how the tourism market is affected by the presence of these mega-firms.

14.2.1.1 The Airline Companies

From the moment when air transport became the most popular form of transport used by international tourism, and from the moment when international tourism was increasing in importance, many airlines changed strategy and made investments in order to satisfy such demand. The joint effect of these factors with the development of ICT and the deregulation of air markets has brought the expansion of low-cost companies and a restructuring of the market through a considerable number of mergers, acquisitions (strategy of horizontal integration), or strategic alliances that involve the major airline companies in the world. Moreover, some companies have also being pursuing a strategy of vertical integration, by buying out tour operators and/or travel agencies.[1]

An important factor driving the process of internationalization is the firm's country of origin, since the airlines with their headquarters in countries generating a high level of international tourism demand have a greater possibility of catching the tourism flows. In the long run, these airlines strengthen their position, their market power, and the share of profits accruing from international tourism.

Low-cost airlines are instead transport companies able to offer flights at prices that are much lower than those set by traditional airlines (for the most successful case in Europe, Ryanair, see Case Study 9.2). The characteristics of low-cost airlines, allowing them to set extremely low prices, are many: technical (for example, the use of an aircraft configuration with a greater number of seats, a more intensive use of the fleet), organizational (for example, multiple duties for employees, flight attendants partially paid in percentage of sales, direct ticket sales by phone or by Internet, self-check-in), economic (for example, routes based on cheaper airports, bulk discounts in purchasing large supplies of fuel, agreements with local firms for additional services, reduction in the number of employees), simplification of the services offered (for example, one ticket class, one type of airplane, elimination of breakfast, lunch and baggage transfer services), regulation (for example, the extra fee to pay for handling in luggage or for reserving a seat), and, finally, marketing (for example, very low prices for early reservations, special sales as promotion tools, and strategies of yield management to deal with the evolution of demand).

At the beginning of the twenty-first century it was possible to count 44 low-cost airlines in Asia; 68 in Europe, of which 14 in the United Kingdom and 11 in Turkey; 30 in the Americas, of which 16 only in the US, 4 in Oceania, and 9 in Africa. The success of the low-cost organizational model has made the traditional airlines rethink their role through the implementation of both strategies of product differentiation in certain routes, market segments, or quality offered and the technical or organizational innovations introduced by the low-cost competitors. Moreover, the concept of low cost has gone beyond the limits of the air market and has quickly spread to other sectors of the economy so that it is now common to refer to the concepts of low-cost economy or low-cost society.

14.2.1.2 International Tour Operators

In the international market tour operators offer all-inclusive tours that involve many countries. As Nowak et al. (2010) clearly point out, the activity of the tour operator is that of assembling the components of a package tour to create a new product. As the many segments of production can be very different from each other in terms of

[1] For example, in the European market the main airline groups are the strategic alliances Air France/KLM, British Airways/Iberia, and Lufthansa, and the low-cost company Ryanair.

technology, skills, factors of production, it seems reasonable to assume that tourism's value added would be internationally split up across different countries, according to varying factors and local comparative advantages (see Sect. 14.3.2). Since we already know (see Sect. 8.2) the economic rationale of the tour operator, here we only discuss the international aspects of its activity. For an international tour operator it is important:

1. To have a continuous update, modification, and expansion of the holiday portfolio, following the evolution of tourists' preferences in the home countries and the economic, social, and geo-political conditions in the destination countries.
2. To pay attention to the peculiar features of the different destinations, focusing on the fiscal advantages, the differences in the legal systems, and the quality of local structures and infrastructures.
3. To evaluate and to forecast the evolution of exchange rates.
4. To diversify the holiday portfolio, in order to meet the tourism demand and to reduce the management risk.
5. To implement an effective policy of commercialization, in order to take advantage from the economies of scale accruing from the international market.

While we leave the feature numbered as 1 and 2 to the sociology and the law of tourism, respectively, let us now consider the economic aspects of the issues numbered as 3, 4, and 5, which we will explain through a few examples.

With regard to the problem of exchange rate evaluation (see issue number 3 above), there exists the possibility for the tour operator to gain from the variation in the purchasing power of different currencies. Let us consider the case of a European tour operator that inserts a holiday to the US in its catalog when the exchange rate is at $1.25 per Euro. The tour operator has to stipulate the contracts with the US service suppliers, for example, with the hotel company, which ask $100 per room. Let us assume that the tour operator charges a markup of 100 %. The strategic decision for the tour operator is on whether to set and publish in the catalog the price of the trip in dollars or in Euros. In the first case, the price is set at $200; in the second case the price is set at 160 € (=200/1.25).

If the exchange rate is predicted not to change, the two prices are equivalent, but if a variation in the exchange rate is foreseen then there are various possibilities: (a) if a depreciation of the dollar to 1.30 is forecast, it is beneficial for the tour operator to set the price of the trip in Euros and pay the supplier in dollars (thus the price in the catalog is set at 160 €, equal to $208 with the new exchange rate, while the contract with the supplier defines the payment of $100, thus realizing a markup of $108, with an extra profit of $8 per reservation); (b) if an appreciation of the dollar to 1.20 is forecast, it is beneficial for the tour operator to set the price of the trip in dollars and pay the suppliers in Euros (thus the price in the catalog is set at $200, equal to 167 € with the new exchange rate, while the contract with the supplier defines the payment of 80 €, equal to $96 at the new exchange rate, thus realizing a markup of $104, with an extra profit of $4 per reservation). The tour operator,

Table 14.1 The diversification of the tour operator's holiday portfolio

	Fiji islands	
Canary islands	High sales (prob = ½)	Low sales (prob = ½)
High sales (prob = ½)	4 + 4	4 + 2
Low sales (prob = ½)	2 + 4	2 + 2

through the careful management of price setting and contracts with suppliers, can therefore get capital gains in the exchange rate, thereby increasing its overall profit.

Moreover, the working on the international market allows the tour operator to reduce the risks involved with its business (see issue number 4 above) through the implementation of a strategy of diversification of its holiday portfolio. Not only such policy meets the tourists' demand for variety but also reduces the risk connected to the fact that the profitability of the trip depends on the matching between the prediction and the effective sales of the trip (see Sect. 8.2.3). Hence, to diversify its holiday portfolio is in the interest of the tour operator. Let us explain it with an example.

Let us assume that a German tour operator decides to offer two sea & sun holidays and that can choose between two destinations to insert in the catalog: the Fiji Islands and the Canary Islands. Each holiday can lead to two possible economic returns: 4 if the sales go well (an event that occurs with a probability of 50 %) and 2 if the sales go poorly (an event that occurs with a probability of 50 %). Moreover, the probability of having good or poor sales in each of the two destinations are independent events. The possible cases are summarized in Table 14.1, which represents the payoff matrix for the international tour operator.

What is the best strategy for the tour operator that wants to offer two holidays in its catalog? Should it offer two holidays in the same destination or diversify the portfolio?

To answer this question we compare the payoffs in the cases of specialization and diversification. We first check what happens when the tour operator is completely specialized, offering two holidays in the Fiji Islands or two holidays in the Canary Islands. Both strategies give an average return of 6 $(=(4 + 4)0.5 + (2 + 2)0.5)$ with a variance of 4 $(=(8 - 6)^2 0.5 + (4 - 6)^2 0.5)$. If we assume instead that the tour operator offers one holiday in the Fiji Islands and one holiday in the Canary Islands, there are many combinations of events that can take place. From Table 14.1 it is easy to check that there is a 2 5 % probability that the trip to Fiji and the trip to the Canary Islands both sell poorly, a 50 % probability that one sells poorly while the other sells well, and finally a 25 % probability that both trips sell well. The average payoff of diversification is still 6 $(=(4 + 4)0.25 + (4 + 2)0.25 + (2 + 4)0.25 + (2 + 2)0.25)$, but its variance is now 2 $(=(8 - 6)^2 0.25 + (6 - 6)^2 0.5 + (4 - 6)^2 0.25)$. Hence, through the diversification strategy the tour operator is faced with a lower level of risk (measured in terms of the variance of the payoff) for the same average payoff. This conclusion is an application of a famous result of financial theory, for which risk-averse agents prefer to diversify their portfolio.

Just as interesting are the results in the case where it is assumed that the payoffs of the two islands are correlated: we will only study the extreme cases, but all the intermediate cases can be traced back to the same conclusions.

The assumption that between the two islands, because they are located in different oceans and latitudes, their tourism flows have a perfect negative correlation is interesting. In this case, the possibilities indicated along the main diagonal of the matrix (Table 14.1) disappear. Therefore, the average payoff of the diversified portfolio is still 6 (=(4 + 2)0.5 + (2 + 4)0.5), with a variance clearly equal to zero, an interesting result when compared to the specialized portfolio, which we know has a variance of 4. Thus, if a perfect negative correlation exists between these events, diversifying the portfolio can totally eliminate the international tour operator's risk. By similarity, if the negative correlation is not perfect, the risk is diminished but not completely eliminated.

On the other hand, if the tourism of the Fiji and the Canary Islands, even though in different oceans, are positively correlated, the sales can either both go well or both go poorly. In this case, the possibilities indicated along the antidiagonal of the matrix (Table 14.1) disappear. Therefore the average payoff of the diversified portfolio is still 6, but with a variance of 4, which is exactly identical to the specialized portfolio of the two holidays in the Fiji Islands or the two holidays in the Canary Islands. Thus, if a perfect positive correlation exists, then diversifying the portfolio does not produce any advantage in terms of risk reduction; the only element to consider, in such case, is the cost of managing a diversified or a specialized portfolio.

Finally, as regards the above point number 5, the commercialization phase represents a part of the production chain on which a relevant share of the tour operators' economic performance depends. For this reason such firms, particularly those that operate in international markets, pay close attention to the achievement of three important objectives: (a) the development of an efficient sales system in different countries, through the implementation of agreements with many travel agencies in different countries; (b) the integration of commercialization efforts with the other firms involved in the production; (c) the development of an effective advertising policy, through the promotion of an internationally recognized brand.

The relevance of these problems is such to convince most of the major international tour operators to enter directly into the retailing sector, by developing or purchasing a chain of travel agencies that exclusively sells their products in the different countries of origin of tourism flows. Moreover, the tour operators can search for other agreements with airlines and hotel chains in order to use their international channels for selling. Overall, these strategies shed light on how the policies of international tour operators can be important for a tourism destination, in some cases even more than its cultural, organizational, or natural resources. The understanding of international markets and firms' strategies is thus able to explain the direction and the size of tourism flows in the international market and the profits generated.

14.2.1.3 International Hospitality Firms

Hotels and other hospitality firms have a key role in the globalization of the tourism sector. In the international market, they are sometimes present as independent operators but more frequently as hotel chains that operate in many different countries. The objective of hotel chains is to offer standardized services to the international traveler, thereby reducing the uncertainty about quality for those booking the hotel from home (see Sect. 6.7.3). Kemmons Wilson, who founded the Holiday Inn chain in 1952, developed this franchising agreement on a large scale in order to connect different hospitality firms in several countries. Holiday Inn and Best Western (Case Study 9.1) were the first examples that encouraged the development of other chains or hotel groups: Hilton, Inter-Continental, Marriott, Sheraton, Starwood. Later, other non-American, European, and Asian firms entered the international tourism market (Accor, Sol Melia, Mandarin Oriental are among the most important), thereby completing the internationalization wave in the hospitality sector. More or less, all these chains are now present in 70–90 countries, with a capacity of around 400,000–500,000 rooms in 3,000–4,000 hotels.

Nowadays, the competition in the hospitality sector mainly develops at the international level, even though we need to recall that hotel chains are not only an international phenomenon; there are in fact chains at the national level and small chains at the local level that offer the standardization of hospitality services at the national and local level, respectively.

14.2.2 The Role of Multinational Companies in Tourism

Since in the international market the development of large and complex corporations has recently taken place, it is now our task to try to understand the key economic features of these companies, which are explicitly called multinational companies in the economics literature. Multinationals can be defined as companies which organization is directed to locating their production activity (or part of it) in different countries, even while maintaining ownership and management in the country of origin.

In addition to the multinational company, in economics there are other definitions: (a) the international firm, that is active in different countries but that keeps the process of decision making in a specific international division coordinated by a group of managers that maintain a national point of view; (b) the transnational firm, that is active in different countries but which management is detached from any type of national link, even with respect to the host country; (c) the supranational firm, the most evolved form of a transnational firm, which has contractual freedom and is developed by agreements between different countries, in order to facilitate a flexible and always updated structure for the company.

The models that explain the rise of multinational companies can be traced back to the following ones: (a) the market power model, which refers to the companies' reaction to the degree of concentration of national markets; (b) the international organizational model, which refers to advantages in terms of transaction costs and international contract costs; (c) the international model of the product life cycle, which refers to a link between the life cycle phases of a product and the location of the company; (d) the technological innovation model, which refers to the center–periphery location of the production of goods with innovative or mature techniques.

Such models have mainly been developed to explain the behavior of manufacturing firms and are not fit for an indiscriminate application to tourism multinationals that are involved in the service sector. It seems more appropriate, though, to use a theoretical interpretation that involves many other factors, which cannot be traced back to the industrial organization models presented earlier. In this perspective, Dunning (1977, 1988) proposed an eclectic theory of multinational firms, which attempted to explain their strategies by using more explanatory factors.

The model is based on the recognition of the alternative methods of involvement of firms in foreign markets: (a) through international trade (for example, exporting goods through foreign partners); (b) through the transfer of know-how, technology, and organizational resources (licensing, technical assistance, franchising, etc.); (c) through foreign direct investments (FDI), by opening departments and carrying out parts of the production process in other countries.

According to Dunning, the reasons behind solution (c), the FDI, are three:

1. *Ownership advantages*, that derive from operating as a foreigner in a country, both for the intangible activities (think of the possibility of engaging in marketing, of using the know-how, of accessing the credit) and for the tangible activities (think of the political pressure that multinational companies can exert over national governments).
2. *Location advantages*, that derive from the firm's location in countries with certain comparative advantages, such as lower costs of production, better access to primary resources, adequate transport and communication networks, tax breaks, and public subsidies, etc.
3. *Internalization advantages*, that derive from the existence of economies in terms of lower transaction costs in purchasing inputs and intermediate goods and in terms of exercising direct control over intangible assets such as the logo and the know-how.

The eclectic theory by Dunning (OLI: Ownership, Location, Internalization) is suitable for interpreting the situation of the tourism market. Tourism multinationals invest abroad due to obvious location advantages (the existence of natural and cultural resources in the destination) and to ownership advantages (the extent and the direction of tourism policies, particularly with respect to economic benefits and direct incentives aimed at foreign firms, such as detaxation of profits). Finally, what is particularly relevant for the case of international tourism is the mobility of tourism flows, therefore firms need to connect countries with tourism resources to countries with strong demand of tourism services (internationalization advantage). Dunning himself, in his work of 1977, considers the hospitality sector (for their resource-based structure) and the sector of production and distribution of package holidays among the sectors that favor multinational firms.

A key issue in the debate on multinationals, which connects FDI to the local development process (see Sect. 13.6), is the role that multinational firms plays in promoting or jeopardizing the development of host country. The economic literature has approached this issue in different ways, arriving at different conclusions.

On one hand, the heterodox and radical perspective affirms that the multinational company, being technologically and organizationally at the forefront, is able to transfer important real and financial resources to the host country (and also vice versa, depending on own profitability and not on the destination's interests), thereby putting competitive pressure on the small local firms and political pressure on local governments. Both aspects lead to relevant negative effects on the process of development of the region and the country. According to this point of view, multinational firms exploit the local resources thus crowding out investment of local firms (see Sect. 13.4) and limiting their economic and political strategies. When this happens, we already know that the tourism sector develops through enclaves with scarce economic impact on the local territory.

On the other hand, the orthodox mainstream perspective considers that the technological gap between multinational and local firms can be, at least partially, filled by the positive externality generated by FDI (technology and know-how transfer, capital inflows, etc.). If this outweighs the negative effects of competitive pressures, the impact on the local territory can be overall positive. It would hence be optimal for the local government to promote and to provide incentives for attracting FDI.

The literature has not been able to verify which of the two positions empirically holds, and even though the mainstream economic thought is theoretically more convincing, it is important to recall that two interpretive models remain at the theoretical level. It must also be said that the effect of multinational firms is not only limited to their contribution to growth, but is also related to aspects of social sustainability, such as inequality and poverty. To this end, the literature shows both theoretical rationales (Feenstra and Hanson 1997) and empirical evidence (Figini and Goerg 1999, 2011) that link FDI with an increase in inequality and poverty. In addition, it is found that the investment in environmental protection depends on the type of firm: Calveras (2003) shows that international hotel chains have, for example, less incentive to invest in the protection of the natural resources than local firms.

Leaving behind these negative effects and focusing instead on the transmission channels of positive externalities, the literature classifies them into horizontal externalities and vertical externalities. The former relate to externalities that are generated if the local firms operate in the same productive sector of the multinational, the latter occur if they operate upstream or downstream in the production process. In any case they deal with: (a) human capital appreciation by imitation (learning by observing) or by experience on the job place (learning by doing); (b) labor mobility; (c) the imitation effects generated by the contact between local producers and the multinational companies; (d) the incentive for local firms to introduce new technologies (Aghion and Howitt 1998).

Although tourism is not explicitly considered in these models, there is no doubt that the above-mentioned effects can be found also in the tourism sector, provided that the tourism goods and services are, as we already know, in a tight relationship, and require a high level of coordination between producers. These sectoral linkages, therefore, develop among workers in the sector, stimulate the creation of by-products or local spin-off, provide incentives for the introduction of new technologies for reservations, marketing, etc.

The attention of the economic literature on the linkages stemming from the entry of a multinational firm has been proposed, among others, by Rodriguez-Clare (1996) and Alfaro et al. (2004). Nevertheless, these models focus on the growth and the variety of local firms that supply intermediate goods to the multinational firm (backward linkages) and on the greater specialization that allows to produce more complex goods (forward linkages).

However, the characteristics of tourism lead to the fact that multinational enterprises have other positive effects on local tourism development. In fact, the tourism product is enriched by the sophistication and the variety of local goods and services included in there, except when tourism demand is concentrated in an enclave. Since the tourism product is composed by the organized mix of many different goods and services, it is important to recall that linkages also work from the output side. If the tourists show appreciation for variety (the Love for Variety Theorem, see Sect. 4.3.2), it can be assumed that the greater the diversification of the bundle of tourism goods offered by the destination, the more valuable the tourism product. Hence, the willingness to pay of the tourist is an increasing function of the degree of variety. In this way, a common interest between multinationals and the destination arises, both being motivated to the completion of the tourism product, the former in terms of increased profits, the latter being able to undertake a strategy of development based on local firms.

It is not possible to determine, however, whether the optimal degree of variety for the multinational company coincides with that of the destination. If this not happens, due to the dynamics of land's price and the barriers to entry faced by local firms, the optimal degree of tourism variety for the multinational company can be higher or (more likely) lower than that of the destination. In such case, a policy intervention might be desirable.

Andergassen and Candela (2011) develop this point by assuming that the multinational firm could have speculative purposes, thus purchasing land not to build tourism structures and infrastructures but for re-selling it at a higher price once the market has grown. In this way, the multinational company gains a profit in its core business (i.e., hospitality) and have a capital gain on the land market. In their paper, Andergassen and Candela show that:

- If the degree of local variety is too high, the speculation activity would reduce the variety supplied, creating a common interest within the multinational firm, between its core business, which aims at a lower level of local tourism production, and its speculative profit.
- If the degree of local variety is too low, it can still be convenient to speculate on land, even if this does not create a common interest with the core business, since it further reduces the local tourism variety.

The two statements taken together affirm that the speculative strategy cannot be excluded, and when this happens there are negative effects on the local development of the destination. In addition, it is shown that the multinational never has an interest in supporting local development, even when the tourism variety is too low. This conclusion implies that the policy maker (the destination management) must intervene to control the multinational's operations and to avoid that their speculative activities are harmful for the local firms. In practical terms, the policy maker might increase the extent of land that is used for the resort or for other tourism purposes, thus facilitating the mobility of tourists within the destination through improvement in the transport system and reclaiming land from other uses. This policy is perfectly in line with the goal of local development, since it contrasts speculation and spreads the benefits of tourism in a larger territory.

Another element of clash between the foreign investors and the local community can emerge in the selection of investments between hotels and holiday homes. In general terms, the investment in hotels is preferred by the destination management, since the tourism multiplier generated by the hospitality sector is supposed to be higher than the multiplier of holiday homes' tourism, while the local real estate and building sector prefer to invest in holiday homes since they provide larger profits per square meter (Candela et al. 2012).

This conclusion deserves attention: small destinations, particularly in developing countries, are the most exposed to speculation by tourism multinationals and are the least protected because their governments do not have the financial resources to invest in infrastructures and because their limited political power is subject to strong pressures coming from the multinationals. Indeed, although describing the role of multinationals with the standard tools of economic theory, our conclusions are partially in line with some critical considerations of the radical economic perspective.

14.2.3 Globalization and Tourism

The term globalization has strongly entered the common language, sometimes with excessive intrusion: everything seems to be globalization and everything, including tourism, seems to be affected by it. Without entering the discussion on what globalization is and whether it has positive or negative effects on a socioeconomic level, it seems necessary to provide, in this context, the key elements needed to analyze the way in which globalization affects tourism and vice versa.

The process of globalization can be defined as the progressive reduction in the cost and in the time needed to cover a given distance: information, people, money, and commodities can move faster and at ever lower costs. Globalization is a historic process that, following successive waves, has been hitting our societies. The rise of the current phase of globalization can be traced back to the 1980s and 1990s and was triggered by the combination of scientific, cultural, political, and economic factors: (a) the information and communication technology revolution well depicted by the evolution of Internet; (b) the fall of socialist countries, which based their economy on central planning by the State, and the resulting reduction of the world, politically, from being bipolar to unipolar; (c) the affirmation of the market economy as the only system to efficiently produce and allocate resources, with the subsequent prevalence of free-market liberal ideology. This last element is so important that the present phase of globalization is often called as *neo-liberal globalization*.[2]

On a strictly economic level (Figini 2005), the key features of globalization are: (a) the increasing opening up of countries to international trade of goods and services; (b) the increasing importance of the role played by finance in the international economy, with its global implications in terms of speculation activities and higher volatility of the economic cycle; (c) the increasing liberalization and deregulation of domestic markets, including the labor market; (d) the increasing importance of strategies such as delocalization of investments and outsourcing of production activities to countries with more favorable economic conditions; (e) the reduction of the role played by the public sector in the economy, implemented both by limiting the economic policy to interventions that remove the obstacles that impede the correct functioning of the market, and through privatization policies; (f) the increasing transferring of national sovereignty, particularly in terms of monetary and fiscal policy, to international (International Monetary Fund) and supranational (European Union) institutions that are not completely democratic.

The process of globalization clearly has strong implications for a mobile phenomenon like tourism, thus affecting the size and the distribution of tourism flows, the organizational structure of tourism firms and markets, and the role played by tourism in contemporary society, with resulting effects on the dynamics of tourism destinations and on the distribution of income. The key elements of these changes can be unfolded as follows.

- The Information and Communication revolution, which is well represented by the development of the Internet, has contributed to lowering the cost of information and to expanding the range of choices and alternatives that can be accessed, making previously far and little-known destinations now well known and closer (see Sect. 12.3.1). Globalization has opened and continues to open new destinations to tourism, and economics should study the key features of this

[2] As regards the role of ideology in Tourism Economics, with particular reference to the effect of globalization, see Tribe (2011, Chap. 18).

widening process. If globalization increases tourism flows rather than only affecting their distribution, the access to new destinations undoubtedly produces a global development of tourism. If, on the contrary, the total number of arrivals and overnight stays remains more or less constant, the process could simply lead to an increase in the degree of competition in the market, with long-run positive effects in terms of efficiency. However, in the short run the redistribution among destinations of the global wealth created by tourism might generate transition problems and social inequalities, sometimes even dramatic if not cautiously dealt with. The question is whether globalization has contributed to accelerating global economic growth or whether the process has increased growth in some countries to the detriment of others. The answer provided by the economics literature has been more of applied than theoretical analysis, looking in the empirical evidence a solution that does not appear to be unequivocal, as it produces different and often non-robust results (Figini and Santarelli 2006, and their bibliography).

- The virtuous circle due to the interaction between the reduction in transport costs and the increase in tourism flows has reduced the relative price of international tourism with respect to domestic tourism, and has favored destinations in emerging countries, with middle-low income and lower cost of living, or in those countries that were previously excluded from tourists' itineraries (for example, Eastern European countries and China), leading to a strong redistribution of global tourism flows. In these emerging countries, globalization has had very important effects on inequality, with some social classes, economic sectors, and production factors gaining and leaving some people and certain economic activities behind. Moreover, if globalization has redistributive effects, a fundamental question cannot be avoided: what are the effects on poverty? Has globalization increased or decreased the number of people living below the line of absolute and relative poverty? Again, faced with the diversity of implications derived from theoretical models, the research provided by economics has mainly been empirical, but the results are once again not robust but rather depend on many factors.[3]
- Tourism destinations often offer similar types of holiday, but never completely the same, since neither the resources nor the cultures are exactly the same across destinations. Nevertheless, tourism firms operating in a global tourism market that has been progressively liberalized have to change their organizational structure and their strategies to stay competitive, choosing policies of standardization and horizontal and vertical integration that frequently lead to the development of multinational firms (see Sect. 14.2.2). The economic and cultural (material and linguistic) process of standardization leads to knock down the differences and to promote a single model of lifestyle, since globalization

[3] For a general discussion on the effects of globalization on poverty, see: Figini and Santarelli (2006) and Lee and Vivarelli (2004). For applications to the tourism sector, see Blake et al. (2008) and Figini and Romaniello (2012).

imposes standard products that are sold in the worldwide market. In this process, the local culture and local products are perceived as limitations to development, to modernization, and to market efficiency. Nevertheless, in the moment when standardization is the norm, the incentive to differentiate arises again, looking for the "uniqueness" of the tourism product or of the destination. Hence, the differentiation of tourism products becomes the way through which the local recognition and identification at the global scale is the strategy for earning back the market power that was lost due to greater international competition. The rediscovering of the local identity in the arena of global competition is the strategy that the media call *glocal.*

On this last point, Candela and Cellini (2006) build a theoretical model to justify the firms' choice between standardization and diversification in the long run. The model assumes the indirect demand function:

$$v_i(t) = A_i - Bx_i - D\sum\nolimits_{i \neq j} x_j, \tag{14.1}$$

where, given n destinations, $v_i(t)$ is the price of the tourism product x_i in the i-th destination at time t; and x_j, for $i \neq j$, are the products offered by the remaining $(n - 1)$ destinations; $B > 0$ measures the price sensitivity to the quantity offered by the i-th destination; $0 \leq D \leq B$ measures the price sensitivity to the quantity offered by the other destinations.

- If $D = 0$, then $v_i(t) = A_i - Bx_i$, the destination's product is completely independent of the others and is offered with the maximum level of diversification.
- If $D = B$, then $v_i = A_i - B\sum_{i=1}^{n} x_i$, the destination's product is perfectly substitutable with the others and is offered with the maximum level of standardization.

In (14.1), the lower D the greater the degree of diversification; the greater D the greater the degree of standardization: this demand function can thus be used to find a theoretical answer to the firm's strategy between the searching for global standards ($\mathrm{d}D/\mathrm{d}t > 0$) and the investment in local diversification ($\mathrm{d}D/\mathrm{d}t < 0$). Candela and Cellini show that, if globalization increases the number of destinations, investment in the diversification of local identity (natural and cultural) is promoted: in fact, if globalization sensibly increases the value of $\sum_{i \neq j} x_i$ so much to sensibly decrease the price, the destination can protect its product by investing in the local identity, thus diminishing the value of D.

Although it is often affirmed that globalization reduces the diversification of the tourism product, mortifying local cultures and identities, this model concludes that, if globalization is sufficiently wide, the degree of diversification of tourism products in the long run might increase. The intuition behind the conclusion is simple: if many homogeneous tourism destinations exist, the degree of competition is very high and thus profits are low, close to zero. Hence, by following the rationale of product differentiation (see Sect. 10.3), the investment in diversification becomes more profitable, even while bearing the costs connected to the promotion of the local brand and of the idiosyncratic characteristics and resources of the territory.

To conclude this short analysis of tourism globalization, we cannot leave out the cultural, economic, and environmental effects on the destination that hosts, in a much more intensive way than in the past, international tourism.

- On the cultural side, the impact is ambiguous. On one hand, global tourism allows to contact different societies and cultures, to appreciate their peculiarities and diversities: hence, it can be an extra instrument in the hands of citizens to understand the complexity of contemporary world. On the other hand, it is also true that much of international tourism takes the form of an "alien guest," where the contact with the local culture is frequently absent or distorted. In this case, the globalization of tourism would not be a tool for cultural growth and opening minds but often a cause of closing minds and reaffirming stereotypes and prejudices. Particularly when the arrival of tourists in a new destination is unexpected and massive, the impact with the tourists' culture can be devastating for the host country: the risk is of losing the local values and culture in order to welcome that of the tourists, thereby erasing the destination's heritage (see Sect. 16.4).
- On the economic side, we already know that tourism can be a factor of development but also a parasitic factor or, in the extreme case of the enclave, can produce no economic returns to the host economy (see Sect. 13.2.2). Unfortunately, in the age of globalization, much of international tourism flows is in the form of preorganized package tours, in which almost everything recalls the tourists' home environment and is detached from the local economy: from the restaurants to the amusements, from the standardized souvenirs to the groceries available in the supermarkets. If this is the case, not only tourism fails to be an engine of local development, but mainly in the case of enclaves located in poor countries, it can become an island of wealth and luxury to the eyes of the local population, thereby increasing the perception of inequality and risking to promote criminality and rebellion, to the point where the coexistence of tourists and the local population is unfeasible. Thus, the lack of economic spillovers to the rest of the economy also becomes a mechanism of social instability.
- On the environmental side, globalization allows tourists to cheaply discover tourism destinations that are still uncontaminated, meeting the growing demand stemming from developed countries for wilderness, adventure, and natural tourism. As it will be highlighted in Chap. 16, this process calls for the implementation of sustainable development policies which, however, are often lacking in developing countries, thus favoring speculation and profits in the short and in the medium run.

In conclusion, the globalization of tourism can have both a positive impact on the destination, if it goes towards social and environmental sustainability, or a negative impact, if it exploits the local resources and pollutes the indigenous culture, with the risk of breaking up the host society. Like with any other thing, also with globalization of tourism it would be incorrect to have an unambiguous position. Examples of balanced paths of development live side by side with cases of exploitation of the local territory or of the population.

Recent studies on the interaction between globalization and tourism are, among the others, Knowles et al. (2001), Wahab and Cooper (2001), Fayed and Fletcher (2002), Hjalager (2007).

14.3 The Real Aspects of International Tourism

In this section we will move to analyze the real aspects of international tourism. We will start by studying the contribution of international tourism to the balance of payments and to national income, to later draw our attention on the driving factors of international tourism and to conclude with an application to tourism of an important economic geography model: the center–periphery model.

14.3.1 Commodities and Tourists in the Balance of Payments

To approach international tourism it is useful to recall that the most relevant economic fact linked to tourism is the expenditure made in a destination by tourists from another country. This expenditure, in fact, constitutes an injection of liquidity into the economic area being considered. For American citizens who travel to Italy, presumably the money available for their spending derives from income earned in the United States, calculated and expressed in dollars. When they spend (after having exchanged their dollars into euros) in Italy, they introduce into the Italian economy additional demand that derives from income that has been produced elsewhere. This tourism expenditure by foreigners represents what is usually called *international tourism receipts* in statistical terms (see Chap. 3) and *tourism exports* of a country in economic terms. This terminology can lead to some confusion, since with the term exports we normally refer to goods leaving the country, like a pair of shoes or a car produced domestically and demanded by consumers of another country, while in tourism exports nothing leaves the country, rather tourists enter it.

Nevertheless, this is not a contradiction of terms. When tourists go to Italy, they not only buy tourism goods and services that are produced and consumed locally, but they also buy other goods (shopping and souvenirs) that return with them to their home country. What is exported with the tourism product, in the end, is an abstract good that we can call *tourism experience*; in addition, from an economic perspective, there is not much difference between, say, a T-shirt exported by an Italian firm and bought by an American citizen in a large store in New York and a T-shirt bought during the holiday in Italy of the American tourist: the only difference is that in the first case the good is moved, in the second case the person moves. But what defines the export is the movement of currency used in the transaction, not of the good: in both cases there is the same movement of currency, that is, dollars leaving the United States and spent as Euros in Italian products.

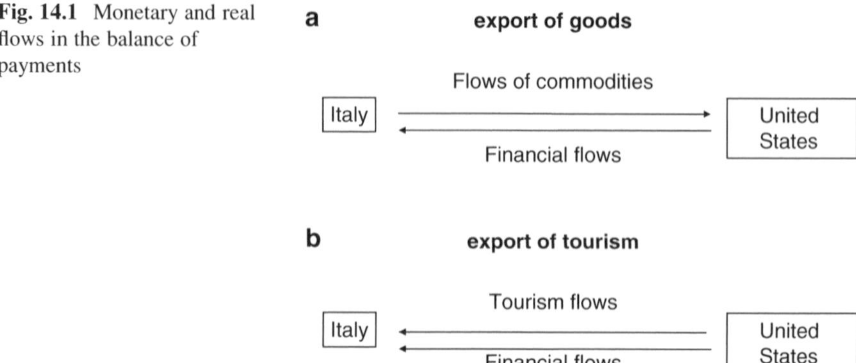

Fig. 14.1 Monetary and real flows in the balance of payments

Figure 14.1 compares the international flows of goods and persons with the corresponding payments and should make the concept clear. When an American tourist travels to Italy and spends money there, he creates an export for Italy (and therefore an import for the US); when an Italian tourist travels to the US and spends money, she creates an import for Italy (and therefore an export for the US). Obviously, tourism flows and international currency flows move in the same direction (payments follow tourists), while the movement of goods and currency flows move in opposite directions. Since currency flows are the flows registered in the balance of payments, it is easy to understand the reason why exports and incoming tourists are assets and imports and outgoing tourists are liabilities in the balance of payments.

The flow of international tourism produces two main economic effects in the host country: the first one is on income and is linked to the effect of the tourism multiplier (already studied in Sect. 13.2); the second one is a stabilizing/destabilizing effect on the balance of payments. International tourism is considered stabilizing if it contributes to the equilibrium of the country's balance of payments, either reducing/eliminating the deficit or reducing/eliminating the surplus. International tourism is considered destabilizing if it worsens the disequilibrium of the country's balance of payments by increasing the deficit or the surplus.

Nevertheless, it may be interesting to distinguish the macroeconomic effect of international tourism in developed countries, that are both recipients of incoming tourism and generators of outgoing tourism, from the effect in developing countries, that are mainly recipients of incoming tourism.

As regards developed countries, the problem can be addressed by recalling the condition (13.3) of equilibrium between national income and aggregate demand, and, for simplicity, assuming $g = 0$:

$$Y = C + I + (X + G) - (Z + H), \tag{14.2}$$

where Y is national income, C is consumption, I is investment, G is incoming tourism expenditure, X is exports, Z is imports, and H is outgoing tourism expenditure.

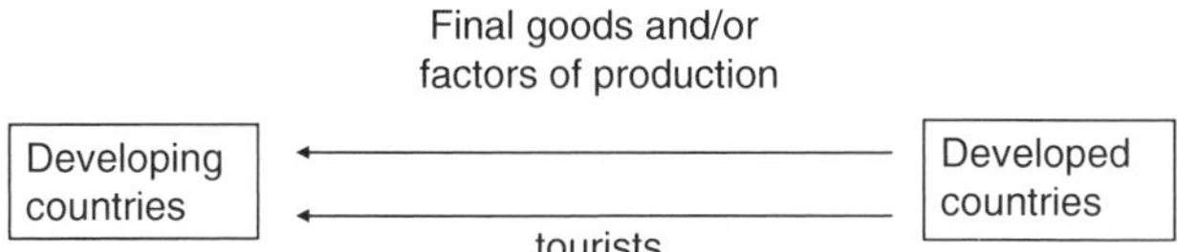

Fig. 14.2 Real flows in a developing country

Being a particular type of exports, countries have a benefit in attracting incoming tourists: tourism receipts G (in addition to export) constitute a positive component of aggregate demand that helps the national economy. On the contrary, outgoing tourism constitutes a negative component of aggregate demand that worsens the national economy. Looking at (14.2) we can understand the stabilizing/destabilizing effect of international tourism and see that if $(Z + H)$ exceeds $(X + G)$, the foreign demand contributes negatively to national income.

For developing countries (14.2) still applies, but something else has to be added under a different perspective. These countries, in fact, often depend on imported foreign goods both for consumption and for investment purposes (including the transfer of technology, see Sect. 14.2.2). Without the positive role played by incoming tourism on the balance of payments, the weight of imports in the balance of payments would be too heavy and would risk to jeopardize the process of development. If we change Fig. 14.1 into Fig. 14.2, which focuses only on the real movements of goods and tourists, we immediately observe that the two movements of tourists and goods, both coming into the country, compensate each other in terms of balance of payments. The currency inflows generated by incoming tourism can hence be used to finance the imports of intermediate and final goods that would otherwise open an important deficit in the foreign accounts. As a matter of fact, incoming tourism can play a key role in a developing country's takeoff, by financing the imports of goods and capital (the TKIG hypothesis, Sect. 13.5) and hence starting a virtuous circle of development.

14.3.2 The Determinants of International Tourism

To identify the factors that determine the extent and the direction of tourism flows between countries, one needs to focus on the local resources, the productive capacity, and on the organizational aspects of the different destinations. In Tourism Economics many models have been proposed to interpret international tourism movements, each one attempting to isolate and capture a particular cause. One theory obviously does not exclude another; therefore, the most plausible explanation for each historical process of tourism development can come from any of the models, but also from their combination. A short description of these theories is hence needed.

14.3.2.1 The Diversity of Environmental and Cultural Resources

According to this theory, the asymmetric distribution of natural and/or cultural resources among countries is a key factor in generating international tourism flows. Since these resources are, within a certain limit, non-reproducible and unique resources, their endowment guarantees an in-kind product differentiation, and to the destination the possibility of having a certain degree of monopolistic or quasi-monopolistic power. However, tourism resources are not forever: some resources are subject to degradation (think of uncontaminated beaches that, due to tourism exploitation, lose this characteristic, or the cultural degradation that follows the development of a mass tourism destination). Other resources can be, in some way, reproduced (think of Disneyland, US, and Disneyland Paris, France). Moreover, the evolution of tourism demand can stimulate, with the generation of new types of tourism, the exploitation of new resources.

Following this theory, international tourism stems from the different production possibilities of the different countries. To illustrate the model, we recall Samuelson and Nordhaus (2009), when stating that countries with tropical weather naturally specialize in the production of coffee, bananas, and beach holidays, while countries with colder climates specialize in maple syrup, salmon, and skiing holidays.

14.3.2.2 The Diversity of Preferences

A second driver of international tourism is the preferences of tourists. Even if the countries were able to produce domestically all the different types of tourism, international tourism would arise should the preferences of their citizens be different. For example, let us assume that France uses the sun and the sea for beach tourism and Sweden uses the snowy lowlands for cross-country skiing. However, the Swedish prefer swimming in the sea and the French cross-country skiing. In this case France and Sweden will exchange tourists, with benefits for both countries. The opening to international tourism, therefore, would increase the satisfaction of tourists in both countries.

14.3.2.3 The Principle of Comparative Advantage

The two determinants of international tourism that have been described so far are of common sense: tourists move where the resources are. Tourism flows between countries (and also between destinations within the same country) can also stem from a less intuitive driver. This very well-known principle of economics is the *theory of comparative advantage*, which when applied to tourism, affirms that a country gains from participating in international tourism even if it has an absolute advantage (i.e., it is always more efficient) with respect to the other country in the production of any type of tourism. The driver of international trade is the comparative, not the absolute advantage.

The model of comparative advantage was firstly formulated in 1817 by David Ricardo and is a strong demonstration that each country specializes in the production and in the export of those goods that is able to produce at a relatively (although not absolutely) lower cost; in which, therefore, it is relatively more efficient than the other country. Similarly, each country imports those goods that are produced at a relatively higher cost; in which, therefore, it is relatively less efficient than the other country. This simple rule, which extends to international trade the principle of the division of labor and of exchange between individuals, is the unshakable foundation of international trade theory. It is hence evident that can also be applied to international tourism flows.

To illustrate the principle of comparative advantage, let us assume the case of two different countries, A and B. Each of the two countries can organize their resources to produce two different types of tourism, mountaineering & skiing tourism (M) and sea & sun tourism (S). The two countries have different endowments of resources, skills, and know-how such as country A can produce a maximum of 12 million overnight stays on the mountains ($N_A^M = 12$) if diverts all its resources on this type of tourism, or a maximum of 4 million overnight stays on the beach ($N_A^S = 4$) if diverts all its resources on this second type of tourism. In this example, the relative price of S with respect to M in country A, p_A^S, is 3 (=12/4). In other words, if the country gives up the production on one unit of tourism S, it saves resources that can be diverted to produce 3 units of tourism M.

Similarly, country B can produce a maximum of three million overnight stays on the mountains ($N_B^M = 3$) if investing all its resources on this type of tourism, or a maximum of three million overnight stays on the beach ($N_B^S = 3$) if diverts all its resources on this second type of tourism. In this example the relative price of S with respect to M in country B, p_B^S, is 1 (=3/3). In other words, if the country gives up the production on one unit of tourism S, it saves resources that can be invested to produce one unit of tourism M.

Finally, let us assume that in both countries the demand of tourists is such as they want to spend the same amount of holiday on the mountains and on the sea: the ratio between mountain and sea tourism is hence 1:1.

Although these assumptions are very basic, they are sufficiently general to explain how the principle of comparative advantage works, when applied to tourism. Firstly, let us observe that country A is more efficient in the production of both types of tourism ($N_A^M > N_B^M$ and $N_A^S > N_B^S$): in other words country A has an absolute advantage in the production of both services. The intuition would suggest that there is no incentive for country A to open to international tourism; however, the economic rationale provides a different solution, the one that specialization and trade is more efficient. To demonstrate it, let us first consider the situation in which countries do not trade tourism, that is, the only possible type of tourism is the domestic one.

Since tourists demand one unit of mountaineering together with one unit of sea & sun holiday, the solution to the production problem is, for country A, to devote three fourths of its resources in the production of S, thereby producing $N_A^S = 3$

$(= 4 \times 3/4)$ and one fourth in the production of M, thereby producing $N_A^M = 3$ $(= 12 \times 1/4)$. It is easy to check that such solution satisfies the demand constraint, and overall tourism production in country A is equal to 6 (=3 + 3) million overnight stays. Similarly, country B should devote one half of its resources in the production of S, thereby producing $N_B^S = 1.5(= 3 \times 1/2)$ and the other half in the production of M, thereby producing $N_B^M = 1.5(= 3 \times 1/2)$. Again, such solution satisfies the demand constraint of country B and its overall tourism production is equal to 3 (=1.5 + 1.5) million overnight stays. The fact that citizens of country A enjoy more holidays than citizens of country B reflects the fact that country A has an absolute productive advantage, that is, country A is richer than country B. Finally, global tourism, composed only of domestic tourism in the two countries, is 9 million overnight stays.

What happens if the two countries open to international tourism? If each country decides to specialize in the production of those services in which owns a comparative advantage an interesting solution applies. Let us start from country B. Clearly country B, although less efficient of A in the production of both services, has a comparative advantage with respect to A in the production of S (in other words, it is "less inefficient"). If B completely specializes in S, can produce three million overnight stays and sell a part for domestic use and the rest to tourists of country A. At what price? To precisely answer this question we need a theory of international prices. To our aims it is sufficient to notice that international trade arises if the price p is in between the relative prices of the two countries: $p_B^S < p < p_A^S$ that is, in our case p has to be higher than 1 and lower than 3. Let us assume for simplicity that $p = 2$. Hence B can sell one unit of S in exchange of two units of M.

With this price, country B has an interest in producing $N_B^S = 3$ million and sell 1 million to tourists of country A in exchange for 2 million of N_A^M. After specialization and trade, tourists of country B can enjoy two million overnight stays on the mountains (spent on the mountains of country A) and two million overnight stays on their own sea, with a total number of four million overnight stays. Tourism flows have indeed grown for country B (in this numerical example the growth rate of tourism in B has been 33.3 % = (4 − 3)/4).

But what about country A, the most efficient country? Does it too have an advantage in specializing and trading? It is easy to demonstrate that also A has an advantage in reducing the amount of resources invested in S and increasing the investment in M: if A invests 56.25 % only of its resources in S can produce $N_A^S = 2.25$ million overnight stays domestically at which the million imported by country B has to be added, with a total of $N_A^S = 3.25$. The remaining 43.75 % of resources is invested in M thus producing 5.25 million overnight stays, of which 2 million are exported to incoming tourists of country B, thus domestically consuming $N_A^M = 3.25$. Tourism flows have indeed grown also for country A, which overall number of overnight stays is now 6.5 million (in this numerical example the growth rate of tourism in country A has been 8.3 % = (6.5 − 6)/6).

This mutual gain is possible only when each country, independently from the presence of any absolute advantage, specializes in the production in which it enjoys a comparative (relative) advantage: mountain tourism for country *A*, sea & sun tourism for country *B*. Through specialization and international trade both countries increase tourism consumption, thus leading to a global increase in tourism: global tourism, now composed of domestic and international tourism, counts 10.5 million overnight stays, with a growth rate of 16.6 % with respect to the previous case.

More generally, the model of comparative advantage states that: (a) specialization in the activity in which each country enjoys a comparative advantage is the efficient solution; (b) through specialization and subsequent trade of products both countries are better off; (c) global welfare in the economic system increases. The principle of comparative advantage holds for countries and for individuals: in the case of tourism the most efficient and welfare-enhancing solution is that countries specialize in the type of tourism in which they are relatively more efficient. This means that countries (like people) specialize in certain tourism activities even if they are less efficient than others in absolute terms, but with mutual gains for everyone.

14.3.2.4 The Hecksher–Ohlin Model and the Endowment of Productive Factors

Also this interpretation of international tourism flows stems from the application of a famous international trade model to tourism: the *Hecksher–Ohlin model*. While in the model of Ricardo the relative advantage from which international trade originates depends on the efficiency of labor, in the Hecksher–Ohlin model the relative advantage stems from the allocation of productive factors, capital and labor, among countries. According to this model, it is more efficient for countries abundant with capital to export goods that are relatively capital intensive and to import, from countries abundant with labor, goods that are relatively labor intensive.

The application of the Hecksher–Ohlin model to international tourism flows assumes the existence of two countries, *A* and *B*, with different endowment of capital and labor and that trade tourism services *Q* (for example hospitality and catering services, which by assumption mostly require lowly qualified labor) and organizational and transport services *R* (for example, booking systems and the production of package tours, which by assumption mostly require capital and highly qualified labor). The conclusion of Hecksher–Ohlin model is that, if country *A* is characterized by a relative abundance of lowly qualified labor with respect to country *B*, *A* will tend to produce and export catering and accommodation services, while *B* will do the same for organizational and transport services. It is easy to recognize in *A* a developing country, a destination receiving international tourism flows and in *B* the developed country, producer of advanced tourism services and generator of international tourism. According to the model such equilibrium is superior to the one in which the two countries cannot specialize and trade: total welfare increases with trade, so as welfare of both countries *A* and *B*.

The distributional consequence of the Hecksher–Ohlin model is interesting, and it is the content of the Stolper–Samuelson theorem: specialization would lead to an increase in the demand of the production factor used intensively in the sector of specialization, thus increasing its price, while the price of the other factor would decrease. If we assume that tourism is abundant of lowly qualified labor, tourism specialization would let the wage of low qualified workers increase, with positive implications in terms of poverty abatement and inequality reduction. The contrary would happen if the tourism is abundant of highly qualified labor: tourism specialization would increase income inequality and poverty.

The application of the Hecksher–Ohlin model to tourism can be difficult since tourism services are not homogeneous and are likely to be produced differently in different countries:

> The capital intensity of tourism varies between countries, and can also vary over time, at different stages of tourism growth. Since tourism is not homogeneous it is likely that it is relatively labor-intensive in countries with a large supply of labor and capital-intensive in countries which are capital-abundant.
>
> (Stabler et al. 2010, p. 241)

Difficulties therefore arise in determining whether the consequences of the Hecksher–Ohlin model hold in a dynamic context: economic growth stemming from international specialization leads to a change in the price of factors, is constrained by the elasticity of international demand, and affected by the presence of economies of scale and other factors. This ultimately leads to the possibility for developing countries to either suffer from *immiserizing growth*, when growth leads to a deterioration of the terms of trade (Bhagwati 1968) or to use tourism as a channel to escape from the poverty trap in which low-income is associated to low quality, low growth and, in turn, low-income again.

14.3.2.5 The Preference for Variety

Another characteristic of international tourism that cannot be integrated into any of the above models is that tourists often show a preference for variety, that is, tourists go to countries that have types of tourism, resources, and destinations similar to those of their home country: Italian tourists can spend their beach holidays in Spain, while Spanish tourists visit the Italian coasts; French tourists can go skiing in Switzerland, while Swiss tourists can go skiing in France. The exchange of international tourism among equivalent types of tourism can be defined *horizontal tourism* or *intra-industry tourism*. Our problem is finding the economic reasons that justify this very particular form of trade between tourists.

Horizontal tourism stems from the interaction between three main factors: (a) the consumer's preference for variety, given that tourists frequently want to repeat the same type of holiday, but not the exact same holiday; thus, although tourists might have a strong preference for a certain type of tourism they often change destination to visit; (b) the existence of economies of scale in production, therefore a destination that is specialized in the production of one particular type of tourism can obtain a large cost advantage from selling on a global rather than on a local scale; (c) the strong reduction in transport costs. In fact, while the factors

(a) and (b) favor intra-industry tourism, the existence of transport costs tends to keep tourists in their home country. Horizontal trade of tourism, therefore, increases with the reduction of transport costs.

It is easy to conclude that tourism is a mirror of the economic integration between countries: the more tightly markets are integrated, the fewer the obstacles to the movement of people, the greater the intra-industry tourism flows. Horizontal tourism dominates when the absence of restrictions on people's movement creates a fully integrated market in which tourists are able to visit a greater variety of destinations at lower costs.

14.3.2.6 The Organizational Skills and the Accessibility of Destinations

Yet, a complete vision of the reasons why tourists travel internationally has not been depicted. Although tourism flows move in search for environmental and/or cultural resources, we must recall that international tourism markets are dominated by few global operators with strong market power. Thus, they have the power to channel tourism demand to those destinations that: (a) are more easily accessible, both because they are close to important airport hubs and because they are served by important carriers; (b) have organizational skills that allow them to offer the leisure services demanded by tourists: amusement parks and other amenities for holiday takers, facilities for conventions, meetings and exhibitions for business tourists, etc.

In a broader perspective, Porter (1990) suggests that there are three channels through which firms (and destinations) can attain a competitive advantage: cost leadership, product differentiation, and market segmentation. The production factors that can be effectively deployed in this process are (Crouch and Ritchie 2006): (a) natural and cultural resources; (b) human resources; (c) capital resources; (d) know-how; (e) infrastructure and organizational resources. According to this approach, Crouch and Ritchie (2006) highlight that the competitiveness of a destination primarily depends on their core resources. However, the core resources act as effective attractors if there are organizational abilities and entrepreneurial skills enabling to develop an environment fit to attract tourists (including the ability to strengthen ties with international tour operators and with markets generating tourism flows); in other words, if there is an efficient destination management with a clear vision about tourism policy and planning (see Sect. 4.3). If this happens, it is possible to convert the comparative advantage of a destination, based on resource endowments, into a sustainable competitive advantage, related to resource deployment (Stabler et al. 2010).

These aspects highlight that tourism is not a specialization precluded for destinations without natural or environmental resources, but that, at least partially, depends on the tourism policy of the destination management and on the entrepreneurial skills of the local population.

14.3.2.7 The Market Factors

Finally, international tourism flows depend on the relative price of the holiday in the destination with respect to the price of its competitors, and on the purchasing power of the tourists that, in turn, depends on their income and on the exchange rate between the home country and the destination. It is therefore important to reaffirm, also for international tourism, the explanatory power of the market factors already introduced in general for tourism demand (see Sect. 4.2). It is mainly on these factors of competitiveness that the economics literature has focused its empirical analysis, and to which we redirect for an in-depth study (for example, see Lim 1997; Sinclair 1998; Dwyer et al. 2000; for a quick introduction, see Notes 14.1).

Notes 14.1. Tourism Demand and the Effect of the Introduction of the Euro on the Competitiveness of European Tourism Destinations

As we recall in the main text, the factors that affect tourism demand (especially on an international level) and its distribution between countries are many and diverse, including sociodemographic, economic, and institutional variables. While the first group (age, gender, education, occupational status) are factors that primarily explain individual demand, the economic and institutional variables are the determining factors on a macroeconomic level.

We have already recalled in Sect. 4.5.3 that the models that are generally used to empirically estimate the impact of these factors on international tourism flows are the so-called Almost Ideal Demand System (AIDS) models, introduced in the literature by Deaton and Muellbauer (1980) and then widely applied to tourism. They are multiple regression systems that estimate the distribution of tourism expenditure of each region of origin among the different destinations. In each equation of the AIDS model, the dependent variable is a measure of tourism flows (tourism expenditure, overnight stays or arrivals) between the region i and the destination j, while the independent variables are: the relative price of the holiday with respect to the other destinations, the relative per capita income of the region of origin with respect to the destination, the transport cost, generally proxied by the geographical distance between the countries, the exchange rate between the currencies, and a series of dummy variables among which we typically find the contiguity between the two regions, whether or not the countries share the same language, the fact of being an island or not, other political-institutional characteristics, etc.

Many works have applied the AIDS models to the analysis of tourism flows. For example, Durbarry and Sinclair (2003) analyze the demand of French tourists in Italy, Spain, and the United Kingdom; Han et al. (2006) estimate the demand of US tourists in some European countries. Both researches find that the variation in relative prices has relevant effects on the distribution of tourism flows; Han et al. (2006) estimate that the price elasticity of American tourists is very high: France, Italy, and Spain are considered substitute destinations, and a change in relative prices produces relevant distributive effects; the same does not happen, on the contrary, for the UK. In addition, as the budget of US tourists increases, France and Italy's market shares tend to increase, while that of Spain and the United Kingdom tends to decrease. On the contrary, Durbarry and Sinclair (2003) do not find any significant effect on tourism flows of changes in French tourists' expenditure.

As we have seen, the exchange rate has a key role in the determination of international tourism flows. The nominal exchange rate, when associated to the price level of the destination, determines the real cost of the holiday for the tourist. It is natural, therefore, to wonder whether the introduction of a common currency, the Euro, has an effect on tourism flows in the European Union. On a theoretical level, the introduction of a single currency in a common economic area can have three effects.

(a) *Intra-area*, the effect is to impede that a country uses depreciation of its currency to make internal holidays cheaper on an international level, and therefore attract a larger share of international tourism flows; from this perspective, the introduction of the Euro makes the internal flows of the region more dependent on real competitive factors.
(b) *Inter-area*, the rise of the Euro as a value reserve leads to its progressive appreciation in international financial markets, making, on the one hand, holidays more expensive in Europe for foreign tourists and, on the other hand, making outgoing holidays by European tourists less expensive; both are negative effects for the tourism balance in the Euro zone (at least in terms of real flows, while the effect on overall expenditure depends on the Marshall–Lerner condition).
(c) On a microeconomic level, the introduction of a single currency has the effect of making prices more transparent to the eyes of consumers, of eliminating transaction costs, and finally, of raising the level of internal competition in the market.

Empirically, Gil-Pareja et al. (2007) attempt to estimate the effect of the introduction of the Euro on tourism. The authors, having controlled for a series of other effects, estimate that the introduction of the Euro has increased internal tourism flows in the Euro zone by roughly 6.3 %, a significant number. Secondly, this positive effect is not driven by the particular performance of any country, but is shared by almost all the countries that have adopted the Euro. Although this work does not analyze the effect on outgoing and incoming flows of the Euro zone, the authors conclude that European tourism has been positively affected by the introduction of the single currency. Santana et al. (2010a) estimate a more sizeable effect (around 12 %) in their analysis of a large panel dataset that includes several experiences of common currencies, not only the Euro. Finally, Santana et al. (2010b), after dividing a sample of 179 countries into three groups by income

(continued)

levels, also show that a considerable effect of common currency on both trade and tourism exists. In fact, they conclude that for the high-income economies in the sample, the estimated effect of the introduction of a common currency is greater on tourism than on trade.

14.3.3 The Center–Periphery Model Applied to Tourism

A model that provides many insights into the understanding of international tourism flows is the center–periphery model developed by Paul Krugman (see Krugman 1991, 1995). The model, here applied to the case of tourism in a very simplified way, proposes an endogenous interpretation of the localization of tourism firms and the movement of tourists in a center–periphery setting.

Let us assume a country with two possible tourism destinations: for example a large country divided into two regions that face two oceans, therefore with an East coast and a West coast with identical quality of beaches and services. The total population of the country, N, is equally divided between the two coasts and their tourism demand is constant (we strongly simplify by leaving out any type of tourism price elasticity). To further simplify the model, we assume that each tourist demands only one unit of tourism product, the holiday. Total tourism demand from the East is therefore $N/2$, the same as from the West. The overall tourism demand in the country is therefore N.

The tourism services that have to be supplied in order to meet the demand of the population can be provided in three different ways: on the East coast only; on the West coast only; in both locations. Indeed, if tourism is provided only on one of the two coasts, the tourists originating from the other coast will have to pay for transport costs. We assume that the transport costs, for each person, are equal to t.

Moreover, we need to introduce some assumptions on the production cost of tourism services: we assume that to build a tourism facility (for example a hotel with beach services) the firm is faced with a fixed cost, equal to F, plus a variable cost of production a for each service provided. Since tourism demand N represents the total number of holidays, the total cost C of the services produced is equal to $C = F + aN$. This linear cost function shows economies of scale, since the average cost of production AC diminishes as production increases: $\text{AC} = C/N = F/N + a$. If we assume that the market structure of tourism in each coast is the monopolistic competition (see Sect. 10.2.3), the long-run equilibrium with free entry results in zero profits for the firms, therefore the price of the holiday v is equal to the average cost of production: $v = \text{AC}(N)$.

We now have all the elements to decide on the location advantage of tourism services. Let us start with the assumption that all the tourism firms are located on the West coast: they supply services for the whole tourism demand, which is hence all directed to this coast. Tourism production in the West is $N_W = N$, its price, equal to the average cost of production is $v = F/N + a$. This price, however, is paid only by the resident population in the West; each resident in the East must also pay for the transport cost of moving to the other coast. Therefore, the price for the tourist that lives in the East, but goes on holiday in the West, is:

$$v_{E;W} = v + t = \frac{F}{N} + a + t. \tag{14.3}$$

We now make an analogous example but assuming that all the tourism firms are located on the East coast: they supply services for the whole tourism demand, which is hence directed to this coast. Tourism production in the East is $N_E = N$, its price, still equal to the average cost of production is, however, paid only by the resident population in the East; each resident in the West must also pay for the transport cost of going to the other coast. Therefore, the price for the tourist that lives in the West, but goes on holiday in the East, is:

$$v_{W;E} = v + t = \frac{F}{N} + a + t. \tag{14.4}$$

Finally, we consider the option that tourism services are provided on both coasts, therefore $N_W = N_E = N/2$. Having two tourism markets allows tourists to save on the transport costs, but it impedes the tourism firms from taking full advantage of the economies of scale. In fact, the price in the West and in the East exclusively depends on the average production costs that, with the simple assumption we have made, are:

$$v_{W;W} = v_{E;E} = 2\frac{F}{N} + a. \tag{14.5}$$

Comparing (14.3), (14.4), and (14.5), we see that there are many possible equilibria. Let us consider the situation in which the whole tourism sector is located on the West coast: what is the condition in order for this equilibrium to be stable? The answer depends on the interaction of two contrasting forces: one is centripetal, due to the economies of scale, the other centrifugal, due to transport costs. Hence, the development of tourism also on the East coast can only take place if there is an incentive for firms to move to the other market and to serve the population of the other coast. In other words, the concentration of tourism firms on the West coast is stable if it is not profitable for any firm to defect from one coast and provide tourism services to the other coast. For the firms concentrated in the West, it is not profitable to change location if the price at which they could offer beach tourism over there is higher than the price at which they can offer it in the West, serving also tourists coming from the East. That is, if $v_{E;E} > v_{E;W}$, therefore $2F/N + a > F/N + a + t$. This condition holds if:

$$\frac{F}{N} > t. \tag{14.6}$$

In other words, if the average fixed cost is greater than the transport cost the firms would continue to serve tourists from the East while remaining located only on the West coast. If the condition (14.6) is satisfied, transport costs are so low, relative to the fixed costs of production, that it is better to take advantage of the economies of scale stemming from concentration on one coast and let the tourists travel from the East.

In the opposite case, if $F/N < t$, the transport costs are sufficiently high to convince tourism firms to open up tourism services on the East coast to provide beach tourism to the East coast's population; the diffusion of tourism firms on both coasts does not achieve full economies of scale but, on the other hand, allow tourists to save on transport costs. Similarly, the same rationale can be applied to the case where the firms' location is initially concentrated on the East coast.

To summarize, the model shows three potentially stable equilibria: all the tourism firms are located on the West coast; all the tourism firms are located on the East coast; tourism firms are distributed equally both on the West coast and on the East coast. The condition of concentration or equal distribution of tourism services depends on the comparison of transport costs and economies of scale.

In the case when the advantages of concentration prevail, $F/N > t$, it remains to determine which equilibrium is verified, concentration on the West or on the East. Such simple model does not provide an answer, in fact the solution depends on where tourism has started: *history decides*![4] However, when the solution of geographic concentration prevails (it does not matter which coast of the country is historically developed), a tourism center and a periphery without tourism structures develop. In the center (the tourism destination) tourism firms are located, from the periphery (the tourism generating region) the tourists travel to spend their holidays.

This simple center–periphery model can be extended in many aspects: (a) assuming a different distribution of the population between two or more regions; (b) assuming that tourism demand is not the same across regions but rather a function of the regional income; and (c) describing the dynamic process driving the movement of tourists and the location of firms on the two coasts.

Nevertheless, the extensions (a) and (b) would only complicate the equilibria (14.3)–(14.5) without substantially change the conclusion. More important is the study of the dynamic process (c) of localization but the analysis would go beyond our needs. It is sufficient to propose some reflections on the process of change.

The relationship between economies of scale and transport costs (14.6) can represent a terribly conservative force, which tend to freeze any historically defined form of relationship between center and periphery: the geographic structure of tourism can remain essentially unchanged for a long period. But nothing is eternal.

---

[4] Clearly, the model holds if tourism production does not depend on environmental or cultural resources. In a more realistic but complex setup, the concentration or the diffusion of tourism firms is not only linked to economies of scale and to transport costs but also to the location of natural and cultural goods. Moreover, the structure of the transport network and hubs can make tourists moving easier in certain directions than in others, as underlined in the previous subsection.

The plurality of the equilibria described earlier suggests that changes are possible when the conditions change. Obviously, a reduction in transport costs (as it has been happening in the last few years) leads to a wider diffusion of tourism and to the multiplication of destinations. Similarly, if a region stops enjoying economies of scale as a consequence of congestion effects or environmental unsustainability, tourism firms might benefit from locating in the other region.

So far, we have described the core–periphery model by considering that the two regions belong to the same country. It is straightforward to interpret the two regions as two countries (W and E) and, hence, the movement of tourists from one coast to the other as international tourism. Therefore, we can describe different configurations of international tourism: a country that is a tourism center, country W, which receives all the incoming tourism, while country E is the periphery and is where all the outgoing tourism originates. In the second case, the tourism center is E, and finally the third case in which the two countries are both tourism producers and consumers; in this last case international tourism flows are negligible and are only generated by the other factors described in Sect. 14.3.2.

Therefore, the center–periphery model shows that countries can assume many configurations in equilibrium: we can find countries that become international tourism centers and in which incoming tourism constitutes the most relevant part of tourism flows; there are countries that become the tourism periphery, in which outgoing tourism constitutes the main part of tourism flows; finally, there are countries with an integrated tourism system, in which outgoing and incoming tourism coexist with domestic tourism.

The center–periphery model is very close to the methodology used in geography, such as this line of research has given birth, in the last decade or so, to a flourishing literature, named as New Economic geography (NEG). As Krugman himself recalls (Krugman 1995), economic geography has long been marginalized in the economic theory but space matters, and the time has come to regain it as one of the most important tools of economic analysis. In fact, the analysis by tourism geographers Dewailly and Flament (1995) makes use of this interpretative model to describe and explain tourism flows:

> Tourism flows are mass movements. However, regardless of their complexity, there are some organizational regularities, such as the opposition between the center and the periphery [. . .] which is evident in the movement on the medium and the long distance.
>
> (Dewailly and Flament 1995 p. 47. *Our translation*)

Dewailly and Flament use this approach to classify the different types of tourism regions according to the characteristics of their tourism flows: hospitality regions, departure regions, and transit regions. With these categories many centers and many peripheries can be clearly identified in the global tourism system.

In conclusion, let us state that the model described in this section is an extreme simplification of the model developed by Krugman to explain manufacturing location in an economy. Nevertheless, Krugman himself proposes the application of the core–periphery model to the services sector, such as tourism, after having observed that the contemporary process of concentration mainly regards services, while the manufacturing industry is moving in the opposite direction. Following this line of research, a few applications to tourism are of interest (Papatheodorou 2003a, 2004).

Hence, the issue of localization remains history driven; in other words, small accidental events give life, in a region, to a cumulative process that, starting from a few firms, moves developing and attracting other firms and workers, evolves with the concentration of an increasing number of firms and workers that react to the economic incentives provided by that localization. The economies of scale and the external economies of production explain the growth of a tourism center, but at the beginning of the process, history and chance play the most relevant role.

14.4 The Monetary Aspects of International Tourism

In Sect. 14.2 we indicated the exchange rate, c_r, as the fundamental variable that allows to distinguish the international from the domestic tourism market. Nevertheless, we have used so far an intuitive concept of exchange rate: it is now time to use a more scientific approach.

14.4.1 The Use of Currency and Financial Markets in Tourism

First of all, let us investigate on the complications arising in passing from domestic to international trade, that is, to an exchange between countries that use different currencies. If a German citizen decides to buy a holiday in the United States from a travel agency in New York, the American travel agency wants to be paid in its national currency, the dollar, while the original currency of the tourist is the Euro. Similarly, if another European tourist buys a *kimono* during a holiday in Japan, the Japanese shop wants to be paid in yen. Analogously, the Americans and Japanese tourists who want to buy goods and services in Europe must use the European currency. Therefore, international trade introduces a new important dimension to the exchange: the price of a country's currency expressed in units of another currency, what is called the exchange rate.

The crucial point of international tourism is therefore the relevance of different currencies: the foreign money is called foreign currency, and the currencies are bought and sold on a specific market, the currency market. The price that is defined by the market is the nominal exchange rate, which expresses the relative price of a currency in terms of another. There are two ways to indicate the nominal exchange rate at time t: (a) indicating the number of units of foreign currency c_t that can be bought with one unit of the national currency; (b) indicating the number of units of national currency E_t that can be bought with one unit of foreign currency. Which of the two methods is commonly used is simply the result of institutional factors or historic uses. The difference is purely formal given that an easy arithmetic operation links the two expressions: one is the reciprocal of the other, $c_t = 1/E_t$. In this section we will express the exchange rate in terms of the national currency, following the definition (b) above (an in-depth study of the interpretation and the use of exchange rates is in Notes 14.2).

Notes 14.2. On the Interpretation and the Use of the Exchange Rate
Let us consider the dollar/Euro exchange rate and take the rate of the dollar from Frankfurt stock exchange at a specific moment in time: "Exchange rate of the $1.2814." This means that in Frankfurt, at that moment, 1 € can buy $1.2814. Its reciprocal, 0.7804, indicates that $1 can buy 0.7804 €.

Given this exchange rate, if we have to convert 1,000 € into dollars in Frankfurt we have to multiply this sum times the exchange rate ($ = 1.2814 × 1,000, where $ is the corresponding sum in dollars), getting $1,281.40. If, instead, we have $1,000 to be converted in Euros we have to divide the sum by the relative nominal exchange rate (€ = 1,000/1.2814, where € is the corresponding sum in Euros), getting 780.40 €.

In the same way if we have to compare the price of 180 € for a hotel room in Frankfurt with the same category hotel room in New York, which price is $120, we have to perform the relative conversions using the nominal exchange rate:

- Convert both prices in Euros: 180 and 120/1.2814 = 93.65
- Convert both prices in dollars: 120 and 180 × 1.2814 = 230.65

Obviously, the two operations are equivalent since, in both cases, the price of the room in Frankfurt results 92.20 % more expensive than the one in New York: the choice of the currency in which to list prices does not affect the real economic variables.

To conclude, let us observe that an increase in the nominal exchange rate, for example to 1.3605, means that the Euro has nominally appreciated, since more dollars are obtained with 1 €; while a depreciation in the nominal exchange rate, for example to 1.2480, means that the Euro has nominally depreciated, since fewer dollars are obtained with 1 €. The appreciation or depreciation of a currency affects the comparison of the two stays in our example. If we convert prices in Euros, in the case of an appreciation of the Euro, the stay in New York becomes even cheaper, 88.20 €, thus the price in Frankfurt is 104.08 % more expensive. In the case of a depreciation, the stay in New York increases in price, 96.15 €, thus the price in Frankfurt is still relatively expensive, the 87.20 % more, but less than before.

This numerical example shows that, from a European perspective, the appreciation of the Euro might shift tourism flows outside Europe, since tourism in Europe becomes more expensive for non-Europeans, while tourism outside Europe becomes cheaper for Europeans. On the contrary, the depreciation of the Euro would shift tourism flows inside Europe, since tourism in Europe becomes less expensive for non-Europeans, while tourism outside Europe becomes more expensive for Europeans.

After this introductory definition, we can now tackle two more specific aspects: the functioning of the currency market and the definition of the real exchange rate.

14.4.1.1 The Functioning of the Currency Market

One of the most interesting aspects of the currency market, both from the researchers' and from the operators' perspective, is the way in which currency transactions take place and how exchange rates are determined.

One method of negotiation requires the immediate delivery of the currency, where by immediate we mean within 48 h after the execution of the exchange contract. This market is called *spot* and responds to the need of settling the immediate need (even in large sums) of foreign currencies. Nevertheless, customers and banks are not always in such conditions of urgency. Therefore there exists another way to operate, the *future* market. When this happens, the currency is delivered and paid for at a future date (much longer than the 2 days mentioned before) at a price fixed today; this price is called the forward exchange rate.

The forward exchange generally has standardized expiration dates (1, 3 or 6 months), but banks, within certain limits, can modify the expiration to which their customers are subject, in exchange for a payment. The difference between a forward and a spot rate is called premium or future discount. For each currency, therefore, at time t there exist at least two prices on the market: the spot rate, E_t, and the forward rate for the delivery in $(t + \tau)$, $E_{t+\tau}$. The premium is therefore given by the following ratio: $(E_{t+\tau} - E_t)/E_t$.

Among currency operators there are commercial banks but also central banks: the rules defining the role of central banks on the currency market allow for the identification of different exchange regimes. The exchange market can function according to two fundamental regimes, the *fixed exchange rate* or the *floating exchange rate*, and to two derivative regimes, the *adjustable peg* and the *dirty fluctuation*.

In the fixed exchange regime, the exchange rates are kept constant by the systematic intervention of the central bank. For example, the central bank announces that it is willing to buy or sell a certain currency at a given rate E^* and, obviously, the exchange rate cannot go below this quote since, if the market were to offer foreign currency at a lower price, the operators would turn to the central bank to buy it; similarly, the rate cannot rise above E^*, since if the market offers a higher price it would be better for the operators to sell the foreign currency directly to the central bank. In carrying out this policy, the central bank uses own foreign currency reserves to keep the rate fixed, and the variation in reserves appears in the country's balance of payments. In a fixed exchange rate system, currencies are exchanged continuously, but changes in the exchange rate are exceptional, only as a consequence of a declaration of the central bank, for reasons of international monetary equilibrium. These changes are defined revaluation (if the exchange rate E decreases) or devaluation (if the exchange rate E increases).

On the contrary, there is a floating exchange regime when the central bank refrains from any currency operation and the exchange rates are freely determined by the market. In a system of floating exchange rates, currencies are exchanged continuously, and the nominal exchange rate changes continuously. Its variations are called nominal appreciation or depreciation. An appreciation of the currency is a decrease in the rate E_t, while a depreciation results in its increase. Obviously, should we adopt the convention of measuring the rate in terms of the national currency c_t we would face the opposite situation: an appreciation is an increase in c_t, while a depreciation is a decrease in c_t.[5]

In addition to these two "extreme" regimes, there also exist *mixed regimes*. If the exchange rate is fixed but variations can occur given certain macroeconomic conditions, such as problems in the management of currency reserves, we have an adjustable pegging system. On the contrary, if the rate is floating but the central bank can intervene by buying or selling foreign currency, even on a daily basis, with the aim of contrasting excessive fluctuations we have a system of dirty fluctuations. These interventions can occur in order to avoid speculation or to correct macroeconomic problems (inflation, unemployment, etc.). After the World War II, the international system is dominated by the mixed regime, although a wide variety of exchange rate systems coexist today.

14.4.1.2 The Real Exchange Rate

The key factor determining the decisions taken by consumers, tourists, and firms at the international level is not the nominal exchange rate but the price of foreign goods in terms of national goods; this relative price is called the real exchange rate.

The real exchange rate is not quoted and is not observable on the currency market, but depends on the combination of the nominal exchange rate and the price level in both countries. It is the real exchange rate, not the nominal one, to affect the behavior of the international operators and tourists. To the German tourist willing to travel to the US, what is relevant is not the quantity of Euros needed to buy $1, but the quantity of goods and services that can be purchased at the destination with a given sum of Euros. Receiving more dollars for 1 € does not mean anything if in the meantime the price of a stay in New York has gone up of the same percentage. This is also true for tourism firms that purchase from abroad, and in general for all household consumption and for all the purchases made by firms.

In order to make economically rational decisions, though, it is necessary to understand the way in which the real exchange rate is built and can be measured. We propose two methods: to start with, we refer to the comparison when only one

[5] Since in textbooks and in practice both relationships are used, for completeness we have shown both. We understand that this is confusing, as it confuses many professional agents, but the notation will become more familiar as the study continues.

good exists; then, we will refer to the comparison between the entire national economies.

As regards one single good, the calculation is immediate. Given the object of study of this book (but the example could be referred to any other good), let us consider an identical (perfectly homogeneous) tourism service that can be purchased in two countries, for example accommodation in hotels of the same international chain.[6] The calculation of the real exchange rate between Germany and the US consists of defining the price of the accommodation, let's say in New York and in Berlin using the same currency. If, at time t, p_t^* is the price of accommodation in dollars and p_t is the price in Euros, the real exchange rate r_t is defined by the ratio:

$$r_t = \frac{p_t^*}{c_t p_t} \quad \text{or} \quad r_t = \frac{E_t p_t^*}{p_t}. \tag{14.7}$$

The real exchange rate is therefore the nominal exchange rate adjusted to take into account the different prices of the good in the two countries.

If $r_t > 1$ then $p_t^* > c_t p_t$, therefore it is advantageous to purchase in the domestic market; if $r_t < 1$ then $p_t^* < c_t p_t$, therefore it is advantageous to purchase from abroad. If demand can move internationally, domestic and international prices will change due to arbitrage operations, until they reach equilibrium, $r_t = 1$. Under this last condition we have $p_t^* = c_t p_t$, therefore prices are equal when expressed in the same currency and the consumers are indifferent about where to buy the good. If there are no limitations to the international trade, the condition of equilibrium states that the exchange rate is determined by the buying power of the currencies: this is the famous *theorem of purchasing power parity*.

$$c_t = \frac{p_t^*}{p_t} \quad \text{or} \quad E_t = \frac{p_t}{p_t^*}. \tag{14.8}$$

Such theorem affirms that, in the long run, the real exchange rate is equal to one, therefore the nominal exchange rate of a currency tends to equalize the ratio between the domestic prices of the good in the two countries. This theorem obviously applies to tradable goods, goods that are both exportable and importable, while this might not be true for those services (non-tradable goods) where international trade is not possible (the hairstyling service is just one of the most obvious examples). Nevertheless, as regards tourism we know that tourists, not the services, freely move (see Sect. 14.3), therefore tourism flows imply a tendency towards the purchasing power parity equilibrium for the apparently non-tradable service of tourism.

[6] The calculation of the real exchange rate requires the identification of the same good in two different countries: a widespread method refers to a famous product that is found all over the world, the Big Mac from McDonald's; the weekly magazine *The Economist* has been computing and publishing for years the real exchange rate using this good, the so-called *Big Mac's Index*.

With reference to the whole national economy, the calculation of the real exchange rate follows the same rationale, although it is more complicated since prices have to be aggregated, for example considering the bundle of goods produced in the US and the bundle of goods produced in Germany. The formula is the same, but in (14.7) an aggregate index of prices in the two countries must be estimated, the so-called GDP deflator: the one for the US in the numerator, the one for Germany in the denominator. The aggregate real exchange rate is then equal to the nominal exchange rate deflated by a general index of prices in the two countries.

The real exchange rate is a pure index, with no meaning in absolute terms, but its fluctuations are important. For the same nominal exchange rate, an increase in the relative price of the foreign goods (the prices in the US increase more than those in Germany) leads to an increase in the real exchange rate, making the US goods relatively more expensive, and vice versa. In fact the real exchange rate measures the relative price of goods, while the nominal exchange rate measures the relative price of currencies. If the relative price remains constant (for example, if inflation in the US is equal to that in Germany) the real and nominal exchange rates are perfectly correlated; if, however, inflation has different trends, then the two exchange rates also move differently.

Finally, we recall that in practice an even more complex aggregation is used when the multilateral real exchange rate instead of the bilateral one is computed. In this case, the aggregate index of prices with respect to that of all the commercial partners of the country under consideration has to be computed, using average values weighted by the share of import or export for each country.

14.4.2 Tourism Operators and the Currency Market

International tourism operators use the currency market daily and are interested in knowing the currency exchange regime of destination countries and the past and expected fluctuations of the exchange rate. In the currency market, both tourism firms (tour operators, travel agencies, transport carriers, and hospitality firms) and tourists operate (although under somewhat different conditions) carrying out two fundamental types of transactions:

1. Transactions between tourism firms, for example a French tour operator that purchases accommodation services from a hotel in California must pay in dollars; analogously, a travel agency that intends to purchase some seats from a Japanese airline must pay in yen.
2. Transactions between tourists and tourism firms, for example a Dutch tourist who decides to spend her holidays in the UK must buy British pounds from her bank (which in turn buys pounds from other financial institutions) and pay in pounds tourism services in the destination.

The transactions between tourism firms often involve large figures, since they refer to the wholesale production of holidays, while the transactions carried out directly by tourists are normally of more modest amount, but they become more relevant when aggregated, due to the large flows of international tourism and the high frequency with which the transactions take place. In both cases, however, knowing the value of the exchange rate allows for taking rational decisions on planning a holiday abroad. Let us assume that the hotel in New York sets a price of $100 for a room with breakfast; the German tourist (or the tour operator) only has to find out the exchange rate of the dollar with the Euro, which for example is equal to $1.2814 for 1 €; thus he asks his German bank to transfer 78 € (= 100/1.2814) from his account to the hotel's account (likely in a bank in New York) in order to pay accommodation in New York. Similarly, this is also the behavior of the Americans who want to travel to Europe.

As regards tour operators, the problem is a bit more complex, since they have to find out the exchange rate at which to convert the price of their all-inclusive trips in the respective national currencies. In fact the tour operators' catalogs are usually published with the prices expressed in the currency of the country in which they are sold. Since the catalogs are usually printed a few months before tourists go on holiday (see Sect. 8.2), the tour operator must find out not only the spot and forward exchange rates, but also information about the currency regime, fixed or flexible, of the country where the offer is directed. In addition, when the expected fluctuation of the exchange rate is very high, it is possible that the tour operator changes the prices, explicitly indicating this clause in the catalog.

14.4.3 The Currency Exchange for Tourism Firms

The deep economic meaning of the exchange rate can fully be grasped when analyzing the strategic content of the decisions of firms operating on the international market.

Those firms usually operate on the currency market because they need a large amount of foreign currency: banks satisfy such requests through the opening of credit lines in currency. In carrying out these operations, both the bank and the tourism firm are exposed, particularly when faced with flexible exchange rate systems, to the risk of unexpected variations. To insure themselves against the risk of economic loss due to unexpected changes in the exchange rate, operators undertake hedging activity, both tourism firms and banks.

When banks carry out their intermediary services they buy important sums of foreign currency and are thus interested in hedging operations on their own account, and not just to cover the clients' demand. If a European bank has a daily exposure, for example, of $10 million, a variation in the exchange rate from 1 € per dollar to 0.99 would cost it 100,000 €. Let us describe how the bank can use the hedging operation to insure against this risk.

The bank just received $10 million from a large international tour operator, but does not want to keep it in its portfolio as liquidity. With a little bit of luck, the bank can find another client that needs to buy spot the same amount, although this is quite unlikely. Hence, the bank has to sell the $10 million on the future currency market. In this way the bank avoids any risk, since the future price to correspond at the delivery date has already been set: whatever happens to the exchange rate from the moment of the stipulation and the conclusion of the future contract does not affect the exchange rate that was agreed upon. In the meantime the bank can transfer the $10 million to the account of an American bank and receive the corresponding interest rate. When the bank contemporaneously makes a spot purchase and a future sale of the currency, it implicitly carries out an operation on the interest rates in the two countries; in this case it is said that it carries out a swap transaction.

Tourism firms undertake hedging operations too. Let us assume that a hotel in Berlin has sold room accommodation through a free sale contract to an American tour operator and that the payment will occur in dollars, at a previously fixed price, in 6 months. In financial jargon one can say that the hotel has a long position in dollars: it owns income in currency as an asset, although the currency is not available yet. In the absence of hedging, if the dollar appreciates in Frankfurt's exchange market, the hotel can receive a larger amount of Euros, but if the dollar depreciates it will obtain a loss that limit the profitability of the stipulated contract with the tour operator. If we assume that the hotel does not want to speculate[7] and that, on the contrary, it aims at eliminating the risk associated with its long position, the dollars can be sold through a future contract to its bank in exchange of a commission, which is the premium paid to the bank to remunerate it for this insurance activity.

Similarly, a European tour operator that buys room accommodation through a free sale contract from a Californian hotel, with payment in dollars in 3 months, finds itself with a short position in dollars. To cover this position (the risk is that the dollar will appreciate and therefore the Euro depreciates in the next 3 months, increasing the cost of the accommodation as measured in the European currency), the tour operator must buy dollars on the forward market with expiration in 3 months.

The commission paid to the bank for these transactions can be interpreted as the premium paid to insure against the risk of having long or short positions. Banks and tourism firms, therefore, can use the future market to cover the risk associated to their positions in the currency market when the exchange rate can fluctuate: the operator with a debt in currency insures itself against exchange rate fluctuations through a future buyout contract; the operator with a credit in currency insures itself with a future sale contract.

Finally, there is another type of instrument, often the least burdensome, that can cover against the risk of exchange rates fluctuations: the option (see Sect. 11.4.2). An option is defined call if the contract allows the owner of the option to buy a certain asset (in our case, a currency) at a predetermined price (strike price) before a future date; an option is called put if the contract allows the owner of the option to

[7] Given that the main source of income for the hotel is the ordinary management of reservations, it does not make sense for the hotel to expose itself to such risks, otherwise the hotel would be considered a sort of gambler.

sell the asset at a predetermined price before a future date. In both cases the owner of the option is not compelled to sell or to buy, and can let the expiration date pass without executing the contract. If the option is not taken up, the owner of the contract loses the commission paid (which becomes a true insurance premium) but, differently from what is provided for by the future contract, it is not obliged to neither buy nor sell currency. The call and put options are executed only if the owner has an advantage to do so; for example the call option on the currency is taken up only if the exchange rate increases more than the strike price.

In conclusion, let us consider again the example of the hotel in Berlin that is waiting for a payment in dollars: it could buy a put option, instead of stipulating a future sale contract, that would be taken up by paying a price to have the right to sell a certain amount of dollars at a predetermined price. If the spot exchange rate of the dollar decreases below the strike price, the hotel, taking up the option, can avoid a great loss. But if the exchange rate of the dollar appreciates above the strike price, the hotel does not take up the option and obtains an extra gain on the payment of the reservation. This is the most interesting aspect of the option contract; it is evident that the right to take up the option has a price: the net gain of the option is determined by subtracting the option price from the gain due to the fluctuation of the exchange rate.

Similarly, the European tour operator that must face a future payment in dollars to an American firm will buy a call option to protect itself from the appreciation of the dollar.

14.4.4 The Currency Exchange for Tourists

Travelers and international tourists frequently operate in the exchange market: the amounts of currency involved in each individual operation are normally small, but the whole volume of their transactions reaches important figures. Banks are still the reference point for the tourist's currency transactions, even if the form that the currency takes can be that of cash, cheques, electronic transactions, or credit cards.

Since the currency demanded is usually limited in quantity, and since currency is needed for paying cash, the tourists are not interested in insuring against the exchange rate fluctuation. Their problem is to identify the best way to carry the necessary currency, enabling them to purchase goods and services and to face emergency expenditure while abroad. Apart from cash, which is always subject to the risk of being lost or stolen, there are many alternatives for the tourist, let us see them briefly.

- *Traveler's cheques*. They are cheques named in foreign currency (usually dollars, Euros, yen), which are bought before the trip in a bank by paying the corresponding money at the current exchange rate. Traveler's cheques can be exchanged in local cash at the destination when the need for money arises. The way they are used is unusual: they are signed by the client at the moment they are withdrawn and signed again when used for payment. The two signatures are the guarantee against being lost or stolen.

- *Credit cards*. They are personal cards that allow to purchase without paying in cash: the amount will be automatically charged to the client's bank account, usually in the month following the purchase. Since there is an elapse of time between the payment and the charge to the bank account, the exchange rate can fluctuate, the bank covers the risk of fluctuation by charging a commission which is added to the market rate. The credit cards can be used, within a monthly spending limit, only if the business has an agreement with the credit card company. Nowadays there are a few internationally well-known credit card companies: Visa, Mastercard, American Express, Diner. Credit cards can also be used to withdraw cash from ATMs (Automatic Teller Machines).
- *Debit cards*. If they are qualified for international withdrawals they permit the withdrawal of cash abroad at any ATM, within certain daily and monthly limits and paying a commission to the bank for the foreign withdrawal.

All these forms of payment abroad are safer than cash, but each one is different for the procedure needed in case they are lost or stolen and for the ease to which they are converted into cash. The benefit of security is naturally paid by the tourist through a commission that is charged by the card company and/or the bank. The choice of the best way to pay while abroad is an economic calculation that takes into consideration the financial situation of the tourists (for example, the credit card limit), the way in which they travel (alone, in a small group, with organized tours; whether they use a hotel or a camping site, etc.), the expected amount of expenditure, the destination country (whether or not the country has a reliable banking system), and, in the end, the probability of having unforeseen expenditures.

14.4.5 The Exchange Rate and the Competitiveness of Destinations

The exchange rate plays a key role in setting the price of the different types of tourism and, as an explanatory variable, in the function of tourism demand; therefore, we must examine the way in which the value of the exchange rate and its fluctuations affect the competitiveness between destinations in the distribution of international tourism flows.

We start by considering the role played by the exchange rate level in the determination of tourism demand. We approach the problem by using a simple example: we assume that tourists in country A can purchase the same holiday, identical in quality and services, within their own country or in a foreign country B. In such decision the level of the exchange rate plays an important role, in fact, it introduces a factor that affects the competitiveness of country B's tourism product. Let us assume that the tourism product of A has a price of 5,000 units of its currency, while the price of the tourism product of *B* has a price of 1,000 units of its currency. Obviously, if the exchange rate is above 5 it is advantageous for the tourists to buy the domestic tourism product, while if the exchange rate is below 5 the tourism product of *B* becomes more competitive. Since the exchange rate determines the price of *B*'s tourism services, it is easy to understand its relevance in the determination of international tourism flows (see Sect. 14.3.1). A similar rationale can be used for the tourists of country *B* with respect to tourism in country *A*.

The fluctuation of the exchange rates modifies the distribution of international tourism flows, changing the competitiveness of the destinations. If the exchange rate of the Euro were to depreciate by 10 % with respect to all the other foreign currencies, all the prices and services for foreign tourists would be reduced by the same percentage, leading European destinations to be more affordable for non-European tourists. For the same reason the price of tourism in non-European destinations would increase for European tourists. Similarly, the same rationale applies if an appreciation of the Euro were to occur.

In this way, the size and the direction of international tourism flows can be affected by the monetary policy implemented in the different destinations. Decisions to let the national currency depreciate normally lead to an increase in incoming tourism flows and to a reduction in outgoing flows; decisions to let the national currency appreciate normally lead to a reduction in incoming tourism flows and an increase in outgoing flows (Notes 14.1).

14.4.6 The Arbitrage Operations by Tourists

A general characteristic of financial markets, and hence also of the currency market, is that operators are continuously searching for opportunities to make profits for themselves and for their customers. In other words, there are arbitrage operations that allow one to make extra profits (although very limited if markets are efficient) through the simultaneous buying and selling of the same (or equivalent) assets in different marketplaces.

There exist different types of arbitrage. *Direct arbitrage* occurs when an operator identifies a spread between the exchange rate of the same currency in two marketplaces: for example, the dollar–Euro rate in Frankfurt is different from the dollar–Euro rate in New York (or in Tokyo). Given that electronic transactions allow for real-time communication between different marketplaces, an operator that has access to both markets, if a spread between two exchange rates is discovered, can buy the currency in the market where it has a lower price and sell it in the market that rates a higher price. However, if everyone behaves this way, the spread in the exchange rate will be absorbed very soon and the exchange rates realigned.

Differently, *triangular arbitrage* takes place when the exchange rates between three currencies are not consistent. For example (Fig. 14.3), if the US dollar is exchanged for 1 € per dollar and the yen is quoted at 120 per 1 €, the yen–dollar exchange rate must also be equal to 120 (= 120 € per yen/1 € per dollar). If this

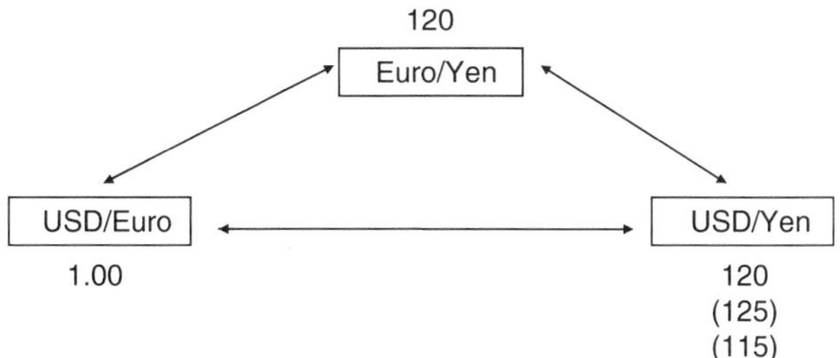

Fig. 14.3 A case of triangular arbitrage

is not the case, a profitable and riskless operation exists. Let us assume that the price of the dollar in yen is 125; an operator could sell 120 yen per 1 € and then exchange 1 € with $1 and then sell the dollar to purchase yen again: however, this triangular activity would conclude with 125 yen, with a profit of roughly 4 %. An exchange rate of 115 yen per dollar would make profitable the exchange in the opposite direction.

Tourists can take advantage of these small earning opportunities by making analogous operations. In fact, they are faced with an arbitrage problem when they wonder what currency is best to travel with. For example, a French tourist traveling to Japan has to calculate whether it is better to arrive in Tokyo having already changed her money in yen, at the exchange rate of Paris, or to bring Euros with her and change them in yen once in Tokyo, at the local exchange rate. The triangular arbitrage of the tourist is not particularly complex and is solved by deciding which currency is better to bring in the purse as she crosses the border.

Similarly, there could be advantages for the French tourist traveling to Japan to buy dollars instead of yen at the exchange rate of Paris and, once in Tokyo, convert the dollars into yen. In this case, the dollar works as a third currency; this lets the tourist perform a triangular arbitrage operation that allows for a saving on the price of tourism in Japan. The US dollar (and other important currencies like the Euro or the yen) is the currency that acts as a *numeraire* for the international tourists, especially when they travel to developing countries.

Chapter Overview

- For the economics of tourism, the distinction between domestic and international tourism stems from the role played by the exchange rate.
- According to the theory of Dunning, the multinational firm is developed to take profit of ownership, internationalization, and location advantages. The multinational activity can be implemented through outsourcing, commercial agreements, or foreign direct investments.
- The current phase of economic globalization is characterized by the opening up of countries to international trade, the liberalization of all markets, privatization policies, policies aimed at reducing the role of the government in the economy, and the transfer of economic sovereignty to international organizations.

- The expenditure of foreign tourists in the country represents what is usually called the tourism exports of the country. What is exported with the tourism product is an abstract good, the tourism experience sold to incoming foreign tourists.
- Incoming tourists can be an important asset in a developing country's takeoff, since the money from incoming tourism can finance the imports of goods, and of factors of production necessary to start the virtuous cycle of development.
- The different models that have been proposed to explain international tourism flows focus on: the diversity in the endowment of natural resources, diversity in preferences, the principle of the comparative advantage, preference for variety, organizational skills and transport system management, advantages in terms of price and of the exchange rate.
- In the center–periphery model, the localization of tourism firms depends on the comparison between the fixed costs of production (therefore on the extent of economies of scale) and transport costs.
- The nominal exchange rate is the price of a foreign currency in terms of the national currency. The real exchange rate is the price of foreign goods in terms of national goods and depends on the combination of the nominal exchange rate and the prices of the goods in the two countries.
- Tourism firms, according to the different exchange regimes (flexible, fixed, or mixed regime) can use existing financial instruments (futures, options) to reduce or to eliminate the risk associated with the fluctuations of the exchange rate or, eventually, to speculate on the expected variations.
- The size and direction of international tourism flows are affected by the monetary policy implemented in the different destinations. Decisions to let the national currency depreciate normally lead to an increase in incoming tourism flows and a reduction in outgoing flows; decisions to let the national currency appreciate normally lead to a reduction in incoming tourism flows and an increase in outgoing flows.

Chapter 15
The State Intervention and the Public Organization of Tourism

Learning Outcomes
By the end of the chapter you will understand:

- The concept of market failure, with particular reference to the externalities and the public good.
- The reasons behind the intervention of the State in the economy, its available instruments, and financing possibilities.
- The organization of tourism on a local, national, and international level.

15.1 Introduction

When speaking of tourism, there exist positive and normative motivations for analyzing those institutions that govern and supervise the economic relationships between tourism operators in the market. An institution can be defined as any organization which is accepted by the members of the society and with the power of regulating the behavior of individuals and to make decisions which consequences fall on the entire community. In fact, as a general rule of the economy, and this is particularly true for the tourism sector, many economic problems can be mainly settled through the intervention of an external authority, either being a voluntary organization (such an association of firms) or a public institution (such a public body), which sets the rules and enables to make them obligatory.

Regarding the positive motivations, the existence of inefficiencies in the free market equilibrium can mainly derive from the presence of public goods in the matrix of the tourism product and from the existence of externalities. We must recall that, even though the focus of this textbook is mainly on the production and the distribution of tourism services, tourism in the destination can develop thanks

G. Candela and P. Figini, *The Economics of Tourism Destinations*,
Springer Texts in Business and Economics, DOI 10.1007/978-3-642-20874-4_15,

to the presence of natural, historical, cultural, organizational, and institutional resources that have the characteristics of public goods (see Sect. 15.2) and produce strong externalities that cannot be efficiently managed by the market itself. In presence of public goods or externalities, the economic theory states that the social optimum is not reached when the decisions about the allocation of resources are left to the market.

For the correct framing of the problem, let us start with a short reminder of the three fundamental reasons that lead the policy maker to intervene in the economy: (a) the *allocation* reason, for which the intervention follows the inability of the market to achieve the efficient equilibrium; (b) the *distribution* reason, for which the policy maker intervenes to redistribute resources and income (through taxation and direct production of goods and services) according to equity criteria; (c) the *stabilization* reason, for which the government intervenes for anticyclical purposes, to reach the optimal level of aggregate demand and to sustain employment trying to avoid, at the same time, problems of inflation.

As far as tourism is concerned, although redistribution issues (in particular between residents and tourists) and stabilization policies (in terms of controlling employment and income effects of seasonality) can be relevant, the main activity is with regard to allocation. The intervention of the *allocation bureau* is necessary since, as recalled many times in this work, the complexity of the tourism phenomenon drives to: (a) coordination problems between firms and markets, due to the strong complementary between the several goods and services included in the tourism product; (b) market failures linked to the incompleteness of information for the tourist, to the external economies connected to the fact that tourism shapes and unfolds in a specific territory, and to the prevalence of monopoly and non-competitive market structures; (c) the key role played by public goods and common resources in the matrix of the tourism product.

Due to their relevance for tourism production, we start with the study of public goods and of what we symmetrically call "public bads," which are exactly their opposites (see Sect. 15.2). Public goods (bads) have the key characteristic that, at the moment when they are produced, they create strong positive (negative) externalities on the rest of the community of tourists and residents. Hence, in Sect. 15.3, we will focus on the phenomenon of tourism-related externalities to later continue, in Sect. 15.4, with the topic of how to regulate the tourism sector and how to finance the public intervention in the economy. In particular, we will focus on the motives as to why tourists can be the target of specific taxes.

Finally, in Sect. 15.5 we will see how public intervention in tourism can be made more efficient through the creation of specific institutional bodies: in fact, although public intervention in tourism is a key feature for any country, many types of bodies, institutions, and organizational structures are possible. In the real world, different organizations, international, national, regional, and local coexist and each country displays different judicial and administrative frameworks. The detailed description of these systems is left to comparative tourism law; our task as economists of tourism is to analyze the content, the aims, and the organizational structure that tourism bodies can take. The need of organization in tourism, finally, is so strong that even self-organized bodies, such as voluntary associations of firms or workers are often at play.

15.2 Public Goods and Public Bads in the Tourism Product

Public goods are goods which benefits are spread over the whole community, regardless of the individual act of purchasing. Technically, a public good differs from a private good (the standard good exchanged in markets) in two characteristics: the *rivalry in consumption* and the *excludability of benefits*. A public good is characterized by:

1. The absence of rivalry in consumption: more than one individual can simultaneously benefit from the good without reducing the utility they get from consumption. Some examples of the non-rivalry of consumption are street lights, university lectures, radio–television transmissions; if the contemporaneous use by many agents leads to a partial reduction in everyone's utility, it is said that the public good is subject to a phenomenon of congestion. A private good, on the contrary, has the property of rivalry in consumption: an example of good with this property is food, if a person eats a sandwich, the same sandwich is not available for consumption to anyone else.
2. The absence of excludability of benefits: if the good is made available to someone, it is not possible, or it is not economically advantageous, to exclude other consumers from the benefits that the good produces; the non-excludability can be technical, linked to the physical characteristics of the good (think of a beach), or economic, if the non-excludability (even if it is technically possible, think of the possibility of encrypting television transmissions to make them available only to those who have a decoder) derives from a cost of exclusion that is too high. Some examples of non-excludability of benefits are street lights, a public square, and the landscape that can be viewed from a mountain. A private good, on the contrary, has the property of excludability of benefits. Recalling the example of the sandwich, the bar that puts the sandwich on sale has all the technical and legal rights to deny consumption to the person who is not willing to pay its price.

If the good has both characteristics of non-rivalry in consumption and non-excludability of benefits is a pure public goods, but intermediate cases are also possible, as illustrated in Table 15.1. Impure public goods are those that allow a certain degree of excludability: for these goods, therefore, it is possible to find a mechanism that allows for providing the services only to a well-identified group of users, excluding the non-participants from the group. James Buchanan calls them *club goods*. The mechanism of exclusion could be technical (like in certain alumni clubs where access is only granted to graduates) or economic (if one pays a subscription fee to access the good or the service, such as pay-tv). Similarly, mixed public goods are those goods in which a certain degree of rivalry in

Table 15.1 The classification of goods according to the characteristics of excludability and rivalry

	Excludability	
Rivalry	Yes	No
Yes	Private good	Mixed good
No	Club good	Public good

consumption is present. In these cases, consumption by an individual can partially reduce the consumption of others, but not completely eliminate it (like in broadband connection, in which the quality of connection depends on the number of other users connected to the network). Finally, in the case in which the good has the characteristics of rivalry in consumption and excludability of benefits, we are faced with a private good.

15.2.1 Public Goods in the Tourism Product

In the matrix of the tourism product (see Sect. 2.5) many public goods are included. Information available over the Internet, most of the cultural heritage of the destination, the city's skyline, even the whole city itself are examples of public goods that enter the matrix of tourism. In addition, also club goods are important in tourism, think of swimming pools, museums, golf courses, where access can be partially limited through the use of various technical or economic mechanisms. Finally, also mixed goods are important if, due to different types of congestion, a rivalry in consumption applies: think of traffic jams on the streets, crowded beaches, etc.

To illustrate the economic problem of public goods in tourism, let us consider the case of a small city that wants to attract tourists, and to this aim, the city council approves the construction of a statue by a famous artist in the city's main square. Being in a public square, the sculpture would be accessible to everyone, tourists and residents, without leading to problems of congestion. According to the above economic definition, the statue is a pure public good. Without losing generality, let us assume that there exist only two families living in the city, A and B, with incomes equal to Y_A and Y_B, respectively. Both families are willing to support the installation of the sculpture both for their personal enjoyment and because it constitutes a tourism attraction but, given that members of A and B are called to finance the cost of the statue, the available income of the households would be reduced. Therefore, each family has to choose between two alternative states of the world: (a) the utility resulting from the provision of the statue, which is associated with less available income; (b) the utility resulting from the full availability of income for other consumption purposes, but associated with no artistic consumption.

The problem of economic policy, therefore, is to determine the social welfare for the community of families in the two alternative cases. What initiatives should the city council take: to buy or not to buy the sculpture? How does the policy maker arrive at the decision?

In the standard case of private goods, with rivalry in consumption and benefits that are excludable through the recognition of property rights, the solution is left to the market. Producers and consumers meet on the market, the equilibrium between demand and supply is achieved through the process of price setting and the good is allocated among different agents. Consistently, different quantities of the private good appear in the individual demand functions, according to respective preferences. From the consumption theory we know that, if the equilibrium price is unique, the allocation of the good is socially optimal (Pareto-efficient), and this solution leads to the equality of the individual weighted marginal utilities.

On the contrary, since the public good is non-excludable and non-rival, it appears with the same value in the utility function of each consumer, and the optimality condition must be modified. We assume, for example, that the availability of the

Theory in Action 15.1. The Optimal Production of a Public Good

The preferences of two families, A and B, are represented by a utility function with arguments the money available for private consumption, respectively M_A and M_B, and a public good G:

$$U_A = U_A(M_A; G); \quad U_B = U_B(M_B; G).$$

The fact that G is present, for the same amount, in the utility function of both families characterizes its nature of public good (its use is non-rival and benefits are not excludable). In order to identify the condition of optimal production for the public good, we need to present two cases, differing according to whether the policy maker intervenes or not in its production.

The Public Sector Defines the Optimal Size of the Public Good

Since the policy maker's aim is the maximization of overall welfare, its objective function, in this simple community composed by two families, can be indicated as the sum of the two utility functions:

$$W = U_A(M_A; G) + U_B(M_B; G). \tag{I}$$

The overall budget constraint is given by the initial endowments of the two families in terms of available income Y_A and Y_B:

$$M_A + M_B + cG = Y_A + Y_B, \tag{II}$$

where c is the price of one unit of the public good.

(continued)

The maximum of (I) subject to the budget constraint (II) leads, for the private good, to the usual condition of equality of the marginal utilities:

$$U'_A(M_A) = U'_B(M_B)$$

while for the public good the condition can be written as:

$$\mathrm{MRS}_A + \mathrm{MRS}_B = c, \tag{III}$$

where the symbols MRS_i for $i = A, B$, indicate the marginal rate of substitution between the public and the private good for each family. Equation (III) is the condition of optimality for the public good, known in the literature as the Samuelson Condition. It affirms that the optimal supply of a public good requires that the sum of the marginal rates of substitution between each pair made up of a private good and a public good, for all individuals, is equal to the price of the public good.

Condition (III), if referred to a public good of continuous size, allows for determining its optimal size; if it is referred instead to a good with a given size, for which the only possible alternative is to produce it or not, condition (III) can be written in this way: if $\mathrm{MRS}_A + \mathrm{MRS}_B \geq c$, the answer is yes, the public good is produced (as in the case described in Sect. 15.2.1); if $\mathrm{MRS}_A + \mathrm{MRS}_B < c$, the answer is obviously no.

The Private Sector Defines the Optimal Size of the Public Good
When the decision about the size of the public good must be directly taken by the private sector, without intervention of the policy maker, each family knows that, following a selfish rationale, its decision G_i depends on the other family's decision. The size of G is therefore:

$$G = G_A + G_B.$$

To illustrate the individual decision, we consider family A, but the same rationale can be also applied to the other family. The optimal size depends on the maximization of the individual utility function:

$$U_A = U_A(M_A; G) = U_A(M_A; G_A + G_B) \tag{IV}$$

subject to the budget constraint:

$$M_A + cG_A = Y_A. \tag{V}$$

It is clear that the solution to this problem strongly depends on the assumption that each individual makes on the choice of the other party:

A makes an assumption on the expected value of G_B. The simplest assumption is to consider the Cournot–Nash solution and assume that such value is given. Thereby, family A's problem goes back to the standard solution of the consumer's equilibrium, in which the marginal rate of substitution between the own share of contribution to the cost of the public good and the private good must be equal to the price of the public good:

$$\mathrm{MRS}_A = c.$$

The same solution applies for family B, with the assumption that the size of G_A is given:

$$\mathrm{MRS}_B = c.$$

Summing the two solutions for A and for B we get the condition of determination of the size of the public good, in the case where the decision is taken by the private sector only:

$$\mathrm{MRS}_A + \mathrm{MRS}_B = 2c$$

from which:

$$(1/2)(\mathrm{MRS}_A + \mathrm{MRS}_B) = c, \qquad \text{(VI)}$$

which expresses the condition that the semisum of the marginal rates of substitution (in general, their arithmetic average) must be equal to the price of the public good.

The two solutions (III) and (VI), with and without the intervention of the public sector, are different and this difference has to be discussed: if one indicates with G^* the optimal size of the public good determined by the public sector, solution (III), and with G^+ the optimal size of the public good determined by the private sector, solution (VI), it is easy to verify (with the usual assumptions on $U_i(.)$ and MRS_i) that $G^+ < G^*$, that is, in the decentralized private solution the public good results undersized with respect to the socially optimal size, achieved with the intervention of the public sector. Without the public intervention, in other words, the market fails.

statue in the square gives each family an increase in utility of two units, while the overall cost of the statue is three units of utility. In these conditions it is immediate to show that the community composed by the two families would receive a net benefit from the acquisition, given that the overall increase in utility is four units while the cost of the statue is three units (this is the Samuelson condition, Theory in Action 15.1).

Table 15.2 Payoff matrix for the public good decision

Vote of A/vote of B	Yes	No
Yes	0.5; 0.5	−1; 2
No	2; −1	0; 0

However, the individual preferences, being private information of each household, are unknown to the city council, which only knows the cost of the statue.

To decide on the purchase, the city council must ask the families to reveal their willingness to pay. Let us imagine that each family can separately vote "yes" or "no" to the purchase, and that the statue is then bought (and paid for) only by those who voted "yes." Table 15.2 presents all the possible results of this game, in the form of a payoff matrix. In each cell we find a pair of numbers to be interpreted as payoffs in terms of the net utility of the two families (which is equal to the monetary value of total utility minus the cost), stemming from the interaction of the two voting strategies that distinguish each cell.

If both families vote "yes," they each have the same payoff of 0.5 units given that they obtain two units of utility with a cost of 1.5 (= 3/2). If only one family votes "yes," a positive payoff (equal to two units) only appears for the family that votes "no," given that they can enjoy the statue without having to pay the cost, while the family that votes "yes" has a loss of one unit since it is called to finance the entire cost of the statue. Finally, if both families vote "no," the purchase does not go through, therefore the payoff is zero for both.

Under these conditions (which typically defines the prisoner's dilemma, see also see Sect. 11.7.2) the dominant strategy for both A and B is to vote "no": if the other family votes "yes" it is better to vote "no," given that the payoff of two is better than 0.5; if the other family votes "no" it is also better to vote "no," since zero is better than −1. Therefore, since it is rational for both families to vote "no," the statue is not purchased. However, the outcome is inefficient, since the solution of purchase with cost borne by the two families would be better for both, leading to a payoff of (0.5; 0.5) higher than the outcome of the game. Moreover, the decision of not purchasing the statue has also a negative effect for tourism, since visitors will not avail of the potentially new tourism attraction.

The solution where the public good is not available in the tourism product of the destination originates from an economically rational behavior of the families. In fact, the citizens do not gain from revealing their true willingness to contribute to the public good. In fact, if they have developed the conviction, as is theoretically correct to happen, that they will be called to pay on the basis of their expressed willingness to pay, then it is rational to undervalue their own real utility stemming from the public good. This selfish behavior, which takes into consideration the opportunity of receiving benefits from what the others do (since the public good is non-excludable and non-rival, they would freely avail of the good without paying its price) is called *free-riding*: the expression refers to a person who uses transportation without paying the ticket, thereby receiving a free ride and counting on the fact that the transportation cost is paid for by the others. However, if each citizen were to hide their own preferences, motivated by this rationale, then the result would be to have a quantity of the public good lower than what is socially optimal, until the extreme case where the public good is not produced at all (like in our example, in which the statue is not purchased by the city council), with economic damage to each individual and for the society as a whole.

Such simple example typically explains the market failure stemming from the characteristics of a public good, for which the market mechanism based on voluntary and decentralized decisions does not lead to an efficient outcome. To avoid such situation, the public authority is called for intervention through: (a) the direct activity of production of the public good; (b) the allocation of the total cost among the community through taxes.

The problem of free riding can be partially resolved in the case of the club good; in fact for this type of goods the benefits are excludable, therefore the fact that individuals can have access to the good only by paying, naturally drives to the revelation of own preferences.

Beyond this example, the model of the public good is sufficiently general to explain why the cultural gatherings in a public square, green areas, or parking lots to access the destination so rarely enter in the offer of package tours. In general one can expect, if the public administration does not intervene, a lower level of public goods in the tourism product of the destination. The result of this inefficiency in the product's structure is the lowering of the quality and of the variety, thereby diminishing the tourist's satisfaction and rendering the destination less attractive and less competitive on the international market.

15.2.2 Public Goods as Factors of Production

In the previous subsection we have considered the public good in relation to the consumption activity by residents (and indirectly by tourists). Nevertheless, it is clear that public goods can also serve as production factors: the tourist information office offered by the destination management, consultancy services to firms, professional education programs, museums, squares, festivals are only a few examples of public goods that enter, as intermediate goods, the production function of the tourism product.

For classification purposes, it is necessary to distinguish two types of public production factors.

1. *Public factors in relation to private production factors.* In this case the public good is available for use by the other production factors, labor or capital, with the effect of increasing their productivity. Examples of this type are the cleared traffic streets for going to work, professional education programs that increase the competency of workers, antipollution programs that render the work

environment healthier, etc. Factors of this type are pure public goods, with no possibility of exclusion, neither for the firms nor for the factors of production. They are called factor augmenting.

2. *Public goods in relation to the firms.* In this case the public good is available for the use by the firm, directly as an additional factor of the production function. Examples of this type are legal and fiscal services provided by professional associations for their own members (this is a typical example of a club good), public watch services, fairs, conventions, etc. They are called firm augmenting.

In tourism production both factor augmenting and firm augmenting public goods are present, but the most important is surely the goods of the latter type: cultural goods or natural resources can be interpreted as production factors that enter as public goods in the tourism product: they can be exploited by several different firms at the same time, tourism and not, without producing excludability or rivalry.

We now focus on the firm augmenting public good, by considering again the example of the previous section and adding that the two families, *A* and *B*, are the owners of two hotels located in the square where the city council has decided to install the sculpture. Since the sculpture can be viewed from the windows of their hotel rooms, the statue enters the production function of the accommodation service in the same way in which the other production factors, capital and labor, appear. Moreover, since the statue is appreciated by the cultural tourists visiting the city, the hotels receive an extra income from having the sculpture as a production factor.

If the number of firms is variable, that is, if the opening of new hotels in the square is possible, the supply of accommodation can increase thus reducing the price until the extra profit is absorbed by the greater degree of competition. In the more realistic example in which the number of firms is fixed and new hotels cannot be opened in the square, the extra income due to the sculpture also remains in the long run. According to the basic principle that production factors must be remunerated, we should expect that the city council, which purchases and takes care of the statue, ask the hotels to pay a contribution to the total cost. This is just an application to public production factors of the general principle of economics that factors are paid according to the value of their marginal contribution to production.

To summarize, the cost of public goods being used for direct consumption by residents or as intermediate goods for tourism firms must be covered. To finance the former, one must turn to the contribution of residents based on their willingness to pay (measured in terms of personal utility stemming from the public good). To finance the latter, one must turn to the contribution of tourism firms (measured in terms of the marginal productivity of the public good).

However, to efficiently apply this principle, each firm should transfer to the city council a payment equal to the surplus received from the contribution of the public good in production. Nevertheless, as in the case of consumers, it is not realistic to assume that this value is identified by the firms themselves: automatic market mechanisms to reveal the contribution of public goods used in production do not exist, leading to free-riding behaviors by firms, which use (and gain from) the public goods in production without paying a price equal to their contribution.

Once again, this rational but selfish behavior by firms drives to the reduction of public goods as production factors in the tourism supply: museums with too short opening hours, dirty squares or beaches, poorly preserved cultural sites, few festivals or live performances, rare exhibitions, etc. are just a few examples of insufficient public goods in the tourism product. To avoid such situation, the public authority is called for intervention through: (a) the direct activity of supplying the public good; (b) the allocation of the total cost through taxes on firms.

15.2.3 Public Bads in the Tourism Product

Public bads can be defined as the damages caused to the entire community and without the possibility of being excluded. It often deals with unwanted by-products of consumption or production activities, such as environmental pollution. Public bads are also of interest for the tourism sector: both the pollution that affects the natural environment and the deterioration of monuments and cultural cities have a general negative effect on tourism.

A symmetrical result to that of the public goods is verified also for the public bads: the maximization of individual goals leads to a socially inefficient outcome. This conclusion is the typical result stemming from many situations of non-cooperative strategic interaction: the condition is well illustrated by the famous prisoner's dilemma game, which we have already used to illustrate the problem of public goods.

As an example of public bads in tourism, let us assume two hotels, *A* and *B*, located on the shores of a mountain lake; each hotel, in order to produce its own hospitality services, pollutes the lake and the forests. If none of the hotels takes the responsibility of financing a project of water purification or trash collection, the environmental degradation drives tourists away, with damage done to nature, to tourism activity, and to the firms' profitability. In this sense, the pollution of the lake and the forests is a public bad, negatively entering the production function. Assume that the two hotels can choose between two forms of using the environment: (a) respect it (we indicate this action with *R*), through developing and managing an environmentally friendly "eco-hotel," and bearing the costs that this attention in terms of environmental quality brings with it; (b) damage it (we indicate this action with *D*), without worrying about the environmental problems and without sustaining cleanup costs.

What is the best strategy to use for each of the two hotels? We indicate in Table 15.3 the payoffs of the two hotels according to the strategies they adopt. In any cell each of the two figures can be interpreted as the long-run profits of each hotel, according to the respective strategy. The first figure in each cell is hotel *A*'s profit; the second figure is hotel *B*'s profit. If both *A* and *B* manage eco-hotels, they obtain the same profit of 50 which stems from the prices paid by their "green" customers; if only one hotel respects the environment and the other does not, and if we assume that this type of degradation of the environment is within the limits of

Table 15.3 The payoff of two hotels in case of strategies of respecting (R) or damaging (D) the environment

	Hotel B	
Hotel A	R	D
R	50; 50	10; 70
D	70; 10	20; 20

natural regeneration, the tourists are satisfied, but the hotel that pollutes will have the advantage of not bearing the costs of environment protection; such hotel can therefore get the highest profit (=70), while all the costs are borne by the other hotel, which gets a low profit (=10). Finally, in the case where both hotels damage the environment the threshold of natural regeneration is bypassed and the degradation of the lake and the forests keeps the best tourists away: long-run profits for both hotels are quite modest in this case (=20).

It is straightforward to observe that there exist a dominant strategy (a strategy that is chosen by a hotel independently of what is the other hotel's strategy) for each hotel: it is better for hotel B to damage the environment both if A plays R (since $70 > 50$) and if A plays D (since $20 > 10$). The same rationale can be used for hotel A. Therefore, since each hotel wants to get the highest profit, it is better for both to adopt strategy D, independently of what its rival decides. Due to the strategic interaction of the two players that follow this rational but selfish behavior, no one decides to manage an eco-hotel, and both hotels end up getting the modest long-run profit of 20, while the public bad of pollution of the lake and the forests emerges.

However, the game would also allow a cooperative solution in which the simultaneous respect for the environment would be more profitable for both hotels. This solution, unfortunately, is not achieved automatically, since it is advantageous for each of the two hotels to shift the environmental costs onto the other. Only the public intervention, through a law of environmental protection and with efficient sanctions that make it a binding commitment, can bring the game to the efficient solution, making the agents leave the rational trap of a Hobbesian solution. Such cooperative equilibrium is beneficial to both hotels, is more satisfying for tourists and more respectful to the environment.

In its simplicity, the example of the two hotels demonstrates that a selfish behavior leads to socially suboptimal results when there are public bads, while the best solution for both hotels and for the environment can be reached only with a binding agreement that economists call *commitment*.[1] In addition, in this payoff structure, the process of investment in the production of public goods and in the elimination of public bads is self-reinforcing. By investing in the quality of the tourism product the willingness to pay of tourists and profits of firms increase, hence enabling the administration to increase fiscal revenue (assuming that taxes

[1] If the game is repeated with an infinite horizon, the *Folk Theorem* states that the cooperative solution may be obtained without public intervention, only through individual strategies.

are proportional to profits) and allowing to finance public investment in the production of public goods (Rigall-I-Torrent and Fluvià 2007).

To conclude this section, we highlight that is the same rational but selfish and non-cooperative behavior that explains why in the composition and structure of the tourism product: (a) public goods are often undersized; (b) public bads are often oversized; (c) the public intervention is necessary to bring the agents to the socially optimal cooperative solution.

15.3 The Externalities in the Tourism Product

Economic theory teaches that the market is able to coordinate individual decisions through its only informative mechanism, the price, and that the perfectly competitive equilibrium is characterized by the property of Pareto optimality.[2] It is well known, however, that efficiency is not reached when the assumptions of perfect competition are not satisfied, that is, when there is asymmetric information, when firms have some degree of monopoly power, when there is strategic interaction among agents, when there is uncertainty in the market conditions, in case of presence of common, merit or public goods and when there are externalities. In the previous section we studied one form of market failure: the presence of public goods (or bads) in the tourism product. The simultaneous presence of the characteristics of non-excludability of benefits and non-rivalry in consumption makes the behavior of an agent (firm or tourist) produce strong externality effects on the behavior of the other agents. Therefore, in this section we discuss the concept of externality, generalizing beyond the definition of public goods (and bads).

An externality is a benefit or a cost not transmitted through the price mechanism. In presence of externalities the economic decision of an agent affects other parties independently of their wills. Externalities can be classified through two different schemes.

The first classification is related to the type of agents producing the externality: (a) *consumption externalities*, when the consumption decisions of an agent affect the utility function of other agents, consumers, or firms; (b) *production externalities*, when the production decisions of a firm affect the output of other firms or the utility of some consumers.

The second classification distinguishes the externalities according to the sign of the effect they produce: (a) *positive externalities* or *external economies*, if they produce a positive effect on the utility or on the output of other agents; (b) *negative externalities* or *external diseconomies*, if they produce a negative effect on the utility or on the output of other agents.

[2] Pareto optimality, also called Pareto efficiency, is a situation in which it is not possible to increase the well-being of an individual without decreasing the well-being of someone else.

Mixing these two classification schemes allows us to say, for example, that smoking or the excessive noisiness of a car are negative externalities of consumption; on the contrary, a well taken care garden is a positive externality of consumption because it increases the well-being of the neighbors. On the production side, the most typical example of negative externality is the manufacturing firm that pollutes the water of a lake, with negative effects on the tourists staying in a nearby campsite. Finally, an example of positive production externality is a modern building designed by a top architect for a firm's headquarter, which attracts tourists to have lunch in a nearby restaurant with view of the building.

The key factor characterizing the externality is that goods (smoke, noise, pollution, a neighbor's garden, etc.) affecting the act of consumption should have a positive economic value but, because of their characteristics or because there is lack of property rights, a market where these goods can be exchanged against a price does not exist. Therefore, when there are externalities, the price mechanism sends incoherent signals with respect to the efficient distribution of resources, with the consequence that the link between competition and optimality is lost. This phenomenon can be classified as another market failure, since the information that the agents receive from the market price is insufficient, or even biased, and does not allow them to efficiently allocate goods or production factors. The fact that the market can fail in certain situations, however, does not mean that it should be totally abandoned:

> However, the existence of externalities does not mean that markets must be disbanded. Abolishing the price mechanism because air pollution is bothersome and because flower gardens are pleasurable would be throwing the baby out with the bath water.
>
> (Feldman and Serrano 2006, p. 146)

What is necessary, hence, is to identify the appropriate instruments of correction of the externality; wherever corrections are not possible or are too costly, the resulting implications of the external economies should be made clear.

In this section we mainly deal with externalities that interest the tourism sector, attempting to identify the policy interventions needed to address these effects. In tourism the most likely situation is that of non-tourism firms that produce a negative externality of production on tourism firms, for example a steel plant that, emitting large quantities of harmful sulfur dioxide smoke, halts any type of tourism development in the destination. Another typical situation is that of the externality induced by tourists on the consumption activity of the local population. In Sect. 15.3.1 we will discuss the negative production externalities, while in Sect. 15.3.2 we will tackle the issue of consumption externalities between tourists and residents, underlining how these can easily switch from positive to negative and vice versa.

15.3.1 Negative Externalities on Tourism Production

To illustrate the first case of market failure caused by negative externalities of production, we consider a manufacturing firm that uses the water of a lake for its production activity. If the water is freely disposable, and in the absence of any type of legislation regarding its protection, the manufacturing firm would dump its production waste in the waters, in order to maintain production costs low and to maximize profits. Let us assume that, on the shores of the lake, there are some hotels and campsites that use the same water as a primary factor of production of holidays and leisure services. It is reasonable to think that the number of overnight stays of tourists (which, we recall, represent the output of the production of tourism services) is negatively correlated with the degree of pollution in the lake and therefore with the amount of dumped waste. In technical terms, the manufacturing firm's activity causes an external diseconomy on the production of the tourism firm.

More formally, the cost of production borne by the manufacturing firm, its private cost, can be expressed in function of the quantity Q of manufactured goods, which we indicate with $C(Q)$, with costs increasing with quantity, $C' > 0$. Nevertheless, the production activity leads to damages for the tourism hotels in the area, in terms of a reduction in overnight stays, N, according to the function, $N = F(Q)$, with $N' < 0$, which can be accounted for as an external cost of manufacturing production, $S(Q)$. Therefore, the total cost of manufacturing production which also takes into account the externality, that we call social cost $C_S(Q)$, is given by the sum of the private cost and the externality:

$$C_S(Q) = C(Q) + S(Q). \tag{15.1}$$

If the manufacturing firm operates in a perfectly competitive market it maximizes its profit by equating the private cost to the product's price, p, obviously not taking into account the external cost of pollution of the lake caused by its activity. Hence, for the manufacturing firm, production is determined by the condition:

$$C'(Q) = p, \tag{15.2}$$

which is satisfied in correspondence with quantity Q^+ in Fig. 15.1. The policy maker is interested in maximizing instead the objective function of the entire community composed by both the manufacturing and the hospitality firms. The optimal production of manufacturing goods has to be determined by taking into account the private cost of production but also the external cost on tourism activities, thus equating the marginal social cost, C'_S, to the price:

$$C'_S(Q) = C'(Q) + S'(Q) = p \tag{15.3}$$

a condition that is satisfied in correspondence with Q^* in Fig. 15.1. Equation (15.3) is strikingly different from (15.2), therefore the socially optimal production, Q^*, certainly does not coincide with that of Q^+ decided by the firm.

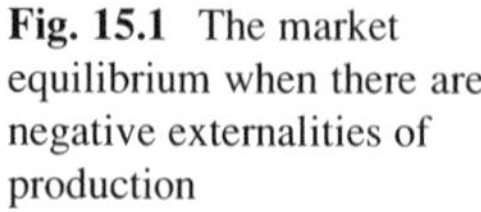

Fig. 15.1 The market equilibrium when there are negative externalities of production

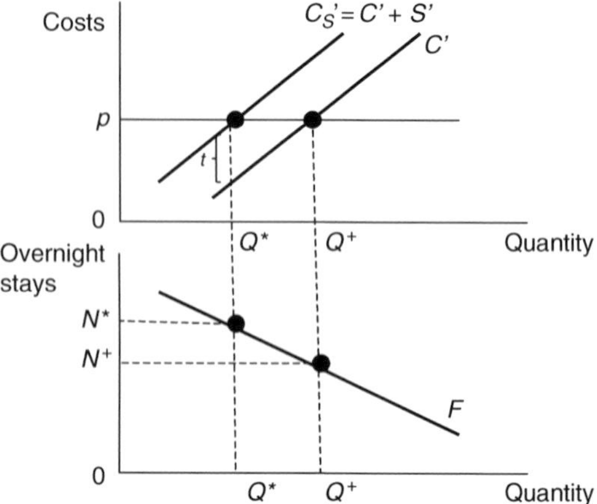

Such situation is depicted in Fig. 15.1 where on the top part the private marginal cost curve, $C'(Q)$, and the social marginal cost curve, $C'_S(Q)$, are shown. $C'_S(Q)$ has been constructed by adding the marginal externality $S'(Q)$, which for simplicity we have considered to be constant, to the private marginal cost. On the bottom part of the figure the tourism production function is shown, where the number of overnight stays depends on the pollution of the lake and, therefore, on industrial production, $N = F(Q)$. If we also indicate the price of the manufacturing product, p, it is easy to graphically determine the solutions Q^* and Q^+. In addition, the graphical solution allows for stating that $Q^+ > Q^*$.

Industrial production, therefore, stays above the socially optimal level, since the manufacturing firm does not internalize in its managerial decision the external cost that pollution produces on overnight stays of the hotels: the bottom part of Fig. 15.1 shows that the market solution the hotels are forced to adopt in the presence of externalities is below the optimum, $N^+ < N^*$. Should the destination be willing to take into account both the manufacturing production and the needs of the tourism sector,[3] it would prefer, according to (15.3), a solution with less manufacturing goods and more tourists. On the contrary the manufacturing firm, which plans its activity according to (15.2), would decide for an overproduction of the good that produces negative externalities. This divergence between the private and the social cost signals a bias in the allocation of resources: a tourism resource (the lake) that becomes too industrial, being polluted beyond its optimal level.

To avoid this suboptimal solution, the public correction is necessary, not only requested by the hotels or by tourism stakeholders, but by the entire community: in fact, solution (15.3) represents the social optimum, not the optimum for the tourism firms only, which would want the lake's water completely clean. In other words, Q^*

[3] Since the manufacturing sector produces income and employment, the socially optimal solution would not be the one in which industrial production is set to zero, as Fig. 15.1 clearly shows.

does not achieve the purity of the water (in which $Q = 0$), but rather its socially efficient level of pollution.

The many tools the policy maker can manage to bring the economy to Q^* can essentially be gathered in two groups: administrative interventions or private methods.

15.3.1.1 Administrative Interventions

The policy maker can impose the solution (15.3) by taking an active role in the market through a direct or indirect activity of control. In the first case (*direct control*) the policy maker uses the power of law, imposing a regulation that can affect the production activity through permits, licenses, or quotas of production. Despite their technical differences, the effect is similar and can be represented through setting a ceiling in manufacturing production. In our example, the appropriate ceiling should be Q^*. In this way the destination would achieve the desirable combination of manufactured goods and overnight stays (Q^*; N^*) and the socially efficient level of pollution of the lake.

Another form of direct control is through setting the standards of production. In this case, the destination management does not tell the firm how to achieve the standard, leaving to the firm, aiming at the maximum profit, the search for it. Nevertheless, the standards are difficult to implement; they require an effective activity of monitoring and an efficient system of punishment in case of breaking the standard. Particularly, the fines and the probability of being caught if breaking the law should be sufficiently high to make abiding by the law the best choice. But if, as often happens, control is difficult to implement and the fines are not that high, the firm can achieve a higher expected profit by not abiding by the law.

In the case of *indirect control*, the policy maker is able to change the cost structure of the manufacturing good through price-based interventions. It can take the form of: (a) taxes or subsidies on the quantity of the manufacturing good; (b) charges or refund schemes based on the quantity of the externality generated. Despite their technical differences, the effect is similar and can be represented through increasing the position of the cost function of manufacturing production (Fig. 15.1). For example, the government can intervene by imposing a tax t, called *Pigou tax*, for each unit of manufacturing production and which amount is equal to the externality. The amount of the tax is therefore added to the marginal cost of production and the new optimality condition for the firm becomes:

$$C'(Q) + t = p. \tag{15.4}$$

If the tax is correctly set by the policy maker we have $t = S'$. Figure 15.1 shows that the externality is internalized and the socially optimal solution is achieved, $Q = Q^*$. In practice, with the introduction of the tax, each unit of the manufacturing good would cost t more. By comparing the new marginal cost (inclusive of the tax) to the price, the firm would not find it anymore profitable to produce Q^+, but would rather prefer to reduce production down to the new point of profit maximization, which is the socially optimal solution Q^*. The hotels would also achieve their optimal level of overnight stays N^*.

And what about the tax revenue tQ^* ? As Pigou suggested in 1920, it could be used to purchase purifiers to clean up the environment (in our case to purify the lake's water) until reaching the level of pollution that is socially optimal.

To conclude, the decision whether to implement a direct or indirect strategy of intervention is a matter of cost–benefit analysis. Economic theory suggests that direct control can be too burdensome, since it affects all the firms without distinguishing their efficiency in production. Moreover, while under deterministic assumptions (as in our example) the two instruments lead to the same result, Q^*, it has been demonstrated that in stochastic scenarios there exist conditions in which the administrative standard is the first best and others in which the Pigou tax is the first best.

15.3.1.2 Private Methods

A completely different method to correct the externality is suggested by the Coase Theorem (1960), according to which in a perfectly competitive market and in the absence of transaction costs, the consequences of externalities are corrected by the market's own mechanism, as long as property rights are clearly defined. As regards our example, the first consideration is that the manufacturing firm can freely pollute the lake only because the property rights on the lake's water are not properly defined. Should the policy maker assign the property rights of the lake to the hotels, they might exchange this right by selling pollution permissions to the manufacturing firm; each permission would allow the buying firm to produce one extra unit of the manufacturing good, with the relative pollution of the lake. Hotels, following a cost–benefit analysis, would continue selling permissions until the revenue compensates, on the margin, the economic damage due to increased pollution, which is represented by the reduction in overnight stays.

In other words, the Coase theorem suggests to create the *missing market* which is, in our example, the market of water. By assigning property rights on the lake's water, as is illustrated in Fig. 15.2, the manufacturing firm would demand water to use (and pollute) it for the production of its goods, while the hotels would supply water and sell it if its price is greater than the damage they receive as a consequence of increased pollution. Like in any other market, an equilibrium price would be set, p_w, when the demand for water (which is decreasing in price) equals the supply (which is increasing in price).

It is straightforward to demonstrate that, if the new market works properly, the equilibrium price of the water is equal to the Pigou tax, $p_w = t^*$. The manufacturing firm now bears a new cost p_w to buy a factor of production that was previously freely available and the new market for water allows to autonomously achieve the socially optimal equilibrium, (Q^*; N^*) without any policy intervention, except the allocation of property rights. According to Coase, the complete definition of

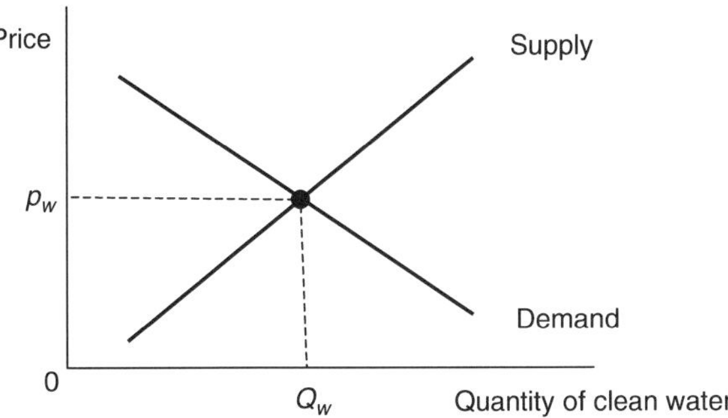

Fig. 15.2 The Coase theorem and the allocation of property rights in the missing market

property rights is a sufficient condition for the market mechanism to restore efficiency and to solve the issue of externalities.

Nonetheless, it is important to underline that hotels could use the revenue from the sale of pollution permissions to buy water cleaners, exactly as in the case with the Pigou tax. Moreover, Coase demonstrates that in terms of efficiency it is indifferent whether the property rights are assigned to the hotels or to the manufacturing firm; in the latter case the hotels would buy permissions to have a clean lake from the manufacturing firm: the efficiency condition would anyway be achieved, with the only difference in terms of distribution of profits.

In practice, the Coase solution has some serious caveats. Firstly, if the externality is spread over a large number of agents, assigning property rights is almost impossible. Secondly, assigning to a particular subject the property rights of a good that is being polluted (or that generates pollution) leads to monopoly power, therefore the price at which the permissions are sold would differ from the perfectly competitive price: an imperfect competition price would not be efficient, leading away from Q^* (Pearce and Turner 1990).

In conclusion, we have analyzed two alternative possibilities of public intervention in order to protect tourism from negative production externalities. In the case of private methods (the Coase theorem), the intervention is implemented at the constitutional level, redesigning the map of property rights, allowing the functioning of a missing market and thus reestablishing the conditions of efficiency. In the case of administrative intervention, through opportune methods of taxation or direct control on quantities, the policy maker modifies the costs of production, making the private choices of firms coherent with the social target. Which alternative is operationally preferred depends on the particular conditions of the market and on the costs associated with the different types of intervention: in some cases a direct administrative intervention may be preferred (e.g., no-smoking laws set the quantity of smoke Q^* equal to zero); in other cases an indirect administrative intervention may be preferred (e.g., the carbon tax on emissions); finally, if transaction costs are low, the Coase solution may be more efficient (e.g., some aspects of the Kyoto Protocol, in which countries can sell or buy permission to emit CO_2 in the atmosphere).

15.3.2 The Externalities Between Tourists and Residents

The relationship between tourists and the local community is a very complicated one. To unfold it, let us continue with the example of Sect. 15.2 and assume that the sculpture installed in the main square allows the city to develop as a tourism destination. The generic improvement of the city's cultural capital and urban architecture, which attracts a growing number of tourists, can either have a positive effect on residents, due to the effect of being in a more lively and attractive city, or a negative effect, if the excessive number of tourists does not allow residents to fully enjoy the attractions of the city. In the first case the presence of tourists goes hand in hand with improvements in the quality of life of residents; in the second case a worsening in their standard of living is recorded.

> The attitude of local residents towards tourists should be carefully taken into consideration: the success of many tourism development programs depends on a local management that is sensitive both to the social impact of tourism on the host population, and able to increase the benefits derived from tourism, by preventing or reducing its negative aspects, also in relations with the mix of the different types of tourism. In particular, the potential trade-off with the local population stems from the fact that the most important resource for tourism – the environment or, more generally, the territory – is to be shared with residents.
>
> (Figini and Vici 2012a, p. 3)

From a technical point of view, however, the two cases of friendly and unfriendly tourism can be classified as, respectively, positive and negative externalities of consumption that tourists produce on residents.[4] We now consider these two cases separately, as each one implies different solutions.

15.3.2.1 The Friendly Tourism Hypothesis

The relationship between tourists and residents can be defined as *friendly* if overnight stays produce a positive externality on the utility of the local population. For example, residents enjoy facilities that are built for the needs of tourists (e.g., tennis courts, parking lots, beach structures, etc.) but that are also used by residents, particularly off the seasonal peaks. In such case, overnight stays, N, in addition to bringing a net private benefit $B(N)$ (measured by profit) to the tour operator and/or the tourism firms located in the destination, also have a positive social effect on the utility of residents, which we assume can be expressed in monetary terms through $U(N)$.

[4] The socioeconomic impact of tourism and the factors affecting residents' attitude towards tourism have received some attention in recent years (Akis et al. 1996; Alberini et al. 2005; Crotts and Holland 1993; Faulkner and Tideswell 1997; Figini et al. 2009; Haralambopoulos and Pizam 1996; Lindberg and Johnson 1997a, b; Lindberg et al. 1999; Concu and Atzeni 2012). In particular, the impact of tourism is often disaggregated into three categories: economic, sociocultural, and environmental effects (Ryan 1991; Williams 1979). Since tourism generally disrupts social, cultural, and environmental local systems, the non-economic impact often tends to be negative as a whole (Liu et al. 1987), while economic effects are perceived as positive.

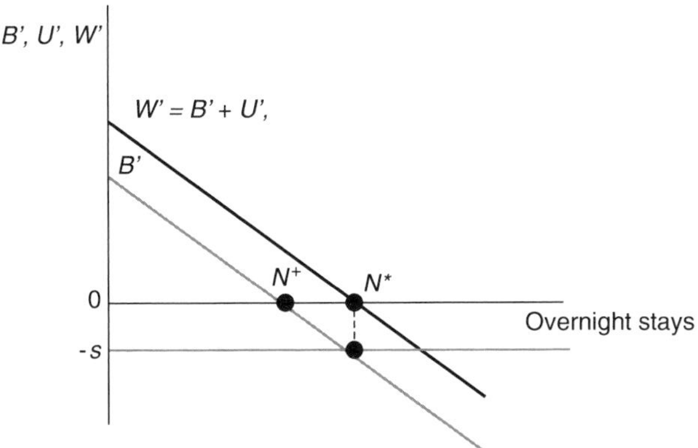

Fig. 15.3 Positive consumption externalities in the friendly tourism hypothesis

Since tourism is friendly, the social welfare stemming from tourism for the destination, W, is defined by the algebraic sum between the net private benefit of the tourism firms and the social external effect of overnight stays:

$$W(N) = B(N) + U(N) \quad \text{with} \quad B'(N) > 0, B''(N) < 0, U'(N) > 0, U''(N) \leq 0 \quad (15.5)$$

The tourism sector decides the optimal amount of overnight stays on the basis of its private benefit, which is maximized at $B'(N^{+}) = 0$ (see Fig. 15.3), while the community evaluates the optimal quantity of overnight stays by solving for the maximum of function (15.5):

$$W'(N^{*}) = B'(N^{*}) + U'(N^{*}) = 0. \quad (15.6)$$

In Fig. 15.3 we show the geometric solution provided by the function $B'(N)$ and function $W'(N)$ (which for simplicity are assumed to be linear) obtained by moving up segment $U'(N)$ (which again, for simplicity, is assumed to be constant). The maximum of function $W(N)$ determines through its abscissa N^{*} the social optimum in terms of overnight stays. It is immediate to verify that $N^{+} < N^{*}$.

By not internalizing the positive external effect on the utility of residents, the tourism sector achieves a number of overnight stays that is lower than what would be optimal for the community. Once again, this is a market failure, and there is room for a proper intervention by the destination management. Since this is the opposite case to the negative externality, also the instrument of intervention is the opposite: that of subsidy, that is, a monetary transfer to the sector. In fact, if the policy maker gives a subsidy s for each day of holiday spent by the tourist in the destination, the private benefit function of the tourism operators must be modified: $B(N) + sN$, in which the maximum at:

$$B'(N) = -s. \quad (15.7)$$

If the per capita subsidy is properly set, that is, if $s = U'(N)$, it is easy to verify (both from condition (15.6) and from Fig. 15.3) that the solution (15.7) corresponds to the number of overnight stays N^* that is socially optimal for residents. Hence, if the subsidy is equal to the marginal social utility, the market failure stemming from the friendly tourism case is solved.

15.3.2.2 The Unfriendly Tourism Hypothesis

The relationship between tourists and residents is *unfriendly* if overnight stays produce a negative effect on the utility of residents. For example, tourists produce too much trash, cause traffic jams and, more in general, tourists enter into conflict with residents in using structures, infrastructures, and services. In such case, overnight stays, N, in addition to bringing a net private benefit, $B(N)$, to the tour operator and/or the tourism firms located in the destination, also have a negative social effect on the utility of residents, which is still assumed to be expressed in monetary terms, through $C(N)$. Since tourism is unfriendly, the social welfare for the destination stemming from tourism, W, is defined by the algebraic sum between the net private benefit of the tourism firms minus the social effect of overnight stays:

$$W(N) = B(N) - C(N) \quad \text{with} \quad B'(N) > 0, B''(N) < 0, C'(N) > 0, C''(N) \geq 0. \tag{15.8}$$

The tourism sector decides the optimal amount of overnight stays on the basis of its private benefit, which is maximized at $B'(N^+) = 0$, while the community evaluates the optimal quantity of overnight stays by solving for the maximum of function (15.8):

$$W'(N^*) = 0 \quad \text{if} \quad B'(N^*) = C'(N^*). \tag{15.9}$$

In Fig. 15.4 we show the geometric solution provided by the function $B'(N)$ and function $C'(N)$ (which for simplicity are still assumed to be linear), obtained by moving down segment $U'(N)$. The maximum of function $W(N)$ determines, through its abscissa, N^*, the social optimum in terms of overnight stays. It is immediate to verify that $N^+ > N^*$.

By not internalizing the negative external effect on the utility of residents, the tourism sector achieves a number of overnight stays that is higher than what would be optimal for the community. Also in this case there is a market failure, and there is room for a proper intervention of the destination management. In this case of negative externality, the instrument of intervention is the tax. In fact, if the policy maker charges a tax, t, for each day of holiday spent by the tourist in the destination, the private benefit function of the tourism operators must be modified: $B(N) - tN$, in which the maximum is at:

$$B'(N) = t. \tag{15.10}$$

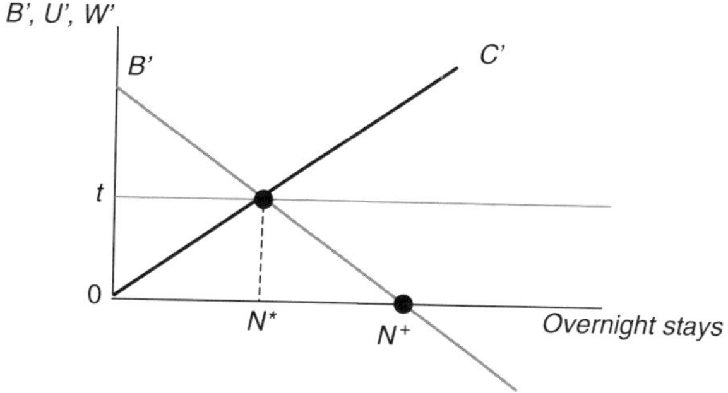

Fig. 15.4 Negative consumption externalities in the unfriendly tourism hypothesis

If the tax is properly set, that is, if $t = C'(N)$, it is easy to verify (both from condition (15.9) and from Fig. 15.4) that the solution (15.10) corresponds to the number of overnight stays N^* that is socially optimal for residents. Hence, if the tax is equal to the marginal social disutility, the market failure stemming from the unfriendly tourism case is solved.

In practice these instruments of intervention are effectively used in tourism. There are local administrations that offer subsidies to airline companies or to tour operators for each route opening at the local airport or each package holiday organized at the destination; there are cities that make tourists pay a fee when they arrive at the destination. In the former case the public authority believes that the destination is living a phase of friendly tourism and tries to subsidize it in order to increase its size; in the latter case the public authority thinks that the destination is living a phase of unfriendly tourism and tries to tax it in order to decrease its size or to compensate for the extra costs borne by residents.

The difficulty for the destination management, other than the (usual) problem of finding the correct amount of the subsidy or of the tax, is the selection of the types of tourism in which an intervention is necessary. In the same destination and at the same time, in fact, some types of friendly tourism and other types of unfriendly tourism can coexist; moreover, a certain type of tourism can be friendly in some destinations while unfriendly in others. Again, a certain type of tourism can be friendly with regards to certain groups of residents and unfriendly with regards to others. The type of relationship depends both on the sociodemographic characteristics of the resident (a leisure type of tourism has probably a positive effect on young residents, and a negative effect on the elderly) and on its employment characteristics (residents who work in the tourism sector attach more importance to the positive effects on their income stemming from tourism, while residents who work in other sectors probably attach more importance to the costs associated to road congestion and to the crowding of the city). Therefore, it is not possible to generalize, and one of the primary needs of the destination management is to select the most effective policy and analyze the implications of tourism policy on the destination.

Three interesting works that analyze the preferences of summer tourists, off-season tourists, and residents in the organization of the territory and of tourism services in the mass destination of Rimini (Italy) are, respectively, Brau et al.

(2009), Figini and Vici (2012a), and Figini et al. (2009). Since these works share the same methodology of investigation (discrete choice experiments, see Theory in Action 6.2), it is possible to highlight the presence of any synergy or trade-off between tourists and residents in the use of the same resources: trade-offs signal that tourists and residents are potentially in an unfriendly relationship; synergies signal a friendly relationship. The implication of this type of analysis for the policy maker is straightforward: it is possible to identify the best configuration of resources for tourists and residents among alternative scenarios and implement those investments that are welfare improving for both populations.

To summarize, the assumptions of friendly and unfriendly tourism can be traced back to the classic hypothesis introduced by Pigou that any production or consumption activity generates positive or negative externalities and that could be denominated as *parallel externalities*. Nevertheless, some tourism flows can generate externalities that in certain conditions are positive and in other conditions are negative: for example, when there is a threshold effect within which tourism produces a positive externality but beyond it produces a negative externality. Candela et al. (2008a) call this hypothesis in which a type of tourism can be at the same time friendly or unfriendly as *intersection externality* (multiple externalities according to Schubert 2010). If in the parallel externalities the choice between the subsidy and the tax depends on the sign of the externality, in the case of an intersection externality the choice is contingent to the particular case, and requires solving an information problem: knowing in detail the micro-effects of tourism flows on the environment of the destination.

15.4 The Taxation of Tourism

In this chapter we have seen (and we will see again in Chap. 16) that the choices made by the private sector in the presence of public goods and bads can lead to: (a) a myopic management of tourism resources, which degree of exploitation might not be environmentally sustainable; (b) an insufficient supply of public goods with respect to what would be socially optimal; (c) an overproduction of public bads with respect to what would be socially optimal.[5] As a consequence, when there are externalities, the market alone is not able to achieve the socially efficient solution, and a regulatory public intervention is advocated.

The destination, without such public management, risks compromising the sustainability of its natural and cultural resources; tourists, when arriving in the host region, risk finding too little public goods and too many public bads; tourism firms risk facing industrial pollution that damages their ability to attract tourists and their profitability; finally, residents cannot make their voice heard to the tourism

[5] Also public bads have an optimal size, which is generally different from zero: think that the absence of pollution, for example, is absence of life.

firms, to remind them of the friendly or unfriendly aspects of tourism. When these conditions of market failure exist, the policy maker must intervene. Hence, in the next subsections we will outline the actions that it can take, by focusing on taxation, the instrument that is operationally most relevant.

15.4.1 The Public Intervention

First of all, the policy maker (which can be the central government, the regional authority, or the destination management, according to the territory taken into consideration and to the organization of the public sector) must define and plan what is the sustainable use of resources from the destination's life cycle perspective (see Sect. 4.5.1) and monitor the effects of tourism on the environment and on the population.

Secondly, the policy maker must identify which public goods and which public bads are of interest for tourism. For public bads, it is necessary to induce the tourism operators to cooperate through the application of laws, regulations, and sanctions. For public goods the intervention is more complex, since the intervention is needed to directly or indirectly produce them (see Sect. 15.2.1) and to find the optimal financial scheme by identifying a fair distribution of taxes among the private sector. We have seen, in fact, that households and firms are willing to reduce their share of payment for the public good, by sending false messages to the policy maker; as a consequence, the production of the public good in the "false but revealed" scenario is at an inferior level than in the "true and desired" scenario.

In the tourism sector there is a further complication. Since the public good is not only used by firms and residents, but also by tourists, the government has to determine: (a) the share of cost of the public good that must be financed by taxes on profits; (b) the share that must be financed by taxes on households' income; (c) the share that might be financed by tourists, through specific taxes (see Sect. 15.4.2).

In addition, the government must correct the negative externalities that other economic sectors cause to tourism through the use of administrative interventions (direct or indirect) or private methods (see Sect. 15.3.1). It must also encourage, through subsidies, friendly tourism and reduce, through taxes, unfriendly tourism (see Sect. 15.3.2). The ability to separate the different effects that tourism generates on the territory is essential for the selection of the optimal intervention by the policy maker.

In the absence of public intervention the market does not guarantee, theoretically and practically, that the solution of the private sector is efficient in the short- and long-run. This need of collaboration between public and private sectors constitutes another form of complexity for the tourism sector and for the organization of tourism destinations, due to the complementarity, in the tourism product, of public and private goods and services. The composition of the tourism product, the protection of the environment, the clash of interests and the synergies between tourists, residents, and firms require the joint action of the private and the public sectors through what we have identified as the destination management (see Sect. 4.3.3).

To minimize the cost of public intervention, however, not only cooperation and coordination between the private sector and the policy maker is needed, but also the development of a real co-entrepreneurship ethics where the firms are committed to "telling the truth," thereby avoiding useless social costs, and the public sector is committed to efficiently producing laws, regulations, and public goods in response to the needs of the tourism product, thereby avoiding waste and disservices. Only through this strong cooperation can a tourism destination offer a tourism product that is respective of the environment, better in quality and competitive in price.

15.4.2 Taxes on Tourists

As previously affirmed, the public authority might gather taxes from firms, the host population, and tourists. Taxes are used to produce public goods, to correct externalities, to approve laws and regulations, to organize the public administration that controls and manages the destination, to monitor and protect the environment, and to finance projects of tourism development in the destination.

Since the population of the destination is composed of tourists (who might be defined as "temporary citizens") and the local population (the permanent residents), the destination management has to bear costs that are much higher than what would have been with the resident population only (e.g., trash collection, streets cleaning, police services, first-aid structures, etc.).

On one hand, it is true that tourism indirectly contributes to the local tax revenues due to the effect of the income multiplier generated by tourism expenditure. Hence, one could conclude that no special taxes on tourists are needed. On top of that, if tourists have a holiday home in the destination, they might be called to directly contribute to local taxes, if specific taxes such as a property tax exist. For both reasons (that have been already outlined in Chap. 13), tourism expenditure contributes to the local public budget and theoretically allows the policy maker to finance the additional expenditure for services imposed by the presence of tourists.

The functioning of this mechanism depends, however, on the country's fiscal system. In fact, the structure of a country's public finance can be organized according to two different criteria: (a) a federal system, in which taxing power is assigned to the local authority; (b) a centralized system, in which taxes are directly collected by the government and then transferred, according to own distribution criteria, to the local authority. It is clear that the more the fiscal system is inspired by the second criteria, the less automatic is the conclusion that taxes raised on the extra income stemming from the tourism multiplier go to the local public budget. This is particularly true when the criteria that determine the local transfers refer only to the resident population.

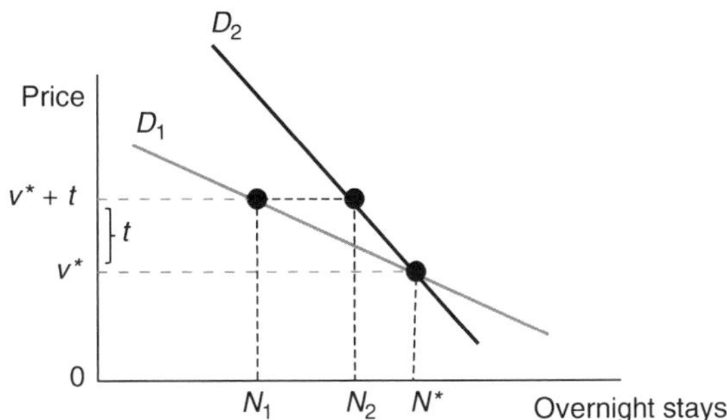

Fig. 15.5 The elasticity of demand and the effect of taxation

Hence, there are a number of motivations in favor of the direct taxation of tourists. The objective of this tax would be that of cashing extra revenue for the destination, with the scope of covering, all or in part, the extra costs that guests impose on their hosts, so that these costs do not completely lie on the local community (Fisch 1982; Hughes 1981; Vaccaro 2007). Taxes on tourists can be classified in:

- A fixed (lump-sum) tax paid by each tourist, which can be defined as a tax on arrivals; taxes of this type are frequently charged to travelers in airports or ports.
- A tax proportional to the length of stay (an excise tax, or duty), which can be defined as a tax on the overnight stays; taxes of this type are sometimes charged in hotels and other hospitality firms.
- A sum proportional to the price paid (an ad valorem tax, or sales tax), which is computed as a percentage of the price paid by the tourist (this is the typical case of the Value Added Tax-VAT paid on tourism services).

In some cases, taxes on tourists can be progressive when their amount changes according to criteria of ability to pay: this happens, for example, when higher fees or tax rates are matched with hotels of a superior category.

To assume that the tourist is the subject who is effectively affected by the tax, the price of the stay in the destination, v, has to increase by the exact value of the tax, t. In such case it is easy to demonstrate that the tax revenue on tourists depends on the elasticity of demand.[6] In Fig. 15.5 we show what happens if a tax t is introduced when two different demand functions, D_1 and D_2, are compared. Let us assume that, before the introduction of the tax, in equilibrium the two functions have the same number of overnight stays, N^*, and the same price of tourism, v^*; if we recall Sect. 4.2, we can affirm that the demand curve D_1 is more elastic than D_2.

The introduction of a tax proportional to the length of stay (but the discussion does not substantially change for the introduction of a VAT) raises the price of the tourism product to $(v^* + t)$. This leads to a reduction in the number of overnight

[6] In the most general case, it is possible to demonstrate that the distribution of the tax between the tourists and the firms depends on the elasticity of demand and the elasticity of supply of the tourism service (Mak and Nishimura 1979).

stays which is larger the more elastic is the demand: in the case of demand D_1 overnight stays become N_1, in the case of demand D_2 overnight stays become N_2. Since the tax revenue is equal to the value of the tax t times the number of overnight stays after its introduction, it is easy to graphically verify that the tax revenue is larger for the least elastic demand: $tN_2 > tN_1$.

However, it is clear that the introduction of the tax, by modifying the relative price of the tourism product, has an effect on the spending decisions of tourists and can alter the competitiveness of the destination. For example, the more elastic in Fig. 15.5 the tourism demand, the greater the degree of substitutability with the tourism product of other competing destinations, the lower the tax revenue. From this perspective, the problem of taxing tourists should not be seen only in terms of local revenue, but should be framed in the wider context of promoting the competitiveness of the destination. Similarly, taxes might be used to discriminate among different types of tourism (see the distinction between friendly- and unfriendly-tourism in Sect. 15.3.2). Figure 15.5 allows to conclude, anyway, that the two goals of increasing tax revenue and discouraging tourism through the introduction of a tax are incompatible with one another. In fact, the aim of increasing revenue reaches its maximum effect when the demand is rigid; the aim of discouraging unfriendly tourism is achieved when the demand is elastic.

The discussion on whether taxes should be introduced on tourists shows its pros and cons. On one hand, Weston (1986) favorably considers such taxes based on the following reasons: (a) they are justified in terms of equity, since they charge the tourists with a share of the cost for the public services provided to them (Gago et al. 2009; Vaccaro 2007); (b) they might be politically more affordable, since they do not affect the local population which is, in the end, the one electing the local government (Fuji et al. 1985); (c) they have low administrative costs and are easy to collect, especially airport fees and custom taxes; (d) they can be a potentially large source of tax revenue, particularly for countries with a strong tourism specialization: see the case of Bahamas or Bermudas (Archer 1977), and the Maldives (Satuiendrakumar and Tisdell 1989).

On the other hand, it is obvious that taxes are unpopular among tourists and tourism firms (Jensen and Wanhill 2002), since they believe, truly or not, to already contribute to the destination's local economy through the price they pay for the holiday and through the taxes raised on profits and incomes. From this point of view, the negative psychological effect of the tax would be minimized should the government tax firms, letting it be them to decide if and how to indirectly pass the extra cost of taxation to the tourists, through an increase in the price of the stay.[7]

[7] Symmetrically, most of these arguments can be used to justify the use of subsidies to promote arrivals at the destination (see the important example of Ryanair, Papatheodorou and Lei 2006) or to contrast crisis management (Faulkner 2001; Blake and Sinclair 2003, for the 9/11 terrorist attack; Pambudi et al. 2009, for the Bali bombings).

Finally, a particular case is the one regarding the taxation of those durable goods that, like holiday homes, permanently link the tourist to the destination (see Sect. 5.6). We just recall that in some countries or regions, in which the tourism of holiday homes is important, the policy maker taxes differently the real estate owned by tourists from that owned by residents.

15.4.3 The Two-Part Tariff

In Sect. 15.4.2 we mentioned the possibility, for the destination, of taxing both the arrivals, with a lump-sum tax, and the overnight stays, with an excise tax. The policy maker, in other words, has two policy instruments with which the destination's optimal policy in terms of length of stay can be implemented, thus being able to affect the arrivals and the overnight stays. The tax on tourists, therefore, could be composed of two parts: a fixed amount tariff paid to accessing the destination and a variable part that depends on the number of services that are effectively bought.

To clarify this concept let us consider the tourism destination as an amusement park where the tourist, in order to enjoy the park, must pay an entrance fee, which can be understood as a tax on arrivals, and a ticket for each service used, which can be understood as a tax proportional to the length of stay. Indeed, the two-part tariff was introduced in the economics literature to explain the optimal pricing policy of amusement parks like Disneyland (Oi 1971); recently, this concept has been applied to the pricing structure of the holiday by Candela et al. (2009b).

If we denote with F the fixed part of the tariff, paid upon arrival at destination, and with t the tax paid for each night spent at the destination, N, the two-part tariff paid by the tourist is: $T = F + tN$. Thus, the unit cost, UC, of a day spent at the destination decreases as the length of stay increases: $\mathrm{UC} = T/N + t$. As a consequence, it is no longer indifferent for the tourist to spend 10 days in the destination during a single trip rather than traveling twice to the destination for 5 days each: this second alternative, for the same price of the tourism product, becomes more expensive due to the two-part tariff.

Hence, by means of fine-tuning the two parts of this tariff, the destination could control, at least partially, the average length of stay of tourists', thus choosing to favor certain types of tourism rather than others. In fact the externalities produced by tourists can be divided into two classes: (a) those that are mainly associated with the movement of tourists, measured by arrivals, like traffic jams, congestion in transport terminals (train stations, ports, airports), etc.; (b) those that are mainly associated with the presence of tourists, like the use of water, the cost of trash collection, etc. If the externalities are mostly of type (a), the destination can impose a relatively high fixed part F with respect to t, in order to discourage "hit and run" tourism or, in the extreme case, that of same-day visitors. If the externalities are mainly of type (b), the destination can weigh more the variable component t with respect to F in order to diminish the average length of stay of tourists that tend to stay much in one place.

15.5 National and International Tourism Organizations

In this section, the different types of organization that are associated with tourism will be classified and described. Firstly, a straightforward classification distinguishes institutions between: (a) public organizations; (b) private organizations. Moreover, institutions can be classified on the basis of their territorial competence: (a) international organizations; (b) national organizations; (c) local organizations.

15.5.1 National Public Organizations

A public tourism organization's general duties include: planning the tourism policy on a medium and long time horizon; promoting the country's image at the international level;[8] setting and controlling the rules; helping the coordination of tourism operators in the supply of the tourism product; completing the tourism product through the offer of infrastructures and general services; protecting the natural and cultural resources used by the tourism sector; assisting the tourist while on holiday; and matching the needs of the local population with the demands of guests, travelers, and visitors.

All these functions of destination management are carried out by the public bodies on three operative levels: local, regional, and national. Nevertheless, the organizational structure of a country's institutions depends on some of its economic and legal characteristics.

Firstly, it is very likely that the tourism organization is affected by the type of economic policy implemented by the country's government, which can be more or less interventionist in economic matters. In addition, if the country's government is centralized, this evidently has an effect on the structure of the tourism organizations, while if we are faced with a federal country it is more likely that the national organization is the result of the cooperation between different regional institutions working at different territorial levels. Secondly, the tourism organization tends to reflect the importance that tourism has in the national economy; in fact it is natural to expect that the public tourism system be more developed where tourism activity is an industry of primary economic relevance.

[8] National organizations, with ad hoc advertising campaigns targeted to selected markets, are able to promote incoming tourism (with the positive macroeconomic effects spreading on the entire economy, Chap. 13) and, indirectly, tourism in the individual destinations.

Thirdly, the public tourism system tends to reflect the state of development of the country: developed and developing countries, in general, cannot guarantee the same organizational and control standards. Finally, there are many other factors that influence the solution adopted by a country; among these, for example, there is the efficiency of its administrative structure and the history of its institutions.

Although these differences, which show us how varied the organizational structure of different destinations can be, there is a general common feature: whatever the type of decentralization achieved, a certain degree of coordination of functions and objectives between the different administrative levels must be guaranteed.

15.5.1.1 The National Level

A key role in the national tourism system is played, evidently, by the national government. The government has to identify the targets of tourism policy and plan it. Tourism policy must define the target growth rate of tourism in the future, the degree of integration of tourism into the national economy, what its objectives are, how the tourism sector is articulated in its national and regional competencies, how it can achieve collaboration between public and private operators, etc. To these aims, the government must identify the instruments through which these targets can be reached and, eventually, delegate to its administration the control on whether the goals have been achieved and how. Frequently, tourism bodies are, partially or totally, independent from the government, and their task is promoting national tourism; for institutions of this type, countries have followed very different approaches.

15.5.1.2 The Local Level

The local level of the public organization has the duty of developing and promoting incoming tourism in those destinations that are located under its jurisdiction. Local institutions have an informational advantage and are therefore more suitable for dealing with the particularities of the territory than the national organization. Moreover, these institutions have the duty of supplying assistance and information to tourists. Local tourism organizations must coordinate the tourism interests among local operators and be involved in the promotion of the different tourism products offered by the territory. They often are the oldest form of public tourism organizations and also collaborate with associations (voluntary or institutional), with the objective of managing common problems of the destination management (see Sect. 4.3) and of externality (see Sect. 15.3).

15.5.1.3 The Regional Level

The regional tourism organization is on an intermediate level between the national and the local level. Usually, these tourism institutions have three tasks: (a) to develop the regional tourism economy; (b) to promote the tourism image of the region; (c) to spread tourism from the tourism centers to the periphery of the region. When one talks of the regional level, the problem is about the correct definition of the area; in fact, the borders of the administrative region may not coincide with those of the tourism destination. This creates the possibility of conflicts and of administrative inefficiency with no easy solution, to which legislation can try to find a remedy.

Administrative decentralization and coordination among bodies at different levels should be characterized by the principle of *subsidiarity*, that is, the principle according to which public decisions must be taken as close to the citizens as possible. From this perspective, the central government intervenes to perform only those tasks that cannot be executed efficiently at a more immediate or local level.

In tourism, subsidiarity essentially means to administrate the single destinations or tourism regions primarily at the local level, since the possession of a better understanding of the territory, of the needs of the resident population, and of the specific features of tourism in the destination allow for a more efficient administration.

15.5.2 International Organizations

The growth of international tourism is reflected by the development of international organizations dealing with tourism. These institutions are born from the need to cooperate and coordinate between citizens, firms, associations, and governments of different countries. International organizations have a long history, and it is interesting to remark that the first ones to appear on the world stage belong to the transport and communication sectors. For example, in the second half of the nineteenth century the Universal Postal Union was born; after the First World War the International Chamber of Shipping and the International Union of Railways were created; immediately after the Second World War the International Civil Aviation Organization was born. The first international institutions involved in tourism rose between the two World Wars, but they largely developed after the Second World War; for example the International Union of Official Travel Organizations was created in the 1920s; the Tourism Committee of the OECD, the European Travel Commission, the Caribbean Tourism, and the Pacific Area Travel Association were born in the 1950s. Finally, the most important tourism organization on the international level, the United Nations World Tourism Organization was born in 1975 (Case Study 15.1).

Case Study 15.1. The United Nations World Tourism Organization

The World Tourism Organization was founded in 1925 with the name of International Congress of Official Tourist Traffic Associations, with the aim of coordinating tourism policies and promoting tourism. It became the World Tourism Organization in 1975, the year in which the organization established its headquarters in Madrid. In 2003 it fully assumed the status as a special agency of the United Nations, changing its name to the United Nations World Tourism Organization (UNWTO). Currently, more than 160 member countries and territories, and more than 370 associated members, representing the private sector, higher education institutions, tourism sector stakeholders, and destination management organizations participate.

The UNWTO is the leading international body in the tourism sector. Article 3 of its statute states that the institution promotes tourism in order to contribute to economic development, the understanding between people, peace, prosperity, universal respect, the observation of human rights and liberty, independently of race, sex, language, or religion. The UNWTO serves as a global forum for tourism and related issues, such as economic development, the diffusion of know-how, the promotion of responsible and sustainable tourism policies. With particular reference to this last aspect, the UNWTO plays a central role, actively promoting sustainable tourism in developing countries (Program ST-EP, Case Study 16.1). Since 1988, the UNWTO has adopted the concept of sustainable development, applying its definition to tourism and actively participating in the United Nations' conferences in Rio de Janeiro (1992) and in Johannesburg (2002).

Moreover, the UNWTO has promoted the world tourism ethical code, with the aim of guaranteeing that member countries, tourism destinations, and firms, beyond the maximization of profits, do not negatively affect the territory and host communities. The aim is to avoid that the economic benefits of tourism operate in a negative way on the social and environmental level or that they are unequally distributed.

Among its other functions, the UNWTO acts as an international statistical office for tourism. It is involved in gathering, harmonizing, and publishing data on tourism flows, mainly international tourism, defining the methodological framework for the sector, offering technical assistance to national statistical offices, particularly those in developing countries, publishing annual reports and quarterly bulletins in which the current and future trends of tourism are discussed (see Sect. 3.6). This analysis is conducted on a global, regional, and national level, and the UNWTO is a rich source of information for whom is involved, as a stakeholder or as a researcher, in international tourism.

The fundamental distinction, which must be referred to in order to classify international tourism organizations, is the one recalling the nature of the parties of the organization. From this point of view we have governmental or non-governmental institutions.

15.5.2.1 Non-governmental Institutions

Non-governmental institutions are created by individuals, firms, or associations; their members are constituted of representatives of these parties and the institutions are voluntary agreements between parent institutions, which normally do not enjoy particular legal privileges and are subject to the laws of the country in which they are located. These organizations can be divided into four main groups, according to their competencies: general, special, regional, and sectoral.

- Institutions with general competency look at tourism as their main object, in all its dimensions, for example the International Association of Scientific Experts in Tourism (AIEST).
- Institutions with specific competency are involved in a specific form of tourism, for example the International Bureau of Social Tourism, recently renamed International Organization of Social Tourism (OITS).
- Institutions with a regional competency deal with tourism in participating regions, for example the European Travel Commission (ETC).
- Institutions with sectoral competency, finally, are involved in the organization of participating firms and industries, for example the International Air Transport Association (IATA), the International Hotel Association and, for the overall tourism sector, the World Tourism and Travel Council (WTTC).

Obviously these are just some examples, since in tourism the classification of non-governmental agencies is evidently very large.

15.5.2.2 Governmental Institutions

The governmental organizations are created by international agreements signed by countries, and their members are delegates from the participating governments. The agreement has to specify what are the functions, goals, and the competencies of these international agencies. In some cases international agencies have the power to obligate member countries to abide the law, with a sharing of sovereignty between the countries and the institution, with the latter assuming the nature of supranational institution: the European Union is one of the most important real-world examples. In all the other cases, which regard international institutions, each decision must be ratified by national governments in order to have legal power.

The governmental organizations can be classified in general, special, and regional.

- General institutions are organizations that are involved in all the relationships that take place between countries: tourism is obviously included. The most important of these institutions is the United Nations Organization (UN).
- The special institutions are limited in the purpose of cooperation, and are created by agreements that have a specific aim, like the Organization for Economic Cooperation and Development (OECD).
- The regional institutions are limited to their territory of reference as a limitation. These institutions normally deal with all the economic and social relationships between participating countries: once again tourism is one of the matters of relevance. An example is the Association of South-East Asian Nations (ASEAN).

The most important special organization that exclusively deals with tourism is the World Tourism Organization, which in 2003 became part of the group of special agencies that constitute the UN, assuming the name United Nations World Tourism Organization (UNWTO). In the world panorama there exist many other special institutions that do not explicitly deal with tourism, but some of them are so close to the topic, both for the issues they deal with (e.g., the International Labour Organization, the World Health Organization, the World Trade Organization) and for the sector they organize (e.g., the International Civil Aviation Organization or the Inter-Government Maritime Consultative Organization).

It has to be highlighted the relevant role played by the World Trade Organization (WTO) in setting the guidelines and the competitive framework of the international economic system. In particular, the WTO aims at promoting trade liberalization and trade expansion and at halting any trade barrier or discrimination between countries as a means of attaining economic growth. In 1995 the WTO approved the General Agreement on the Trade of Services (GATS), which has important consequences also for tourism and travel-related services. The GATS may be promoting international tourism by removing restrictions associated with tourism flows (e.g., visa requirements) and discriminatory and anticompetitive national practices and policies (e.g., air accessibility denied to foreign airlines).

As regards the European Union (EU), tourism is dealt with through the Directorate-General Enterprise and Industry (Tourism unit). Among the main duties of the tourism unit is the promotion of European tourism and the coordination of the other European departments so that the interests of tourism are taken into consideration in the general legislative activity of the EU. In the last few years, the activity of the EU in the tourism sector has led to the identification of some strategic objectives: in particular the EU aims at promoting the growth and the competitiveness of the whole sector and, above all, at promoting sustainable tourism (see Sect. 16.3).

15.5.3 Non-profit and Voluntary Organizations in Tourism

Non-profit organizations are institutions lying between the public and the private sector (private firms are mainly driven by the goal of profit maximization and are also called forprofit firms), which supply public goods and services under the condition that they cannot make profits. Non-profit firms are commonly called voluntary associations or moral bodies. All together they are defined as the "third sector," with the aim of shedding light on their alternative function with respect to the private and the public sector. Like the firms driven by profit, non-profit firms are organized and controlled through initiatives of a private nature but, in contrast to these, they do not aim at making profits and they are subject to the restriction of not transferring monetary benefits to the owners. On the other hand, contrary to what happens in public administration, their activity is not driven by the political process, nor is it financed by taxes. Their social role is acknowledged by the fact that in many legal systems they enjoy fiscal benefits.

The theory of non-profit firms has shed light on the fact that they are particularly important in those services sectors characterized by asymmetric information. In this context, in fact, they contribute to resolving the problem of market failure: due to the lack of incentives in taking advantage of their own informational advantages (that is, they cannot share profits) they enjoy a higher reputational capital and are more trusted by the citizens. Moreover, the voluntary organization can constitute a valid source of additional supply with respect to the services provided by the government. Since we know that tourism is essentially an experience good, characterized by important informational asymmetries, it is evident that the non-profit firms can play a key role in the integration between the public and the private organizations.

Voluntary tourism associations were created in the nineteenth century in France, Switzerland, Italy, and Austria with different denominations to dedicate their activity to the promotion of the destination. In the Italian experience, all these associations were unified in 1920 with the definitive denomination of *Pro Loco*.

In tourism, there are also many voluntary organizations composed by tourism stakeholders, participating either on a personal or a professional level. These organizations can be local, regional, or national. The main types of organization that people voluntarily adhere to are the professional associations and the trade unions.

Professional associations are institutions that organize individuals employed in specific activities, which require specific skills, developed over a long period of learning and training. These associations have the aim of guaranteeing the standards and the value of the services offered by their members, even through the use of tests that regulate admission. They act, therefore, by defining the minimum standard of quality (usually based on the level and the type of education and on previous working experience) and by controlling and monitoring that the requirements are reached by the new members and are maintained by those who are already members. The economic rationale of these professional organizations is to supply reliable signals to the market (in order to reach separating equilibria, see Sects. 10.4 and 11.5.4). In this way, however, the professional associations contribute, at least implicitly, to increasing the degree of monopoly power of their members, thereby strengthening entry barriers to the profession.

Also trade unions are associations that group people together, in this case workers. Their aim is to protect working conditions, to promote workers' rights, and to bargain their salary. Given the heterogeneous nature of the tourism product many agreements signed by trade unions have relevant effects on tourism, not only those that are specific for the workers of tourism firms (tour operators, travel agencies, hospitality firms, restaurants, transport firms, museums, and cultural sites, etc.). With regards to these firms, nevertheless, the role of trade unions is important since they can impose, through collective bargaining, minimum salaries, rights for workers, and operational requirements for the tourism firms, hence determining production costs. Their role in tourism, in the end, is fundamental also for the function that the unions have with regards to the protection of atypical workers, which is important in tourism production, and in the way they regulate the use of workers in facing the problem of seasonality.

The organizations to which firms voluntarily adhere are usually called business unions, but in practice they are indicated with the name of association, consortium, or confederation. Symmetrically to trade unions, also business unions group together firms that belong to the same sector or groups of firms that have common interests. Their immediate function is of representation, since they act as a channel of communication with the government on one side and other organized groups (including trade unions) on the other side. Moreover, business associations provide important information, assistance, and business services to their members. In some cases these associations also have the power to regulate the competition within the sector.

Chapter Overview

- Public goods are characterized by non-rivalry in consumption and non-excludability of benefits. For public goods, benefits are spread over the whole community, independently on the price effectively paid. For public goods there is an individual incentive to free ride, that is, to not reveal own willingness to pay: hence there is a market failure and the public sector is called to produce the public good and pay for it through tax collection.
- There are externalities when the utility of some agent is affected, negatively or positively, by the consumption or production choices of other agents, without the effect being internalized in the price mechanism. In presence of externalities, the quantity produced in the market is beyond (negative externality) or below (positive externality) the optimal social quantity, since the firm does not have incentives to internalize the external cost (benefit) generated on other agents.
- To internalize the externalities, the policy maker can intervene in different ways: through direct control (limiting or prohibiting by law), through indirect control (a Pigou tax or subsidy of an amount equal to the externality), or with private methods (the definition of property rights, according to the Coase theorem).
- Taxes on tourists are mainly motivated by the need, for the destination, to finance the extra cost associated to the greater amount of services that have to be offered to cover the needs of tourists. They can be a lump sum (tax on arrivals), an excise (tax on overnight stays), or ad valorem (VAT).

Chapter 16
Sustainable Tourism

Learning Outcomes
After reading this chapter you will understand:

- The complexity of the relationship between tourism and the environment.
- The concept of sustainability, with its economic, environmental, and social dimensions, and its application to tourism.
- The relevance of the different forms of ethical and responsible tourism in contemporary world.

16.1 Introduction

The relationships among biological and anthropic phenomena stemming from the economic activity of human beings are complex, and the environment is a system in which natural and human resources (social, economic, and cultural) have to coexist. Like any other human activity, also tourism is twisted around the environment: tourism affects and is affected by the environment and in this chapter we will try to analyze in greater detail the key issues of this complex relationship.

The tourism sector consumes natural resources in the same way such as any other economic activity. Moreover, given that tourists have to travel to the destination to enjoy the holiday, it is inevitable that they have an impact on the social, cultural, and natural environment of the host region. Such impact is also empirically relevant, if it is recalled that the tourism sector contributes roughly to the 10 % of the income produced globally.

From the economics perspective, the key issue of the relationship between tourism and the environment is that most of their complex interactions do not pass through the market and its price mechanism. Many of the diverse resources (natural, cultural, social) that compose the tourism product are public goods and, once available, they can be freely used by anyone: tourists, residents, firms. As we have seen in Chap. 15, this situation signals the existence of strong externalities, leading the market away from the social optimum.

G. Candela and P. Figini, *The Economics of Tourism Destinations*,
Springer Texts in Business and Economics, DOI 10.1007/978-3-642-20874-4_16,

Table 16.1 Sustainability and the two dimensions of externalities generated by tourists

The timing of externalities	The subjects of externalities	
	Tourists on tourists	Tourists on residents
At the same time	Elite tourism/mass tourism	Friendly tourism/Unfriendly tourism
In the future	Environmental (un)sustainability	Sociocultural (un)sustainability

The concept of externality can hence be used to introduce the link between tourism and the environment and to define sustainability. The externalities generated by tourists can unfold around two dimensions: the space, thereby affecting other subjects in the destination (either other types of tourists or the host community); the time, thereby affecting subjects who use the environment either at the same time or in the future. This framework can be represented by a two-entry matrix (Table 16.1) and allows for identifying four different types of externality.

- *At the same time, between different types of tourism*, for example between mass tourism and elite tourism. This interaction is central to the tourism policy of the destination and has already been addressed in Sect. 4.4. It is worth to recall that, should the pricing policy of the destination increase tourism flows, for example to attract mass tourism with a lower willingness to pay, it could produce some negative effects due to the lower quality of the tourism experience in the crowded destination. On the contrary, should the pricing policy of the destination reduce tourism flows, for example to defend an elite-cultural tourism with higher willingness to pay, it could produce some negative effects due to the denial of the cultural experience to mass tourists.
- *At the same time, between tourists and residents*. This externality, which can be positive in the case of friendly tourism and negative for unfriendly tourism, is the typical consumption externality and has already been studied in Sect. 15.3.2.
- *Inter-temporal, between present and future tourists*. In the case where the behavior of the tourist today, excessively consuming the environmental resources, should not allow for the repetition of the same tourism experience in the future, there is environmental unsustainability of the tourism phenomenon. As we will see in this chapter, the concept of sustainable tourism pivots around this type of externality.
- *Inter-temporal, between present tourists and the future host community*. In the case where the behavior of the tourist today, excessively consuming the sociocultural resources of the destination, should not allow the host community to defend its own cultural and social values, jeopardizing their survival, there is social unsustainability of the tourism phenomenon. In such cases the tourism experience increases prostitution, corruption, crime, or the distribution of earnings generates injustice, inequality, and lack of poverty reduction.

According to the previous classification, while in Chap. 15 we have analyzed the two cases of externality at the same time, in this chapter we are left with analyzing the two forms of inter-temporal externality, those that deal with a development process that is either environmentally or socially unsustainable. Even though these two dimensions of sustainability are strongly interrelated, when one talks about sustainability the emphasis is usually put on the natural environment, which constitutes the main resource, without which tourism (at least the leisure type of tourism) cannot develop.

The recognition of the links between tourism and the environment, which today seems so evident, was affirmed with difficulty and only recently. The study of the impact of the economy on the natural environment is indeed relatively recent and the first economic models were provided only in the 1970s by Boulding (1972), Forrester (1971), and Meadows et al. (1972). In more recent years, also the relationship between tourism and the environment was finally recognized by environmental economists, who have also been studying those natural resources that are a source of leisure, and by tourism economists, who have been placing the environment and its preservation at the core of the tourism studies.

Moreover, for both environmental and tourism economists, the question of the relationship between the economy and the environment is the key issue, since the standard economic theory shows that the market is not able to solve the problem of environmental conservation. Pearce and Turner (1990) concluded that also tourism has to deal with this inefficiency, which is perhaps more relevant than for any other economic activity both because tourism takes place in the territory and because the environment is the key resource for the tourism product.

It is important to highlight that the environment has to be understood in a holistic sense (Green and Hunter 1992; Cooper et al. 2008) including:

(a) The natural environment, which includes the different physical characteristics of the atmosphere, land, water, climate, wildlife, vegetation, etc.
(b) The human-made environment, which includes the urban and industrial architecture, the historical and artistic heritage, monuments, public infrastructures, the skyline of the city, etc.
(c) The sociocultural environment, which includes the dialects, traditions, arts, in other words the culture and the social organization of the local community in the most profound meaning.

Aspects (a) and (b) constitute the natural and cultural resources around which the destination's environment pivots. Although in this chapter we will mainly refer to the natural resources when talking about environmental sustainability, we have to highlight that cultural resources can be implicitly treated in the same manner: cultural resources are demanded by some types of tourism, they can be classified according to the same schemes (in terms of appropriability or depletion, for example, see Sect. 16.3), their carrying capacity (see Sect. 16.4) can be identified and measured. Aspect (c), on the contrary, is key to the concept of social sustainability, which pivots around the relationship between the host population and their guests: the tourists.

As a final note, in the age of globalization, the environmental economists understand that sustainability and the environmental impact of economic activities are to be considered as global externalities, and tourism is not an exception to this rule (Hall and Higham 2005; Gössling and Hall 2006): for example, think about the global externality produced by intercontinental air transport. Along this perspective, one has to distinguish between local and global sustainability of tourism.

The chapter is organized as follows: in Sect. 16.2 the evolution of the relationship between tourism and the environment will be briefly recalled; Sect. 16.3 will deal with the concept of sustainability in its environmental dimension, which is linked to the exploitation of natural and cultural resources for tourism purposes, and in its social dimension, also introducing the concepts of ethical and responsible tourism. The issue of sustainability also calls for defining and measuring the carrying capacity of a territory in its different dimensions (see Sect. 16.4) and controlling and monitoring the effects of the tourism activity on the state of the environment (see Sect. 16.5).

16.2 The Evolution of the Relationship Between Tourism and the Environment

The relationship between tourism and the environment is complex, in the sense that it can assume different forms, and dynamic, in the sense that the same forms can change and evolve over time. Theorizing the complexity of this relationship originates from the work of Budowski (1976), who was the first to explicitly affirm that there exist three different types of relationship between the tourism activity and the environment: (a) the coexistence, in the sense that tourism and the environment are separated and with very few marginal connections; (b) the conflict, if there is interaction and tourism damages the environment; (c) the symbiosis, when tourism and the environment receive benefits one from each other.[1] Budowski's categories were conceived for the natural environment but can also be interpreted to study the relationship between the social environment and tourism. In this sense, the conditions of symbiosis and conflict introduced by Budowski recall the distinction between the positive and negative externalities attached to friendly and unfriendly tourism (see Sect. 15.3.2).

There is symbiosis when tourism increases the value of the territory: in this case tourism provides a value of existence to the environment of the destination. On the other hand, the relationship of conflict is explained with the simple observation that an excessive tourism load can lead to the natural degradation of the mountains, countryside, coasts, towns, etc. Budowski believed that the relationship of conflict is more common than that of symbiosis, but he thought that the recognition of the possibility of symbiosis is relevant when planning and implementing environmental

[1] Among the many works on the relationship between tourism and the environment, see Shaw and Williams (1990, 2002), Hardy et al. (2002), Teo (2002), Liu (2003), Farrell and Twining-Ward (2004, 2005), Miller and Twining-Ward (2005), Bramwell (2007), and Moscardo (2008). Specific case studies are analyzed, for example, by Bramwell and Lane (2000).

protection policies. He affirmed that tourism brings arguments in favor of environmental protection programs, since they develop educational, scientific, and recreational resources which become objects of attraction for many more tourists and for many different types of tourism (Budowski 1976).

Finally, the observation that the relationship between tourism and the environment is dynamic is simply demonstrated by the history of tourism development (Dowling 1990).

16.2.1 The Early Visions: The 1950s and the 1960s

In these years the main vision was that tourism had little effect on the natural environment. In 1952, Zierer affirmed that an important characteristic of the tourism and recreational sector is that it does not contribute or it should not contribute to the destruction of natural resources (Zierer 1952). Nevertheless, professional tourism scholars (working for international tourism organizations) started to recognize the possibility of perverse impacts of tourism on the environment and in the 1960s the first empirical research on the environmental effects of tourism began. The results convinced the World Tourism Organization to pay attention to the problem. In the *Conference on the Human Environment*, organized by the UN in Stockholm in 1972, the condition that any type of tourism development must adhere with and respect the local, natural, and cultural resources was firstly stated. A few years later also the World Bank adopted this line of thought, strengthening it with the request that the leisure activities of tourism should also bring benefits to the local population.

16.2.2 The Beginning of the Debate: The 1970s

In this decade, the complexity of the tourism–environment link was underlined by the analysis of different case studies. While in some cases tourism was clearly providing an incentive for environmental conservation (specifically as regards to natural parks), in other case studies (Young 1973) tourism was found to strongly increase pollution and to damage the local flora and fauna. In the last part of the 1970s, the attention of scholars on the environmental impact of tourism became nearly systematic. In particular, Cohen (1978) was able to identify a series of factors through which environmental degradation depends on tourism: (a) the intensity of the tourism exploitation of natural resources; (b) the resiliency of the ecosystem, that is, the ability of adapting and maintaining constant the productivity level, when it is subject to pressure or exogenous shocks; (c) the economic time horizon of local decision makers, public and private; (d) the evolution of tourism demand. Cohen concluded by indicating the need to protect the environment "from tourism and for tourism".

16.2.3 The Core of the Debate: The Early 1980s

In the 1980s, the attention to the conservation of the environment became central. In September 1980, the *Manila Declaration* was approved and published by the World Tourism Organization, based on the recognition of the environmental damage that can be provoked by tourism; it focused on recognizing a conflict between tourism and the environment, the latter now fully understood in a broader sense. Immediately after, the OECD published a report specifically created to study the environmental effects of tourism. The conclusion was that, since tourism was involving more and more people and becoming a mass phenomenon, its uncontrolled expansion could seriously damage the environment (OECD 1980).

As the attention to the environment and to its relations with all the economic activities grew in the academic and political agenda, the concept of eco-compatible development was introduced. Not much time passed when this concept was also applied to tourism (Mathieson and Wall 1982).

16.2.4 From Idealism to Realism: The Late 1980s

In the late 1980s, the complexity of the relationship between tourism and the environment was fully unfolded. In the economic studies, along with the environmental damages provoked by tourism, the original idea of Budowski was acknowledged, with explicit reference to the potential cooperation between tourism and the conservation of the environment. In this way, tourism became an argument to favor conservation, and a strong support for the request to give funds and resources for recuperating and preserving the environment was recognized (Phillips 1985). At the end of the 1980s it was clear that tourism itself could play an important role as a factor of environmental protection (against the multiplication of industrial activities with the related growing gas emissions) and, at the same time, the recognition of the environmental damages generated by tourism was also evident.

16.2.5 The Idea of Sustainability in the 1990s

In the 1990s it became clear that the three relationships indicated by Budowski could simultaneously coexist in destinations and different types of tourism (Hall 1991): think that the love for green and ecological tourism was born in the 1990s, in a period of strong development of mass tourism in many destinations. In 1987 the World Commission on Environment and Development of the United Nations, directed by Gro Harlem Brundtland, produced a report entitled *Our Common Future* that definitively caught the attention of economists, ecologists, and policy makers on the definition, for the first time official, of sustainability:

> Sustainable development is development that meets the needs of the present without compromising the ability of future generations to meet their own needs.
>
> (WCED 1987)

The Brundtland Report was based on the idea that "we do not inherit the earth from our ancestors; we borrow it from our children." The definition of sustainability could similarly be applied to the relationship between tourism and the environment, giving birth to the concept of sustainable tourism (see Sect. 16.4). The most popular definition of sustainable destination requires that tourism demand be satisfied in a way to continue to attract tourism flows but also to respect the needs of the local population, thereby safeguarding the natural environment of the destination.

In 1992, the United Nations Conference on Environment and Development held in Rio de Janeiro and commonly known as "Earth Summit" gave another push to the concept of sustainability by launching the *Agenda 21*, an agreement that proposed a global strategy for moving towards sustainable development in the twenty-first century, understood not only in the environmental sense but also in a more comprehensive way, including the aim of reducing inequalities between the North and the South of the world and of promoting the broader concept of human development. The Agenda 21, which included a general program of environmental protection that had to be adopted by the 182 nations that signed it, nevertheless remained, as often happens with many decisions by the United Nations, prevalently a declaration of principles. By emphasizing the peculiarity of each development path, the Agenda 21 was also suggesting that the local authorities all over the world should define and approve Agendas 21 at the local level, that would identify the process of partnership through which the local public bodies could cooperate with the private sector, with the aim of defining action plans directed to achieving sustainability at the local level.

The idea of sustainable development quickly conquered many and invaded every economic activity, from production to consumption, with also the need to apply it to tourism.[2] The problem lies in the way in which a declaration of principle can be applied as a political objective (Candela et al. 1995). In fact the idea of sustainable development became of common use in policy reports and in studies by environmental economists, so much as to generate a sort of confusion and to dilute its relevance: in fact Pearce and Turner (1990) observed that only 2 years after the Brundtland Report there were more than 300 alternative definitions of sustainability, thus creating misunderstandings among scholars and between professional operators and politicians.

16.2.6 At the Beginning of the Twenty-First Century

After the first decade of the twenty-first century, international politics still has a significant delay in effectively dealing with the unsustainability of the present model of development, being only able to declare a wide and sharable series

[2] As previously reported in Chap. 15, two international institutions mainly promote local and global sustainability of tourism, the UNWTO (see also the Case Study 16.1), and the WTTC, an international organization of travel industry executives promoting travel and tourism worldwide.

of objectives. The most important example is the Millennium Development Goals (MDG), a series of eight general development objectives (elimination of poverty, reduction in emissions, reduction in gender discrimination, reduction in child mortality, etc.) that should be met by 2015. The MDG were approved in 2000 at the Millennium Summit of the United Nations in New York but, in the absence of precise political strategies and without the identification of the instruments to be used to reach these targets, they risk becoming, as what happened with the Agenda 21, mere declarations of principle.[3]

However, the novelty of the last decade is the success of the concept of socially responsible tourism, that is, individual behaviors that spontaneously defend the natural and social environment (Cater and Cater 2007; Fennell 2007). These behaviors can be distinguished between:

(a) The so-called Corporate Social Responsibility (CSR), the proactive behavior of companies in searching for environmental protection and in favor of the local community and the consumers. It is a form of business self-regulation to adhere to ethical codes, to voluntary eliminate harmful practices from the public sphere, to social and environmental certifications, to social accounting and reporting (for the application to the tourism sector, see Baldarelli 2009 and Kang et al. 2010).
(b) The ethical consumption, that is the direct demand expressed by consumers for products and services which satisfy ethical and environmental standards. In this way, through their own consumption choices, tourists (and consumers more in general) become responsible with regards to the physical and social quality of the destination thus demanding a tourism product that has a greater ethical, social, and environmental content. Born in the 1990s, it is at the beginning of the new century that the forms of eco-tourism, green tourism, and responsible tourism gain relevance.

Therefore, it is not the public sector only, through its policy decisions, that must guarantee the sustainability of tourism; tourists and companies themselves become aware that sustainability is indispensable for the enjoyment of future tourists and for maintaining profit opportunities over time. Firms respond to these new needs of tourism demand by offering holidays and trips with a lower environmental impact, respecting the ecosystem and in harmony with the host population.

Then, the sustainability of tourism develops both from the behavior of businesses with long-run economic horizons and from the growth of a new awareness in consumers who *vote with their trolley*: tourists who respect the environment and the social ethics.

---

[3] Among the many issues developed by the specific literature (for a comprehensive survey, see Stabler et al. 2010, p. 344) see the effects of the World Bank economic policy on tourism (Hawkins and Mann 2007); the relationship between tourism and poverty (Blake et al. 2008; Scheyvens 2011; Figini and Romaniello 2012); the role of women (Scheyvens 2002); the ethical principles of tourism (Page and Dowling 2002; Fennel 2007; Wheeler 1994; Buckley 2003); and the project "debt for nature" applied to tourism (Holden 2007).

Faced with the profound economic crisis that hit many countries in the world since the second half of 2008, the search for sustainable and green economy could also become an opportunity of economic growth, in addition to being an environmental safeguard. However, in order for this opportunity to become a reality, together with the change in the paradigms of individual behavior by firms and consumers, a strong action of economic policy in tourism as in the rest of the economy is needed (Figini 2008).

The evolution of the relationship between tourism and the environment allows to affirm, as was stated by Budowski, that the effects produced by tourism on the environment can be both positive and negative.

Among the positive effects there are the preservation and the restoration of the destination's cultural heritage (monuments, historic and cultural sites and buildings) and the creation of natural parks and protected areas, among which mountains, beaches, and lakes.

Among the negative effects the most important is the depletion of the territory due to the exploitation of its resources. Examples are the destruction of bays with dynamite to develop beaches for tourists, as happened in some of the Mauritius Islands, and the quantity of waste spread around the base camp on Mount Everest, due to climbing. This last example is very important since it allows to conclude that no type of tourism is, in itself, sustainable; in fact even the presence of a few tourists can endanger the destination if it is a weak environment. Any type of tourism, any single tourist can be a source of pollution or environmental over-exploitation. This is, in fact, the true meaning of the complex relationship between tourism and the environment; Alexander Langer wrote that:

> Tourism is compatible with the environment only in homeopathic doses. The reciprocity aspect and the relationship with the indigenous community are essential. Otherwise, even the keenest of the ecotourists can easily become an annoying, irritating and harmful Jiminy Cricket.
>
> (Langer, quoted by Canestrini 2002. *Our translation*)

Nowadays, the great availability of data, the easiness of diffusion of information, and the application of Tourism Satellite Accounting (see Sect. 3.4) allow to use sophisticated methods of analysis (such as the Computable General Equilibrium) to help unfold the complexity of these relationships (Casagrandi and Rinaldi 2002; Costantino and Tudini 2005; Johnston and Tyrell 2005, 2008).

16.3 Sustainable Tourism

Recalling from Sect. 16.2 the concept of sustainability, we can define sustainable tourism as:

> those activities able to meet the present needs of tourists, of the tourism sector and of the host community without compromising the ability of future generations to meet their own needs.

Swarbrooke (1999) defines sustainable tourism as:

> [That type of] tourism which is economically viable but does not destroy the resources on which the future of tourism will depend, notably the physical environment and the social fabric of the host community.
>
> (Swarbrooke 1999, p. 13)

As it has been remarked recently, sustainability can be understood in a weak sense or in a strong sense. Sustainability in the weak sense, the first one to be introduced in the literature, gave birth to the concept of Sustainable Tourism Growth (STG) and refers to the search of the maximum rate of economic growth which is compatible with the sustainable use of resources. Sustainability in the strong sense gave birth instead to the concept of Sustainable Tourism Development (STD) and refers to a wider (holistic) vision of tourism that, together with economic growth, also considers the environmental, social, and cultural effects of tourism development in the destination.

As we have seen in the previous section, sustainable tourism is a pretty recent concept; it originates both from the deterioration of natural and cultural resources, which are the main attractions of many tourism destinations, and from the effects of economic development and globalization. Economic development and globalization have in fact determined a more than proportional increase in tourism demand, which has also spread to countries and environments untouched by tourism until a few years ago.

Although in common language the term sustainability is used to indicate environmental and natural resource problems, the concept of sustainability is multifaceted and comprises different dimensions, often interconnected one to each other (Swarbrooke 1999):

(a) An *environmental dimension*, which deals with both natural resources and the cultural and historic heritage.
(b) A *social dimension*, which deals with the social and cultural impact on the host population.
(c) An *economic dimension*, which deals both with the positive aspect of income and employment growth generated by tourism (through the multiplier, Sect. 13.2) and the negative aspects of diverting resources from alternative uses towards tourism (the crowding out effect, see Sect. 13.4).

While the dimension (c) is a typical economic problem, which we have already dealt with in Chap. 13, in the two following subsections we will discuss the relationship between the environmental dimension and tourism (see Sect. 16.3.1) and between the social dimension and tourism (see Sect. 16.3.2).

16.3.1 Environmental Sustainability and the Tourism Exploitation of Natural Resources

In general, economists approach the concept of environment in the destination in terms of stock of total capital, which can be decomposed in three distinct elements

(Cater and Cater 2007): natural capital, physical capital, and human capital. As we have discussed the concepts of physical and human capital many times in this book, it is now time to focus on natural capital (which can also identify cultural capital, as it has been highlighted in Sect. 16.1). Therefore, in this section we will describe in a more technical way the relationship between tourism and the exploitation of the natural capital of the destination. To start with, we define as natural resources the consumption goods or the factors of production that are not reproducible, that is, that are not obtainable in the economic process of production, given the present technological frontier. This definition does not exclude that the natural resources are biologically producible, but their reproduction occurs naturally and not as the result of a production process.

Natural resources can be classified according to different aspects that are also relevant for tourism:

- According to their availability, natural resources can be divided into exhaustible and inexhaustible resources.
- According to the natural process of replenishment, natural resources can be divided into renewable and non-renewable resources.
- According to the law, natural resources can be divided into appropriable or inappropriable resources; the latter are also called common goods.

Since all these definitions pivot around the relationship between tourism and the exploitation of the resource, we try to discuss the issue by dividing it into two parts: in the first one, we consider the classifications related to availability and replenishment; in the second one we discuss the economic model referring to the state of appropriation of the resource and by introducing an important economic effect linked to the exploitation of natural resources: the tragedy of the commons.

Mixing the classification of the natural resources according to availability and replenishment, we identify four categories, each one leading to a specific consequence in terms of tourism exploitation of the resource. If we indicate with $X(t)$ an index that measures the quantity of natural resource X available at time t, we can analyze the implications of these four different cases.

16.3.1.1 Inexhaustible and Non-renewable Natural Resources

A natural resource is inexhaustible and non-renewable if its exploitation does not modify in any way its future availability. Traditional examples of this type of resource are the sun or the earth itself, including the sea. If $X(t)$ is the quantity of the resource, the assumption of inexhaustibility and non-reproducibility can be expressed in the following differential equation:

$$\frac{\mathrm{d}X}{\mathrm{d}t} = 0, \qquad (16.1)$$

which defines the state of the resource that does not change over time. The examples already given for beach tourism (which is indeed called sea&sun

tourism), but others can easily be made, immediately convince us that resources of this type are found in many types of tourism. These resources do not display problems of sustainability, if their exploitation is below a certain threshold, the so-called carrying capacity (see Sect. 16.4).

16.3.1.2 Exhaustible and Non-renewable Natural Resources

A resource is exhaustible and non-renewable if its use partly destroys it: the classic example is that of mines, including carbon and oil. In the case of tourism we can assume that the depletion of the resource depends on the number of overnight stays N at time t, according to the function $g(N_t) = aN_t$ assumed as linear for simplicity. Therefore, the state of the resource can be described by the following differential equation:

$$\frac{dX}{dt} = -g(N_t) = -aN_t, \tag{16.2}$$

which defines that the state of the resource decreases with its exploitation, which is proportional to the number of overnight stays.

Since the economic issue related to this type of resource (for example, the barrier reef that is being destroyed by tourists, each one bringing home a piece of coral as a souvenir, but many cultural and artistic resources are of this type) is that they will be exhausted in the long run, hence a problem of inter-temporal utilization is at work. In fact, the higher the number of overnight stays for the present generation, the lower the available resource for future tourism. The way in which the exhaustible resource is used shows a problem of social optimum between generations: this is at the heart of the sustainability model that we will analyze in detail in the next section.

The practical difficulty in determining a solution to the inter-temporal problem obviously lies in the attribution of a value to the temporal preference (the rate of inter-temporal discount, Theory in Action 16.1), but the true political problem is the fact that the value is set by the current generation, and no mechanism exists to avoid the opportunistic tendency of assigning a too low value for the consumption preference of future generations that, not being born yet, cannot reveal their true

Theory in Action 16.1. The Inter-generational Exploitation of a Non-renewable and Exhaustible Resource

Let us assume a natural resource of amount S that must be entirely consumed in a given time horizon. Since the period has a finite length, we can simplify, without any loss in generality, assuming two periods only, time 1 and time 2, which can easily be interpreted as today and tomorrow, or as the present and the future. Assume that the social preferences of the community are known and that: (a) the function $U(.)$ measures the utility that each generation receives from the tourism (and non-tourism) use of the resource; (b) the inter-temporal rate of discount σ measures the importance that the current generation attributes to the future generation's utility.

In such model, the inter-temporal welfare function can be written as follows:

$$W = U(C_1) + \sigma U(C_2),$$

where C_1 and C_2 represent consumption by the first and the second generation. Obviously, $C_i = aN_i$ with $i = 1, 2$ where N_i is the number of overnight stays in the i-th period. The interpretation of σ, the parameter measuring the relative weight of the utility of future generations in the function $W(.)$, is important:

- If $\sigma > 1$, the current generation has a strong preference towards the future use of the resources; the current generation takes into consideration the future generation: they love their offspring.
- If $\sigma < 1$, the current generation has a strong preference towards the present use of the resources; the current generations does not take into consideration the future generation: they leave their offspring with nothing.
- If $\sigma = 1$, current consumption and future consumption are perfectly substitutable.

Moving to the solution for the optimal exploitation of the resource S over the two periods, it is sufficient to compute the first-order condition for $W(.)$:

$$\frac{\partial W}{\partial C_1} = \frac{\partial U(C_1)}{\partial C_1} + \sigma \frac{\partial U(C_2)}{\partial C_2} \frac{\mathrm{d}C_2}{\mathrm{d}C_1} = 0.$$

Since $C_2 = S - C_1$, then $\mathrm{d}C_2/\mathrm{d}C_1 = -1$, and the condition of optimality becomes

$$U'(C_1) - \sigma U'(C_2) = 0,$$

from which

$$U'(C_1) = \sigma U'(C_2).$$

If $\sigma = 1$, then the straightforward solution is $C_1 = C_2 = (1/2)S$, that is, the two generations enjoy an equal division of the resource and can equally benefit from the exploitation of tourism.

(continued)

If $\sigma < 1$, then $C_1 > C_2 = S - C_1$, and the current generation exploits the resource relatively more for current tourism, leaving less of it to the future use.

Finally, if $\sigma > 1$, then $C_1 < C_2 = S - C_1$, and the future generation will exploit the resource relatively more for future tourism activities.

preferences. This tendency can open the door to the madcap exploitation of exhaustible resources by the tourism sector in order to maximize the present gains.

The limitation in the use of this type of resource can be relaxed by technological progress: through innovations that allow to save the resource (e.g., through recycling it or by developing green technological processes: in this sense, tourism is progressively becoming a technological sector, see Sect. 7.6); through the responsible behavior of tourists and firms; through the policy of sustainability of the destination (Kuniyal 2005). An example related to cultural resources is the introduction of a controlled atmosphere (in terms of temperature and humidity) in the museum where an art masterpiece is shown to visitors. Technically, in all these cases the rate of exploitation a of the resource becomes a function of time, $a(t)$, with $\mathrm{d}a/\mathrm{d}t < 0$.[4]

16.3.1.3 Exhaustible and Renewable Natural Resources

Some natural resources, subject to exhaustion by exploitation, are however able to regenerate: the typical example of this type of resource is to be found in the biotic components of nature, like fish and birds, but the same criteria can refer to natural resources such as woods and forests. The state of these resources can be described through the following differential equation:

$$\frac{\mathrm{d}X}{\mathrm{d}t} = n - g(N_t) = n - aN_t, \tag{16.3}$$

where $g(N_t) = aN_t$ still measures the exploitation due to overnight stays and n is the natural growth rate of the resource, assumed for simplicity to be constant.[5]

The observation of the dynamic law (16.3) immediately clarifies that each state of the resource $X(t)$ can be indefinitely maintained if the depletion of the natural

[4] If the green innovations have an imitation effect among the destinations, they can produce a global effect: this is the so-called California effect or Porter hypothesis (Porter 1990; Huybers and Bennet 2003; Razumova et al. 2009).

[5] The most general biotic case is where the growth rate of the resource depends on the size of its population: $n = cX^2 - bX$ represents the growth rate of the resource according to the logistic function. Using this function would complicate the algebra without substantially changing the conclusions.

resource due to the presence of tourism is less or equal than the resource's ability to regenerate. The linear approximation allows for easily getting the level of overnight stays that is compatible with the conservation of the environmental state:

$$\frac{dX}{dt} = 0 \quad \text{if} \quad N^* = \frac{n}{a}. \tag{16.4}$$

The tourism exploitation of the natural resource with a level N^* of overnight stays stabilizes the resource to the initially observed condition. This condition allows for the conservation of the resource in any desired state: (a) if the initial condition $X(0)$ is less than the desired X^* it is sufficient to exploit the resource for a value $N < N^*$, in order for it to increase by natural reproduction until reaching X^* in t^+; after t^+ if the resource is exploited for a value of overnight stays N^*, the desired state can be maintained forever; (b) if the initial condition $X(0)$ is greater than the desired X^*, it is sufficient to exploit the resource for a value $N > N^*$, in order for it to diminish until reaching X^* in t^+; after t^+ if the resource is exploited for a value of overnight stays N^* the desired state can be maintained forever.

Tourism can show, for this type of resource, also a more complicated solution. In fact, given that tourism is usually a seasonal phenomenon, the period in which the natural resource is exploited is more limited than (a fraction of) its period of reproduction. Therefore, the condition of equilibrium for the resource not only depends on the number of overnight stays but also on the length of the peak season. In this case, there might be a trade-off between the amount of overnight stays and the length of the season (for analogous considerations on the undesired effects of seasonality, see Sect. 7.5.4).

16.3.1.4 Inexhaustible and Renewable Natural Resources

This is the most optimistic case (although the rarest) of natural resources: these resources do not deplete with their use and grow at the natural rate n. The equation describing the evolution of these resources becomes, assuming n as constant:

$$\frac{dX}{dt} = n. \tag{16.5}$$

It is immediately clear that the resource does not put any constraint of depletion on the tourism exploitation of the destination, but presents instead another important economic problem: that of the usage rate. In fact, if the usage rate of the resource at time t is defined as $N(t)/X(t)$, the steady state condition for this relationship requires that the growth rate of overnight stays be equal to the natural reproduction rate of the resource: $(dN/dt)/N = n/X$. If overnight stays lag behind the growth rate of the resource, it will progressively become more unused until, in the limit, it will become a free good. The growth in overnight stays is the effective constraint that follows the presence of renewable and inexhaustible resources of which the progressive abandonment has to be avoided. In these terms, the condition of equality between the growth rates of income and of the population, $\gamma = n$ (see Sect. 13.3.2, eq. 13.16, $\lambda \equiv 0$) can be interpreted as the condition for maintaining full employment in a population that grows at rate n; the human population, therefore, can be considered a *sui generis* resource of this type.

To conclude the analysis of natural resources and of the different problems stemming from their exploitation, we observe that a few rules to deal with sustainable tourism can be identified. In general terms, the management of sustainability implies the solution of complex dynamic programs of optimal control in an overlapping generations setting (Candela et al. 1995), but there are also some simple golden rules that identify in the steady state of the resource the condition of sustainability. By looking at the inexhaustible and non-renewable resources and at the exhaustible and renewable resources it is possible to list these simple rules of sustainability:

- Do not exceed the carrying capacity of the inexhaustible resources in order not to compromise their quality.
- Avoid the exploitation of exhaustible and non-renewable resources.
- Limit the exploitation of renewable resources to a level approximately equal to their natural rate of reproduction.

Finally, it can be useful to quote an interesting approach to the identification of the level of sustainability: the ecological footprint (Rees 1992; Rees and Wackernagel 1994).

> Ecological footprint analysis is an accounting tool that enables us to estimate the resource consumption and waste assimilation requirements of a defined human population or an economy in terms of corresponding productive land area.
>
> (Wackernagel and Rees 1996, p. 9)

The ecological footprint can be interpreted as the equivalent portion of the earth's surface that is consumed by a specific lifestyle: if the portion consumed is greater than what is available, the lifestyle is not sustainable; if instead it is less than, or equal to, what is available, the lifestyle is sustainable. In short, by using the ecological footprint it is possible to estimate how many *planets earth* would be needed to sustain a certain lifestyle (currently on a global level 1.8 earths would be needed relative to the one that we have available: our current lifestyle is therefore unsustainable).

Leaving the in-depth analysis of the concept of ecological footprint to the specific literature, it is necessary to underline in this context that the relevance of the ecological footprint in tourism has been affirmed (Hunter and Shaw 2007). These authors, in addition, affirm that such an indicator would allow us to leave behind the provincialism linked to measuring sustainability in the destination only and to provide an overall estimate of the global impact of tourism on the planet's resources.

16.3.1.5 Appropriability of the Resource and Common Goods

Finally, we move to the last classification of resources from which we started this analysis, the one relating to the state of appropriability of the resource. This concept is of great importance for tourism, since it distinguishes between the economic utilization of a resource with the characteristics of a private good and that of a natural resource with the characteristics of a common good. To this aim we examine a particular type of market failure, known in the literature as the tragedy of the commons (Hardin 1968); we will paraphrase the original example that deals with open grazing in a prairie.

Let us consider a seaside resort in which people want to open kiosks on the beach, to sell drinks. Let us assume the two alternative appropriability mechanisms: the first one is based on the common property of the beach, that is, the beach has free access to everyone without any restrictions; the second one is based on the private property of the beach, that is, only one subject (that can be a private firm or a public body) decides how many kiosks to open. We also assume that managing the kiosk costs a. Finally, we assume that the overall spending of tourists $S(.)$ increases with the number of kiosks x located on the beach, but expenditure increases at a decreasing rate, for example: $S(x) = -mx^2 + nx$. The economic problem for the local economy is to define the optimal number of kiosks that have to be opened in order to satisfy the demand of tourists.

- We begin by assuming that the beach is a common good. In this case each person can freely decide whether or not to open a kiosk; new kiosks open as long as they are profitable: that is, until the revenue generated by the kiosk is greater than its cost. Since the average revenue for each kiosk is $S(x)/x$, the equilibrium number of kiosks is given by the condition:

$$\frac{S(x)}{x} = a, \quad \text{that is} - mx + n = a, \quad \text{from which}\, x^\circ = \frac{n-a}{m}. \tag{16.6}$$

  Note that this is also the zero profit condition (i.e., the long-run equilibrium) of a perfectly competitive market: $\pi = S(x) - ax = 0$.
- In the alternative case let us assume that the beach is property of the public sector that autonomously decides how many licenses to assign for opening bars. It is clear that the policy maker allows to open a number of kiosks so as to maximize the overall economic profit:

$$\max_x \pi = S(x) - ax = -mx^2 + nx - ax$$

  the first-order condition of which is

$$\frac{\mathrm{d}S(x)}{\mathrm{d}x} - a = 0, \quad \text{that is,} - 2mx + n - a = 0, \quad \text{from which}\, x^* = \frac{n-a}{2m}. \tag{16.7}$$

Comparing solutions (16.6) and (16.7) it is easy to verify that, given the analytical properties of $S(x)$, it is always true that $x^\circ > x^*$; in our example in particular, it is true that $x^\circ = 2x^*$. Therefore, with the assumption of common property, the number of kiosks is greater than what would be optimal for the amount of available resource, that would automatically be realized should the property be centralized. It is important to underline that the tragedy of the commons (i.e., the over exploitation of the resource stemming from the lack of property rights) does not necessarily imply that common goods should be managed by the public sector; this is a possible interpretation, but in general the model only implies that the calculation of (16.7) should be done by the government or by its local bodies in the public's interest. Managerial and policy aspects might then lead to the situation in which the management of the common resource either remains in the hands of the public monopolist or is given to one or more private agents through a license mechanism.

> Of course, private property is not the only social institution that can encourage efficient use of resources. For example, rules could be formulated about how many *kiosks can be opened* on the *beach*. If there is a legal system to enforce those rules, this might be a cost-effective solution to providing an efficient use of the common resource.
>
> (Varian 1996, p. 574. *The italics is ours*)

In any case, the general conclusion is that the common property of the beach leads to an excessive tourism exploitation. Such "tragedy" is a key characteristic of natural resources exploited by tourism, especially in destinations where the public intervention is weak.

16.3.2 Social Sustainability

The other aspect that is left to deal with is the sociocultural dimension of sustainability:

> The only sustainable tourism is the one not jeopardizing the life and the culture of the host community.
>
> (Simonicca 2002, p. 4. *Our translation*)

Tourism pivots around the meeting of two cultures and two social models: the tourists' and the indigenous' ones. In tourism, like in any human experience, the meeting with the *Other* is always an experience that changes the *Self*; any economic activity, tourism included, modifies the sociocultural structure and is itself modified by it. It is not about avoiding any contact and change, which would inevitably lead to inaction and underdevelopment, but to underline the characteristics that the relationship between peoples and cultures should have to be socially sustainable. Without entering into the problems that belong to the sociology and the anthropology of tourism (see for example Apostolopoulos et al. 1996; Nash 1996; Smith and Brent 2001; Dann and Liebman Parrinello 2009), we would only wish to underline that, when tourism tends to repeat a model of dependence or, even worse, of new colonialism (as sometimes happens in mass tourism), then socioeconomic sustainability is difficult to achieve.

The meeting of the tourist with the host population can theoretically be synergistic but, more commonly, it will be the more problematic the greater the differences in terms of income and culture. The attention is then on the social unsustainability raised with the spreading of tourism to developing countries, but this is not the only relevant case. Just think of the social impact that tourism can have in a mountain community of a developed country when the territory is exploited as a tourism destination.

In addition, the meeting between the visitor and the host can have positive or negative effects in both directions, in the sense that the tourism experience not only modifies the local population but also the tourists themselves. The tourists can in fact assume, in a positive or negative way, the habits of the country being visited: for example an English tourist that, returning from a holiday in a Mediterranean country, changes the own diet.

Similarly to the classification of Budowski recalled earlier, the effects of the tourist on the local population can be: (a) positive, like the preservation and recovery of traditions, the conservation of ceremonies or craftsmanship, the restoring of historic buildings or artistic sites; (b) negative, like the commodification of local behaviors or traditions; (c) potentially neutral, like assuming certain dress codes or food habits, that do not enter in conflict with the local traditions.

Such classification obviously implies a value judgment that can be agreed upon or not. However, if we share the approach of sustainable tourism, we must at least agree upon the most evident cases: it is very difficult, for example, to admit that child prostitution stemming from sexual tourism leads to socially sustainable development.[6]

The sociocultural impact of tourism obviously also depends on the type of tourism hosted by the destination. According to the classification by Smith (1989) we can distinguish: (a) the *explorers*, elite and anticonformist tourists that, being in a limited number and able to adapt well to the local norms, come into contact with the local population in a discrete manner; (b) the *mass tourists*, numerous and in a continuous flow, that visit the destination and search for the typical features of the local culture; (c) the *charter tourists*, they arrive and leave in mass, they demand a cultural environment that is almost identical to that of their own country. Clearly, moving from the explorer to the charter tourist there is a process of tourism development (about the phases of the destination life cycle, see Sect. 4.5), in which the risk of sociocultural unsustainability increases.

In addition, for Cohen (1988), the relationship between tourism and local culture can assume different forms: (a) the commodification, in which the traditions and the culture of the local population are commercialized and standardized in order to gain from tourism; (b) the authenticity show, in which simulations of events are presented to satisfy the demand of new experiences by tourists and, at the same time, the host population preserves, saving it from contamination, the cultural riches of its own tradition; (c) the search for authenticity, typical of the elite and anticonformist tourists who require, in order to satisfy their own cultural demand, entering into contact with different environments and cultures.

---

[6] It is evident the relevance of tourism onto the degradation of the local culture, the handicraft sector, and local uses and traditions, especially in tourism destinations located in developing countries and hosting important tourism flows originating from the Western World. Doxey (1975) suggests that the impact of tourism flows on local cultures interests various *Irritation Indexes* (Irridex) that signal the phases of euphoria, boredom, antagonism, and saturation.

Sustainable tourism, therefore, requires on one hand the maximization of the objective function of the current generation, subject to the constraint of maintaining the same stock of resources for future generations (environmental sustainability), and on the other hand the involvement of the host population in the planning and development of the destination (social sustainability). Recalling Sect. 16.1, sustainability can indeed be treated as a policy choice problem in two dimensions: an inter-temporal dimension (between the present and the future generations of tourists) and a distributive dimension (between the tourists and the host population).

To be more precise, the distributive conflicts are two: the first is between the tourists and the host population, of which we have talked about at length in this section and in Sect. 15.3.2 when dealing with friendly and unfriendly tourism; the second distributive conflict is between different stakeholders in the host population. Not all the residents have the same interests with regards to tourism, nor are they economically involved in the same way. To define social sustainability it is therefore not possible to go beyond the identification of a general principle of equal distribution of the benefits stemming from tourism between tourists and residents on one side and, within host population, between those who work and earn in the tourism sector and those who are instead not linked to the tourism sector (Figini et al. 2009). The core of social sustainability, as recalled by Costa et al. (2001), is in the definition of equity:

> [Sustainability] has to benefit the local community and hence the choice is primarily political, and regards the distribution of costs and benefits between different stakeholders and between different periods. Clearly, there can be diverging interests [...] if the main goal is to maximize the rate of tourism exploitation in the short run.
>
> (Costa et al. 2001, p. 124. *Our translation*)

To conclude, the role played by the local population is crucial to solving the problem of sustainability: without the participation of the host community in the strategic decisions regarding tourism development, environmental protection, and social organization it is difficult to conceive a type of development that is authentically sustainable. This statement is strengthened the further tourism moves into the age of globalization (see Sect. 14.2.3). Since the globalization of tourism renders easier to delocalize, that is, to easily switch tourism flows from one destination to another, the involvement of local actors in the decision process can play a fundamental role in how the advantages and disadvantages of tourism development are to be shared. In other words, the search for sustainability can lead to a self-centered local development model.

16.3.3 The Different Aspects of Responsible Tourism

As underlined before in this chapter, sustainable tourism is not only based on its recognition on the part of local stakeholders, practitioners, and researchers, but also on the environmental and sociocultural consciousness by a growing number of tourists. A new demand for responsible tourism has then been imposing, thus driving public intervention towards targets of sustainability (Case Study 16.1) and pushing destinations to compete in the environmental and social quality of their tourism product.

Case Study 16.1. The UNWTO Programs on Social Sustainability (ST-EP) and Environmental Sustainability (Tourism and Climate Change)
At the Millennium Summit in 2000 the United Nations identified the fight against poverty as one of the biggest challenges of the new millennium. In that occasion the ambitious objective of eliminating extreme poverty by 2015 was announced and the World Tourism Organization became the promoter of the ST-EP program (Sustainable Tourism-Eliminating Poverty) that was presented at the World Summit on Sustainable Development held in Johannesburg in 2002.

The ST-EP program is the attempt to provide a long-term operational framework that is able to promote sustainable tourism, understood in the broadest sense and hence connected to its economic, social, and environmental dimensions. Through the ST-EP program, the UNWTO has created a structure aimed at alleviating poverty through the development of tourism, especially for those communities and people that live on less than $1 a day. For example, programs have been started for the training of local tourist guides and workers for the hospitality sector in poor countries. Moreover, programs aiming at the inclusion of the local community in ecotourism activities, in the management of cultural heritage sites, and programs of enhancement of tourism entrepreneurship on a national or regional level have been promoted.

In addition to programs to combat poverty, the UNWTO is also supporting projects aimed at protecting the environment and fighting the climate change. Also in this case the UNWTO strategy is part of a wider strategy brought forward by the UN: the 2002 was proclaimed the International ecotourism year by the United Nations, and the UN commission for Environmental Protection (UNEP) invited tourism operators and policy makers to collaborate with the goal of encouraging sustainable tourism. The sensibility to environmental issues has also pushed the UNWTO to pay attention to climate change, aware that it can cause dramatic changes in specific and delicate areas. At the same time, tourism is among the sectors that contribute the most to greenhouse gas emissions, through the means of transportation used by travelers.

The first conference dealing with the relationship between climate change and tourism took place in Djerba, in Tunisia, in 2003, and on that occasion the need to reduce the impact of tourism on the environment and climate was declared for the first time. More recently, the former general secretary of the United Nations, Ban Ki-Moon, insisted on the need for a common action by governments and by

(continued)

international organizations in defense of the climate, a strategy that must be in tight coordination with the actions against poverty, already taken in the domain of the UN Millennium Development Goals. The UNWTO is responsible for the task of ensuring that the fight against poverty and the environmental policies is applied to the tourism sector in a coordinated manner. This is particularly relevant for poor and developing countries, for which the natural environment constitutes the main tourism resource they avail for.

When talking about responsible tourism there is often much confusion about terms: the concept is sometimes identified with ecotourism, some other times with social tourism, etc.

> In tourism literature there has been much confusion as how to describe what has been given various labels, the most frequently quoted being: adapted; adventure; alternative; appropriate; community-based; conservation; cultural; ecological; ethical; fair-trade; green; high-value; natural area; nature-aware; nature-based; popular ecotourism; responsible; self-reliant; small group; soft; social; sustainable; and wildlife tourism. Three terms have assumed prominence, 'ecotourism', 'geotourism', and 'sustainable tourism', of which the first has been widely adopted.
>
> (Stabler et al. 2010, p. 359)

While we redirect to the specific bibliography for the precise definitions and the comparison of the different concepts (Hultsman 1995; Garrod and Fyall 1998; Diamantis 1999; Fennell 2001; Page and Dowling 2002; Buckley 2003; and in particular the review article by Doan 2000), in what follows we propose a remark on the differences between these terms, bringing forward our way of classification.

With the term *responsible tourism* we define the process of self-selection, on the part of the tourist, of tourism activities that are sustainable and respectful of the environment; therefore it can be seen as the expression, on the demand side, of the need of sustainable tourism. It is a type of ethical consumption that goes beyond the simple holiday experience and can also be expressed through the activities of boycotting destinations for environmental, social, or political reasons.

With the term *ecotourism* we recall two definitions:

> [Ecotourism] is the desire to view ecosystems in their natural state, both in terms of wildlife and the indigenous population. However ecotourism is often understood to be something more, linked to the desire of preserving the ecosystem and improving the quality of life of the local community.
>
> (Swarbrooke 1999, p. 318)

> Ecotourism is a sustainable, non-invasive form of nature-based tourism that focuses primarily on learning about nature first-hand and which is ethically managed to be low impact, non-consumptive and locally oriented (control, benefit and scale). It typically occurs in natural areas, and should contribute to the conservation of such areas
>
> (Fennell 2007, p. 24)

In the last few years many ecotourism projects have been developed, mainly in protected areas where the tourists satisfy their own adventure and exploration demand in (almost) uncontaminated sites, and where they are willing to pay a higher price for the holiday, implicitly including the cost of protecting the environment.

A positive effect of ecotourism, as Tisdell and Wilson (2001) show, is that the holiday experience increases the tourists' willingness to contribute to the conservation of the environment also when the trip is over, thus beginning a virtuous circle of tourism development and environmental sustainability.

The critics of ecotourism, like Swarbrooke, underline that also small projects of tourism development in protected areas may not be sustainable and can break the fragile equilibrium of the ecosystem. In fact, the aim of the ecotourists is not sustainability in itself but rather the desire to live the natural ecosystem: the tourism activity is respectful, but invading unexplored areas risks putting its sustainability in danger.[7]

> To counter environmentally destructive mass tourism, the Tourism Authority of Thailand (TAT) launched the concept of ecotourism [...] but tour companies seem to have their own ideas of what being green is [...]. Ideally, ecotourism is environmentally-friendly and sustainable tourism which also benefits the local communities. But in fact, many ecotourism ventures all over the country are destroying the very ecosystems they claim to protect.
> (Cooper et al. 1998, p. 164)

Even though the definitions overlap and often have different meanings in different languages, with the term *social tourism* we indicate those tourism activities that favor the meeting and the socialization between people and among social groups (even those that are disadvantaged), responding to a widespread need of social interaction. Among social tourism, there are trips organized by non-governmental organizations in developing countries but also skiing weeks organized by workers' clubs.

The demand for sustainable, responsible, eco and social tourism all pushed tourism operators and destinations to offer higher quality standards; to select the search for ethnicity, wildlife, and true cultural experiences as marketing tools; and to introduce ethical and environmental quality certifications (see Sect. 16.5). Strategies of sustainability such as demarketing and smoothing seasonality (see Sect. 7.5.4) have been introduced to move tourism flows towards less crowded areas and periods of the year.

The rise of the demand and the supply of ethical tourism pushed the request to identify the rights of the different actors and stakeholders involved in tourism (tourists, the host community, firms) and to give tourism an ethical code. This request met an institutional answer in the *Global Code of Ethics for Tourism*, approved by the World Tourism Organization in 1999 (UNWTO 1999). This code aims at promoting a global tourism system that is fair, responsible, and sustainable, and respects the fundamental principles established by the most important international declarations, such as the *Universal Declaration of Human Rights* in 1948 and the *Rio Declaration on Environment and Development* in 1992.

[7] There are many case studies in the literature: marine tourism (Cater and Cater 2007; Garrod and Wilson 2003); island tourism (Briguglio et al. 1996; Robinson 2001); and community-based tourism (Stem et al. 2003; Mowforth and Munt 2003; Hall and Richards 2000).

The fundamental principles of the Global Code of Ethics for Tourism are:

- The recognition of tourism as a factor of mutual understanding and respect between people and societies and as a vehicle for individual and collective fulfillment; it is therefore the responsibility of tourists, tour operators, and the authorities to respect the human rights, the culture, the traditions, and the laws of the destination; to prohibit the exploitation of human beings; and to guarantee the safety of tourists.
- The recognition of fundamental rights for the workers of the tourism sector, particularly in relation to the high degree of seasonal and temporary jobs; the recommendation to the multinational firms to not abuse their positions and to commit, in exchange for economic freedom, to local development while respecting the native culture.
- The recognition of biodiversity and the importance of natural, cultural, and artistic resources for tourism, as humanity's common heritage, which must be protected and enhanced in a sustainable development perspective.
- The recognition of the right for the host community to have access in a fair manner to the benefits stemming from tourism.
- The implementation of a World Committee on Tourism Ethics, able to resolve the controversies related to the application and interpretation of the code.

In conclusion, the ethical feature of tourism can be seen as an attempt to abandon the prevalent model of the tourist as a customer, who lives the tourism experience as a consumption good that is later thrown away, to rather impose the model of the tourist as a traveler (Zamagni 1999).

16.4 The Carrying Capacity

The concept of *carrying capacity* was developed in engineering to indicate the weight that a structure can bear before collapsing; analogously it has been applied in economics, when dealing with territorial planning, to identify the threshold to not exceed for the protection of resources (Coccossis and Nijkamp 1995; Farrell and Runyan 1991). The same concept, applied to tourism, can be understood as the maximum number of tourists that a resource can bear without deteriorating its quality and leading to a contraction in overnight stays. Hence, it can provide a measure to determine when the process of tourism development changes from being sustainable to unsustainable.

Recalling the several dimensions of sustainability, the carrying capacity can be defined both in a social and in an environmental sense. In a social sense because the overload of tourism flows can produce negative effects on the culture and on the social fabric of the host community, particularly in developing countries (see Sect. 16.3 and Iorio and Sistu 2002). In an environmental sense because the overload of tourism flows can produce physical effects that alter the state of sustainability of the natural (and cultural) resources.

16.4.1 The Environmental Carrying Capacity

With reference to tourism, Mathieson and Wall (1982) applied the physical concept of carrying capacity to the whole territory. In fact, they define the carrying capacity of the destination as:

> the maximum number of people who can use a site without an unacceptable alteration in the physical environment and without an unacceptable decline in the quality of the experience gained by visitors.
>
> (Mathieson and Wall 1982, p. 21)

This definition has successively been improved and completed by the UNWTO, for which the carrying capacity of a tourism destination is the maximum number of people that visit it at the same time without compromising its environmental, physical, economic, and sociocultural characteristics and without reducing the level of satisfaction of tourists. This definition widens the concept of carrying capacity to the whole range of sociocultural and physical alterations that an overload of tourism flows can produce on the destination, that is, on its environmental, psycho-sociological, and urban dimensions.

> The identification of the carrying capacity is not an easy task. Its value depends on the complex interaction between different variables: the researcher's perception, the properties of the ecosystem, the development target and its monitoring, the types of tourism hosted by the destination and their seasonal distribution, the expectations of tourists, residents and tourism operators. These interactions and their feedback impede to provide a unique and steady estimate of the carrying capacity. If any of those variables changes, the carrying capacity will change too.
>
> (Iorio and Sistu 2002, p. 242–3. *Our translation*)

Therefore, such a general concept becomes very complex to measure, since it is necessary to identify many indicators (a vector of indexes) of the carrying capacity according to the different types of resources in the destination: for example, a mountain destination has different carrying capacities, one referred to the access roads, another one referred to the skiing slopes, another one to the ski lifts, etc.

The need to identify and classify the different dimensions of the carrying capacity then becomes necessary:

- *The ecological dimension* refers to the physical environment of the destination and identifies the ecological threshold as the resiliency of the ecosystem, in connection both with the tourism activity (with particular reference to its concentration in space and time) and with the coexistence in the same destination of more types of tourism. Specific components of the general ecosystem like the water pollution, the greenhouse gas emissions, the biodiversity, the geology, etc. and the specific ecosystems like the coasts, the islands, the lakes, and the parks are included in this dimension.
- *The physical-structural dimension* refers to the destination's system of structures and infrastructures (from the transport network to waste collection and water services) that are used by tourists and residents. In general, it refers to any human-made environment: cities, monuments, public goods, etc.

- *The psycho-social dimension* identifies a threshold, which is highly subjective, above which the level of crowding is perceived as intolerable by visitors or residents.
- *The economic dimension*, finally, refers to the ability of the local economic system to meet, with its own production, the demand by tourists without being subject to pathological alterations in terms of allocation of resources and prices.

Obviously, each dimension of the carrying capacity is interrelated with the others and has to be measured through one or more indicators of fruition in order to monitor the use of the resource. These indicators must be easily measurable, representative of the phenomenon to be checked, sensitive to changes in the socioeconomic and environmental scenarios, and must allow for predicting future scenarios (Iorio and Sistu 2002). With respect to their use, the indicators must allow for different monitoring states: (a) indicators of response, (b) indicators of impact, (c) indicators of alarm, (d) indicators of stress.

The methodology behind the measurement of carrying capacity has been set by the United Nations (United Nations Environmental Programme, UNEP), and in particular by the Priority Actions Programme/Regional Activity Centre (PAP/RAC), through a series of directives adopted in 1997. These guidelines indicate that the carrying capacity must become an essential part of the process of tourism policy and planning. The methodology includes the following phases: (a) data analysis and their graphical representation; (b) definition of the sustainability indexes for the tourism resources; (c) analysis of the present tourism scenario; (d) definition of future tourism development scenarios; (e) definition of the method to compute the carrying capacity.

The monitoring of the indicators is controlled in the first place by the local authorities and policy makers and in the second place by the different tourism stakeholders: hotels, tourism firms, consumer associations, and also tourists themselves. Recently, the work of monitoring the carrying capacity and the sustainability of the tourism development process has lead to the publication by the UNWTO of an operational manual for destination managers (UNWTO 2008b). In the report, numerous sustainability and carrying capacity indexes are introduced, and the methodology for the gathering of data and for the construction of indexes, which diverge depending on the type of destination, is described.

The carrying capacity is a problem specifically referred to inexhaustible and non-renewable resources, for which it is important to define a threshold of exploitation beyond which the risk of qualitative deterioration is high. Nevertheless, this concept is sufficiently general to be applied to the management of any type of resource, with the aim of controlling not only its quality but also the dangers of its depletion.

Through the carrying capacity, tourism destinations can calculate the hospitality load, defined as the maximum number of tourists that the destination can host, naturally identified with reference to the most binding constraint among those expressed by different carrying capacities. Hence, the problem becomes more complicated the more dimensions a destination's carrying capacity has. Therefore, for explanatory reasons, it may be opportune to first consider a destination specialized in a single type of tourism that shows a carrying capacity in only one dimension, to later move on to the problem of the carrying capacity with more than one dimensions.

16.4.1.1 The Carrying Capacity in One-Dimensional Problems

For specialized destinations, which only have one resource and host one type of tourism only, the carrying capacity is represented by one index, the threshold value of the overnight stays N°. Therefore, to maintain the quality of tourism, it is reasonable to assume that the destination management aims at reaching that size of tourism flows that is not greater than the carrying capacity of the resource, $N \leq N^\circ$.

In such case, it is sufficient to monitor the flow of overnight stays. If $N > N^\circ$, the destination would face a deterioration in the quality of its tourism that can lead to serious economic problems, since tourists can "vote with their feet," going on holiday elsewhere, and "vote with their wallet," showing their disapproval by a reduction in tourism spending.

> Visitor satisfaction surveys are frequently undertaken by many destinations to monitor acceptability. Furthermore, if the carrying capacity is exceeded, tourists will vote with their cheque book and go elsewhere.
>
> (Cooper et al. 1998, p. 188)

To avoid this outcome, the tourism policy can intervene with instruments of direct or indirect control. Instruments of direct control are those that limit the access, impose prohibitions and regulations in using the resource. Instruments of indirect controls are those that are able to modify the individual decisions in terms of arrival and length of stay without imposing an explicit restriction, mainly by using the price system (for example, by introducing taxes on tourists, see Sect. 15.4.2).

16.4.1.2 The Carrying Capacity in Two-(or More-) Dimensional Problems

If the destination has to deal with a carrying capacity composed of more than one dimension, as regards resources and types of tourism, the monitoring becomes more complex. For simplicity, we consider a beach resort with a carrying capacity in two physical dimensions that are easily measurable: for example, assume to have an index of carrying capacity for the beach, which supports up to N_B° people, and an index of carrying capacity for the sea water, with a maximum value of N_W°.

If the destination receives just one type of tourism (sea&sun), it is clear that the overall carrying capacity of the destination is bounded by the minimum of the two values. The activity of monitoring and controlling just verifies whether or not the condition $N \leq \min\,[N_B^\circ; N_W^\circ]$ is satisfied, which is just a little more general than the condition indicated in the previous case of one-dimensional problems. In this case, the destination's carrying capacity is defined with respect to a single dimension, the one with the strictest carrying capacity.

The problem becomes more complex if the destination hosts at least two types of tourism, $N = N_1 + N_2$, which utilize the two resources differently. In fact, the

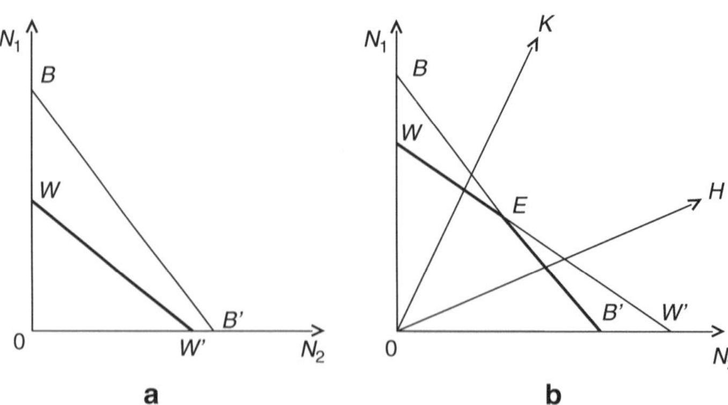

Fig. 16.1 The carrying capacity in a two-dimensional problem

selection of the strictest carrying capacity could depend on the consumption habits of the two types of tourism.[8] We assume that tourists of type one prefer diving and swimming and use, for each day at the resort, fewer beach services b_1 with respect to water services w_1, while tourists of type two prefer sunbathing and use the beach and its services b_2 relatively more than the sea water w_2. Given these hypotheses, the following property is verified between the coefficients: $w_1/b_1 > w_2/b_2$, therefore $w_2/w_1 < b_2/b_1$. Therefore, the thresholds for the carrying capacity are as follows:

$$N^{\circ}_{\mathrm{W}} \geq w_1 N_1 + w_2 N_2 \quad \text{therefore} \quad N_1 \leq \frac{N^{\circ}_{\mathrm{W}}}{w_1} - \left(\frac{w_2}{w_1}\right) N_2, \tag{16.8a}$$

$$N^{\circ}_{\mathrm{B}} \geq b_1 N_1 + b_2 N_2 \quad \text{therefore} \quad N_1 \leq \frac{N^{\circ}_{\mathrm{B}}}{b_1} - \left(\frac{b_2}{b_1}\right) N_2. \tag{16.8b}$$

Figure 16.1 represents the two thresholds for the carrying capacity, developing two hypotheses that differ according to the assumptions on the value of the abscissa at the origin $N^{\circ}_{\mathrm{W}}/w_2$ with respect to $N^{\circ}_{\mathrm{B}}/b_2$. In Fig. 16.1a the constraint stemming from the beach resource BB' is dominated from the bottom by the one stemming from the water resource WW', therefore the carrying capacity of the destination is, in this case, determined solely by this last factor and the problem is similar to the one-dimensional problem. Even though there are more dimensions in the carrying capacity, the destination management only needs to control the total overnight stays ($N = N_1 + N_2$), independently of the composition of the types of tourism.

[8] Moreover, the consumption habits of the host population should also be added, if they compete with tourists in the use of the same resources.

Figure 16.1b, on the contrary, assumes that the two constraints intersect at point *E*. Obviously, the overall carrying capacity of the destination is now determined by the area defined by the minimum envelope between the two constraints, that is, the area $0WEB'$ in the figure. The mix of tourism hosted by the resort determines which constraint of the carrying capacity is binding; in fact along the expansion path of tourism *K*, which sees a relatively larger presence of the tourists of type one, the water constraint crosses before the beach constraint, while along the expansion path of tourism *H*, which sees a relatively larger presence of tourists of type two, the beach constraint crosses before that of the water. As a consequence, if the mix of tourism hosted by the destination changes overtime, the constraint defining its overall carrying capacity changes as well.

> The carrying capacity, in its different formulations, depends on the specific targets of sustainable development: a natural park used as a natural reserve should have a lower density of visitors of the same park if used as an amusement park.
>
> (Costa and Manente 2000, p. 259. *Our translation*)

In the case analyzed in Fig. 16.1b, therefore, the activity of monitoring becomes difficult, since the carrying capacity does not only depend on the overall number of overnight stays but also on its distribution among different types of tourism. In fact, the destination that plans its tourism policy based on the carrying capacity of the waters, WW', does fine until the expansion path of tourism follows the vector *OK*, but it would commit a serious mistake should the structure of tourism change following the vector *OH*, thus leading to the deterioration of the beach. The case in Fig. 16.1b shows how the carrying capacity is a dynamic concept that can change also in the short run following the dynamics of the tourism mix in the destination.[9]

The importance that the carrying capacity has in tourism planning and policy is now clear. In fact, through the monitoring of the carrying capacity both the preservation of the quality of existing resources and the optimal level of investment in these resources (if they can be produced, such as public or private goods in the tourism product) can be addressed.

16.4.2 The Social Carrying Capacity

The social carrying capacity measures the destination's sustainability, not in relation to the physical limit of the natural resources as shown in Fig. 16.1, but rather on the effect that crowding has on the relationship between residents and visitors.

[9] Since the degree of utilization of each resource depends on the different types of hosted tourism, only a complex model of optimization can solve both the issue of identification of the binding constraints and the issue of identification of the tourism mix that maximizes profits. The problem can be formulated as a dynamic optimization program, linear or non-linear, subject to a set of constraints expressed as weak inequalities. The solution can be found by applying the Kuhn–Tucker method (Theory in Action 6.1).

From this perspective, the social carrying capacity can be studied according to two different approaches: the Marzetti–Mosetti model (2004), in which a voting system is used to determine the optimal load factor, and the Bimonte–Punzo model (2007), in which the optimal load factor is determined as the result of a free exchange between tourists and residents. Both models are based on the observation that tourists and residents compete for the same local resources.

16.4.2.1 Voting on the Social Carrying Capacity

The social carrying capacity can be measured both from the tourist and the resident points of view, since both have an opinion on the threshold of the crowding, in terms of overnight stays N. Each tourist compares the utility accruing from the holiday with the disutility stemming from crowding, thus identifying a maximum level of acceptable crowding, $N_{i\mathrm{T}}$, referred to the i-th Tourist; the resident compares the utility attached to the share of income generated by the tourism activity with the cost of not using the local resources, thus identifying a maximum level of acceptable crowding, $N_{j\mathrm{R}}$, referred to the j-th Resident.

Since the individual optimal values expressed in the group of tourists and in that of residents are many and diverse, the model assumes a voting system to determine, for each of the two groups, the preferred carrying capacities, respectively N_{T}^{*} and N_{R}^{*}. The voting mechanisms analyzed in the theory of social choice are mainly two, exit and voice:

(a) Exit is the expression of one's own preferences by moving away from the territory that is disliked and moving to the one that is preferred: this possibility is also called "voting with the feet"
(b) Voice is the expression of one's own preferences by making one's voice heard through the democratic system: this possibility is also called "voting with the voice"

Marzetti and Mosetti (2004) affirm that tourists and residents use two different voting mechanisms. The former, which are temporary residents, vote with their feet, by eventually deciding to leave the territory for other tourism destinations; the latter, which are permanent residents, vote with their voice, through the democratic process.

The voting system of tourists automatically determines the equilibrium level N_{T}^{*}: tourists with lower optimal values leave the destination, while only the n tourists which have preferences for crowding that are more than or equal to N_{T}^{*} stay.

To determine N_{R}^{*} we need instead to describe an explicit voting mechanism. The most common assumption is that the deliberation be taken by majority rule. The result hence depends on the assumptions we make on the distribution of residents preferences and also on their voting strategy. Under the usual assumptions of the Median Voter Theorem (Black 1948) we assume that the individual preferences of residents are single peaked, where those not working in the tourism sector but competing for the local resources obviously prefer less crowding, $N_{1\mathrm{R}}$, while those marginally working in the tourism sector prefer a medium level of crowding, $N_{2\mathrm{R}}$,

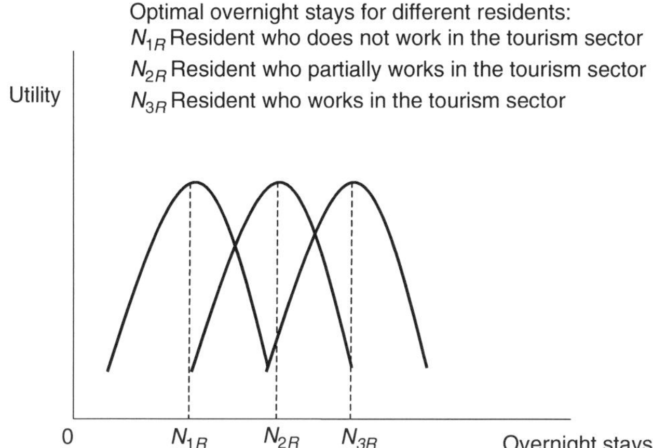

Fig. 16.2 Individual preferences of residents and the voting mechanism

and finally those receiving the most important share of their income from tourism prefer a high level of crowding N_{3R}. Figure 16.2 illustrates this situation.

In addition we assume that abstention is not allowed and that each resident votes sincerely, therefore choosing the closest alternative to own absolute preference. Given these assumptions, the majority voting rule always determines a social result, which is identified by the preference of the median voter N_{MR}, that is, the voter that, being in the median position, is able to convert each minority into the majority. The application of the median voter theorem to our problem implies that the carrying capacity chosen by the local community coincides with the preference of the median voter, the resident with subscript 2: $N_R^* = N_{2R}$.

This result is robust to different voting procedures and to the different distributions of preferences: for example, we assume that the number of voters is 21 and, in the limit case, they are equally distributed between the three alternatives: seven prefer N_{1R}, seven prefer N_{2R}, and seven prefer N_{3R}. Voting N_{1R} against N_{2R}, N_{2R} would win for 14 votes against 7; voting N_{2R} against N_{3R}, N_{2R} would win again for 14 votes against 7.

Such model allows to highlight that the problem of carrying capacity is not only a technical problem, but also a political issue, involving the search for an equilibrium among the local community in function of the economic participation of residents in the tourism sector. Social sustainability depends indeed on the distribution of earnings from tourism among the different groups of residents, as already stated in Sect. 16.3.2.

As a final comment on the Marzetti–Mosetti model, we observe that if $N_T^* = N_R^*$ there is perfect empathy between tourists and residents. In the more general case, when the two values differ, we can have the following situations: (a) if $N_T^* < N_R^*$, the binding constraint is the one set by tourists, who impose their decision by leaving the destination; (b) if $N_T^* > N_R^*$, the binding constraint is the one set by residents, who will ask the destination's management, democratically elected, to limit the size of tourism flows by using the direct and indirect instruments of control studied in Chap. 15.

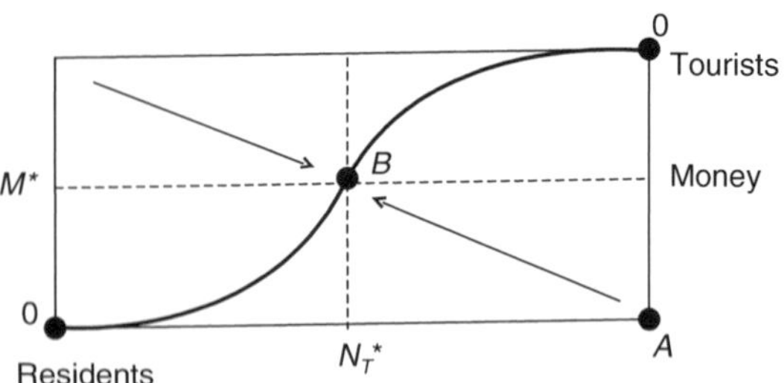

Fig. 16.3 The carrying capacity as a social exchange between money and territory

16.4.2.2 The Social Carrying Capacity as a Social Exchange

Before the development of the region as a tourism destination the local community has the complete availability of the resources, but residents do not enjoy the economic gains stemming from tourism. On the contrary, with the development of the tourism destination the host community has an economic windfall, but residents must share the resources with tourists. In this sense, tourism can be understood as the exchange between money and territory. The Bimonte–Punzo model (2007) interprets the carrying capacity of the destination as the equilibrium that is determined in this social exchange between tourists and residents.

If R indicates the available amount of the resource, which is used with intensity N_{H} by the host community and N_{T} by tourists, we have a competition in its use, $N_{\mathrm{H}} + N_{\mathrm{T}} \leq R$. To put it differently, the host community must make room in the use of the resource in exchange for money that it receives from tourists. This trade-off can be represented with the standard tools of economics by the marginal rate of substitution, $\mathrm{MRS_H}$, the ratio between the marginal utility of money and the marginal utility of the resource they give up.

Similarly, tourists transfer money M to gain the right of using the resource, in function of their marginal rate of substitution, $\mathrm{MRS_T}$, defined over the same variables. Since the exchange is voluntary, the general equilibrium between tourists and residents is efficient and is determined on the contract curve, shown in black in the Edgeworth Box of Fig. 16.3. Beginning with the initial condition in which all the available resource is used by the host community with a utility $U_{\mathrm{H}}(R; 0)$ and all the money is in the hands of tourists, $U_{\mathrm{T}}(0; M)$, that is from point A in the figure, the efficient equilibrium is determined when the allocation of the resource lies on the contract curve, such as at point B in Fig. 16.3 where $\mathrm{MRS_H} = \mathrm{MRS_T}$.

The carrying capacity of the destination is therefore the efficient result of this exchange, $(N_{\mathrm{T}}^*; M^*)$ in which both the equilibrium of residents $U_{\mathrm{H}}\left(R - N_{\mathrm{T}}^*; M^*\right)$ and that of tourists $U_{\mathrm{T}}\left(N_{\mathrm{T}}^*; M - M^*\right)$ are satisfied.

In conclusion, even though the result of the social exchange is conceptually different from the political economy model of Marzetti–Mosetti, also the Bimonte–Punzo model affirms that the carrying capacity of the destination is not only a technical-engineering problem but a social issue involving the host population. The carrying capacity depends in fact on the life style of the local community, which competes with tourists in the consumption of the same resource.

16.5 Methods of Environmental Monitoring

If any economic activity, including tourism, has an environmental impact, it is necessary to perform continuous environmental monitoring, in a way to guarantee that the exploitation of resources does not exceed the environmental carrying capacity and hence that the development process remains within the limits of sustainability. The fundamental problem of environmental monitoring deals with the different nature of the costs and benefits associated with tourism. While the benefits are prevalently monetary, and easily appropriated by the private sector, the costs are prevalently public, spread throughout the community, and often not easily measurable. Moreover, while the benefits usually spillover to the rest of the economy through the income and the employment multipliers, the environmental and sociocultural costs are often concentrated in specific areas or groups.

The instruments of environmental control developed by the specific literature are: the Cost–Benefit Analysis (CBA), which also includes the Planning Balance Sheet Analysis (PBSA), the Community Impact Analysis (CIA), the Community Impact Evaluation (CIE); the Cost Effectiveness Analysis (CEA) which is more operational than the CBA since it does not consider non-market goods; the Multiple Criteria Analysis (MCA); the Multiple Criteria Division Analysis (MCDA) which extends the MCA to some non-monetary impacts; the Strategic Environmental Analysis (SEA); the Resource Impact Analysis (RIA); the Damage Assessment (DA); the Computational General Equilibrium (CGE), the Input–Output Analysis (I–O), the Tourism Satellite Accounting (TSA) already discussed in other parts of the book and the Environmental Impact Assessment (EIA) which will be analyzed in Sect. 16.5.1. Although many other assessments are also carried out through non-scientific approaches, stimulated by business reasons rather than scientific research, the availability of adequate tools for assessing the optimal exploitation of tourism resources is a "necessary choice":

> However, they are feasible methods that the sector could and should employ given that the human-made and human environments constituting the tourism product are vital to the survival of tourism destinations
>
> (Stabler et al. 2010, p. 325)

In what follows we focus on the most relevant method of environmental monitoring and control, the EIA.

16.5.1 The Environmental Impact Assessment

The EIA is used to estimate the impact on the environment of a specific development project, industrial, infrastructural, or tourism-related. The principal aims of the EIA are of: (a) anticipating any potential environmental impact, in order to avoid or just to measure the cost of a subsequent correction; (b) evaluating the future contraction in tourism flows following the depletion of the tourism resources; (c) widening the analysis of a project beyond purely economic terms, in order to include the overall effects on the surrounding environment.

The EIA is multidimensional, since it can include non-monetary aspects, for example the impact that the construction of a tourism resort has on the local social organization, and monetary aspects, for example the estimation of the costs of reclaiming land to the project or the purification of the environment, as well as the opportunity cost due to the crowding out of other alternative projects. The EIA is therefore an indispensable instrument for choosing the optimal allocation of (scarce) environmental resources between different alternative uses.

For the purpose of tourism economics, the EIA is interesting since it allows both to estimate the environmental impact of a tourism project and to estimate the impact of a non-tourism project on the environment and, indirectly, also on tourism. In both cases, it is necessary to estimate the direct, indirect, and induced impact of the project, following the income multiplier model (see Sect. 13.2).

The methods used to implement the EIA are essentially two.

1. *The control list.* Natural and anthropological variables that might be at risk as a consequence of the project are identified; this list is then used to construct an evaluation matrix on which the effects of the proposed projects are computed on each of the variables. To evaluate these effects some environmental indicators have been proposed (OECD 1994; UNWTO 2008b) to measure, for example, the climate impact, the waste production, the quality of the urban environment, the future availability of natural resources, etc.
2. *The input–output approach.* Fletcher (1994) proposed an approach similar to EIA that uses the Input–Output model (see Sect. 3.3.2) through a series of quantifiable environmental indicators, thus analyzing the economic relationships between the different sectors. In this way it is possible to estimate the overall environmental effect and therefore to allocate the resources among alternative projects (not only tourism related) in order to minimize the environmental impact.

In applied economics many methods and approaches have been introduced to measure the value of the environment and to quantify the effect of alternative interventions, with many applications to tourism. The *Total Economic Valuation* (TEV) estimates the value of a natural resource as the sum of the many components defining it: the market value, the consumers' surplus, the option value (use and non-use values), the pure existence value.

> It must be recognized that virtually all resources used by tourists and tourism businesses have other uses [...] Where tourism can co-exist with other uses, the question arises as to what the level of usage ought to be to optimize the use and nonuse value gained.
>
> (Stabler et al. 2010, p. 377)

The most popular methods used in tourism economics are: the Contingent Valuation Method (CVM), the Choice Modeling (CM), the Hedonic Price Method (HPM), the Travel Cost Method (TCM), and any combination between them, the Production Cost Method; the Dose–Response Function; the Avoid Cost and Averting Expenditure Method; the Opportunity Cost Method; the Replacement Cost Method, the Provision Cost Method, and the Delphi technique. Some of these methods have been discussed before (CM and HPM are outlined in Theory in Action 6.2) while the Delphi technique is recalled in Sect. 4.5. For a comprehensive introduction, see Stabler et al. (2010, Chapter 10, and cited bibliography).

16.5.2 The Environmental Audit

The audit was created in the business sector as a certification process for the achievement of qualitative standards. Differently from EIA, which is a preventative study on the impact of the development project, the environmental audit is a continuous and systematic process of environmental monitoring and certification of the project under development. So far, the audit is a voluntary process that allows for individual firms to control the attainment of environmental standards and can contribute to communicating to the tourist a better image of itself. Nevertheless, its use on a wider scale in the future is hoped; a big leap surely happened upon the introduction of two specific environmental management and certification schemes on an international level:

- *ISO*. It is a voluntary and totally private scheme, approved and managed by the ISO (International Standard Organization) in September 1996 after an important work of implementation of the principles included in Agenda 21 (see Sect. 16.2). The ISO introduced a series of quality standards and other criteria for improving the management of firms and organizations.
- *EMAS*. It is a voluntary scheme of environmental audit, but it was instituted by a EU regulation in 1993 and represents the strong commitment of the EU in favor of sustainable development, not only through instruments and methods of control but also through a process of responsibility of firms, organizations, and local bodies.

Therefore, the environmental audit is a continuous and systematic monitoring process, providing environmental certifications or ecolabels. As previously affirmed on a theoretical level, also in practice the environment has to be understood in a holistic sense, thus it has to include the issues of ethical behavior and social responsibility of the firm. From this perspective, such certifications require specific management systems of social and environmental performance, and include continuous monitoring and improvement processes. There is a wide range of available certifications, and we just recall the main ones:

- ISO 14001 (which replaced the ISO 14000) is an international certification dealing with the environmental management system ISO and is granted by qualified certifying organizations.
- SA (Social Accountability) 8000 is the ethical certification of excellence; it corresponds to an international standard that has nine types of social management requirements.
- ISO 26000 is an ISO international standard that is in the process of being defined and provides the guidelines for organizing processes of social responsibility within the firm.

As was stated before, these processes of certification assign labels, among which we recall the European Ecolabel, which is granted by the EU together with the European Environmental Agency (EEA). The Ecolabel attests the environmental performance of products, services, and firms, and their adherence to the principles of ecological quality stated in the Environmental Management System of the EEA.

The economic effects of certifications and labels, which are costly investments, must be assessed and compared to benefits in terms of the image and communication strategies of the firm: (a) within the firm, by improving the employees' motivation and the workplace's conditions; (b) outside the firm, by increasing the credibility and the reputation for the products and services offered.

Today, the main tourism services that are certified in Europe are hospitality services. The ECOLABEL is granted to hotels and other hospitality structures for the quality of the service provided in terms of energy efficiency, schemes of water reduction, waste reduction and recycling, the use of local products and organic food, and the promotion of eco-friendly behaviors among customers, etc. While in economic terms these certifications and labels have the rationale of signaling and of investment in reputation by the firm (see Sects. 10.4.2 and 10.4.3), the detailed analysis of these procedures is mainly a subject for business studies. To our aims, therefore, this short discussion can be considered sufficient to conclude this book. That's all, folks.

Chapter Overview

- Sustainable development meets the needs of the present generation, without compromising the ability of future generations to meet their own needs. Sustainability is a multifaceted concept, with an environmental, a social, and an economic dimension.
- Tourism is sustainable if the activities are able to meet the present needs of tourists, of the tourism sector, and of the host community without compromising the satisfaction of the needs of future generations.
- There can be coexistence, conflict, or symbiosis between tourism and the environment. Such a relationship is complex, in the sense that it can shape differently, and dynamic, in the sense that the relationship can change and evolve over time.
- Natural resources are production factors or consumption goods that are not obtainable through an economic process of production. As regards availability, resources can be exhaustible or not; as regards natural reproduction, resources can be renewable or not; as regards property rights, resources can be private or common goods.
- For common goods, the economic rationale leads to an excessive exploitation of the resource. If the laws and regulations in terms of property rights are ineffective it is likely that the "tragedy of the commons" will take place.
- The key issue of sustainability lies in the role played by the local community: without its participation in the strategic planning of tourism development, in

environmental protection, and in social self-organization it is difficult to conceive the development as an authentically sustainable process.
- The demand of sustainable, responsible, eco-friendly, and social tourism has stimulated tourism operators and the destinations to put into action socially responsible behaviors and offer tourism products of higher environmental and ethical quality.
- The carrying capacity can be defined as the maximum number of tourists that a tourism resource can carry without causing a deterioration in its quality and a reduction in tourism flows.
- When the destination has many resources and hosts many types of tourism, the carrying capacity can be determined by the mix of tourism and by the characteristics of the host community: a change of the mix over time will change the constraint that defines the carrying capacity.
- The main method of environmental monitoring is the EIA, which estimates the environmental impact of a development project; the eco-audit, instead, is a continuous and systematic process of setting and controlling the environmental standards.

References

Aghion, P., & Howitt, P. (1998). *Endogenous growth theory*. Cambridge: MIT Press.

Agliardi, E. (1988). La segmentazione delle scelte turistiche: la teoria neo-classica e la scelta direzionale. In G. Candela (Ed.), *Contributi all'analisi economica del turismo*. Bologna: CLUEB.

Agnew, D., & Viner, D. (2001). Potential impact of climate change on international tourism. *Tourism and Hospitality Research, 3*, 37–59.

Aguilò, E., Alegre, J., & Sard, M. (2003). Examining the market structure of the German and UK tour operator industries through an analysis of package holiday prices. *Tourism Economics, 9*, 255–278.

Akerlof, G. (1970). The market for "lemons": quality uncertainty and the market mechanism. *Quarterly Journal of Economics, 84*, 488–500.

Akis, S., Peristianis, N., & Warner, J. (1996). Residents' attitudes to tourism development: the case of Cyprus. *Tourism Management, 17*, 481–494.

Aktas, G., & Gunlu, E. A. (2005). Crisis management in tourism destinations. In W. Theobald (Ed.), *Global tourism*. Burlington: Elsevier.

Alberini, A., Rosato, P., & Zanatta, V. (2005). Combining actual and contingent behaviour to estimate the value of sport fishing in the lagoon of Venice. *Ecological Economics, 61*, 530–541.

Alchian, A., & Demsetz, H. (1972). Production, information costs, and economic organization. *American Economic Review, 62*, 777–795.

Alegre, J., & Juaneda, C. (2006). Destination loyalty: consumers' economic behaviour. *Annals of Tourism Research, 33*, 684–706.

Alegre, J., Mateo, S., & Pou, L. (2011). A latent class approach to tourists' length of stay. *Tourism Management, 32*, 555–563.

Alegre, J., & Pou, L. (2006). The length of stay in the demand for tourism. *Tourism Management, 27*, 1343–1355.

Alfaro, L., Rodríguez-Clare, A., Hanson, G. H., & Bravo-Ortega, C. (2004). Multinationals and linkages: an empirical investigation. *Economía, 4*, 113–169.

Almeida, A., & Correia, A. (2010). Tourism development in Madeira: an analysis based on the life cycle approach. *Tourism Economics, 16*, 427–441.

Alvarez-Albelo, C. D., & Hernandez-Martin, R. (2009). *The commons and anti-commons problems in the tourism economy. Document de treball XREAP, 2009–16*. Spain: University of La Laguna.

Andergassen, R., & Candela, G. (2011). *LDCs, tourism investments and local economic development*. Bologna: University of Bologna. Mimeo.

Andergassen, R., & Candela, G. (2012). Development strategies for tourism destinations: tourism sophistication vs. resource investments. *Economia Politica – Journal of Analytical and Institutional Economics*, forthcoming.

G. Candela and P. Figini, *The Economics of Tourism Destinations*, Springer Texts in Business and Economics, DOI 10.1007/978-3-642-20874-4,

Andergassen, R., Candela, G., & Figini, P. (2012). *An economic model for tourism destinations: product sophistication and price coordination*. University of Bologna. Mimeo.

Apostolakis, A., & Shabbar, J. (2005). Stated preferences for two Cretan heritage attractions. *Annals of Tourism Research, 32*, 985–1005.

Apostolopoulos, Y., Leivadi, S., & Yiannakis, A. (1996). *The sociology of tourism*. Abingdon: Routledge.

Arana, J. E., & Leon, C. J. (2008). The impact of terrorism on tourism demand. *Annals of Tourism Research, 35*, 299–315.

Archer, B. H. (1977). *Tourism in the Bahamas and Bermuda: two case studies. Occasional Papers in Economics*. UK: University of Wales.

Arvanitis, P., & Zenelis, P. (2008). Africa. In A. Graham, A. Papatheodorou, & P. Forsyth (Eds.), *Aviation and tourism: implications for leisure travel*. Aldershot: Ashgate.

Ashworth, G. J. (1989). Urban tourism: an imbalance in intention. In C. P. Cooper (Ed.), *Progress in tourism, recreation and hospitality management*. London: Belhaven.

Bagella, M., & Becchetti, L. (2000). *The competitive advantage of industrial districts: theoretical and empirical analysis*. Heidelberg: Physica Verlag.

Balaguer, J., & Cantavella-Jordà, M. (2002). Tourism as a long-run economic growth factor: the Spanish case. *Applied Economics, 34*, 877–884.

Baldarelli, M. G. (2009). Le dimensioni della responsabilità sociale: riflessioni su miti e paradossi in una prospettiva economico-aziendale. *Rivista Italiana di Ragioneria e di Economia Aziendale, 1–2*, 59–69.

Banerjee, A. V. (1992). A simple model of herd behavior. *Quarterly Journal of Economics, 107*, 797–818.

Bank, M., & Wiesner, R. (2011). Determinants of weather derivatives usage in the Austrian winter tourism industry. *Tourism Management, 32*, 62–68.

Baretje, R., & Defert, P. (1968). *Aspects économiques du tourisme*. Aix-en-Provence: Berger-Levrault.

Bar-On, R. R. V. (1989). *Travel and tourism data – a comprehensive research handbook on the world travel industry*. London: Euromonitor.

Bates, J. M., & Granger, C. W. J. (1969). The combination of forecasts. *Operational Research Quarterly, 20*, 451–468.

Battilani, P. (2001). *Vacanze di pochi, vacanze di tutti*. Bologna: Il Mulino.

Baum, T., & Lundtrop, S. (2001). *Seasonality in tourism*. Oxford: Pergamon.

Baumol, W., Panzar, J., & Willig, R. (1982). *Contestable markets and the theory of industry structure*. San Diego: Harcourt, Brace and Jovanovic.

Becattini, G. (1987). *Mercato e forze locali: il distretto industriale*. Bologna: Il Mulino.

Becattini, G. (2000). *Distretti industriali e sviluppo locale*. Torino: Bollati Boringhieri.

Becattini, G. (2004). *Industrial districts. A new approach to industrial change*. Cheltenham: Edward Elgar.

Beriman, D. (2003). *Restoring tourism destination in crisis: a strategic marketing approach*. Cambridge: CABI Publishing.

Bhagwati, J. N. (1968). Distorsions and immiserizing growth: a generalization. *Review of Economic Studies, 35*, 481–485.

Bikhchandani, S., Hirshleifer, D., & Welch, I. (1992). A theory of fads, fashion, custom, and cultural change as informational cascades. *Journal of Political Economy, 100*, 992–1026.

Bikhchandani, S., Hirshleifer, D., & Welch, I. (1998). Learning from the behavior of others: conformity, fads, and informational cascades. *Journal of Economic Perspectives, 12*, 151–170.

Bimonte, S., & Punzo, L. (2007). The evolutionary game between tourist and resident populations and tourist carrying capacity. *International Journal of Technology and Globalization, 3*, 73–87.

Black, D. (1948). On the rationale of group decision-making. *Journal of Political Economy, 56*, 23–34.

Blake, A. T., Durbarry, R., Eugenio-Martin, J. L., Gooroochurn, N., Hay, B., Lennon, J., Sinclair, M. T., Sugiyarto, G., & Yeoman, I. (2006a). Integrating forecasting and CGE models: the case of tourism in Scotland. *Tourism Management, 27*, 292–305.

Blake, A. T., Gillham, J., & Sinclair, M. T. (2006b). CGE tourism analysis and policy modelling. In L. Dwyer & P. Forsyth (Eds.), *International handbook on the economics of tourism*. Cheltenham: Edward Elgar.

Blake, A. T., Saba Arbache, J., Sinclair, M. T., & Teles, V. (2008). Tourism and poverty relief. *Annals of Tourism Research, 35*, 107–126.

Blake, A. T., & Sinclair, M. T. (2003). Tourism crisis management: US response to September 11. *Annals of Tourism Research, 30*, 813–832.

Blake, A. T., Sinclair, M. T., & Sugiyarto, G. (2003). Quantifying the effect of food and mouth disease on tourism and the UK economy. *Tourism Economics, 9*, 449–465.

Bocksteal, N. E., & McConnell, K. E. (1981). Calculation equivalent and compensation variation for natural resource facilities. *Land Economics, 56*, 56–63.

Bocksteal, N. E., & McConnell, K. E. (1983). Welfare measurement in the household production framework. *American Economic Review, 73*, 806–814.

Bonham, C., Edmonds, C., & Mak, J. (2006). The impact of 9/11 and other terrible global events on tourism in the United States and Hawaii. *Journal of Travel Research, 45*(1), 99–110.

Boniface, B., & Cooper, C. (2009). *Worldwide destinations casebook. The geography of travel and tourism*. Butterworth-Heinemann: Oxford (second edition).

Boulding, K. E. (1972). Toward the development of a cultural economics. *Social Science Quarterly, 53*, 267–284.

Bowdin, G., Allen, J., O'Toole, W., Harris, R., & McDonnell, I. (2010). *Events Management*. Abingdon: Routledge.

Boyd, A. (1998). Airline Alliance Revenue Management. *OR/MS Today*, 25 October.

Bramwell, B. (2007). Opening up new spaces in the sustainable tourism debate. *Tourism Recreation Research, 32*, 1–9.

Bramwell, B., & Lane, B. (2000). *Tourism collaboration and partnerships, politics, practice and sustainability*. Clevedon: Channel View.

Brau, R., Lanza, A., & Pigliaru, F. (2007). How fast are small tourism countries growing? Evidence from the data for 1980–2003. *Tourism Economics, 13*, 603–613.

Brau, R., Scorcu, A. E., & Vici, L. (2009). Assessing visitor satisfaction with tourism rejuvenation policies: the case of Rimini, Italy. *Journal of Environmental Planning and Management, 52*, 25–42.

Briassoulis, H., & van der Streaten, J. (1992). *Tourism and environment*. London: Kluwer.

Briguglio, L., Archer, B., Jafari, J., & Wall, G. (1996). *Sustainable tourism in islands and small states: issues and policies*. London: Pinter.

Bronner, F., & de Hoog, R. (2011). Vacationers and eWOM: who posts, and why, where, and what? *Journal of Travel Research, 50*, 15–26.

Bruni, L., & Sugden, R. (2007). The road not taken: how psychology was removed from economics, and how it might be brought back. *Economic Journal, 117*, 146–173.

Buckley, R. C. (2003). *Case studies in ecotourism*. Wallingford: CABI.

Budowski, G. (1976). Tourism and environmental conservation: conflict, coexistence or symbiosis? *Environmental Conservation, 3*, 27–31.

Buhalis, D. (2006). The impact of information technology on tourism competition. In A. Papatheodorou (Ed.), *Corporate rivalry and market power: competition issues in the tourism industry*. London: I.B. Tauris.

Buhalis, D., & Costa, C. (2006). *Tourism management dynamics: trends, management and tools*. Oxford: Elsevier Butterworth-Heinemann.

Buhalis, D., Karcher, K., & Brown, M. (2006). TISCOVER: development and growth. In B. Prideaux, G. Moscardo, & E. Laws (Eds.), *Managing tourism and hospitality services: theory and international applications*. Wallingford: CABI Publishing.

Buhalis, D., & Law, R. (2008). Progress in information technology and tourism management: 20 years on and 10 years after the Internet—The state of eTourism research. *Tourism Management, 29*, 609–623.

Buhalis, D., & Licata, M. C. (2002). The future e-tourism intermediaries. *Tourism Management, 23*, 207–220.

Burkart, A. J., & Medlik, S. (1974). *Tourism. Past, present and future*. London: Butterworth Heinemann.

Butler, R. W. (1980). The concept of a tourism area life cycle of evolution. *Canadian Geographer, 24*, 5–12.

Butler, R. W. (1994). Seasonality in tourism: issues and problems. In A. Seaton, C. Jenkins, R. Wood, P. Dieke, M. Bennet, L. McLellan, & R. Smith (Eds.), *Tourism: the state of the art*. Chichester: Wiley.

Butler, R. W. (2001). Seasonality in tourism: issues and implications. In T. Baum & S. Lundtrop (Eds.), *Seasonality in tourism*. Oxford: Pergamon.

Butler, R. W. (2006). *The tourism area life cycle. Vol. 2: conceptual and theoretical issues*. Clevedon: Channel View.

Calveras, A. (2003). Incentives of international and local hotel chains to invest in environmental quality. *Tourism Economics, 9*, 297–306.

Calveras, A., & Orfila, F. (2007). *Intermediaries and quality uncertainty: evidence from the hotel industry*. Spain: University of Balearic Islands. Mimeo.

Candela, G. (1988). *Contributi all'analisi economica del turismo*. Bologna: CLUEB.

Candela, G. (1996). *Manuale di economia del turismo*. Bologna: CLUEB.

Candela, G., & Castellani, M. (2008). *Stagionalità e destagionalizzazione*. In A. Celant & M.A. Ferri (Eds.), *Il declino economico e la forza del turismo*. ROMA: Marchesi Grafiche Editoriali.

Candela, G., Castellani, M., & Dieci, R. (2008a). Economics of externalities and public policy. *International Review of Economics, 55*, 285–311.

Candela, G., Castellani, M., & Mussoni, M. (2009a). Tourism investments under uncertainty: an economic analysis of "eco-monsters". *Tourism Economics, 15*, 671–688.

Candela, G., Castellani, M., & Mussoni, M. (2012). Clashes and compromises. *Economics, 6(2012–23)*, 1–25.

Candela, G., & Cellini, R. (1997). Countries' size, consumers' preferences and specialization in tourism: a note. *Rivista Internazionale di Scienze Economiche e Commerciali, 44*, 451–457.

Candela, G., & Cellini, R. (1998). I mercati dei beni di qualità esogena. *Politica Economica, 14*, 217–244.

Candela, G., & Cellini, R. (2006). Investment in tourism market: a dynamic model of differentiated oligopoly. *Environmental and Resource Economics, 35*, 41–58.

Candela, G., Cellini, R., & Scorcu, A. E. (2003). Comportamenti d'impresa e informazione del consumatore: un'analisi empirica sui prezzi del pernottamento turistico. *Politica Economica, 19*, 441–465.

Candela, G., Fabbri, P., & Nardini, F. (1995). I programmi di un'economia sostenibile. *Rivista di Politica Economica, 85*, 69–82.

Candela, G., & Figini, P. (2003). *Economia del turismo*. Milan: McGraw-Hill.

Candela, G., & Figini, P. (2005). *Economia dei sistemi turistici*. Milan: McGraw-Hill.

Candela, G., & Figini, P. (2009). Tourism economics: a discipline of economics. *AlmaTourism, 0*, 7–18.

Candela, G., & Figini, P. (2010a). *Economia del turismo e delle destinazioni*. Milan: McGraw-Hill.

Candela, G., & Figini, P. (2010b). Destination unknown. Is there any economics behind tourism areas? *Review of Economic Analysis, 2*, 256–271.

Candela, G., Figini, P., & Scorcu, A. E. (2008b). The economics of local tourist systems. In R. Brau, A. Lanza, & S. Usai (Eds.), *Tourism and sustainable economic development: macroeconomic models and empirical methods*. Cheltenham: Edward Elgar.

Candela, G., Figini, P., & Scorcu, A. E. (2009b). Destination management and tourists' choice with a two-part tariff price of the holiday. *Rivista di Politica Economica, 99*, 107–125.

Candela, G., & Scorcu, A. E. (2004). *Economia delle arti*. Bologna: Zanichelli.

Canestrini, D. (2002). *Etica e turismo: l'Associazione Italiana Turismo Responsabile*. Unimondo

Casagrandi, R., & Rinaldi, S. (2002). A theoretical approach to tourism sustainability. *Conservation Ecology, 6*, 13–27.

Castellani, M., & Mussoni, M. (2007). An economic analysis of the tourism contract: allotment and free sale. In A. Matias, P. Nijkamp, & M. Sarmento (Eds.), *Advances in modern tourism research*. Heidelberg: Physica-Verlag.

Cater, C., & Cater, E. (2007). *Marine ecotourism: between the devil and the deep blue sea*. Wallingford: CABI.

Cavour, C.B. (1939). *Discorsi parlamentari*, vol. VIII. In A. Omodeo (Ed.) Firenze: La Nuova Italia.

Cerina, F. (2007). Tourism specialisation and environmental sustainability in a dynamic economy. *Tourism Economics, 13*, 553–582.

Chen, C. F., & Rothschild, R. (2010). An application of hedonic pricing analysis to the case of hotel rooms in Taipei. *Tourism Economics, 16*, 685–694.

Cheong Kon, S., & Turner, L. W. (2005). Neural network forecasting of tourism demand. *Tourism Economics, 11*, 301–328.

Choi, S., Lehto, X. Y., & Oleary, J. T. (2007). What does the consumer want from a DMO website? A study of US and Canadian tourists' perspectives. *International Journal of Tourism Research, 9*, 59–72.

Christaller, W. (1964). Some considerations of tourism location in Europe. *Papers of the Regional Science Association, 12*, 95–105.

Chu, F. L. (1998). Forecasting tourism demand in Asian Pacific countries. *Annals of Tourism Research, 25*(3), 597–615.

Clawson, M., & Knetsch, J. L. (1969). *Economics of outdoor recreation*. London: John Hopkins Press.

Clerides, S., Nearchou, P., & Pashardes, P. (2008). Intermediaries as quality assessors: tour operators in the travel industry. *International Journal of Industrial Organization, 26*, 372–392.

Clewer, A., Pack, A., & Sinclair, M. T. (1992). Price competitiveness and the inclusive tour holidays in European cities. In P. Johnson & B. Thomas (Eds.), *Choice and demand in tourism*. London: Mansell.

Coase, R. (1937). The nature of the firm. *Economica, 4*, 386–405.

Coase, R. (1960). The problem of social cost. *Journal of Law and Economics, 3*, 1–44.

Coccossis, H., & Nijkamp, P. (1995). *Sustainable tourism development*. Aldershot: Avebury.

Cohen, E. (1978). The impact of tourism on physical environmental. *Annals of Tourism Research, 5*, 215–237.

Cohen, E. (1988). Authenticity and commodization in tourism. *Annals of Tourism Research, 15*, 371–386.

Concu, N., & Atzeni, G. (2012). Conflicting preferences among tourists and residents. *Tourism Management*. doi:10.1016/j.tourman.2011.12.009.

Cooper, C.P. (1990). Il ciclo di vita delle località turistiche. *Politica del turismo*, 5.

Cooper, C. P., Fletcher, J., Gilbert, D., Shephard, R., & Wanhill, S. (1998). *Tourism. Principles and practice* (2nd ed.). New York: Longman.

Cooper, C. P., Fletcher, J., Gilbert, D., Shephard, R., & Wanhill, S. (2008). *Tourism. Principles and practice* (4th ed.). New York: Longman.

Copeland, B. R. (1991). Tourism, welfare and de-industrialization in a small open economy. *Economica, 58*, 515–529.

Cortés-Jiménez, I. (2008). Which type of tourism matters to the regional economic growth? The cases of Spain and Italy. *International Journal of Tourism Research, 10*, 127–139.

Cortés-Jiménez, I., & Blake, A. T. (2011). Tourism demand modelling by purpose of visit and nationality. *Journal of Travel Research, 50*, 408–416.

Cortés-Jiménez, I., Durbarry, R., & Pulina, M. (2009). Estimation of outbound Italian tourism demand: a monthly dynamic EC-LAIDS model. *Tourism Economics, 15*, 547–565.

Costa, P., & Manente, M. (2000). *Economia del turismo*. Milan: Touring Club Italiano.

Costa, P., Manente, M., & Furlan, M. C. (2001). *Politica economica del turismo*. Milan: Touring Club Italiano.

Costa, P., & Rispoli, M. (1992). *Dimensioni dell'industria italiana dei viaggi e del turismo*. Rome: SIPI.

Costantino, C., & Tudini, A. (2005). How to develop an accounting framework for ecologically sustainable tourism. In A. Lanza, A. Markandaya, & F. Pigliaru (Eds.), *The economics of tourism and sustainable development*. Cheltenham: Edward Elgar.

Cross, R. G. (1997). *Revenue management: hard-core tactics for market domination*. New York: Broadway Books.

Crotts, J. C., & Holland, S. M. (1993). Objective indicators of the impact of rural tourism development in the state of Florida. *Journal of Sustainable Tourism, 1*, 112–120.

Crouch, G. I., & Louviere, J. J. (2004). The determinants of convention site selection: a logistic choice model from experimental data. *Journal of Travel Research, 43*, 118–130.

Crouch, G. I., & Ritchie, J. R. B. (1999). Tourism competitiveness and social prosperity. *Journal of Business Research, 44*, 137–152.

Crouch, G. I., & Ritchie, J. R. B. (2006). Destination competitiveness. In L. Dwyer & P. Forsyth (Eds.), *International handbook on the economics of tourism*. Cheltenham: Edward Elgar.

Cuccia, T., & Santagata, W. (2004). Adhesion-exit: incentivi e diritti di proprietà collettivi nei distretti culturali. *Studi economici, 80*, 5–29.

D'Aspremont, C., Gabszewicz, J. J., & Thisse, J. F. (1979). On Hotelling's stability in competition. *Econometrica, 47*, 1045–1050.

D'Elia, A. (2007). *Economia e management del turismo*. Milan: Il Sole 24 Ore.

Dann, G., & Liebman Parrinello, G. (2009). *The sociology of tourism: European origins and developments*. Bradford: Emerald.

Darbellay, F., & Stock, M. (2011). Tourism as complex interdisciplinary research object. *Annals of Tourism Research, 39*, 441–458.

Daveri, F. (2002). The new economy in Europe. *Oxford Review of Economic Policy, 18*, 345–362.

Davidson, R., & Maitland, R. (1997). *Tourism destinations*. London: Hodder & Stoughton.

De Cantis, S., Ferrante, M., & Vaccina, F. (2011). Seasonal pattern and amplitude – a logical framework to analyse seasonality in tourism: an application to bed occupancy in Sicilian hotels. *Tourism Economics, 17*, 655–675.

De Mello, M., & Nell, K. S. (2005). The forecasting ability of a cointegrated VAR system of the UK tourism demand for France, Spain and Portugal. *Empirical Economics, 30*, 277–308.

De Oliveira Santos, G. E., Ramos, V., & Rey-Maquieira, J. (2011). A microeconomic model of multidestination tourism trips. *Tourism Economics, 17*, 509–529.

Deaton, A., & Muellbauer, J. (1980). An almost ideal demand system. *American Economic Review, 70*, 312–326.

Deaton, A., & Muellbauer, J. (1989). *Economics and consumer behavior*. Cambridge: Cambridge University Press.

Delbono, F., & Ecchia, G. (1988). Asimmetrie informative e qualità del prodotto nel mercato turistico. In G. Candela (Ed.), *Contributi all'analisi economica del turismo*. Bologna: CLUEB.

Dewailly, J. M., & Flament, E. (1995). *Géographie du tourisme et des loisirs*. Sedes: CDU.

Deyak, T., & Smith, V. K. (1978). Congestion and participation in outdoor recreation: a household production function approach. *Journal of Environmental Economics and Management, 5*, 63–80.

Diamantis, D. (1999). The concept of ecotourism: evolution and trends. *Current Issues in Tourism, 2*, 93–122.

Dickens, P. (2003). Changing our environment, changing ourselves: critical realism and trans-disciplinary research. *Interdisciplinary Science review, 28*, 95–105.

Dillon, T. (2000). Employment and wages: the travel industry in Montana. *Technical Report 2000-1*, Missoula University Travel Research Program.

Divisekera, S., & Kulendran, N. (2006). Economic effects of advertising on tourism demand: a case study. *Tourism Economics, 12*, 187–205.

Dixit, A. K., & Stiglitz, J. E. (1977). Monopolistic competition and optimum product diversity. *American Economic Review, 67*, 297–308.

Doan, T. M. (2000). The effects of ecotourism in developing nations: an analysis of case studies. *Journal of Sustainable Development, 8*, 288–304.

Doganis, R. (2005). *The Airline Business*. London: Routledge.

Donald, J. (1986). Knowledge and the university curriculum. *Higher Education, 14*, 267–282.

Dowling, R. K. (1990). Tourism and environmental integration: the journey from idealism to realism. In C. P. Cooper & A. Lockwood (Eds.), *Progress in tourism, recreation and hospitality management*. London: Belhaven.

Dowling, R. K. (2006). *Cruise ship tourism*. Wallingford: CABI.

Doxey, G. V. (1975). *A Causation theory of visitor-resident irritants. Proceedings of the Travel Research Association*. San Diego: Travel Research Association.

Dritsakis, N. (2004a). Tourism as a long-run economic growth factor: an empirical investigation for Greece using causality analysis. *Tourism Economics, 10*, 305–316.

Dritsakis, N. (2004b). Cointegration analysis of German and British tourism demand for Greece. *Tourism Management, 25*, 111–119.

Dunning, J. H. (1977). Trade, location of economic activity and the multinational enterprise: a search for an eclectic approach. In B. Ohlin, P. Hesselborn, & P. Wijkman (Eds.), *The international allocation of economic activity*. London: McMillan.

Dunning, J.H. (1988). The eclectic paradigm of international production: a restatement and some possible extensions. *Journal of International Business Studies*, Spring:1–31.

Durbarry, R. (2004). Tourism and economic growth: the case of Mauritius. *Tourism Economics, 10*, 389–401.

Durbarry, R., & Sinclair, M. T. (2003). Market shares analysis. The case of French tourism demand. *Annals of Tourism Research, 30*, 927–941.

Dwyer, L., & Forsyth, P. (2008). Economic measures of tourism yield: what markets to target? *International Journal of Tourism Research, 10*, 155–168.

Dwyer, L., Forsyth, P., Madden, J., & Spurr, R. (2003a). Inter-industry effects of tourism growth: implications for destination managers. *Tourism Economics, 9*, 117–132.

Dwyer, L., Forsyth, P., & Rao, P. (2000). The price competitiveness of travel and tourism: a comparison of 19 destinations. *Tourism Management, 21*, 9–22.

Dwyer, L., Forsyth, P., & Spurr, R. (2004). Evaluating tourism's economic effects: new and old approaches. *Tourism Management, 25*, 307–317.

Dwyer, L., Forsyth, P., Spurr, R., & Van Ho, T. (2003b). Tourism's contribution to a state economy: a multi-regional general equilibrium analysis. *Tourism Economics, 9*, 431–438.

Espinet, J. M., Saez, M., Coenders, G., & Fluvià, M. (2003). Effect on prices of the attributes of holiday hotels: a hedonic prices approach. *Tourism Economics, 9*, 165–177.

Etzioni, A. (1993). Andare oltre le preferenze esogene: un compito urgente per la ricerca socio-economica. In M. Franzini & M. Messori (Eds.), *Impresa, istituzioni e informazione. Letture di microeconomia non tradizionale*. Bologna: CLUEB.

Eurostat (2011). *Glossary: satellite account*. Eurostat: Statistics Explained (http://epp.eurostat.ec.europa.eu).

Evans, N., & Stabler, M. J. (1995). A future for the package tour operator in the 21st century? *Tourism Economics, 1*, 245–263.

Fabbri, P. (1988). Le ferie e il mercato turistico: un problema di politica economica. In G. Candela (Ed.), *Contributi all'analisi economica del turismo*. Bologna: CLUEB.

Falk, M. (2008). A hedonic price model for ski lift tickets. *Tourism Management, 29*, 1172–1184.

Farrell, D. H., & Runyan, D. (1991). Ecology and tourism. *Annals of Tourism Research, 18*, 26–40.

Farrell, B. H., & Twining-Ward, L. (2004). Reconceptualising tourism. *Annals of Tourism Research, 31*, 274–295.

Farrell, B. H., & Twining-Ward, L. (2005). Seven steps towards sustainability: tourism in the context of new knowledge. *Journal of Sustainable Tourism, 13*, 109–122.

Faulkner, B. (2001). Towards a framework for tourism disaster management. *Tourism Management, 22*, 135–147.

Faulkner, H. W., & Tideswell, C. (1997). A framework for monitoring community impacts of tourism. *Journal of Sustainable Tourism, 5*, 3–28.

Fayed, H., & Fletcher, J. (2002). Globalization of economic activity. Issues for tourism. *Tourism Economics, 8*, 207–230.

Feenstra, R. G., & Hanson, G. H. (1997). Foreign direct investment and relative wages: evidence from Mexico's maquilladoras. *Journal of International Economics, 42*, 371–393.

Feldman, A. M., & Serrano, R. (2006). *Welfare economics and social choice theory* (2nd ed.). New York: Springer.

Fennell, D. A. (2001). A content analysis of ecotourism definitions. *Current Issues in Tourism, 4*, 403–421.

Fennell, D. A. (2007). *Ecotourism*. London: Routledge.

Fernandez-Barcala, M., Gonzales-Diaz, M., & Prieto-Rodriguez, J. (2010). Hotel quality appraisal on the Internet: a market for lemons? *Tourism Economics, 16*, 345–360.

Field, D., & Pilling, M. (2003). Privatised airports blasted. *Airline Business, 19*, 10.

Figini, P. (2005). La politica economica della globalizzazione. *Sistemaeconomico, 10*, 3–21.

Figini, P. (2008). Impugnare il mercato dalla parte del manico. Ovvero, giocare con l'economia per imparare a difendersi. *Sociologia Urbana e Rurale, 30*, 57–68.

Figini, P., Castellani, M., & Vici, L. (2009). Estimating tourist externalities on residents: a choice modelling approach to the case of Rimini. In A. Matias, P. Nijkamp, & M. Sarmento (Eds.), *Advances in tourism economics new developments*. Berlin: Springer-Verlag.

Figini, P., & Goerg, H. (1999). Multinational companies and wage inequality in the host country: the case of Ireland. *Weltwirtschaftliches Archiv, 1999*, 594–612.

Figini, P., & Goerg, H. (2011). Does foreign direct investment affect wage inequality? An empirical investigation. *The World Economy, 34*, 1455–1475.

Figini, P., & Romaniello, L. (2012). *Poverty and tourism specialization*. Bologna: University of Bologna. Mimeo.

Figini, P., & Santarelli, E. (2006). Openness, economic reforms and poverty: globalization in the developing countries. *Journal of Developing Areas, 39*, 129–151.

Figini, P., & Vici, L. (2010). Tourism and growth in a cross-section of countries. *Tourism Economics, 16*, 789–805.

Figini, P., & Vici, L. (2012a). Off-season tourists and the cultural offer of a mass tourism destination: the case of Rimini. *Tourism Management, 33*, 825–839.

Figini, P., & Vici, L. (2012b). *Tourists are a flock of sheep! Herd behaviour in purchasing tourism services*. Bologna: University of Bologna.

Fisch, M. (1982). Taxing international tourism in West Africa. *Annals of Tourism Research, 9*, 91–103.

Fletcher, J. (1994). Economic impacts and input-output analysis. In S. F. Witt & L. Moutinho (Eds.), *Tourism marketing and management handbook*. Cambridge: Prentice Hall.

Forrester, J. W. (1971). *World dynamics*. Cambridge: MIT Press.

Frechtling, D. C. (2010). The tourism satellite account. A primer. *Annals of Tourism Research, 37*, 136–153.

Fuchs, M., Eybl, A., & Hoepken, W. (2011). Successfully selling accommodation packages at online auctions – The case of eBay Austria. *Tourism Management, 32*, 1166–1175.

Fuji, E., Khaled, M., & Mak, J. (1985). The exportability of hotel occupancy and other tourist taxes. *National Tax Journal, 38*, 169–177.

Gabszewicz, J., & Thisse, J. F. (1979). Price competition, quality and income disparities. *Journal of Economic Theory, 20*, 340–359.

Gabszewicz, J., & Thisse, J. F. (1980). Entry (or exit) in a differentiated industry. *Journal of Economic Theory, 22*, 327–338.

Gago, A., Labandeira, X., Picos, F., & Rodriguez, M. (2009). Specific and general taxation of tourism activities: evidence from Spain. *Tourism Management, 30*, 381–392.

Gandolfi, B. (2008). *Innovare il turismo. Metodologie e tecniche per lo sviluppo*. Bologna: CLUEB.

Garcia, D., & Tugores, M. (2006). Optimal choice of quality in hotel services. *Annals of Tourism Research, 33*, 456–469.

Gardini, A. (1986). *Caratteri strutturali e dimensioni macroeconomiche del turismo in Emilia-Romagna*. Bologna: University of Bologna. Mimeo.

Garín-Muñoz, T. (2006). Inbound international tourism to Canary Islands: a dynamic panel data model. *Tourism Management, 27*, 281–291.

Garrod, B., & Fyall, A. (1998). Beyond the rhetoric of sustainable tourism? *Tourism Management, 19*, 199–212.

Garrod, B., & Wilson, J. C. (2003). *Marine ecotourism. Issues and experiences*. Clevedon: Channel View.

Georgescu-Roegen, N. (1936). The pure theory of consumer's behaviour. *Quarterly Journal of Economics, 50*, 545–593.

Giannoni, S., & Maupertuis, M. A. (2007). Environmental quality and optimal investment in tourism infrastructures: a small island perspective. *Tourism Economics, 13*, 499–513.

Gil Molto, M.J., & Piga, C. (2007). Entry and exit in a liberalised market. *Rivista di Politica Economica*, 3–38.

Gilbert, E. W. (1939). The growth of inland and seaside health resorts in England. *Scottish Geographical Magazine, 55*, 16–35.

Gilbert, D. C. (1990). Conceptual issues in the meaning of tourism. In C. P. Cooper (Ed.), *Progress in tourism. Recreation and hospitality management*. London: Belhaven.

Gil-Pareja, S., Llorca-Vivero, R., & Martinez-Serrano, J. A. (2007). The effect of EMU on tourism. *Review of International Economics, 15*, 302–312.

Glaesser, D. (2006). *Crisis management in the tourism industry*. Oxford: Butterworth-Heinemann.

Goeldner, C. R., Ritchie, J. R. B., & McIntosh, R. W. (2005). *Tourism: principles, practices and philosophies*. Chichester: Wiley.

Gössling, S., & Hall, C. M. (Eds.). (2006). *Tourism and environmental change: ecological, social economic and political relationships*. London: Routledge.

Graham, A. (2008). *Managing airports: an international perspective*. Oxford: Butterworth-Heinemann.

Green, H., & Hunter, C. (1992). The environmental impact assessment of tourism development. In P. Johnson & B. Thomas (Eds.), *Perspectives on tourism policy*. London: Mansell.

Greene, W. H. (2003). *Econometric analysis*. London: Prentice-Hall.

Greenidge, K. (2001). Forecasting tourism demand: an STM approach. *Annals of Tourism Research, 28*, 98–112.

Griffiths, W. E., Carter Hill, R., & Judge, G. G. (2000). *Learning and practicing econometrics*. New York: Wiley and Sons.

Gunadhi, H., & Boey, C. K. (1986). Demand elasticities of tourism in Singapore. *Tourism Management, 7*, 239–253.

Gunduz, L., & Hatemi, A. (2005). Is the tourism-led growth hypothesis valid for Turkey? *Applied Economics Letters, 12*, 499–504.

Gunn, C. (1987). A perspective in the purpose and nature of tourism and hospitality research methods. In J. Ritchie & C. Goeldner (Eds.), *Travel, tourism and hospitality research*. Chichester: Wiley.

Hall, C. M. (1991). *Introduction to tourism in Australia: impacts, planning and development*. Melbourne: Longman Cheshire.

Hall, C. M. (2011). Publish and Perish? Bibliometric analysis, journal ranking and the assessment of research quality in tourism. *Tourism Management, 32*, 16–27.

Hall, C. M., & Higham, J. (Eds.). (2005). *Tourism, recreation and climate change*. Clevedon: Channel View.

Hall, C. M., & Page, S. (2006). *The geography of tourism and recreation: place, space and environment*. London: Routledge.
Hall, D., & Richards, D. (Eds.). (2000). *Tourism and sustainable community development*. London: Routledge.
Han, Z., Durbarry, R., & Sinclair, M. T. (2006). Modelling US tourism demand for European destinations. *Tourism Management, 27*, 1–10.
Haralambopoulos, N., & Pizam, A. (1996). Perceived impacts of tourism: the case of Samoas. *Annals of Tourism Research, 23*, 503–526.
Hardin, G. (1968). The tragedy of commons. *Science, 162*, 1243–1247.
Hardy, A., Beaton, R. J. S., & Pearson, L. (2002). Sustainable tourism: an overview of the concept and its position in relation to conceptualisations of tourism. *Journal of Sustainable Tourism, 10*, 475–496.
Haroutunian, S., Mitis, P., & Pashardes, P. (2005). Using brochure information for the hedonic analysis of holiday packages. *Tourism Economics, 11*, 69–84.
Haugland, S. A., Ness, H., Gronseth, B. O., & Aarstad, J. (2011). Development of tourism destinations. An integrated multilevel perspective. *Annals of Tourism Research, 38*, 268–290.
Hawkins, D., & Mann, S. (2007). The World Bank's role in tourism development. *Annals of Tourism Research, 34*, 348–363.
Hayes, D. K., & Ninemeier, J. D. (2006). *Hotel operations management*. New York: Prentice Hall.
Haywood, K. M. (1986). Can the tourist area life cycle be made operational? *Tourism Management, 7*, 154–167.
Heath, E., & Wall, G. (1992). *Marketing tourism destinations*. New York: Wiley.
Heller, M. A. (1998). The tragedy of the anticommons: property in the transition from Marx to markets. *Harvard Law Review, 611*, 621.
Heller, M. A. (1999). The boundaries of private property. *Yale Law Review, 108*, 1163–1223.
Henscher, D., & Brewer, A. (2001). *Transport: an economics and management perspective*. Oxford: Oxford University Press.
Hinch, T. D., & Higham, J. E. S. (2001). Sport tourism: a framework for research. *International Journal of Tourism Research, 3*, 45–58.
Hirst, P. (1965). Liberal education and the nature of knowledge. In A. Archmbault (Ed.), *Philosophical analysis and education*. London: Routledge and Kegan Paul.
Hirst, P. (1974). *Knowledge and the curriculum*. London: Routledge and Kegan Paul.
Hjalager, A. M. (2007). Stages in the economic globalization of tourism. *Annals of Tourism Research, 34*, 437–457.
Hoerner, J. M. (2000). The recognition of tourist science. *Espace, 173*, 18–20.
Holden, A. (2007). *Environment and tourism*. London: Routledge.
Holloway, J. C., & Taylor, N. (2006). *The business of tourism*. Harlow: Prentice Hall.
Hotelling, H. (1929). Stability in competition. *Economic Journal, 39*, 41–57.
Hughes, H. L. (1981). A tourism tax The case for and against. *International Journal of Tourism Management, 2*, 196–206.
Hultsman, J. (1995). Just tourism. An ethical framework. *Annals of Tourism Research, 22*, 553–567.
Hunter, C., & Shaw, J. (2007). The ecological footprint as a key indicator of sustainable tourism. *Tourism Management, 28*, 46–57.
Huybers, T. (2005). Destination choice modelling: what's in a name? *Tourism Economics, 11*, 329–350.
Huybers, T., & Bennet, J. (2000). Impact of the environment on holiday destination choices of prospective UK tourists: implications for Tropical North Queensland. *Tourism Economics, 6*, 21–46.
Huybers, T., & Bennet, J. (2003). Environmental management and the competitiveness of nature-based resource destinations. *Environmental and Resources Economics, 24*, 213–233.
Hylleberg, S. (1992). *Modelling seasonality*. Oxford: Oxford University Press.

Iatrou, K., & Oretti, M. (2007). *Airline choices for the future: from alliances to mergers*. Aldershot: Ashgate.
Ingold, A., McMahon-Beattie, I., & Yeoman, I. (2000). *Yield management*. London: Thomson.
Inkeles, A. (1964). *What is sociology*. New Jersey: Englewood Cliffs.
Ioannides, D., & Petridou-Daugthrey, E. (2006). Competition in the travel distribution system: the US travel retail sector. In A. Papatheodorou (Ed.), *Corporate rivalry and market power: competition issues in the tourism industry*. London: I.B. Tauris.
Iorio, M., & Sistu, G. (2002). Sviluppo turistico e capacità di carico ambientale in Sardegna. In R. Paci & S. Usai (Eds.), *L'ultima spiaggia. Turismo, economia e sostenibilità ambientale in sardegna*. CUEC: Cagliari.
Jafari, J. (1977). Editor's page. *Annals of Tourism Research, 6*, 6–11.
Jantsch, E. (1972). *Technological planning and social figure*. London: Cassel.
Jehle, G. A., & Reny, P. J. (2000). *Advanced microeconomic theory*. New York: Pearson.
Jensen, C. M., & Wanhill, S. (2002). Tourism's taxing times: value added tax in Europe and Denmark. *Tourism Management, 23*, 67–79.
Johnston, R. J., & Tyrell, T. J. (2005). A dynamic model of sustainable tourism. *Journal of Travel Research, 44*, 124–134.
Johnston, R. J., & Tyrell, T. J. (2008). Tourism sustainability, resiliency and dynamics: towards a more comprehensive perspective. *Tourism and Hospitality Research, 8*, 14–24.
Juaneda, C., Raya, J. M., & Sastre, F. (2011). Pricing the time and location of a stay at a hotel or apartment. *Tourism Economics, 17*, 321–338.
Kahn, R. (1931). The relation of home investment to unemployment. *Economic Journal, 41*, 173–198.
Kaldor, N. (1950). The economic aspects of advertising. *Review of Economic Study, 18*, 1–27.
Kaldor, N. (1957). A model of economic growth. *Economic Journal, 67*, 591–624.
Kang, K. H., Lee, S., & Huh, C. (2010). Impacts of positive and negative corporate social responsibility activities on company performance in the tourism industry. *International Journal of Hospitality Management, 29*, 72–82.
Katircioglu, S. T. (2009). Revisiting the tourism-led-growth hypothesis for Turkey using the bounds test and Johansen approach for co-integration. *Tourism Management, 30*, 17–20.
Keynes, J. M. (1936). *The general theory of employment, interest and money*. London: McMillan and Palgrave.
Kihlstrom, R., & Riordan, M. (1984). Advertising as a signal. *Journal of Political Economy, 92*, 427–450.
Kim, H. J., Chen, M. H., & Jang, S. S. (2006). Tourism expansion and economic development: the case of Taiwan. *Tourism Management, 27*, 925–933.
Kimes, S. E. (2000). A strategic approach to yield management: strategies for the service industries. In A. Ingold, U. McMahon-Beattie, & I. Yeoman (Eds.), *Yield management: strategies for the service industries*. London: Thomson.
King, A. R., & Brownell, J. A. (1966). *The curriculum and the disciplines of knowledge: a theory of curriculum practice*. New York: Wiley.
Klein, B., Crawford, R., & Alchian, A. (1978). Vertical integration, appropriable rents, and the competitive contracting process. *Journal of Law and Economics, 21*, 297–326.
Knowles, T., Diamantis, D., & El-Mourhabi, J. (2001). *The globalization of tourism and hospitality: a strategic perspective*. London: Continuum.
Koenig-Lewis, N., & Bishoff, E. E. (2005). Seasonality research: the state of the art. *International Journal of Tourism Research, 7*, 201–219.
Kotler, P., Bowens, J. T., & Makens, J. C. (2009). *Marketing for hospitality and tourism*. New York: Prentice Hall.
Krugman, P. (1990). *Rethinking international trade*. Cambridge: MIT Press.
Krugman, P. (1991). Increasing returns and economic geography. *Journal of Political Economy, 99*, 483–499.
Krugman, P. (1995). *Development, geography and economic theory*. Cambridge: MIT Press.

Kulendran, N., & Witt, S. (2001). Cointegration versus least squares regression. *Annals of Tourism Research, 28*, 291–311.

Kuniyal, J. C. (2005). Solid waste management in the Himalayan trails and expedition summits. *Journal of Sustainable Tourism, 13*, 391–410.

Lambertini, L. (1994). Equilibrium location in the unconstrained Hotelling game. *Economic Notes, 3*, 438–446.

Lamminmaki, D. (2007). Outsourcing in Australian hotels: a transaction cost economics perspective. *Journal of Hospitality and Tourism Research, 31*, 73–110.

Lancaster, K. (1971). *Consumer demand: a new approach*. New York: Columbia University Press.

Lancaster, K. (1979). *Variety, equity and efficiency*. New York: Columbia University Press.

Lanza, A., & Pigliaru, F. (1995). Specialization in tourism: the case of small open economy. In H. Coccossis & P. Nijkamp (Eds.), *Sustainable tourism development*. Aldershot: Avebury.

Lanza, A., & Pigliaru, F. (2000). Tourism and economic growth: does country's size matter? *Rivista Internazionale di Scienze Economiche e Commerciali, 47*, 77–85.

Law, R. (2000). Back propagation learning in improving the accuracy of neural network based tourism demand forecasting. *Tourism Management, 21*, 331–340.

Laws, E. (2000). Perspectives on pricing decision in the inclusive holiday industry. In A. Ingold, I. Yeoman, & U. McMahon-Beattie (Eds.), *Yield management: strategies for the service industries*. London: Thomson.

Ledesma-Rodríguez, F. J., Navarro-Ibánez, M., & Pérez-Rodríguez, J. V. (2001). Panel data and tourism: a case study of Tenerife. *Tourism Economics, 7*, 75–88.

Lee, E., & Vivarelli, M. (2004). *Understanding globalization, employment and poverty reduction*. Geneve: Palgrave & ILO.

Leibenstein, H. (1950). Bandwagon, snob and Veblen effects in the theory of consumers' demand. *Quarterly Journal of Economics., 64*, 183–207.

Leiper, N. (1981). Towards a cohesive curriculum in tourism: the case of distinct discipline. *Annals of Tourism Research, 8*, 69–83.

Leiper, N. (1990). *Tourism systems, Occasional Papers 2*. Auckland: Massey University.

Leiper, N. (2000). An emerging discipline. *Annals of Tourism Research, 27*, 805–809.

Li, S., Blake, A. T., & Cooper, C. (2010). China's tourism in a global financial crisis: a computable general equilibrium approach. *Current Issues in Tourism, 13*, 435–453.

Li, G., Song, H., & Witt, S. F. (2005). Recent developments in econometric modeling and forecasting. *Journal of Travel Research, 44*, 82–99.

Li, G., Wong, K. G., Song, H., & Witt, S. (2006). Tourism demand forecasting: a time varying parameter error correction model. *Journal of Travel Research, 45*, 175–185.

Lim, C. (1997). Review of international tourism demand models. *Annals of Tourism Research, 24*, 835–849.

Lindberg, K., Dellaert, B. G. C., & Rassing, C. R. (1999). Resident trade-offs. A choice modelling approach. *Annals of Tourism Research, 26*, 554–569.

Lindberg, K., & Johnson, R. L. (1997a). The economic values of tourism's social impacts. *Annals of Tourism Research, 24*, 90–116.

Lindberg, K., & Johnson, R. L. (1997b). Modelling resident attitudes toward tourism. *Annals of Tourism Research, 24*, 402–424.

Liu, Z. (2003). Sustainable tourism development: a critique. *Journal of Sustainable Tourism, 11*, 459–475.

Liu, J., Sheldon, P., & Var, T. (1987). A cross-national approach to determining resident perceptions of the impact of tourism on the environment. *Annals of Tourism Research, 14*, 17–37.

Loeb, P. D. (1982). International travel to the United States: an econometric evaluation. *Annals of Tourism Research, 9*, 7–20.

Loomes, G., & Sugden, R. (1986). Regret theory: an alternative theory of rational choice under uncertainty. *Economic Journal, 92*, 805–824.

Louvière, J. J., Hensher, D. A., & Swait, J. D. (2000). *Stated choice methods*. Cambridge: Cambridge University Press.

Lozano, J., Gomez, C. M., & Rey-Maquieira, J. (2008). The TALC hypothesis and economic growth theory. *Tourism Economics, 14*, 727–749.

Lucas, R. E. (1988). On the mechanics of economic development. *Journal of Monetary Economics, 22*, 3–42.

Lundberg, D. E. (1976). *The tourism business*. Boston: CBI Publishing.

Lundberg, D. E., Krishnamoorthy, M., & Stavenga, M. H. (1995). *Tourism economics*. New York: Wiley.

Lyssiotou, P. (2000). Dynamic analysis of British demand for tourism abroad. *Empirical Economics, 15*, 421–436.

Machina, M. (1987). Choice under uncertainty: problems solved and unsolved. *Journal of Economic Perspectives, 1*, 154–167.

Maggioni, M. A., & Merzoni, G. S. (2002). L'economia politica e la nuova economia: fondamenti analitici e paradigmi interpretativi. In L. Prosperetti (Ed.), *La new economy: aspetti analitici e implicazioni di policy*. Bologna: Il Mulino.

Mak, J., & Nishimura, E. (1979). The economics of a hotel room tax. *Journal of Travel Research, 17*, 2–6.

Mallen, C., & Adams, L. J. (2008). *Sport, recreation and tourism event management*. Amsterdam: Elsevier.

Manning, R. E., & Poewers, L. A. (1984). Peak and peak-off use: redistributing the outdoor recreation tourism load. *Journal of Travel Research, 23*, 25–31.

Marcoullier DW (1996) *The seasonality of labour use in rural tourism regions*. Mimeo

Marshall, A. (1920). *Principles of economics*. London: McMillan.

Marzetti, S., & Mosetti, R. (2004). *Sustainable tourism development and social carrying capacity: a case-study on the North-Western Adriatic Sea*. In: *Sustainable Tourism*. Southampton: Wit Press.

Mas-Colell, A., Whinston, M. D., & Green, J. R. (1995). *Microeconomic theory*. Oxford: Oxford University Press.

Masters, E. L. (1915). *Spoon river anthology*. London: McMillan.

Mathieson, A., & Wall, G. (1982). *Tourism: economic, physical and social impacts*. Harlow: Longman.

Mathisen, T. A., & Solvoll, G. (2007). Competitive tendering and structural changes: an example from the bus industry. *Journal of Transport Policy, 15*, 1–11.

Mazzanti, M. (2003). Discrete choice models and valuation experiments. *Journal of Economic Studies, 30*, 584–604.

McConnell, K. E. (1985). The economics of outdoor recreation. In A. V. Kneese & J. L. Sweeney (Eds.), *Handbook of natural resource and energy economics*. Amsterdam: Elsevier.

McIntosh, R. W., Goeldner, C. R., & Ritchie, J. R. B. (1995). *Tourism. Principles, practices, philosophies*. New York: Wiley.

McKercher, B. (1999). A chaos approach to tourism. *Tourism Management, 20*, 425–434.

McKinsey (2007) How businesses are using Web 2.0: a McKinsey global survey. *The McKinsey Quarterly*, Special Edition 4.

Meadows, D. H., Meadows, D. L., Randers, J., & Behrens, W. W. (1972). *The limits to growth*. New York: Universe Books.

Medlik, S. (1988). *What is tourism? Teaching tourism into the 1990s, International Conference for Tourism Education, July 1988*. Guildford: University of Surrey.

Michelman, F. I. (1982). Ethics, economics, and the law of property. In J. R. Pennock & J. W. Chapman (Eds.), *Nomos XXIV: ethics, economics and the law*. New York: New York University Press.

Milgrom, P., & Roberts, J. (1992). *Economics organization and management*. New York: Prentice Hall.

Miller, G., & Twining-Ward, L. (2005). *Monitoring for a sustainable tourism transition: the challenge of developing and using indicators*. London: CABI.

Mintel (2007). European cruises. *Travel and Tourism Analyst*, August

Moore, K., Cushman, G., & Simmons, D. (1995). Behavioral conceptualization of tourism and leisure. *Annals of Tourism Research, 22*, 67–85.

Morgan, N., Pritchard, A., & Pride, R. (2004). *Destination branding*. Oxford: Elsevier.

Morley, C. (2000). Demand modeling methodologies: integration and other issues. *Tourism Economics, 6*, 5–19.

Moscardo, G. (2008). Sustainable tourism innovation: challenging basic assumptions. *Tourism and Hospitality Research, 8*, 4–13.

Motta, M. (2004). *Competition policy*. Cambridge: Cambridge University Press.

Mowforth, M., & Munt, I. (2003). *Tourism and sustainability: new tourism in the third world*. London: Routledge.

Murthy, B., & Dev, C. S. (1992). Average daily rate. In A. Khan, M. D. Olsen, & T. Var (Eds.), *NVR's encyclopedia of hospitality and tourism*. New York: Van Nostrand Reinhold.

Nash, D. (1996). *Anthropology of tourism*. New York: Pergamon.

Nelson, P. (1970). Information and consumer behaviour. *Journal of Political Economy, 78*, 311–329.

Nelson, P. (1974). Advertising as information. *Journal of Political Economy, 82*, 729–754.

Nicolau, J. L. (2010). Variety-seeking and inertial behaviour: the disutility of distance. *Tourism Economics, 16*, 251–264.

Nijkamp, P., Bruinsma, F., & Kourtit, K. (2010). An agent-based decision support model for the development of e-services in the tourist sector. *Review of Economic Analysis, 2*, 232–255.

Nowak, J. J., Petit, S., & Sahli, M. (2010). Tourism and globalization: the international division of tourism production. *Journal of Travel Research, 49*, 228–245.

Nowak, J. J., Sahli, M., & Cortés-Jiménez, I. (2007). Tourism, capital good imports and economic growth: theory and evidence for Spain. *Tourism Economics, 13*, 515–536.

Nowotny, H. (2003). *The potential of transdisciplinarity*. Paris: Rethinking Interdisciplinarity.

Nwosu, N. P. (2008). *L'importanza dell'informazione per il turista-consumatore. Analisi dei diversi canali distributivi di una vacanza in Messico*. Bologna: University of Bologna. Mimeo.

O'Connor, W. E. (2000). *An introduction to airline economics*. Westport, CT: Praeger.

O'Connor, P., & Frew, A. (2001). Expert perceptions on the future of hotel electronic distribution channels. In P. J. Sheldon, K. W. Woeber, & D. R. Fesenmaier (Eds.), *Information and communication technologies in tourism 2001*. New York: Springer.

OECD. (1980). *The impact of tourism on the environment*. Paris: OECD.

OECD. (1994). *Environmental indicators*. Paris: OECD.

Oh, C. O. (2005). The contribution of tourism development to economic growth in the Korean economy. *Tourism Management, 26*, 39–44.

Oi, W. (1971). A disneyland dilemma: two-part tariffs for a Mickey Mouse monopoly. *Quarterly Journal of Economics, 85*, 77–96.

Page, S. J., & Dowling, R. K. (2002). *Ecotourism*. Harlow: Prentice Hall.

Pak, K., & Piersma, N. (2002). *Airline revenue management: an overview of OR techniques 1982–2001. ERIM Report Series, 12*. Rotterdam: Erasmus University.

Palmer, A., Montano, J. J., & Sesé, A. (2006). Designing an artificial neural network for forecasting tourism time series. *Tourism Management, 27*, 781–790.

Pambudi, D., McCaughey, N., & Smith, R. (2009). Computable general equilibrium estimates of the impact of the Bali bombing on the Indonesian economy. *Tourism Management, 30*, 232–239.

Papatheodorou, A. (1999). The demand for international tourism in the Mediterranean region. *Applied Economics, 31*, 619–630.

Papatheodorou, A. (2003a). Modelling tourism development: a synthetic approach. *Tourism Economics, 9*, 407–430.

Papatheodorou, A. (2003b). Corporate strategies of British tour operators in the Mediterranean region: an economic geography approach. *Tourism Geographies, 5*, 280–304.

Papatheodorou, A. (2003c). Do we need airport regulation? *Utilities Journal, 6*, 35–37.

Papatheodorou, A. (2004). Exploring the evolution of tourist resorts. *Annals of Tourism Research, 31*, 219–237.

Papatheodorou, A. (2006). The cruise industry. An industrial organization perspective. In R. Dowling (Ed.), *Cruise ship tourism*. Wallingford: CABI.

Papatheodorou, A. (2008). The impact of civil aviation regimes on leisure travel. In A. Graham, A. Papatheodorou, & P. Forsyth (Eds.), *Aviation and tourism: implications for leisure travel*. Aldershot: Ashgate.

Papatheodorou, A., & Lei, Z. (2006). Leisure travel in Europe and airline business models: a study of regional airports in Great Britain. *Journal of Air Transport Management, 12*, 47–52.

Papatheodorou, A., & Platis, N. (2007). Airline deregulation, competitive environment and safety. *Rivista di Politica Economica, I–II*, 221–242.

Pareto, V. (1911). Economie mathématique. In Gauthier-Villars (Ed.) *Encyclopedie des sciences mathematiques*.

Parisi, F., Depoorter, B., & Schultz, N. (2000). Duality in property: commons and anticommons. *Law and Economics Research Paper Series*, N. 00-32, University of Virginia School of Law.

Parisi, F., Schultz, N., & Depoorter, B. (2004). Simultaneous and sequential anticommons. *European Journal of Law and Economics, 17*, 175–190.

Pasqualoni, P. (2008). *La gestione delle prenotazioni delle compagnie aeree. Un esperimento sulla tratta Parigi – New York*. Bologna: University of Bologna. Mimeo.

Pattie, D. C., & Snyder, J. (1996). Using a neural network to forecast visitor behaviour. *Annals of Tourism Research, 23*, 151–164.

Pearce, D. G. (2005). Advancing tourism research: issues and responses. In W. Alejziak & R. Winiarski (Eds.), *Tourism in scientific research*. Krakow: Academy of Physical Education.

Pearce, D. W., & Turner, R. H. (1990). *Economics of natural resources and the environment*. New York: Harverster Wheatsheaf.

Pestana Barros, C., & Pinto Machado, L. (2010). The length of stay in tourism. *Annals of Tourism Research, 37*, 692–706.

Phelps, E. S. (1988). *The economics of imperfect information*. Cambridge: Cambridge University Press.

Phillips, A. (1985). Opening address. In *Tourism, Recreation and Conservation in National Park and Equivalent Reserves, A European Heritage Landscapes Conference*, Derbyshire: Peak National Park Centre

Phlips, L., & Thisse, J. F. (1982). Spatial competition and the theory of differentiated markets: an introduction. *Journal of Industrial Economics, 31*, 1–9.

Piga, C. (2003). Territorial planning and tourism development tax. *Annals of Tourism Research, 30*, 886–905.

Pigliaru, F. (2002). Economia del turismo: crescita e qualità ambientale. In R. Paci & S. Usai (Eds.), *L'ultima spiaggia. Turismo, economia e sostenibilità ambientale in Sardegna*. Cagliari: CUEC.

Pintassilgo, P., & Silva, J. A. (2007). Tragedy of the commons in the tourism accommodation industry. *Tourism Economics, 13*, 209–224.

Plog, S. C. (1974). Why destination areas rise and fall in popularity. *Cornell Hotel and Restaurant Quarterly, 14*, 43–45.

Pollack, R. A. (1978). Endogenous tastes in demand and welfare analysis. *American Economic Review, 68*, 374–379.

Pollock, A. (1998). Creating intelligent destinations for wired consumers. In A. M. Tjoa & J. Jafari (Eds.), *Information communication technologies in tourism*. Vienna: Springer.

Porter, M. E. (1980). *Competitive strategy: techniques for analysing industries and competitors*. New York: Free Press.

Porter, M. E. (1990). *The competitive advantage of nations*. New York: Free Press.

Porter, M.E. (1998). Cluster and the new economic competition. *Harvard Business Review*, 77–90.

Prud'homme, R. (1985). Il futuro industriale di Venezia. In OECD (Ed.), *Rapporto sulla rigenerazione industriale di Venezia*. Paris: OECD.

Przeclawski, K. (1993). Tourism as the subject of interdisciplinary research. In D. Pearce & R. Butler (Eds.), *Tourism research: critiques and challenges*. London: Routledge.

Pulina, M., & Cortés-Jiménez, I. (2010). Have low-cost carriers influenced tourism demand and supply? The case of Alghero, Italy. *Tourism Analysis, 15*, 617–635.

Punzo, L., & Usai, S. (Eds.). (2007). *L'estate al mare. Residenti e turisti in alcune destinazioni italiane*. Milan: McGraw-Hill.

Raffestin, C. (1986). Nature e culture du lieu touristique. *Méditerranée*, 3.

Razumova, M., Rey-Maquiera, J., & Lozano, J. (2009). Is environmental regulation harmful for competitiveness? The applicability of the Porter hypothesis to tourism. *Tourism Analysis, 14*, 387–400.

Rees, W. E. (1992). Ecological footprints and appropriated carrying capacity: what urban economics leaves out. *Environment and Urbanization, 4*, 121–130.

Rees, W. E., & Wackernagel, M. (1994). Ecological footprints and appropriated carrying capacity: measuring the natural capital requirements of the human economy. In A. M. Jansson, M. H. Hammer, C. Folke, & R. Costanza (Eds.), *Investing in natural capital: the ecological economics approach to sustainability*. Washington: Island Press.

Richards, G. (2002). Tourism attraction systems: exploring cultural behavior. *Annals of Tourism Research, 29*, 1048–1064.

Rigall-I-Torrent, R., & Fluvià, M. (2007). Public goods in tourism municipalities: formal analysis, empirical evidence and implications for sustainable development. *Tourism Economics, 13*, 361–378.

Ritchie, B. W. (2004). Chaos, crisis and disasters: a strategic approach to crisis management in the tourism industry. *Tourism Management, 25*, 669–683.

Robinson, J. (2001). Socio-cultural dimension of sustainable tourism development: achieving the vision. In H. Varma (Ed.), *Island tourism in Asia and the Pacific*. Madrid: UNWTO.

Rodriguez-Clare, A. (1996). Multinationals, linkages and economic development. *American Economic Review, 86*, 852–873.

Ropero, A. (2011). Dynamic pricing policies of hotel establishments in an online travel agency. *Tourism Economics, 17*, 1087–1102.

Rosen, S. (1974). Hedonic prices and implicit markets: product differentiation in pure competition. *Journal of Political Economy, 82*, 34–55.

Rosselló Nadal, J., Riera Font, A., & Sansó Rosselló, A. (2004). The economic determinants of seasonal patterns. *Annals of Tourism Research, 31*, 697–711.

Roth, A.E., & Ockenfels, A. (2000). *Last minute bidding and the rules for ending second-price auctions: theory and evidence from a natural experiment on the Internet*. Working Paper 7729, National Bureau of Economic Research.

Russell, R., & Faulkner, B. (1997). Chaos and complexity in tourism: in search of a new perspective. *Pacific Tourism Review, 1*, 93–102.

Russell, R., & Faulkner, B. (1999). Movers and shakers: chaos makers in tourism development. *Tourism Management, 20*, 411–423.

Russell, R., & Faulkner, B. (2004). Entrepreneurship, chaos and the tourism area life cycle. *Annals of Tourism Research, 31*, 556–579.

Rutherford, D. G., & O'Fallon, M. J. (2006). *Hotel management and operations*. New York: Wiley & Sons.

Ryan, C. (1991). *Recreational tourism: a social science perspective*. London: Routledge.

Ryan, C. (1997). Tourism: a mature discipline. *Pacific Tourism Review, 1*, 3–5.

Sacco, P. L., & Ferilli, G. (2006). *Il distretto culturale evoluto nell'economia post industriale, DADI Working Paper n. 4/06*. Venice: IUAV.

Salò, A., & Garriga, A. (2011). The second-home rental market: a hedonic analysis of the effect of different characteristics and a high-market-share intermediary on price. *Tourism Economics, 17*, 1017–1033.

Samuelson, P. A., & Nordhaus, W. D. (2009). *Economics* (19th ed.). New York: McGraw-Hill.

Santagata, W. (2005). I distretti culturali nei paesi avanzati e nelle economie emergenti. *Economia della Cultura, 2*, 141–152.
Santana-Gallego, M., Ledesma-Rodriguez, F., & Perez-Rodriguez, J. (2010a). Exchange rate regimes and tourism. *Tourism Economics, 16*, 25–43.
Santana-Gallego, M., Ledesma-Rodrìguez, F., Pérez-Rodrìguez, J., & Cortés-Jiménez, I. (2010b). Does a common currency promote countries' growth via trade and tourism? *The World Economy, 33*, 1811–1835.
Satuiendrakumar, R., & Tisdell, C. (1989). Tourism and the economic development of the Maldives. *Annals of Tourism Research, 16*, 254–269.
Scheyvens, R. (2002). *Tourism and development: empowering communities*. Harlow: Pearson.
Scheyvens, R. (2011). *Tourism and poverty*. London: Routledge.
Schmalensee, R. (1978). A model of advertising and product quality. *Journal of Political Economy, 86*, 485–503.
Schubert, S. (2010). Coping with externalities in tourism: a dynamic optimal taxation approach. *Tourism Economics, 16*, 321–343.
Schumpeter, J. A. (1934). *The theory of economic development*. Cambridge: Harvard University Press.
Schumpeter, J. A. (1975). *Capitalism, socialism and democracy*. New York: Harper. (Original publication 1942.
Schwartz, Z., Stewart, W., & Backlund, E. A. (2012). Visitation at capacity-constrained tourism destinations: exploring revenue management at a national park. *Tourism Management, 33*, 500–508.
Selten, R. (1975). Re-examination of the effectiveness concept for equilibrium in extensive games. *International Journal of Game Theory, 4*, 25–55.
Sequeira, T. N., & Macas Nunes, P. (2008). Does tourism influence economic growth? A dynamic panel data approach. *Applied Economics, 40*, 2431–2441.
Shaked, A., & Sutton, J. (1982). Relaxing price competition through product differentiation. *Review of Economic Studies, 49*, 3–13.
Shaked, A., & Sutton, J. (1983). Natural oligopoly. *Econometrica, 51*, 1468–1484.
Shapiro, C. (1984). Premiums for high quality products as returns to reputation. *Quarterly Journal of Economics, 98*, 659–679.
Shaw, M. (1992). Hotel pricing. In A. Khan, M. D. Olsen, & T. Var (Eds.), *VNR's encyclopedia of hospitality and tourism*. New York: Van Nostrand Reinhold.
Shaw, G., & Williams, A. M. (1990). Tourism, development and the environment: the eternal triangle. In C. P. Cooper & A. Lockwood (Eds.), *Progress in tourism, recreation and hospitality management*. London: Belhaven.
Shaw, G., & Williams, A. M. (2002). *Critical issues in tourism*. Oxford: Blackwell.
Shaw, G., & Williams, A. M. (2004). *Tourism and tourism spaces*. London: Sage.
Sheldon, P. J. (2006). Tourism information technology. In L. Dwyer & P. Forsyth (Eds.), *International handbook on the economics of tourism*. Cheltenham: Edward Elgar.
Sheldon, P. J., & Dwyer, L. (2010). The global financial crisis and tourism: perspectives of the academy. *Journal of Travel Research, 49*, 3–4.
Shih, D. (1986). VALS as a tool of tourism market research. *Journal of Travel Research, 24*, 2–11.
Shy, O. (2008). *How to price. A guide to pricing techniques and yield management*. Cambridge: Cambridge University Press.
Sigala, M. (2004). Collaborative supply chain management in the airline sector: the role of global distribution systems (GDS). *Advances in Hospitality and Leisure, 1*, 103–121.
Simon, H. (1991). Organization and market. *Journal of Economic Perspectives, 5*, 25–44.
Simonicca, A. (2002). *Turismo, ambiente e culture locali. Note antropologiche*, Mimeo.
Sinclair, M. T. (1998). Tourism and economic development: a survey. *Journal of Development Studies, 34*, 1–27.
Sinclair, M. T., Clewer, A., & Pack, A. (1990). Hedonic prices and the marketing of package holidays: the case of tourism resorts in Malaga. In G. Ashworth & B. Goodall (Eds.), *Marketing tourism places*. London: Routledge.

Sinclair, M. T., & Stabler, M. (1997). *The economics of tourism*. London: Routledge.

Smith, A. (1776). *The Wealth of Nations*.

Smith, S. L. J. (1988). Defining tourism: a supply-side view. *Annals of Tourism Research, 25*, 179–190.

Smith, V. L. (1989). *Hosts and guests: the anthropology of tourism*. Philadelphia: University of Pennsylvania Press.

Smith, S. L. J. (1995). *Tourism analysis. A handbook*. Essex: Longman.

Smith, V. L. (1998). War and tourism: an American ethnography. *Annals of Tourism Research, 25*, 202–227.

Smith, V.L., & Brent, M. (2001). *Hosts and guests revisited: tourism issues of the 21st century*. Cognizant Communication

Solow, R. (1956). A contribution to the theory of economic growth. *Quarterly Journal of Economics, 70*, 65–94.

Solow, R. (1987). We'd better watch out. *New York Times Book Review*, July 12th:36.

Song, H., & Li, G. (2008). Tourism demand modelling and forecasting. A review of recent research. *Tourism Management, 29*, 203–220.

Song, H., & Turner, L. (2006). Tourism demand forecasting. In L. Dwyer & P. Forsyth (Eds.), *International handbook on the economics of tourism*. Cheltenham: Edward Elgar.

Song, H., Witt, S. F., & Li, G. (2003). Modelling and forecasting the demand for Thai tourism. *Tourism Economics, 9*, 363–987.

Song, H., Witt, S. F., & Li, G. (2008). *The advanced econometrics of tourism demand*. London: Routledge.

Song, H., & Wong, K. F. (2003). Tourism demand modeling: a time-varying parameter approach. *Journal of Travel Research, 42*, 57–64.

Sonmez, S. F. (1998). Tourism, terrorism and political instability. *Annals of Tourism Research, 25*, 416–456.

Sonmez, S. F., & Graefe, A. R. (1998). Influence of terrorism risk on foreign tourism decisions. *Annals of Tourism Research, 25*, 112–144.

Spence, M. (1974). *Market signaling*. Cambridge: Harvard University Press.

Spurr, R. (2006). Tourism satellite accounts. In L. Dwyer & P. Forsyth (Eds.), *International handbook on the economics of tourism*. Cheltenham: Edward Elgar.

Stabler, M. J., Papatheodorou, A., & Sinclair, M. T. (2010). *The economics of tourism* (2nd ed.). London: Routledge.

Statistics Canada. (2007). *Canadian tourism satellite account handbook*. Ottawa: Statistics Canada.

Stem, C. J., Lassole, J. P., Lee, D. R., & Deshler, D. J. (2003). How "eco" is ecotourism? A comparative case study of ecotourism in Costa Rica. *Journal of Sustainable Tourism, 11*, 322–347.

Stigler, G. J. (1961). The economics of information. *Journal of Political Economy, 69*, 213–225.

Sutcliffe, C. M., & Sinclair, M. T. (1980). The measurement of seasonality within the tourist industry: an application to tourist arrivals in Spain. *Applied Economics, 12*, 429–441.

Swann, P. G. M. (2010). The rise, fall and renaissance of the resort: a simple economic model. *Tourism Economics, 16*, 45–62.

Swarbrooke, J. (1999). *Sustainable tourism management*. New York: CABI.

Talluri, K. T., & van Ryzin, G. (2005). *The theory and practice of revenue management*. Heidelberg: Springer.

Taylor, P. (1995). Measuring changes in the relative competitiveness of package tour destinations. *Tourism Economics, 1*, 169–182.

Teo, P. (2002). Striking the balance for sustainable tourism: implications for the discourse on globalization. *Journal of Sustainable Tourism, 10*, 459–474.

Thompson, A. (2011). Terrorism and tourism in developed versus developing countries. *Tourism Economics, 17*, 693–700.

Tisdell, C., & Wilson, C. (2001). Wildlife-based tourism and increased support for nature conservation financially and otherwise: evidence from sea turtle ecotourism at Mon Repos. *Tourism Economics, 7*, 233–249.

Toulantas, G. (2001). Valuing tour operators during volatile times. *Deloitte and Touche Leisure Review, 4*, 5–11.
Toulmin, S. (1972). *Human understanding*. Oxford: Clarendon.
Tremblay, P. (1998). The economic organization of tourism. *Annals of Tourism Research, 25*, 837–859.
Tribe, J. (1997). The indiscipline of tourism. *Annals of Tourism Research, 24*, 638–657.
Tribe, J. (2004). Knowing about tourism. Epistemological issues. In J. Phillipmore & L. Goodson (Eds.), *Qualitative research in tourism*. London: Routledge.
Tribe, J. (2011). *The economics of recreation, leisure and tourism* (4th ed.). Oxford: Butterworth-Heinemann.
Tribe, J., & Xiao, H. (2011). Developments in tourism social science. *Annals of Tourism Research, 38*, 1–26.
UNWTO. (1999). *The global code of ethics for tourism*. Madrid: UNWTO.
UNWTO. (2003). *Tourisme y atenuacion de la pobreza*. Madrid: UNWTO.
UNWTO. (2007). *2008 international recommendations for tourism statistics*. Madrid: UNWTO.
UNWTO. (2008a). *2008 tourism satellite account: recommended methodological framework*. Madrid: UNWTO.
UNWTO. (2008b). *Indicators of sustainable development for tourism destinations*. Madrid: UNWTO.
UNWTO. (2010). *Tourism highlights* (2010th ed.). Madrid: UNWTO.
UNWTO. (2011a). *World tourism barometer, January 2011*. Madrid: UNWTO.
UNWTO. (2011b). *Technology in tourism*. Madrid: UNWTO.
Uysal, M., & Crompton, J. L. (1984). Determinants of demand for international tourist flows in Turkey. *Tourism Management, 5*, 288–297.
Uysal, M., & El Roubi, M. S. (1999). Artificial neural networks vs. multiple regression in tourism demand analysis. *Journal of Travel Research, 38*, 111–118.
Uysal, M., Muzaffer, X., & Crompton, J. L. (1985). An overview of approaches used to forecast tourism demand. *Journal of Travel Research, 23*, 7–15.
Vaccaro, G. (2007). Pro e contro un'imposizione fiscale sui turisti. *Studi e Note di Economia, 11*, 257–282.
Van Doorn, J. W. M. (1986). Scenario writing: a method for long term tourism forecasting? *Tourism Management, 7*, 33–49.
Vanhove, N. (2005). *Economics of tourism destinations*. London: Butterworth-Heinemann.
Var, T., & Lee, C. K. (1992). Tourism forecasting: state-of-the-art techniques. In A. Khan, M. D. Olsen, & T. Var (Eds.), *NVR's encyclopedia of hospitality and tourism*. New York: Van Nostrand Reinhold.
Varian, H. R. (1996). *Intermediate microeconomics. A modern approach*. London: Norton & Company.
Varian, H. R., Farrell, J., & Shapiro, C. (2004). *The economics of information technology*. Cambridge: Cambridge University Press.
Varni, A., & Negri Zamagni, V. (Eds.). (1992). *Economia e società a Rimini tra '800 e '900*. Rimini: Cassa di Risparmio di Rimini.
Vila, N., & Corcoles, M. (2011). Yield management and airline strategic groups. *Tourism Economics, 17*, 261–278.
von Ungern-Sternberg, T., & von Weizsäcker, C. C. (1985). The supply of quality on a market of 'experience goods'. *Journal of Industrial Economics, 33*, 531–540.
Wachsman, Y. (2006). Strategic interaction among firms in tourist destinations. *Tourism Economics, 12*, 531–541.
Wackernagel, M., & Rees, W. E. (1996). *Our ecological footprints: reducing human impact on the earth*. Gabriola Island: New Soviet Publishing.
Wahab, S. (1975). *Tourism management*. London: Tourism International Press.
Wahab, S., & Cooper, C. (2001). *Tourism in the age of globalization*. London: Routledge.
Wall, G., & Mathieson, A. (2006). *Tourism: change, impacts and opportunities*. Harlow: Pearson and Prentice Hall.

Wang, Y., & Pizam, A. (2011). *Destination marketing and management: theories and applications*. London: CABI.

Wanhill, S. R. C. (1980). Tackling seasonality: a technical note. *International Journal of Tourism Management, 1*, 243–245.

WCED. (1987). *Our common future*. Oxford: World Commission on Environment and Development and Oxford University Press.

Weitzman, M. L. (1998). Recombinant growth. *Quarterly Journal of Economics, 113*, 331–360.

Wensveen, J. G. (2007). *Air transportation: a management perspective*. Aldershot: Ashgate.

Werther, H., & Klein, S. (1999). *Information technology and tourism – A challenging relationship*. Vienna: Springer.

Weston, R. (1986). The ubiquity of room taxes. *Tourism Management, 4*, 194–198.

Wheeler, M. (1994). The emergence of ethics in tourism and hospitality. *Progress in Tourism, Recreation and Hospitality Management, 6*, 647–654.

White, P. R. (2008). *Public transport: its planning, management and operations*. London: Routledge.

Williams, T. A. (1979). Impact of domestic tourism in host population: the evolution of a model. *Tourist Recreation Research, 4*, 15–21.

Williams, A. M., & Shaw, G. (1991). *Tourism and economic development: Western European experiences*. Chichester: Wiley.

Wilton, D., & Wirjanto, T. (1998). *An analysis of the seasonal variation in the national tourism indicators: a report prepared for the Canadian Tourism Commission*. Waterloo: University of Waterloo.

Wolf, H. (2004). Airport privatization and regulation. Getting the institutions right. In P. Forsyth, D. Gillen, H. M. Niemeier, & D. Starkie (Eds.), *The economic regulation of airports*. Aldershot: Ashgate.

WTTC. (2011). *Tourism satellite accounting tools*. London: World Travel and Tourism Council.

Xiang, Z., & Gretzel, U. (2010). Role of social media in online travel information search. *Tourism Management, 31*, 179–188.

Young, G. (1973). *Tourism: blessing or blight?* Harmondsworth: Penguin.

Zamagni, S. (1999). Verso il superamento della concezione economicistica del turismo. In V. Negri Zamagni, M. Mussoni, & G. Benzi (Eds.), *Per un turismo autenticamente umano*. Fara Editore: Rimini.

Zehrer, A., Crotts, J. C., & Magnini, C. P. (2011). The perceived usefulness of blog postings: an extension of the expectancy-disconfirmation paradigm. *Tourism Management, 32*, 106–113.

Zenelis P, Papatheodorou A (2008). Low cost carriers' penetration: a comparative case study of Greece and Spain. Mimeo

Zierer, C. M. (1952). Tourism and recreation in the West. *Geographical Review, 42*, 463–475.

Zirulia, L. (2011). *Should I stay or should I go? Weather forecasts and the economics of "short-breaks"*. Bologna: University of Bologna. Mimeo.

Index

G. Candela and P. Figini, *The Economics of Tourism Destinations*, Springer Texts in Business and Economics, DOI 10.1007/978-3-642-20874-4,